SOCIOLOGY

An Introduction to Sociology

SOCIOLOGY
An Introduction to Sociology

Roshni Jain
M.A., Ph.D.
Utkal University, Orissa

AITBS PUBLISHERS, INDIA
J-5/6, Krishan Nagar, Delhi-110051 (INDIA)
Tel.: 011-40167052, 49067602; Fax: 011-22009074
Email: aitbsindia@gmail.com & aitbsindia@hotmail.com

First Edition : 2012
Second Edition : 2022

ISBN: 978-93-7473-496-4

Published by:
Virender Kumar Arya for
AITBS Publishers, India
J-5/6, Krishan Nagar, Delhi-110051 (INDIA)
Tel.: 011-40167052, 49067602; Fax: 011-22009074
Email: aitbsindia@gmail.com & aitbsindia@hotmail.com

Printed by AITBS, Delhi

PREFACE

Sociology, the scientific study of human social behavior. As the study of humans in their collective aspect, sociology is concerned with all group activities: economic, social, political and religious. Sociologists study such areas as bureaucracy, community, deviant behavior, family, public opinion, social change, social mobility, social stratification, and such specific problems as crime, divorce, child abuse and substance addiction.

Sociology tries to determine the laws governing human behavior in social contexts. Sociology is a science which attempts the interpretive understanding of social action to arrive at a casual explanation of its course and effects. Sociology seeks to formulate type concepts and generalized uniformities of empirical processes. History, on the other hand, is interested in the causal analysis of particular events, actions or personalities.

Action is human behavior to which the acting individual attaches subjective meaning. It can be overt or inward and subjective. Action is social when, by virtue of the subjective meaning attached to it by the acting individual(s), it takes account of the behavior of others and is thereby guided. Social action may be oriented to past, present or predicted future behavior of others. Others may be concrete people or indefinite pluralities.

This book is applied to modern social problems, for use in institutions where but a short time can be given to the subject, in courses in sociology where it is desired to combine it with a study of current social problems on the one hand, and to correlate it with a course in economics on the other.

We acknowledge the inspiration and blessings of our parents from the core of our heart and extend thanks to my husband and our family members for their moral support which helped us in the successful completion of this book. Our gratitude is due to a large number of writers and authors of books on Sociology, whose ideas and thoughts have imperceptibly influenced us in the preparation of this book.

We are also thankful to Virender Kumar Arya and his team at AITBS Publishers, Delhi, for their meticulous efforts in the direction of bringing out this book on time.

—Author

Contents

INTRODUCTION TO SOCIOLOGY

Introduction: *Science, Natural Sciences, Social Science, Sociology as a Social Science, Sociological Positivism, Antipositivism, Sociology of Science.* ***Meaning and Definition of Sociology. Nature of Sociology. Characteristics of Sociology. Sociology is both Dynamic and Static. Areas of Sociology. Origins of Sociology. In the Beginning****: Auguste Comte.* ***Scope of Sociology:*** *Formal School of Sociology, Synthetic School of Sociology.* ***Development of Sociology, The Use of Concepts in Sociology. Major Perspectives in Sociology:*** *Functionalism, Symbolic Interactionism, Conflict Theory.* ***Importance of Sociology. Career in Sociology.***

INTRODUCTION

Sociology is a social science which studies society and the human beings in perspective of society. Sociology is concerned with all group activities: economic, social, political and religious. As described by *Giddens*, "Sociology is the study of human social life, groups and societies. It is a dazzling and compelling enterprise, having as its subject matter our own behaviour as social beings. The scope of sociology is extremely huge, ranging from the analysis of passing encounters between individuals in the street up to the investigation of world-wide social processes". Sociology helps us to determine the laws governing human behaviour in social contexts.

SCIENCE

Science refers to a way of acquiring knowledge. This system uses observation and experimentation to describe and explain natural phenomena.

The term science also refers to the organized body of knowledge people have gained using that system. Less formally, the word science often describes any systematic field of study or the knowledge gained from it. Fields of science are commonly classified along two major lines:

— Natural sciences, the study of the natural world.

— Social sciences, the systematic study of human behaviour and society.

NATURAL SCIENCES

Natural science refers to a naturalistic approach to the study of the universe, which is well known as obeying rules or laws of natural origin. Overall, natural science is the core of all sciences. The natural sciences are astronomy, biology, chemistry, earth science and physics. There are also cross-disciplines such as biophysics which integrate between sciences.

SOCIAL SCIENCE

Social science is, in its broadest sense, the study of society and the manner in which people behave and impact on the world around us. The social sciences are one of three divisions of science, along with *natural science* and *formal science*. Social science is related with human aspects of the world, like the arts and humanities, although social science places more effort on experimentation and the scientific method.

The social sciences include anthropology, economics, education, geography, history, law, linguistics, political science, psychology, sociology, communication studies, development studies, information science and sociobiology.

SOCIOLOGY AS A SOCIAL SCIENCE

Sociology is the study of human societies. It is a social science which uses various methods of empirical investigation and critical analysis to develop and refine a body of knowledge on human social activity, often with the goal of applying such knowledge to the pursuit of social welfare. As much of what humans do fits under the category of social structure and agency, sociology has gradually expanded its focus to further subjects, such as medical, military and penal organizations, the internet and even the role of social activity in the development of scientific knowledge.

SOCIOLOGICAL POSITIVISM

In social science, sociological positivism refers to an epistemological approach, closely associated with naturalism and the scientific method, which attempts to analyse the social realm through empirical means. Positivist methods are in this sense predominantly "quantitative", producing numerical data to draw inferences across a population and establish correlations.

Positivism started from the original sociology of *Auguste Comte*, but has since modified many different meanings and interpretations. In spite of philosophical connotations relating to scientism, any simple test of a population to derive statistical data may be regarded as an exercise of positivist research. Antipositivists, by contrast, reject statistical methods and instead prefer interpretative (or qualitative) analysis. Both perspectives, however, involve a systematic (and to some extent subjective) interaction between theory and data. In practice, quantitative and qualitative methods are often combined.

ANTIPOSITIVISM

Antipositivism is the view in sociology that academics must necessarily reject empiricism and the scientific method in the conduct of social theory and research. In practice, non-positivist (or qualitative) research is often coupled with positivist (or quantitative) techniques.

Antipositivism holds there is no methodological unity of the sciences: the three goals of positivism—*description*, *control*, and *prediction*—are incomplete, since they lack any understanding. Some argue that, even if positivism were correct, it would be dangerous. Science aims at understanding causality so that control can be exerted. If this succeeded in sociology, those with knowledge would be able to control the ignorant and this could lead to social engineering. The perspective, however, has led to controversy over how one can draw the line between subjective and objective research, much less draw an artificial line between environment and human organization and influenced the study of hermeneutics. The base concepts of antipositivism have expanded beyond the scope of social science, in fact, phenomenology has the same basic principles at its core.

SOCIOLOGY OF SCIENCE

The sociology of scientific knowledge is the study of science as a social activity, especially dealing "with the social conditions and effects of science, and with the social structures and processes of scientific activity." Sociologists of scientific knowledge study the development of a scientific field and attempt to identify points of contingency or interpretative flexibility where ambiguities are present. Such variations may be linked to political, corporate or economic factors.

MEANING AND DEFINITION OF SOCIOLOGY

Sociology is the branch of philosophy that treats of the constitution, phenomena, and development of human society.

Sociology is the scientific study of society or the science of social phenomena. In other way, we can say that "Sociology is the name applied to a somewhat inchoate mass of materials which embodies our knowledge about society."

A number of people define sociology, but unsatisfactory in many ways, like 'the science of social process' and 'the science of social relation.' Better than these are, "Sociology is the study of men considered as affecting and as affected by association," or, "the study of human association, including whatever conduces to it or modifies it." Formal definitions that have been given by Scientific men, none is more comprehensive than that of Professor Giddings, which follows : "Sociology is an attempt to account for the origin, growth, structure, and activities of society by the operation of physical, vital, and psychical causes working together in a process of evolution." While it is difficult to give a brief comprehensive definition of sociology that will prove entirely satisfactory through all of the changes of a developing science, Professor Giddings's definition is of great service to one who wishes a clear understanding and a precise view of the nature and purposes of the science. An adequate knowledge of the true nature and import of sociology, however, may be better obtained by a careful consideration of the underlying principles of the science, than by an attempt to follow any carefully formulated definition. Sociology treats of the phenomena of society arising from the association of mankind. It includes a body of classified knowledge relating to society and a number of principles and laws. It investigates causes and effects, discovers social forces, and formulates laws of control, or rules of action.

NATURE OF SOCIOLOGY

The foregoing statements represent partially and in brief the complex material with which the science of society must deal. It must consider social facts of all kinds and arrange and classify these facts and deduce therefrom universal principles or laws relating to the growth and activity of human society. The difficulty in bringing such diverse groups of phenomena into logical order and giving a scientific basis to this order is not easily overcome. Sociology is the most difficult of all the social sciences. It deals with material which has existed from the beginnings of human association, but proposes to establish the most general fundamental truths concerning its existence. Now a days Sociology represents the results of studies of different scientists sometimes along parallel lines, in other instances along converging lines and in still others, along trajectories which have crossed. Each science views society from a different standpoint, and sociology will not become a compact, well-defined science until sociologists are able to generalize the truths discovered by those approaching social phenomena from various points of view and to agree more or less closely upon the subject matter and the method of treatment.

CHARACTERISTICS OF SOCIOLOGY

Much of the confusion concerning this science has arisen from books whose writers fail to acknowledge that science has a subjective as well as an objective boundary. It is the aim of a science, the course of reasoning and the end to be sought as much as the phenomena with which it deals that give it its distinctive mark as a science. For instance, botany and chemistry may be dealing with the same material in a certain sense, but with entirely different aims. However, added to this is the fact that in the scientific sense the "material" with which each deals is quite distinct. The chemist is dealing chiefly, though not wholly, with inorganic matter and is interested primarily in molecules and atoms of different kinds and their relations to each other. The botanist, on the other hand, is interested in molecules and atoms only incidentally. He is studying organic matter primarily and is concerned with cells and the forms into which they build themselves. Both are studying matter, but quite different aspects thereof, and in widely varied relations. Therefore, sociology, ethics, economics, politics, and history; while they all deal with the same thing in a broad sense, viz., human society, each is interested in a different aspect of social relationships.

In the history of the natural sciences biology was the latest to develop. It is a general science, in the sense that it deals with facts and principles which underlie all the special sciences concerned with various forms of life, such as botany, zoology, anthropology, etc. While biology rests on all these special biological sciences in the sense that they provide facts and principles upon which larger generalizations can be made, yet its field is not precisely that of any of these special sciences. It deals with fundamentals common to them all.

Although economics, politics, history, anthropology, and all the rest deal with particular aspects of human association, sociology is the science which investigates the regularities of human association in all its varied aspects. The special social sciences take as presuppositions the general aspects which are the objects of sociology. Take, for instance, the trust and consider all the facts and phenomena of society that arise out of it. If we consider it from an economic standpoint, we shall be determining how the trust increases the development of wealth, its effect on wages or on general distribution of products, and many other economic questions. It is evident that we are working within the province of economics.

If we think the moral conduct of the individual interested in the trust, and its general effects on the morals of the community, we shall be studying ethics. If, however, we consider what legislation may be brought to control or regulate the trust, we shall be in the realm of political science.

If, finally, we consider trust-phenomena in relation to their effects on the homes and migrations of people, the dispersion and concentration of social groups, in fact, the general effect on the social standard, we shall be in the realm of sociology.

So we shall find, so far as the material field of operation is concerned, that all sciences cross each other more or less, and we must not forget that in reality there is but one science—the science of the universe—and that the division of this science into groups and individual branches is merely a matter of convenience and pedagogical relationships.

SOCIOLOGY IS BOTH DYNAMIC AND STATIC

These terms are derived from mechanics and in a measure have the same meaning in sociology as in mechanics. However, the meaning of these terms in sociology is modified to suit the requirements of a science dealing with human beings with will power as against a science dealing with inanimate matter. Dynamic sociology refers to development or progress and static refers to relationship. We should have the basis of the latter if we were to take an instantaneous view of all society with its various co-relationships in respect to structure or activity. If now we could consider society moving forward and its various relationships changing at each successive stage, we should have the dynamic conception. In the static conception the comparison of relationships might be referred to some ideal standard which would lead us to an ethical basis of society. Some writers, carrying over into sociology the terminology of physics, have introduced the terms "social kinetics" and "social statics" as subdivisions of social dynamics. This terminology, however, as in the use of biological terms in sociology, is helpful only if clearly recognized as borrowed and not as exactly fitting social phenomena unless the terms are redefined. At the most they only serve to call attention to two different ways of looking at social phenomena. For, if we consider society at all, it is always developing or changing. Only for an instant do relationships continue until they are suddenly changed into new relationships by the process of social development. This constant changing of society enables us to establish general laws of social order, but not to determine a permanent status of society. Therefore, social statics would give us a picture of society at consecutive stages of its development, but considered together, this series of snap shots would be a moving picture of social development, that is, of social dynamics. Therefore it seems better to speak of social dynamics, and then subdivide it into social statics and social kinetics, the former dealing with social movements which are not changing in rate or direction, and the latter with those which change in rate or direction or both.

AREAS OF SOCIOLOGY

Sociologist is one who has earned advanced degrees or pursued other advanced studies in sociology and is engaged in teaching, research or other professional work in the field of sociology. The careless use of the term sociologist is very common. Magazine and newspaper writers, social workers, labour leaders, government officials, social critics etc. may be described incorrectly as sociologist. Sociology concentrates its study upon the group life of human beings and the product of their group living. The sociologist is especially interested in customs, traditions and values which emerge from group living and in the way group living is in turn affected by these customs, traditions and values. Sociology is interested in the way groups interact with one another and in the processes and institutions which they develop. Sociology is subdivided into many specialized fields of which some of are:

- — Applied sociology
- — Collective behaviour
- — Community
- — Comparative sociology
- — Crime and delinquency
- — Cultural sociology
- — Demography
- — Deviant behaviour
- — Formal and complex organizations
- — Human ecology
- — Industrial sociology
- — Law and society
- — Marriage and family
- — Medical sociology
- — Military sociology
- — Political sociology
- — Sociology of religion
- — Urban sociology
- — Social psychology
- — Social control
- — Rural sociology
- — Sociological theory
- — Sociology of education

Sociology is only one of the most popular social sciences and other disciplines share its interest in many fields. Its interest in communication and public opinion is shared by psychology and political science, criminology is shared with psychology, political science and law and police science. Sociology is especially close to psychology and anthropology and overlaps them constantly.

ORIGINS OF SOCIOLOGY

The formal study of sociology started in the nineteenth century as an attempt to make sense of great changes that were sweeping over Western Europe at that time. European societies were industrialising and there was a mass movement of people from the rural to the urban areas. Traditional institutions of power and control, such as the Church and landed aristocracy, were losing much of their influence. The late eighteenth and nineteenth centuries were times of reform and revolution and new sources of power, such as the property-owning capitalist class and organised labour movements were beginning to emerge. The fact that societies could be transformed so dramatically in such a comparatively short space of time led scholars to start exploring the sources of social order and change, and the subject we now know as sociology was born.

These early sociologists tried to make sense of this new industrial age by identifying what they believed were its essential characteristics and comparing them with what had gone before.

For *Karl Marx* (1818–1883), whose ideas were later to transform the world, the modern age was characterised, above all, by a new form of free market economy that he called industrial capitalism. Marx was very critical of capitalism. He argued that most of the wealth it created remained in the hands of the small owning class who made their profits by exploiting the labour power of the workers. However, capitalist societies were constantly changing, and Marx was optimistic that they were sowing the seeds of their own destruction. The injustices they produced, and people's increasing awareness of them, would lead to revolutionary change and the creation of what Marx believed would be fairer communist societies where resources would be distributed to people according to their needs.

Max Weber (1864–1920), another key founder of sociology, took a different and altogether more pessimistic view. He argued that the modern age was characterised by a process of increasing rationalisation. By rationalisation he meant the change from doing things because they had always been done that way (traditional action) to identifying outcomes and calculating the most efficient means of achieving them (rational action). Other examples of the rationalisation of life included the substitution of religion by science as the major source of intellectual authority, the displacement of elites based on birth by ones based on qualifications, and the increasing bureaucratic administration of life.

Weber was concerned that the remorseless spread of rational bureaucracy was stifling individual initiative, creativity and imagination. He called this the 'iron cage' of rationality. Weber believed that Marx could be right about capitalism being replaced by communism. However, unlike Marx, Weber did not think this would be any liberation. In fact he thought it would almost certainly lead to an even more bureaucratic state having more control over people's lives. For Weber there was no way out of the 'iron cage'.

IN THE BEGINNING

Political arithmetic started in Great Britain in the 1600s. As demographic and census activity increased, data became available on the nature of social problems. From 1815–1848, public hygienists and medical reformers became increasingly concerned with the condition of the working and lower classes in the urban, industrial environment. Moral statisticians could use demographic and other census data to generate theories to explain population and social problems including crime, suicide, and pauperism. As interest grew, there was increased demand for more detailed data sets and for scholars to interpret them. In its beginning, sociology was most concerned with solving immediate, highly visible urban problems.

AUGUSTE COMTE

Between (1830–1842), Auguste Comte's Curs de Philosophie Positive gave sociology a name and place among the academic disciplines. Comte, long interested in the history of human society, saw sociology as the master science of human behaviour which would discover the laws of human society just as natural science discovered the laws of nature. There was considerable emphasis on morality and moral progress. Scientific thought would guide social planning. Sociology would organize and systematize all human knowledge. Knowledge gained from sociological research would render government and human affairs more efficient. Society was seen as a set of functional relationships. Comte's most important colleagues was Henri de Saint-Simon who was one of the founders of socialism.

Auguste Comte (1798–1857)

Towards the end of the 19th century, sociology was increasingly recognized as an academic discipline in Europe. Emile Durkheim became highly visible and promoted sociological research. He established the Annee Sociologique, the first French social science periodical. Increasingly, sociology focused on "human behaviour as structure and process," discensus, control and power in human affairs, and society as a "set of functional relationships."

SCOPE OF SOCIOLOGY

There are two schools of thought with different viewpoints regarding scope and subject matter of sociology—*formal school* and *synthetic school.*

According to formal school sociology was conceived to be a social science with a specifically defined field. This school had George Simmel, Ferdinand Tonnies, Alfred Vierkandt and Leopord Von Wiese as its main advocates. On the other hand, the synthetic school with Durkheim, Hobhouse and Sorokin advocated a synthesis in form of coordination among all social sciences.

FORMAL SCHOOL OF SOCIOLOGY

Formal school argued in favour of giving sociology a definite subject matter to make it a distinct discipline. It emphasized upon the study of forms of social relationships and regarded sociology as independent. According to *Simmel* sociology is a specific social science which describes, classifies, analyses and delineates the forms of social relationships or in other words social interactions should be classified into various forms or types and analysed. *Simmel* argued that social interactions have various forms. He bore out studies of such formal relationships as cooperation, competition, sub and super ordinate relationships and so forth. He said however diverse the interests are that give rise to these sociations; the forms in which the interests are realized may yet be identical. He emphasized on the process of abstraction of these forms from human relationship which are common to diverse situations.

Vierkandt maintained that sociology should be concerned with ultimate forms of mental or psychic relationship which knit the people together in a society. According to *Von Wiese* there are two kinds of fundamental social processes in human society. Firstly, the associative process concerning contact, approach, adaptation etc. and secondly disassociate processes like competition and conflict. Apart from these two processes a mixed form of the associative and disassociative also exists. Each of these processes has sub-classes which in totality give around 650 forms of human relationships. Sociology should confine itself to the discovery of the fundamental force of change and persistence and should abstain from a historical study of concrete societies. Tonnies divided societies into two groups namely *Gemeinschaft* (community) and *Gesellschaft* (association) on the basis of degree of intimacy among the members of the society. He has on the basis of forms of relationship tried to differentiate between community and society.

Max Weber also makes out a definite field for sociology. According to him the aim of sociology is to interpret or understand social behaviour. But social behaviour does not cover the whole field of human relations. Indeed not all human interactions are social. Sociology is concerned with the analysis and classification of types of social relationships.

CRITICISM OF FORMAL SCHOOL

Formal school has been criticized on the issue that it has emphasized on merely abstract forms and neglected the concrete contents of social life. Abstract forms separated from concrete relations cannot be studied. Ginsberg says that the study of social relationships would remain barren if it is conducted in the abstract without the full knowledge of the terms to which in concrete life they relate. Sociology does not alone study the forms of social relationship. Political science, International law also studies forms of social relationship. The conception of pure sociology is not practical as no social science can be studied in isolation from other social sciences.

SYNTHETIC SCHOOL OF SOCIOLOGY

Synthetic school wanted sociology to be synthesis of the social sciences and thus wanted to widen the scope of sociology. According to Durkheim, sociology has three principal divisions' namely—Social morphology, social physiology and general sociology. Social morphology is concerned with geographical or territorial basis of life of people such as population, its size, density and distribution etc. It can be done at two levels—analysis of size and quality of population which affects the quality of social relationship and social groups. Secondly, the study of social structure or description of the main forms of social groups and institutions with their classification. Social physiology deals with the genesis and nature of various social institutions namely religion, morals, law and economic institutions etc. In general sociology the main aim is to formulate general social laws. Attempt is made to find out if there are links among various institutions which would be treated independently in social physiology and in the course to discover general social laws. Hobhouse perceived sociology as a science which has the whole social life of man as its sphere. Its relations with the other social sciences are considered to be one of mutual exchange and mutual stimulation. Karl Mannheim's divides sociology into two main sections—systematic and general sociology and historical sociology. Systematic sociology describes one by one the main factors of living together as far as they may be found in every kind of society. The historical sociology deals with the historical variety and actuality of the general forms of society. It falls into two sections—comparative sociology and social dynamics. Comparative sociology deals specially with the historical variations of the same phenomenon and tries to find by comparison general features as separated from industrial features. Social dynamics deals with the interrelations between the various social factors and institutions in a certain given society for example in a primitive society. Ginsberg has summed up the chief functions of sociology as it seeks to provide a classification of types and forms of social relationships especially of those which have come to be defined institutions and associations. It tries to determine the relation between different parts of factors of social life for example the economic and political, the moral and the legal, the intellectual and the social elements. It endeavours to disentangle the fundamental conditions of social change and persistence and to discover sociological principles governing social life.

CONCLUSION

Thus, it is based on viewpoints of different sociologists we can get a general outline of the scope of sociology. First, the analysis of various institutions, associations and social groups which are results of social relationships of individuals should be the concern of sociology. Second, the links among different parts of society should be studied. This objective is dealt with justice by functionalist school of sociology and Marxist school also gives importance to this viewpoint. Thus social structure should be given adequate importance in subject matter of sociology. Third, sociology addresses itself to the factors which contribute to social stability and social change. Fourth, sociology should also explain the trend of the changing pattern and the aftermath of the changes in the society.

DEVELOPMENT OF SOCIOLOGY

Sociology is the youngest of the recognized social sciences. Auguste Comte in France coined the word 'sociology' in his Positive Philosophy published in 1838. He believed that a science of sociology should be based on systematic observation and classification not on authority and speculation. This was a relatively new idea at that time. Herbert Spencer in England published his Principles of Sociology in 1876. He applied the theory of organic evolution to human society and developed a grand theory of social evolution.

Lester F. Ward

Lester F. Ward an American published his Dynamic Sociology in 1883 calling for social progress through intelligent social action which sociologists should guide. All these founders of sociology were basically social philosophers. They proclaimed that sociologists should collect, organize and classify factual data and derive sound social theories from these facts. Although they called for scientific investigation they did relatively little of it themselves.

Emile Durkheim gave the most notable early demonstration of scientific methodology in sociology. In his Rules of Sociological Method published in 1895, he outlined the methodology which he pursued in his study 'Suicide' published in 1897. Inplace of speculating upon the causes of suicide, he first planned his research design and then collected a large mass of data on the characteristics of people who commit suicide and then derived a theory of suicide from these data.

Courses in sociology implemented in many universities in the 1890s. The American Journal of Sociology began publication in 1895 and the American Sociological Society was organized in 1905. Whereas most of the early European sociologists came from the fields of history, political economy or philosophy many of the early American sociologists had been social workers, ministers and nearly all were from rural backgrounds.

Emile Durkheim (1858-1917)

Urbanization and industrialization were creating grave social problems and these early sociologists were looking for scientific solutions. They felt sociology as a scientific guide to social progress. The early volumes of the American Journal of Sociology contained relatively few articles devoted to scientific description or research but carried many sermons filled with advice etc.

By 1930s the several sociological journals were well filled with research articles and scientific descriptions. Sociology was gradually becoming a body of scientific knowledge with its theories based upon scientific observation rather than upon impressionistic observation.

THE USE OF CONCEPTS IN SOCIOLOGY

Every field of study makes the student memorize many words to which the field attaches special meanings. It is done because precise concepts are necessary. First we need carefully expressed concepts to carry on a scientific discussion. The sociological concepts are necessary for a clear discussion of social phenomena. The formulation of concepts leads to increased knowledge. Some accurate descriptive knowledge must be organized before a concept is framed. Then the analysis and criticism of this new concept point up the gaps and errors in present knowledge. Use of the concept often calls attention to the facts and relationships which may have been overlooked. While studying migration *Park* framed the concept of the marginal man who is on the fringes of two groups or two ways of life while fully belonging to neither.

The use of this concept quickly led to the recognition that there were many kinds of marginal persons—the persons of mixed racial ancestry who belongs clearly to neither race, the supervisor who is clearly either management or labour the ambitious climber no longer in the lower class yet not securely a middle class person and many others. Concepts like marginality lead to increased knowledge. Concepts are useful as verbal shorthand. The term control group replaces an entire sentence. Every discipline develops concepts as time savers. Most of the concepts of sociology are expressed in words which also have a popular meaning. Every science appropriates some common words and makes them into scientific concepts by giving them a specific definition and sociology is no exception.

MAJOR PERSPECTIVES IN SOCIOLOGY

FUNCTIONALISM

Functionalism is the oldest, and still the dominant, theoretical perspective in sociology and many other social sciences. This perspective is built upon twin emphases: application of the scientific method to the objective social world and use of an analogy between the individual organism and society.

The emphasis on scientific method leads to the assertion that one can study the social world in the same ways as one studies the physical world. Thus, Functionalists see the social world as "objectively real," as observable with such techniques as social surveys and interviews. Furthermore, their positivistic view of social science assumes that study of the social world can be value-free, in that the investigator's values will not necessarily interfere with the disinterested search for social laws governing the behaviour of social systems. A number of ideas go back to *Emile Durkheim* (1858-1917), the great French sociologist whose writings form the basis for functionalist theory. Durkheim was himself one of the first sociologists to make use of scientific and statistical techniques in sociological research (1950).

The second emphasis, on the organic unity of society, leads functionalists to speculate about needs which must be met for a social system to exist, as well as the ways in which social institutions satisfy those needs. A functionalist might argue, for instance, that every society will have a religion, because religious institutions have certain functions which contribute to the survival of the social system as a whole, just as the organs of the body have functions which are necessary for the body's survival.

This analogy between society and an organism focuses attention on the homeostatic nature of social systems: social systems work to maintain equilibrium and to return to it after external shocks disturb the balance among social institutions. Such social equilibrium is achieved, most importantly, through the socialization of members of the society into the basic values and norms of that society, so that consensus is reached. Where socialization is insufficient for some reason to create conformity to culturally appropriate roles and socially supported norms, various social control mechanisms exist to restore conformity or to segregate the nonconforming individuals from the rest of society. These social control mechanisms range from sanctions imposed informally—sneering and gossip, for example—to the activities of certain formal organizations, like schools, prisons, and mental institutions.

SYMBOLIC INTERACTIONISM

Symbolic interactionism, or interactionism for short, is one of the major theoretical perspectives in sociology. This perspective has a long intellectual history, beginning with the German sociologist and economist, *Max Weber* (1864–1920) and the American philosopher, *George H. Mead* (1863–1931), both of whom emphasized the subjective meaning of human behaviour, the social process, and pragmatism. Although there are a number of versions of interactionist thought, some deriving from phenomenological writings by philosophers, the following description offers a simplified amalgamation of these ideas, concentrating on points of convergence. *Herbert Blumer*, who studied with Mead at the University of Chicago, is responsible for coining the term, "symbolic interactionism," as well as for formulating the most prominent version of the theory.

Interactionists focus on the subjective aspects of social life, rather than on objective, macro-structural aspects of social systems. One reason for this focus is that interactionists base their theoretical perspective on their image of humans, rather than on their image of society (as the functionalists do). For interactionists, humans are pragmatic actors who continually must adjust their behaviour to the actions of other actors. We can adjust to these actions only because we are able to interpret them, i.e., to denote them symbolically and treat the actions and those who perform them as symbolic objects. This process of adjustment is aided by our ability to imaginatively rehearse alternative lines of action before we act. The process is further aided by our ability to think about and to react to our own actions and even our selves as symbolic objects. Thus, the interactionist theorist sees humans as active, creative participants who construct their social world, not as passive, conforming objects of socialization.

For the interactionist, society consists of organized and patterned interactions among individuals. Thus, research by interactionists focuses on easily observable face-to-face interactions rather than on macro-level structural relationships involving social institutions. Furthermore, this focus on interaction and on the meaning of events to the participants in those events (the definition of the situation) shifts the attention of interactionists away from stable norms and values toward more changeable, continually readjusting social processes. Whereas for functionalists socialization creates stability in the social system, for interactionists negotiation among members of society creates temporary, socially constructed relations which remain in constant flux, despite relative stability in the basic framework governing those relations.

These emphases on symbols, negotiated reality, and the social construction of society lead to an interest in the roles people play. *Erving Goffman* (1958), a prominent social theorist in this tradition, discusses roles dramaturgically, using an analogy to the theater, with human social behaviour seen as more or less well scripted and with humans as role-taking actors. Role-taking is a key mechanism of interaction, for it permits us to take the other's perspective, to see what our actions might mean to the other actors with whom we interact. At other times, interactionists emphasize the improvisational quality of roles, with human social behaviour seen as poorly scripted and with humans as role-making improvisers. Role-making, too, is a key mechanism of interaction, for all situations and roles are inherently ambiguous, thus requiring us to create those situations and roles to some extent before we can act.

Ethnomethodology, an offshoot of symbolic interactionism, raises the question of how people who are interacting with each other can create the illusion of a shared social order even when they don't understand each other fully and in fact have different points of view. *Harold Garfinkel*, a pioneer in these investigations, demonstrated the problem by sending his students out to perform "experiments in trust," called breaching experiments, in which they brought ordinary conversations to an abrupt halt by refusing to take for granted that they knew what the other person was saying, and so demanded explanations and then explanations of the explanations. More recently, ethnomethodologist researchers have performed minutely detailed analyses of ordinary conversations in order to reveal the methods by which turn-taking and other conversational maneuvers are managed.

Interactionists tend to study social interaction through participant observation, rather than surveys and interviews. They argue that close contact and immersion in the everyday lives of the participants is necessary for understanding the meaning of actions, the definition of the situation itself, and the process by which actors construct the situation through their interaction. Given this close contact, interactionists could hardly remain free of value commitments, and, in fact, interactionists make explicit use of their values in choosing what to study but strive to be objective in the conduct of their research.

Symbolic interactionists are often criticized by other sociologists for being overly impressionistic in their research methods and somewhat unsystematic in their theories. These objections, combined with the fairly narrow focus of interactionist research on small-group interactions and other social psychological issues, have relegated the interactionist camp to a minority position among sociologists, although a fairly substantial minority.

CONFLICT THEORY

The several social theories that emphasize social conflict have roots in the ideas of *Karl Marx* (1818–1883), the great German theorist and political activist. The Marxist, conflict approach emphasizes a materialist interpretation of history, a dialectical method of analysis, a critical stance toward existing social arrangements, and a political program of revolution or, at least, reform.

Karl Marx
(1818–1883)

The materialist view of history starts from the premise that the most important determinant of social life is the work people are doing, especially work that results in provision of the basic necessities of life, food, clothing and shelter. *Marx* thought that the way the work is socially organized and the technology used in production will have a strong impact on every other aspect of society. He maintained that everything of value in society results from human labour. Thus, Marx saw working men and women as engaged in making society, in creating the conditions for their own existence.

Marx summarized the key elements of this materialist view of history as follows—

> *In the social production of their existence, men inevitably enter into definite relations, which are independent of their will, namely relations of production appropriate to a given stage in the development of their material forces of production. The totality of these relations of production constitutes the economic structure of society, the real foundation, on which arises a legal and political superstructure and to which correspond definite forms of social consciousness. The mode of production of material life conditions the general process of social, political and intellectual life. It is not the consciousness of men that determines their existence, but their social existence that determines their consciousness (Marx 1971:20).*

Marx divided history into several stages, conforming to broad patterns in the economic structure of society. The most important stages for Marx's argument were—*feudalism*, *capitalism*, and *socialism*. The bulk of Marx's writing is concerned with applying the materialist model of society to capitalism, the stage of economic and social development that Marx saw as dominant in 19th century Europe. For Marx, the central institution of capitalist society is private property, the system by which capital (that is, money, machines, tools, factories, and other material objects used in production) is controlled by a small minority of the population. This arrangement leads to two opposed classes, the owners of capital (called the bourgeoisie) and the workers (called the proletariat), whose only property is their own labour time, which they have to sell to the capitalists.

Owners are seen as making profits by paying workers less than their work is worth and, thus, exploiting them. (In Marxist terminology, material forces of production or means of production include capital, land, and labour, whereas social relations of production refers to the division of labour and implied class relationships.)

Economic exploitation leads directly to political oppression, as owners make use of their economic power to gain control of the state and turn it into a servant of bourgeois economic interests. Police power, for instance, is used to enforce property rights and guarantee unfair contracts between capitalist and worker. Oppression also takes more subtle forms: religion serves capitalist interests by pacifying the population; intellectuals, paid directly or indirectly by capitalists, spend their careers justifying and rationalizing the existing social and economic arrangements.

In sum, the economic structure of society molds the superstructure, including ideas (e.g., morality, ideologies, art, and literature) and the social institutions that support the class structure of society (e.g., the state, the educational system, the family, and religious institutions). Since the dominant or ruling class (the bourgeoisie) controls the social relations of production, the dominant ideology in capitalist society is that of the ruling class. Ideology and social institutions, in turn, serve to reproduce and perpetuate the economic class structure. Thus, Marx aimed the exploitative economic arrangements of capitalism as the real foundation upon which the superstructure of social, political, and intellectual consciousness is built.

Marx's aim of history might seem completely cynical or pessimistic, were it not for the possibilities of change revealed by his method of dialectical analysis. (The Marxist dialectical method, based on Hegel's earlier idealistic dialectic, focuses attention on how an existing social arrangement, or thesis, generates its social opposite, or antithesis, and on how a qualitatively different social form, or synthesis, emerges from the resulting struggle.) Marx was an optimist. He believed that any stage of history based on exploitative economic arrangements generated within itself the seeds of its own destruction.

For instance, feudalism, in which land owners exploited the peasantry, gave rise to a class of town-dwelling merchants, whose dedication to making profits eventually led to the bourgeois revolution and the recent capitalist era. Similarly, the class relations of capitalism will lead inevitably to the next stage, socialism. The class relations of capitalism embody a contradiction: capitalists need workers, and vice versa, but the economic interests of the two groups are fundamentally at odds. Such contradictions mean inherent conflict and instability, the class struggle. Adding to the instability of the capitalist system are the inescapable needs for ever-wider markets and ever-greater investments in capital to maintain the profits of capitalists. Marx expected that the resulting economic cycles of expansion and contraction, together with tensions that will build as the working class gains bigger understanding of its exploited position (and thus attains class consciousness), will eventually culminate in the socialist revolution.

Despite this sense of the unalterable logic of history, Marxists see the need for social criticism and for political activity to speed the arrival of socialism, which, not being based on private property, is not expected to involve as many contradictions and conflicts as capitalism. Marxists believe that social theory and political practice are dialectically intertwined, with theory enhanced by political involvement and with political practice necessarily guided by theory. Intellectuals ought, therefore, to engage in praxis, to combine political criticism and political activity. Theory itself is seen as necessarily critical and value-laden, since the prevailing social relations are based upon alienating and dehumanizing exploitation of the labour of the working classes.

Marx's ideas have been applied and reinterpreted by scholars for over a hundred years, starting with Marx's close friend and collaborator, *Friedrich Engels* (1825–95), who supported Marx and his family for many years from the profits of the textile factories founded by Engels' father, while Marx shut himself away in the library of the British Museum. Later, *Vladimir I. Lenin* (1870–1924), leader of the Russian revolution, made several influential contributions to Marxist theory. In recent years Marxist theory has taken a great variety of forms, notably the world-systems theory proposed by *Immanuel Wallerstein* (1974, 1980) and the comparative theory of revolutions put forward by *Theda Skocpol* (1980). Marxist ideas have also served as a starting point for many of the modern feminist theorists. Despite these applications, Marxism of any variety is still a minority position among American sociologists.

IMPORTANCE OF SOCIOLOGY

(1) *Sociology makes a scientific study of society*: Prior to the emergence of sociology the study of society was carried on in an unscientific manner and society had never been the central concern of any science. It is through the study of sociology that the truly scientific study of the society has been possible. Sociology because of its bearing upon many of the problems of the present world has assumed such a great importance that it is considered to be the best approach to all the social sciences.

(2) *Sociology studies role of the institutions in the development of the individuals:* It is through sociology that scientific study of the great social institutions and the relation of the individual to each is being made. The home and family, the school and education, the church

and religion, the state and government, industry and work, the community and association, these are institutions through which society functions. Sociology helps these institutions and their role in the development of the individual and suggests suitable measures for restrengthening them with a view to enable them to serve the individual better.

(3) *Study of sociology is indispensable for understanding and planning of society:* Society is a complex phenomenon with a multitude of intricacies. It is difficult to understand and solve its numerous problems without support of sociology. It is rightly said that we cannot understand and mend society without any knowledge of its mechanism and construction. Without the investigation carried out by sociology no real effective social planning would be possible. It helps us to determine the most efficient means for reaching the goals agreed upon. A certain amount of knowledge about society is necessary before any social policies can be carried out.

(4) *Sociology is of great importance in the solution of social problems*: The modern world is suffering from many problems which can be solved through scientific study of the society. It is the task of sociology to study the social problems through the methods of scientific research and to find out solution to them. The scientific study of human affairs will ultimately provide the body of knowledge and principles that will enable us to control the conditions of social life and improve them.

(5) *Sociology has drawn our attention to the intrinsic worth and dignity of man*: Sociology has been instrumental in changing our attitude towards human beings. In a specialized society we are all limited as to the amount of the whole organization and culture that we can experience directly. We can hardly know the people of other areas intimately. In order to have insight into and appreciation of the motives by which others live and the conditions under which they exist a knowledge of sociology is essential.

(6) *Sociology has changed our outlook with regard to the problems of crime etc.*: It is through the study of sociology that our whole outlook on various aspects of crime has change. The criminals are now treated as human beings suffering from mental deficiencies and efforts are accordingly made to rehabilitate them as useful members of the society.

(7) *Sociology has made great contribution to enrich human culture:* Human culture has been made richer by the contribution of sociology. The social phenomenon is now understood in the light of scientific knowledge and enquiry. According to Lowie most of us harbour the comfortable delusion that our way of doing things is the only sensible if not only possible one. Sociology has given us training to have rational approach to questions concerning oneself, one's reli-

gion, customs, morals and institutions. It has further taught us to be objective, critical and dispassionate. It enables man to have better understanding both of himself and of others. By comparative study of societies and groups other than his existence, his life becomes richer and fuller than it would otherwise be. Sociology also impresses upon us the necessity of overcoming narrow personal prejudices, ambitions and class hatred.

(8) *Sociology is of great importance in the solution of international problems:* The progress made by physical sciences has brought the nations of the world nearer to each other. But in the social field the world has been left behind by the revolutionary progress of the science. The world is divided politically giving rise to stress and conflict. Men have failed to bring in peace. Sociology helps us in understanding the underlying causes and tensions.

(9) *The value of sociology lies in the fact that it keeps us update on modern situations:* It contributes to making good citizens and finding solutions to the community problems. It adds to the knowledge of the society. It helps the individual find his relation to society. The study of social phenomena and of the ways and means of promoting what Giddens calls social adequacy is one of the most urgent needs of the modern society. Sociology has a strong appeal to all types of mind through its direct bearing upon many of the initial problems of the present world.

CAREER IN SOCIOLOGY

A student who becomes interested in a subject may wonder what possibilities it holds for a career. A combination of courses which constitutes an undergraduate minor or major in sociology is not in itself preparation for a professional career as a sociologist. Undergraduate majors and minors are useful mainly as background preparation for other careers. In social work the better jobs demand a graduate degree in social work and a strong post graduate degree in social work/sociology is usually recommended. In the professions like in medicine and law there is some scope for sociology as they give better perspective to the students. Secondary schools/colleges present some demand for sociology teachers.

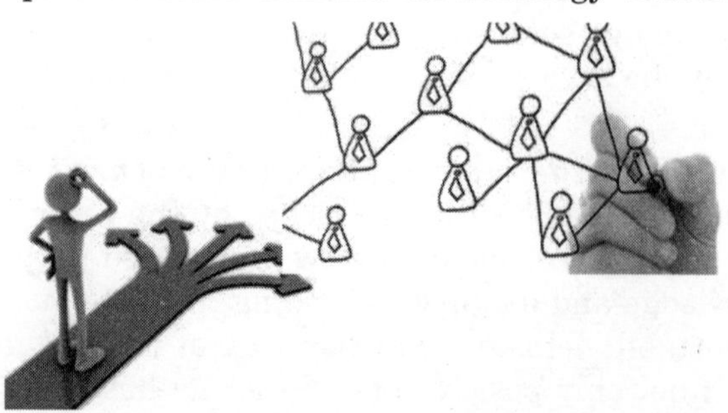

Choice of career in sociology.

Civil service positions often include sociology as one of the subjects for sitting in the examination. Sociologists are employed in small numbers by industry, trade, associations, labour unions, foundations and in fairly large numbers by research organizations in wide variety of positions very often in the administration and conduct of research. Presently emergent careers in many sorts of action programs have developed in recent years like training programs, foreign aid programs and in Humanitarian Organizations like UN.

Basic Sociological Terms

Aspects of the Social Sciences. Social System: *Origin, Concepts and Meaning of Social System.* ***Social Organization or Social Institution. Institutions. Association or Organization. Organization or Association v/s Institution. Status and Role:*** *Ascribed Statuses, Achieved Statuses, Characteristics of Role.* ***Social Change:*** *Factors of Social Change.* ***Sexual Foundations of Society. Power. Class. Status Groups and Honour. Discrimination. Deviance. Social-Conflict. Social Work. Sociology and Social Work. Social Structure. Social Indicators. Types of Social Indicators:*** *Criterion Indicators, Life Satisfaction and Happiness Indicators, Descriptive Social Indicators.* ***Social Perception.***

ASPECTS OF THE SOCIAL SCIENCES

Although institutions tend to appear to people in society as part of the natural, unchanging landscape of their lives, study of institutions by the social sciences tends to reveal the nature of institutions as social constructions, artifacts of a particular time, culture and society, produced by collective human choice, though not directly by individual intention.

The relationship of institutions to human nature is a foundational question for the social sciences. Institutions may be seen as "naturally" arising from, and conforming to, human nature—a fundamentally conservative view—or institutions can be seen as artificial, almost accidental, and in need of architectural redesign, informed by expert social analysis, to better serve human needs—a fundamentally progressive view. Adam

Smith anchored his economics in the supposed human "propensity to truck, barter and exchange". Modern feminists have criticized traditional marriage and other institutions as part of an oppressive and obsolete patriarchy. The Marxist feels that the human nature as historically 'evolving' towards voluntary social cooperation, shared by some anarchists, is that supraindividual institutions such as the market and the state are incompatible with the individual liberty which would obtain in a truly free society.

Economics has used as game theory to study institutions from two perspectives. First, how do institutions survive and evolve? In this perspective, institutions arise from Nash equilibria of games. For example, whenever people pass each other in a corridor or thoroughfare, there is a need for customs, which avoid collisions. Such a custom might call for each party to keep to their own right (or left—such a choice is arbitrary, it is only necessary that the choice be uniform and consistent). Such customs may be supposed to be the origin of rules, such as the rule, adopted in many countries, that requires driving automobiles on the right side of the road.

Second, how do institutions affect behaviour? In this perspective, the main focus is on behaviour arising from a given set of institutional rules. In these models, institutions determine the rules (i.e., strategy sets and utility functions) of games, rather than arise as equilibria out of games. For example, the Cournot duopoly model is based on an institution involving an auctioneer who sells all goods at the market-clearing price. Although it is always possible to analyse behaviour with the institutions-as-equilibria approach instead, it is much more complicated.

In political science, the effect of institutions on behaviour has also been considered from a meme perspective, like game theory borrowed from biology. The "memetic institutionalism" has been proposed that institutions provide selection environments for political action, whereby differentiated retention arises and thereby the Darwinian evolution of institutions over time.

Public choice theory, another branch of economics with a close relationship to political science, considers how government policy choices are made, and seeks to determine what the policy outcomes are likely to be, given a particular political decision-making process and context.

Sociology traditionally analysed social institutions in terms of interlocking social roles and expectations. Social institutions created and were composed a number of roles, or expected behaviours. The social function of the institution was executed by the fulfilment of roles. Basic biological requirements, for reproduction and care of the young, are served by the institutions of marriage and family, for example, by creating, elaborating and prescribing the behaviours expected for husband or father, wife or mother, child, etc.

In history, a distinction between eras or periods, implies a major and basic change in the system of institutions governing a society. Political and military events are judged to be of historical significance to the extent that they are associated with changes in institutions. In European history, particular significance is attached to the long transition from the feudal institutions of the Middle Ages to the modern institutions, which govern contemporary life.

SOCIAL SYSTEM

Social system is a central term in sociological systems theory. The term drives from ecosystem, biological organisms, psychical systems and technical systems. They all form the environment of social systems. Minimum requirements for a social system is interaction of at least two personal systems or two persons acting in their roles. In sociological systems theory there is a controversy what kind of structural elements a social system consists of. For Talcott Parsons it is actions, while Niklas Luhmann considers communication processes which constitute a social system. Though communication is also an action (e.g., speech acts) and on the surface this seems to be a discussion about terms only, the selection of basic terms has theoretical and empirical consequences. There are multiple methods of measuring participation within a social system. Reach, engagement, frequency of participation—all tell something about the success of a social system.

Social system in sociology.

All social systems have commonalities. One is that they become more fun and interesting as more people play and participate. Another is that with each iteration, or version, very quickly the population or interest reaches a plateau.

ORIGIN, CONCEPTS AND MEANING OF SOCIAL SYSTEM

A social system basically consists of two or more individuals interacting *directly* or *indirectly* in a bounded situation. It may be *physical* or *territorial boundaries*, but the fundamental sociological point of reference is that the individuals are oriented, in a whole sense, to a common focus or interrelated foci. Thus it is appropriate to regard such diverse sets of relationships as small groups, political parties and whole societies as social systems. Social systems are open systems, exchanging information with, frequently acting with reference to other systems.

Modern conceptions of the term may be identified to the leading social analysts of the nineteenth century, notably *Auguste Comte, Karl Marx, Herbert Spencer* and *Emile Durkheim*; each of whom elaborated in some form or other conceptions of the major units of social systems (mainly societies) and the relationships between such units—even though the expression social system was not a key one.

Thus, in Marx's theory, the major units or components of the capitalist societies with which he was principally concerned were socioeconomic classes, and the major relationships between classes involved economic and political power. The most influential conceptualisation of the term has been that of Talcott Parsons. Parsons' devotion to this issue has two main aspects.

First, what is called the problem of social order; i.e. the nature of the forces giving rise to relatively stable forms of social interaction and organization, and promoting orderly change. *Parsons* took *Thomas Hobbes Leviathan*, 1651, as his point of departure in this part of his analysis. *Hobbes* had maintained that man's fundamental motivation was the craving for power and that men were always basically in conflict with each other.

Thus, order could only exist in powerfull government. To counter this *Parsons* invoked the work of *Max Weber* and, in particular, *Durkheim*, who had placed considerable stress on the functions of normative, factors in social life, such as ideals and values. Factors of this kind came to constitute the mainspring in Parsons Delineation of a social system.

Thus, in his major theoretical work, The Social system, 1951, he defines a social system as consisting in a plurality of individual actors interacting with each other in a situation which has at least a physical or environmental aspect, actors, who are turned in terms of a tendency to the optimization of gratification and whose relations to their situations, including each other, is defined and mediated in terms of a system of culturally structured and shared symbols.

The major units of a social system are said to be collectivities and roles (i.e., not individuals as such) and the major patterns or relationships linking these units are values (ends or broad guides to action) and norms (rules governing role performance in the context of system values). *Parsons* second major interest has been to make sociology more scientific and systematic, by developing abstract conceptions of the social system; one of this points being that even though Weber placed much emphasis upon normative factors as guiding action, there was in Weber's sociology no elaboration of a theoretically integrated total system of action.

In this way, the attempt to combine in one framework both a conception of actors in social situations and an overall, highly abstract, outside view of the major factors involved in a social system as a going concern. Various points in Parsons' formulation have been criticized. Notably, objections have been made to the emphasis upon normative regulation, and it has been alleged that Parsons neglected social conflict under the pressure of his systematic perspective; i.e., preoccupation with systemness and analytical elegance which blinds the sociologist to disconsensus in real life and spurs him to stress integrative phenomena in his analyses.

However, it is widely agreed that sociologists should explain with some clearly defined conception of what constitutes a social system. Thus, for many sociologists the term social system is not by any means restricted to those situations where there is binding normative regulation; but in order to qualify as social system it must involve a common focus, or set of foci, or orientations and a shared mode of communication among a majority of actors. Thus, on this basis there can be a system of conflict.

SOCIAL ORGANIZATION OR SOCIAL INSTITUTION

Social organization or social institution, indicates to a group of social positions, connected by social relations, performing a social role. It is defined in a narrower sense as any institution in a society that works to socialize the groups or people in it. The common examples include education, governments, families, economic systems, religions, and any people or groups that you have social interaction with. It is a major sphere of social life organized to meet some human needs.

They are patterns of relationships (Role, Status) which is expected to be maintained as per certain rules and regulations, with a focus and functions to be performed, and to bring about social change/order. For example, family, religion, economy and polity.

A social organisation

Social organizations can take many forms, depending on the social context. For example, for family context the corresponding social organization is the extended family. In the business context a social organization may be an enterprise, company, corporation, etc. In the educational context, it may be a school, university, etc. In the political context it may be a government, political party, etc. Commonly, experts officially recognize these five major social institutions that have been evident in some way in every civilization in history: government, religion, education, economy and family.

To give a simple example like productive institutions are dependent on educational institutions for a skilled workforce, educational institutions are dependent on the government for their funding, and government institutions, in turn, rely on productive institutions to create wealth to finance government spending. Sociologists call this institutional interdependence.

Max Weber concluded that in the history of mankind, organizations evolved towards rationalization in the form of a rational-legal organization, like bureaucracy.

INSTITUTIONS

The term "institution" is commonly applied to customs and behaviour patterns important to a society, as same as to particular formal organizations of government and public service. As structures and mechanisms of social order among humans, institutions are one of the principal objects of study in the social sciences, including sociology, political science, and economics. Although individual, formal organizations, commonly identified as "institutions," may be deliberately and intentionally created by people, the development and functioning of institutions in society in general may be regarded as an instance of emergence; that is, institutions arise, develop and function in a pattern of social self-organization, which goes beyond the conscious intentions of the individual humans involved.

Institutions are structures and mechanisms of social order and cooperation governing the behaviour of a set of individuals within a given human collectivity. Institutions are identified with a social purpose and permanence, transcending individual human lives and intentions, and with the making and enforcing of rules governing cooperative human behaviour. Institutions are a central concern for law, the formal mechanism for political rule-making and enforcement. The creation and evolution of institutions is a primary topic for history.

Different institutions

As mechanisms of social cooperation, institutions are manifest in both objectively real, formal organizations, such as the U.S. Congress, or the Roman Catholic Church, and, also, in informal social order and organization, reflecting human psychology, culture, habits and customs. Most important institutions, considered abstractly, have both objective and subjective aspects: examples include money and marriage. The institution of money encompasses many formal organizations, including banks and government treasury departments and stock exchanges, that can be termed, "institutions," as same as subjective experiences, which guide people in their pursuit of personal well-being. Powerful institutions are able to imbue a paper currency with certain value, and to induce millions into cooperative production and trade in pursuit of economic ends abstractly denominated in that currency's units. The subjective experience of money is so pervasive and persuasive that economists talk of the "money illusion" and try to disabuse their students of it, in preparation for learning economic analysis.

Marriage and family, as a set of institutions, also encompass formal and informal, objective and subjective aspects. Both governments and religious institutions make and enforce rules and laws pertaining to marriage and family, create and regulate various concepts of how people relate to one another and what their rights, obligations and duties may be as a consequence. Culture and custom permeate marriage and family. In the United States and Western Europe, a transition from a conception of marriage, as license for sexual intercourse granted by Church and State, to a conception of marriage as a form of contract, freely entered into, has occasioned momentous social and political controversies pertaining to laws and customs governing the freedom of women, divorce, cohabitation outside marriage, contraception, and homosexuality.

ASSOCIATION OR ORGANIZATION

In sociology "organization" is understood as planned, coordinated and purposeful action of human beings to construct or compile a common tangible or intangible product. This action is usually framed by formal membership and form (institutional rules).

"An Association or an organization is a social arrangement which pursues collective goals, which controls its own performance, and which has a boundary separating it from its environment."

In the social sciences, organizations are studied by researchers from several disciplines, the most common of which are sociology, economics, political science, psychology, management, and organizational communication. The broad area is commonly referred to as organizational studies, organizational behaviour or organization analysis. Therefore, a number of different theories and perspectives exist, some of which are compatible,

(a) Organization – *process-related*: an entity is being (re-)organized (organization as task or action).

(b) Organization – *functional*: organization as a function of how entities like businesses or state authorities are used (organization as a permanent structure).

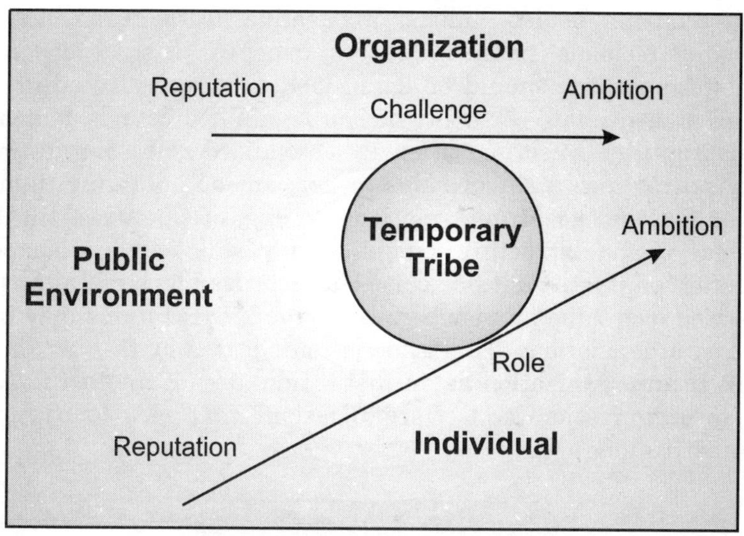

A Pattern of Association or Organization

(c) Organization – *institutional*: an entity is an organization (organization as an actual purposeful structure within a social context).

Sociology distinguishes the term organization into planned formal and unplanned informal (i.e., spontaneously formed) organizations. Sociology analyses organizations in the first line from an institutional perspective. In this sense, organization is a permanent arrangement of elements. These elements and their actions are determined by rules so that a certain task can be fulfilled by a system of coordinated division of labour.

An organization is defined by the elements that are part of it (who belongs to the organization and who does not?), its communication (which elements communicate and how do they communicate?), its autonomy (Max Weber termed autonomy in this context: Autocephaly)(which changes are executed autonomously by the organization or its elements?) and its rules of action compared to outside events (what causes an organization to act as a collective actor?).

ORGANIZATION OR ASSOCIATION V/S INSTITUTION

The term organization is in sociology sometimes used interchangeably with the term institution, as when referring to a formal organization like a hospital or a prison. In other parts of sociology, such as the sociology of organizations and especially new institutionalism (also new institutional economics in economics and historical institutionalism in political science), 'organization' and 'institution' refer to two different phenomena. Organizations are a group of individuals pursuing a set of collective goals with established roles, methods of coordination, procedures, culture and space.

Organizations can include political bodies (political parties, Congress, Department of Corrections), social groups (churches, clubs, athletic associations), economic bodies (unions, cooperatives, corporations) and educational bodies (schools, training centers, colleges). Institutions are ideas about how something should be done, look or be constituted in order to be viewed as legitimate. Institutions can be defined as a "stable collection of social practices consisting of easily recognized roles coupled with underlying norms and a set of rules or conventions defining appropriate behaviour for, and governing relations among, occupants of these roles". Institutions provide structure, guidelines for behaviour and shape of human interaction. Institutions are also characterized by social practices that are repeated over time by members of a group. Institutions may be or not be involved organizations. This issue is complicated by the fact that is one may talk of an organization as an institution, and of the institutions that govern an organization, and of organizations that seek to strengthen or destroy institutions.

STATUS AND ROLE

R. Linton (1936) defined "status" simply as a position in a social system, such as child or parent. Status denotes to what a person is, whereas the closely linked notion of roles denotes to the behaviour expected of people in a status. Status is also used as a synonym for honour or prestige, when social status denotes the relative position of a person on a publicly recognized scale or hierarchy of social worth.

This is the first meaning of the term status, status as position, that we are going to refer to in the following passages. Status as honour or prestige is a part of the study of social stratification.

As described by *Linton*, status is associated with distinctive beliefs about the expectations of those having status, as for example, the status of children. Other common bases for status are age, sex, birth, genealogy and other biological constitutional characteristics. Status is only a phenomenon, not the intrinsic characteristic of man but of social organization. What matters is not what you really are, but what people believe you to be. At times, some confuse the two terms, status and role. Status defines who a person is, as for example, he is a child or a Negro, or a doctor; whereas, role defines what such a person is expected to do, as for example, he is too young to work, he should care about parents etc.

A common method of identifying the status in a social system is to discover the list of status designators, as for example, kinship status typically begins with a list of kin terms and their usage. One other characteristic feature of status, as understood today, is that any person can have more than one status. Generally, no status in any social situation encompasses one person. Also, it has to be kept in mind those statuses and persons are not only distinct concepts but also at distinct levels of analysis. Besides, in sociology it is status, rather than person, which is more useful as a tool of analysis.

Why we should treat these two terms as separate can be argued on various grounds. First, two persons having quite different characters may possess similar observable conduct if they have the same status, as for example, very acquisitive and very altruistic doctors may behave in much the same way. Second, two persons having the same character, very often, have different observable conduct because of having two different statuses. Third, even two persons having similar characters but having two different statuses show very often different observable conduct, as for example, a docile son and a kind father.

Hence, in society, which in reality is a *social system* where interaction occurs between actors, status but not person in important. If we treat person as the unit of such a system we must discover a basic personality structure which is an impossible task. On the other hand, it is easy to comprehend status although it is an abstract concept. Status is the most elementary component of the social system which is equally abstract.

Interaction between two actors occurs not as persons but as two having statuses. A social position is always defined in relation to a counter position, as for example, a doctor to a patient, to a nurse, and to the hospital administrator. In other words, the basic unit of analysis for social system is not status itself but the relation of two statuses. The first writer to do considerable work in this field was Merton in 1957. According to him, there are three aspects of status. To illustrate, Mr. Pandey is a doctor must have social relations with nurses, patients, other doctors, hospital administrators, and so on, that is, a role set. If Mr. Pandey is also a husband, a father, a member of Hare-Krishna cult and a municipal councilor, it is a status set. And the process, by which Mr. Pandey became a doctor, required that he first be a medical student, then an intern and then a resident, that is, a status sequence. Since what is known as status is related to other statuses, the interaction of statuses is a very crucial one. Stable interaction systems depend on the emergence of normative expectations. Once it emerges, such expectations are not created anew every time. Two new actors encounter each other. The idea underlying this statement is that every actor is sensitive to the attitudes others will have towards him. Every actor, therefore, tends to feel tense and upset if he is unable to define the social situation in such a way that the behaviour of the other is predictable.

A more dynamic feature of this series of *social interactions* is the idea that each action implies a status and each status action. Therein each actor reveals how he defines a situation by the way he behaves, and thus provides other actors with cues to their own statuses in the situation.

Although the interaction of statuses is normally satisfactory, at times, confusion might arise owing to status ambiguity. If, however, an actor has more than one status, the attitudes of any two statuses may be either compatible or incompatible with their demands on the person. If two statuses that are activated in the same situation are incompatible it would be difficult for each status occupant to know how to interact with the other, because it will be difficult for him to know which status is the basis of their interaction. Such ambiguities are a source of strain and discomfort and people either get out of such situations or wish that they be changed.

The term *social role* is borrowed by social scientists originally from the Greek Drama. The word person derived from the Latin word persona, which originally meant a mask. Greek actors wore masks when they performed in their drama. It leads us directly to the definition of the concept of social role. The social role is a group of social norms that govern a person's behaviour in a group and determine his relationships with other group members. Put somewhat differently a role is the expected pattern of behaviour associated with a given social status. Status and role are reciprocal aspects of the same phenomenon. Status, or position, is the static aspect that fixes the individual's position in a group; role is the dynamic behavioural aspect that defines how the person who occupies the status should behave in different situations.

Social Role of Mass Media with courses that teach students

Individuals in a society behave according to certain standard patterns of behaviour or roles. These standard patterns of behaviour are determined by the social position or the status which the individual occupies in society because it is these social positions which lay down norms by indicating which individual should observe which norms. In other words, status refers to a collection of norms; and each society classifies its members into a more or less elaborate system of statuses. Each of the statuses involves a role, set of behaviour or action-patterns that people belonging to a given status are expected to perform. One plays as many roles as he has statuses. A given man may both concurrently and sequentially enact the roles of husband, father bread-winner, and football fan and so on. Social roles may be linked to blue-prints for behaviour that are handed to the individual, hypothetically, when he becomes a member of a group. As such these constitute the group's expectations concerning how one would behave. Thus, whereas the status of a person tells us what he is, his role will tell us what he does as a member of a status group. Instead of this fundamental difference between the two, statuses and roles are very closely interlinked. There are no roles without statuses and no statuses without roles. Indeed, there are some exceptions. Though all statuses imply some role or roles, it is not always possible to infer people's statuses from what they do, as for example, two persons, who bear the title of knighthood and thus holding same social positions, might be performing completely different roles. Also, many statuses are wholly or partly defined with reference to roles which their occupants are expected to perform like policemen, poets, etc.

The importance of role was recognized from 1936 when Linton presented the first systematic statement identifying role as a segment of culture. He also held the view that role was related to social status. Much work has been done after Linton in the form of experimental study. Many studies have shown that lack of clarity and consensus in role conceptions is a contributory factor in reducing organizational effectiveness and morale.

A status is simply a rank or position that one holds in a group. One occupies the status of son or daughter, playmate, pupil, radical, militant and so on. At last one occupies the statuses of husband, mother breadwinner, cricket fan, and so on, one has as many statuses as there are groups of which one is a member. For analytical purposes, statuses are divided into two basic types:

ASCRIBED STATUSES

Ascribed statuses are those which are fixed for an individual at birth. Ascribed statuses that exist in all societies include those based upon sex, age, race ethnic group and family background.

Equally, power, prestige, privileges, and obligations always are differentially distributed in societies by the age of the participants. It has often been said about the youth culture in the U.S. because of the high value Americans attach to being young. Pre-modern China, by contrast, attached the highest value to old age and required extreme subordination of children. The perquisites and obligations accompany age change over the individual's lifetime, but the individual proceeds inexorably through these changes with no freedom of choice.

As the discussion implies, the number and rigidity of ascribed statuses vary from one society to another. Those societies in which many statuses are rigidly prescribed and relatively unchangeable are called caste societies, or at least, caste like. Among major nations, India is a caste society. In addition to the ascribed statuses already discussed, occupation and the choice of marriage partners in traditional India are strongly circumscribed by accident of birth. Such ascribed statuses stand in contrast to achieved statuses.

ACHIEVED STATUSES

Achieved statuses are those which the individual acquires during his or her lifetime as a result of the exercise of knowledge, ability, skill and/or perseverance. Occupation provides an example of status that may be either ascribed or achieved, and which serves to differentiate castelike societies from modern ones. Societies vary in both the number of statuses that are ascribed and achieved and in the rigidity with which such definitions are held. Both ascribed and achieved statuses exist in all societies. However, an understanding of a specific society requires that the interplay among these be fully understood. For *Weber* class is a creation of the market situation. Class operates in society independently of any valuations. As Weber did not believe in the economic phenomena determining human ideals, he distinguishes status situation from class situation.

CHARACTERISTICS OF ROLE

Sociologists are agreed to the following characteristics of role. It is believed that when roles are stabilized, the role structure persists regardless of changes in the actors. In some families when the parents become disorganized and become childish, a child suddenly blossoms into responsibility and helps to supply the family leadership. As the roles get stabilized, an individual adopts a given role; and if he fails to fulfill the role expectation, he will be pertained as a violator of the terms of interaction.

The above functioning of the role is determined, to some extent, by the organizational setting which supplies both direction and constraint to the working of the as for said processes. If the role structure is incorporated in an organizational setting, the latter's goals tend to become the crucial criteria for role differentiation, legitimacy of expectation, and judgments of adequacy.

Second, depending on the level of integration with the organizational setting, roles get linked with statuses in the organization.

Third, depending on the extent to which the roles are incorporated with an organizational setting, each tends to develop a pattern of adaptation to incorporate other roles. A teacher in a public school must incorporate within his role pattern, his role adaptations to pupils, parents, other teachers and the principal. Merton describes several mechanisms that are employed to minimize conflict in the role-set.

Fourth, when roles are incorporated with the organisational setting they persist as tradition and formalization. Finally, the place of role is determined by society itself; for, society is based on accommodation among many organizations. Society introduces multiple organisational references for roles, and multiplies roles for the actor. A view from society's perspective shows that roles in different contexts tend to become merged. One example is our tendency to speak of male and female roles of heroic and unheroic roles while seeking meaning and order in simple human interactions. According to the perspective of society, differentiation of roles gets linked with social values. If the societies and the individuals' assigned roles are consistent with each other the roles tend to get merged with social values. A glaring example is our tendency to use age, sex and occupation as qualifying criteria for the allocation of other roles.

At last we have to say that it is an actor who faces the strain; for the dynamic hinges on his management of the several roles in his repertoire. It may come about through failure of role cues, gross lack of consensus and so forth. This situation results in an individual adopting his own repertoire of role relationship as a framework for his own behaviour and as a perspective for the interpretation of the behaviour of others. When the individual forms a self-conception by selective identification of certain roles as his own to be held in his repertoire, the individual is said to develop a sense of personal prestige, which is likely to be reflected in his bearing, his self-assurance and other aspects of his interpersonal relations.

Generally, the concept of role is crucial in all sociological analyses which attempt to link the functioning of the social orders with the characteristics and behaviour of the individuals who belong to that order. A study of roles provides a comprehensive pattern of social behaviour and attitudes. It constitutes a strategy for coping with a recurrent type of situation. It is socially identified as an entity. It can be played recognizably by different individuals, and it supplies a major basis for identifying and placing persons in a society.

SOCIAL CHANGE

Social change is ubiquitous. While earlier social scientists often treated stability as normal and significant social change as an exceptional process that required a special explanation, scholars now expect to see change at all times and in all social organizations. A number of this type of change is continuous; it occurs in small increments and reveals long-term patterns such as growth. Discontinuous changes, however, are more common than has been assumed. By the perspective of individual organizations, these changes are relatively common and often result in sharp departures from previous states such as when corporations are created, merged, or terminated. By the perspective of larger populations of such organizations, relatively few discontinuous changes result in comparably sharp departures from long-term patterns and trends. Even revolutions that result in dramatic changes of political and legal institutions generally do not transform all of society equally. Some previous patterns continue; others are restored.

Cumulative social change must be distinguished from recurrent fluctuations and the processual aspect of all social life. Both sociologists and historians study the latter by focusing on those dynamic processes through which the social lives of particular individuals and groups may change even though overall patterns remain relatively constant. Marriages and divorces are huge changes in social relationships, but a society may have a roughly constant marriage or divorce rate for long periods. Similarly, markets involve a continuous flow of changes in regard to who possess money or goods, who stands in the position of creditor or debtor, who is employed or unemployed, and so forth. These specific changes, however, generally do not alter the nature of the markets. Researchers both study the form of particular transactions and develop models to describe the dynamics of largescale statistical aggregations of such processes.

Cumulative social change

FACTORS OF SOCIAL CHANGE

There are many factors of social change. Some more powerful than others. Among the more significant factors of social change are new technologies, new ideas, economic power, times of extreme crisis, empowering visions, persuasive skill, new forms of organization, and conditions of systemic collapse. But perhaps the most potentially powerful factors of social change are masses of oppressed and marginalized people with a deeply held determination to become the key factors of social change for the common good.

Meanwhile the mass of marginalized people there arises from time to time the "divine discontent" that becomes a vision for social change, the motivation to mobilize, energy for action, determination to persevere, and the steadfast commitment to pay the price for being one of the primary factors of social change. When such a body of people is driven by a vision for social justice they can overcome all other forms of power that resist social change and become the largest factors of social change.

Religious collaboration becomes one of these powerful factors of social change when it is rooted in deeply held values, enables diverse groups with different viewpoints to find common ground, motivates the sharing of resources, promotes patient and careful planning, and builds strategic action with a long-range perspective. As one of the factors of social change, religious collaboration becomes especially powerful when it is embodied in an organization of people who have suffered the consequences of injustice and have discovered that they can become the change that they seek.

SEXUAL FOUNDATIONS OF SOCIETY

Sexual foundation of society.

The sex drive is one of the building blocks of human social life. Although no inborn drive compels humans to act in any particular way, each drive consists of a set of recurrent tension states which impels people to some kind of activity to relieve the tension. Sexuality involves all the feelings and behaviour added to sex through either biology or social learning. The human shares with the anthropoids the biological fact of continuous sexuality meaning that the female may be sexually active at any time. The human female passes through no biological cycles of sexual acceptance and rejection. There are some species whose males and females associate continuously while mating only seasonally. Continuous sexuality therefore is not necessary for continuous association but it is a guarantee that the sexes will associate continuously. This makes continuous sexuality a part of the biological basis for human social life.

Thus human sex drive is notable for continuous sexuality which ensures the continuous association of the sexes, desire for continuity which makes for enduring sexual partnerships, the desire for variety that conflicts with the desire for continuity and remarkable pliability with sex interest channelled through whatever patterns a society has established as normal.

POWER

Power is the "chance of a man or a number of men to realize their own will in a social action even against the resistance of others who are participating in the action."

The role of power.

Power may rest of a variety of bases, and can be of differing types. "Economically conditioned power is not identical with power. The emergence of economic power may be the consequence of power existing on other grounds. Man does not strive for power only to enrich himself economically. Power, including economic power, may be valued for its own sake. Very frequently the striving for power is conditioned by the social honour it entails. Not all power entails honour." Power is not the only basis of social honour, and social honour, or prestige, may be the basis of economic power.

"Power, as same as honour, may be guaranteed by the legal order, but. The legal order is not their primary source. The legal order is rather an additional factor that enhances the chance to hold power or honour; but it cannot always secure them."

CLASS

Class is defined in terms of market situation. A class exists when a number of people have in common a specific casual component of their life chances in the following sense: this component is represented exclusively by economic interests in the possession of goods and opportunities for income under conditions of the commodity or labour markets.

When market conditions prevail (e.g., capitalism), property and lack of property are the basic categories of all class situations. However, the concept of class-interest is ambiguous. Collective action based on class situations is determined by the transparency of the connections between the causes and the consequences of the class situation. If the contrast between the life chances of different class situations is merely seen as an acceptable absolute fact, no action will be taken to change the class situation.

A class in and of itself does not constitute a group (Gemeinschaft). "The degree in which social action and possibly associations emerge from the mass behaviour of the members of a class is linked to general cultural conditions, especially those of an intellectual sort". "If classes as such are not groups, class situations emerge only on the basis of social action."

STATUS GROUPS AND HONOUR

Unlike classes, status groups do have a quality of groups. They are determined by the distribution of social honour. A specific style of life is shared by a status group, and the group itself is defined by those with whom one has social intercourse. Economic elements can be a sort of honour; however, similar class position does not necessitate similar status groups. People from different economic classes may be members of the same status group, if they share the same specific style of life. The way in which social honour is distributed in the community is called the status order. Criteria for entry into a status group may take forms such as the sharing of kinship groups or certain levels of education. The most extreme of a status system with a high level of closure (that is, strong restriction of mobility between statuses) is a caste system. Status distinctions are guaranteed not only by law and convention but also by religious sanctions.

Status groups can sometimes be equal to class, sometimes be broader, sometimes more restrictive, and sometimes bear no relation to class. In most cases, status situation is the apparent dimension of stratification: "stratification by status goes hand in hand with a monopolization of ideal and material goods or opportunities."

Class situation can take precedence over status situation, however. "When the bases of the acquisition and distribution of goods are relatively stable, stratification by status is favoured". Technological and economic changes threaten stratification by status, and "push class situation to the foreground.... Every slowing down of the change in economic stratification leads, in due course, to the growth or status structures and makes for a resuscitation of the important role of social honour."

DISCRIMINATION

Discrimination, in its sociological meaning, involves highly complex social processes. The term derives from the Latin discriminatio, which means to perceive distinctions among phenomena or to be selective in one's judgment. Cognitive psychology retains the first of these meanings, popular usage the second. Individual behavior that limits the opportunities of a particular group is encompassed in many sociological considerations of discrimination. But exclusively individualistic approaches are too narrow for robust sociological treatment. Instead, sociologists understand discrimination not as isolated individual acts, but as a complex system of social relations that produces intergroup inequities in social outcomes.

The definitional expansion transforms "discrimination" into a truly sociological concept. But in its breadth, the sociological definition leaves room for ambiguity and controversy. Obstacles to consensus on what constitutes discrimination stem from two sources—one empirical, the other ideological and political. First, deficiencies in analysis and evidence limit our ability to trace thoroughly the dynamic web of effects produced by discrimination. Second, because social discrimination is contrary to professed national values and law, a judgment that unequal outcomes reflect discrimination is a call for costly remedies. Variable willingness to bear those social costs contributes to dissension about the extent of discrimination.

The broadest sociological definitions of discrimination assume that racial minorities, women, and other historical target groups have no inherent characteristics that warrant inferior social outcomes. Thus, all inequality is seen as a legacy of discrimination and a social injustice to be remedied. By contrast, political conservatives favor a far narrower definition that limits the concept's scope by including only actions intended to restrict a group's chances. For solid conceptual reasons, sociologists seldom follow suit (see Burkey 1978, p. 79). First, an intentionality criterion returns the concept to the realm of psychology and deflects attention from restraining social structure. Second, the invisibility of intentions creates insuperable obstacles to documenting discrimination.

DEVIANCE

Deviance is any behavior that violates cultural norms. Deviance is often divided into two types of deviant activities. The first, crime is the violation of formally enacted laws and is referred to as formal deviance. Examples of formal deviance would include: robbery, theft, rape, murder, and assault, just to name a few. The second type of deviant behavior refers to violations of informal social norms, norms that have not been codified into law, and is referred to as informal deviance. Examples of informal deviance might include: picking one's nose, belching loudly (in some cultures), or standing too close to another unnecessarily (again, in some cultures).

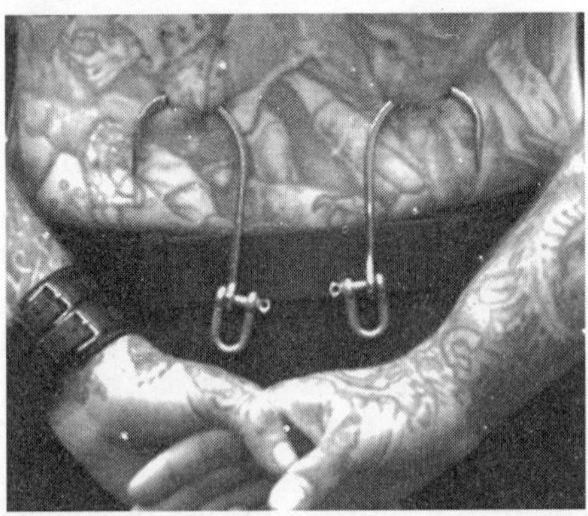

Deviance for its own sake is reactionary, not rebellious

There are many scholars conducting fascinating research about deviance. For example, Dr. Karen Halnon of the Pennsylvania State University has examined how some people exercise informal deviance in the United States in recent years. She has focused on what she calls "deviance vacations" where people of certain socioeconomic status descend to lower strata. For instance, heterosexual white males may become drag queens on the weekend. It is a vacation because heterosexual white males can afford to descend temporarily and then return to the advantages of their true socioeconomic status. Other examples include white hip-hop acts like Eminem and Nu-Metal bands like Limp Bizkit that mimic lower or middle class people in order to use their socioeconomic credentials for profit, despite their true socioeconomic status.

Sociological interest in deviance includes both interests in measuring formal deviance (statistics of criminal behavior, see below) and a number of theories that try to explain both the role of deviance in society and its origins. This chapter will cover the theories of deviance used by sociologists and will also cover current crime statistics.

SOCIAL-CONFLICT

The social-conflict approach to deviance views deviance, as it does with most things, as a power struggle. The power struggle when it comes to deviance is framed in reference to the deviant and the non-deviant. But it is important to understanding that, according to the socialconflict approach, the determination of what is deviant and what is not deviant is closely tied to the existing power structure of a society. For instance, laws in capitalist countries tend to reflect the interests of the wealthy and powerful. Laws that codify one's right to private property will tend to favor those with property and disfavor those without property (who might be inclined to take property). The social-conflict approach takes this idea to the next step by arguing that the powerful and wealthy are able to avoid being labeled deviant by actually changing what is considered deviant so they are not included in that classification. In short, the social-conflict approach to understanding deviance argues that deviance is a reflection of the power imbalance and inequality in society.

SOCIAL WORK

Social work has been defined as being concerned with the interactions between people and their social environment which affect the ability of people to accomplish life tasks, alleviate distress, and realize their aspirations and values. The purpose of social work therefore is to:

(a) enhance the problem-solving and coping capacities of people,
(b) link people with systems that provide them with resources, services, and opportunities,
(c) promote the effective and humane operation of these systems, and
(d) contribute to the development and improvement of social policy'.

A key difference between social work and sociology lies in the emphasis placed on intervention in social work. A social worker expects to be actively involved in the amelioration of social problems, while a sociologist typically focuses on understanding the nature and extent of social issues. Social workers establish a helping relationship with a client system (individual, family, small group, community), using their assessment skills and knowledge of helping resources to identify alternatives that may improve a situation.

SOCIOLOGY AND SOCIAL WORK

After a long time the link between social work and sociology has been strong, although the two fields have grown increasingly distant. There can be little doubt, however, regarding the importance of sociological theory and research for the development of the knowledge and theoretical base of social work practice. For example, social stratification, conflict theory, deviance, organizational theory, community development and dynamics, family studies, occupational sociology, criminology, and life-span theories are only a few areas of sociological theory development and research that have informed and directly influenced both the theory and the practice of social work. Landmark social program evaluation studies were undertaken by sociologists, some of whom were members of faculties of social work, in the late 1950s and 1960s.

Clearly, social work and sociology are related, although there are fundamental differences. Sociologists study and analyze social organizations and institutions. The emphasis has been on theory development, primarily through positivistic approaches, focusing on measurement and design issues. Although the development of grounded theory (Glaser and Strauss 1967) has been a major conceptual contribution in sociology, it has not been the dominant influence. Although there are reform-minded, "radical" sociologists, they are a minority. Sociologists are interested in understanding the "why" of human interaction. Sociology observes; it maintains a detached posture.

Social workers participating in a rally

In contrast, social workers attempt to apply theories of social organization and interaction to improve social functioning. Social workers go beyond understanding social problems in their efforts to improve social functioning; social work intervenes. The goal is engendering progressive social change, improving social conditions, creating more humane delivery systems, and problem solving with individuals, families, groups, communities, and organizations and in public policy. Social workers develop and implement interventions in the form of programs, policies, and services in the context of public funding and demands for professional accountability. The orientation is toward outcomes, cost-effectiveness, and cost-benefit analyses.

There has been and continues to be tension in the relationship. Heraud notes that "the social worker may be able to participate actively in policy making through social science research; there is considerable need for research related to both intended and unintended consequences of social policy . . . there is considerable need in the initial stages of such research for intuition and speculation. Instead of only using the sociologist at this stage, who may be a distant figure, the social worker may have an important role to play". A few years earlier, Halmos noted that social workers could function "as an intelligence agent of the sociologist and of the policy maker, and a trusty pilot of the sociological researcher". Although these attitudes may be antiquated, elements of such elitism remain, particularly in sociology's limited interest in applied social research.

Some attention has been paid to the development of so-called applied sociology. While the main body of sociological thought focuses on exploratory, descriptive, and explanatory theory; modeling; and empirical testing, "applied sociology" briefly emerged in response to the increasing interest in social program evaluation and the limited supply of trained methodologists who could design and execute well-formulated evaluative studies. Thus, applied sociology could provide an alternative, public-policy-oriented career path for sociologists, since the preferred, higher-status university-based employment opportunities were limited.

After completing the last twenty five years, however, social work researchers have become key players in the design, implementation, and analysis of applied social research, particularly through their involvement in federally funded demonstration projects. In this period, there has been a proliferation of journals of social work, including research journals (Social Work Research and Abstracts, Research on Social Work Practice), as well as a range of specialty journals (Gerontological Social Work, Health and Social Work, Child Welfare, School Social Work), which provide publication outlets for researchers and practitioners.

At one time, social work education occurred within the social sciences, frequently attached to sociology. More recently, social work has emerged as an independent professional discipline, forming alliances with a variety of other professions, such as law, education, business, and nursing. Increasing numbers of pragmatic students have been attracted to social work because of the ability of graduates to find employment.

SOCIAL STRUCTURE

Social structure is a general term for any collective social circumstance that cannot be altered by isolated actions and thus is fixed or given for the individual. It thus provides a context, environment, or fixed backdrop for action. The size of organizations, the distribution of activities in space, shared language, and the distribution of wealth all might be regarded as social structural circumstances that set limits on feasible activities for individuals.

Social structure is objective in the sense that it is the same for everyone and is beyond the capacity for alteration by any individual. Accordingly, social structure often is spoken of in the singular and as a thing apart, as if there were only one from whose effects no one can escape. This usage masks disagreement about the exact extension of the term but reflects the intention of authors to highlight abstract patterns as an inflexible collective circumstance to which individuals must adapt.

Social structure, or the weaker structural regularities, arises because of the prevalence of social routine. Many social patterns change very slowly either through unmotivated inertia, through willful efforts to renew or reproduce them, or as a collective consequence of individual efforts undertaken for independent reasons. An image or picture, such as a map colored by the linguistic practices of the inhabitants of geographic areas, will lose accuracy slowly and often would remain largely accurate after a century or more. Such substantial durability, along with the accompanying slow continuous change, suggests the possibility of regularities or even scientific laws governing the phenomena that underlie the description.

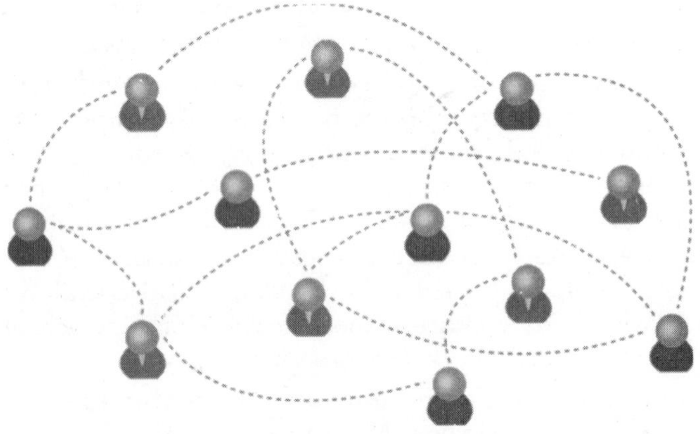

Social structure

Routines endure and structural regularities persist for at least three general reasons. Social life is subject to physical constraints such as distance. Thus, most people live close to where they work or do both at one place. For related reasons, many persons maintain stable residences. Furthermore, many people need or desire the company or cooperation of representative social types, such as those who share their religious convictions, or particular work skills. As usual, one can associate social attributes with geographic maps. It was a central activity of the Chicago school of sociology (Park and Burgess 1924) and gave rise to the perspective of human ecology (Hawley 1986). The specialization of social types and activities in space is subject to powerful incentives that induce similarity in the face of turnover among individuals. For example, ethnic concentrations result in specialized facilities, such as food shops, that attract replacements that conserve the ethnic character. Such patterns often persist beyond the lifetimes of the people who initiated them.

A second source of routine is limited learning capacity or the complexity of many social activities. Linguistic rules, moral codes, and work skills illustrate social capacities whose acquisition requires considerable time and effort. This socialization often requires extended exposure to others who know the routines well, especially when the delicate skills of interpretation are involved.

SOCIAL INDICATORS

Social indicators are statistical time series that are "used to monitor the social system, helping to identify changes and to guide intervention to alter the course of social change" (Ferriss 1988, p. 601). Examples are unemployment rates, crime rates, estimates of life expectancy, health status indices such as the average number of "healthy" days (or days without activity limitations) in the past month for a specific population, school enrollment rates, average achievement scores on a standardized test, rates of voting in elections, and measures of subjective well-being such as satisfaction with life as a whole.

TYPES OF SOCIAL INDICATORS

CRITERION INDICATORS

Based on the premise that social indicators should relate directly to social policymaking considerations, an early definition by the economist Mancur Olson, the principal author of Toward a Social Report, characterized a social indicator as a "statistic of direct normative interest which facilitates concise, comprehensive and balanced judgments about the condition of major aspects of a society." *Olson* stated that such an indicator is in all cases a direct measure of welfare and is subject to the interpretation that if it changes in the "right" direction while other things remain equal, things have gotten better or people are better off. Accordingly, by this definition, statistics on the number of doctors or police officers could not be social indicators, whereas figures on health or crime rates could be.

In the language of policy analysis, social indicators are target or output or outcome or end-value variables toward changes in which a public policy (program or project) is directed. This use of social indicators requires that:

(a) society agree about what needs improving

(b) it be possible to decide unambiguously what "getting better" means, and

(c) it be meaningful to aggregate the indicators to the level of aggregation at which the policy is defined.

LIFE SATISFACTION AND HAPPINESS INDICATORS

Another class of social indicators has its roots in the work of Campbell and Converse in the early 1970s. In 'The Human Meaning of Social Change' (1972), they argued that the direct monitoring of key social-psychological states (attitudes, expectations, feelings, aspirations, and values) in the population is necessary for an understanding of social change and the quality of life. In this approach, social indicators are used to measure psychological satisfaction, happiness, and life fulfillment by employing survey research instruments that ascertain the subjective reality in which people live. The result may be termed life satisfaction, subjective well-being, or happiness indicators.

DESCRIPTIVE SOCIAL INDICATORS

Building on Ogburn's legacy of research on social trends, a third approach to social indicators focuses on social measurements and analyses designed to improve the understanding of what the main features of society are, how they interrelate, and how these features and their relationships change. This produces descriptive social indictors—indices of the state of society and the changes taking place within it. Although descriptive social indicators may be more or less directly (causally) related to the well-being goals of public policies or programs and thus include policy or criterion indicators, they are not limited to such uses. For instance, in the area of health, descriptive indicators may include preventive indicators such as the percentage of the population that does not smoke cigarettes as well as criterion indicators such as the number of days of activity limitations in the past month and an index of selfreported satisfaction with health. Ferriss published a compilation of descriptive indicators for the United States at the end of the 1980s; regularly published national social indicator compilations for other nations also contain numerous examples.

The various statistical forms descriptive social indicators can take are described by *Land*. These forms can be ordered by degree of abstraction from those which require only one or two data series and little processing (e.g., an agespecific death rate) to those which involve more complicated processing into a single summary index (e.g., years of life expectancy at a given age and years of active or disability free life expectancy at a given age). Descriptive social indicators can be formulated at any of these levels of abstraction. Moreover, as described in Juster and Land, these indicators can, at least in principle, be organized into demographic or time-budget based systems of social accounts.

SOCIAL PERCEPTION

Social perception theories and investigations deal with the nature, causes, and consequences of perceptions of social entities, including one's self, other individuals, social categories, and aggregates or groups to which one may or may not belong. The content of a perception can be virtually any property. Individual attributes may include personality traits, behavioural dispositions, physical characteristics, and ability evaluations. Group attributes can include properties such as size, cohesiveness, cultural traits, stratification patterns, network patterns, legitimacy, and historical elements. With some notable exceptions, however, the field of social perception traditionally has emphasized the micro side, focusing on individual inferences regarding one individual or a very small number of other individuals.

Social perception is the best viewed as an umbrella label that covers a range of loosely related and usually loosely formulated theoretical conjectures and associated research. Now-a-days social cognition may be the more popular label, subsuming theory and research indexed under numerous other headings: person perception, social judgment, social representation, schema theory, reference group theory, impression formation, attribution theory, and more.

BRANCHES OF SOCIOLOGY

Introduction. Historical Sociology. Rural Sociology: *Origin and Development of Rural Sociology; Main Features of Rural Society.* ***Sociology of Education. Industrial Sociology:*** *Objectives.* ***Sociology of Law. Human Ecology:*** *Society for Human Ecology (SHE).* ***Political Sociology. Economic Sociology. Sociology of Religion. Urban Sociology. Medical Sociology. Sociology of Knowledge. Military Sociology. Clinical Sociology. Environmental Sociology.***

INTRODUCTION

Sociology linked the family of social sciences relatively at a later stage, i.e., in the 19th century, for it had no independent existence before. In fact, sociology began to emerge as an independent and separate discipline only around the middle of the 19th century. It took almost fifty years before the subject began to assume scientific character that it has today. Prior to the middle of the 18th century, the study of society was dominated by social philosophers rather than by social scientists. These philosophers were less concerned about what society actually like, than what they thought it ought to be like. But in a relatively short period this emphasis was completely reversed. Hence study of society became more scientific than philosophical.

HISTORICAL SOCIOLOGY

It is used as a category to identify social scientific research that constructs or illustrates theory by careful attention to culturally, geographically, and temporally located facts, historical sociology (or from the historian's vantage point, sociological history) exists as a self-conscious research orientation within both of its parent disciplines.

Popular assertions in the 1950s and 1960s that history involved the study of particular facts while sociology involved the formulation of general hypotheses had turned around by the early 1980s, at which time Abrams claimed that "sociological explanation is necessarily historical." While this integrative interpretation of the two disciplines reflects the attitudes of many researchers in the respective disciplines, a few persons remain extremely cautious about the merits of integrating them.

Abrams's claim is true for much of sociological theorizing, and sociologists realize that seminal research in their discipline has been informed by careful attention to historical information. Nonetheless, fundamental differences exist between history and sociology regarding the choice of research strategies and methodologies. Historical research emphasizes the sociocultural context of events and actors within the broad range of human culture, and when examining events that occurred in early periods of the human record it borrows from archaeology and cultural anthropology, two companion disciplines. Historians, therefore, who examine premodern material often borrow anthropological rather than sociological insights to elucidate areas where the historical record is weak, under the assumption that preindustrialized societies share basic similarities that sociological theory rarely addresses. Historians are likely to choose research topics that are culturally and temporally delimited and that emerge "from the logic of events of a given place and period."

In contrast, sociological research stresses theory construction and development, and its heavy emphasis on quantification limits most of its research to issues that affect societies after they begin to modernize or industrialize (and hence develop accurate record keeping that researchers can translate into data). Many of their methodological techniques—including surveys, interviews, qualitative fieldwork, questionnaires, various statistical procedures, and socialpsychological experimentation—have little if any applicability to historians. Interestingly, however, a number of historical sociologists are utilizing narratives to elucidate sociologically traditional issues like capital–state relations and urban development. Given their orientation toward theory, sociologists are likely to choose research topics that are "rooted in and generated by some conceptual apparatus". Their data sources infrequently involve archival searches or heavy dependence on primary texts. Sociologists seem more willing than historians both to "undertake comparative analysis across national and temporal boundaries" and to present generalizations that relate to either a number of cases or universal phenomena. Reflecting these basic differences, social history, which developed out of the historical discipline, concentrates on speaking about lived experiences, while traditional historical sociologists concentrate on analysing structural transformations. Although some historical sociological studies attempt either to refine concepts or rigorously to test existing theoretical explanations, more often they attempt "to develop new theories capable of providing more convincing and comprehensive explanations for historical patterns and structures." When testing existing theories, historical sociologists argue deductively (by attempting to locate evidence that supports or refutes theoretical propositions), case comparatively by (juxtaposing examples from equivalent units), or case-illustratively by comparing cases to a single theory or concept. Both case comparisons and case illustrations can show either that cases share a common set of "hypothesized causal factors" that adequately explain similar historical outcomes or that they contain crucial differences that lead to divergent historical results. In any case, historical sociologists occasionally need reminding that, in both their quantitative and qualitative research, they must avoid the "common tendency . . . to play fast and loose with time" (Jensen), since the temporal dimensions of events have profound implications for the validity of comparisons.

Underappreciated by theorists of historical sociology is the growing number of studies that apply sociological categories and concepts to the emergence and development of historically significant religious traditions. By doing so, these scholars have surpassed the traditional sociological and historical colleagues who limit their efforts primarily to political and structural issues, especially ones arising during the late eighteenth to twentieth centuries. Swanson, for example, coded material on fifty hunting and gathering societies in an effort to connect religion and magic to social structure, and subsequently analyzed relationships between constitutional structures and religious beliefs around the period of the Protestant Reformation. The emergence and early development of major religious traditions has received considerable sociological attention. They include, for example, analyses of early Christianity as a social movement, as a millenarian movement, and as a dramatically expansive young religion during the first centuries of the Common Era. Concepts from sociological studies of modern sectarianism have informed historical studies of Mahayana Buddhism and Valentinian Gnosticism. Weberian examinations continue to influence historically grounded studies of numerous world religions, including ancient Judaism, Islam, and other religious traditions from around the world. On a grand scale, religion figures prominently in the work of globalization theorist Roland Robertson.

The historically grounded research in the sociology of religion, along with the works of Eisenstadt and others, suggests that future historical sociological studies will continue pushing beyond the confines of modern, macrosociological topics and into a wide range of premodern historical areas. Likewise, historical issues likely will become more consciously developed in microsociological studies, and there will appear more sociologically informed historical examinations of cultural development. Nonetheless, considerable macrosociological research still needs to be performed on historical issues affecting preindustrializing and Third World countries as well as on recent international realignments between forms of capitalism and communism.

Sometimes coupled with communism's collapse is the reappearance of nationalism and ethnic violence in various parts of the world. The deterioration of the Balkans in what (under Soviet influence) was Yugoslavia, for example, prompted Veljko Vujacic to develop "a comparative examination of contemporary Russian and Serbian nationalism" by attempting "to demonstrate the usefulness of some of Weber's key theoretical ideas on nations, nationalism, and imperialism." Specifically, he tried "to show how long-term historical and institutional legacies, shared memories, and defining political experiences, played themselves out in the contemporary period, influencing the different availability of mass constituencies in Russia and Serbia for nationalist mobilization under the auspices of new "empire-saving coalitions." Despite being faced with the difficult task of utilizing Weberian theory in this comparative context, Vujacic warned, "there is no need to gloss over the frequently bloody and unpredictable consequences of (people's) struggles with unduly abstract sociological generalizations. Instead, we should theorize our narrative, while giving contingency its place." In essence, narrative accuracy must not be compromised by the demands of theory building.

RURAL SOCIOLOGY

Rural sociology is a part of sociology associated with the study of life in small towns and the country. It is a scientific study of social arrangements and behaviour amongst peoples that are distanced from points of concentrated activity. Much of rural sociology involves the examination of statistical data. Sociologists define rural as those areas which are not urban. Rural sociology, then, contrasts with urban sociology. Urban areas are usually defined in terms of size and population density. The line between urban and rural is quite arbitrary. However, rural settlement patterns tend to be, relatively, small in scale and low in density.

Rural scciology

According to A.R. Desai rural sociology should be to make a systematic, scientific and comprehensive study of the rural social organization of its structure, function and objective tendencies of development and on the basis of such a study to discover the laws of its development.

T.L. Smith says that some investigators study social phenomena that are present only in or largely confined to the rural environment to persons engaged in agricultural occupation.

Such sociological aspects and principles as one derived from the study of rural social relationships may be referred to as rural sociology. Bertrand has observed that in the broadest definition rural sociology is the study of human relationships in rural environment.

Rural sociology is a holistic study of rural social setting. It provides us with valuable knowledge about the rural social phenomena and social problems which helps us in understanding rural society and making prescriptions for its all round progress and prosperity.

ORIGIN AND DEVELOPMENT OF RURAL SOCIOLOGY

Rural sociology is a new branch of sociology with studies being carried out from 19th century. The prominent scholars engaged in rural sociology during this period were—Sir Henry Maine, Etton, Stemann, Baden Powell, Slater and Pallock etc.

The period of 1890–1920 in America saw the rural societies facing many socio-economic problems which attracted the attention of the intelligentsia thus establishing study of rural society as an academic discipline. The appointment of Country life Commission by *Theodore Roosevelt* was an important landmark in the history of rural sociology. In 1916 the first textbook on sociology was published by J.N. Gillettee.

Development of rural sociology

The Second World War caused heavy destruction and damage to human society which needed reconstruction. As a result rural sociology got an impetus in USA. The main concern of rural sociology came to be the understanding and diagnosing of the social and economic problems of farmers. More emphasis was placed on issues such as the internal structures of community life and the changing composition of rural populations than on their relationships with land or the social aspects of agricultural production. Theoretically rural sociology remained caught up in bipolar notions of social change whereas rural often got defined as the opposite of urban. Rurality was conceptualized as an autonomous sociological reality. The identification of rural sociology with rural society has also raised questions about its relevance in the western context where no rural areas were left anymore and almost the entire population had become urbanized.

In response to these critiques of rural sociology a new sub-discipline of sociology emerged that operated largely within the functionalist paradigm and was preoccupied with the study of the community life of rural people. This sub-discipline known as sociology of agriculture focused its attention on understanding and analyzing the social framework of agricultural production and the structures of relations centered on land. It raised questions about how and on what terms the agrarian sector was being integrated into the system of commodity production and about the unequal distribution of agricultural incomes and food among the different social categories of people.

The sociology of agriculture also distinguished itself from peasant studies on the grounds that its focus was on capitalist farming where the production was primarily for the market, not on peasants producing for their own consumption by using family labour. Thus it claimed more kinship with the tradition of the political economy of agriculture or agrarian studies. At the methodological level, historical inquiries became as relevant as ethnographic/empirical studies. This conceptual shift during the early 1970s also helped in bringing sociologists working on agrarian issues in the western countries closer to those concerned with agrarian transformations in the third world.

MAIN FEATURES OF RURAL SOCIETY

Village is a community: The village satisfies all their needs in the village. They have a sense of unity and a feeling of amiability towards each other.

Village is a institution: The development of villages is influenced considerably by the life of the village. In this way village is a primary institution.

Religiosity: Faith in religion and universal power is found in the life of the villages.

The major occupation is agriculture which involves dependence on nature. Farmers worship forces of nature. They have not much amount to spend on agriculture forming. The life of the village is the joint family system.

Family has a strict control and administrative powers over the individual. All the members of the family share the burden of the family occupation. In this way of working together the villagers maintain sense of cooperation among themselves. In the life of the villagers group feeling occupies an important place. They respect the judgment and obey the orders of their elders and the panchayats. Society, caste and panchayat have control over the individual.

SOCIOLOGY OF EDUCATION

Sociology of education is a philosophical as well as a sociological concept, denoting ideologies, curricula, and pedagogical techniques of the inculcation and management of knowledge and the social reproduction of personalities and cultures. In practice, the sociology of education is mostly concerned with schooling, and especially the mass schooling systems of modern industrial societies, including the expansion of higher, further, adult, and continuing education. School organization and pedagogy has drawn upon at least four competing educational philosophies: élitist or Platonic, open or encyclopaedic, vocational and civic (as exemplified by American pragmatist education for democracy and the polytechnic school systems of Marxist state socialism). Sociologists argue that the power structure and needs of individual societies determine which of these is emphasized.

Systematic sociology of education can be traced to *Émile Durkheim's* pioneering studies of moral education as a basis for organic solidarity and Max Weber's analysis of the Chinese literati as an apparatus of political control. But the first major expansion of the subject after the Second World War was associated with technological functionalism in America, egalitarian reform of opportunity in Europe, and human-capital theory in economics. These all asserted a causal linkage between amounts of schooling and the economic advancement of both individuals and societies. They also implied that, with industrialization, the need for technologically educated labour progressively undermines class and other ascriptive systems of stratification, and that educational credentialism promotes social mobility.

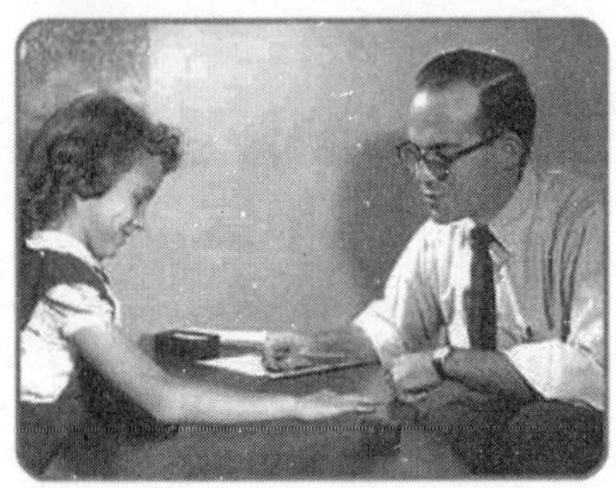

Sociology of education

However, statistical and field research in numerous societies uncovered a persistent link between social class origins and achievement, and suggested that only limited social mobility occurred through schooling. As a result, intense controversy developed over the determinants of the educability of groups disadvantaged by class and ethnic background.

Sociological studies pointed to a wide range of material, cultural, and cognitive factors likely to depress intellectual development. Other work showed how patterns of schooling reflected, rather than challenged, class stratification and racial and sexual discrimination.

That school learning is an unmitigated good was even more profoundly challenged with the general collapse of functionalism from the late 1960s onwards. *Neo-Marxists* argued that school education simply produced a docile labour-force essential to late-capitalist class relations. Advocates of deschooling argued that, for the world's poor, schools merely created institutional dependence on professional educators. In particular, the deschoolers drew on a growing research literature revealing numerous counter-productive effects of human-capital-inspired development programmes for the Third World. An analogous challenge, combining research and ideology, was mounted against human-capital compensatory programmes for the urban poor of the industrialized West. Phenomenological and interactionist perspectives emphasized several important dimensions of knowledge management through schooling—in school classroom interaction; by the professionalizing of the teaching process; through the bureaucratization of school organization; and, at the cultural level, where the links between the sociology of education and the sociology of knowledge are more immediately visible.

INDUSTRIAL SOCIOLOGY

The industrial sociology concerns itself with two basic characteristics of industry and the workplace. It examines the production of goods and services in society, and specifically the nature of the social relations involved in the production process.

These social relations may be of a harmonious nature, or they may create conditions of conflict. The second element is the analysis of the tasks that individuals perform in the workplace to see if these tasks provide for the satisfaction of human needs.

Industrial sociology

Industrial relations constitute one of the most delicate and complex problems of the modern industrial society that is characterised by rapid change, industrial unrest and conflicting ideologies in the national and international spheres. It is a dynamic concept that depends upon the pattern of the society, economic system and political set-up of a country and changes with the changing economic and social order. It is an art of living together for the purposes of production, productive efficiency, human well-being and industrial progress. It comprises of a network of institutions, such as, trade unionism, collective bargaining, employers, the law, and the state, which are bound together by a set of common values and aspirations. Knowledge of such institutions is important if we are to understand every day industrial relations phenomena. These institutions are a social network of organisations, participants, processes and decisions: all of which interact and inter-relate together within the industrial relations environment and even beyond it.

OBJECTIVES

Apart from the primary objective of bringing about sound and healthy relations between employers and employees, industrial relations aim:

(i) to facilitate production and productivity;
(ii) to safeguard the rights and interests of both labour and management by enlisting their co-operation;
(iii) to achieve a sound, harmonious, and mutually beneficial labour management relations;
(iv) to avoid unhealthy atmosphere in the industry, especially work, stoppages, goslows, gheraos, strikes, lockouts; and
(v) to establish and maintain industrial democracy.

The state endeavours to correct, through effective industrial relations, an imbalanced, disordered and maladjusted social and economic order with a view to reshaping the complex socio-economic relationships following technological and economic progress. It also controls and disciplines the parties concerned and adjusts their conflicting interests. In this process, it protects some and restrains others, depending upon the situation.

SOCIOLOGY OF LAW

Sociology of law refers to both a sub-discipline of sociology and an approach within the field of legal studies. Sociology of law is a diverse field of study which examines the interaction of law with other aspects of society, such as the effect of legal institutions, doctrines, and practices on other social phenomena and vice versa. Some of its areas of inquiry include the social development of legal institutions, the social construction of legal issues, and the relation of law to social change. Sociology of law also intersects with the fields of jurisprudence, economic analysis of law and more specialized subjects such as criminology. The legal philosophy "sociological jurisprudence" is an approach to adjudication that views law as a means to promote social welfare, requiring legislators and judges who will make law in light of society's constantly evolving needs and interests.

Sociological jurisprudence involved a three-part program. First, since the purpose of law was to satisfy community needs and desires, a study of the "social facts" of American society was required as a step toward making appropriate law.

Sociology of law

Second, sociological jurists analyzed the actual social effects of legal rules rather than their logical symmetry. Sociological jurists thought legal rules should be considered from the point of view of how they functioned. Law must effectively influence social life in desirable directions.

Third, sociological jurists insisted that every legal case required individualized consideration to take account of the diverse circumstances of each dispute. Law should be premised not on strictly drawn rules but on ambiguous standards, such as "good faith" and "reasonableness." Standards made the prediction of case outcomes less certain, but fairer.

HUMAN ECOLOGY

The branch of ecology that considers the relations of individual persons and of human communities with their particular environment. The study of how the distributions and numbers of humans are determined by interactions with conspecific individuals, with members of other species, and with the abiotic environment. Human ecology encompasses both the responses of humans to, and the effects of humans on, the environment. Human ecology today is the combined result of humans' evolutionary nature and cultural developments.

Humans' strong positive and negative emotional responses to components of the environment evolved because our ancestors' responses to environmental information affected survival and reproductive success. Early humans needed to interpret signals from other organisms and the abiotic environment, and they needed to evaluate and select habitats and the resources there. These choices were emotionally driven. Humans will continue to exert powerful influences on the functioning of the Earth's ecological systems. The human population is destined to increase for many years. Growing affluence will be accompanied by increased consumption of resources and, hence, greater appropriation of the Earth's primary production. Nevertheless, many future human ecology scenarios are possible, depending on how much the human population grows and how growth is accommodated, the efficiency with which humans use and recycle resources, and the value that people give to preservation of biodiversity.

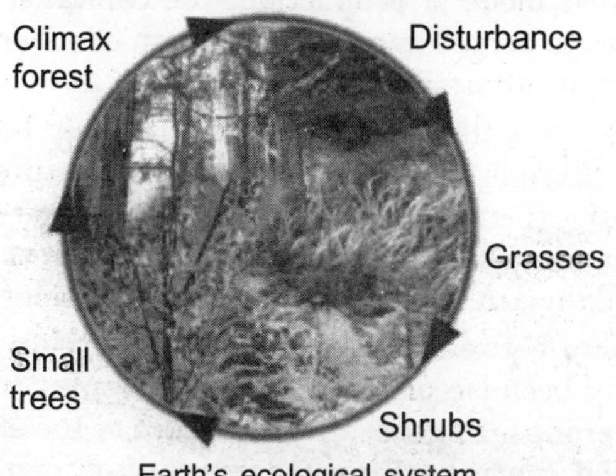

Earth's ecological system

SOCIETY FOR HUMAN ECOLOGY (SHE)

The Society for Human Ecology (SHE) is an international interdisciplinary professional society that promotes the use of an ecological perspective in research, education, and application. These are the following goals of SHE's:

(a) Provide a forum through which scientists, scholars, educators, and practitioners may exchange ideas and information.

(b) Promote the advancement of an ecological perspective in interdisciplinary studies and practice.

(c) Identify problems, discover their origins, examine possible solutions and their implications, and then make recommendations for implementing those solutions.

(d) Look ahead to the consequences of human action on our social, natural, and built environments.

(e) Build co-operative arrangements among human ecology programs and organizations throughout the world.

(f) Facilitate the exchange of this information throughout an international network of individuals interested in human ecology.

The Society holds regular conferences, conducts workshops and symposia, and co-sponsors a variety of related activities to further integrate work among professionals in fields pertaining to human ecology.

POLITICAL SOCIOLOGY

Political science becomes a subfield of sociology. It analyzes the operation of power in social life, examining the distribution and machination of power at all levels—*individual*, *organizational*, *communal*, *national*, and *international*.

In the 1980s and 1990s political sociologists focused on social movements, the state, and institutions. According to Marx and Engels, economic structure and class relations are the basis for all political activity. The dominant mode of production determines who wields power in society. Under the capitalist mode of production, the capitalist class controls the state, which serves to perpetuate its domination of subordinate classes and manage "its common affairs."

More generally, it is the study of the relationship between politics and society. Although there is debate as to the precise nature of the discipline's proper focus, most experts agree that the idea of power, i.e., who holds, wields, achieves, and seeks power, particularly within the state and/or civil society—is a fundamental concern of political sociology.

The relationship between the state and civil society is often seen as a key point of study because of the constant interplay and power struggle between the two groups. In general, the concept of the state takes the form of government and centralized power, most often denoted by its militarized and legislative authority, while civil society often refers to organizations such as businesses, churches, and unions. Also of consideration is the role of the individual and the concept and interplay of power between the state and civil society.

The role of political sociology in a state and civil society

The principal theories within political sociology include social class theory, elite theory, and pluralism. Social class theory is often associated with Marxist theory, in which power is examined in terms of which societal class controls the prevailing means of economic production. Elite theory is a theory in which power is viewed as being concentrated in elite groups and societies. In pluralism, power is seen to be spread and shared throughout society and institutions.

ECONOMIC SOCIOLOGY

A branch of sociology called *economic sociology* deals with the social aspects of economic life. The battle as to which should be given precedence, sociology or economics, is present in these two disciplines also. However attempts have been made to link the two disciplines. One extreme position has been adopted by Marxists. According to them the understanding of the super structure consisting of various social institutions can never be complete unless seen in the context of economic substructure. Thus economic behaviour of man is viewed as a key to understand social behaviour of man or economics is given precedence over sociology. On the other hand sociologists have criticized the economic theory as being reductionist in nature and according to them the economist's conception of man ignores the role of various social factors which influence the economic behaviour. Thus various sociologists have tried to show that economics cannot be an entirely autonomous science.

Economic sociology

A. Lowie considers that two sociological principles underlie the classical laws of the market: the economic man and the competition or mobility of the factors of production. A contemporary of Durkheim argues that since the first principles of economics are hypothesis they can be tested only by a sociological enquiry. In recent times Parsons and Smelser attempted to show that economic theory is a part of the general sociological theory. In actual practice there are a number of sociological studies which are concerned with problems of economic theory. Of late, the interaction between two disciplines has been on the increase. Barbara Cotton analyses the classical economic theory of Wages and presents a sociological analysis of the determinations of wages and salary differences based on British data. Sociologists have explored the aspects of economic behaviour neglected or treated in a hurried manner by economists such as Marx, Max Weber and Hobson.

In recent times there are many studies in the same field like those of Schimpeter, Strachey, Galbraith, Gunnar Myrdal and Raymond Aron. Apart from this contribution; sociologists have also studied particular aspects of economic organization like the property system, the division of labour and the industrial organization.

Economics would lay emphasis on relations of purely economic variables- relations of price and supply, money flows, input-output, etc. Whereas sociology would study the productive enterprises as a social organization the supply of labour as affected by values and preferences, influences of education on economic behaviour; role of caste system in economic development and so on. Thus sociology and economics meet in a number of areas of knowledge. The factors that contributed for this convergence are two. Economists are no longer interested only in market mechanism but also in economic growth, national product and national income and also development in underdeveloped regions. In all these areas the economist has either to necessarily collaborate with the sociologist or he himself has to become a sociologist.

SOCIOLOGY OF RELIGION

The sociology of religion concerns the practices, social structures, historical backgrounds, developments, universal themes and roles of religion in society. There is particular emphasis on the recurring role of religion in all societies and throughout recorded history. Crucially the sociology of religion does not involve an assessment of the truth-claims particular to a religion, although the process of comparing multiple conflicting dogmas may require what Peter L. Berger has described as inherent 'methodological atheism'. Sociologists of religion attempt to explain the effects of society on religion and the effects of religion on society; in other words, their dialectical relationship. It may be said that academic sociology began with the analysis of religion in Durkheim's 1897 study of suicide rates amongst Catholic and Protestant populations.

At the simplest level religion is the belief in the power of supernatural. These beliefs are present in all the societies and variations seem endless. A belief in the supernatural almost always incorporates the idea that supernatural forces have some influence or control upon the world. The first indication of a possible belief in the supernatural dates from about 60,000 years ago. Archaeological evidences reveal that Neanderthal man buried his dead with stone tools and jewellery. Religion is often defined as people's organized response to the supernatural although several movements which deny or ignore supernatural concerns have belief and ritual systems which resemble those based on the supernatural. However these theories about the origin of religion can only be based on speculation and debate.

Sociology of Religion concerns the Practices, Social structures, Historical backgrounds, Developments, Universal themes and Roles of Religion in Society.

Though religion is a universal phenomenon it is understood differently by different people. On religion, opinions differ from the great religious leader down to an ordinary man. There is no consensus about the nature of religion. Sociologists are yet to find a satisfactory explanation of religion.

Durkheim in his *'The Elementary Forms of the Religious Life'* defines religion as a unified system of beliefs and practices relative to sacred things that is to say things set apart and forbidden. *James G. Frazer* in his *The Golden Bough* considered religion a belief in powers superior to man which are believed to direct and control the course of nature and of human life. Maclver and Page have defined religion as we understand the term, implies a relationship not merely between man and man but also between man and some higher power. According to *Ogburn* religion is an attitude towards superhuman powers. *Max Muller* defines religion as a mental faculty or disposition which enables man to apprehend the infinite.

To answer the question how did religion begin – two main theories *animism* and *naturism* were advanced. The early sociologists, adhering to evolutionary framework, advocated that societies passed through different stages of development and from simplicity to complexity is the nature of social progress. The scholars who have contributed to the field of magic, religion and science can broadly be divided into four different types such as:

- Evolutionary scholars
- Fundamentalist
- Symbolic theorists
- Analytical functionalists.

URBAN SOCIOLOGY

Urban sociology is the sociological study of social life and human interaction in metropolitan areas. It is a normative discipline of sociology seeking to study the structures, processes, changes and problems of an urban area and by doing so providing inputs for planning and policy making.

Urban Sociology

Urban sociology is sociological concern with urbanization began with sociology itself, for it was the rapidly growing nineteenth-century industrial cities that first supported those social relationships and structures which inspired the new discipline. Most early sociologists shared the anti-urban bias of much Victorian thought and writing—and a correspondingly romanticized view of rural life. A key concern was the apparent breakdown of community and social control consequent upon urbanization. Like most areas of sociology, urban sociologists use statisticial analysis, observation, social theory, interviews and other methods to study a range of topics, including migration and demographic trends, economics, poverty, race relations, economic trends, etc.

After the industrial revolution, sociologists such as Max Weber, and particularly Georg Simmel in works such as *The Metropolis and Mental Life* (1903), focused on the increasing process of urbanization and the effects it had on feelings of Social alienation and anonymity. The Chicago School is a major influence in the study of urban sociology. Many of their findings have been refined or rejected, but the lasting impact of the Chicago School can still be found in today's teachings.

MEDICAL SOCIOLOGY

Over the past several decades medical sociology has become a major subdiscipline of sociology, at the same time assuming an increasingly conspicuous role in health care disciplines such as public health, health care management, nursing, and clinical medicine. The name medical sociology garners immediate recognition and legitimacy and, thus, continues to be widely used—for instance, to designate the Medical Sociology Section of the American Sociological Association—even though most scholars in the area concede that the term is narrow and misleading. Many courses and texts, rather than using the term "sociology of medicine," refer instead to the sociology of health, health and health care, health and illness, health and medicine, or health and healing. The study of medicine is only part of the sociological study of health and health care, a broad field ranging from:

Medical Sociology

(1) social epidemiology, the study of socioeconomic, demographic, and behavioral factors in the etiology of disease and mortality; to

(2) studies of the development and organizational dynamics of health occupations and professions, hospitals, health maintenance and long-term care organizations, including interorganizational relationships as well as interpersonal behavior, for example, between physician and patient; to

(3) the reactions of societies to illness, including cultural meanings and normative expectations and, reciprocally, the reactions of individuals in interpreting, negotiating, managing, and socially constructing illness experience; to

(4) the social policies, social movements, politics, and economic conditions that shape and are shaped by health and disease within single countries, as well as in a comparative, international context.

The rise of contemporary medical sociology can be traced back to the immediate post-World War II period, when science and medicine were dominant cultural forces, fueling a modern optimism that many of society's ills could be eliminated. Several key contributions during the 1950s gave credibility and spurred scholarly interest in the newly developing subfield. Koos's The *Health of Regionville* (1954) and Hollingshead and Redlich's *Social Class and Mental Illness* (1958) addressed the connections between social circumstances and health status, and were instrumental in establishing a strong tradition of sociological research focusing on the social determinants of health. The finding that individuals in the lower socioeconomic levels of society experience greater morbidity and mortality has turned out to be one of the most consistent of these patterns. Also during this time, a number of sociology's most prominent theorists turned their attention to health and health care. They approached the topic not because their primary interest was in health care or medicine, but out of a generic interest in authority and the maintenance of social order. Robert Merton, Everett Hughes, and Anselm Strauss all studied professional organizations and socialization during the 1950s, focusing primarily on physicians and the process of medical education.

The theoretical work of the 1950s most influential for medical sociology was undoubtedly Talcott Parsons's 'The Social System' (1951). In it, Parsons recognized illness as a major threat to the stability and productivity of societies and introduced the "sick role" concept to describe the social regulation of sickness and explain the mechanism through which individuals are induced to return to productive activity. Parsons argued that because sick persons were unable to perform their expected social roles, they were subject to being negatively sanctioned. On the other hand, if they had not intended to become ill and were motivated to get well, then, according to Parsons's analysis, they could claim and be granted temporary exemption without blame from normally expected role responsibilities. Rather than being held accountable for failure to perform, they would be excused as sick. Parsons's work generated enormous sociological interest because of its analysis of illness and medical care in terms of their broad social consequences and because of its focus on the structure and functions of social roles. His work also expanded the theoretical foundations of medical sociology by provoking equally compelling work from contrasting perspectives. Elliot Freidson in Profession of Medicine (1970) analyzed the dominance of the medical profession, suggesting that power relations in health care were fundamentally contentious. He saw physicians as rising to dominate health care through a process of struggle with competitors in which they prevailed largely because they gained the support of political institutions, limiting the role of competing occupations. In contrast to the fixed roles in structural-functional theory, Freidson argued that illness definitions and illness behavior were socially constructed through a process of negotiation. The debate over structure and agency represented in these early contributions laid theoretical pathways for subsequent scholarship and solidified medical sociology's ties to some of the central issues of the discipline.

Medical sociology became established in only a few sociology departments during its early years, typically in elite universities. It was not until the 1970s that most graduate departments of sociology began to offer medical sociology. Today, sociology courses on health and medicine can be found in nearly every graduate program in the United States as well as in many other nations, notably the United Kingdom and Germany (Bloom 1986). Research funding to support the growth of medical sociology in many countries has come from government sources. In the 1960s and 1970s, U.S. medical sociology expanded in part because social science research was held in favor by the federal government as well as by influential private foundations. Major funding sources at that time included the National Institute of Mental Health (NIMH) and, later, the National Center for Health Services Research (NCHSR).

SOCIOLOGY OF KNOWLEDGE

The sociology of knowledge as a subdiscipline in sociology deals with the social and group origins of ideas. In its brief history as a field of study, it has included the entire ideational realm (knowledge, ideas, theories, and mentalities), in an attempt to comprehend how that realm is related to particular social and political forces and how the mental life of a group of people arises within the context of the groups and institutions in which those people live and act. More recently, its subject matter has included not only a society's authoritative ideas and formal knowledges but also those which operate in the realm of everyday life: informal knowledges.

Sociology of Knowledge.

The term "sociology of knowledge" (Wissenssoziologie) was first used in 1924 and 1925 by Scheler (1874–1928) (Scheler [1924] 1980, 1992) and Mannheim (1893–1947) (Mannheim [1924] 1952). From its inception, it described a field of inquiry closely linked to problems of European philosophy and historicism. In several important respects, this is an accurate description, for the sociology of knowledge reflected the nineteenth century German philosophical interest in problems surrounding relativism that were linked to the legacies of Karl Marx, Friedrich Nietzsche, and the historicists, whose cultural philosophy of worldviews (Weltanschauungs philosophie) was influential in German social science from the 1890s to the 1930s. Each of these developments was concerned in different ways with the determinate relationship between thought and society, between knowledge and social structure. For Scheler and Mannheim, Wissens-soziologie would serve as an empirical and historical method for resolving the intense conflicts of ideologies in Weimar Germany that followed political and social revolutions of the nineteenth and early twentieth centuries and produced warring groups whose battles were manifestly ideational and grounded in conflicting worldviews. Sociology of knowledge would provide a method, outlined in early statements by Scheler and Mannheim, for unmasking the assumptions of political ideologies and indicating their truth content. However much Scheler and Mannheim differed about the nature of truth within relativism, both agreed that truths do not exist apart from historical and social processes. As members of a postwar generation of European intellectuals, they also shared a sense that they were witnessing the gradual disappearance of epistemology and its replacement by the sociology of knowledge as a foundational discipline for all philosophy. As participants in this historical process, they also believed, as did their contemporaries, that intellectuals play a vital role in thought and politics.

The excitement and urgency with which the framers of Wissenssoziologie approached the study of the social origins of ideas has been replaced by a widespread acceptance of their premises concerning the social origins of ideas, ideologies, and worldviews. To borrow Weber's term, the sociology of knowledge was "rountinized" into the established structures and practices of modern social science. Many of the positions advanced by Scheler, Mannheim, and other early writers in this field (e.g., in the United States by Florian Znaniecki, C. Wright Mills and Edward Shils) operate today as working propositions for a range of social scientists as well as for specialists in other disciplines, including the subfields of the history of ideas, social psychology, social studies of science, feminist theory and cultural studies. Even the urgency, expressed by Mannheim, surrounding the problem of relativism as a "contemporary predicament" has been transformed into a commonplace fact. Today, this is certainly the case in the academic world, whereas in the past, the sociology of knowledge provided the occasion for intense controversies about the postulate of the essential "sociality of mind".

MILITARY SOCIOLOGY

Military sociology has been a relatively minor field in American sociology. Few sociologists conduct research and write on military topics, and few university departments offer courses of study in this field. To the layperson this circumstance may seem rather curious, given the sheer size and complexity of the military enterprise and the effects of war on individual societies and on the world order as a whole. The Vietnam War of the 1960s and the Persian Gulf War of 1991 are reminders of the impact that military institutions and operations have on American society.

There is no single reason for this lack of emphasis. One reason may be ideological aversion to military matters. Most sociologists fall on the liberal side of the political spectrum, which has tended to emphasize the peace rather than the war aspect of international relations. Another reason may be that support for most military research requires clear policy applications, and applied research is of less interest to the majority of sociologists. Unlike other social sciences, sociology has not developed a sizable cadre of practitioners who conduct research and policy studies in those nonacademic settings where most military research takes place.

There are notable exceptions. One is the classic work of Samuel Stouffer and colleagues during World War II, The American Soldier (1949). Its studies of cohesion, morale, and race relations among combat units made critical contributions to both sociological theory and military personnel policies. The work of Morris Janowitz on organizational and occupational changes in the military is also a significant exception to the rule (Janowitz 1960). Charles Moskos at Northwestern University and David and Mady Segal at the University of Maryland are upholding this tradition today, and their universities are among the few that offer courses on military sociology.

Role of Military Sociology in Countries

In recent years most of the studies that could be classified as military sociology have been carried out in private research institutes or in military agencies, such as the Rand Corporation, the Brookings Institute, the Human Resources Research Organization (HumRRO), the Army Research Institute and the Office of the Secretary of Defense. Study teams are generally interdisciplinary, with the fields of psychology, economics, political science and management frequently represented. While these studies have a sociological complexion, they are not limited to sociological concepts or theory, and they usually have a military policy focus.

Much of the published work in this field consists of reports from these various organizations and agencies. No journal is devoted specifically to military sociology, although there is an American Sociological Association Section on Peace and War. Armed Forces and Society is an interdisciplinary journal that focuses on social science topics in the military, and Military Psychology, published by the Division on Military Psychology of the American Psychological Association, also covers topics of sociological interest.

CLINICAL SOCIOLOGY

Clinical sociology is a humanistic, multidisciplinary specialization that seeks to improve the quality of people's lives. Clinical sociologists assess situations and reduce problems through analysis and intervention. Clinical analysis is the critical assessment of beliefs, policies, and/or practices with an interest in improving a situation. Intervention, the creation of new systems as well as the change of existing systems, is based on continuing analysis.

Clinical sociologists have different areas of expertise--such as health promotion, sustainable communities, social conflict, or cultural competence—and work in many capacities. They are, for example, community organizers, sociotherapists, mediators, focus group facilitators, social policy implementers, action researchers, and administrators. Many clinical sociologists are full-time or part-time university professors, and these clinical sociologists undertake intervention work in addition to their teaching and research.

Clinical Sociologists have different Areas of Expertise.

The role of the clinical sociologist can be at one or more levels of focus from the individual to the intersocietal. Even though the clinical sociologist specializes in one or two levels of intervention (e.g., marriage counseling, community consulting), the practitioner will move among a number of levels (e.g., individual, organization, community) in order to analyze or intervene or both.

ENVIRONMENTAL SOCIOLOGY

Environmental sociology is a relatively new area of inquiry that emerged largely in response to increased societal recognition of the seriousness of environmental problems. Many areas of sociology have similarly arisen as a result of societal attention to problematic conditions, including poverty and inequality, racial and gender discrimination, and crime and delinquency. Environmental sociology is unique, however, in that sociological attention to environmental problems had to overcome strong disciplinary traditions that discouraged giving attention to nonsocial conditions such as environmental quality. Consequently, the growth of sociological work on environmental issues has been accompanied by a critique and reassessment of core sociological assumptions and practices, with the result that environmental sociology has a somewhat ambivalent stance toward its parent discipline.

Environmental Sociology.

We begin with a brief examination of the nature and evolution of environmental problems, in order to clarify the kinds of issues that are of concern to environmental sociologists. Then we describe the emergence of societal attention to environmental problems, highlighting sociological work on environmental activism and related topics. Next we describe sociology's response to the increased salience of environmental problems, including the development of environmental sociology as an area of inquiry as well as its critique of mainstream sociology's neglect of environmental issues. Then we review some important emphases of the field, including analyses of the causes of environmental problems, examinations of the social impacts of these problems, and analyses of solutions to such problems.

SOCIOLOGICAL THEORIES

What is Theory? Importance of Theory. Sociological Theories: *Conflict Theory, Convergence Theories, Critical Theory, Dependency Theory, Deviance Theories, Diffusion Theories, Feminist Theory, Mate Selection Theories, Metatheory, Modernization Theory, Rational Choice Theory, Social Exchange Theory, Realism, Positivism, Interpretivism, Methodology, Ontology, Epistemology.* ***Theory and Proof: Testing a Hypothesis. Theoretical Paradigms:*** *Salient Paradigms.*

WHAT IS THEORY?

Sociology as a discipline emerged out of a series of debates begun during the period of the Enlightenment between philosophers, scientists and other intellectuals about the origins and nature of human societies. The important thing for us to grasp here is that sociological thinking emerged out of a series of debates. Questions began to be asked during the period of the Enlightenment about what societies are and how they function; about the relationship between individuals and societies, and about social change. However, these questions did not immediately lead to a single set of conclusions. Rather, different perspectives and different ideas emerged in response to these questions and these were often vigorously debated between people holding competing views.

This remains the case today and it is important to grasp this point as it allows us to recognise that the systematic attempt to answer complex questions is bound to lead to different solutions, in other words to different theories of what societies are and how they work.

Sociological theory is closely related to other forms of social theory. As we will see, sociology as an academic discipline emerged in the later part of the nineteenth century. From the beginning, it attempted to define itself against other forms of explanation, including other types of social theory.

IMPORTANCE OF THEORY

In the theory proposed above, the astute reader will notice that the theory includes two components. The data, the correlation between ice cream consumption and crime rates, and the proposed relationship. Data alone are not particularly informative. In fact, it is often said that 'data without theory is not sociology'. In order to understand the social world around us, it is necessary to employ theory to draw the connections between seemingly disparate concepts.

Take, for instance, Emile Durkheim's class work Suicide. Durkheim was interested in explaining a social phenomenon, suicide, and employed both data and theory to offer an explanation. By aggregating data for large groups of people in Europe, Durkheim was able to discern patterns in suicide rates and connect those patterns with another concept (or variable): religious affiliation. Durkheim found that Protestants were more likely to commit suicide than were Catholics. At this point, Durkheim's analysis was still in the data stage; he had not proposed an explanation of the relationship between religious affiliation and suicide rates. It was when Durkheim introduced the ideas of anomie (or chaos) and social solidarity that he began to formulate a theory. Durkheim argued that the looser social ties found in Protestant religions lead to weaker social cohesion and social solidarity and result in increased social anomie. The higher suicide rates were the result of weakening social bonds among Protestants, according to Durkheim.

While Durkheim's findings have since been criticized, his study is a classic example of the use of theory to explain the relationship between two concepts. Durkheim's work also illustrates the importance of theory: without theories to explain the relationship between concepts, we would not be able to understand cause and effect relationships in social life or otherwise gain better understandings of social activity (i.e., Verstehen).

SOCIOLOGICAL THEORIES

Sociological theory emerges out of attempts to provide explanatory frameworks that link specific aspects of the social world to larger processes, thus helping us to contextualise them and to understand them. William Skidmore suggests that most sociological theories are developed out of a desire to find solutions to 'theoretical problems'. For Skidmore, 'theoretical problems' are questions about how we might understand problematic aspects of the social world. For example, how do we explain social disintegration or the maintenance of social stability, the persistence of poverty, the rise and fall of the suicide rate or the birth rate, for example? Skidmore argues that the 'solutions' to these problems usually involve the creation of 'additional related concepts' through which the first problem can be understood.

Sociological theory is developed at multiple levels, ranging from grand theory to highly contextualized and specific micro-range theories. There are literally thousands of middle-range and micro-range theories in sociology. Because such theories are dependent on context and specific to certain situations, it is beyond the scope of this text to explore each of those theories. The purpose of this chapter is to introduce some of the more well-known and most commonly used grand and middle-range theories in sociology.

CONFLICT THEORY

Conflict theory explains social structure and changes in it by arguing that actors pursue their interests in conflict with others and according to their resources for social organization. Conflict theory builds upon Marxist analysis of class conflicts, but it is detached from any ideological commitment to socialism. Max Weber generalized conflict to the arenas of power and status as well as economic class, and this multidimensional approach has become widespread since the 1950s.

For Marx and Engels, a society's conflicting interests derive from the division between owners and nonowners of property. Dahrendorf proposed that conflicts are based on power, dividing order-givers, who have an interest in maintaining the status quo, from order-takers, who have an interest in changing it. Property is only one of the bases of power conflict, and conflicts can be expected inside any type of organization, including socialist ones. In the Weberian model there are even more types of conflict, since every cultural group (such as ethnic, religious, or intellectual groups) can also struggle for advantage. In addition, economic conflict takes place in three different types of market relations, pitting employers against workers, producers against consumers, and lenders against borrowers (Wiley 1967). Gender stratification produces yet another dimension of conflict.

CONVERGENCE THEORIES

The idea that societies move toward a condition of similarity—that they converge in one or more respects—is a common feature of various theories of social change. The notion that differences among societies will decrease over time can be found in many works of eighteenth and nineteenth century social thinkers, from the prerevolutionary French philosophes and the Scottish moral philosophers through de Tocqueville, Toennies, Maine, Marx, Spencer, Weber and Durkheim. More recently, the study of "postindustrial" society and the debate over "postmodernist" aspects of contemporary society also reflect to some degree the idea that there is a tendency for broadly similar conditions or attributes to emerge among otherwise distinct and dissimilar societies.

In sociological discourse since the 1960s, the term convergence theory has carried a more specific connotation, referring to the hypothesized link between economic development and concomitant changes in social organization, particularly work and industrial organization, class structure, demographic patterns, characteristics of the family, education, and the role of government in assuring basic, social and economic security. The core notion of convergence theory is that as nations achieve similar levels of economic development they will become more alike in terms of these (and other) aspects of social life. In the 1950s and 1960s, predictions of societal convergence were most closely associated with modernization theories, which generally held that developing societies will follow a path of economic development similar to that followed by developed societies of the West. Structural-functionalist theorists, such as Parsons and Davis, while not actually employing the terminology of convergence theory, paved the way for its development and use in modernization studies through their efforts to develop a systematic statement of the functional prerequisites and structural imperatives of modern industrial society; these include an occupational structure based on achievement rather than ascription, and the common application of universalistic rather than particularistic evaluative criteria. Also, beginning in the 1960s, convergence theory was invoked to account for apparent similarities in industrial organization and patterns of stratification found in both capitalist and communist nations.

CRITICAL THEORY

The term critical theory was used originally by members of the Institute for Social Research in Frankfurt, Germany, after they emigrated to the United States in the late 1930s, following the rise of Hitler. The term served as a code word for their version of Marxist social theory and research. The term now refers primarily to Marxist studies done or inspired by this so-called Frankfurt School and its contemporary representatives such as Jurgen Habermas. Critical sociologists working in this tradition share several common tenets including a rejection of sociological positivism and its separation of facts from values; a commitment to the emancipation of humanity from all forms of exploitation, domination, or oppression; and a stress on the importance of human agency in social relations.

DEPENDENCY THEORY

Conceived in the 1960s by analysts native to developing countries, dependency theory is an alternative to Eurocentric accounts of modernization as universalistic, unilinear evolution. Instead, contemporary under-development is seen as an outgrowth of asymmetrical contacts with capitalism. The thesis is straightforward: Following the first wave of modernization, less-developed countries are transformed by their interconnectedness with other nations, and the nature of their contacts, economies, and ideologies. Interaction between social orders is never merely a benign manifestation of economic or cultural diffusion. Rather, both the direction and pace of change leads to internal restructuring designed to bolster the interests of the more powerful exchange partner without altering the worldwide distribution of affluence.

Widely utilized as both a heuristic and empirical template, dependency theory emerged from neo-Marxist critiques of the failure of significant capital infusion, through the United Nations Economic Commission for Latin America, to improve overall quality of life or provide significant returns to countries in the region. Dependency theory quickly became an instrument for political commentary as well as an explanatory framework as it couched its arguments in terms of the consequences of substituting cash crops for subsistence farming and replacing local consumer goods with export commodities destined for developed markets. Frank, an early proponent, established the premise for dependency theory; contemporary underdevelopment is a result of an international division of labor exploited by capitalist interests.

DEVIANCE THEORIES

Since its inception as a discipline, sociology has studied the causes of deviant behaviour, examining why some persons conform to social rules and expectations and why others do not. Typically, sociological theories of deviance reason that aspects of individuals' social relationships and the social areas in which they live and work assist in explaining the commission of deviant acts. This emphasis on social experiences, and how they contribute to deviant behavior, contrasts with the focus on the internal states of individuals taken by disciplines such as psychology and psychia-try.

Sociological theories are important in understanding the roots of social problems such as crime, violence, and mental illness and in explaining how these problems may be remedied. By specifying the causes of deviance, the theories reveal how aspects of the social environment influence the behaviour of individuals and groups. Further, the theories suggest how changes in these influences may yield changes in levels of deviant behaviours. If a theory specifies that a particular set of factors cause deviant behaviour, then it also implies that eliminating or altering those factors in the environment will change levels of deviance. By developing policies or measures that are informed by sociological theories, government agencies or programs focused on problems like crime or violence are more likely to yield meaningful reductions in criminal or violent behaviour.

Despite their importance, deviance theories disagree about the precise causes of deviant acts. Some look to the structure of society and groups or geographic areas within society, explaining deviance in terms of broad social conditions in which deviance is most likely to flourish. Others explain deviant behaviour using the characteristics of individuals, focusing on those characteristics that are most highly associated with learning deviant acts. Other theories view deviance as a social status conferred by one group or person on others, a status that is imposed by persons or groups in power in order to protect their positions of power. These theories explain deviance in terms of differentials in power between individuals or groups.

DIFFUSION THEORIES

The concept of diffusion inherently focuses upon process. Diffusion refers to the dissemination of any physical element, idea, value, social practice, or attitude through and between populations. Diffusion is among the rare concepts used across the physical, natural, and social sciences, as well as in the arts. Diffusion is most closely associated with the social sciences, particularly rural sociology, anthropology, and communication. Diffusion thinking offers a logic through which to describe and perhaps explain myriad types of change that involve equally diverse foci, ranging from the adoption of internet technology, to the spread of belief systems.

Work connected to the concept of diffusion is arguably structured as theory. Certainly there is no single, unified, deductively structured collection of propositions, widely regarded by social scientists as identifying the principal mechanisms of diffusion that could be employed across all substantive areas. There are however, many distinct collections of propositions, a few well-tested over decades, that describe different diffusion phenomena in different content areas. Indeed, in the area of innovation diffusion, Everett Rogers produced a formal theory that is broadly recognized, often tested, and that has been adapted to other content areas including disaster research and technology transfer. Part of the problem in formalizing diffusion theories is that the concept does not inherently specify content (rather a framework or process to structure thinking). However, it cannot be examined empirically without tying it to some substance. That is, studies of diffusion focus on something (a technology, idea, practice, attitude, etc.) that is being diffused. Consequently, the research on diffusion that would drive theory building has remained scattered in the literatures of different sciences and as such it is not readily pulled together. These conditions do not facilitate ready assembly of information that would encourage creation of a general theory of diffusion.

FEMINIST THEORY

The term feminist theory is an invention of the academic branch of the mid-and late twentieth century feminist movement. It refers to generating systematic ideas that define women's place in society and culture, including the depiction of women—large questions, indeed. The task of feminist theorists is necessarily monumental. It requires the wisdom, courage, and perseverance that Penelope displayed as she wove and unwove her tapestry to trick the suitors who sought to appropriate her kingdom and so steal her child's birthright.

For many reasons the task of feminist theorists is difficult. First, it is interdisciplinary. Literary critics, art historians, musicologists, historians, and philosophers—to name some specialists associated with the humanities—have all offered powerful and sometimes conflicting ideas about women in society and culture. So have sociologists, anthropologists, economists, psychologists, and psychoanalysts. Although the biological and physical sciences do not usually make fruitful contributions to contemporary debates about social and cultural issues, feminist scientists have posed questions that challenge the presuppositions of their own fields. They, too, have augmented the scope of feminist theory. Indeed, specialists in so many disciplines have offered apt ideas that no one essay or writer can even pretend to outline the scope of contemporary feminist theory. This presentation will concentrate on ideas developed in the social sciences.

Second, because feminist theory has its basis in the current women's movement, it is necessarily infused with the political concerns of the contemporary era. (Any system of arranging facts, including the writing of history, is necessarily influenced by the dominant concerns and ideologies of its times.) The most important of these is the relationship among race (ethnicity), gender and class, both cross-culturally and historically. For even as Americans and Europeans have sought to confront institutionalized racism and sexism, as well as the unequal distribution of income and wealth in their own nations, women in developing nations have posed issues regarding the application of generalizations based on those experiences to their own situations. So, too, historical research has raised the challenge of process—namely, the problem that any particular historical outcome is not predetermined, so that the development of relationships among gender, class and race or ethnicity may vary greatly. Such variations make the act of generalizing hazardous, if not foolhardy.

Third, feminist theory has not merely existed in a sociopolitical context but has been informed by it. This means that many theorists realize that their ideas have been influenced by their own material conditions and cultures. Thus, they have had to confront epistemological issues, including the meaning of objectivity and the way male dominance has shaped notions important to all branches of human inquiry.

MATE SELECTION THEORIES

Social scientists who study the family have long been interested in the question "Who marries whom?" On one level, the study of mate selection is conducted from the perspective of family as a social institution. Emphasis is placed on the customs that regulate choice of mates. A counterperspective views the family as an association. This perspective centers instead on the couple and attempts to understand the process of marital dyad formation. Both of these perspectives generate an abundance of knowledge concerning mate selection. Beginning primarily in the 1920s, theoretical and empirical work in the area of mate selection has made great advances in answering the fundamental question "Who marries whom?"

METATHEORY

Metatheory in sociology is a relatively new specialty that aims to describe existing sociological theory systematically, and also, to some degree, to prescribe what future sociological theories ought to be like. It leaves to other specialties—most notably the sociology and history of sociology and the logic of theory construction—the problems of explaining and predicting how such theories have been, and can be, formulated.

There are two broad varieties of metatheory. One variety, synthetic, classifies whole theories according to some overarching typology; the other variety, analytic, first dissects theories into their underlying constituents and then classifies these constituents into types.

Some typologies encountered in synthetic metatheory refer to the time periods when the theories were originated, for example, forerunner, classical, and contemporary. Some refer to the places where the theories were originated, for example, France, Germany Italy, and the United States. Some refer to the substantive themes of the theories, for example, structural-functional, evolutionist, conflict, and symbolic interactionist. Some refer to the ideologies supported by the theories, for example, pro-establishment and anti-establishment. Some refer to various combinations of all the above differences.

Analytic metatheory is divisible into two broad classes: one in which the constituents of theories are required to have empirical referents, either directly or indirectly, and another in which these constituents are required or permitted to have nonempirical referents. Thus, one sociologist claims our theory should be brought "closer to nonempirical standards of objectivity", while another claims "sense-based inter-subjective verification is indispensable [to sociology]". (This difference in kind of analytic metatheory reflects an applicability of the synthetic-analytic distinction to metamethod in sociology: In the synthetic variety of metamethod, whole methods are characterized as empirical or nonempirical, positivistic or hermeneutical, experimental or participant-observational, and so on. In the analytic variety, such methods are dissected into their underlying constituents, which are then classified as measurement, interpretation, speculation, comparison, test, generalization, specification, deduction, induction, and so on.)

MODERNIZATION THEORY

Modernization theory is a description and explanation of the processes of transformation from traditional or underdeveloped societies to modern societies. In the words of one of the major proponents, "Historically, modernization is the process of change towards those types of social, economic, and political systems that have developed in Western Europe and North America from the seventeenth century to the nineteenth and have then spread to other European countries and in the nineteenth and twentieth centuries to the South American, Asian and African continents". Modernization theory has been one of the major perspectives in the sociology of national development and underdevelopment since the 1950s. Primary attention has focused on ways in which past and present premodern societies become modern (i.e., Westernized) through processes of economic growth and change in social, political, and cultural structures.

In general, modernization theorists are concerned with economic growth within societies as indicated, for example, by measures of gross national product. Mechanization or industrialization are ingredients in the process of economic growth. Modernization theorists study the social, political, and cultural consequences of economic growth and the conditions that are important for industrialization and economic growth to occur. Indeed, a degree of circularity often characterizes discussions of social and economic change involved in modernization processes because of the notion, embedded in most modernization theories, of the functional compatibility of component parts.

RATIONAL CHOICE THEORY

Rational choice theory is typically seen as the use of economic reasoning in contexts that were traditionally the concern of disciplines other than economics, especially of political science, sociology, and anthropology. If we take a more nuanced historical view, however, we might as soon see mainstream economics as the stepchild of the kind of reasoning about larger social institutions, norms, behaviours, and so forth that was central to the Scottish Enlightenment in the works of David Hume, Adam Smith and many others. The genius of these thinkers was to make sense of such institutions, norms, and so forth as the products of individuals acting from their own private incentives. Their concern was that of James Coleman, to explain macrophenomena from microchoices. Through most of the past two centuries, economists increasingly focused such reasoning on explaining the nature and working of the market, for example on prices and conditions for an equilibrium of supply and demand, and the earlier concern with broader sociological issues faded. The great classical economists, such as Smith, Alfred Marshall, and Vilfredo Pareto, were interested not only in the market but also in broader social institutions and practices. Much of their work can readily be counted among the great contributions to sociology in their eras.

Contemporary rational choice theory represents a resurgence of such earlier efforts. The efflorescence of such theory in our time has followed on the development of game theory by John von Neumann and Oskar Morgenstern, Kenneth Arrow's demonstration that individual preferences do not aggregate into analogous collective preferences and Anthony

Downs's analysis of democratic participation. The largest bodies of contemporary work are those on the study of group behaviour, under the rubric of Mancur Olson's logic of collective action and on political participation, which in part can be seen as merely a special case of collective action. Perhaps the fastest-growing area of inquiry today is in the analysis of institutions, much of it focused on historical institutions, as in the work of Douglass North.

SOCIAL EXCHANGE THEORY

Social exchange theory is a major theoretical perspective in sociology. Within this framework, social behaviour is viewed primarily in terms of the pursuit of rewards and the avoidance of punishment and other forms of cost. Individuals engage in interaction to meet their needs. The basic unit of analysis is the relationship between actors. Thus, exchange theorists view social relations and the social structures generated by the ties that bind people in different forms of association as the central object of sociological inquiry. Major topics of study within this tradition of research include the nature and effects of the interconnections among actors and the distribution of power within exchange structures. Power and status relations among actors in different types of social structures are considered key forces in determining the nature of structural change over time. The major exchange theorists all have treated power, structural sources of power, and the dynamics of power use as primary in their theoretical formulations.

Social exchange theory derives from several distinct lines of theoretical work in the social sciences, including social behaviourism, utilitarianism, and functionalism. Major proponents of the social exchange perspective within sociology include Homans, Blau, and Emerson. Within psychology, the work of Thibaut and Kelley bears a strong resemblance to social exchange theory in its emphasis on the interdependence of actors and the social implications of different forms of interdependence. Anthropologists such as Malinowski, Mauss, Schneider, and Levi-Strauss have contributed in different ways to the emergence of this theoretical perspective. In addition, the foundation of microeconomics has much in common with some variants of social exchange theory. This affinity is clearest in Blau's Exchange and Power in Social Life and in subsequent theoretical developments. The breadth of the intellectual heritage of social exchange theory accounts in part for its continued significance in the social sciences.

REALISM THEORY

Realist theory, like positivism, holds that sociology can, and should, follow the logic and methods of the natural sciences. Where realism differs from positivism is in its interpretation of science. Realists question positivism's empiricist interpretation of the basis of scientific knowledge.

They argue that no form of science relies exclusively on observable empirical evidence. There are always aspects of any form of reality that remain hidden beneath the surface of what can be observed. According to realists, the aim of scientific work—rather than looking at relationships between observable phenomena as positivists argue—is to uncover the underlying causal mechanisms that bring about observable regularities.

The idea of medical viruses was originally constructed to explain infections that could not be explained as a result of bacteria or germs. Thus, while the causal mechanisms were unobservable or 'hidden' they were nonetheless real and observable in the effect of the viruses.

Realism has become quite fashionable in sociology. However, like positivism and interpretivism, it has a long history. For example, there were strong realist elements in the work of Karl Marx.

Marx was particularly interested in the analysis of capital accumulation and the process of change. However, he argued that the observable features of capitalist society, such as economic fluctuation, capital growth and massive inequalities, could only be explained in terms of something called the mode of production; that is the relationship between how goods are produced and how production is organised. (However, the mode of production was a theoretical construct that could not be observed directly. Thus, for Marx, to understand how capitalism worked, you had to look beneath the surface.)

The development of a clear, realist epistemology is comparatively recent in sociology and owes much to 'new realist' writers like Bhaskar and Pawson. The key to realist epistemology is that it is theory-driven and non-empiricist.

Realists do not make the clear separation between theory (ideas) and observation (facts) found in positivism. In positivist research theories are tested against observations and found to be 'true' or 'false' or somewhere in between. In simple terms, the 'facts' are the judge of the theory.

Realists do not make this clear-cut separation because they do not believe that 'observations' can be separated from 'theories'. For realists, all data is theory-dependent.

POSITIVISM

Positivism originated as a philosophy of science. Its key idea is unity of scientific method. This means that although the content of the various sciences is obviously very different, the form of all scientific enterprise is essentially the same. Scientific inquiry is based on the systematic accumulation of 'facts' rather than on belief, opinion, tradition or divine revelation.

Many of the early sociologists writing in the nineteenth century, such as Auguste Comte and Herbert Spencer believed that by applying the principles and practices that had worked so well in natural sciences (especially physics, chemistry and biology), sociology could discover the 'laws' that explained how societies worked and changed.

Most modern sociologists do not have such grand ambitions and tend to write about 'trends' or 'probabilities' in particular societies rather than 'scientific laws' of social development of all societies. However, a great deal of research in sociology (and other social sciences) is underpinned by positivist assumptions, so it is important to identify some of the most important ones.

INTERPRETIVISM

The interpretivist tradition in sociology developed largely as a criticism of the dominant theory of positivism. Interpretivist sociologists do not necessarily reject the positivist account of scientific knowledge, but what they do question is the idea that the logic and methods of natural science can be imported into the study of societies. Max Weber (1864–1920) was one of the main influences on the interpretivist tradition in sociology. For him, 'natural science' and 'social science' are two very different enterprises requiring a different logic and different methods.

The key idea of interpretivist ontology is that there is a fundamental difference between the natural world and social world. The social world is meaningful.

As *Schutz*, one of the most important influences on interpretive sociology, argued:

The world of nature, as explored by the natural scientist, does not 'mean' anything to molecules, atoms and electrons therein. The observational field of the social scientist, however, namely the social reality, has a specific meaning and relevance structure for beings living, acting and thinking therein. (Schutz, 1954)

As people engage in conscious, intentional activities and attach meanings to their actions, human societies are essentially subjective realities. Social institutions—the subject matter of sociology—cannot be divorced from the subjective understanding that people (including sociologists) have of them.

Interpretivists argue that the positivist idea of a chain of causation is quite logical in the natural world where a particular stimulus consistently produces a given effect, but does not apply in the social world. People do not merely react to stimuli.

METHODOLOGY

- Methods are the tools sociologists use to collect data.
- Methodology is the study of sociological research methods.

It is also helpful to remember that although research seems to be something only undertaken by specialists, at various times in our everyday lives, most of us do it.

As *Pawson* has observed, the assertion that sociology provides some authoritative understanding of the working of the social world is based on usage of some special tools of inquiry. The 'special tools of inquiry' involve a combination of thinking skills and practical skills. Methodology is the analysis of these skills. The practical skills—involve things like gaining access to research sites and selecting the right methods for the research problem. The thinking skills—that we shall be more concerned with in this section—involve things like excavating the underlying theoretical assumptions on which research is based, subjecting them to critical scrutiny and considering alternatives.

ONTOLOGY

The term ontology originated in philosophy and is concerned with the essential nature of what is being studied. Therefore, an ontological question in sociology addresses the essential nature of human societies. It is concerned with what societies are, what units make them up and how these units relate to each other.

Sociologists who favour structural approaches conceptualise societies primarily as networks of social institutions and patterns of social relationships that are comparatively long lasting. Sociologists adopting this approach try to show the ways that different social structures shape the behaviour of the individuals living within them. Thus the focus tends to be on large-scale, or macro, social processes.

From this point of view, there are similarities between the natural world and the social world. Both are 'external realities' that constrain people's actions in various ways. Just as gravity limits our power of movement, the societies in which we live influence and constrain how we think and act. For example, the wealth of a society, its productive processes and its customs and values shape people's life experiences irrespective of their conscious wishes.

Many of those whose work helped to 'found' sociology in the nineteenth century viewed societies as social structures. For Marx, the key to understanding societies lay in their economic structures. This is known as a materialist view of societies. Marx claimed that social change was caused primarily by changes and resulting tensions in the underlying economic structures of societies rather than by the outcomes of battles or the decisions of a few powerful people, as history books led people to believe.

Durkheim took a different view of social structures. He saw the morals and values of a society, transmitted from one generation to the next, as social forces that regulate people's behaviour and bind them to each other through shared membership of social institutions. Sociological approaches that see values and beliefs as the 'core' elements of societies are called idealist.

A cluster of approaches in sociology, loosely described as social action theories, view the relationships between the individuals and societies rather differently. Action theorists argue that as societies are produced by the intentional activities of people, sociologists should begin by studying individual social action and the meanings people give to these actions. Action theorists sometimes suggest that structural theories reduce people to the mere puppets of societies.

EPISTEMOLOGY

Epistemology is another term from philosophy. An epistemology is a theory that presents a view of what can be regarded as knowledge rather than belief. In more simple terms, it explores the basis for knowledge – how we know what we know.

Therefore, it follows that epistemological questions in sociology are investigations into how sociologists justify the knowledge they are providing of social life.

Again, sociologists have different views on this. A major epistemological debate in sociology concerns the similarity of sociological knowledge and scientific knowledge.

This point of view holds that, as far as possible, sociology can develop methods of investigation based on the logic of experimentation and measurement found in the natural sciences.

On the other hand, there are those – sometimes referred to as anti-naturalists – who argue that because nature and society are completely different from each other, the principles and methods of the natural sciences have little or no application to the study of social life. Sociologists study people and, unlike the matter studied by most natural scientists, people are reflective and try to make sense of the situations in which they find themselves. Therefore, sociology requires a very different approach from that of the natural sciences, one where researchers transcend their subjectivity by interpreting the subjectivity of the people they are studying. In between these extremes there are a variety of positions that accept the principles of scientific inquiry to a limited degree in relation to specific research questions.

However, before looking at these theories, it is important to put them into perspective, as it would be quite wrong to see sociology as divided into three distinct and entirely separate approaches.

- First, few sociologists would describe themselves as a positivist, interpretivist or realist. These are terms used primarily by methodologists and social theorists to try to describe and evaluate the theoretical assumptions underlying different approaches to research.
- Second, many studies in sociology use a combination of positivist, interpretivist and, more recently, realist ideas, just as they use different research methods.

- Third, positivism, interpretivism and realism are very general descriptive terms and there are many different theoretical approaches within the general framework of each one.

For example, some interpretivists (following Weber) believe that understanding the meanings that people give to their actions is the first step towards explaining their behaviour. However, others (following Schutz) argue that sociology cannot move beyond people's subjective meanings.

THEORY AND PROOF: TESTING A HYPOTHESIS

Another key point to note here is how Durkheim's general theory of the primacy of society over the individual generates a concrete hypothesis in relation to the problem of suicide. A hypothesis is a testable statement, which sometimes takes the form of a prediction, about a relationship between two or more ideas or classes of phenomena. In Durkheim's case, we can see that the purpose of his study of suicide is to demonstrate a relationship between social solidarity and individual behaviour. We have already seen how in the natural sciences, theory is often (although not always) developed through empirical observation and study, experimentation and so on through a process of generalisation from particular examples. This process is known as induction. When we come to think about hypotheses we can see this process in reverse; this is called deduction. Here, reasoning is from the general to the particular. That is, from a general statement or rule we move to down to a specific example. The specific example is then demonstrated to be an example of the workings of the general rule. The two are thus directly related to one another.

For example, Durkheim's general theory, developed over a number of studies, maintains that the individual is entirely dependent on society for all aspects of life. The collective entity that we refer to as 'society' gives us our identity and a sense of belonging. If the social bonds are sufficiently robust, social solidarity will be relatively highly developed and the individual will be integrated into the social order. In order for Durkheim to demonstrate this general theoretical proposition, he needed to prove a definite relationship between social solidarity and individual behaviour. In order to do this, Durkheim needed 'concrete indications' of both social solidarity and individual behaviour. Durkheim had collected statistical data about an apparently supremely individual act (suicide). He also noted that stronger forms of social solidarity were provided by the Catholic faith and weaker ones by the Protestant, which is a much more individualistic religious tradition.

Durkheim's hypothesis therefore was 'that in areas of Europe where Catholicism was strong, suicide rates would be lower than in areas where Protestantism was predominant' (Skidmore). Durkheim expected a relationship to exist between suicide rates and religious affiliation precisely because he had derived his hypothesis from a general theoretical understanding of the relationship between social solidarity and individuality.

As Skidmore argues, 'the fact that Durkheim's concrete prediction (his hypothesis) was by and large confirmed suggested that the theoretical scheme from which it derived also was valid.' The apparent fact that suicide rates are higher in Protestant countries appeared to provide empirical evidence proving the validity of the general theory. In this case, therefore, we can see that a very important aspect of theoretical work is that it makes general propositions about the nature of the social world that we inhabit and it also attempts to validate these propositions through use of specific, empirically verifiable examples. The testing of hypotheses is one part of this process.

THEORETICAL PARADIGMS

Theory is a statement of how and why specific facts are related. The job of sociological theory is to explain social behaviour in the real world. For example why some groups of people have higher suicide rates than others?

In building theory, sociologists face two basic facts: What issues should we study? How should we connect the facts? How sociologists answer these questions depends on their theoretical "road map" or paradigm. (It is pronounced as para-daia-um.)

Paradigm is a basic image of society. A theoretical paradigm provides a basic image of society that guides thinking and research. For example: Do societies remain static? Do they continuously keep changing? What keeps them stable? What makes societies ever changing?

SALIENT PARADIGMS

Sociology has three major paradigms reflecting different images of society:

1. The Structural-Functional
2. The Social-Conflict
3. The Symbolic-Interaction

1. The Structural-Functional Paradigm:

It is a framework for building theory that sees society as a complex system whose parts work together to promote solidarity and stability.

The paradigm is based on the idea that:

1. Our lives are guided by social structure, i.e., relatively stable patterns of social behaviour. Social structure gives our lives shape, whether it be in families, the workplace, or the classroom.
2. Social structures can be understood in terms of their social functions, or consequences for the operation of society as a whole. All social structures – from simple handshake to complex religious rituals – function to keep society going. All social structures contribute to the operation of society.

Herbert Spencer compared society to the human body. The structural parts of human body—the skeleton, muscles, and various internal organs—show interdependence, each contributing to the survival of the entire organism. Similarly various social structures, such as the family, educational system, and the economy are interdependent, working in concert to preserve the society.

Talcott Parsons saw society as a system, and sought to identify the basic tasks that any and all societies must perform to survive and the way they accomplish these tasks.

Robert K. Merton looked at functions in a different way:

1. The consequences of any social pattern are likely to differ for various categories of people. For example conventional family pattern provides for the support and development of children, but it also confers privileges on men while limiting the opportunities for women.
2. People rarely perceive all the functions of a social structure. He therefore distinguishes between manifest functions–the recognized and intended consequences of a social pattern–and latent functions–the largely unrecognized and unintended consequences. Manifest functions of educational institution–imparting knowledge, preparing young people for job market—Latent function could be keeping so many young people out of the labor market.
3. Not all the effects of any social system benefit everyone in society. There could be social dysfunctions, i.e., undesirable consequences for the operation of society. Not everyone agrees on what is beneficial and what is harmful. Is women empowerment functional?

Critical Evaluation

The chief characteristic of structural-functional paradigm is its vision of society as orderly, stable, and comprehensible. Goal is to figure out 'What makes the society tick.'

How can we assume that society has a "natural" order? If that is natural then there should be no variation in the social pattern of people at different places, and there should be no change over time.

2. The Social-Conflict Paradigm

The social conflict framework sees society as an arena of inequality that generates conflict and change. Unlike structural-functional paradigm, which emphasizes solidarity, this approach highlights division based on inequality.

Factors like gender, ethnicity, social class, and age are linked to the unequal distribution of money, power, education and social prestige.

A conflict analysis suggests that, rather than promoting the operation of society as a whole, social structure typically benefits some people while depriving the others. There is an on-going conflict between dominant and disadvantaged categories of people–rich and poor, white and the colored, men in relation to women.

- People on top strive to protect their privileges, while the disadvantaged try to gain more resources for themselves.
- Schooling perpetuates inequality by reproducing the class structure in every new generation.
- Who goes to school, to college, to university, to vocational training institution?

How do the structural-functionalists look at the above analysis? Structural-functionalists assert that such tracking benefits all of society because students receive training that is appropriate to their academic abilities.

Conflict sociologists counter the argument saying that 'tracking' often has less to do with talent than with a student's social background, so that the well to do are placed in higher tracks and the poor children end up in lower tracks.

Young people from privileged families gain the best schooling, and, when they leave college, they pursue prestigious, higher income careers. That is not the case for children from poor families. In both cases the social standing of one generation is passed on to another, with the schools justifying the practice in terms of individual merit.

Conflict sociologists not only try to understand the inequality in society but also try to influence to reduce inequality in society. They want to change the system.

Critical Evaluation

This school of thought has a large critical evaluation, which are as follows:

- This paradigm highlights inequality and division in society, but it largely ignores how shared values and interdependence can generate unity among members of a society.
- To a great extent, this paradigm has political goals, therefore it cannot claim objectivity.
- Conflict theorists counter that all approaches have political consequences.

3. The Symbolic-Interaction Paradigm

The structural-functionalists and social-conflict paradigms share a macro-level orientation, meaning a focus on broad social structures that shape society as a whole. The symbolic interaction paradigm provides a micro-level orientation, meaning a focus on social interaction in specific situations. The symbolic-interaction paradigm sees society as the product of the everyday interactions of individuals. "Society" amounts to the shared reality that people construct as they interact with one another.

- Human beings are the creatures who live in the world of symbols, attaching meaning to virtually everything.

- Symbols attached to reality (material or nonmaterial).
- Meanings attached to symbols.
- Symbols are the means of communication.
- Symbols as the basis of social life.
    - Without symbols we would have no mechanism of perceiving others in terms of relationships (aunts and uncles, employers and teachers). Only because we have these symbols like aunts and uncles that define for us what such relationships entail. Compare these symbols with symbols like boyfriend or girlfriend; you will see that the relationships change quite differently.
    - Without symbols we cannot coordinate our actions with others; we would be unable to plan for a future date, time, and place. Without symbols there will be no books, movies, no schools, no hospitals, and no governments. Symbols make social life possible.
    - Even self is symbol, for it consists of the ideas that we have about who we are. May be changing.

As we interact with others we may constantly adjust our views of the self, based on how we interpret the reactions of others. We define our realities. The definitions could vary. The definitions could be subjective. For example who is a homeless? Who is a police officer – a provider of security or creator of anxiety. It has a subjective meaning.

Max Weber is an exponent of this paradigm. He emphasized the need to understand any social setting from the point of view of the people in it. A person is the product of his experiences with others.

Critical Evaluation

Without denying the usefulness of abstract social structures like the family, and social class this paradigm reminds us that society basically amounts to people interacting. How individuals experience society. This approach ignores the widespread effects of culture as well as factors like social class, gender, and race.

SOCIOLOGICAL RESEARCH

***Introduction:** Influences on Researchers' Choices of Design and Method. **Aims and Criteria in Research:** From Subjectivity to Objectivity, Standardisation, Reliability, Transparency, Validity. **The Study of Social Relationships. Social Institutions. Research Design:** Concepts and Conceptual Thinking, Descriptive and Explanatory Research Designs, Quantitative and Qualitative Research Designs. **The Expected and the Unexpected in Social Research. Major Research Designs in Sociology:** Surveys Method, Sampling Method, Longitudinal Approaches, Experimental and Evaluative Research. **Ethnography. Research Methods for Collecting Data:** Primary Research Methods, Semi-structured Interview, Unstructured Interviews, Limits of All Interview Methods, Observational Methods, Comparative Research.*

INTRODUCTION

The discipline of sociology is based on the claim that sociologists offer some kind of expert understanding of social life. To evaluate this claim, we need to know how this 'expert knowledge' is generated, how well it stands up to critical scrutiny and what assumptions it makes about the nature of the social world. This is why understanding social research is such a central part of understanding sociology.

The discipline of sociology is based on the claim that sociologists offer some kind of expert understanding of social life. To evaluate this claim, we need to know how this 'expert knowledge' is generated, how well it stands up to critical scrutiny and what assumptions it makes about the nature of the social world. This is why understanding social research is such a central part of understanding sociology.

The process of undertaking sociological research is broadly similar. There are usually three key stages:

1. *Formulation and design:* research begins with questions that then need to be translated into a researchable form.
2. *Data collection:* the research has to be organised and data collected through various research strategies and methods.
3. *Data interpretation:* the information that is collected has to be presented, analysed and related to the question that is being investigated.

It is clear that sociological research also involves a number of particular decisions, such as working out how research questions can be translated into a researchable project, deciding how data is to be collected and organised, and thinking about how it is to be interpreted.

Doing sociological research, then, is a reflexive process. It involves the researcher not only looking out at the part of the social world being studied, but also looking inwards and continually reflecting on the processes by which the research is being undertaken. In planning and carrying out research, sociologists are confronted by a number of choices and each choice brings advantages and limitations. The analysis of these choices and their consequences is what we mean by methodology.

INFLUENCES ON RESEARCHERS' CHOICES OF DESIGN AND METHOD

Some of the most important influences on researchers' choices of design and method are:

- *The nature of the problem being investigated*: Some research techniques are more appropriate than others to particular research problems. For example, researching the distribution of income in a whole society will require a different research design and different methods from a project exploring how a particular organisation works.
- *Practical considerations*: The researcher must work out what is possible in terms of such things as the amount of time and money available, access to sources of data and the requirements of those funding the research.
- *Existing research*: Much research is undertaken to extend, check or question existing work in the field.
- *Theoretical considerations:* Sociologists have different theoretical ideas about the nature of human societies and the best ways of generating knowledge about them, and these theoretical preferences influence their choice of research methods.

The consequence of these choices and constraints is that there is no single 'correct way' of doing sociological research. Rather there are a number of different ways, each with their benefits and costs and their advocates and critics. Therefore, understanding sociological research, and giving good answers to 'theory and methods' questions, involves being able to compare and contrast different approaches.

AIMS AND CRITERIA IN RESEARCH

FROM SUBJECTIVITY TO OBJECTIVITY

The general aim of sociological research (and indeed all research) is to try to move from a subjective understanding to a more objective understanding of what we are studying. Subjectivity and objectivity are very important terms in sociology.

Subjective knowledge is literally knowledge belonging to the subject. It refers to individual's perceptions, including their values, opinions and preferences. There is nothing 'wrong' with subjective knowledge and understanding. Everyone – including the sociologist – draws on their subjective understanding to make sense of the world around them. However, to justify itself as an academic subject, sociologists have to provide knowledge of societies that is something more than their own opinions and prejudices. This is where objectivity comes in.

Objective knowledge is knowledge that is more than personal perceptions; it is knowledge that is free from bias, opinion and prejudice. The scientific laboratory experiment is typically seen as the ideal form of generating objective knowledge. Scientists are emotionally detached from the objects of their research, sociologists should aim to do the same.

However, even if sociology cannot be truly objective, as most sociologists believe, objectivity remains a goal of sociology and research has to provide an understanding of societies that goes beyond mere subjectivity.

The aim of social research is to move from a subjective understanding to a more objective understanding of how societies work. However, this raises the question of how researchers try to be more objective.

STANDARDISATION

Your mother is complaining about your behaviour again and she brings in evidence to support her complaints. She tells you that you are not working hard enough at college and you are rude to your father. All that she says, may be true, but her use of evidence is highly selective. She only refers to things that support the point she is making. This is typical of the way we behave in everyday life. We tend to look mainly for things that confirm what we believe.

Sociological research cannot (or certainly should not) be carried out in this way. If sociologists simply grab at evidence that supports their favourite point of view then their accounts of social life would be highly subjective. One way of trying to avoid such subjectivity is to standardise the collection and organisation of data by making research as systematic and consistent as possible. This means that rather than having their views consistently confirmed by the evidence, sociologists may be surprised by what they discover, even to the point of having their favoured theories challenged or overturned.

We can illustrate this point from our earlier example of studying sociology students. The researcher will have to make compromises when doing research. If we use a questionnaire and give it to all students taking sociology, the data collection is standardised: that is, it is done in a consistent fashion. This means there is less opportunity for the researchers simply to take data that suits their own point of view. So if, for example, a majority of students tell me that they dislike sociology and find it 'very boring' one is stuck with the results, even though his subjective view is that sociology is a fascinating subject and they should all love it.

However, supposing we choose an alternative method and, instead of giving out questionnaires, we observe sociology classes and talk informally to students. Here, even if we record our observations as systematically as we can, the data collection will be less standardised than the questionnaire data. We won't be able to remember everything and we can't even write down everything we do remember. Therefore, there is more risk of our subjective view influencing the data.

However, although this observational approach does not do so well in terms of the criterion of standardisation, it does not necessarily make it the 'wrong' choice. It may well bring benefits, such as knowledge of how students actually behave in class, that would not be obtained by a standardised questionnaire-based study.

So, just as a person choosing friends may have to sacrifice one desired criterion, such as kindness, in order to obtain others, such as a sense of humour and lots of money, sociologists may also have to compromise on key research criteria.

RELIABILITY

Reliability is concerned with the question of whether research is repeatable and is most commonly used in relation to quantitative research. The reliability of a test employed in research is the extent to which repeated measurements using this test (under the same conditions) produce the same results. This criterion is important because people have more confidence in research that can be repeated and the results checked out.

If the research is repeatable and produces the same results each time, this suggests that researchers have been able to detach themselves from the object of their research – indicating objectivity. Replication, which is very close to reliability, is when one researcher chooses to repeat the research of another. There are many reasons for doing this. The findings of the original research may be unusual, or a researcher may want to find out if the same results still apply after a time lag.

TRANSPARENCY

Transparency means that a researcher has shown exactly how the research was done. For example, if interview methods were used, the research methods are transparent if the researcher has provided the questions, explained how they were asked, indicated the numbers of people who replied and so on. If possible, the transcriptions or tape recordings should also be available. It is now common practice for many researchers to leave the various records of their work in research archives for other researchers to examine and possibly replicate. For research to be reliable and replicable the research methods must be transparent.

VALIDITY

The textbooks and your Statistics unit will list many forms of validity but in everyday language something is valid if it is believed to be reasonable or well founded. In sociology it has a slightly more specific meaning. The issue of validity is concerned with the correspondence between a piece of data and the conclusions that are drawn from it. In other words, how justified are we in drawing these conclusions from this data?

From this basis we can distinguish between *construct validity*, *internal validity* and *ecological validity*.

Construct validity is concerned with whether data represents what it is supposed to represent. At first reading, this may seem a strange criterion. How can data not be what it is? After all, facts are facts, aren't they? The data that sociologists (and other researchers) collect is not simply 'discovered'. Rather, it is constructed through the ideas being used by the researcher, and these ideas are open to question.

Internal validity is concerned with whether the conclusion that is drawn about the relationship between two or more different things is justified. For example, a researcher may claim that (a) causes (b). However, the relationship between (a) and (b) may be the result of something else.

Ecological validity is the criterion of ecological validity is concerned with whether the results of social scientific research are actually applicable to the reality of people's everyday lives. This is a criterion that is much more specific to sociology than to the other social sciences.

THE STUDY OF SOCIAL RELATIONSHIPS

The word sociology comes from a combination of the Latin *socius* (meaning 'companion') and the Greek logos (meaning 'the study of'), so the word literally means the study of companionship, or social relations.

Sociologists are primarily interested in all that happens to people in terms of their relationships with others. These may be:

- *Personal relationships* with people we know well, such as family members, friends and people we know at work or college

- *Impersonal relationships*, such as those we have with people who serve us in shops, take away our rubbish or drive the taxi we are in
- *Indirect relations* with people we neither know nor see, but whose actions influence our lives.

Sociologists are interested in the study of individuals' personalities and behaviour but they are also interested in how they relate to other people. Therefore, the word relationship is very important in sociology. All sociology is about relationships of one sort or another: for example, relationships between different societies, between different parts of a society and between individuals and societies.

The fact that sociology is about social relationships that can take many different forms means that its scope is very wide. It can range from things that affect large parts of the world over long periods of time, such as industrialisation or globalisation, to the study of specific social organisations, such as schools or families, right down to two people having a brief conversation in an elevator.

Thus it is very difficult to give a precise definition of sociology because it operates at different levels. However, the key idea in all sociological research is that people's lives and behaviour cannot be understood apart from the social contexts in which they participate, directly or indirectly.

SOCIAL INSTITUTIONS

Social relationships are rarely random. Normally they are organised in various ways. Sociologists refer to these patterns of behaviour as social institutions. Types of family life, education and religious practice are examples of social institutions, where behaviour tends to be regular or patterned. What we loosely refer to as a 'society' is actually a complex of many social institutions. In contemporary industrial societies we find, for example, political, family, economic, educational, legal and religious institutions. Although these institutions seem to be separate and distinct they are also related to each other in various ways.

To give a simple example: productive institutions are dependent on educational institutions for a skilled workforce, educational institutions are dependent on the government for their funding and government institutions, in turn, rely on productive institutions to create the wealth to finance government spending. Sociologists call this institutional interdependence.

RESEARCH DESIGN

It's very rare just to drop everything and dash off on holiday. Holidays are usually planned in advance. Similarly a sociologist can't just suddenly start doing research. Research journeys also need to be planned and organised in advance. Although doing sociological research never felt much like a holiday to me, there are similarities between going on holiday and doing research. Both of them usually involve going on a 'journey' to somewhere different. Holidays begin with a desire to take time out and go somewhere, and research begins with the desire to find something out.

Research always begins with questions. Sociologists ask all sorts of questions about social life, such as why societies are different from each other, why social groups within the same society have different life chances, or why societies change in the way they do. It is the researcher's questions that give research its sense of purpose and direction.

Social Institutions.

However, the sociologist's general questions need to be narrowed down into something that can actually be researched. For example, a sociologist who is interested in how a society has changed in the last 25 years cannot possibly study every change. They will have to narrow this down into something manageable by focusing on specific changes in particular institutions, such as family life, work and leisure activities.

What we call a research design is the process of translating a researcher's original ideas and interests into a researchable 'journey'. It involves making a number of strategic decisions and provides an overall framework for the research, in the same way as travel itineraries provide frameworks for holidays.

CONCEPTS AND CONCEPTUAL THINKING

If you were asked to write an account of a particular day at your college, your account would actually be a simplified version of what 'really' went on. This is because there are many things you would simply not know about. Your account would also be very different from those of other students. You might choose to write about different things, depending on what you felt was important and, even when you were writing about the same incident, you would probably interpret it differently. Therefore, people's accounts of things tend to be different because they are selective reconstructions of a set of real events, and the selection process is shaped by people's subjective views of what they consider to be important and interesting.

It is much the same for researchers. They also have to select evidence in their accounts of social life and, like everyone else, they are influenced by their subjective views. However, as we have already observed, researchers have to move beyond their own subjective views and provide more objective accounts of social life. This means they have to find ways of making the selection process more systematic and standardised. One of the ways they try to do this is by using theoretical categories called ***concepts***.

Concepts are the theoretical tools sociologists use to describe and explain the social world. They are clearly defined categories given to aspects of the social world that have significant common features. Concepts are the most important tools of social research. They are the building blocks around which theory and research are organised.

Social class is one of the concepts used in sociology to simplify the infinite complexities of social inequalities. Social classes are groups of people who share a similar economic position in a society. Different social class groupings can be identified in a society and this can provide a basis for exploring patterns of inequality. For example, sociologists have explored relationships between people's social class and their values, political beliefs, educational achievements and life expectancy.

However, social class is an abstract, theoretical term and sociologists wanting to do quantitative research have to find ways of measuring, or operationalising, the concept, in much the same way that the mercury in the thermometer measures the concept of temperature. These operationalising devices are called ***indicators***.

For example, a sociologist wanting to explore the relationship between the concepts of 'class' and 'educational achievement', would have to find indicators of these concepts. As occupation is the major source of income for most people, most sociologists have typically used various forms of 'occupational ranking' as indicators of class, whereas attendance, reports and academic qualifications gained at school can be used as indicators of educational success.

Concepts are the most important aspect of research design. They define what the sociologist studies and provide the basis for organising and presenting data. The important thing to understand here is that concepts do not just reflect data, they shape it and this is one of the main ways that theory is linked to research. In this context, it is important to note that concepts are contested categories. That is, sociologists do not all agree about how things like 'class' should be defined or measured.

DESCRIPTIVE AND EXPLANATORY RESEARCH DESIGNS

Research designs have many different purposes but an important distinction is whether the research is descriptive or explanatory.

Descriptive research is about trying to construct a much clearer and more comprehensive picture of how something works, often on the basis of earlier exploratory studies. For example, a descriptive study of social change might ask how family life, work and leisure have changed over the last 25 years. Descriptive research studies are more likely to be inductive; this means that a researcher may draw out possible explanations from their observations.

Explanatory research asks why something happens and identifies possible 'causal mechanisms'. For example, an explanatory research study of social change might ask why family life, work and leisure have changed in the last 25 years. Explanatory research studies are more likely to be deductive; this means that a researcher is testing a theory, or hypothesis, against the data.

Although there are sociological studies that are either purely deductive or inductive, many move between the two. For example, a descriptive study might suggest explanations that are then 'tested' by further explanatory research.

QUANTITATIVE AND QUALITATIVE RESEARCH DESIGNS

Another important distinction is between quantitative and qualitative research designs. In very simple terms, quantitative data can be measured whereas qualitative data cannot, but the term has much wider implications. Sometimes a researcher's decision to use quantitative or qualitative designs is shaped by the nature of the problem being researched. For example, studying poverty levels in a society will almost certainly require a quantitative research design, whereas exploring the inner world of a religious cult or a criminal gang will almost certainly require a qualitative design.

However, the decision to use quantitative or qualitative data does not just depend on the nature of the problem being investigated, it can also reflect different theoretical approaches to sociological research. Quantitative data is closer to the scientific ideal of research. Quantitative designs usually mean researchers are relatively detached from the people they are studying and it is less likely that their values will influence the research process.

Quantitative research designs have a number of important advantages.

- enable relationships between variables to be documented systematically
- are more likely to fulfil the key criteria of standardisation, reliability and transparency.
- give data more authority, especially with government departments and the media.

Stop and think for a moment: If quantitative research designs have all these advantages why is not all sociological research quantitative? After all, measurement is synonymous with science and some social sciences, such as economics and psychology, are based almost exclusively on quantitative methods.

The simple answer to this question is that there are many important sociological questions that simply cannot be answered with quantitative methods. We can illustrate this point by returning to our earlier example of the relationship between social class and educational achievement.

A *quantitative research design* using concepts and indicators in the way described above can provide valuable data about relationships between class background and education. But when it comes to trying to explain this relationship there are some questions that cannot be answered very well by quantitative research designs. For example, what is it actually like to be brought up in relative poverty or in relative affluence? How do pupils and teachers interact with each other in the classroom? These kinds of questions can really only be examined by qualitative research designs and strategies – such as making detailed observations of school life or interviewing people at great length – that bring researchers into much closer contact with those they are studying.

THE EXPECTED AND THE UNEXPECTED IN SOCIAL RESEARCH

Where we started it by comparing the holiday and the research project. There is usually a sense of adventure about going on holiday. You may be going to an unfamiliar place and unexpected things can, and often do, happen. Much the same is true of research. You are often surprised by some of the things you discover.

However, by planning a holiday and deciding to stay in a particular place at a given time of year, most holidaymakers narrow the possibilities of what might happen. Therefore, the holiday experience is a product of the unexpected and the expected. The plans made in advance provide a framework for what actually happens. Much the same is true of research. Sociologists' research designs provide the framework for the things they find out about social life. So just as the holidaymaker expects certain things from their holiday, such as sandy beaches or snowy mountains, sociologists usually have some idea of what they are going to find from their research.

The really important lesson to learn from this comparison is that researchers are not just giving us information about what is happening in the social world. They are doing much more than this. They are shaping and organising it for us. Our brief trip through research designs has shown that what emerges as data in a research project is a product of the relationship between the researcher's design and the intrinsic nature of what is being researched.

MAJOR RESEARCH DESIGNS IN SOCIOLOGY

The major research designs, or approaches, in sociology are:

SURVEYS METHOD

In everyday language to survey something is to take a general view. In geography, for example, surveys map out a landscape or a town. Similarly, in social sciences, surveys try to map out aspects of the social world. Surveys offer breadth of view at a specific point in time, rather like a photograph of a landscape or townscape from a distance. Surveys are usually – but not necessarily – quantitative. They are used for simply collecting information, testing peoples' opinions or attitudes and mapping out relationships between things in a quantifiable form.

Survey data are most commonly collected by asking people questions, usually administered by questionnaires or face-to-face interviews. However, the survey is a research design or strategy and not a research method, and survey data can be collected through other methods such as using documents or making observations.

SAMPLING METHOD

Survey research is usually undertaken in relation to large populations, and researchers cannot collect data from everyone in the population. Therefore they use a sample: this is a part of a population being studied.

Probability sampling means that the sample has been selected randomly.

Simple random sampling means that everyone in the population has an equal (non-zero) chance of being selected.

Stratified random sampling is a special case of sampling, which means that every member of a population being studied has an equal chance of being selected in relation to their representation within the general population. For example, if females outnumber males by four to one in a population then stratified random sampling will ensure that 80 per cent of those sampled are female. The more the sample surveyed represents the population being studied, especially in terms of key variables such as age, class, ethnicity, gender and professional status, then the more confident the researcher will feel in generalising from the results.

Non-probability sampling means that the sample has not been selected using a random selection method and cannot be taken to represent the population as a whole. The main reason for non-probability sampling is that the researcher does not have enough information about the population being studied to construct a sampling frame as, for example, in studies of drug use, crime and self-harm. In non-probability sampling researchers will simply contact whom they can and this is known as convenience sampling.

Snowball sampling is a form of convenience sampling that is often used in research into very sensitive areas such as health problems or criminal activities, where a researcher makes contact with a small group, gains their confidence and uses that to make further contacts and enlarge the sample.

A *quota sample* represents a group of people that a sociologist wants to make statements about. They divide the population into parts on the basis of the population. Therefore if we were researching a school and we knew the population of the school contained 55 per cent of girls and 44 per cent of boys we would select a sample in proportion to these percentages, for example choosing any 110 girls and 88 boys.

LONGITUDINAL APPROACHES

A longitudinal research design involves collecting data from the same source at intervals over time. It is not really a design in itself but is rather an addition to an existing design and is most frequently used in survey research when the samples being investigated are interviewed at different times. Taking a longitudinal approach is one of the ways sociologists document changes in individuals and organisations over time and is most frequently used in areas like child development, health and educational research.

EXPERIMENTAL AND EVALUATIVE RESEARCH

The laboratory experiment is the key method in scientific research. In the experiment a possible causal influence, called an independent variable, is manipulated under controlled conditions to see if it produces a change in another factor, called a dependent variable.

Smoking	Cancer
Independent variable	Dependent variable

Laboratory experiments are rare in sociology. Nonetheless the classic experimental design is seen by some researchers as an important yardstick against which other methods can be assessed. Field, or *quasi-experimental*, research designs that attempt to explore relationships between independent and dependent variables in more natural settings are becoming increasingly common in sociology, particularly in evaluative research. The aim of evaluative research is to examine different social programmes, such as crime prevention strategies or health promotion policies, to see if they 'work' or to find out if one works better than another.

The most common type of experimental research design uses a control group. This involves establishing two broadly similar populations and introducing an independent variable to one group (the experimental group) but not to the other (the control group). The aim is to see if there are differences in the behaviour of the experimental group and the control group.

ETHNOGRAPHY

The key idea behind ethnography is that as human behaviour is intentional, research should be orientated towards understanding the reasoning behind people's actions. This is sometimes referred to as 'verstehen', a German word meaning empathetic understanding.

Ethnography is usually based on detailed case studies of particular groups, organisations or individuals, and uses methods such as observations, long conversational interviews and personal documents, that bring researchers into close contact with the everyday lives of those they are studying. Research reports are in the form of a narrative, with key evidence, such as detailed descriptions of particular episodes being reproduced to illustrate the point the researcher is making.

RESEARCH METHODS FOR COLLECTING DATA

Research methods are techniques used for collecting data. There are many different types of data in sociological research, but an important distinction is between primary and secondary data. Primary data is information that researchers collect for themselves by, for example, interviewing people or observing them. Secondary data is information that is already in existence before the research starts. For example, a researcher may make use of government statistics or monitor the content of newspapers, magazines or TV programmes.

Although some sociology textbooks use the umbrella term 'Methods' to describe the entire research process, it is important to distinguish between research design and research methods. Sociologists have a range of research methods to choose from, each with their advantages and limitations, and they have to work out which methods best fulfil the aims of their research design.

Methods are about the practical part of research, and sociologists do not just have to work out what method they are going to use. They also have to work out how best to implement it. For example, suppose I have decided to use an interview method. I still have to decide if I'm going to do it by telephone or face-to-face. If it's face-to-face, I still have to work out how to record the data. If I'm constantly scribbling notes or using a tape recorder it may intimidate interviewees and prevent them from saying what they really think. But if I conduct the interview more like a natural conversation, it may be difficult to recall enough of what the interviewees say.

However – and this is important and less obvious – sociologists' decisions are not just influenced by practical or technical concerns. They are also influenced by theory. This is because methods are not simply neutral research tools, as if they were methodological hammers or screwdrivers.

PRIMARY RESEARCH METHODS

Asking People Questions in Social Research

One of the ways sociologists try to find out about the social world is to ask people questions. This can be done by:

- asking people to fill in questionnaires.
- telephone or Internet.
- formal face-to-face interviews.
- asking questions informally in the context of field work.

There are many different types of interview methods in sociology but the most important distinction is between structured and unstructured interviews. Although sociologists sometimes use a combination of interview methods in their research, we shall look at them separately to clarify the distinctions between them.

Structured Interviews and Questionnaires

Structured interviews are built around an already prepared interview schedule. You ask the questions as they appear in the schedule, and also record the answers. You are, however, expected to provide explanations, wherever necessary, to clarify the questions. You may also do some probing and ask the respondent to explain the answers, if found vague.

When the answers to a question are in the form of alternatives as given in the following example, you either read these out or hand over a card on which these are printed, and ask the respondent to choose the one which is appropriate in his or her opinion.

Q: If you do not take bath daily, what could be your reasons

1. I do not find time.
2. There is scarcity of water.
3. Have to fetch water from a long distance.
4. Lack of privacy for taking bath.
5. Any other reason.

Through prompting, you can make sure that the respondent has fully considered all possibilities before replying to the question.

This is good for getting information about prevalence and distribution of an issue from large numbers of people and the resulting data are quantitative. The interview can be completed rapidly in the field, and less skill in required on the part of the interviewers in such cases.

At the same time, much skill is needed to create the questionnaire or interview schedule. It requires much time for pre-testing of the questionnaire, and also training the field staff. Highly structured questionnaires yield little insight into how people feel about the issues involved.

SEMI-STRUCTURED INTERVIEW

Semi-structured interview provides greater scope for discussion and learning about the problem, opinions and views of the respondents. While there are some fairly specific questions (closed questions) in the interview schedule, each of which may be probed or prompted, there are lot more questions which are completely open-ended. The latter questions mainly serve to explore different facets of the issue. The information thus collected is both qualitative and quantitative.

UNSTRUCTURED INTERVIEWS

One way round some of the limitations of the structured interview is to use an unstructured interview. Unstructured interviews are more like ordinary conversations; there is no set interview structure and interviewees answer in their own words. Unstructured interviews are sometimes used in survey designs, but they are most frequently used in ethnographic research.

The effectiveness of unstructured, qualitative interviews often depends on the rapport and trust that is built up between researcher and respondent. The aim of such interviews is to allow respondents to reconstruct their experiences in as much detail as possible, giving the researcher, and ultimately the reader, an insight into how they experienced particular events.

Unstructured interviews have more depth and flexibility than structured interviews. They are also normally more valid as they give greater insight into the meanings of a subject's experiences. However, they also have important limitations. The data collection is not standardised and is thus hard to generalise from and, as there is usually far too much data to reproduce in full, readers are dependent on the researcher's selection of data. Unstructured interviews are also less reliable than structured interviews as the results cannot be quantified and re-tested.

LIMITS OF ALL INTERVIEW METHODS

Some sociologists use a combination of structured and unstructured interviews in their research on a 'horses for courses' principle, using structured questions to obtain factual information, such as age or income, and unstructured questions to probe deeper into people's experiences. Alternatively, they may use semi-structured interviews where the questions are closed, but interviewees are given space (in questionnaires) or time (in face-to-face interviews) to elaborate on their answers.

However, despite their many benefits, there are certain limitations with all interview methods.

- People may simply have problems in recalling information accurately. A great deal of psychological research has shown just how unreliable memory can be.

- There is something known as the interview effect. This means that interviewees may give the more 'socially acceptable' answer, or they answer a question in the way they think the interviewer wants.
- With all interviews (structured, unstructured or semi-structured) researchers are dependent on what people tell them. If researchers want to find out how people really behave in their daily lives, then they have to go and take a look.

OBSERVATIONAL METHODS

Watching people is another important way that sociologists find out about social life. Researchers using observational methods do not have to rely on what people say they do. They can see for themselves.

Like interviews, observation can be structured or unstructured, or semi-structured, that is, it uses a combination of both. Structured observations are most commonly associated with experimental or evaluative research designs. For example, subjects may be given certain tests or tasks to do as part of an experiment and the researcher systematically records the results. Structured observation can also take place in naturalistic settings. For example, as part of her research on gender and schooling, Michelle Stanworth (1983) systematically recorded the amount of direct contact time teachers give to male and to female students.

However, the vast majority of observational research studies in sociology are unstructured, and most of them use a method called participant observation where the researcher participates directly in the life of the people being studied.

This technique was first used by Western anthropologists who joined tribal societies, learning their language and customs in order to document ways of life that were disappearing with colonisation and the relentless advance of industrialisation. Like anthropologists, sociologists have to find ways of getting into the groups or organisations they wish to study and this may take a lot of friendly persuasion, persistence and the cultivation of helpful contacts. Once established, the research work involves detailing observations, listening to what is being said and asking questions. This is easier said than done. It requires both an attachment to and a detachment from those you are studying.

Participant observation is the method most commonly used in ethnographic research designs and you will find that some textbooks treat ethnography and participant observation as if they were the same. However, this is not strictly accurate. Participant observation can be used in experimental designs and ethnographic research can, and sometimes has to, be done by other methods, such as unstructured interviews or documents.

There is a richness of detail in participant observation research that tends to be lacking in other methods and one have to confess it has always been his favourite research method. Some of the most vivid and interesting studies in sociology have used participant observation. For example, sociologists have worked in factories, offices, schools, prisons and mental hospitals; they have made observations in clinics, clubs, call centres, on street corners and in public toilets; and they have joined political parties, criminal gangs and religious cults, all in the name of research.

In participant observation sociologists are able to see for themselves how people behave in their natural contexts. This authentic knowledge and the depth and detail it provides mean that data from participant observation usually fulfils the key criterion of validity far better than data obtained from other methods. It also offers flexibility and can provide the basis for inductively generating new theoretical explanations.

COMPARATIVE RESEARCH

Comparative research is a research methodology in the social sciences that aims to make comparisons across different countries or cultures. A major problem in comparative research is that the data sets in different countries may not use the same categories, or define categories differently (for example by using different definitions of poverty).

Comparative research, simply put, is the act of comparing two or more things with a view to discovering something about one or all of the things being compared. This technique often utilizes multiple disciplines in one study. When it comes to method, the majority agreement is that there is no methodology peculiar to comparative research. The multidisciplinary approach is good for the flexibility it offers, yet comparative programs do have a case to answer against the call that their research lacks a "seamless whole".

There are certainly methods far more common than others in comparative studies, however. Quantitative analysis is much more frequently pursued than qualitative, and this is seen in the majority of comparative studies which use quantitative data. The general method of comparing things is the same for comparative research as it is in our everyday practice of comparison. Like cases are treated alike, and different cases are treated differently; the extent of difference determines how differently cases are to be treated. If one is able to sufficiently distinguish two cases, comparative research conclusions will not be very helpful.

Secondary analysis of quantitative data is relatively widespread in comparative research, undoubtedly in part because of the cost of obtaining primary data for such large things as a country's policy environment. This study is generally aggregate data analysis. Comparing large quantities of data (especially government sourced) is prevalent. A typical method of comparing welfare states is to take balance of their levels of spending on social welfare.

In line with how a lot of theorizing has gone in the last century, comparative research does not tend to investigate 'grand theories', such as Marxism. It instead occupies itself with middle-range theories that do not purport to describe our social system in its entirety, but a subset of it. A good example of this is the common research program that looks for differences between two or more social systems, then looks at these differences in relation to some other variable coexisting in those societies to see if it is related. The classic case of this is Esping-Anderson's research on social welfare systems. He noticed there was a difference in types of social welfare systems, and compared them based on their level of decommodification of social welfare goods. He found that he was able to class welfare states into three types, based on their level of decommodification. He further theorized from this that decommodification was based on a combination of class coalitions and mobilization, and regime legacy. Here, Esping-Anderson is using comparative research: he takes many western countries and compares their level of decommodification, then develops a theory of the divergence based on his findings.

Comparative research can take many forms. Two key factors are space and time. Spatially, cross-national comparisons are by far the most common, although comparisons within countries, contrasting different areas, cultures or governments also subsist and are very constructive, especially in a country like New Zealand, where policy often changes depending on which race it pertains to. Recurrent interregional studies include comparing similar or different countries or sets of countries, comparing one's own country to others or to the whole world.

The historical comparative research involves comparing different time-frames. The two main choices within this model are comparing two stages in time (either snapshots or time-series), or just comparing the same thing over time, to see if a policy's effects differ over a stretch of time.

When it comes to subject matter of comparative inquiries, many contend there is none unique to it. This may indeed be true, but a brief perusal of comparative endeavours reveals there are some topics more recurrent than others. Determining whether socioeconomic or political factors are more important in explaining government action is a familiar theme. In general, however, the only thing that is certain in comparative research issues is the existence of differences to be analysed.

6

CHAPTER

Individual, Society and Community

Introduction to Individual:** Individualism and Society, What is a Society?, Meaning of Society, Definitions of Society. **Types of Societies:** Tribal Society, Characteristics of Tribal Society, Agrarian Society, Characteristics of Agrarian Societies, Industrial Society, Characteristics of Industrial Society, Post-Industrial Society, Western Society, The Royal Society, The Fabian Society, Society of Friends. **Community. Nature of Communities. Characteristics of the Community:** Historical Factors, Social Factors, Economic Factors, Cultural Factors. **Difference Between Community and Society.

INTRODUCTION TO INDIVIDUAL

An individual is a person or any specific object in a collection. In the 15th century and earlier, and also today within the fields of statistics and metaphysics, individual means "indivisible," typically describing any numerically singular thing, but sometimes meaning "a person." From the 17th century on, individual indicates separateness, as in individualism. Individuality is the state or quality of being an individual; a person separate from other persons and possessing his or her own needs, goals, and desires. According to *Anatman*, the individual is really a series of interconnected processes that, working together, give the appearance of being a single, separated whole.

Individualism is the moral stance, political philosophy, ideology, or social outlook that stresses "the moral worth of the individual." Individualists promote the exercise of one's goals and desires and so independence and self-reliance while opposing most external interference upon one's choices, whether by society, or any other group or institution.

Individualism makes the individual its focus and so it starts "with the fundamental premise that the human individual is of primary importance in the struggle for liberation." Human rights and freedom are the substance of these theories. Liberalism, existentialism and anarchism are examples of movements that take the human individual as a central unit of analysis.

It has also been used as a term denoting "The quality of being an individual; individuality" related to possessing "An individual characteristic; a quirk." Individualism is thus also associated with artistic and bohemian interests and lifestyles where there is a tendency towards self creation and experimentation as opposed to tradition or popular mass opinions and behaviors as so also with humanist philosophical positions and ethics.

INDIVIDUALISM AND SOCIETY

An individualist enters into society to further his or her own interests, or at least demands the *right* to serve his or her own interests, without taking the interests of society into consideration. The individualist does not lend credence to any philosophy that requires the sacrifice of the self-interest of the individual for any higher social causes. Societies and groups can differ, in the extent to which they are based upon predominantly "self-regarding" (individualistic and arguably self-interested) rather than "other-regarding" (group-oriented and group or society-minded) behavior. The extent to which society, or groups are "individualistic" can vary from time to time, and from country to country.

Individualism, sometimes closely associated with certain variants of anarchism or liberalism, typically takes it for granted that individuals know best and that public authority or society has the right to interfere in the person's decision-making process only when a very compelling need to do so arises (and maybe not even in those circumstances). This type of argument is often observed in relation to policy debates regarding regulation of industries, as well as in relation to personal choice of lifestyle.

SOCIETY?

Society is a historically developed complex of relations between people that are based on constant changes of forms and conditions of their activity. It is a fundamental category of philosophy and sociology. Philosophical and theoretical analysis of society is possible only on the basis of research of its' ideal form. During the whole history of humanity there were a constant search for this perfect model and attempts to describe it. That is why different sociologists and researches give various definitions to the notion of society although there is one general and accepted variant of society definition.

Society is generally a group of people who share a common culture, occupy a particular territorial area, and feel themselves to constitute a unified and distinct entity. *Norbert Elias* was one of the sociologists where his work became relatively neglected in his life time. Elias developed his social theory in a relatively modest way, without explicitly presenting himself as 'theorist.' He placed more emphasis on the empirical investigation of particular historical and sociological questions because he was concerned to transcend the division between social theory and social research.

Simmel conceives sociology as the science of social forms. He makes use of a helpful analogy of geometry as the study of forms (i.e., shapes) which may exist in an unlimited variety of physical materials. Simmel believes that sociology should leave the examination of the content of societal interaction to other sciences (such as psychology or economy) in the way that geometry leaves content analysis to the physical sciences.

Simmel discovered various forms of social interaction when researching individuals on society. Simmel views exchange as the purest and most concentrated form of significant human interaction. In fact, much action that may initially appear to be unilateral actually involves reciprocal effects (i.e., is a form of exchange) and generally all interactions may more-or-less be conceived of as exchange. One characteristic of exchange is that the sum of values (of the interacting parties) is greater afterward than it was before, i.e., each party gives the other more than he had himself possessed.

MEANING OF SOCIETY

The term society is most fundamental to sociology. It is derived from the Latin word socius which means companionship or friendship. Companionship means sociability. According to George Simmel it is this element of sociability which defines the true essence of society. It indicates that man always lives in the company of other people. Man is a social animal said Aristotle centuries ago. Man needs society for his living, working and enjoying life. Society has become an essential condition for human life to continue. We can define society as a group of people who share a common culture, occupy a particular territorial area and feel themselves to constitute a unified and distinct entity. It is the mutual interactions and interrelations of individuals and groups.

DEFINITIONS OF SOCIETY

More broadly, a society is an economic, social or industrial infrastructure, made up of a varied collection of individuals. Members of a society may be from different ethnic groups. A society may be a particular ethnic group, such as the Saxons; a nation state, such as Bhutan; a broader cultural group, such as a Western society. The word society may also refer to an organized voluntary association of people for religious, benevolent, cultural, scientific, political, patriotic, or other purposes. A "society" may even, though more by means of metaphor, refer to a social organism such as an ant colony.

August Comte, the father of sociology, saw society as a social organism possessing a harmony of structure and function.

Emile Durkheim, the founding father of the modern sociology, treated society as a reality in its own right.

According to *Talcott Parsons,* "Society is a total complex of human relationships in so far as they grow out of the action in terms of means-end relationship intrinsic or symbolic."

G.H. Mead conceived society as "an exchange of gestures which involves the use of symbols."

Morris Ginsberg defines society as "a collection of individuals united by certain relations or mode of behaviour which mark them off from others who do not enter into these relations or who differ from them in behaviour."

Cole sees society as "the complex of organized associations and institutions with a community."

According to *MacIver* and *Page* "society is a system of usages and procedures of authority and mutual aid of many groupings and divisions, of controls of human behavior and liberties. This ever changing complex system which is called society is a web of social relationship."

TYPES OF SOCIETIES

Sociology recognises many types of Society and defines these types of society in a very clear manner. Following are some of those types of Society and their characteristics:

TRIBAL SOCIETY

According to Ralph Linton: tribe is group of bands occupying a contiguous territory or territories having a feeling of unity deriving from numerous similarities in culture, frequent contacts and a certain community of interests. Ghurye calls the tribal of India as imperfectly segment of the Hindus. D.N. Majumdar defines tribe as a social group with territorial affiliation endogamous with no specialization of functions ruled by tribal officers hereditary or otherwise united in language or dialect recognizing social distance with other tribes. A large section of tribal population depends on agriculture for survival. The examples of agricultural tribes are: Oraons, Mundas, Bhils, Santhals, Baigas, and Hos etc. The Toda furnish classic example of pastoral economy. Their social and economic organization is built around the buffaloes. They obtain their living through exchange. In some parts of India the tribal people are engaged in shifting cultivation.

It is known by different names—Nagas call it Jhum, Bhuiya call it Dahi and Koman, Maria of Bastar call it Penda, Khond refer to it as Podu and Saiga call it Bewar. Many subsidiary occupations like handicrafts are undertaken in the various tribal zones. These include basket-making, spinning and weaving. For example, Tharu depend upon furniture making, musical instruments, weapons, ropes and mats. The Korw and Agaria are well known iron-smelters producing tools for local use.

The Tribal Society in India is a very Close-knit one, with Unity Surviving in Diversity.

CHARACTERISTICS OF TRIBAL SOCIETY

The tribe inhabits and remains within definite and common topography. The members of a tribe possess a consciousness of mutual unity. The members of a tribe speak a common language. The members generally marry into their own group but now due to increased contact with outsiders there are instances of tribal marring outside as well. The tribes believe in ties of blood relationship between its members. They have faith in their having descended from a common, real or mythical, ancestor and hence believe in blood relationships with other members.

Tribes follow their own political organization which maintains harmony. Religion is of great importance in the tribe. The tribal political and social organization is based on religion because they are granted religious sanctity and recognition.

AGRARIAN SOCIETY

The invention of plough marked the beginning of agrarian societies 6000 years back. According to Collins, 'Dictionary of Sociology', Agrarian society refer to any form of society especially so traditional societies primarily based on agricultural and craft production rather than industrial production. Wallace and Wallace describe agrarian societies as "employing animal drawn ploughs to cultivate the land." The mode of production of the agrarian society that is cultivation distinguishes it from the hunter-gatherer society which produces none of its food. The theories of Redfield and Tonnies are considered important. Robert Redfield talks about folk-urban continuum and little tradition and great tradition as his paramount focus in rural studies. Tonnies on the other hand discuss concepts of Gemeinschaft and Gesselschaft.

Nature of Human Society to an Individualistic Agrarian Society.

CHARACTERISTICS OF AGRARIAN SOCIETIES

Cultivation of land through the plough as this invention enabled the people to make a great leap forward in food production. It increased the productivity of land through the use of animals and bringing to the surface the nutrients of the soil. Combining irrigation techniques with the use of the plough increased the productivity and the crop yield. It also brought fallow land under cultivation. The size of the agricultural societies increased as it lessened the burden of large number of people who engaged themselves in other activities. Agricultural societies lead to the establishment of more elaborate political institutions like formalized government bureaucracy assisted by the legal system. It also leads to the evolution of distinct social classes—those who own the land and those who work on the other's land. Land is the major source of wealth and is individually owned.

This creates major difference between the social strata. Agricultural societies provide the basis for the establishment of economic institutions. Trade becomes more elaborate and money is medium of exchange. It also demands the maintenance of records of transaction, crop harvest, taxation, governmental rules and regulations. Religion becomes separate institution with elaborate rituals and traditions. The agricultural societies support the emergence of arts and cultural artifacts due to surplus food production people tend to divert their attention to other recreational activities. There is far more complex social structure. According to Ian Robertson the number of statuses multiplies, population size increases, cities appear, new institutions emerge, social classes arise, political and economic inequality becomes inbuilt into the social structure and culture becomes much more diversified and heterogeneous.

INDUSTRIAL SOCIETY

The Industrial mode of production began some 250 years ago in Britain and from there it spread to the entire world. In the simplest sense an industrial society is a social system whose mode of production focuses primarily on finished goods manufactured with the aid of machinery. According to Wallace and Wallace in industrial societies the largest portion of the labour force is involved in mechanized production of goods and services. The term 'industrial societies' originated from Saint Simon who chose it to reflect the emerging central role of manufacturing industry in the 18th century Europe in contrast with previous pre-industrial and agrarian society.

CHARACTERISTICS OF INDUSTRIAL SOCIETY

Industrial society is associated with the emergence of industrialization which transformed much of Europe and United States by replacing essentially agriculture based societies with industrial societies based on the use of machines and non-animal sources of energy to produce finished goods. Industrial societies are in a continual state of rapid change due to technological innovations. The high level of productivity in industrial societies further stimulates population growth where people start living in cities and urban areas.

An Industrial Society.

New medical technologies and improved living standards serve to extend life expectancy. The division of labor becomes complex with the availability of specialized jobs. The statuses are achieved rather than ascribed. The family and kinship as social institutions are relegated to the background. It is becomes a unit of consumption. There is breakup of joint family system and nuclear family units become prominent. The influence of religion diminishes as people hold many different and competing values and beliefs. State assumes central power in the industrial societies. Industrialism is associated with the widening gap between two social classes of 'haves' and 'have nots'. The rich or the capitalist class is seen as exploiting class and the poor class known as working class is seen as exploited. However in most of the industrial societies there is steady reduction in social inequalities. Industrial societies have given rise to number of secondary groups such as corporations, political parties, business houses and government bureaucracies, cultural and literary associations. The primary groups tend to lose their importance and secondary groups come to the prominence.

POST-INDUSTRIAL SOCIETY

The concept of Post-Industrial society was first formulated in 1962 by D. Bell, and subsequently elaborated in his seminal work 'Coming of Post Industrial Society'. It describes the economic and social changes in the late twentieth century. According to Bell, in modern societies theoretical knowledge forms the axial principle of society and is the source of innovation and policy formulation. In economy, this is reflected in the decline of goods production and manufacturing as the main form of economic activity, to be replaced by services. With regard to the class structure, the new axial principle fosters the supremacy of professional and technical occupations which constitute a new class, in all spheres economic, political and social decision making is influenced by new intellectual technologies and the new intellectual class. Other writers have also commented on the growing power of technocrats in economic and political life. G.K. Galbraith believes that power in the United States economy and therefore in American society as a whole lies in the hands of a technical bureaucracy of the techno-structure of large corporations, A. Jouraine suggests similar technocratic control of French economic and political life.

WESTERN SOCIETY

The development of the Western world has brought with it the emerging concepts of Western culture, politics and ideas, often referred to simply as Western society. Geographically, it covers at the very least the countries of Western Europe, North America, Australia and New Zealand and sometimes also includes South America and Israel. The cultures and lifestyles of all of these stem from Western Europe. They all enjoy relatively strong economies and stable governments, allow freedom of religion, have chosen democracy as a form of governance, favor capitalism and international trade, are heavily influenced by Judeo-Christian values, and have some form of political and military alliance or cooperation.

Ideals of Western Society Reflect an Intuitively Accurate Grasp.

THE ROYAL SOCIETY

The Royal Society, officially the Royal Society of London for the Improvement of Natural Knowledge, is a learned society for science that was founded in 1660 and is considered by most to be the oldest such society still in existence. Fellowship, granted for life, is awarded to scientists after their election by existing fellows, and is considered a great honour. Fellows must be citizens or residents of a member of the Commonwealth of Nations or the Republic of Ireland, while the smaller number of Foreign Members are drawn from other countries.

The Royal Society of London for improving natural knowledge.

THE FABIAN SOCIETY

Britain's best-known socialist society is the Fabian Society, a membership organization affiliated with the Labour Party. It was founded in 1884, some years before the creation of the Labour Party itself. Although membership is relatively small (around 7,000), the society is very influential.

The Fabian Society.

It is best known for its ground-breaking work from the late 19th century until World War I. The society laid many of the foundations of the Labour Party. Today, it is a vanguard "think tank" of the New Labour movement.

SOCIETY OF FRIENDS

The Society of Friends is a Christian organization whose members are commonly known as Quakers. It was founded in 17th century England by George Fox who called for a radical, egalitarian, spirit-filled Christianity that would not be oppressive of people on account of race, sex, or class. Women and men were given equal status as all were children of God. A person should not set himself up with honors and distinctions as these were meaningless in the sight of God.

Quakers maintain that the teaching of Jesus is a practical method for the guidance of the world today and that religion is concerned with the whole of life. Friends World Committee for Consultation (FWCC) is the International Quaker Organization which loosely unifies the diverse groups of Friends from around the world.

COMMUNITY

A body of people having common rights, privileges, or interests, or living in the same place under the same laws and regulations; as, a community of monks. Hence a number of animals living in a common home or with some apparent association of interests.

A group of people having ethnic or cultural or religious characteristics in common; "the Christian community of the apostolic age"; "he was well known throughout the Catholic community".

It was *Aristotle* who first defined the word "community" as a group established by men having shared values. That initial definition has been refined and expanded through the years. We have come, for example, to recognize that people can belong to a number of different "communities" simultaneously—communities of place; cultural communities; communities of memory, in which people who may be strangers share "a morally significant history"; and psychological communities "of face-to-face personal interaction governed by sentiments of trust, co-operation, and altruism".

The world, we are repeatedly reminded, has contracted into a "global village." One effect of this contraction is the bringing together of hitherto isolated peoples, allowing for the development of new patterns of civilization—but also creating new tensions. Thus, challenges now confront communities at local, national, and global levels. For example, new information technologies have created "networks" and "cybercommunities" in the world of the Internet that link individuals and organizations around the globe without regard for national boundaries; small communities around the planet are affected by urban migration or by degradation of the natural and built environment; the existence of national communities—nation states—is under threat from assaults by ethnic or tribal enclaves. Ironically, while the emergence of a global community wielding effective power is seen by many as a necessity in order to combat the ill effects of unfettered market economics, the whole idea that a real global community can ever come into existence is met with deep misgivings or complete skepticism by others. How, then, can we understand "community" at the end of the twentieth century—and what will its future be in the next millennium?

A number of significant challenges to community have arisen from developments in global information technologies. While pundits ponder whether or not Internet users form any kind of viable community as they sit at their computers in farflung corners of the world, a deeper and more serious issue is the manner in which the entire structure of computer networks undermines more traditional kinds of community organization.

Mathews raises important questions: What kind of community can be forged in an internetted world, where the structure of the technology promotes anarchy, with its emphasis on complete freedom of expression and lack of regard for authority? Does this spell the end of the nation-state and, if so, what other kind of political entity might arise in its stead? The challenges posed by the new information technologies may generate significant crises felt throughout the world, but such a development looms on the horizon.

World-connect-people-community.

There are, however, a number of current crises facing community. Loss of the sense of community based on "place" is a worldwide phenomenon. Millions of people all over the planet are being displaced from their homes. Some are refugees fleeing escalating political strife. Others are forced from their homes by economic necessity, such as farmers from rural China who are migrating to cities in vast numbers, searching for factory work. Such movement destroys families, undermines the traditional sense of trust found in community, increases feelings of isolation and dislocation, and creates a host of social problems.

Even where people still maintain their homes, there are challenges to the sense of place. A case in point is America, where planners are in revolt against the manner in which the built environment of communities has been shaped in the latter part of the twentieth century. A movement widely known by the name "new urbanism" protests against the "fantastic, awesome, stupefying ugliness" of "the gruesome, tragic suburban boulevards of commerce" so common in American towns and cities, contending that "this ugliness is the surface expression of deeper problems" and contributes substantially to the widely expressed sense of "loss of community" felt throughout the society.

The new urbanists posit that going back to the planning and design principles that shaped the traditional neighborhoods of America is a way of recapturing this lost sense of place and community, of reversing a pattern of development they see as "economically catastrophic, an environmental calamity, socially devastating, and spiritually degrading." Discarding the zoning laws that segregate various activities, they seek to create neighborhoods (or hamlets or villages) of manageable size which, when clustered together, become towns and cities. Each neighborhood is constructed on a "human scale"; it contains both residential and commercial property and provides housing for people of different levels of income. The proposal is not fantastic. Many traditional European towns, for example, have preserved this element of "human design." But to make such a change, citizens everywhere must take an active role in decisions regarding the environment in which they live.

Human settlements are like living organisms. They must grow, and they will change. But we can decide on the nature of that growth—on the quality and the character of it—and where it ought to go. We do not have to scatter the building blocks of our civic life all over the countryside, destroying our towns and ruining farmland.... It is within our power to create places that are worthy of our affection.

Such loss of "community of place" can also bring loss of communities of memory and communities governed by trust. In the late nineteenth century Ferdinand Tönnies theorized that in the development of systems of culture, communities invariably move from a period of Gemeinschaft, where shared experience and likeness are most important, toward a period of Gesellschaft, where individuals exist in isolation from each other, there is a strong sense of competition, relationships are contractual, and monetary values prevail. Such a progression has been noted by others as well.

NATURE OF COMMUNITIES

Like most things in the social sciences, community does not fit into a nice neat package. We use the word a lot, but in this training it is important to ask more seriously what it is.

First, let us note that a "community" is a construct, a model. We can not see a whole community, we can not touch it, and we can not directly experience it. Like the words "hill" or "snowflake," a community may come in one of many shapes, sizes, colours and locations, no two of which are alike.

More importantly, a community is not just the people who are in it. A community usually was already existing when all of its current residents were not yet born, and it will likely continue to exist when all of the people in it have left. It is something that is beyond its very components, its residents or community members. A community may have members who have temporarily moved to other locations. They may wish to eventually return, but not all do.

A "community" in some senses may not even have a physical location, but be demarcated by being a group of people with a common interest. In the training material here, however, the "community" which is the object of a mobilizer's attention, is usually one with a physical geographic location.

CHARACTERISTICS OF THE COMMUNITY

The characteristics discussed below are some that may be useful in identifying incentives to good resource management in communities. The list in no way attempts to be comprehensive since there are innumerable characteristics that might in different circumstances play a role in communities' abilities to work together on resource management activities. Nor are the categories intended to be mutually exclusive. One might list ethnicity or language under cultural factors just as well as under social factors, where they are placed in this analysis. The categories are simply a convenience that may help in thinking through some of the issues that are likely to be among the most important determinants of social cohesion and the ability to collaborate on forestry activities.

HISTORICAL FACTORS

Communities are a product of their past: current development activities take place against a historical backdrop. Historical factors may hinder or help the implementation of community forestry projects; what is undisputable is that they will have some impact on the success of those projects.

Among the historical factors that play a key role in community cohesion and resource management are:

- population and settlement history; and
- conflict history.

The population history reflects the ancestral origins of the community. In some cases all present members of the village may be descended from a single ancestor or family. This may be an important factor in current social cohesion. In other cases families may have divided or new families may have joined the community. If so, it is important to try to understand the basis on which the more recent members were admitted into the community.

The sequential arrival of families, lineages and clans may give rise to distinctions between founders and first settlers on the one hand, and later arrivals or even 'stranger' families on the other. Alternatively some founding families can be subjugated by later, more numerous and more powerful arrivals. Whatever their relative status, the two groups often view public issues quite differently. Their resource use patterns often reflect attempts to overcome perceived injustices in the historical distribution of resources. Newcomers may attempt to use a community forestry project to gain access to resources otherwise denied them. Founding families may try to use the project to maintain their traditional dominance. These are examples of historically based incentives influencing certain behaviours that can affect the implementation of community forestry activities.

The community's experience with conflict and the way it has managed conflict in the past greatly influence its present degree of social cohesion and its willingness to engage in cooperative resource management activities. Old cases of land tenure disputes, violent confrontations and contested divorces or adultery may appear to have been settled, but they may leave a residue of resentment in the community. Past conflicts often determine trust levels between members of the community and the willingness of the population to delegate decisions or responsibilities to subgroups or individuals. Bitterness that has existed for decades, even centuries, may create strong disincentives to collective action. At the very least such old sources of conflict may make arriving at a consensus very time-consuming and may even make it impossible.

SOCIAL FACTORS

There are numerous issues related to the social structure of the community that affect its cohesion and the kinds of interests different groups may wish to protect as they seek solutions to resource management problems. Some of the most salient include:

- Ethnicity and language;
- Family structure;
- Caste and other social divisions; and
- Gender relations.

While ethnicity is not necessarily a divisive factor in communities, it certainly can have a divisive effect. It may be compounded by other issues such as the ways different ethnic groups pursue their livelihoods. One ethnic group may make its living principally from herding, for example, while another practises cultivation or fishing.

Other potentially divisive factors include religion and language. In each of these cases a key question is whether a particular local population's allegiances lie primarily with the community in which it lives, or whether it identifies more closely with interests outside the community. A particular religious sect, for example, may be more readily prepared to follow directives of its religious leader than to follow directives from within the community. Some ethnic groups may feel greater affinity to people of their own ethnicity who live outside the community than to their immediate neighbours. In such cases community organization for the purpose of governing resources can be difficult. In other cases, however, this is not an issue and all the inhabitants of a community share overriding common interests despite their differences. Sometimes the divisive factors work primarily inside a community. Factions within the community may be organized according to affiliation with a religion, caste or ethnic group. Even when they do not have strong ties outside the village, these factions can have different interests and concerns that make collective action more difficult.

Family structures often play an important role in creating or limiting social cohesiveness. When intermarriage is common in a community, a vast network of relationships is created that may (but does not necessarily) contribute to a common sense of identity and purpose. This is less likely to take place when other factors such as caste, ethnicity, cultural taboos or family histories discourage such intermarriage.

Gender considerations are also a key to understanding whether communities will be able to organize action in response to some of the more complex resource governance problems. It is clear that both men and women need to be integrally involved in resource management whenever, as is usually the case, both are active participants in the harvesting, transformation and use of tree products. If one group (more often women) feels that its interests are not represented when decisions are made about rules for resource access or use, it is less likely to follow the rules and to participate in enforcing them. Conversely if both men and women feel that their concerns are reflected in resource governance agreements, they will have a stronger incentive to participate in making the management plans work.

ECONOMIC FACTORS

The preceding section described several social factors that can affect whether members of a community are more willing or less willing to work together to solve their resource management concerns. Economic factors can also play a role in determining whether people have similar or divergent interests concerning how resources should be managed. Two salient issues are:

- differences or similarities in livelihood strategies; and
- the degree of economic stratification in the community.

People's perceptions of resources and their attitudes toward those resources will differ depending on how resources fit into their individual livelihood strategies. Some people may depend almost entirely on tree and plant resources. This would be the case of someone who specializes in the preparation of medicines or teas from plants, for example, or a charcoal maker. For others tree products may be an important input into their activities if they use tree products to feed animals or to provide fencing or fuel-wood. Others, such as shopkeepers, may have relatively little direct use for tree products.

These economic interests provide various incentives to protect, invest in and exploit tree resources. As an agriculturist Maman had an incentive to protect and maintain trees in his field in order to promote crop productivity. On the other hand, the herder who cut his trees had an incentive to lop off branches for animal feed and was not concerned with what happened to the soil under the gawo trees he cut. Both of them were trying to look out for their families' economic well-being, but with dramatically different effects on the sustainable use of resources.

People's interest in the resource base also varies depending on their level of economic well-being. There is now considerable evidence to suggest that poor people often depend more heavily on forest resources to meet their subsistence needs than do people who are more wealthy. Poor people, for example, may not be able to afford gas for cooking or modern pharmaceuticals. Instead they depend on forest products for fuel and medicine. Because of this they may face very different incentives for their own use of resources and they may have strong opinions about what the rules for access and exploitation should be. As with the gender considerations above, if these concerns are not reflected in the management plans devised by the community, the incentives for some groups not to comply with the regulations are likely to be strong.

The success of many collective community forestry activities depends on people's perceptions that they want to stay in a community and are willing to make investments in it. Conversely if they expect to leave (or think that their children will do so) their interests may be divergent from those of the rest of the community. In such cases they may even destroy forestry resources in order to finance their departure.

CULTURAL FACTORS

Many cultural factors affect the incentives people face in protecting and exploiting their tree and forest resources. Some of them are related to religion. People sometimes believe in the power of a religious item such as a fetish or the Quran or other holy book to seek out and punish transgressors of local rules regarding tree use or activities in forests. Such beliefs may reduce the need to monitor the behaviour of local people although there may still be a need to use other means to control access by people who do not accept these beliefs.

Cultural beliefs also play a profound role in people's sense of ownership of resources. In some communities it is unthinkable that an individual might be considered the owner of a tree or forest since people believe that those resources are only in the temporary stewardship of the current generation, which manages them on behalf of the ancestors and future generations. This creates incentives that are very different from those in another culture where people believe that trees can be property like anything else, and that the owner has absolute rights to decide what should be done with that property.

DIFFERENCE BETWEEN COMMUNITY AND SOCIETY

The difference between community and society becomes more visible these moments of economic and financial crisis, when the role of the state increases, as compared with the role of the private sector. A "new" type of capitalism, implying a reconfiguration of the state and its national communities, mirrors the manner in which the artificial society of transnational type, without borders, makes room for the natural community.

The antagonistic pair studied by Tönnies allows for de-potency of the concept of 'community', absorbed by society, at a time when globalization becomes manifest. Under these circumstances, community has begun to characterize a decaying social organization type, whereas 'soceity' has imposed the over-national integration trend. The generalized conflict of identities, as reaction of communities towards a monopolizing society, was interpreted in consensus with the theoretical de-valorization of the idea of a nation. Soceity has replaced the community's system of values with the individual, selfish values stock of an isolated civilization within the whole that has stolen its cultures. Communities managed to survive by opposing the culture of the conquering civilization and offering as an alternative to integration through differentiation, the integration through identity expression. The community, which proved to be not only a concept to characterize the delayed nations, has imposed the logic of organic integration, by manifesting its identity and by appreciating common values. A new model of organic integration, by appealing to the expression of identity, is provided by the united Europe, regarded as unit as multiplex.

HEREDITY AND ENVIRONMENT

Introduction. Meaning of Heredity. Effects of Heredity. Twins. Chromosome. Genes. Meaning of Environment: *Definition of Environment, Types of Environment.* ***Relationship Between:*** *Heredity and Environment, Hereditary and Environment are Not Separable.* ***Personality, Work Environment and Performance. Environment and Heredity: Physical Growth and Motor Skills. Heredity, the Environment and Development.***

INTRODUCTION

Heredity is very complex and a geneticist cannot possibly analyse all the traits of an organism at once. Instead, he studies only a few traits at a time. Many other traits are present. As the geneticists work out the solution to each hereditary mystery, the geneticist must not forget that all organisms live in a complex environment.

The environment may affect the degree to which a hereditary trait develops. The geneticist must try to find out which of the many parts of the environment may affect his results. The factors must be kept as constant as possible by using controlled experiments. Only then can he tell that the differences observed are due to heredity.

Heredity determines what an organism may become, not what it will become. What an organism becomes depends on both its heredity and environment. The modern science of genetics started with the work of *Gregor Mendel*. He found that a certain factor in a plant cell determined the traits the plant would have. Thirty years after his discovery this determines was given the name gene. Of the traits Mendel studied, he called *dominant* those at showed up in the offspring and *recessive* those. In most organisms, including man, genetics information is transmitted from mother to daughter cells and from one generation to the next by deoxyribonucleic acid (DNA).

MEANING OF HEREDITY

Man's behavior is influenced by two forces: heredity and environment. The biological or psychological characteristics which are transmitted by the parents to their offspring are known by the name of heredity. Heredity is a biological process of transmission of certain traits of behavior of the parents to their children by means of the fertilized egg. Hereditary traits are innate, they are present at birth.

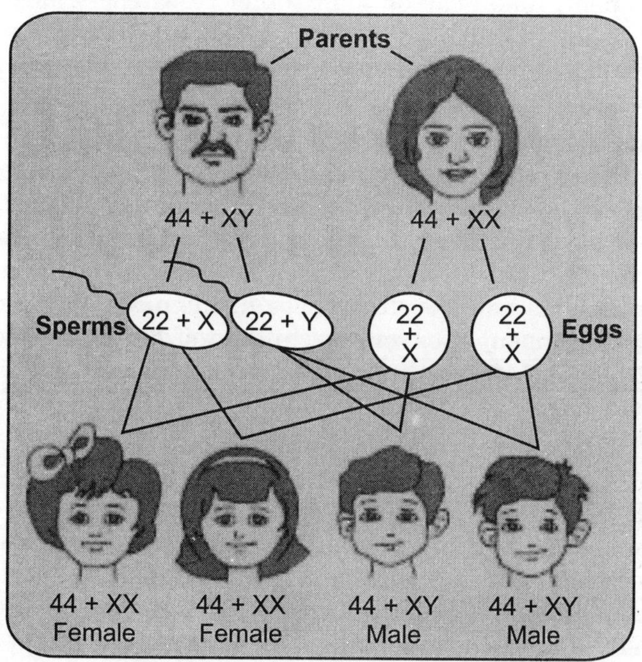

Sex Determination in Human Being.

The human individual is the progeny of two parent cells that come together when a male sperm fertilizes a female egg. In the nuclei of these parent cells are certain hair like substances called chromosomes. The chromosomes contain chemical substances called gene. These basic substances chromosomes and genes determine characteristics of the individual.

The essential chara-cteristics inherited by all human beings are physical structure, reflexes, innate drives, intelligence and temperament. There are some scholars who explain that the variations of human beings and the societies are due to differences in environment. A debate has been going on about the relative importance of hereditary and environment in determining the behavior of individuals and groups.

EFFECTS OF HEREDITY

Some of the scholars who supported heredity theory are Galton, Karl Pearson, Mc Doughall while the champions of the environment have been G.B. Watson and other behaviourist authors. Gallon in his pioneer work on hereditary genius has sought to show that the probability of the occurrence of greatly gifted children is vastly higher when the fathers have superior intelligence. Karl Pearson had also concluded that the influence of the environment is far less than that of heredity in determination of importance of human differences. According to him it was possible to measure the relative efficiency of the two.

He had given evidence to show that for people of the same race within a given community hereditary is more than seven times more important than environment. Like Pearson many other researchers have shown that the groups within the higher social or intellectual rating have produced more persons of genius or distinction. For instance royal families produce in proportion more geniuses than others.

The sociologists have been making controlled experiments to solve the nature—nurture problem and to ascertain the influence of environment over heredity or vice versa. They have held one of the factors as constant and the other varied on the principle that the differences so revealed can be attributed solely to the variant factor. Twins have been put under different environments and the differences in their behavior have been attributed to environment. Conversely children of different heredities have been placed together under the same environment and the differences in their behavior have been attributed to their hereditary differences.

TWINS

It is difficult to sort out the effect of genetic inheritance from the effect of the environment, particularly in human genetics. Studies of identical twins provide geneticists with the opportunity to examine the influences of heredity (nature) and environment (nurture). The study of twins offer bountiful material with which to study many of the most detailed aspects of human heredity.

Identical Twins.

Identical twins develop when the cells arising from a single fertilized egg separate and two complete embryos form. These embryos have exactly the same genetic information. If identical twins exhibit the same expression of a trait, then it would appear that the trait is heavily influenced by the environment. The message from such studies is that both genes and environment are important.

Fraternal twins, on the other hand, are the product of two entirely different eggs simultaneously matured by the mother and fertilized, approximately at the same time, by two entirely different sperms. They carry quite different genes, and need be no more alike than any other non twin siblings in the same family, as often as not, in fact, being of opposite sex.

In other words, identical twins are from the standpoint of heredity, exactly the same individual in duplicate. Fraternal twins are two entirely different individuals who merely through chances were born together.

By comparing the twins with regards to many characteristics known to be definitely inherited or influenced by heredity, they can tell whether or not the degree of resemblance or correlation is high enough to stamp them as identical among the characteristics used for comparison are blood groups, blood pressure, pulse, respiration, and brain wave patterns, eye color, and vision, palm, sole and finger patterns: skin color, hair color, hair form and various minor hereditary abnormalities where present. The correlation in those characteristics is so much greater between any two identical twins that there is virtually no possibility of confusing their relationship.

In as much as identical twins have exactly the same heredity, whatever differences there are between them must be due to environment. But when identical twins are reared in different environments, there being instances of such separation in infancy and nonetheless develop marked similarities of any kind, these might be ascribed to heredity.

The study of fraternal twins takes a different direction. In their case, as they have much more similar environment in prenatal life and often thereafter than singly born individuals, the question is how much more alike this will tend to make them.

If heredity were everything, then identical twins would be exactly the same in all respects, even if reared apart. But a number of studies show that they are never exactly alike, even though they do have remarkable similarities in most respects.

On the other hand, if environment were everything, then fraternal twins, reared under the same conditions, would also be alike, regardless of how different were their genes. But here we find that although they show a closer resemblance to each other than do non-twin brothers and sisters, “fraternal,” even when of the same sex are very much alike than are “identical” reared apart.

Thus, the various studies of twins have comprised an important source of evidence for geneticists. No identical twins are really identical because they cannot possibly have had identical environments, even before birth.

If all human traits behaved in the clear-cut Mendelian fashion that *Albinism* and *Huntington's chorea* do, twin studies would not be necessary as an aid in unraveling the complications that the environment often superimposes upon a Mendelian pattern of heredity. There seems to be a rule that the most common defects have the largest environmental component, which makes it difficult to tell whether their hereditary basis for the abnormality is a simple dominant or recessive. The environment acts to suppress the expression of the abnormal gene in some cases but fails to do so in others! It can be appreciated that this unpredictable behaviour of environmental factors would upset the classic orderly Mendelian ratios, especially if they are the complicated ones that result when more than one gene pair is involved.

Pairs of twins are useful in detecting the relative effectiveness of heredity and environment upon the expression of a disease or trait. If a trait is highly hereditary, both members of a pair of identical twins will be expected to show the trait. If one identical twin shows the trait and the other member of the pair does not, the disagreement must be due to environmental differences between the two twins, because the genes of one are exactly the same as the genes of the other.

We know that the heredity of blood groups behaves according to the Mendelian rules and that environment seems to have no affect on the kind of blood group a person has. Identical twins both have exactly the same blood group. Tuberculosis is a good example of a disease in which an hereditary susceptibility and an environmentally favourable situation are both necessary for the appearance of the active disease. A comparison of the behaviour of identical and fraternal, and for susceptibility to tuberculosis, where heredity and environment share the responsibility.

CHROMOSOME

In the nucleus of each cell, the DNA molecule is packaged into thread-like structures called **chromosomes.** Each chromosome is made up of DNA tightly coiled many times around proteins called *histones* that support its structure.

Chromosomes are not visible in the cell's nucleus—not even under a microscope—when the cell is not dividing. However, the DNA that makes up chromosomes becomes more tightly packed during cell division and is then visible under a microscope. Most of what researchers know about chromosomes was learned by observing chromosomes during cell division.

Each chromosome has a constriction point called the centromere, which divides the chromosome into two sections, or "arms." The short arm of the chromosome is labelled the "p arm." The long arm of the chromosome is labelled the "q arm." The location of the centromere on each chromosome gives the chromosome its characteristic shape, and can be used to help describe the location of specific genes.

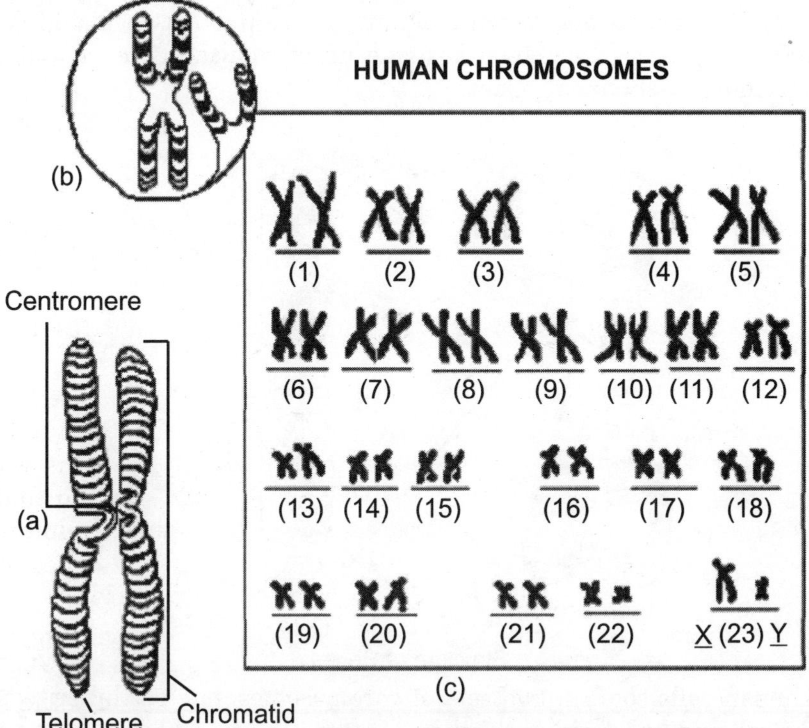

Representation of the 23 Paired Chromosomes of the Human.

GENES

Genes are working subunits of DNA. DNA is a vast chemical information database that carries the complete set of instructions for making all the proteins a cell will ever need. Each gene contains a particular set of instructions, usually coding for a particular protein.

DNA exists as two long, paired strands spiraled into the famous double helix. Each strand is made up of millions of chemical building blocks called bases. While there are only four different chemical bases in DNA (adenine, thymine, cytosine and guanine), the order in which the bases occur determines the information available, much as specific letters of the alphabet combine to form words and sentences.

DNA resides in the core, or nucleus, of each of the body's trillions of cells. Every human cell (with the exception of mature red blood cells, which have no nucleus) contains the same DNA. Each cell has 46 molecules of double-stranded DNA. Each molecule is made up of 50 to 250 million bases housed in a chromosome.

The DNA in each chromosome constitutes many genes (as well as vast stretches of noncoding DNA, the function of which is unknown). A gene is any given segment along the DNA that encodes instructions that allow a cell to produce a specific product—typically, a protein such as an enzyme—that initiates one specific action. There are between 50,000 and 100,000 genes, and every gene is made up of thousands, even hundreds of thousands, of chemical bases.

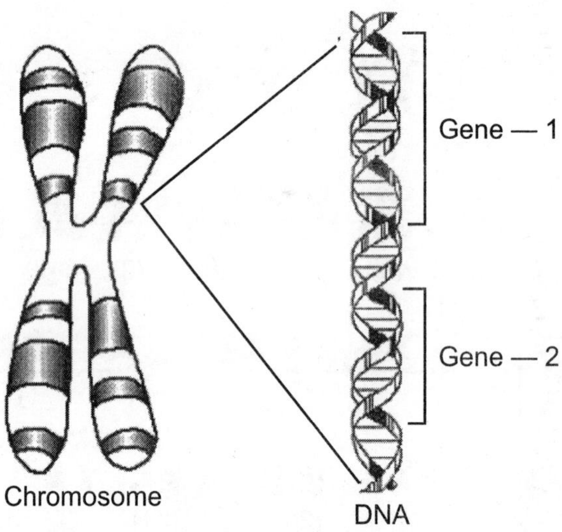

Structure of Genes.

Human cells contain two sets of chromosomes, one set inherited from the mother and one from the father. (Mature sperm and egg cells carry a single set of chromosomes.) Each set has 23 single chromosomes—22 autosomes and an X or Y sex chromosome. (Females inherit an X from each parent, while males get an X from the mother and a Y from the father.) These are working subunits of DNA. DNA is a vast chemical information database that carries the complete set of instructions for making all the proteins a cell will ever need. Each gene contains a particular set of instructions, usually coding for a particular protein.

The problem of nature versus nurture defies satisfactory solution. As a matter of fact it is futile to ask which of two factors, heredity or environment is more important. According to Maclver every phenomenon of life is the product of both, each is as necessary to the result as the other, neither can ever be eliminated and neither can be isolated.

MEANING OF ENVIRONMENT

Environmental factor is the most important factor for planet, earth and living beings. This text involves different types of environment, the definition of environment and the importance of environment for living beings.

Factors Responsible for the Degradation of the Environment.

DEFINITION OF ENVIRONMENT

'Environment', this word has a great importance in our life. The simple definition of environment is the 'surrounding'. It is what surrounds a thing. We can also define it as "environment is the combination of all of physical and organic factors that act on a living being, residents, or ecological society and power its endurance and growth".

It could be a physical component, which is known as physical environment or a-biotic environment that includes the built environment. The natural surroundings like air conditions, water, land, atmosphere etc. are also the part of physical environment but they are commonly known as natural environment. People surrounding the item or thing, this type of environment is known as human environment. This is also known as the social environment and includes elements like the religious environment, emotional environment, residence, relations etc.

TYPES OF ENVIRONMENT

There are mainly three types of environment:

1. The Physical or Abiotic Environment

It is also known as *natural environment*. The meaning of 'abiotic' or 'physical' is non-living like land, water, air conditions atmosphere which constitutes of soil. So we can say that physical or abiotic environment is the environment which includes nonliving or physical things which are constitutes of soil and affect the living things. The physical or abiotic environment also includes the climatic factors such as sunbeams, rainwater, precipitation, moisture, pressure and wind speed.

The Importance of Physical Environment

- Just think, the most important thing to make house is residential space, and for residential space, we need land area. The land area is included in physical environment. So it is responsible for the residential for living beings.
- The abiotic environment like soil, water and air are the necessary nutrients element provider for the living beings.

- All of living beings are surrounded by atmosphere; it is the combination of different types of gases. The living beings take oxygen and other gases from the atmosphere.
- The abiotic environment also controls the climatic factors like weather.
- The physical environment also includes the soil which is responsible for the works and food crops for the living beings. It also provides different types of minerals which are very necessary for growth of life.
- Water is one of the most necessary things for living beings. Physical environment also deals with the water factor of the earth.

2. Biotic Environment

It is also known as biological environment and organic environment. In the opposite side of the physical environment, the biotic or biological environment is responsible for the living beings. You have already understood that the meaning of 'biological' is living things. So, the biological environment is the environment which involves the living part of the earth.

The Importance of Biotic Environment

- In this type of environment includes the plants, trees, animals, mammals, underwater living beings including human beings and microorganisms like bacteria and fungi.
- There is a concept which is necessary to understand. The living beings are highly dependent to each other. For example humans are highly depend upon plants and trees for food and oxygen, and plants and trees are also depend upon humans and animals because of CO_2.

3. Social or Cultural Environment

This type of environment involves the culture and life style of the human beings. The social or cultural environment means the environment which is created by the man through his different social and cultural activities and thinking. The historical, cultural, political, moral, economic aspects of human life constitute to the social or cultural environment.

The Importance of Social or Cultural Environment

- Culture involves the religion of the human, relations with each other etc. In a society there involve different types of people, they have different religion, different thinking, which has culture of its own and posses people having their own life style.
- The social or culture environment affects the social culture of human beings and hence it has the great importance.
- The development of a child is highly depends upon culture and society.

RELATIONSHIP BETWEEN HEREDITY AND ENVIRONMENT

Organisms can transmit some hereditary conditions to their offspring even if the parents do not show the trait. In the small, familiar fruit fly. Drosophila, there is a hereditary trait in which the wings curl up sharply if the files are raised at a temperature of 25°C. If, however, the files are raised at a lower temperature, such as 16°C then the trait rarely appears. The wings seem to be straight, and the flies look normal. The genetic trait is there, however, and will reappear in the next generation if the temperature returns to 25°C.

A similar type of inheritance appears in plants. In some types of corn the kernels will remain yellow until they are exposed to sunlight. Once exposed, the kernels become various shades of red and purple. Some traits do not appear to be affected by the environment. One of the first hereditary traits studied in humans was polydactyly. An individual with polydactyly has more than ten figures or toes. This trait does not seem to be affected by the environment at all. Other human traits like color blindness, baldness, blood type, skin color, the ability to taste certain substances, the presence or absence of hairs on the middle of the fingers, and free or attached ear lobes do not seem to be influenced by the environment.

HEREDITARY AND ENVIRONMENT ARE NOT SEPARABLE

No society is a product of environment alone for men inherit physical heritage. There is incessant interaction between the two. They are inseparable. One man is a law-abiding citizen, another is a criminal; one is militarist and another pacifist. It is difficult to indicate any genetic basis for these variations and in many cases it is almost impossible to assess properly the relative role of heredity and environment in producing these differences. Both have been operative to produce every particular situation since time immemorial.

In no case of personality development can we properly attribute any characteristic to heredity or to environment alone. A given result is always produced by the interaction of gene substance and their environment. We should therefore be interested in asking about the absolute contribution of either factor as a whole. The conclusions that can be drawn is that the question which is more important, heredity or environment wrongly assumes that environment and heredity are opposed so that if one is important the other cannot be. All the qualities of life are in the heredity all the evocations of qualities depend on the environment. In other words heredity has potentiality and environment offers it a chance of bringing them out. It also follows from this principle that the higher the potentiality, the greater is the demand made on environment.

Thus more subtle differences in environment may have little effect on those of low potentiality while the same differences may be vastly significant for those who have higher potentiality. For instance a minor change in a situation say a rebuff may prove decisive to a sensitive nature while it may not affect a thick skinned man. Lastly, the more elastic the life the more is it at the mercy of environment. That is why environment affects us most in the earlier years of our life when we are most impressionable. It is clear that heredity and environment—the two ultimate determinants of every living being are of co-equal importance and that none is more potent than the other.

PERSONALITY, WORK ENVIRONMENT AND PERFORMANCE

According to Schneider, "the people make the place," and people are differentially attracted to, differentially selected, and differentially leave organizations. Costa, McCrae and Holland assert that people begin this process by selecting into vocations that match their personalities. Similarity between a job applicant's values and the values of recruiters and employees within organizations has been shown to result in improved work attitudes and increased performance after organizational entry. Research by Cable and Judge and Judge and Cable provides evidence that applicants pro-actively choose such organizational environments based on individual preferences, as they found that job candidates seek organizations with reward systems and cultures that fit their personalities. Of even greater significance is the possibility that the relationship between personality characteristics and specific work environments may influence performance.

The general trend in the research has been towards increased optimism regarding the utility of personality tests in personnel selection with the goal of ultimately enhancing job performance. The general consensus has been that personality holds utility as a predictor of job performance, specifically the conscientiousness dimension. Research has also provided evidence of linkages between personality dimensions with narrower facets of performance. Research by Motowidlo and Van Scotter; Van Scotter and Motowidlo, suggests that personality has a larger impact on contextual (as opposed to task-oriented) dimensions of performance; specifically, extraversion and agreeableness were more strongly related to interpersonal facilitation. *Hurtz* and *Donovan* found that emotional stability and agreeableness were also significant predictors of interpersonal facilitation, and emotional stability was a predictor of task performance.

However, a number of different studies have begun to illustrate that the effects of personality on performance may be more indirect than bivariate. Recent research indicates the intervening effects of performance expectancies, self-efficacy, and goal-setting on the relationship between conscientiousness and performance. These studies illuminate a significant gap in the literature—that the research to date has disproportionately focused on the direct linkage between personality and performance, and "... if we are to truly understand the relationship between personality and job performance, we must move beyond this bivariate relationship and toward specifying the intervening variables that link these domains". Although specific personality traits like conscientiousness have been linked to a variety of employee outcomes, what remains unclear is the nature of the relationship between personality, work environment preferences, and such outcomes. It is possible that personality is primarily expressed in individual preferences for work environments, and that the direct effects of personality on workplace outcomes are fully or partially mediated by such preferences. Thus, we may find that specific work environment preferences may be more substantial predictors of employee outcomes in organizations than Big Five personality factors.

This study utilizes Barrick and Mount's Big Five factors of personality, and Moos' conceptualization of work environments as the theoretical bases for the constructs of personality and work environments. Barrick and Mount's Big Five factors represent a widely accepted approach to conceptualizing personality, as meta-analyses consistently support the construct validity of this approach.The Big Five factors consist of an individual's openness to experience (proactive seeking, toleration for and exploration of the unfamiliar), conscientiousness (thorough approach, hard-working, organized), extraversion (the need for stimulation, desire for activity levels with interpersonal interaction), agreeableness (cooperative nature, likeability) and emotional stability (calm and secure, low in anxiety).

According to Moos, work environment preferences can be measured using three dimensions of work environment settings: system maintenance, goal orientation, and relationship dimensions. System maintenance refers to how orderly and organized the work setting is, how clear it is in its expectations, and how much control it maintains. Goal orientation assesses the degree to which an environment encourages or stifles growth through providing for participation in decision making and autonomy, maintaining a task orientation, and providing job challenge and expectations for success and accomplishment. The relationship dimension measures the degree of interpersonal interaction in a work environment, such as the social communication exchanges and cohesion among workers, and the friendship and support provided by co-workers and management. These work environment preferences have been shown to affect individuals' personal functioning at work (Billings and Moos, 1982). Examination of work environment preferences can help identify organizational factors that may be problematic, and can guide interventions aimed at reducing employee stress in a variety of work settings.

ENVIRONMENT AND HEREDITY: PHYSICAL GROWTH AND MOTOR SKILLS

Environmental and hereditary elements that affect physical growth and motor skills development in early childhood are:

- Heredity affects physical growth by regulating production of hormones.
- Extreme emotional deprivation interferes with production of growth hormones.
- Disease can lead to malnutrition, which affects a child's development.
- Smoking — can lead to increase in infections, sinuses, and lungs.
- Parents can encourage their children to participate in physical activity.

HEREDITY – THE ENVIRONMENT AND DEVELOPMENT

The first individual to systematically study the human behaviour and heredity was Sir Francis Galton. Heredity is basically concerned with biological variation. On the other hand, behavioral genetics is concerned with two things, that is, how genetics and the environment interrelate to influence the behavior of a human being. However, according to *Kail et al.* behavioral genetics is complicated by the inherent difficulty to come up with a definition of the behavior under consideration. For example, intelligence is itself hard to define. The question of how heredity and environment may act to influence an individual's behavior development with regard to intelligence may be hard to answer as intelligence has no assigned meaning.

Behavioural genetics is further complicated by multiple genes. This trait has been cited as frustrating efforts to pinpoint genetic contributions. Another aspect that *Kail et al.* cites as making behavioral genetics a difficult subject to explore is the requirement and need to carry out an analysis of populations as well as families. This enhances measures to compare those with and without the trait under consideration.

With regard to genetic and evolutionary concepts, development is set from the beginning to the end and hence it can be said to be largely predetermined. This is what is referred to as genetic determination. In this view, the various development levels are determined by information contained in the genes. This development levels could span across the various organs all the way to the characteristics of a psychological nature.

According to *Shaffer*, it is important to note that not all psychological characteristics are subject to information carried in the genes. At times, it has been noted that certain psychological characteristics are subject to variations over time as a result of changes that can be attributed to the environment as well as various experiences based on individual's interaction with one another. This points out that, organisms in a continuous basis adapt to their environment and therefore the theory regarding to genetic determination is not conclusive and hence adaptability should be described using systems that are adaptable.

Several factors with regard to the influence of the environment can be mapped out in an infant's physical growth and development. An example of such a factor is nutrition. A mother's inadequate diet and nutritional intake can have an effect in an infant and risk the occurrence of such things as still birth and congenital defects. A pregnant mother's exposure to severe emotional stress can contribute in a big way to a premature delivery or even result in a miscarriage. According to Shaffer, an infant's prenatal development can be influenced by a wide range of factors other than maternal issues. These other factors may include diseases, exposure to radiation and other environmental agents.

According to Shaffer, a child's development and how it is influenced by the environment is called *nurture*. This may include a love for the movies etc. As a child develops, he or she is inclined to avoid things that result in punishment and on the other hand he is influenced to do things which he is rewarded for. To fully comprehend the nature of a child's development, we must first understand the complicated interrelation between environment and heredity.

Kalat notes that a child's development is both affected by nurture and nature. While this interaction is vital with regard to psychological development, they lead to a more complicated way of identifying the various causes of development. With that in mind it therefore follows that not all aspects of psychological characteristics acquisition can be understood in the framework of genetic determination and in such a case, it may be useful to consider using epigenetic models which are more complex.

With regard to the theory of social construction as was advanced by Vygotsky, Kail et al. notes that in line with the acquisition of cultural tools, a child acquires the various models of social interaction. To explain this in a clearer way, the following scenario may be useful. The child's use of a spoon over time can be used to explain the child's gain of this cultural tool. In a child's first interaction with a spoon, he may tend to hold it just as he would hold any other object.

However a parent's intervention may over time influence the way the child holds the spoon. The child is taught that that is the right manner in which a spoon should be held so as to reflect good mannerisms.

Kail et al. notes that a child holding the spoon as it should be cannot be accounted for by genetics alone but rather by the various environmental factors such as the parent's interference.

CULTURE

Introduction. Meaning of Culture. The Development of Culture. Characteristics of Culture: *Culture is Learned, Culture is Non-instinctive, Culture is Cumulative, Culture is Based on Symbols, Culture is Integrated, Culture is Dynamic.* ***Basic Elements of Culture. Functions of Culture. Culture Contents:*** *Material Culture, Non-material Culture.* ***Cultural Growth:*** *Cultural Diffusion, Types of Cultural Diffusion, Cultural Invention.* ***Changing Concept of Culture. Causes of Cultural Change:*** *A Global Culture.* ***Components of Culture. Social Values and Norms. Culture by Social Class:*** *Sub-Culture, Multiculturalism, Counter Culture, Cultural Change, Cultural Lag.* ***Subculture. Monochronic and Polychronic Cultures. High-context and Low-context Cultures. Cultural Relativism. Civilisation. Culture and Civilization.***

INTRODUCTION

As Homo sapiens, evolved, several biological characteristics particularly favourable to the development of culture appeared in the species. These included erect posture; a favourable brain structure; stereoscopic vision; the structure of the hand, a flexible shoulder; and year round sexual receptivity on the part of the female. None of these biological characteristics alone, of course, accounts for the development of culture. Even in combination, all they guarantee is that human beings would be the most gifted members of the animal kingdom.

The distinctive human way of life that we call culture did not have a single definite beginning in time any more than human beings suddenly appearing on earth. Culture evolved slowly just as some anthropoids gradually took on more human form. Unmistakably, tools existed half a million years ago and might be considerably older. If, for convenience, we say that culture is 500,000 years old, it is still difficult day has appeared very recently.

The concept of culture was rigorously defined by *E.B. Taylor* in 1860s. According to him, culture is the sum total of ideas, beliefs, values, material cultural equipment and non-material aspects which man makes as a member of society. Taylor's theme that culture is a result of human collectivity has been accepted by most anthropologists. Tylarian idea can be discerned in a modern definition of culture—*culture is the man-made part of environment.*

From this, it follows that culture and society are separable only at the analytical level: at the actual existential level, they can be understood as the two sides of the same coin. Culture, on one hand, is an outcome of society and, on the other hand, society is able to survive and perpetuate itself because of the existence of culture. Culture is an ally of man in the sense that it enhances man's adaptability to nature. It is because of the adaptive value of culture that Herskovits states that culture is a screen between man and nature. Culture is an instrument by which man exploits the environment and shapes it accordingly.

Culture can be conceived as a continuous, cumulative reservoir containing both material and non-material elements that are socially transmitted from generation to generation. Culture is continuous because cultural patterns transcend years, reappearing in successive generations. Culture is cumulative because each generation contributes to the reservoir.

An inherent paradox exists within the social heritage where culture tends to be both static and dynamic. Humans, once having internalized culture, attach positive value judgments to it and are more or less reluctant to change their established ways of life. Through most of recorded history men have apparently considered that change per say is undesirable and that the ideal condition is stability. The prospect of change can seem threatening, yet every human culture is subject to and does experience change. Those who speak of a generation gap portray two generations at odds with each other. According to this view, the parent generation embodied the dynamic dimension. We contend that if, in fact, a generation gap does exist in modern societies, and the differences are of degree and not of substance. Part of the social heritage of almost every modern society is the high value placed on progress. Parents encourage young people to seek progress and progress is a form of social change. Debates between generations in modern societies are seldom about whether any change should occur. The debates are usually about how such change should occur, how fast it should occur, and which methods should be used for bringing about change enduring sexual partnerships, the desire for variety which conflicts with the desire for continuity and remarkable pliability with sex interest channeled through whatever patterns a society has established as normal.

MEANING OF CULTURE

Culture refers to the pattern of human activity and the symbols that give significance to these activities. Culture manifests itself in terms of the art, literature, costumes, customs, language, religion and religious rituals. The people and their pattern of life make up the culture of a region. Cultures vary in the different parts of the world. They are different across the land boundaries and the diversity in cultures results in the diversity in people around the world. Culture also consists of the system of beliefs held by the people of the region, their principles of life and their moral values. The patterns of behaviour of the people of a particular region also form a part of the region's culture. The word 'culture' that hails from the Latin word, 'cultura' derived from 'colere', means, 'to cultivate'. Hence the way in which the minds of the masses inhabiting a particular region are cultivated, in someway determines the culture of a region. Let us look at the basic characteristics of culture and its fundamental elements.

THE DEVELOPMENT OF CULTURE

The distinctive human way of life that we call culture did not have a single definite beginning. This is to say that human beings did not suddenly appear on earth. Culture evolved slowly just as anthropoids gradually took on more human form. The earliest tools cannot be dated precisely. Australopithecus may have used stones as weapons as long as five million years ago. Stones that have been used as weapon do not differ systematically from other stones, however, and there is no way to tell for sure. The first stones that show reliable evidence of having been shaped as tools trace back some 500,000 to 600,000 years. The use of fire can be dated from 200,000 to 300,000 years ago. Tools of bone had come into existence by 100,000 B.C. the age of Neanderthals. The Neanderthals also apparently had some form of languages and buried their deal with an elaborateness that indicates the possibility of religious ceremonies. Cro-Magnon, dating from 35,000 years ago, was a superior biological specimen and had a correspondingly more elaborate culture. Their cave paintings have been found. They also made jewellery of shells and teeth, and carved statuettes of women that emphasized pregnancy and fertility. They made weapons of bone, horn and ivory, and used needle in the fabrication of garments.

Thus, a striking parallel appears between the evolution of Homo sapiens and the development of culture. The parallel cannot be drawn in detail because all inferences to the period before the dawn of history must be made from material artifacts, and these tell little about the total way of life of the people who used them. Moreover, the parallel between biological and cultural evolution should not be overdrawn. Cro-Magnon's brain capacity, for example, was large, but factors having to do with the growth of culture itself were sufficient to prevent any quantum leap in the development of learned behaviour.

CHARACTERISTICS OF CULTURE

Culture is shared, by which we mean that every culture is shared by a group of people. Depending on the region they live in, the climatic conditions they thrive in and their historical heritage, they form a set of values and beliefs. This set of their principles of life shapes their culture. No culture belongs to an individual. It is rather shared among many people of a certain part of the world. It belongs to a single community and not to any single human being.

CULTURE IS LEARNED

Culture is learned, not biologically inherited. The process whereby culture is passed from one generation to the next is called enculturation. Children begin learning their cultures the moment they are born. Parents and extended family teach children what is expected of them in terms of familial duty and contributions to the household.

The members of a culture share certain ideals, which shape their lives. Generations learn to follow these ideals and principles. Culture propagates through generations, which adopt their old customs and traditions as a part of their culture. The ideals they base their lives on is a part of their culture. Cultural values are imparted from one generation to another, thus resulting in a continual of traditions that are a part of culture. The language, the literature and the art forms pass across generations. Culture is learned, understood and adopted by the younger generations of society. No individual is born with a sense of his/her culture. He/she has to learn it.

A gradual change is characteristic to almost every culture. Cultures are subject to change. Culture loses some of its traits and gains new ones. The aspects of culture that change vary across societies. With the passage of time, new technologies emerge, new modes of work come up, social thinking undergoes transitions and so does culture. Every culture changes in time although the rate of change of every culture varies.

CULTURE IS NON-INSTINCTIVE

Human infants come into the world with basic drives such as hunger and thirst, but they do not possess instinctive patterns of behaviour to satisfy them. Likewise, they are without any cultural knowledge. However, they are genetically predisposed to rapidly learn language and other cultural traits. New born humans are amazing learning machines. Any normal baby can be placed into any family on earth and grow up to learn their culture and accept it as his or her own. Since culture is non-instinctive, we are not genetically programmed to learn a particular one.

CULTURE IS CUMULATIVE

Every human generation potentially can discover new things and invent better technologies. The new cultural skills and knowledge are added onto what was learned in previous generations. As a result, culture is cumulative. Due to this cumulative effect, most high school students today are now familiar with mathematical insights and solutions that ancient Greeks such as Archimedes and Pythagoras struggled their lives to discover.

CULTURE IS BASED ON SYMBOLS

Much of human behaviour is mediated by symbols—signs, sounds, emblems, and other things that represent meaningful concepts. For instance, the religious symbols found in most Oaxacan homes (city situated in Mexico) represent a particular belief system and are used to remind people of their faith and their moral code. The most important symbolic aspect of culture is language. Language represents the most pervasive use of symbols in a culture because it uses symbols to represent objects and ideas.

CULTURE IS INTEGRATED

The foundation of culture includes three structural elements that work together to keep the culture strong. An infrastructure provides the basic necessities of life, a social structure determines how people interact with one another, and a superstructure, or worldview, provides a belief system that helps people identify themselves, their society, and the world around them. It is apparent in the video that the infrastructure in Oaxaca is changing, which affects the other layers of structural elements as well.

CULTURE IS DYNAMIC

When one element within the system shifts, the entire system shifts to accommodate it. When the women of Oaxaca leave their cultural homeland and flock to the city to work, they provide an example of the dynamic nature of culture. They and their families must adapt to new circumstances without losing their cultural identities.

BASIC ELEMENTS OF CULTURE

The language, other forms of expression as also the thoughts and emotions of the people, their social and cultural norms, their principles and beliefs are the basic elements of culture. For an effective transfer of culture from one generation to another, it has to be translated in terms of symbols, which represent the cultural values of a community. Language, art and religion form the system of symbols that render a deep meaning to culture.

Despite the efforts of the older generations to transfer their cultural values to the forthcoming generations, many tend to remain unaware of their culture. People are often found to have an incomplete knowledge of their culture. People seldom know their culture completely.

FUNCTIONS OF CULTURE

Culture carries with it a framework of meaning and interpretation that enables participants to integrate themselves and their activities into a meaningful whole.

Culture provides reasons for participants to be willing to devote energy and loyalty to the organization. It provides reasons for sacrifice and investment of self in the future of the organization.

Culture legitimates the structure of authority and organization that control activities within the organization. Myth, ritual, and symbol provide explanations for activities and thus help to reconcile differences between ideals and actual behaviour.

Culture can also be seen to play a specific function in social life. According to *Griswold*, "The sociological analysis of culture begins at the premise that culture provides orientation, wards off chaos, and directs behaviour toward certain lines of action and away from others". *Griswold* reiterates this point by explaining that, "Groups and societies need collective representations of themselves to inspire sentiments of unity and mutual support, and culture fulfills this need."

In other words, culture can have a certain utilitarian function; the maintenance of order as the result of shared understandings and meanings (this understanding of culture is similar to the Symbolic Interactionist understanding of society).

CULTURE CONTENTS

Culture is a socially learned and transmitted behaviour. Ideas, norms, values and beliefs are largely dependent on the kind of culture we belong to as the products of this culture. A culture is the collective manifestation of human intellectual achievement, and relates to the accomplishments and attitudes of a people of a particular time.

MATERIAL CULTURE

Material culture includes all of the physical objects that people create and give meaning to. These are houses, food items, factories, raw materials technologies, cars, clothing, schools, computers, and books would be examples. An object only becomes part of culture after meaning have been given to it. A rock in a field has no meaning until it is used as a tool or to build a fence.

A material culture places emphasis on objects, material accomplishments; the acquisition of material wealth; skill and productivity in arts and crafts; technology; fine buildings and displays of material prosperity.

NON-MATERIAL CULTURE

Non-material culture consists of thoughts and behaviour that people learn as part of the culture they live in. It includes politics, economics, language, rules, customs, family, religion or beliefs, values, and knowledge.

The non-material aspects of any culture are its beliefs, customs, philosophy, patterns and ways of communication (verbal and non-verbal) and its government. Every culture is the product of this interaction between its' material and non-material aspects. A non-material culture values 'abstract/intangible' things more highly than objects, e.g., things such as ideas; the things of the mind; philosophy; metaphysics; spirituality; values; beliefs; relationships between god and man; being, etc.

CULTURAL GROWTH

CULTURAL DIFFUSION

The process of knowledge, skills, and technology being spread from one society to another, from one place to another place in a due course of time, although during the process of cultural diffusion a drift in the culture at the new place may occur, like change in style of clothing and change in style of transport and change in style of hunting and food habits etc. cultural diffusion is mainly done in order to prevent starving in a group.

Inter-cultural diffusion can happen in many ways. Migrating populations will carry their culture with them. Ideas can be carried by trans-cultural visitors, such as merchants, explorers, soldiers, diplomats, slaves, and hired artisans. Technology diffusion has often occurred by one society luring skilled scientists or workers by payments or other inducement. Trans-cultural marriages between two neighbouring or interspersed cultures have also contributed. Among literate societies, diffusion can happen through letters or books (and in modern times, through other media as well).

TYPES OF CULTURAL DIFFUSION

- **Expansion diffusion:** An innovation or idea that develops in a source area and remains strong there, while also spreading outward to other areas.
- **Relocation diffusion:** An idea or innovation that migrates into new areas, leaving behind its origin or source of the cultural trait.
- **Hierarchical diffusion:** An idea or innovation that spreads by moving from larger to smaller places, often with little regard to the distance between places, and often influenced by social elites.
- **Contagious diffusion:** An idea or innovation based on person-to-person contact within a given population.

CULTURAL INVENTION

A cultural invention is any new or useful innovation developed by people that is not of a physical construct. Cultural inventions include sets of behaviour adopted by groups of people as useful. They are perpetuated by being passed on to others within the group or outside it. They are also passed on to future groups and generations.

Examples are:

- Languages
- Legal systems
- Political systems
- Scientific method
- Sports.

CHANGING CONCEPT OF CULTURE

Today most social scientists reject the cultured vs. uncultured concept of culture and the opposition of culture to human nature. They recognize that non-elites are as cultured as elites (and that non-Westerners are just as civilized); they are just cultured in a different way.

During the Romantic Era, scholars in Germany, especially those concerned with nationalism, developed a more inclusive notion of culture as worldview. That is, each ethnic group is characterized by a distinct and incommensurable world view. Although more inclusive, this approach to culture still allowed for distinctions between civilized and primitive or tribal cultures.

By the late 19th century, anthropologists had changed the concept of culture to include a wider variety of societies, ultimately resulting in the concept of culture outlined above - objects and symbols, the meaning given to those objects and symbols, and the norms, values, and beliefs that pervade social life.

This new perspective has also removed the evaluative element of the concept of culture and instead proposes distinctions rather than rankings between different cultures. For instance, the high culture of elites is now contrasted with popular or pop culture. In this sense, high culture no longer refers to the idea of being cultured, as all people are cultured. High culture simply refers to the objects, symbols, norms, values, and beliefs of a particular group of people; popular culture does the same.

India is a country of multitudes of religions with varied rituals and practices. Even Hinduism which is followed by many has gone through changes according to the regional practices pertaining to climate, habits and linguistics. Cultural changes happen according to the needs of socio economic trends. In the olden days importance was given to the elders whose blessings were sought by the youngsters. Sumptuous food was prepared at home and every one sat together to eat and enjoyed the family union at such gatherings. Festivals were always celebrated in groups either with their families or community. Some visited the temples also. In recent times, festivals are celebrated in star hotels, discothques and cinema halls. The elders too celebrate but in old age homes with their collegues.

In the past 50 years India has undergone a terrific change due to the British and Western influences. Birthdays, wedding days are celebrated by lighting candles, cutting cakes, hosting parties. Ushering in the new year in January is done with great fun and fare. Surprisingly there is no objections to these celebrations. Infact the real significances of celebrating the festivals are forgotten. People watch special programmes in Television or go to theatres to watch newly released films on these occasions. Late night parties and special events on dance floors are order of the day.

In India, these festivals and occasions are also celebrated but there is so much hue and cry for Valentines day being celebrated. It has been concluded that people object to the unruly and indecent behaviour of some teenagers or unmarried lovers who view this day as a license given to them to do anything they want. Disciplined celebrations are appreciated in India but we should draw a line between immoral and decent behaviour.

CAUSES OF CULTURAL CHANGE

Cultures are internally affected by both forces encouraging change and forces resisting change. These forces are related to both social structures and natural events, and are involved in the perpetuation of cultural ideas and practices within current structures, which themselves are subject to change.

Social conflict and the development of technologies can produce changes within a society by altering social dynamics and promoting new cultural models, and spurring or enabling generative action. These social shifts may accompany ideological shifts and other types of cultural change. Environmental conditions may also enter as factors. For example, after tropical forests returned at the end of the last ice age, plants suitable for domestication were available, leading to the invention of agriculture, which in turn brought about many cultural innovations and shifts in social dynamics. Cultures are externally affected via contact between societies, which may also produce—or inhibit—social shifts and changes in cultural practices. War or competition over resources may impact technological development or social dynamics. Additionally, cultural ideas may transfer from one society to another, through diffusion or acculturation. In diffusion, the form of something (though not necessarily its meaning) moves from one culture to another. For example, hamburgers, mundane in the United States, seemed exotic when introduced into China. Stimulus diffusion (the sharing of ideas) refers to an element of one culture leading to an invention or propagation in another. "Direct Borrowing" on the other hand tends to refer to technological or tangible diffusion from one culture to another.

Diffusion of innovations theory presents a research-based model of why and when individuals and cultures adopt new ideas, practices, and products.

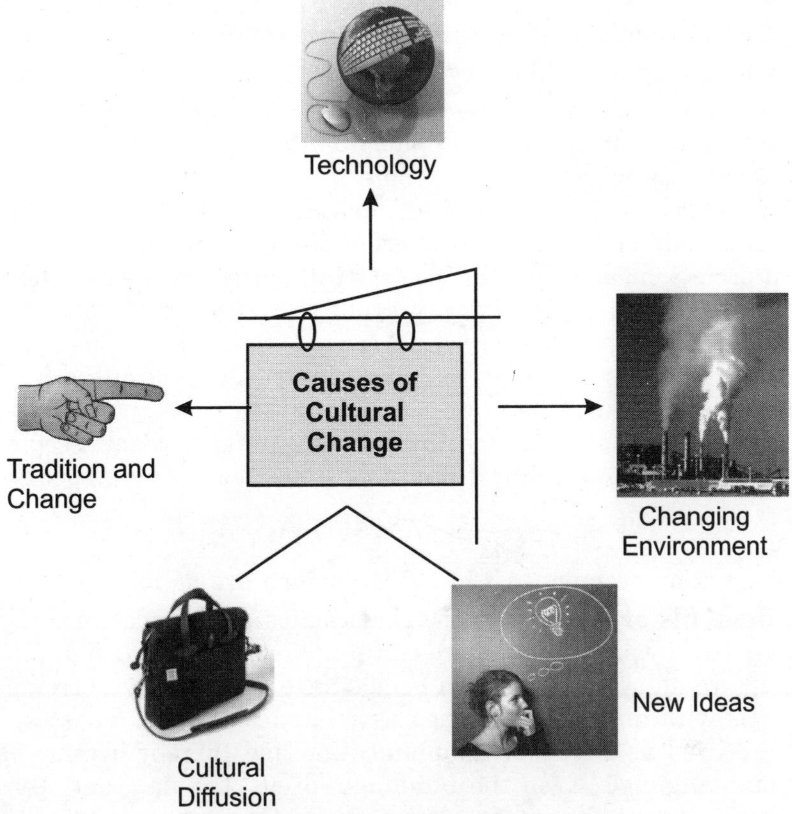

Causes of Cultural Change.

Acculturation has different meanings, but in this context refers to replacement of the traits of one culture with those of another, such has happened to certain Native American tribes and to many indigenous peoples across the globe during the process of colonization. Related processes on an individual level include assimilation (adoption of a different culture by an individual) and transculturation.

A GLOBAL CULTURE

Today, more than ever before, we can observe many of the same cultural practices being followed the world over. We find people wearing jeans, hear the familiar music, and see advertising for many of the same products in different countries. People learn some international language for purposes of communication.

Are we moving toward the single global culture?

Societies now have more contact with one another than ever before, involving the flow of goods, information and people. We are globally connected through:

- The global economy: the flow of goods.
- Global communication: the flow of information.
- Global migration: the flow of people.

These global links make the cultures of the world more similar. But there are three limitations to the global culture thesis. First, the global flow of goods, information, and people is uneven. Generally speaking, urban areas have stronger ties to one another, while many rural villages remain isolated. Then the greater economic and military power of the Western society means that this society influences the rest of the world more than happens the other way around. Second, the global culture thesis assumes that people everywhere are able to afford various new goods and services. That is not so as the poor countries cannot afford it. Third, although many cultural practices are now found throughout the world, people everywhere do not attach the same meaning to them. People have to interpret the other's cultural practices from their own perspective.

COMPONENTS OF CULTURE

There are various components of cuture, which are as follows:

- **Symbols or sign:** Anything that carries a particular meaning recognized by people who share culture. Whistle, flashing light, thumbs up are all symbols. Human beings have the capacity to create symbols with different meanings associated with each. These symbols are used as means of communication and thereby become part of our language. Even the buildings, dress, the flag, and a type of colour may be taken as symbols indicating some aspect of human behavior as well as society's outlook. Red, green, white, blue, pink, each of the colors stands for something in the society. Blue jeans are quite commonly used in Pakistan.
- **Language:** System of symbols that allows members of a society to communicate with one another. Symbols may be oral and these could be written words. We have oral cultural traditions. Human beings have developed different alphabet as part of written language. Language is the major means of cultural transmission. Is language uniquely human?
- **Values:** Culturally defined standards of desirability, goodness, and beauty that serve as broad guidelines for social living. What ought to be. Values are abstract standard of goodness, while beliefs are particular matters that individuals consider to be true or false.

  Examples of values: Equal opportunity; Achievement or success; Material comfort; Activity and work; Science; Freedom; Physical fitness; Health; Punctuality; Wealth; Education; Competition and

Merit; Honesty; Dignity of Labour; Patriotism; Justice and Democracy; Environmental Protection; Charity and Development. Sometimes there could be inconsistency in the values which can lead to a great conflict.

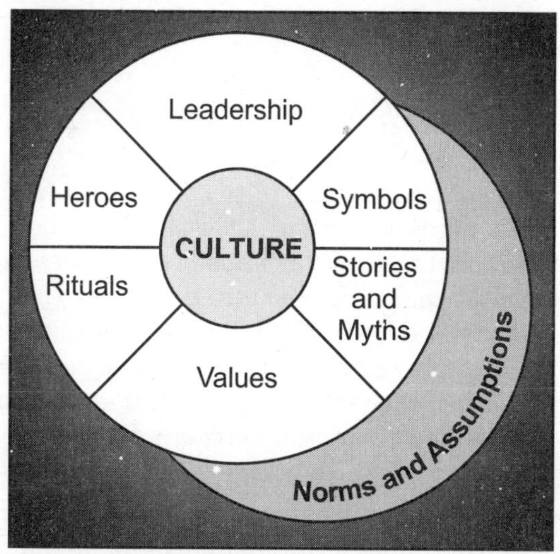

Components of Culture.

— **Beliefs:** Specific statements that people hold to be true. Values are broad principles that underlie beliefs.

— **Norms:** Rules and expectations by which a society guides the behavior of its members. These are the shared expectations of the people that govern their behavior.

- *Proscriptive norms:* Mandating what we should not do. Forbidding from certain actions.
- *Prescriptive norms:* What we should do.

— **Mores and Folkways:** W.G. Sumner gave these concepts

- *Mores (MORE-ays):* Society's standards of proper moral conduct. Such standards have been considered as essential to maintaining a way of life. These are the notions of right or wrong developed by society. Violation of mores brings a strong reaction from others.
- *Folkways:* Society's customs for routine, casual interaction. These are of less moral significance. Examples can be: proper dress, appropriate greetings, and common courtesy. People usually ignore the violation of folkways.

— **Ideal Culture and Real Culture:** These are as follows—

- *Ideal culture*—Social patterns that are mandated by cultural values and norms. The ideal values and norms, which are prevalent in the society.

- *Real culture*—Actual social patterns those only approximate cultural expectations. The norms and value that people actually follow. It can also be how many people follow these cultural patterns. Or how much a person observes a cultural pattern. Since this can be explained in numbers therefore it may also be called a statistical norm.

SOCIAL VALUES AND NORMS

Values and norms are evaluative beliefs that synthesize affective and ***cognitive elements*** to orient people to the world in which they live. Their evaluative element makes them unlike existential beliefs, which focus primarily on matters of truth or falsehood, correctness or incorrectness. Their cognitive element makes them unlike motives that can derive from emotions or psychological drives. Values and norms involve cognitive beliefs of approval or disapproval. Although they tend to persist through time and therefore faster continuity in society and human personality, they also are susceptible to change (Moss and Susman 1980; Alwin 1994).

The evaluative criteria represented in values and norms influence the behavior of subject units at multiple levels (e.g., individuals, organizations, and societies) as well as judgments about the behavior of others, which also can influence behavior. For example, values and norms affect the evaluation of individuals as suitable marriage partners and in that way influence marital behavior. Values and norms also affect evaluation of the governing policies and practices of societies and thus have an impact on diplomatic relations and the policies of one society's government toward other societies.

CULTURE BY SOCIAL CLASS

Cultural diversity can involve social class. In everyday life, we usually use the term "culture" to mean art forms such as classical literature, music, dance, and painting. We describe people who regularly go to the theater

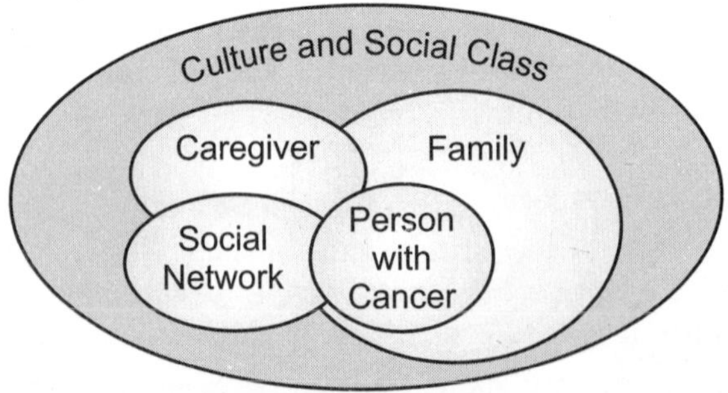

Culture by Social Class.

as "cultured," because we think they appreciate the "finer things in life." We speak less generously of ordinary people, assuming that everyday culture is somehow less worthy. Such judgements imply that many cultural patterns are readily accessible to only some members of society. This is how particular cultural patterns are associated with certain classes. We can further stretch the argument to other components of culture for finding variations in different classes.

People often divide society in different social classes and find that each class represents differences in their norms, values, beliefs, attitudes, and thinking. These norms, values, and attitudes may relate to the institutions of marriage and family, religion, education, earning a living, or their political behavior, one could find the differences. In this perspective culture is often divided into as:

- *High culture*: Cultural patterns that distinguish a society's elite.
- *Popular culture:* Cultural patterns those are widespread among a society's population.
- *Culture of poverty*: Cultural patterns shared by the poor.

SUB-CULTURE

Cultural patterns that set apart some segments of a society's population. Cluster of patterns which both are related to the general culture of the society yet distinguishable from it. The example could be: student subculture, business sub-culture.

MULTICULTURALISM

A policy followed by some governments whereby they recognize cultural diversity in the society and promote the equality of all cultural traditions. Canadian government is following such a policy.

COUNTER CULTURE

It is a subculture, which is in active opposition to the dominant culture. Cultural patterns that strongly oppose widely accepted patterns within a society. Example could be of hippies and drug users.

CULTURAL CHANGE

Cultural change is the process of alteration of culture over time. Any difference in a particular pattern between two points in time may be called cultural change. This may be a change in the family pattern, which is changing from 'joint family system' to a 'nuclear family system' in Pakistani society.

CULTURAL LAG

All parts (elements) of culture do not change at the same rate; some of them change faster than the other.

For example, material culture may change faster than the non-material culture. We often see it is difficult to change the habits quickly.

The different rate of change in the two integrated elements of culture can result in one element lagging behind the other. William F. Ogburn called this gap between the two parts of culture as 'cultural lag'. Such a cultural lag usually disrupts the system. For example we see so many automobiles on the road. There is an increase in their speed as well. There is a sharp increase in mobility. Let us look at another related aspect; these automobiles need a similar change in the quality of roads, which has not changed accordingly or you can say that it has lagged behind. Resultantly there is a lot of disruption leading to traffic jams, accidents, and pollution. You can also look at the 'traffic sense' among the public, be they the drivers, the passengers, the cyclists, or the pedestrians. This lag between the increase in automobiles and the inculcation of traffic sense in public also creates disruption in the system.

SUBCULTURE

"A cultural subgroup differentiated by status, ethnic background, residence, religion, or other factors that functionally unify the group and act collectively on each member." In sociology, anthropology and cultural studies, a subculture is a group of people with a culture (whether distinct or hidden) which differentiates them from the larger culture to which they belong. If a particular subculture is characterized by a systematic opposition to the dominant culture, it may be described as a counterculture. In his 1979 book 'Subculture the Meaning of Style', *Dick Hebdige* argued that a subculture is a subversion to normalcy. He wrote that subcultures can be perceived as negative due to their nature of criticism to the dominant societal standard. Hebdige argued that subcultures bring together like-minded individuals who feel neglected by societal standards and allow them to develop a sense of identity.

Subcultures can be distinctive because of the age, ethnicity, class, location, and/or gender of the members. The qualities that determine a subculture as distinct may be linguistic, aesthetic, religious, political, sexual, geographical, or a combination of factors. According to Dick Hebdige, members of a subculture often signal their membership through a distinctive and symbolic use of style, which includes fashions, mannerisms, and argot. They also live out particular relations to places; Ken Gelder talks about "subcultural geographies" along these lines.

The study of subcultures often consists of the study of symbolism attached to clothing, music and other visible affectations by members of subcultures, and also the ways in which these same symbols are interpreted by members of the dominant culture. Subcultures have been chronicled by others for a long time, documented, analysed, classified, rationalised, monitored, scrutinised. In some cases, subcultures have been legislated against, their activities regulated or curtailed.

MONOCHRONIC AND POLYCHRONIC CULTURES

Monochronic cultures (e.g., the United States) handle information in a direct, linear fashion. Schedules, punctuality, and a sense that time forms a purposeful straight line are indicators of such cultures.

In *polychronic cultures* (e.g., Japan), people work on several fronts simultaneously instead of pursuing a single task.

HIGH-CONTEXT AND LOW-CONTEXT CULTURES

In *high-context cultures* (e.g., Japan), the context of communication is high because, in addition to the verbal part, it includes a great deal of extra information, such as the message sender's values, position, background, and associations in the society. As such, the message cannot be understood without its context. One's individual environment (i.e., physical setting and social circumstances) determines what one says and how one is interpreted by others.

In *low-context cultures* (e.g., the United States), messages are explicit and clear in the sense that actual words are used to convey the main part of information in communication. The words and their meanings, being independent entities, can be separated from the context in which they occur.

CULTURAL RELATIVISM

This is a method whereby different societies or cultures are analyzed objectively without using the values of one culture to judge the worth of another. We cannot possibly understand the actions of other groups if we analyse them in terms of our motives and values. We must interpret their behaviour in the light of their motives, habits and values if we are to understand them. Cultural relativism means that the function and meaning of a trait are relative to its cultural setting. A trait is neither good nor bad in itself. It is good or bad only with reference to the culture in which it is to function. Fur clothing is good in the Arctic but not in the tropics. In some hunting societies which occasionally face long periods of hunger to be fat is good; it has real survival value and fat people are admired. In our society to be fat is not only unnecessary but is known to be unhealthful and fat people are not admired.

The concept of cultural relativism does not mean that all customs are equally valuable, nor does it imply that no customs are harmful. Some patterns of behaviour may be injurious everywhere, but even such patterns serve some purpose in the culture and the society will suffer unless a substitute is provided. The central point in cultural relativism is that in a particular cultural setting certain traits are right because they work well in that setting while other traits are wrong because they would clash painfully with parts of that culture.

CIVILISATION

The word civilisation comes from the Latin civilis, meaning civil, related to the Latin civis, meaning citizen, and civitas, meaning city or city-state. Civilisation (or civilization) is a sometimes controversial term which has been used in several related ways. Primarily, the term has been used to refer to human cultures which are complex in terms of technology, science, politics, and division of labour. Such civilisations are generally urbanized. In classical contexts civilized peoples were called this in contrast to "barbarian" peoples, while in modern contexts civilized peoples have been contrasted to "primitive" peoples.

An Ancient Civilisation.

In modern academic discussions however, there is a tendency to use the term in a more neutral way to mean approximately the same thing as "culture" and can therefore refer more broadly to any important and clearly defined human society, particularly in historical discussions. Still, even when used in this second sense, the word is often restricted to apply only to societies that have attained a particular level of advancement, especially the founding of cities, with the word "city" defined in various ways. The level of advancement of a civilization is often measured by its progress in agriculture, long-distance trade, occupational specialization, and urbanism. Aside from these core elements, civilisation is often marked by any combination of a number of secondary elements, including a developed transportation system, writing, standards of measurement (currency, etc.), contract and tort-based legal systems, characteristic art styles (which may pertain to specific cultures), monumental architecture, mathematics, science, sophisticated metallurgy, politics and astronomy.

Settlement Pattern of Civilisation.

Social scientists such as V. Gordon Childe have named a number of traits that distinguish a civilization from other kinds of society. Civilizations have been distinguished by their means of subsistence, types of livelihood, settlement patterns, forms of government, social stratification, economic systems, literacy, and other cultural traits.

All human civilizations have depended on agriculture for subsistence. Growing food on farms results in a surplus of food, particularly when people use intensive agricultural techniques such as irrigation and crop rotation. Grain surpluses have been especially important because they can be stored for a long time. A surplus of food permits some people to do things besides produce food for a living: early civilizations included artisans, priests and priestesses, and other people with specialized careers. A surplus of food results in a division of labour and a more diverse range of human activity, a defining trait of civilizations.

Civilizations have distinctly different settlement patterns from other societies. The word civilization is sometimes simply defined as "living in cities." Non-farmers tend to gather in cities to work and to trade.

As we know that civilizations have a more complex political structure, namely the state. State societies are more stratified than other societies; there is a greater difference among the social classes. The ruling class, normally concentrated in the cities, has control over much of the surplus and exercises its will through the actions of a government or bureaucracy. Morton Fried, a conflict theorist and Elman Service, an integration theorist, have classified human cultures based on political systems and social inequality.

This system of classification contains four categories, which are as follows:

- Hunter-gatherer bands, which are generally egalitarian.
- Horticultural/pastoral societies in which there are generally two inherited social classes; chief and commoner.
- Highly stratified structures, or chief-doms, with several inherited social classes: king, noble, freemen, serf and slave.
- Civilizations, with complex social hierarchies and organized, institutional governments.

Economically, civilizations display more complex patterns of ownership and exchange than less organized societies. Living in one place allows people to accumulate more personal possessions than nomadic people. Some people also acquire landed property, or private ownership of the land. Because a percentage of people in civilizations do not grow their own food, they must trade their goods and services for food in a market system, or receive food through the levy of tribute, redistributive taxation, tariffs or tithes from the food producing segment of the population. Early civilizations developed money as a medium of exchange for these increasingly complex transactions. To oversimplify, in a village the potter makes a pot for the brewer and the brewer compensates the potter by giving him a certain amount of beer. In a city, the potter may need a new roof, the roofer may need new shoes, the cobbler may need new horseshoes, the blacksmith may need a new coat, and the tanner may need a new pot. These people may not be personally acquainted with one another and their needs may not occur all at the same time. A monetary system is a way of organizing these obligations to ensure that they are fulfilled fairly.

Writing, developed first by people in Sumer, is considered a hallmark of civilization and "appears to accompany the rise of complex administrative bureaucracies or the conquest state." Traders and bureaucrats relied on writing to keep accurate records. Like money, writing was necessitated by the size of the population of a city and the complexity of its commerce among people who are not all personally acquainted with each other.

Aided by their division of labor and central government planning, civilizations have developed many other diverse cultural traits. These include organized religion, development in the arts, and countless new advances in science and technology.

Through history, successful civilizations have spread, taking over more and more territory, and assimilating more and more previously-uncivilized people. Nevertheless, some tribes or people remain uncivilized even to this day. These cultures are called by some "primitive," a term that is regarded by others as pejorative. "Primitive" implies in some way that a culture is "first" (Latin = primus), that it has not changed since the dawn of mankind, though this has been demonstrated not to be true. Specifically, as all of today's cultures are contemporaries, today's so-called ***primitive cultures*** are in no way antecedent to those we consider civilized. Many anthropologists use the term "non-literate" to describe these peoples. In the USA and Canada, where many people of such cultures were displaced by European settlers, the term "First Nations" is used. Generally, the First Nations of North America had hierarchical governments, religion, a barter system, and oral transmission of their traditions, cultures, laws, etc. Respect for the wisdom of elders and for their natural environment (7th Generation decision-making) sustained these cultures for over 10,000 years.

Civilization has been spread by colonization, invasion, religious conversion, the extension of bureaucratic control and trade, and by introducing agriculture and writing to non-literate peoples. Some non-civilized people may willingly adapt to civilized behaviour. But civilization is also spread by the technical, material and social dominance that civilization engenders.

CULTURE AND CIVILIZATION

"Civilization" can also refer to the culture of a complex society, not just the society itself. Every society, civilization or not, has a specific set of ideas and customs, and a certain set of manufactures and arts that make it unique. Civilizations tend to develop intricate cultures, including literature, professional art, architecture, organized religion, and complex customs associated with the elite.

The intricate culture associated with civilization has a tendency to spread to and influence other cultures, sometimes assimilating them into the civilization (a classic example being Chinese civilization and its influence on nearby civilizations such as Korea, Japan and Vietnam). Many civilizations are actually large cultural spheres containing many nations and regions. The civilization in which someone lives is that person's broadest cultural identity.

Many historians have focused on these broad cultural spheres and have treated civilizations as discrete units. One example is early twentieth-century philosopher Oswald Spengler, even though he uses the German word "Kultur," "culture," for what we here call a "civilization." He said that a civilization's coherence is based on a single primary cultural symbol. Civilizations experience cycles of birth, life, decline, and death, often supplanted by a new civilization with a potent new culture, formed around a compelling new cultural symbol.

This "unified culture" concept of civilization also influenced the theories of historian *Arnold J. Toynbee* in the mid-twentieth century. Toynbee explored civilization processes in his multi-volume A Study of History, which traced the rise and, in most cases, the decline of 21 civilizations and five "arrested civilizations." Civilizations generally declined and fell, according to Toynbee, because of the failure of a "creative minority", through moral or religious decline, to meet some important challenge, rather than mere economic or environmental causes.

SOCIAL GROUPS

Introduction: *Definition.* ***Features of Social Groups. Types of Social Groups:*** *Ingroup, Outgroup, Primary Group, Importance of Primary Groups, Secondary Group, Importance of Secondary Group, Difference between Primary and Secondary Groups, Reference Group, Peer Group, Club, Community, Voluntary and Involuntary Groups, Formal groups, Informal groups, Ethnic Group, Non-kinship Based Social Groups, Gender-based Groups.* ***Importance of Social Groups:*** *Social Groups are Needed to Survive, Friends Make a Social Group, Communicating Promotes well being, Families are a form of Social Groups, Social Groups take many Forms, Society has many Social Groups in Coexistence.* ***Group Functions. Social Characteristics of a Group. Negative Effects of Social Groups. Objectives of Social Groups. Group Culture. Group Norms. Sources of Pressures to Conform in Groups. The Structure of Groups:*** *Boundaries: Members and Non-members, Clarity and Openness, Voluntary and Involuntary Membership, In-Groups and Out-Groups, Role and Sociometric Structures, Power and Leadership, Types of Group Leaders, When are Leaders Necessary?, Where Do Leaders Come From?, The Power of Groups.* ***Bureaucracies:*** *The Birth of a Bureaucracy, Characteristics of Ideal-Typical Bureaucracy, Problems of Bureaucracy, Bureaucratic Alienation, Bureaucratic Inefficiency and Ritualism, Bureaucratic Inertia.* ***Group Effectiveness:*** *Individual Versus Group Effectiveness, Effectiveness and Group Culture, Effectiveness and Group Size, Effectiveness, Roles and Leadership, Effectiveness and Communication.* ***Individuals, Freedom, and Life in Groups. Social Structure, Groups and Individuals. Relationship between the Formal and Informal Organization.***

INTRODUCTION

A *group* is a collection of two or more individuals who have developed a common social identity relating to some object of activity. *Social group* is a group of people or organizations who share common interests, views or visions that ties them together. Social group can exist in our towns, colleges etc. People in social groups get along with each other for variety of reasons. Sometimes these groups are of Emotional support for them and sometimes of Professional. Social groups serves as life and blood of society bringing people closer and forming societies either good or bad.

The group is a basic unit of sociological analysis for several reasons. We orient most of our lives to groups, from the intimacy of romantic couples to the overwhelming complexity of bureaucracies. We experience our most intense desires to "belong" in relation to groups, our greatest fears of rejection, and our deepest conflicts as we perform roles in exchange for the privileges of membership. Some groups are like tiny islands — havens in which we are known and accepted or prisons from which there is no escape — whereas others are so large and complex that we feel lost and insignificant in them.

Groups meet many of our needs, including those for approval, acceptance, protection, safety, and support for our values. We use reference groups to define important parts of who we are and to establish and maintain our self-esteem. We grow up in groups, learn, earn livings, and practice religion in them. It is through them that societies govern and defend themselves, distribute justice, heal the sick, distribute rewards, and inflict punishments. Groups are also a source of social conflict and problems. Persecution, discrimination, oppression, and warfare are often based on relationships between groups.

A social group is an organization of people or groups. It is to keep a couple of groups or people in an order for the sake of a single or many purposes. It cannot take those people or groups who are irrelevant. This group can be done for the sake of social participations. Its activity and durability is dependent upon the work they do. They become a family with the passage of time. They find themselves able to understand one another. This can be further elucidated by the help of an example.

This example is about an organization who is working for the benefit of women in a specific area. Those who are a part of this organization will be able to give rise to a social group. Those who will be off the view to save women in that area will become a part of that group. All of them must work for the prosperity of women with one another. Social groups can be of many types and they can be ramified on the basis of their needs in an area.

DEFINITION

A social group can be defined as any two or more people in social interaction who share expectations and responsibilities to the group and who share a unifying characteristic or sense of purpose.

It represents Particular Social Groups/ages (ages 30 onwards) because of its contents and choice of Music etc.

The study of social groups is conducted by sociologists who analyze behavior and interactions among people and show how these interactions shape societies. Social groups are groups of three or more people that are primarily focused on social activities, as opposed to tasks, and help humans develop identity and self esteem. Most people belong to more than one social group.

FEATURES OF SOCIAL GROUPS

According to social scientists, two or more people make up a group when five things are true. These five things are as follows:

- *People in group interact.* That is, the behavior of each member of a group affects the behaviour of the other members.
- *The members of group depend each other for the fulfillment of their primary and secondary needs.* They are interdependent.
- *Members of group share common goals or interests.* Group always originates, starts and proceeds with common interests.
- *They share meanings.* In other words, each members. Each member understands the rules of the group. Each member knows how to behave.
- *The members of group develops a strong sense of "we feeling" and "consciousness of kind".* It is psychological awareness of belonging to one another and is a proof of their being social.

TYPES OF SOCIAL GROUPS

There are two main types of social groups: primary and secondary. ***Primary groups*** are usually *kinship* based, though not necessarily, and they are long lasting. ***Secondary groups*** are larger, formal groups based on common interests, backgrounds, goals or roles. Some examples of secondary groups include clubs, communities, gangs, teams and platoons. While secondary groups can be long lasting, they can also quickly form and almost immediately disband, as is the case with mobs. Sometimes small groups of people within the secondary group will form a new primary group. For example, if two people from the same chess club choose to get married, they are still members of the secondary group, the chess club, but they are also now members of a *new primary group*, the family.

- *Kinship Groups*: Kinship groups are family-based units and are generally the first social group a person will belong to. Families are the primary basis for developing a sense of self.
- *Age Groups*: As people progress through life, they invariably become associated with others of the same age. For instance, during the school years, a person is classified as a first-grader or a fifth-grader. Later, the same person will become a teenager.
- *Gender Groups:* People are classified into groups based on their gender, male or female, or their sexual preference, including heterosexual, homosexual or bisexual.
- *Cultural Groups:* Another common form of classification in society is based on cultural or ethnic background. For instance, a person can be classified as Hispanic or Asian, or more specifically as Mexican or Japanese.
- *Interest Groups:* Individuals can also belong to interest- and faith-based groups or clubs, like the Freemasons or Girl Scouts. People can be categorized as Democratic or Republican, Catholic or Protestant, and many other social classifications, as well.

INGROUP

In sociology and social psychology, an *ingroup* is a social group towards which an individual feels loyalty and respect, usually due to membership in the group. This loyalty often manifests itself as an ingroup bias. Commonly encountered ingroups include family members, people of the same race, culture, gender or religion, and so on. Research demonstrates that people often privilege ingroup members over outgroup members even when the ingroup has no actual social standing; for instance, a group of people with the same color shirts, when the other group has another color of shirt.

OUTGROUP

In sociology, an *outgroup* is a social group towards which an individual feels contempt, opposition, or a desire to compete. Members of outgroups may be subject to outgroup homogeneity biases, and generally people tend to privilege ingroup members over outgroup members in many situations.

PRIMARY GROUP

One of the most widely utilized concepts of sociological groups is that developed by *Charles Horton Cooley* of the "primary group". Cooley defines a primary group as being a "small intimate, face to face association..." of individuals who share some type of common group identity. *Cooley* goes on to say that the development of this common group identity lead the members of the primary group to naturally identify themselves as "we or us." Cooley described five characteristics of the primary group:

(1) It has face to face interaction.

(2) It is unspecialized; that is, it exists not for specific purpose but to fulfill wide range of personal needs.

(3) It is relatively permanent.

(4) It is small.

(5) It is intimate.

The group is characterized by a sense of "weakness", an emotional commitment to the whole rather than to other individuals or to the specific goals of a given members. The group itself is a goal.

According to Cooley, family, play-group, and neighbourhood are primary groups whereas Dexter, another sociologists adds "peer group". Thus we can say that there is greater degree of intimacy, love, unity and emotional attachment in the members of primary groups.

IMPORTANCE OF PRIMARY GROUPS

Primary groups are fundamental in forming the social nature and ideals of the individual. The result of primary association, psychologically, is a fusion of individualities in a common whole, so that an individual's life is aligned with the common life and purposes of the group.

It should not be assumed that the unity of the primary group is one of harmony and love. It is always a differentiated and can be a competitive unity. The individual may be ambitious, but the chief object of his ambition will be some desired place in the thought of the others, and he will feel allegiance to common goals of the group. For example, a boy may dispute with his fellows a place on the team, but will place above such disputes the group goal of winning the game.

The most important spheres of this intimate association and cooperation are the family, the peer groups of children, and the neighborhood or community group of elders. These are practically universal, belonging to all time periods and all stages of development. Human nature is not something existing separately in the individual, but a group-nature or primary phase of society, a simple and general condition of the social mind. It is something more than mere instinct and something less than the more elaborate development of ideas and sentiments that make up institutions (Cooley, 1962).

SECONDARY GROUP

The term secondary group has come into use in sociology to describe any group which lacks one or more of the elements that go together to characterize a primary group. In general, a secondary group is composed of individuals who lacks strong emotional ties one another. In these groups, people do not always interact closely and directly. They may know each other only as people who are salesmen o secretaries, or the next person on the assembly line. Unlike members of primary groups, family etc. members of secondary group know very little about each other's feelings and likes and dislikes. Secondary means "second in importance", therefore, the type of relationship is formal, indirect, and impersonal.

Like primary group, secondary group is of special significance in modern society, and of which the large scale organisation is the most outstanding example. A secondary group is one which is large in size, such as, city, nation, political party, labour union etc. In this the relation of the members is limited in scope and exerts only indirect influence over the other. In this group co-operation among the members is indirect and very seldom comes face-to-face with them.

IMPORTANCE OF SECONDARY GROUP

The primary groups have an important place in a simple and small society but in modern society the trend is towards secondary groups. The small community has given way to large communities. Population has moved from village to city. The cottage industries are replaced by giant corporations. Man now depends more on secondary group for his needs. Most of the needs which were previously satisfied in the village is now satisfied in the cities. Not only the members but the variety of secondary groups are increasing. The importance of the secondary groups are as follows:

(i) The secondary groups have opened *channels of opportunity*. They provide a greater chance to develop individual talents. In earlier times there were only a handful of pursuits like agriculture and small trades. But now-a-days there are thousands of occupations which open the way for specialized careers.

(ii) A secondary group is marked by clear cut *division of labour*. There are sets up rules to regulate it. A formal authority is set up with the responsibility of managing the organisation efficiently. The great advances in material comfort would be impossible without the rise of goal-directed secondary organizations.

(iii) A secondary group *broadens the outlook* of its members. In a primary group the outlook of its members gets narrowed because they think of their limited interests. But a secondary group has to accommodate a large number of individuals which widens the outlook of its members.

Today, our life to a *great extent is controlled* by secondary group. It becomes a necessity for the labourer to join the other to protect his rights and fulfill his interests. The secondary groups have entered almost all the parts of our life—political, economic, commercial, educational, religious etc.

DIFFERENCE BETWEEN PRIMARY AND SECONDARY GROUPS

Primary relationships are most common in small and traditional societies. A primary group is a group in which one exchanges implicit items, such as love, caring and concern. Primary groups are composed of people who are emotionally closed, concerned for each other's welfare and share a sense of "We".

Secondary relationships are composed of people who have little personal knowledge of each other, do not share an amount of concern, have weak emotional ties and share a specific interest or activity.

A primary group is based on intimate, face to face interaction whereas a secondary group is less cohesive, more formal and less supportive of members.

Both primary group and secondary group differ from each other in certain respects.

(1) **Difference in size:** The size of the primary group is small as it consists of few members. Small size of the primary group helps its members to develop personal relations among themselves. On the other hand, secondary group is large in size. It consists of large number of people who are scattered all over the country. Due to its large size the members do not have personal relations among themselves.

(2) **Difference in physical proximity:** Physical proximity refers to physical closeness or physical nearness. Members of a primary group are physically close to each other and personally known to each other. There exists a face-to-face contact among the members of a primary group. But in a secondary group the face-to-face contact is not found among the members. Physical distance is a characteristic feature of secondary group.

(3) **Difference in relationship:** The relationship of the members of a primary group is primary relationship which are direct, personal, cordial, close, intimate, face-to-face and informal in nature. For example, family, play group, neighborhood etc. But, on the other hand, the relationship of the members of a secondary group is secondary relationship which are indirect, impersonal, formal, lacks face-to-face, lacks cordiality and less intimate. For example, political parties voluntary organisations, trade union etc.

(4) **Difference in nature of control:** Primary group controls the behaviour of its members through informal means such as customs,

traditions, folkways, mores, norms, beliefs, suggestions etc. Secondary groups control the behaviour of its members by formal means such as law, police, court, jail, army etc.

(5) **Difference in goals:** The goals or the aims and objectives of the members of a primary group is same and the persons take other's interest as their own. The main purpose of a primary group is to fulfill all the needs of the members. But in secondary groups the aims or goal are not same. Every one ties to fulfill his self-interest. Secondary groups satisfy the specific need or interest of the members.

(6) **Difference in means and ends:** Primary group is characterized by the primary relationship and this is not as a means to an end, but an end in itself. This relationship is spontaneous. On the other hand, the secondary relationship is considered not as an end in itself but as a means to an end.

(7) **Difference in structure:** The structure of primary group is rigid and guided by some rigid informal means of customs, traditions, folkways, mores and norms. But the structure of secondary group is very flexible and regulated by a set of formal rules.

(8) **Difference in membership:** The membership of a primary group is permanent and compulsory because man lives, grows and dies within it. But the membership of the secondary group is temporary and voluntary. People may join secondary groups according to their will, and also withdraw their membership at anytime without any reason. That is why secondary groups are known as 'Special Interest Groups'.

(9) **Difference in type of co-operations:** In the primary groups the co-operation among the members is always direct and intimate. So the primary relations are inclusive. But in secondary groups there is only indirect type or co-operation among the members because the functions are based on division of labour and specialization of work.

(10) **Difference in position:** In primary groups, the position or status of a person is fixed according to his birth, age and sex. For example, in family the position of father is based upon his birth, and age. But in secondary groups, the position of a person is determined by his roles. For example, in a trade union the position of the president depends upon the roles he plays in the union.

REFERENCE GROUP

A reference group is composed of individuals possesing a set of similar characteristics which are used as standards by other individuals in evaluating their own behavior. Reference groups in many cases are not true groups in that the individuals who make up the reference group may not share the common identity characteristic of groups.

It is a group with which individual identifies himself because of having been socialized in it, For example, a person residing in America may be conforming to "Islam". His ideas and attitudes may be different from American society and culture but to Islamic society or culture with which he attaches or identifies himself. In this way he refers to an Islamic group which can called his reference group.

An individual though identifies himself with his reference group, yet not necessarily becomes its acting member nor wish to join it and nor his conception of reference group be accurate. The reference group is a social category but it also represents value system and traditions shared by its members.

Reference groups are used in order to evaluate and determine the nature of a given individual or other group's characteristics and sociological attributes. It is the group to which the individual relates or aspires to relate himself or herself psychologically. It becomes the individual's frame of reference and source for ordering his or her experiences, perceptions, cognition, and ideas of self. It is important for determining a person's self-identity, attitudes, and social ties. It becomes the basis of reference in making comparisons or contrasts and in evaluating one's appearance and performance.

PEER GROUP

A peer group is made up of individuals of relatively equal status with whom the individual interacts frequently.

CLUB

A club is a group, which usually requires one to apply to become a member. In narrow sense, a club is an association of two or more people united by a common interest or goal. A service club, for example, exists for voluntary or charitable activities; there are clubs devoted to hobbies and sports, social activities clubs, political and religious clubs, and so forth.

COMMUNITY

A "community" has been defined as a group of interacting people living in a common location. The word is often used to refer to a group that is organized around common values and is attributed with social cohesion within a shared geographical location, generally in social units larger than a household.

VOLUNTARY AND INVOLUNTARY GROUPS

Groups may be classified according to how members become members. If an individual select to become a member of a group then that group can be referred to as a *voluntary group*. On the other hand, if an individual becomes a member of a group, as a result of factors over which he/she has no control, then the group may be referred to as an *involuntary group*.

FORMAL GROUPS

Those groups set up by the management of an organization to undertake duties in the pursuit of organizational goals.

- They are created to fulfill specific goals or undertake specific tasks.
- They have a formal status and role conferred by the organisation.
- They have definite structures with prescribed leadership and established rules, processes and roles.
- They tend to be permanent.

INFORMAL GROUPS

Those grouping which the employees themselves have developed in accordance with their own needs. Every organization has these kind of groups. Researches say these are very important to organisation's effectiveness.

- They are created by the individual members for the purpose of sharing a common interest or meeting a shared need.
- They emerge from organisational interactions and may be contained within formal task groups.
- They exist for as long as they serve a common interest or fulfill a common need.
- Elton Mayo in the Hawthorne studies demonstrated the potential power of the informal workgroup.

In order to fulfill the basic needs and promote diverse interests of men, a large number of organizations have come up in the modern complex societies. These organizations are of two kinds—the formal organization and the informal organization.

The modern industrialized, urbanized and civilized societies of the world consist of a large number of formal organizations. Due to the complexity in the growth of societies, the number and size of the formal organizations have increased. They are found in the economic, political, educational, industrial and other fields. Formal organizations represent those organizations which are characterized by a specific function, division of labour, a hierarchy of authority, rationality and a proper arrangement of statuses and role. They are carefully planned and systematically worked out.

It was *Max Weber* who for the first time made a sociological analysis of formal organization. In his book "Bureaucracy, Organization, Theory of Social and Economic Organization", *Max Weber* has provided his conception of formal organization particularly of bureaucracy. The term bureaucracy assumed sociological importance due to efforts of Max Weber at the beginning of the 20th century.

According to *Talcott Parsons* bureaucracy represents one of the most salient structural characteristics of the modern western society. The relatively large scale organizations with specialized functions can be called bureaucracies.

According to *Blau* the term bureaucracy has a restricted meaning. They have stated in their formal organizations that the term bureaucracy must be used neutrally to refer to the administrative aspects of organizations.

By definition, primary groups have an informal structure in which relationships are flexible and norms are rarely stated explicitly. Although this is true of some secondary groups (social clubs), most have a formal structure that clearly defines role relationships (see following Table).

Primary groups are always informal, but as these examples show, secondary groups can be either formal or informal.		
Primary	**Informal** Family Close friends Small commune	**Formal** None
Seondary	Trial jury Tupperware party College class	Bureaucracy Surgery team Airline crew

In informal groups, relationships among group members change with varying circumstances, and the terms that guide their interactions are always open to negotiation. An act that is punished in one situation may be overlooked in another: friends may tolerate silly, disruptive, behavior one day, but not the next. Informal groups are identified by implicit understandings of norms rather than by explicit statements and by flexible relationships among group members.

In groups with specific goals, however, it is difficult to coordinate people's behavior in predictable ways. Especially when groups have many members who specialize in a variety of tasks, they cannot depend on members to negotiate the terms of their relationships as they go along (*Simmel*, 1950). A response to this problem is the formal organization, in which relationships are regulated by clearly stated, rigid norms oriented to the achievement of specific goals.

ETHNIC GROUP

A group is different from the groups from the point of view of "cultural patterns" and "racial traits", such a group may have its own religion, customs and language. However, language occupies high importance in ethnic groups. The term is different from racial groups. Though it is not impossible, yet an ethnic group is not always racial group nor a religious group. For example, a Christian living in Punjab or in Urban Sindh speaks Punjabi or Urdu respectively. They constitute and identify themselves with their lingual groups. Similarly, a Hindu living in Sindh speaks Sindhi language and identifies himself with Sindhi ethnic group. It shows that for ethnic groups area and its language are highly important.

NON-KINSHIP BASED SOCIAL GROUPS

All societies classify people to some degree based on their age. In North America, for example, we generally label people as children, teenagers, adults, middle aged, and elderly or senior citizens. Such age-based categories are referred to by anthropologists as age grades. They are in a sense both achieved and ascribed statuses. People become senior citizens simply by living long enough. In other words, they have achieved this status through longevity. On the other hand, grandchildren cannot achieve elder status at the same time as their grandparents because they were born much later—there is an ascribed difference between them. In time, however, they also can become senior citizens.

In some societies, age grades are clearly recognized as distinct identifiable groups of people. Anthropologists refer to these groups as age sets. They are people of similar age and usually of the same gender who share a common identity and maintain close ties throughout their lives. They also pass through age-related statuses together as a group. The transition between these statuses is usually marked by a rite of passage.

Age sets are especially common in sub-Saharan Africa. Among the 1/4 million Masai click this icon to hear the preceding term pronounced cattle herding people of southern Kenya and northern Tanzania, for instance, male age-sets have been traditionally very important. The Masai strongly differentiate three major age-based male groups—*boys*, *warriors*, and *elders*. The latter two groups are also informally divided into *junior* and *senior warriors* and *junior and senior elders*.

From the age of 6-8, Masai boys spend much of their time on their own, away from the community, sharing the work of herding cattle owned by their parents. At this time they develop the close male relationships that will last throughout their lives. When they are 12-14, boys are circumcised together in a ritual that marks their transition to a new status—they become morans click this icon to hear the preceding term pronounced, or warriors. In Masai culture, only morans are allowed to have long hair. They also dress differently and spend much of their time away from the community in a hidden training camp. They no longer herd cattle but now are responsible for their defense against predators such as lions and people who might steal them. While boys are not allowed to carry spears, morans do. They must remain unmarried during the 7 years that they are morans, but some of them secretly have girlfriends. In their twenties, the moran once again go through a rite of passage together. It marks their transition to the elder status and role within society. They reinforce their camaraderie at this time by drinking the blood of a freshly killed cow that has been specially sacrificed for the purpose, and their long hair is shaved off by their mothers to signify their new status. They are no longer warriors but are becoming respected decision makers and spokesmen for their families and communities. As elders, they are now allowed to get married when they can acquire sufficient numbers of cattle to pay a bride price. In Masai society girls usually marry in their teens and men in their thirties and later. Middle aged and older men typically have several wives.

GENDER-BASED GROUPS

In addition to age, gender is also a universal basis for organizing social groups. While both men's and women's groups occur, men's associations are more common around the world. When gender-based groups exist in small-scale societies, every adult of the same gender is usually a member. In large-scale societies, gender-based groups become more institutionalized and membership is usually not mandatory. Typical gender-based groups in North America include the Boy Scouts and Girl Scouts, fraternities, sororities, and lodges (e.g., Elks, Masons, etc.).

IMPORTANCE OF SOCIAL GROUPS

Social groups are important for many reasons. A social group is, "A group of two or more people who interact with one another and who recognize themselves as a distinct social unit." Further, social groups play an important role in daily life.

Social Groups are Needed to Survive

Social groups fulfill one of the basic psychological needs for survival, belonging. Feeling needed and wanted psychological motivates a person to stride forward and stay mentally healthy. An example of belonging is found in Maslow's psychological hierarchy of needs.

Friends Make a Social Group

A social group is not always made up of friends, however, friendships may form within a group. Spending a lot of time with people builds relationships and friendships. All members of a group have at least one thing in common otherwise the group would not form.

Communicating Promotes Well Being

Social groups is a form of communication amongst friends or peers. Communication plays an essential and vital role in life. Communication has many forms and is used on a daily basis in one form or another. Again, it is not mentally healthy to be alone all the time as it often leads to inverted personality traits and depression.

Families are a Form of Social Groups

Social groups do not just consist of friends. Families are also a form of social groups. Families play a vital role by teaching other family members acceptable behavior and beliefs to live by.

Social Groups take many Forms

Social groups act as a great support system when needed. Groups can identify and unify to help solve another members problems or anguish. A good example of a support group is any addiction rehabilitation program.

Society has Many Social Groups in Coexistence

In society social groups exist for many reasons. Take protesters for example; they unite to express personal beliefs towards an opposing group or force. The purpose of the protest is to accomplish a unified goal. Accomplishing goals resonates in all occupations.

GROUP FUNCTIONS

Group functions may be divided into two types and a balance of both is required:

(i) ***Task functions***—required to achieve the group's purpose and objectives and include:

- Formulating objectives and setting targets.
- Seeking opinions and exchanging information to facilitate task achievement.
- Reinforcing, confirming and clarifying information.
- Assessing brainstormed ideas and selecting ideal solutions.

(ii) ***Maintenance functions***—of the viability of the group by establishing norms, and a sense of purpose.

- Conflict resolution and ensuring harmonious relationships.
- Creating opportunities for participation and member contribution.
- Assessing group effectiveness and initiating any required remedial action.

SOCIAL CHARACTERISTICS OF A GROUP

The social characteristics of groups affect the way they achieve their goals as well as their success in doing so. Social life centers on groups, and by understanding how they work, we can better understand ourselves as participants. We can also understand how groups affect the welfare of society itself: the ability of families to raise children, of governments to govern, of criminal justice systems to control crime, of hospitals to provide health care-all are vitally important.

A group is basically a collection of individuals contributing to some common aim under the direction of a leader, and who shares a sense of common identity. Groups also provide Stimulus, Protection and other Psychological requirements to its members. The characteristics of a Group are as follows:

- Members engaged in frequent interaction;

- Those involved define themselves as group members;
- Others define members as belonging to a particular group;
- They share common norms and mutual interests;
- They identify with one another and share values;
- They feel a sense of collective responsibility;
- They act in a unified way towards the organisation.

NEGATIVE EFFECTS OF SOCIAL GROUPS

While social groups provide support and identity to people, there is also evidence that these groups can sometimes be hotspots for discrimination, prejudice and elitism. For example, if it is acceptable within the group to discriminate against a certain race, religion or lifestyle, members of the group will likely conform to fit this model of behavior and remain within the group. Social Identity Theory, developed by Tajfel and Turner, says that people in a social group, the "in-group" will sometimes act at the expense of people not in the group, the "out-group" to save face and remain in the in-group. Not all social groups experience this, but many fall prey to this type of thinking.

OBJECTIVES OF SOCIAL GROUPS

Social groups exist to give people a sense of common identity and belonging. Social groups make accomplishing goals much easier and more efficient since a social group can bring people together to work on a task instead of each person working individually. Social groups provide a network of support for people and help give people a collective voice in society. An organized group with many members will typically get more attention than individuals; therefore grouping together to achieve goals is beneficial. Evolutionary speaking, humans probably first formed social groups because it was safer than being alone. The more people there are working together to protect a common interest, the more likely they are to succeed. This mentality, which developed early in the history of humanity, still holds true in modern society.

GROUP CULTURE

All groups are based on shared cultural ideas. Stein and his colleagues argue that whites often exclude nonwhites from groups not only because of race, but because they assume that nonwhites do not share their values and beliefs.

Researchers asked white high school students to answer questions about their values—the desirability of having school spirit, being intelligent, neat, and attractive, or being concerned about other people. They then used these responses to create for each student descriptions of two pairs of fictitious teenagers. One pair of teenagers shared the respondent's values, whereas the second did not. In each pair, one of the teenagers was black, and the other was white.

Respondents were then asked how interested they would be in different kinds of contact with the teenagers, such as inviting them home to dinner, going to a party together, attending the same school, belonging to the same group, living in the same building, or working together on the same committee. Although the willingness for close contact was negatively affected by race, a wide range of contact was not. What did make a difference in these cases was the respondents' perception of shared values.

GROUP NORMS

The power of group norms is illustrated by a study of workers who built telephone switchboards at the Hawthorne plant of Western Electric. In trying to find how to increase productivity, researchers were surprised to discover that workers often violated company norms (trading jobs) and seemed unaffected by company rewards for increased production. They worked quickly in the mornings, but slowly in the afternoons, and never reported fellow workers who failed on the job. Men who worked too hard were labelled "rate busters," whereas those who worked too slowly were "slackers."

By working together, these men formed a sub-group with its own subculture that affected their behavior more strongly than the company's norms and values. That this subculture supported violations of company rules stems in part from sharing a common position in relation to the company and society as a whole. As members of the working class, they shared a long-standing tradition of resistance against the attempts of management to extract as much work from them as possible.

The common circumstances of these workers help explain the formation of their subgroup and the conformity of members to its norms; but in many groups, individuals conform even when they do not want to. What conditions allow groups to exert such power over their members?

SOURCES OF PRESSURES TO CONFORM IN GROUPS

Pressures to conform in groups have three sources:

First, by defining reality and expectations, group culture specifies requirements for membership. Whether we value a group for itself or as a means for achieving personal goals, conformity is the surest way to remain members: we conform to keep our jobs, to stay in school, or to keep the love and respect of family members.

Second, we conform to the cultural ideas of reference groups whether or not we are members. Our admiration and affection for the members of a close- knit work group will lead us to use them as models, and when such models are part of our social identity, conformity to the ideas that make up their culture is important if we are to maintain a stable sense of who we are. When we have "heroes and heroines" we often adopt their standards of behavior as our own.

Third, we depend on one another to support our perceptions of reality. If you sit with friends and suddenly smell gas, you are most likely to turn to other people for confirmation: "Do you smell gas?" If they do not support us, we are likely to conclude that our perceptions are faulty; but if they do support us, we are far more likely to act on our perceptions as if they were accurate.

The pressures to conform are illustrated by an experiment in which eight-member groups were shown a series of sets of four lines for which they were asked to judge which of three lines was the same length as a fourth "standard" line.

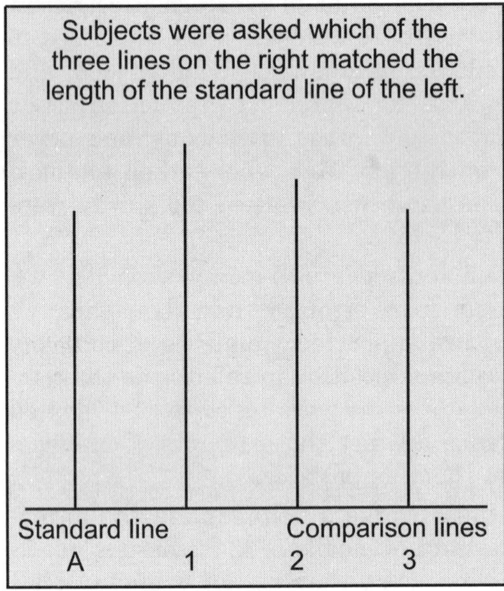

Lines presented to subjects an Asch's Experiment.

Look at adjoing figure and imagine that you participated. Each member makes a judgment out loud, and you go last. With the first two sets of lines everyone agrees on which line is the same length as the "standard," but, with the third set, you hear the first person match the standard line with line 1, which is obviously not the same length. As you think about what a big mistake that was, you hear the second member make the same error, then the third, the fourth, and all the rest. Now it is your turn. Do you agree with the group's unanimous judgment or insist on your own?

Asch found that chances are quite good that you would agree with the majority even though their judgments are clearly wrong. Faced with overwhelming opposition, only 20 percent of *Aschs* subjects openly disagreed with the group. Those who conformed reported afterward that they feared ridicule ("Every time I disagreed I was beginning to wonder if I looked funny") and doubted their own perceptions ("May be where I'm sitting is making me see the lines wrong").

Fear of ridicule and social isolation are especially important, as *Asch* (1952) discovered in a later experiment. This time, only one of the eight people was employed by Asch and instructed to make errors. As the lone confederate made wrong judgments, the volunteer subjects laughed and expressed disbelief and sarcasm. As one subject said later, "I felt the person was attempting a stupid joke.... Then I felt sorry for a person with such poor eyesight." Other studies found similar effects of group pressure on individuals.

Groups exert strong pressures to conform, especially on people who are attracted to them (Kelley, 1952). Such pressures are particularly important for moral questions that rest less on fact than on values and abstract principles of right and wrong. These studies help us appreciate how extraordinary it is for individuals to defy majority judgments, and how difficult it is to maintain a sense of who we are and what we "know" in group contexts.

THE STRUCTURE OF GROUPS

Social relationships have many structural characteristics that affect what goes on in them. Groups differ in the boundaries that define membership, and in the number and content of the roles their members are expected to perform. They have patterns of affection that may bind some members more closely to one another than to the group as a whole.

Groups differ in the amount of power they have in relation to other groups and the ways in which power and prestige are distributed among their members. Patterns of communication describe which members interact, with whom, how often and for what length of time.

Groups such as families and friendship groups are primary, existing for their own sake, enduring through time, and involving members in many aspects of one another's lives. Others—such as work groups—are secondary, limited to specific goals that, once reached, usually end a member's involvement in the group. Groups may be informal, relying on folkways to control behavior, or they may be formal, with specific rules that rigidly define and control role relationships.

BOUNDARIES: MEMBERS AND NON-MEMBERS

All groups have boundaries that distinguish non-members from members. Norms define not only who is eligible for membership, but how long the group is expected to exist and individuals are expected to belong.

Membership takes different forms that depend on participation. Students who rarely talk during class are peripheral, for although they are subject to group norms, their interaction with others is minimal. Those who regularly skip classes are nominal members, for although their names are on the class list, the norms that guide classroom interaction do not affect them.

There are also different kinds of non-members. Some are eligible to belong whereas others are not; and some want to belong more than others. A large pool of eligible members who refuse to join a group can harm it by raising questions about its attractiveness. In this sense, groups have relationships not only among their members, but with non-members as well.

Time, Space and Boundaries: Time is used to define group boundaries. Whereas some groups exist only briefly, others survive across many generations of members. Individual membership also varies in duration from a few hours to a lifetime. Some groups literally use time to define themselves, such as "the college class of 1993."

If you listed the members of your family, you would probably include only living relatives. A family tree, however, spans hundreds of years and includes both living and deceased members. We expect membership in a family to endure for a lifetime, and the family itself to endure long after we die. Such expansive time boundaries give us a sense of permanence, continuity, and stability, and make the family the most important group in our lives.

In contrast, work groups are defined primarily by time and place; and, although the groups may survive indefinitely, their members generally do not stay very long, which makes it difficult to maintain a strong commitment of members to the group.

CLARITY AND OPENNESS

All groups and organizations need to have clear boundaries in order to tell who is a member and who is not, and all vary in the degree to which their boundaries are open or closed. Intelligence services such as the CIA go to great lengths to ensure that their members are not actually enemy spies, and when a spy (often called a "mole") is discovered, it triggers a period during which members cannot be sure of who is a "real" member and who is not.

Groups draw boundaries in ways that restrict membership. College fraternities and sororities discriminate on the basis of gender, and on many campuses, they have come under pressure to drop this restriction. In some cases, they have given in to this pressure but insisted on maintaining a sem- blance of their old boundaries. In one college, a fraternity agreed to admit women, but male members reinforced their gender boundary by insisting that female members be referred to as "brothers."

In her study of corporations, Kanter found that since women almost always constitute a tiny minority at middle and upper job levels, men try to "heighten" group boundaries in order to exclude women as outsiders. The men were more likely to make sexual remarks in front of women than in front of other men. At meetings, they sometimes apologized for an off-color expression they were about to use and then went ahead and used it anyway. This simple act singles women out as outsiders who interfere with what is defined as the normal functioning of the group. By making the presence of "token" women more visible, men increased their solidarity with one another by heightening their own visibility as the dominant members.

VOLUNTARY AND INVOLUNTARY MEMBERSHIP

People often join groups because they value the group as an end in itself. Many people are church members because they enjoy the ritual of the services and the contact with other people who share their faith. Similarly, many people attend college because they enjoy learning, or work because they find it satisfying.

In other cases, individuals join groups as a means to an end. Some people attend church to avoid damnation, to make business contacts, or to impress their neighbors. Almost a fifth of all people employed in the U.S. work only to earn money and say they would quit if they won the lottery. Students often attend college not to satisfy a desire to learn, but to earn the degrees required for good jobs.

Whereas membership in some groups is voluntary, in others—mental hospitals, prisons, and elementary schools—it is not. In such cases, membership is a means to someone else's end. Involuntary membership not only ensures a group's survival, but also gives it more control over its members who are deprived of the right to make many decisions and are vulnerable to abuse and exploitation by those whose ends their membership serves.

The draft illustrates the importance of involuntary membership for the survival of groups, for many argue that without it the military cannot get the number of members it needs to achieve its goals. While ensuring a sufficiently large membership, however, the draft is dysfunctional for social cohesion. People who are forced to join have a low commitment to the organization, which can have disastrous consequences in combat. The draft also raises important questions about individual rights, as it forces young men to kill and risk their lives for goals they do not choose.

In voluntary groups, members sometimes develop a strong sense of loyalty that may lead them to adopt hostile, superior attitudes toward nonmembers, and these can be an important part of group boundaries.

IN-GROUPS AND OUT-GROUPS

William Graham Sumner believed that groups become in-groups by developing a strong sense of "we-ness" and hostile attitudes toward out-groups. "Loyalty to the group, sacrifice for it, hatred and contempt for outsiders ... all grow together, products of the same situation". There are many examples of this: the hostility of students toward "arch rival" schools, intense hatreds between nations, and the hostility that underlies the use of hundreds of slurs and epithets that different racial and ethnic groups apply to one another.

In the late 1970s a religious cult called the People's Temple formed around a single man, the Reverend *Jim Jones*, and settled in the South American country of Guyana. While the cult gave many down- trodden people a sense of purpose, it maintained its boundaries by requiring such intense in-group loyalty that members had to cut their ties with all outsiders, fearing out-groups as "the enemy," and labeling criticism from the outside as lies.

When a congressman, several journalists, and concerned relatives visited the colony, Jones convinced his followers that the visitors wanted to destroy the cult. Not only were several of the visitors murdered, but over 900 members obeyed Jones' command to commit suicide, accepting his belief that the only alternative was the destruction of their colony.

Although there is ample evidence that groups develop a strong sense of in-group loyalty and a hostile superior attitude toward non-members, such attitudes are by no means inevitable (Merton, 1968). Many groups are subgroups of larger groups. Members of college athletic teams may, have a strong sense of group loyalty, but they are "also members of other groups—forms, fraternities, sororities, and classes on whom they depend for support.

ROLE AND SOCIOMETRIC STRUCTURES

As groups develop, members take on different roles that form a role structure, which includes task and expressive roles (Bales, 1950). Members of families perform many roles in addition to those of parent, adult, child, and sibling. Parents often divide task and expressive roles, as when wives take responsibility for "kinkeeping," or keeping family members in touch with one another (Rosenthal, 1985). Children may perform several different roles-caring for a lonely or alcoholic parent or younger children, or soothing conflicts between parents.

Role structures differ in content and complexity. A married couple has two statuses (wife and husband), whereas a group of workers may include hundreds. Large groups are usually more complex than smaller ones, but this is not always true, for a family consisting of two parents, a daughter, and a son has eight statuses (husband, wife, mother, father, son, daughter, brother, and sister), but a college freshman English course has only two: teacher and student.

The complexity of groups is reflected not only in the diversity of roles their members play, but also in the emergence of subgroups based on ties of affection. Even in groups with as few as five or six people; members often form "friendship cliques." The patterns of affection that define a group's sociometric structure reveal that members frequently value subgroups more than the group as a whole. Office workers may become good friends and value being with one another at least as much as they value the achievement of organizational goals. Subgroups often develop their own cultures and share a sense of common destiny.

POWER AND LEADERSHIP

Who controls groups, and why are some groups more powerful than others? Groups distribute power in distinct ways, and sociologists are interested in the effects of this distribution on groups and their members. Power differences between groups are also important, for groups are often a source of social conflict.

Members who are able to define a group's culture have considerable control over group life. In Jones' town, he had the power to define all non-members as "enemies," and his control over group beliefs and values resulted in mass obedience to his command to commit suicide. Individuals derive power from their ability to control resources: when children play baseball, it is not unusual for the—one who supplies the bat and ball to have a disproportionate share of power to decide which rules to play by. Control over patterns of communication is an additional source of power: committee chairpersons decide who talks during meetings, and can use their power to stifle dissenting points of view. Those who perform roles that are important to a group or organization—and who perform them well—also tend to have a relatively large share of power.

In *democratic* groups, power is distributed evenly among members, but in authoritarian groups, power is concentrated in the hands of a relative few. Most groups are neither purely democratic nor purely authoritarian, but fall somewhere in between.

A group has a leadership structure when power is assigned according to norms, and, therefore, takes the form of authority. Leaders perform a variety of roles: coping with external and internal threats, maintaining unity and order, managing anxiety and conflict among members and motivating them to participate. As *Whyte* observed in his study of urban gangs, some groups depend on leaders for their very identity as a group.

The leader is the focal point for the organization of his group. In his absence, members of the gang are divided into a number of small groups. There is no common activity or general conversation. When the leader appears ... the small units form into one large group.... The leader becomes the focal point in the discussion. A follower starts to say something, pauses when he notices that the leader is not listening, and begins again when he has the leader's attention. When the leader leaves the group, unity gives way to the divisions that existed before his appearance.

TYPES OF GROUP LEADERS

There are *three basic types of group leaders*, and they have different effects on how groups function (Lippitt and White, 1947).

Authoritarian leaders dominate group interactions and generally do not participate in group activities.

Democratic leaders act as guides who give advice and suggest alternatives, but leave decisions to the group. ***Laissez-faire*** (a French phrase meaning "allow to act") leaders rarely participate unless asked to by the group and withhold positive or negative evaluations of the group and its members.

Many groups do not have leaders, but even in those that do, authority is not necessarily concentrated in a few hands. This is particularly true in complex organizations. The presidents of corporations are clearly the most powerful leaders; and yet their effectiveness depends on hundreds if not thousands of employees organized into small work groups. Leaders depend on their followers to perform their roles and keep them informed of what is happening in the organization. The ability of followers to withhold or distort information gives them considerable power in spite of their low position in leadership structures.

Different leaders strongly affect how groups function. A study of adult leaders in children's groups found that members are more dependent on authoritarian leaders, demand more attention, and take less initiative. They also are more critical of the leader and less friendly and confiding.

With democratic leaders, members work more independently, are less critical of and more friendly toward the leader, and are more likely to work together as a group. Laissez-faire groups, however, generate anxiety from members who are far more likely to ask for guidance and suggestions.

Some groups (such as friends) have no leadership structure, whereas others have a pluralistic structure, in which authority in specific areas is assigned to specialists. In colleges and universities the administration is responsible for financial decisions, admissions, and financial aid, and the faculty controls what goes on in classrooms.

WHEN ARE LEADERS NECESSARY?

Although people are generally reluctant to surrender individual freedom by giving power to a leader, several social conditions prompt the emergence of leaders.

First, members often give power to leaders in order to achieve highly valued goals. A group of friends usually lacks specific goals, and, therefore, has no leader; but people adrift in a lifeboat share a deep commitment to survival and are far more likely to appoint one.

Second, the more complex a group's role structure is, the more it needs a leader to coordinate the different roles its members perform. Students working on a project may not need a leader until they divide tasks.

Third, regardless of complexity, large groups are more likely to have leaders than small ones are. Studies of groups of varying sizes reveal that regardless of members' personalities, as size increases, a few members tend to dominate group interaction.

Finally, leaders tend to emerge when a crisis threatens the group. Many nations and organizations have given enormous power to leaders during crises: *Robespierre* during the French Revolution, *Adolph Hitler* in Germany, *Stalin* after the Russian Revolution, *Franklin Roosevelt* during the Great Depression, and *Lech Walesa* during the labor crises in Poland in the 1980s. For this reason, times of crisis are particularly dangerous for groups, because leaders are in a position to abuse the power given to them by their members.

WHERE DO LEADERS COME FROM?

Crises, group size and complexity, and a commitment to common goals help explain why groups have leaders, but how do members decide who will lead them? Professors are not hired by the students they teach; nor do workers appoint managers. In such cases, the selection of leaders depends on norms, and from a sociological point of view, such processes are straightforward and of relatively little interest. A more interesting case is the emergence of leaders in groups that initially lack a leadership structure. How are such leaders selected?

During the 1930s and 1940s, researchers identified personality characteristics shared by leaders, including self-confidence, intelligence, dominance, empathy, and an outgoing personality. Their research methods were so varied and ambiguous, however, that later research found many contradictions: traits that were related to leadership in one study were unrelated in others. Although personality certainly makes a difference (shy, retiring people are unlikely to become leaders), the personality approach was abandoned in the 1950s as researchers focused on behavior in groups (Bass, 1960).

One factor that affects the rise of individuals to leadership is their rate of participation in group interactions: the more members talk, the more influence they tend to have. Even shy people can become leaders if they are encouraged to participate. In an experiment, *Hastorf* asked small groups to discuss case studies; during the first session, he identified individuals whose participation was next to the lowest. In the second phase, members were separated by panels equipped with green and red lights. Participants were told that experts on group interaction controlled the lights, that "green" encouraged talk, while "red" advised silence.

During this phase, the lights were used to encourage the previously silent members to talk, and their contributions jumped by 50 percent. In the third phase, discussion continued without the lights, yet these members continued to talk the most; and in members'final ratings of one another's contributions, the initially silent member moved from third to second place.

Apparently, under the right circumstances, anyone has the potential to play a leadership role. People who cannot imagine themselves as leaders may find that merely by speaking up, they acquire surprising levels of power. This underscores the fact that leadership is a social status, that leaders are those whom group members identify as leaders.

From this perspective, it is easier to see how "unlikely people"—Presidents Harry Truman and Lyndon Johnson—who are thrust into leadership positions during crises can perform very well. It is also easier to understand how people who are unfit for leadership nonetheless attain positions of authority through frequent, highly visible participation in group activities.

A second factor in leader selection is latent statuses that have no recognized role in group activities. In newly formed groups, members lack specific information about one another and therefore tend to rely on their general expectations and judgments of other, nongroup statuses such as race, gender, occupation, and age. On juries men and those with high-prestige occupations will tend to be given greater credibility and have more influence than women and those with lower-prestige occupations.

Conformity to norms is a third factor in the selection of leaders, especially in a group's early stages. *Hollander* planted confederates in problem-solving groups and supplied them with the correct answers to the problem. The groups established norms, which the confederates violated (by speaking out of turn) at different stages of the meeting.

Although the confederates always offered the correct solution to the problem, when they spoke out of turn at the beginning of the session they were generally ignored; when they obeyed the rules until mid-ways in the meeting, the confederates' influence was greater; and when they conformed until the meeting was nearly over, their influence reached a maximum. Members initially identified as nonconformists are unlikely to become leaders regardless of their contributions.

Ridgeway used a similar experiment and found that the effect of conformity may not be as simple as Hollander suggests. She found that nonconformity can increase influence by attracting the attention of other members, but that this can be tricky since nonconformists may be seen as caring more about themselves than the group. Nonconformity was particularly dangerous for members who occupy latent statuses that are relatively low in prestige. Ridgeway concluded that the most important factors in determining influence are other people's perceptions of a member's motivation and competence in performing group tasks.

THE POWER OF GROUPS

Group power depends on culture and social structure. Like individual members, groups may exercise authority that rests on norms in the surrounding society. Police departments, the Internal Revenue Service, and employers all hold power over others by virtue of socially defined authority.

Groups also draw power from their structural position in relation to other groups and valued resources. Undergraduate college students conform to professors' demands not only to maintain their membership in undergraduate classes, but also because professors occupy a key position between undergraduate colleges and graduate schools.

The control of valued resources is also a major source of power. Employment, professions, governments, and universities are controlled by people who are white, middle-aged, male, and wealthy, and this gives them power over nonwhites, women, the poor, and the elderly, whom they can exclude from socially legitimate avenues to money, power, and prestige.

Groups draw power from culturally based authority as well as structural positions in the surrounding society. This power is then distributed among group members, whose roles and power affect their position in prestige structures that rank members in terms of the respect they receive from others.

BUREAUCRACIES

Bureaucracy is an organizational model rationally designed to perform complex tasks efficiently. In a bureaucratic business or government agency, officials deliberately enact and revise policy to make the organization as efficient as possible. The ideal bureaucracy is a set of formal secondary relationships rationally organized to achieve specific goals. People specialize in roles that are narrowly and rigidly defined. Power is distributed in a hierarchy, and administrators oversee other people's role behavior to ensure that everything works as it is supposed to.

Bureaucracies are organized around cultural ideas that distinguish them from informal groups. Whereas informal groups place a high value on the welfare of their members, bureaucracies value the organization and its goals most highly, and place a premium on technical efficiency, rationality, precision, speed, reliability, strict obedience, and the highest possible production at the lowest possible cost.

Bureaucracies also rest on beliefs that the best decisions are made by experts (without regard for feelings) and that efficiency is highest when leaders are authoritarian and members are motivated by the desire to maximize their own rewards, rather than by ties of love and affection. A bureaucracy is a partic- ularly passionless organization that tries to rely exclusively on rationality, impersonal relationships, inequality, specialization, and loyalty based on calcu- lations of individual self-interest.

Tumin (1964) argued that bureaucracies also rest on beliefs that protect them from external threats. Because the organization is valued more highly than its individual members, for example, bureaucracies share what Tumin called "the myth of infallibility" Businesses, Tumin noted, rarely admit violations of the law, no matter how compelling the evidence; and prosecutions of large organizations usually end not in criminal convictions, but in settlements by which the company agrees to "stop doing what it never admitted to doing in the first place." When bureaucracies cannot defend themselves in this way, they usually use individuals (or "the computer") as scapegoats, preserving the integrity of the organization itself.

Bureaucracies are unique in the norms that structure relationships among their members. The ideal bureaucracy rests solely on norms that clearly specify how roles are assigned, how power and rewards are distributed, and how decisions are made. Such norms specify what members should do in every situation and forbid the use of personal feelings and individual discretion: decisions are made "by the book," not on a case-by-case basis. Expectations are loose in informal groups, and each member has some power over group interactions ("You can't do that." "Who says?"). In a bureaucracy, however, even the most powerful member is limited by clear norms that anyone can refer to ("According to the bylaws, you can't do that").

In a bureaucracy, individual members are easily replaced, for unlike informal groups, bureaucracies do not depend on particular individuals for their survival. Whereas a family is a group of specific individuals, a bureaucracy is a collection of social statuses whose relationships are structured not to benefit individuals, but to achieve goals within a rigid, stable set of mutual expectations among members. The bureaucratic ideal represents a complete submersion of individuals in a social organization and the resulting irrelevance of individual feelings and needs.

THE BIRTH OF A BUREAUCRACY

Whyte's (1950) study of restaurants shows how bureaucracies emerge as groups grow larger and more complex. Suppose two people decide to open a small restaurant. In its early stages, the structure is informal and may have some of the characteristics of a primary group. Everyone is identified as an individual; shares specific tasks such as cooking and serving food, paying bills and ordering supplies; and handles crises as they arise. Because they interact continually with each other, they can negotiate responsibilities as they go along.

Business booms and they add several employees to cook and serve the food. The owners now face the problem of coordinating the activities of several different people. This requires them to create formal expectations about work hours, dress, and conduct on the job. If their business is highly successful, they might open several restaurants, or perhaps expand into a chain extending across many states. Now they must hire managers to direct each restaurant, accountants to keep the books, and, if they sell stock in their company, a board of directors to oversee the entire operation.

What began as a small informal group grows into a large bureaucracy in which relationships are formally defined. The company becomes more important than its members, any of whom can be replaced with relative case. Although the original members had equal levels of power, the more complex, formal organization has a clearly defined hierarchy of power and prestige, with directors at the top and dishwashers at the bottom.

The structural complexity represented by modern bureaucracies is rooted in the development of more complex societies over the last 1,000 years. Murdock's data on preindustrial societies (1967) show that only 29 percent of villages in advanced horticultural societies were autonomous, free of dominating governments above them, whereas in simple horticultural societies, fully 79 percent were governed solely at the local level. The establishment of central governments spawned increasingly complex societies with formal legal codes, standing armies, and thousands of administrators.

The Industrial Revolution gave the growth of bureaucracy an enormous boost by bringing together large numbers of people with specialized roles. The increased scale and the complexity of production changed the organization of society itself as governments, schools, hospitals and other organizations adopted the bureaucratic model (Zucker, 1983). The bureaucratic ideal has influenced criminals, for although organized crime once revolved around primary family ties, it now operates much like large corporations.

CHARACTERISTICS OF IDEAL-TYPICAL BUREAUCRACY

1. **Specialization:** There is division of labor in the bureaucracy and each member has a specific task to fulfill. All the tasks are coordinated to accomplish the purpose of the organization.
2. **Hierarchy of offices:** Bureaucracies arrange the personnel in a vertical ranking. Each person is supervised by 'higher ups' and in turn supervising others in lower positions. Usually with fewer people in higher positions, the structure takes the form of a bureaucratic 'pyramid'. In this hierarchy *assignments flow downward and accountability flowing upward*. Each level assigns responsibilities to the level beneath it, while each lower level is responsible to the level above for fulfilling these assignments.
3. **Written rules and regulations:** Rationally enacted rules and regulations control not only the organization's own functioning but also its larger environment. In general, the longer a bureaucracy exists and the larger it grows, the more written rules it has.
4. **Technical competence:** A bureaucratic organization expects its officials and staff to have the technical competence to carry out their duties, and regularly monitors worker performance. Evaluation is based on performance and not on favoritism.
5. **Impersonality:** Rules take precedence over personal whims. Members of a bureaucracy owe allegiance to the office, not to a particular person. The impersonality ensures that the clients as well as workers are all treated uniformly. Each worker in bureaucracy becomes a small cog in a large machine. Each worker is a replaceable unit, for many others are available to fulfill each particular function. From this detached approach stems the notion of the "faceless bureaucrat."
6. **Formal, written communication:** Heart of bureaucracy is not people but paperwork. Rather than casual, verbal communication,

bureaucracy relies on formal, written memos and reports. Over time, this correspondence accumulates into vast *files.*

PROBLEMS OF BUREAUCRACY

Bureaucracy can dehumanize and manipulate individuals and it poses a threat to personal privacy and political democracy.

BUREAUCRATIC ALIENATION

Efficiency vs. potential to dehumanize the people it is supposed to serve. The very same impersonality that fosters efficiency keeps officials and clients from responding to each other's unique, personal needs. Follow bureaucratic procedure. Bureaucratic environment gives rise to alienation where a human being is reduced to a part (cog) of big bureaucratic machinery.

BUREAUCRATIC INEFFICIENCY AND RITUALISM

Red tape—The tedious preoccupation with organizational routine and procedures. Rule is a rule. Bureaucratic ritualism (Merton): Preoccupation with rules and regulations to the point of thwarting an organization's goals. Ritualism stifles individual's creativity and strangles organizational performance.

Modest salary–No stake to perform efficiently – no incentive – all ritualism – and the resultant corruption.

BUREAUCRATIC INERTIA

Bureaucratic inertia refers to the *tendency of the bureaucratic organizations to perpetuate them.*

If bureaucrats have little motivation to be efficient, they certainly have every reason to protect their jobs.

Thus the officials typically strive to perpetuate their organization even when its purpose has been fulfilled.

GROUP EFFECTIVENESS

Groups confront a variety of tasks. Factory workers produce goods, and universities produce graduates and research. Groups of scientists solve problems involved in sending a rocket to a distant planet, and families figure out how to balance their budgets and keep everyone happy. Research teams judge the effectiveness of new drugs and juries judge the guilt or innocence of defendants in criminal trials.

Most group work involves one or more of these areas: balancing a family budget requires judgment (estimates of future needs and income) and problem solving (how to raise income or cut spending). Regardless of the mix of tasks involved, all groups must cope with the problems of keeping their members satisfied and maintaining the commitment of their members to the group.

The sociological study of group performance grew out of the Industrial Revolution and the concentration of production in larger and more complex groups. Although early research focused on finding ways to increase productivity (and profits), the study of group performance now includes many groups, such as schools, government bureaucracies, the military, and scientific research laboratories. The settings vary, but the sociological question remains the same: How do the cultural, structural, and ecological characteristics of groups influence their performance? Before describing the importance of such characteristics, we should first examine a fundamental question: Do groups perform better than individuals?

INDIVIDUAL VERSUS GROUP EFFECTIVENESS

"Two heads are better than one," the poet *John Heywood* wrote, and most research comparing the performance of individuals and groups bears the poet out. Individuals usually learn better and faster in the presence of others (Perlmutter and Montmillin,1952), and groups solve puzzles more quickly than individuals do. When Warnik and Sanders (1980) asked groups and individuals to recall details of a videotape portraying a crime, the groups produced more accurate and more detailed accounts.

Although two heads are often better than one, are they twice as good? Research suggests they are not, because individuals tend to reduce their effort as a group grows in size (Harkins, 1981; Harkins, Latan and Williams, 1980). In one experiment, Moede (1927) asked men to pull as hard as they could on a rope attached to a machine that, unknown to them, measured their pull. By themselves, men pulled twice as hard as they did in groups of eight.

Although groups are.generally more effective than individuals, they do have their disadvantages, especially when they are small and members want to maintain group harmony at all costs. When the desire for unity is strong, individuals are less likely to object to poor decisions and suggest alternatives. Groups, in other words, are vulnerable to what Irvingjanis (1968, 1982) called groupthink, in which the desire for consensus overpowers group members' better judgement.

Hall and Watson (1970) asked groups of management trainees to decide what equipment would be needed in order to live on the moon. "Consensus groups" were instructed to reach a collective solution, whereas "conflict groups" were told to avoid changing views simply for the sake of harmony, to views differences of opinion as healthy and constructive, and to not use majority votes to reduce conflict.

Groups tend to be more effective than individuals in achieving goals, but the results depend on the task and the size of the risks involved. Groups differ not only from individuals, however, but from one another, and such differences strongly influence their effectiveness.

EFFECTIVENESS AND GROUP CULTURE

Norms are supposed to help groups achieve their goals, they sometimes have just the opposite effect. Bureaucratic norms cannot anticipate all possible situations, and yet members are expected to obey the rules no matter what. Soldiers are required by law to obey the orders of their commanders, no matter how foolish those orders may appear to be.

Bureaucratic norms often become ends in themselves, obeyed not because they help accomplish group goals, but because "a rule is a rule." Procedures that work in one situation, however, may be totally inappropriate in another. In such cases, highly disciplined training becomes what *Vehien* called a "trained incapacity." During the Japanese attack on Pearl Harbor in 1941, some U.S. officers refused to issue weapons to soldiers without "proper written authorization" from the commander, even though they were being shot at by enemy planes.

In some cases, the content of norms affects group performance. In bureaucracies members are supposed to ignore feelings as they make decisions, to deal with each person as a "case," not as an individual. This often causes the arrogance, abruptness, and coldness so often associated with "bureaucrats," and creates hostile attitudes between bureaucracies and those they serve.

EFFECTIVENESS AND GROUP SIZE

Larger groups tend to perform better than smaller ones when problems require a large number of skills or have a single solution (Watson, 1928). Small groups, however, tend to be more stable (Dames, 1951) and their members can communicate more easily. Small groups perform better when tasks require a limited range of skills and more creative solutions.

Small groups also appear to be better at satisfying their members, but this can be deceiving. Slater (1958) gave problems to 24 groups ranging in size from two to seven members and afterward asked members if they thought their group was too small or too large. The proportion responding "too small" decreased steadily with greater size, whereas the proportion of "too large" responses increased.

Only in groups of five members did no one feel the group was either too large or too small. In addition, members of large groups were more likely to complain about the group and its members, whereas those in the smallest groups expressed no complaints at all. Why should size have this effect?

One might argue that in small groups we feel more important and freer to speak our minds. Yet, when Bales and Borgatta (1955) examined Slater's data, they found that in smaller groups members rarely showed tension or anger, whereas in larger groups anger and disagreement were common.

Bales and Borgatta explained these findings by suggesting that as groups increase in size, some problems are diminished while new ones emerge. The smallest groups depend on agreement and harmony for their survival (Simmel, 1950) and although they may lack the resources they need to accomplish a task, members are likely to conceal disagreement and anger and give a rosy picture of group life.

Large groups, however, have more resources and do not need the agreement of all their members in order to survive or reach a decision. Members feel freer to disagree and show anger because this poses a less serious threat to the group and their standing in it. This suggests that whereas physical freedom (to talk) is greater in small groups, psychological freedom (to express unpopular opinions) is greater in large groups (Mullen, 1983).

This contradicts the common belief that small groups are the only places where we can truly be ourselves. Large groups limit our participation, but small ones limit expression of feelings and outrageous impulses (Simmel, 1950). Whereas large groups tend to make us feel insignificant and lost, small groups tend to inhibit us by making us feel highly visible.

EFFECTIVENESS, ROLES AND LEADERSHIP

The more complex a group is, the better it accomplishes complicated tasks that require a wide range of skills. Complex groups, however, also find it more difficult to coordinate and control their members' behavior.

Group complexity creates problems when it becomes an end in itself. The essence of a bureaucracy is the management of some members by others. In order to demonstrate their importance, bureaucrats often create work that requires assistants, which results in more paperwork as assistants report to their bosses. More assistants are then added, and the organization continues to grow, using more and more resources to manage its mushrooming staff (Parkinson, 1957).

Other problems arise from the ways in which groups decide who plays which roles. Bureaucracies try to secure the loyal, devoted service of their members by offering them job security and clear lines of promotion so long as they obey the rules. This causes three problems.

(i) First, members may use their security to do no more than what the norms require of them. College professors are often criticized for working less after achieving the security of tenure.

(ii) Second, because advancement in bureaucracies requires obedience to norms, people may become timid and overly conservative, afraid to show initiative for fear of risking their promotion to higher positions (Merton, 1968).

(iii) Third, in bureaucracies people tend to be promoted to higher positions on the basis of performance in lower positions. Inevitably, members reach positions that are beyond their abilities and there they stay, unable to perform well enough to reach the next rung on the ladder.

Peter and Hull (1969) called this phenomenon the *Peter Principle*: "In a hierarchy each employee tends to rise to his level of incompetence; every post tends to be occupied by an employee incompetent to execute its duties." They suggested that the only reason top positions are sometimes occupied by competent people is that "there are not enough ranks for them to have reached their level of incompetence: in other words, in that hierarchy there is no task beyond their abilities."Although complex role structures increase group effectiveness in many ways, they also produce unanticipated negative consequences that affect their members and interfere with group performance.

Social situations affect not only the emergence and selection of leaders in groups, but their effectiveness as well. Task leaders are most effective in extreme situations—when groups verge on falling apart during disasters or when they are cohesive and strong. Expressive leaders, however, are more effective than task leaders in less extreme circumstances, when members have less need of a task leader and are in a stronger position to question a leader's authority. A leader who improves group performance in one situation may damage it in another.

EFFECTIVENESS AND COMMUNICATION

Communication patterns affect both success at different tasks and member satisfaction. When members can interact freely with one another (a "circle"), groups have more difficulty solving puzzles with single solutions than they do with tasks having many workable solutions (Shaw, 1954). In addition, although groups that channel communication through a single member (a "wheel") are efficient problem solvers, their members are less satisfied.

From this point of view, it is easier to see why large numbers of people with free and open communication structures (such as street mobs) are inefficient at solving problems. It is also easier to see why bureaucracies have so much trouble satisfying their members and performing efficiently. Their communication structures often leave members feeling insignificant and powerless. They also make it difficult for one part of the organization to know what other parts are doing, for each piece of information must pass through many hands before reaching its ultimate destination.

We have seen, then, that the ability of groups to achieve goals depends on their cultural and structural characteristics. No group, however, can perform well or even survive if it cannot maintain its members' loyalty. All groups must continually cope with the problem of social cohesion.

INDIVIDUALS, FREEDOM AND LIFE IN GROUPS

The social characteristics of groups affect societies and their people. Groups are capable both of supporting and protecting their members and of corrupting and harming them. Through groups, human beings have accomplished stunning and wonderful things, but groups are also the source of our most astonishing cruelty and destruction. How do groups and organizations affect us?

Perhaps one of the most significant cultural changes during the last 2,000 years has been the enormous increase in the social value of individuals and their freedom in relation to groups. Durkheim (1893) went so far as to suggest that in the simplest societies with their uncomplicated divisions of tabor, the idea of an "individual" simply did not exist. The group, he argued, was everything, and it never occurred to people to stand apart from it as unique individuals.

From Durkheim's point of view, "individuality" cannot exist without supporting cultural beliefs (such a thing is possible), values (the individual is important), and norms (individuals have rights in relation to groups); and these ideas are relatively new in history. In this sense, if sociology had existed thousands of years ago, it would not even have identified the effects of groups on individuals as a problem.

Issues on which Large-Group members agreed more often than Small-Group members'

1.	The time available to solve the problem is insufficient.
2.	This group doesn't make the best use of its time.
3.	This group needs somebody to keep it on track.
4.	Some people in this group talk too much.
5.	Some people in this group are crowded out of the discussion.
6.	Some people in this group should participate more.
7.	There are considerable differences of ability and competence between members of this group.
8.	There is too much competition among members in this group.
9.	This group is not accomplishing as much as it could. Small groups have 2, 3 or 4 members, large groups 5, 6 or 7.

The social value of individuals has reached its highest point in complex industrial societies. As societies raise the value of individuals, people are less vulnerable to being "buried" in the group, to having no right to stand apart and celebrate their uniqueness. This, however, creates the danger of being isolated from groups.

In industrial societies, we spend increasingly large portions of our lives in groups and organizations that value efficiency, precision, speed, control, pro- duction, and obedience more than they value the happiness and satisfaction of their members. In addition, Slater (1971) argued that an extreme emphasis on individuals and their uniqueness creates a cultural environment that frustrates basic human needs to trust and cooperate with others, to deal directly with interpersonal problems, and to share responsibility for the conduct of our lives.

In short, Slater argued that modern cultures not only raise the social value of individuals to new heights, but also create unprecedented levels of isolation and loneliness. "Who am I?" is perhaps the most common and disturbing question individuals face in modern cultures, because simple group membership is no longer a complete basis for our existence. Whereas ties between individuals and groups may have been too strong in the simplest societies, in complex societies they are in danger of being too weak.

Such cultural changes, however, do not simply "happen" by accident; they are often responses to changing social structures that define relationships. *Weber* and *Durkheim* saw in the Industrial Revolution a threat to human welfare. What changes in the structure of group life did they see and why were they so concerned?

SOCIAL STRUCTURE, GROUPS AND INDIVIDUALS

Gemeinschaft societies are held together by a common culture, and groups tend to be small, informal, and primary. Work, family, and religion form a unified whole. Those who share in the culture and obey its norms have a secure place in the social world.

The Industrial Revolution, however, accelerated a long-term change in which social relationships became increasingly rational, secondary, and formal in Gesellschaft societies based less on shared culture than on rational calculations of individual self-interest. This change resulted from the rise of the bureaucracy as a model of social organization.

In complex industrial societies, we are known as individuals, and as individuals, we are known primarily by the social statuses we occupy. Children no longer grow up confident of their place in society, knowing exactly what is expected of them, what roles they will play as adults. To survive in modern societies, each of us must achieve a place for ourselves somewhere in the complex division of labor.

Nowhere are the consequences of these structures clearer than in bureaucracies with their formal rules, rigidly defined relationships, and inattention to individual feelings and needs. Argyris (1957) suggested that bureaucracies actually interfere with the needs of healthy people. Maturity includes the ability to act and make judgments independently, to think abstractly and in terms of long-term consequences of behavior. Bureaucracies encourage dependency and timidity, short-term thinking and ignorance of long-term consequences.

Argyris concluded, "Formal organizations are willing to pay high wages and provide adequate seniority if mature adults will, for eight hours a day, behave in a less mature manner."As a result, we often feel frustrated and helpless because we have little control over our environment, goals, or behavior, and the lack of control creates anxiety and uncertainty. *Karl*

Marx described the resulting feelings of being lost and insignificant as alienation—a feeling of helplessness and detachment in relation to work and its results.

Unlike primary groups, bureaucracies do not derive their security from the welfare of their members. We may be fired when it is no longer in an employer's "best interests" to keep us, regardless of our abilities. Middle-aged executives often lose jobs because they are too experienced and too capable and therefore command higher salaries than younger employees.

Some people defend themselves by leaving the organization (a risky choice), or by achieving more powerful positions within the organization. Others, however, who can neither advance nor afford to leave, retreat into apathy and daydreams, or create informal groups that support their feelings of alienation.

The rational basis of bureaucracy leads many to participate in order to achieve personal—not organizational—goals, the most important of which is earning a living (Moore, 1962). We can work in a bureaucracy without valuing its goals or liking our jobs or other workers. This often minimizes feelings of loyalty to large organizations and encourages members to exploit every opportunity for personal gain—whether on the large scale of criminal embezzlement or the small scale of stealing office supplies and equipment, padding expense accounts, or using company cars for personal trips—a clear example of social factors that foster criminal behaviour.

As bureaucracy spreads, we find ourselves with fewer and fewer groups in which we are known and valued as individuals. We spend increasing portions of our lives in secondary groups that involve limited parts of ourselves, and our lives are divided into separate spheres of family, work, friendships, and religion that have little if any connection to one another. In such environments, it is difficult to maintain a sense of "wholeness" about our lives; rather, we tend to feel torn in many directions at once as we divide our time, energy and loyalty between family, friends, and the formal demands of work.

The structures of complex societies create feelings of insignificance and rootlessness in their members, yet how do they differ from Durkheim's vision of simple societies in which individuals are indistinguishable from their groups? Is it not true that individuals have little significance in both simple Gemeinschaft societies and the bureaucracies of modern Geselischaft societies?

Although individuals tend to be "lost" in both types of societies, there is an enormously important difference between the two. In the simple societies Durkheim referred to, individuals had no need to stand apart from their groups, because groups and their members depended on each other for their survival. There was a close connection between the welfare of groups and the welfare of their members.

A bureaucracy, however, uses people as a means for achieving goals that they neither determine nor control, and may not even share. In a bureaucratic society, individuals cannot afford to place their welfare in the hands of organizations that can and often do quickly dispense with them. It is no accident of history that as social structures become increasingly bureaucratic, concern for the rights and welfare of individuals grows stronger. As groups become more exploitative, members must establish new sources of protection and security, and aside from the family, the individual is the last line of defense.

The increased size, complexity, and formality of groups and organizations also affect the welfare of entire societies, for although bureaucracies support efficiency, control, and complex divisions of labour, they also oppose the strong emotional ties that are the basis of human morality, compassion, and empathy. In bureaucracies we are supposed to simply do our jobs and leave the establishment of group goals to our leaders. This gives bureaucracies what Sabini and Silver (1982) have called "a genius for organizing evil".

Nazi Germany was a model of bureaucratic efficiency, and prided itself on the strict format organization of its society. When Adolph Eichmann managed the railway systems that transported millions of people to their deaths in concentration camps, he behaved as a model bureaucrat, carrying out his orders quickly, efficiently, and without question. In the final chaotic months of World War II, when Germany was defending itself on three fronts, Eichmann's proudest achievement was his astonishing ability to keep the trains running on time.

Marx believed that bureaucracy turns individuals into cogs in machines and that as we are more alienated from our work and its results, we are also more alienated from one another. In bureaucratic societies, in which organizations and their rules assume primary importance, it is not surprising that we are often motivated by rational self-interest ("What's in it for me?") and insensitive to the fate of others.

Groups will always be a part of human life, and it is for this reason that decisions about their structures and cultures are so important. We cannot survive alone, and the characteristics of groups set the terms on which we live our lives in relation to other people.

RELATIONSHIP BETWEEN THE FORMAL AND INFORMAL ORGANIZATION

The formal and informal organizations are inter-related. They are not mutually exclusive. There exist many informal organizations simultaneously with the formal organizations. A single formal organization like the state, the university, the industry, the church etc., may consist of several informal organizations in the form of gangs, friendship groups' etc. The line separating formal and informal organization is not always clear. Any formal organization functions best when the informal organization supports it. The most orderly and efficient structure does not automatically produce a successful organizational administration if the members have no goodwill towards one another and have only personal hostilities. On the contrary, the best goodwill in the world will be insufficient for the successful pursuit of an organizational activity if the formal organization is deficient.

The most efficient and satisfactory organization is the one in which formal organization is supported the informal organization. The relationship between the formal and informal organizations is always subtle always complicated and always interesting. According to Page, the continuous interaction and association among the members of formal organization result in the emergence of informal structure of roles and relationships. He calls such informal structure consisting of primary group relations, friendships and cliques, ties of mutual obligations of aid and assistance.

According to Charles Bernard the informal organizations are necessary to the operation of formal organizations as a means of communication of cohesion and of protecting the integrity of the individual.

CASTE SYSTEM

Introduction. Meaning and Concept of Caste System. Historical Backgrounds of the Indian Caste System: *Varna and Jati.* ***Characterisitcs of Caste System. Challenges of the Caste System:*** *The Dysfunctions.* ***Dominant Caste. Caste and Social Status. Caste Mobility. Reforms in Caste System. Caste System During the British Rule. India Since Independence. Modern Status of the Caste System:*** *Scheduled Castes (SC), Scheduled Tribes (ST), Other Backward Classes (OBC), Indian Anti-reservation Protests, Caste System Among Non-Hindus.* ***Caste-related Violence. Caste Politics. Class System:*** *Criterion of Class—Marxian Analysis.* ***Distinction Between Caste System and Class System. Characteristics of Social Class.***

INTRODUCTION

The word caste is derived from the spanish word *casta* which means breed, race, strain or hereditary complex of hereditary qualities. The Portuguese used this word for classes of people. In India known by the term *jati*. Herbert Risley has defined caste as a collection of families or group of families bearing a common name; claiming a common descent from a mythical ancestor, human or divine, professing to follow the same hereditary calling and regarded by those who are competent to give an opinion as forming a single homogenous community. Lundberg defined caste as a merely rigid social class into which members are born from which they can withdraw or escape only with extreme difficulty.

MEANING AND CONCEPT OF CASTE SYSTEM

In ancient India there developed a social system in which people were divided into separate close communities. These communities are known in English as caste. The origin of the caste system is in Hinduism, but it affected the whole Indian society.

The *caste system* in the religious form is basically a simple division of society in which there are four castes arranged in a hierarchy and below them the outcast. But socially the caste system was more complicated, with much more castes and sub-castes and other divisions. Legally the government disallows the practice of caste system but has a policy of affirmative discrimination of the backward classes.

In modern India the term caste is used for Jat and also for Varna. The term, caste was used by the British who ruled India until 1947. The British who wanted to rule India efficiently made lists of Indian communities. They used two terms to describe Indian communities: Castes and Tribes. The term caste was used for Jats and also for Varnas. Tribes were those communities who lived deep in jungles, forests and mountains far away from the main population and also communities who were hard to be defined as castes for example communities who made a living from stealing or robbery. These lists, which the British made, were used later on by the Indian governments to create lists of communities who were entitled for positive discrimination.

HISTORICAL BACKGROUNDS OF THE INDIAN CASTE SYSTEM

There is no universally accepted theory about the origin of the Indian caste system. The Indian classes are similar to the ancient Iranian classes (pistras), wherein the priests are Athravans, the warriors are Rathaestha, the merchants are Vastriya, and the artisans are Huiti.

VARNA AND JATI

The most peculiar characteristic of the Hindu society is the system called varna and jati. Varna is caste on the basis of position in the society and jati a sub-caste. (Varna in Sanskrit actually means colour.) Varna is the positional label imposed upon different castes as a yardstick for social classification. It was this discrimination, exploitation and human right violations on the basis of the varna-jati classification that the reformist movements opposed the most. The varnas are four in number: brahamanas, kshatriyas, vaishyas and shudras. The Bhagavad Gita says varnas are decided based on Guna and Karma. Manusmriti and some other shastras mention four varnas: the Brahmins (teachers, scholars and priests), the Kshatriyas (kings and warriors), the Vaishyas (agriculturists and traders) and Shudras (service providers and artisans).

This theoretical system postulated Varna categories as ideals and explained away the reality of thousands of endogamous *Jatis* actually prevailing in the country as being the historical products of intermarriage among the "pure" Varnas – Varna Sankara. All those, including foreigners, tribals and nomads, who did not subscribe to the norms of the Hindu society were contagious and untouchables.

Another group excluded from the main society was called Parjanya or Antyaja. This group of former "untouchables" (self described as Dalits), i.e., downtrodden, was considered either the lower section of Shudras or outside the caste system altogether. Passages from scriptures such as Manusmriti indicate that the varna system was originally non-hereditary. Different critics of Hinduism state that the caste system is rooted in the varna system mentioned in the ancient Hindu scriptures. However, many groups, such as ISKCON, consider the modern Indian caste system and the varna system as two distinct concepts.

The Role of Vedas is very Important on Caste System.

Many European scholars from the colonial era regarded the Manusmriti as the "law book" of the Hindus, and thus concluded that the caste system is a part of Hinduism, an assertion that is rejected by many Hindu scholars, who state that it is an anachronistic social practice, not a religious one. Although many Hindu scriptures contain passages that can be interpreted to sanction the caste system, they also contain indications that the caste system is not an essential part of Hinduism. The Vedas place very little importance on the caste system, mentioning caste only once (in the Purush Sukta) out of tens of thousands of verses. B.R. Ambedkar believed that even this is a much later interpolation and gave evidence to support his conclusion. In the Vedic period, there was no prohibition against the Shudras listening to the Vedas or participating in any religious rite.

'Varna' did not have any particular use in the operations of the social system, nor had it a built-in power for that. But the most important factor was the caste or jati. Jati denoted a particular community with a definition on customs by and large, having a particular profession hereditarily and, inclusive marriage rights. Each varna would contain several jatis each of which had its own customs and practices. Saint Auvaiyaar has stated that there are only two castes in the world: those who contribute positively and those who contribute negatively. From these, it can be inferred that the caste system is more of a socio-economic class system.

CHARACTERISITCS OF CASTE SYSTEM

A caste system is a type of social structure which divides people on the basis of inherited social status. Although many societies could be described in this way, within a caste system, people are rigidly expected to marry and interact with people of the same social class. India has a well known example of a caste system, although various forms of caste systems can be found in many other cultures as well.

Several characteristics distinguish a caste system. The first is the tendency toward endogamy, meaning that people marry within the same caste exclusively. Caste mobility is also extremely rare; one cannot transform from a laborer to a scholar except in very rare circumstances, for example. Higher castes traditionally hold all of the political power, and the castes may be divided further through language, culture, and economics. Within a caste system, each member generally knows his or her place, and your social status is usually apparently to others as well.

Although people associate the caste system with India, the world is actually borrowed from the Portugese. By 1555, English speakers were using the word to refer to a race of men, adopting the Portuguese word casta. Although the word was used in English to describe race or breeding, in Portuguese it was more widely used in reference to the stratified society of Portugal. When the Indian social system was encountered in the 1600s, it came to be described as a caste system in the Portuguese sense.

The roots of the Indian caste system can be found in the Hindu scriptures, although the caste system was adopted by other religions in India as well. According to scripture, Indian society could be broken down into a number of different groups, known as Varnas. Brahmins, the highest caste, were scholars and priests, while Kshatriya were warriors, rulers, and landlords. Vaisya were merchants, while Sudra were manual laborers. Beyond there four basis Varnas are the Untouchables or Dalit, and the system also has a space for outsiders and foreigners who do not conform with the system.

Within each Varna there are hundreds of Jati, individual endogamous groups. India's extremely refined and complex caste system began to be reformed during the push for independence, and technically discrimination on the basis of caste status is not allowed in modern India. However, the remains of the caste system can still be seen in the way that Indians move through and interact with their society. Many people of lower caste, for example, face legal barriers and difficulty when they try to enter Indian politics.

A sense of highness and lowness or superiority and inferiority is associated with this gradation or ranking. The Brahmins are placed at the top of the hierarchy and are regarded as pure or supreme. The degraded caste or the untouchables have occupied the other end of the hierarchy. The status of an individual is determined by his birth and not by selection nor by accomplishments. Each caste has its own customs, traditions practices and rituals. It has its own informal rules, regulations and procedures. The caste panchayats or the caste councils regulate the conduct of members. The caste system has imposed certain restrictions on the food habitats of the members these differ from caste to caste. In North India Brahmin would accept pakka food only from some castes lower than his own. But he would not accept kachcha food prepared with the use of water at the hands of no other caste except his own. As a matter of rule and practice no individual would accept kachcha food prepared by an inferior casteman. The caste system put restriction on the range of social relations also. The idea of pollution means a touch of lower caste man would pollute or defile a man of higher caste. Even his shadow is considered enough to pollute a higher caste man. The lower caste people suffered from certain socio-religious disabilities. The impure castes are made to live on the outskirts of the city and they are not allowed to draw water from the public wells.

In earlier times entrance to temples and other places of religious importance were forbidden to them. Educational facilities, legal rights and political representation were denied to them for a very long time. If the lower castes suffer from certain disabilities some higher caste like the Brahmins enjoy certain privileges like conducting prayers in the temples etc.

There is gradation of occupations also. Some occupations are considered superior and sacred while certain others degrading and inferior. For a long time occupations were very much associated with the caste system. Each caste had its own specific occupations which were almost hereditary. There was no scope for individual talent, aptitude, enterprise or abilities. The caste system imposes restrictions on marriage also. Caste is an endogamous group. Each caste is subdivided into certain sub-castes which are again endogamous. Intercaste marriages are still looked down upon in the traditional Indian society.

CHALLENGES OF THE CASTE SYSTEM

The caste system is credited to ensure the continuity of the traditional social organization of India. It has accommodated multiple communities including invading tribes in the Indian society. The knowledge and skills of the occupations have passed down from one generation to the next. Through subsystems like Jajmani system the caste system promoted interdependent interaction between various castes and communities with in a village. The rituals and traditions promoted cooperation and unity between members of the different castes.

The origins of the Indian caste system remain shrouded in mystery. The myth reveals that the four varnas (social classes) into which the Indian society is divided have its source in the sacrifice of the original Brahman. Some researchers conclude that the intermingling of different varna members gave rise to a number of castes (social units). Debatable or not as this argument might render itself, the fact remains that the caste system in India has existed there since time immemorial. What is it about the present age with 50 past years in particular then that threatens the status of the Indian caste?

The new democratic government represents one of the major factors that weaken the role of the caste. The Indian nation consists of, as Furnivall called them, "plural societies." Each caste takes care of itself, lives by its own laws and imposes each its own sanctions for breaking them. For a long time this situation did not allow the development of a common economic spirit or common social demands or values. Every caste has definite benefits for its members but the advantages of individual castes all living to themselves come at a price for the nation as a whole.

With the arrival of democracy and the greater focus on the country as a common land, the monopolies of individual castes become less and less relevant. The democratic constitution, which came into effect in 1950, aimed at providing all citizens "equality of status and opportunity." In addition to this, the government in 1955 set up the Untouchability (Offences) Act against discriminating anyone on the basis of their "untouchability." Laws like these heavily impede the carefree expression of caste customs.

P.N. Bose stated that the caste system had been essential to raise the minds from savagery but now it stops them half-way through the progress. To push the Indian society through this progress, the modern government makes attempts at working out the ways so that education remains relatively equally accessible to all castes, another area that significantly challenges the strength of castes. The spread of education definitely contributes to the diminishing of the discrimination between classes and castes. The studies prove that the level of education greatly increases the liberal attitudes toward the caste principles. The modern ways bring the education and the occupational opportunities to the lower classes enabling them to raise their status (sanskritization), a process previously hardly ever possible.

The urbanization of the country weakens the castes as well. With more and more people moving and working in big cities the old caste attitudes are bound to collapse. As the research shows, the city citizens do not identify themselves with their caste origin as much as the villagers do. Democracy, industrialization and education all increase the sense of the individual achievement rather than that of the caste.

Furthermore, the industry in India opens its door to a variety of new jobs and methods, "ritually neutral," which brings members of different castes together decreasing their previous concerns about the mutual contact and pollution.

In regards to the pollution, in the industrialized society where the means of communication and travel require the close contact between people, the laws concerning not touching members of other classes and castes lose their effect. Despite the old commensality and craft exclusiveness rules, modern Indians become more and more liberal toward eating together and changing their occupations.

There exist a number of other dimensions that seriously challenge the survival of the caste system. All of them gradually and persistently, consciously or unconsciously, aim at the elimination of the old system that many people view as unjust and oppressive. The castes stand firm but the security of their future remains threatened. What will be of castes in 50, 100, or 500 years? And will it turn out for better or maybe for worse? Only time will reveal.

THE DYSFUNCTIONS

Caste system promoted untouchability and discrimination against certain members of the society. It hindered both horizontal and vertical social mobility forcing an individual to carry on the traditional occupation against his or her will and capacity. The status of women was affected and they were relegated to the background. The caste system divided the society into mutually hostile and conflicting groups and subgroups.

DOMINANT CASTE

This concept given by M.N. Srinivas holds that a caste is dominant when it is numerically higher than the other castes. In the Mysore village he described the peasant Okkalinga composed of nearly half of the population made up of nineteenth jati group. The Okkalinga were the biggest land owner. The chief criteria of domination of a caste are

1. Economic strength
2. Political power
3. Ritual purity
4. Numerical strength

The dominant caste also wields economic and political power over the other caste groups. It also enjoys a high ritual status in the local caste hierarchy. The dominant caste may not be ritually high but enjoy high status because of wealth, political power and numerical strength. The presence of educated persons and high occupation rate also play an important role in deciding its dominance over other caste groupings. Sometimes a single clan of dominant caste controls a number of villages in areas. The dominant caste settle dispute between persons belonging to their own and other jati. The power of the dominant caste is supported by a norm discouraging village from seeking justice from area, Govt.

official, court or police located outside the village. The members of the dominant caste particularly those from the wealthy and powerful families are representative of this village in dealing with the officials.

CASTE AND SOCIAL STATUS

Traditionally, although the political power lay with the Kshatriyas, historians portrayed that the Brahmins as custodians and interpreters of Dharma enjoyed much prestige and many advantages.

Fa Hien, a Buddhist pilgrim from China, visited India around 400 AD. "Only the lot of the Chandals he found unenviable; outcastes by reason of their degrading work as disposers of dead, they were universally shunned... But no other section of the population were notably disadvantaged, no other caste distinctions attracted comment from the Chinese pilgrim, and no oppressive caste 'system' drew forth his surprised censure." In this period kings of Sudra and Brahmin origin were as common as those of Kshatriya varna and caste system was not wholly prohibitive and repressive.

The castes did not constitute a rigid description of the occupation or the social status of a group. Since British society was divided by class, the British attempted to equate the Indian caste system to their own social class system. They saw caste as an indicator of occupation, social standing, and intellectual ability. Intentionally or unintentionally, the caste system became more rigid during the British Raj, when the British started to enumerate castes during the ten year census and codified the system under their rule.

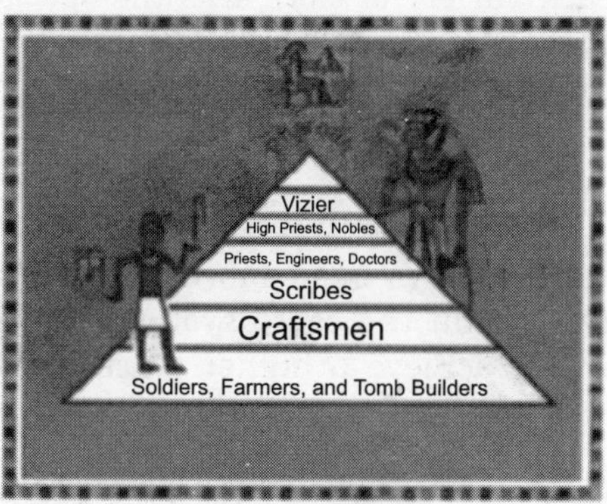

The Social Pyramid.

The Dalits, or the people outside the varna system, had the lowest social status. The Dalits, earlier referred to as "untouchables" by some, worked in what were seen as unhealthy, unpleasant or polluting jobs. In the past, the Dalits suffered from social segregation and restrictions, in addition to extreme poverty. They were not allowed temple worship with others, nor water from the same sources. Persons of higher castes would not interact with them. If somehow a member of a higher caste came into physical or social contact with an untouchable, the member of the higher caste was defiled, and had to bathe thoroughly to purge him or herself of the impurity. Social discrimination developed even among the Dalits. Sub-castes among Dalits, like dhobi, nai etc., would not interact with lower-order Bhangis, who were described as "outcasts even among outcastes".

Sociologists have commented on the historical advantages offered by a rigid social structure, such as the caste system, and its lack of usefulness in the modern world. Historically, the caste system offered several advantages to the population of the Indian subcontinent. While Caste is nowadays seen by instances that render it anachronistic, in its original form, the caste system served as an important instrument of order in a society where mutual consent rather than compulsion ruled; where the ritual rights as well as the economic obligations of members of one caste or sub-caste were strictly circumscribed in relation to those of any other caste or sub-caste; where one was born into one's caste and retained one's station in society for life; where merit was inherited, where equality existed within the caste, but inter-caste relations were unequal and hierarchical. A well-defined system of mutual interdependence through a division of labour created security within a community. In addition, the division of labour on the basis of ethnicity allowed immigrants and foreigners to quickly integrate into their own caste niches. The caste system played an influential role in shaping economic activities. The caste system functioned much like medieval European guilds, ensuring the division of labour, providing for the training of apprentices and, in some cases, allowing manufacturers to achieve narrow specialisation. For instance, in certain regions, producing each variety of cloth was the speciality of a particular sub-caste. Also, philosophers argue that the majority of people would be comfortable in stratified endogamous groups, and have been in ancient times.

CASTE MOBILITY

In practice, there have always been more possibilities for upward (or downward) movement within the caste system than the classic rules of varna would suggest. To achieve a higher place in the social hierarchy,

Rally against Caste System.

the members of a jati often take the following steps: enter an occupation that involves less contact with pollution; follow stricter rules of purity in daily life; and learn Sanskrit, the classic language of the holy scriptures.

As we know that some scholars believe that the relative ranking of other castes was fluid or differed from one place to another prior to the arrival of the British. Sociologists such as Bernard Buber and Marriott McKim describe how the perception of the caste system as a static and textual stratification has given way to the perception of the caste system as a more processual, empirical and contextual stratification.

However, in relation to upward mobility, the downward mobility of individual was the norm. All the outcastes descended to fifth stratum so that purity of society could be maintained; the dastardly caste Panchayat was the tool for this. The Hindu society contains an inordinately large numbers of untouchables. Every fifth Hindu is untouchable. All the untouchables are supposed to provide unclean goods and services to rest of the society. This means that 20 percent of Hindu population or labour force is meant to provide these unclean goods and services. By no measurement or by no stretch of imagination any society needs 20 percent of its strength for such purposes. These so many untouchables are not needed though some people call caste system a specialization of labor. Then what explains their numbers? In ancient times nearly 10 percent of population was employed in the army. So all of them had to be Kshatriyas. With an average family of five, the fifty percent of population had to be Kshatriya. Now they are barely five percent. Where have they gone? The Vaisyas of ancient Hindu society were engaged in agriculture and cattle rearing. These formed about 90 percent of the total productive activities. There should have been about 40 percent Vaisyas but they are barely five percent. For Shudras there was no proper occupation; they were not connected with agriculture and cattle rearing which was then the work of the Vaisyas. Thus they were insignificant in numbers where as they are now about 60 percent of Hindu population. Where have they come from? This means that there have been large scale but slow degradations in the Hindu society. One of the degradation was the degradation of the occupations of agriculture and cattle rearing. These occupations were degraded from Vaisya level to Shudra level thus degrading a very large number of people. Or the Shudras in new Vedic areas engaged in these jobs were not upgraded.

Y.B. Damle, another sociologist, have applied theoretical models to explain mobility and flexibility in the caste system in India. As per the researches made these scholars, groups of lower-caste individuals could seek to elevate the status of their caste by attempting to emulate the practices of higher castes. Flexibility in caste laws permitted very low-caste religious clerics such as Valmiki to compose the Ramayana, which became a central work of Hindu scripture.

As per some psychologists, mobility across broad caste lines may have been "minimal", though sub-castes (jatis) may change their social status over the generations by fission, re-location, and adoption of new rituals. Sociologist M.N. Srinivas has also debated the question of rigidity in Caste. In an ethnographic study of the Coorgs of Karnataka, he observed considerable flexibility and mobility in their caste hierarchies. He asserts that the caste system is far from a rigid system in which the position of each component caste is fixed for all time. Movement has always been possible, and especially in the middle regions of the hierarchy. It was always possible for groups born into a lower caste to "rise to a higher position by adopting vegetarianism and teetotalism," i.e., adopt the customs of the higher castes. While theoretically "forbidden," the process was not uncommon in practice. The concept of sanskritization, or the adoption of upper-caste norms by the lower castes, addressed the actual complexity and fluidity of caste relations. Historical examples of mobility in the Indian Caste System among Hindus have been researched. There is also precedent of certain Shudra families within the temples of the Sri Vaishnava sect in South India elevating their caste.

The fact that many of the dynasties were of obscure origin suggests some social mobility: a person of any caste, having once acquired political power, could also acquire a genealogy connecting him with the traditional lineages and conferring Kshatriya status. A number of new castes, such as the Kayasthas (scribes) and Khatris (traders), are mentioned in the sources of this period. According to the Brahmanic sources, they originated from intercaste marriages, but this is clearly an attempt at rationalizing their rank in the hierarchy. Many of these new castes played a major role in society. The hierarchy of castes did not have a uniform distribution throughout the country. Khatri appears to be unquestionably a Prakritised form of the Sanskrit Kshatriya.

REFORMS IN CASTE SYSTEM

Inevitably, there were certain people who failed to live up to their caste dharma or who violated the rules concerning marriage between castes. Such people and their children were considered outcasts from Hindu society. They had to live apart from other castes and were given the jobs that no one else wanted to perform. Because of their contact with things considered unclean or polluted, the outcasts were believed to be deeply tainted. They came to be thought of as "untouchable" because people believed that their touch—or even the sight of them—would compromise a brahman's purity. The untouchables were not admitted into Hindu temples and instead formed religious sects of their own. Over the centuries, they also organized into sub-castes much like those of orthodox Hindu society. In the 20th century, Mahatma Gandhi made it one of his life's goals to bring the untouchables back into Hindu society. He renamed them the harijans, or "children of God," and tried to convince orthodox Hindus to admit them into their temples and their everyday lives. However, other leaders doubted that upper-caste Hindus would ever treat the harijans as equals. Dr. B.R. Ambedkar, a distinguished scholar who had been born an "untouchable," was a leading spokesman for this view. He used the term scheduled castes when referring to this group, for he believed that the term harijans was demeaning. The scheduled castes, he said, should withdraw from Hinduism altogether and join another religion, such as Buddhism, which does not recognize caste distinctions. After India became an independent nation in 1947, its new constitution outlawed the practice of "untouchability." The constitution also established affirmative action programs to ensure that the scheduled castes would have access to higher education and better jobs. In contrast to similar legislation in the United States, these clauses actually guarantee that a certain percentage of university and job openings will be assigned to disadvantaged groups. Because of these programs, there has been a marked improvement in the status of the scheduled castes. Yet discrimination continues, and the condition of the former "untouchables" is still a major social issue today.

CASTE SYSTEM DURING THE BRITISH RULE

By the time of British rule, starting from around the seventeenth century to not in print version 1947, the caste system had evolved and expanded into some 3000 different castes. The caste system although underwent great changes throughout this period but strictly speaking, never effectively eradicated. Interestingly, the first effect that the British had on the caste system was to strengthen rather than undermine it, for the British gave the Brahmans back certain special privileges which under Muslim had been withdrawn from them. On the other hand, the British legislators did not agree that the members of the lower-caste should receive greater punishment than members of the upper-caste for committing the same offense.

Under British rule, the untouchables and low-caste Indians enjoyed an improvement of their social standings. For example, with wealth and education, they could pass as members of higher castes from some distant area. The strict restrictions on social contacts became harder to enforce as members of different castes mingled increasing. The newly educated and affluence middle class in the cities mixed socially with people based on their financial position and class and not caste. Under the British, it was wealth and education, which determines a person's social status not caste.

By the end of the Raj, traditional Indian society began to break down into a westernized class system. A rising strong middle class with a heightened sense of Indian nationalism evolved out of the caste system allowing men of low castes to rise to high ranks and positions of power, previously closed to them. The moderation of the caste system was largely due to British rule and a man named not in print version Mahatma Gandhi (1869-1948), a product of the British education system. But the degree to which the caste system is successfully challenged by British rule is questionable. Although castes are now prohibited by law in India, they have not totally vanished in practice. Till today, some untouchables still do the dirty work as their forefathers had done so for centuries.

INDIA SINCE INDEPENDENCE

India was a British colony. It earned its independence from the British on 15th August, 1947. Day before that Pakistan which was created as a result of partition of British India was established and flanked on two sides of India: West Pakistan which is called today Pakistan, and east Pakistan, now an independent state called Bangladesh. After its independence, the political leaders of India adopted the liberal democratic system for the country.

Since its independence, India has transformed a lot. When India attained independence in 1947, its population was around 400 million people. Now there are billion people in India. India is the largest democracy in the world. It has the biggest number of people with franchise rights and the largest number of political parties, which take part in election campaign.

Before its independence, India was never a single country but a bunch of different entities. Many predicted that India, because of diversities in its cultures, religion, languages, castes, manners, local histories, nationalities and identities, would not survive as a single democratic country, but would break up into smaller countries.

Since independence, India had many political problems. During independence the most burning issues were the riots between the Hindus and Muslims while the Sikhs were siding with Hindus. Another issue was convincing the Princely states not to declare independence or join Pakistan but to join the Indian Union. India also had a few wars with its neighbors on border issues.

India also has many internal problems. Different communities with different identities—regional, language, caste, religion—demanded different rights for their communities. Some communities demanded more autonomy for their cultures within the Indian states. Others demanded autonomous states within the Indian Union, while the others demanded to be independent from India. With all its problems India survives as a single state with democratic character.

MODERN STATUS OF THE CASTE SYSTEM

The caste system is still intact today but the rules are not as rigid as they were in the past. Because of western education, contact with foreigners, media, and modern communications, people are progressive in many aspects. In 1962, a law was passed making it illegal to discriminate against the untouchable castes. In practice however, discrimination still continues today. In the past, when Brahmins and Chetris came in contact with Sudras, they used to bathe. Now, some people just sprinkle water on their body and some do not even care at all.

Today, Brahmins have land, work in the field and are involved in government service. Some Baisya and Sudra caste people are teachers, high officials, and successful politicians. Previously, Brahmins were not subject to the death penalty and were instead given the same status as cows in the Hindu religion. But now, all castes are equally treated by the law. Education is free and open to all castes. Discrimination is only done socially. The leaders of independent India decided that India will be democratic, socialist and secular country. According to this policy there is a separation between religion and state. Practicing untouchability or discriminating a person based on his caste is legally forbidden. Along with this law the government allows positive discrimination of the depressed classes of India.

In general the urban people in India are less strict about the caste system than the rural. In cities one can see different caste people mingling with each other, while in some rural areas there is still discrimination based on castes and sometimes also on untouchability. Sometimes in villages or in the cities there are violent clashes which, are connected to caste tensions. Sometimes the high castes strike the lower castes who dare to uplift their status. Sometimes the lower caste get back on the higher castes.

In some rural areas and small towns, the caste system is still very rigid. Caste is also a factor in the politics of India. The Government of India has officially documented castes and subcastes, primarily to determine those deserving reservation (positive discrimination in education and jobs) through the census. The Indian reservation system, though limited in scope, relies entirely on quotas. The Government lists consist of Scheduled Castes, Scheduled Tribes and Other Backward Classes:

SCHEDULED CASTES (SC)

Scheduled castes generally consist of former "untouchables" (the term "Dalit" is now preferred). A Dalit — formerly known as untouchable or *achuta* — is a person outside of the four Varnas and considered below of all and polluting. Dalits include people as leather-workers, scavengers, tanners, flayers, cobblers, agricultural labourers, municipal cleaners, gymnasts, drum beaters, folk musicians and street handicraft persons. Like upper castes, Dalit are also divided into various sub-castes or jatis.

The present population is 16% of the total population of India (around 160 million). For example, the Delhi state has 49 castes listed as SC. Until the late 1980s they were called Harijan, meaning children of God. This title was given to them by Mahatma Gandhi who wanted the society to accept untouchables within them. According to the 2001 Census, the Scheduled Castes population in India is 166,635,700 persons, constituting

16.2 per cent of the country's total population. Being rural people, four-fifth (79.8 per cent) of them live in rural areas and rest one-fifth (20.2 per cent) live in urban areas. The sex ratio of 936 females per thousand males is slightly higher than national average of 933 sex ratios.

The highest percentage of Scheduled Castes population to the total Scheduled Castes population of the country live in Uttar Pradesh (21.1 per cent) followed by West Bengal (11.1 per cent) and Bihar (7.8 per cent), Andhra Pradesh (7.4 percent) and Tamil Nadu (7.1 percent). In fact, more than 57 per cent of total Scheduled Castes population inhabit in these five States. Proportionately, the largest proportion of population of the Scheduled Castes to total population of the State is in Punjab (28.9 per cent), followed by Himachal Pradesh (24.7 per cent) and West Bengal (23 per cent). In Andhra Pradesh, Karnataka and Puducherry proportion of SCs population is exactly equal to the National average of 16.2 per cent. The smallest concentration of the Scheduled Castes population is in the North-Eastern tribal States such as Mizoram (with negligible or only 272 persons) followed by Meghalaya (0.5 per cent) and Arunachal Pradesh (0.6 per cent).

As per the 2001 Census, there are 22 districts where the Scheduled Castes population is 30 per cent or more. In majority of the districts (i.e., 273 districts) the concentration of SCs population to the total population is between 10 to 20 per cent. In Nagaland, Lakshadweep and Andaman & Nicobar Islands, no Scheduled Caste is notified.

SCHEDULED TRIBES (ST)

Scheduled tribes generally consist of tribal groups. The present population is 7% of the total population of India i.e. around 70 million. This category includes in it those communities who did not accept the caste system and preferred to reside deep in the jungles, forests and mountains of India, away from the main population. The Scheduled Tribes are also called Adivasi, meaning aboriginals.

According to the 2001 Census, the total population of the Scheduled Tribes in India is 84,326,240 persons, constituting 8.2 per cent of the total population of the country. 91.7 per cent of them lives in rural areas, whereas, only 8.3 per cent inhabit in urban areas. The sex ratio of Scheduled Tribes population at 978 females per thousand males is higher than that of the total population of the country as well as that of Scheduled Castes.

Madhya Pradesh accounts for the highest percentage of Scheduled Tribes population to total STs population of the country (14.5 per cent) followed by Maharashtra (10.2 per cent), Orissa (9.7 per cent), Gujarat (8.9 per cent), Rajasthan (8.4 per cent), Jharkhand (8.4 per cent) and Chhattisgarh (7.8 per cent). In fact, 68 per cent of the country's Scheduled Tribes population lives in these seven States only. The proportion of the Scheduled Tribes to the total population of the States/Union territories is highest in Mizoram (94.5%) and Lakshadweep (94.5%) followed by Nagaland (89.1%), Meghalaya (85.9%). Within the major states Chhattisgarh (31.8%) has the highest percentage of Scheduled Tribes population followed by Jharkhand (26.3%) and Orissa (22.1%). These proportions are in the lowest in Uttar Pradesh (0.1%), Bihar (0.9%), Tamil Nadu (1.0%) and Kerala (1.1%).

As per the 2001 Census, there are 75 districts where Scheduled Tribes population is 50 per cent or more as per the 2001 Census. In majority of the districts (i.e., 403 districts), the concentration of Scheduled Tribes population to its total population is less than 20 percent.

OTHER BACKWARD CLASSES (OBC)

Where did these OBCs come from? Well, they were created in 1990s by Vishwanath Pratap Singh, the former Prime Minister, to create a vote bank of his own. He listed all those vote bank classes who were not listed under SC/ST as OBC and created another section of caste based vote bank, and the Congress is determined to continue this to keep itself in power

Why were they created in 1990s almost 45 years after the independence. In fact after so many years of Independence, the rulers of this country should have created social equality so that even existing caste based reservations for SC/ST should have been abolished.

There could be only two reasons for the creation of OBC in 1990s.

1. The great people who created our constitution in 1950 failed to identify other backwards sections of the society.
2. After ruling the country for 45 years since independence, Congress had ruined and looted the country so much and created so much more backwardness in the country that in 1990s it became necessary to create another section of backward classes in the name of OBC.

Here the reason number one is appropriate because experts from all sections of the society worked on the constitution keeping in view the then social setup and the future of this country. Great experts like Ambedkar would not have missed the needs of any section of the society. Even otherwise it would not have gone unidentified for 45 long years.

So the only reason for creating OBC is reason number two, the Congress which ruled India for 45 years created more backwardness in India... thats the reason why even today more and more castes are being categorized as backward in this country. While the original list of OBC was created it had about 200 castes in it, today its more than 2000.

The Mandal Commission covered more than 3000 castes under OBC Category and stated that OBCs form around 52% of the Indian population. However, the National Sample Survey puts the figure at 32%. There is substantial debate over the exact number of OBCs in India. It is generally estimated to be sizable, but many believe that it is lower than the figures quoted by either the Mandal Commission or the National Sample Survey.

INDIAN ANTI-RESERVATION PROTESTS

The caste-based reservations in India have led to widespread protests, with many complaining of reverse discrimination against the forward castes (the castes that do not qualify for the reservation). The 2006 Indian anti-reservation protests are one major example. Many view negative treatment (or hatred) of forward castes as socially divisive and just as wrong. Blaming reservations for the dilution of efficiency and merit has no force. In fact, it is entirely selfish not to share the fruits of development and state resources with the deprived. The grounds of opposition of the protesting students are merit and economic criterion. So far, more than 80 per cent of seats in medical, engineering and management courses are available on merit, then why have these students not distinguished themselves in a single 'invention', 'research' or 'technology'. There is no reservation in sports, yet the country of a population of one hundred crore has not secured a single gold medal in Olympics!

It is noteworthy that doctors employed in rural areas hardly serve there and prefer to stay in cities. Is not it degrading the profession? Nursing homes charge high fee and do not spare even the poor. As for engineering students, they first use IITs, where the Government of India spends an average of two lakhs rupees per student per year, then they condemn the facilities available in India and take up jobs in the Silicon Valley for earning in dollars. The argument of merit in this case, then, is only a pretext.

The doctors revealed their mindset when they protested with brooms in their hands, as if carrying brooms is a Dalit's job. Thus, they showed no respect for physical labour. The lack of dignity of labour has failed India in every field. We cite the examples of Europe and the USA for work culture, discipline, technology, financing management, etc. but avoid social obligations borne by industries and educational institutions in those societies. In fact, affirmative action is needed more in India than in the USA, because caste is worse than apartheid. There are 75 chief executive officers from among the people of colour in the USA. On the contrary, there is no Dalit CEO in India.

The scene in educational institutes there also has some encouraging examples. Harvard University is considered to be the Mecca of learning. It has the affirmative action in medicine faculty in favour of the people of colour, women and the people of Asian ethnicities up to 50 per cent, yet it enjoys the highest standards of knowledge sharing and has given the maximum number of Nobel laureates to the world. The white population is satisfied with the remaining seats there. This is the sprit needed in India as well, which unfortunately is missing.

Another relevant example from Michigan University will reveal the largesse of the white population of the USA. In June 2004 a student of colour secured admission in its law college with less marks and was challenged by the affected white student in a court of law. Almost all universities and the industry argued in favour of the student of colour in the Supreme Court and finally his admission was justified.

Closer home, in 1902 Shahuji Maharaj introduced reservation in the Kolhapur state. The state of Mysore did the same. Still the standard of education and administration is better in South India than North India. Thus, it proves that sharing resources with the deprived does not hamper the quality and efficiency in a system.

It is being talked that reservation will stifle the growth of India. In fact, there is a latent and unconstitutional reservation in the spheres of knowledge, status, spirituality and wealth, and this is still far more powerful than the constitutional one, because human beings are governed more by social traditions and customs than by the state law. There is no doubt that Dalits and the backwards are not fit for entrepreneurship compared to Baniyas, because they were trained and groomed in this role for centuries. If Dalits and the OBCs are not given opportunities they will remain behind in future as well.

If the opponents of reservation policy are really serious about their arguments they should have opposed the admission in medical and engineering colleges on the basis of capitation fee. There is murmuring that if foreigners were given these seats the protesting students of today might have boasted that even foreigners were looking towards India.

Every society which has progressed is known for adjustment in social policy and sharing its wealth and respect with various social groups. The objective of reservation policy is not mainly to eliminate poverty but to bring the warring social groups closer to each other. Therefore, the visionary framers of the constitution of India based the policy of reservation on educational and social backwardness.

Wherever caste contradiction is sharper Dalits and the most backward castes have taken up guns and joined the bogey of Maoists, which leads to bad law and order situation. The merit mongers should realise that in these circumstances neither the quality educational institutions can exist nor investment can come to India. Who will be the final loser in such a case? : definitely the merit mongers. In Delhi the total seats in all five medical colleges add up to 360 and if 27 per cent of it is bagged by the OBCs it is not going to disturb the scenario of unemployment among the upper castes in a city whose total population is more than one crore.

Admittedly, the institutes like IITs and IIMs have produced good engineers and business managers who are capable of taking up good jobs overseas and in private companies. The money earned by them has hardly to do with the growth of economy: it only helps their kith and kin. The private sector is better than them, because it contributes more to the growth of economy without using much government resources.

In fact, it is not merit and efficiency which is at peril but the interest of elite among the upper castes. Actually, the elite doctors and engineers are not fighting for their society but for themselves. Their agitation may lead to a chain reaction on the other side and finally different warring groups may create a situation where the government jobs and seats in educational institutions are proportioned according to the population of each caste.

At present, even after reservation the upper castes will enjoy 50 per cent of the total seats, which is enough for them to prove merit and share the fruits of state resources. Thus, they should call off their agitation and let others also come up the social ladder. If they do not do so they will harm themselves in future.

CASTE SYSTEM AMONG NON-HINDUS

Curiously, non-Hindu populations in India sometimes organized themselves into castes as well. After the introduction of Islam on the subcontinent, for example, Muslims were divided into classes such as the Sayed, Sheikh, Mughal, Pathan, and Qureshi. These castes are drawn from several sources—the Mughal and Pathan are ethnic groups, roughly speaking, while the Qureshi name comes from the Prophet Muhammad's clan in Mecca. Small numbers of Indians were Christian from C. 50 CE onward, but Christianity expanded after Portuguese arrived in the 16th century. Many Christian Indians still observed caste distinctions, however.

Caste system among non-Hindus.

Religiously anyone who does not belong to the four Varnas is an outcast and untouchable. It means, all foreigners and non-Hindus are all supposed to be untouchables. But in reality neither all foreigners nor non-Hindus were treated as untouchables. Foreigners and non-Hindus were treated differently in different parts of India. Some of the foreigners adopted Hinduism and integrated in the upper level of the Hindu hierarchy.

The Rajputs of Rajasthan belong to the Kshatria Varna (warrior castes). The Rajputs, more than any other Indian Jat, represent the warrior castes of India. Almost any Indian community which claims to be a warrior community, claims a Rajput ancestry. But it is believed that many foreign invaders of ancient India, like Scythians; Huns; Greeks and others, who adopted Hinduism, integrated in the Rajput community and acquired a Kshatria status.

The Konkanash Brahmans of west India are also believed to have non-Indian descent. According to a Hindu legend, an incarnation of Lord Vishnu, Parsuram, found on the Konkan beach some dead bodies which were washed to the shore. In order to cremate them Parsuram gathered them on a pyre. These dead bodies woke up on pyre, probably because they were not dead in the first place but were only unconscious. Parsuram converted these people to Hinduism and made them Brahmans. There are other theories about the origins of these Kokanasth Brahmans. Many of these Brahmans have gray-green eyes. Some claim them to be Vikings or of other European origin. In the Konkan coast there is Jewish community called Bene Israel. Some claim that these Jews are from the 'Lost Tribes'. These Jews who arrived in India after their ship-wrecked near the Konkan coast claim that they and the Kokanastha Brahmans are descendants of the survivals from the same ship. And in their version, it was not an incarnation of Lord Vishnu who converted the Kokanastha Brahmans but a local Brahman. Anyway these Jews do not have gray-green eyes like the Kokanastha Brahmans.

Different religion followers got different status in different parts of India. The Jews of west India (called Bene Israel) had a different status from Jews of south India (Cochini Jews). The Bene Israels professed oil pressing and they had a status equal to a Hindu Jat called Somvar Teli, which also professed oil pressing and were part of Sudra Varna. Some orthodox Hindus treated anyone who was a non-Hindu or doing any type as polluting job as untouchable and therefore treated the Jews as untouchables. But even though the Jews in west India had low status there were among them some who were landlords, businessmen and high rank officers in local armies.

Different religion followers got different status in different parts of India.

Comparing to the Bene Israels, the Jews in south India had higher status. The Jews in Kerala were the business community of Kerala. They even ruled a small kingdom. They had aristocratic rights, such as use of elephants and sedans. They even had servants whose job was to announce their coming to the streets so that the low castes could move away from their way.

The relations between the Jewish communities of India are sometimes explained as affected by the Indian caste system but these relations can also be explained according to Jewish religious laws. There were three main Jewish communities in India. The Baghdadis, the Bene Israels and Cochinis. The Baghdadi Jews were much strict about religious laws than the Bene Israel Jews. The Baghdadis did not mingle with Bene Israel Jews. The Baghdadis did not allow marriages between their children and the children of Bene Israel. They did not eat food prepared by Bene Israel and they refused to count the Bene Israel as part of the Minyan (the ten necessary to start a Jewish prayer). Many explain these relations as an influence of the Indian caste system on the Jewish communities. According to this explanation, the Baghdadi Jews referred to themselves as higher caste than the Bene Israel Jews and therefore did not mingle with them. But these relations between the Jewish communities can also be explained according to the Jewish Halacha laws. The Baghdadi Jews who were much strict about Jewish laws and diet did not mingle with the Bene Israels because the Bene Israels were secular Jews and they perceived in Bene Israel Jews as impure Jews.

The Muslims who arrived in India were strong and powerful to be treated as untouchables. Not only were they strong in the military sense, they also tried to enforce their religion on the Indians. The Indians who converted to Islam in most of the cases remained in the same social status as they had before their conversion to Islam. Hindus from the higher Varnas remained at the higher levels of Indian society. Hindus from the lower levels of the hierarchy thought that by converting to Islam they would come out from the Hindu hierarchy system, but in most of the cases they remained in the same hierarchy level after they converted. Among the Muslims of India there has developed a two-tier hierarchy. The upper class, called Sharif Jat, includes Muslims who belonged to the higher levels in caste hierarchy and also Muslims who arrived to India from foreign countries. The lower class, called Ajlaf Jat, includes Muslim converts from lower castes. As in the world, the upper classes do not have close social relations with lower classes, the same way the Sharif Jat do not normally have close social relations with Ajlaf Jat.

The different Christian communities of India were treated in different ways in different parts of India. The Syrian Christians of Kerala had a high status. Along with the Jews, they were the business communities of Kerala and they too had aristocratic rights. The Indians who were baptized from the 16th century by Christian missionaries remained mostly in the same status they had before. As in the Muslim community of India, the Christians also have a two-tier social hierarchy. Many untouchables who converted to Christianity are still treated as untouchables, sometimes by other Christians.

The European Christians are also supposed to be untouchables to Hindus. Some Europeans in the 17th and 18th century even claimed that they were treated as untouchables. But later on with British rule over India it were the upper level Hindu castes, specially the Brahmans, who adopted the European democratic philosophy according to which all are equal and they introduced it to other Indians.

Other religions which were established in India—Buddhism, Jainism and Sikhism—also have some marks of caste system, even though they oppose caste system. Sikhism rejects caste system. But different Jats who adopted Sikhism act according to traditional Jat lines. The different Jats normally marry within caste lines. The Jats which were the elite of the Punjab and converted to Sikhism do not give equal respect to Sikhs who belong to the lower levels of Indian hierarchy. The Jains also have separate communities who marry within the community lines. The Buddhist in India have a two-tier hierarchy and just like in the cases of Christians and Muslims it is also related to the status of the community to whom the person belongs. On the other hand, the Mahar community of west India, who were untouchables and converted mostly to Buddhism, prefer, because of different political reasons to recognize themselves as Mahars and not always as Buddhists.

Not all residents of India were part of the caste system. About 7% of India's population are referred to as tribes and not as castes or Jats. These tribes are scattered all around India and they are descendants of communities who were not interested in the Varna hierarchy. They preferred to live away from the main societies deep in the jungles, forests and mountains of India. They survived mostly on fishing, hunting or simple agriculture, and also from stealing, robbing and plundering. These tribes had different religious beliefs and different gods. Some of them had simple beliefs, but others use to sacrifice human beings in their ceremonies. One such tribe, called Gond, had a strong kingdom in central India. Most of the tribes adopted Hinduism, others adopted Islam or Christianity. Some tribes in East India claim to Jewish origin.

CASTE-RELATED VIOLENCE

Independent India has witnessed considerable amount of violence and hate crimes motivated by caste. Caste related violence is not restricted merely to 'improper' relations but encompasses all manner of brutal discrimination.

Caste-related violence.

In 1999, a handicapped Dalit woman was paraded naked through the streets of her village by members of the local *khap panchayat*. In January 2006, Dalit labourer Bant Singh, seeking justice against the people who gang raped his daughter, was beaten so severely that he had to have both arms and one leg amputated. In 2007 a Dalit woman, 55 years of age was stripped and tied to a tree, displayed and ashamed publicly because her nephew had eloped with a girl from the same 'gotra' (hereditary group/ community)

Ranvir Sena, a caste-supremacist fringe paramilitary group based in Bihar, has committed violent acts against Dalits and other members of the scheduled caste community.

Phoolan Devi, who belonged to Mallah lower-caste, was mistreated and raped by upper-caste Thakurs at a young age. She then became a bandit and carried out violent robberies against upper-caste people. In 1981, her gang massacred twenty-two Thakurs, most of whom were not involved in her kidnapping or rape. Throughout the mid to late 1900s, Phoolan Devi, of the lower 'mallah' (boatmen) caste, affectionately known as 'the Bandit Queen' committed violent robberies on members of the upper castes in retaliation to being gang raped and beaten repeatedly as a young girl by upper caste men.

Phoolan Devi: The Bandit Queen.

Her Robin Hood-like escapades gained her fame and respect and she became a politician in the 1980s before being assassinated in 2001 by Sher Ringh Rana who claimed to be avenging the deaths of Kshyiartas who had been massacred by her gang in 1981.

Over the years, various incidents of violence against Dalits, such as Kherlanji Massacre have been reported from many parts of India. At the same time, many violent protests by Dalits, such as the 2006 Dalit protests in Maharashtra, have been reported as well.

CASTE POLITICS

In India today, Politics had ceased to be a Public Service, and Politicians are no more Public Servants or Peoples' Representatives. Politics today, has become an Exclusive Business, and a full-time Employment for many without any business. Going with the character of Business and Employment in India, Politics had become an exclusive caste, of the modern day. Once a Politician, always a Politician! And true to the characteristic of Castes in India, the sons, daughters, sons-in law, daughters-in-law and other-in-laws, dominate Politics in India. These had effectively stopped evolution of real Democracy in the Country, and frustrate the Republican forms of Govt.

Caste Politics.

As everyone knows, India is a Nation of Castes. And it always remains in the firm grip of the brahmins. So, the Country remained under the influence of the brahmin-based castes, brahmanic values, and brahmanism. That was always true even during the Rule of not only the Moghuls and British or other Continental People, but also earlier during the times of Huns, Kushans etc. As a result of these, the mainstream brahmin-baniya Parties, and kshatriya-kayasth combinations, were always at the helm of affairs. And even otherwise, the Govt. is always run by the bureaucracy, all contentious issues are arbitrated and decided by the Judiciary, and widespread opinions are made by the Media. All of these are dominated by the brahmins and their sister dominant castes. Hence, all these decades, the Govts. in India meant only brahmanic rule. Therefore, all the decisions taken in whatever forms and fora those may be, were brahmanic. They were taken, solely to protect, safeguard, and to further the brahmanic interests, brahmin welfare, brahmanic growth, and to continue the brahminic rule.

In the absence of Democracy in content, the massive numbers of SC & ST Dalits, Backwards and Minorities, could naturally never understand their intrinsic capacities, the strengths of their massive numbers, and the power of cohesive and collective campaigns. That is the main reason, for the frittering away of opportunities, and wastage of emerging opportunities. The emergence of small splinter Dalit Parties that can not hold together, is therefore natural. That is why we see today, various shades of Republican Parties, Dalit Panthers of Maharashtra, BSP, Pudhiya Tamizhagam (New Tamil Nadu) and Vidudhalai Siruthaigal (Liberation Cheetahs) of Tamil Nadu, Ambedkar Samaj Party, Lok Jan Shakthi, Justice Party and so on. While some of them are of historical repute, had also garnered some International Recognition, National Followings, Regional Parties with Representations in the Assemblies, many others are only making some ripples in the street, some noise on the stage here and there. Some of them are of doubtful backgrounds, and their motives are suspect.

The Mandal Commission was established in 1979 to "identify the socially or educationally backward," and to consider the question of seat reservations and quotas for people to redress caste discrimination. In 1980, the commission's report affirmed the affirmative action practice under Indian law whereby members of lower castes were given exclusive access to a certain portion of government jobs and slots in public universities. When V.P. Singh Government tried to implement the recommendations of Mandal Commission in 1989, massive protests were held in the country. Many alleged that the politicians were trying to cash in on caste-based reservations for purely pragmatic electoral purposes.

In 1990s, many parties Bahujan Samaj Party (BSP), the Samajwadi Party and the Janata Dal started claiming that they are representing the backward castes. Many such parties, relying primarily on Backward Classes' support, often in alliance with Dalits and Muslims, rose to power in Indian states. At the same time, many Dalit leaders and intellectuals started realizing that the main Dalit oppressors were so-called Other Backward Classes, and formed their own parties, such as the Indian Justice Party. The Congress (I) in Maharashtra long relied on OBCs' backing for its political success. Bharatiya Janata Party has also showcased its Dalit and OBC leaders to prove that it is not an upper-caste party. Bangaru Laxman, the former BJP president (2001-2002) was a former Dalit. Sanyasin Uma Bharati, former CM of Madhya Pradesh, who belongs to OBC caste, was a former BJP leader. In 2006 Arjun Singh cabinet minister for MHRD of the UPA Government was accused of playing caste politics when he introduced reservations for OBCs in educational institutions all around.

The Dalits in India still have no land, no wealth, no riches, no properties, and in fact most of the times, no houses. They continue to wallow in misery and penury even today in the twenty-first century.

Hence, Dalits as a Community and Individuals have nothing to loose, and can become entrepreneurs in any field they want to and can enter. Without much of the risks, they can try their hands and test their capacity and resilience to survive and succeed, in the chosen fields. Hence wherever Indians had moved out of their rural homes and urban slums, and whatever they may be, those are their gains – however small or a little that may be.

CLASS SYSTEM

The class system is universal phenomenon denoting a category or group of persons having a definite status in society which permanently determines their relation to other groups. The *social classes* are de facto groups (not legally or religiously defined and sanctioned) they are relatively open not closed. Their basis is indisputably economic but they are more than economic groups. They are characteristic groups of the industrial societies which have developed since 17th century. The relative importance and definition of membership in a particular class differs greatly over time and between societies, particularly in societies that have a legal differentiation of groups of people by birth or occupation. In the well-known example of socioeconomic class, many scholars view societies as stratifying into a hierarchical system based on occupation, economic status, wealth, or income.

According to *Ogburn* and *Nimkoff* a *social class* is the aggregate of persons having essentially the same social status in a given society. *Marx* defined class in terms of the extent to which an individual or social group has control over the means of production.

CRITERION OF CLASS—MARXIAN ANALYSIS

In Marxist terms a class is a group of people defined by their relationship to the means of production. Classes are seen to have their origin in the division of the social product into a necessary product and a surplus product. Marxists explain history in terms of a war of classes between those who control production and those who actually produce the goods or services in society (and also developments in technology and the like). In the Marxist view of capitalism this is a conflict between capitalists (bourgeoisie) and wage workers (proletariat). Class antagonism is rooted in the situation that control over social production necessarily entails control over the class which produces goods – in capitalism this is the exploitation of workers by the bourgeoisie. *Marx* saw class categories as defined by continuing historical processes. Classes, in Marxism, are not static entities, but are regenerated daily through the productive process. Marxism views classes as human social relationships which change over time, with historical commonality created through shared productive processes. A 17th century farm labourer who worked for day wages shares a similar relationship to production as an average office worker of the 21st century. In this example it is the shared structure of wage labour that makes both of these individuals "working class."

Maclver and *Page* defines social class as any portion of the community marked off from the rest by social status.

Max Weber suggest that social classes are aggregates of individuals who have the same opportunities of acquiring goods, the same exhibited standard of living. He formulated a three component theory of stratification with social, status and party classes (or politics) as conceptually distinct elements.

- *Social class* is based on economic relationship to the market (owner, renter, employee, etc.)
- *Status class* has to do with non-economic qualities such as education, honour and prestige.
- *Party class* refers to factors having to do with affiliations in the political domain.

According to *Weber* a more complex division of labour made the class more heterogeneous. In contrast to simple income—property hierarchies, and to structural class schemes like Weber's or Marx's, there are theories of class based on other distinctions, such as culture or educational attainment. At times, social class can be related to elitism and those in the higher class are usually known as the "social elite". For example, Bourdieu seems to have a notion of high and low classes comparable to that of Marxism, insofar as their conditions are defined by different habitus, which is in turn defined by different objectively classifiable conditions of existence. In fact, one of the principal distinctions Bourdieu makes is a distinction between bourgeoisie taste and the working class taste. Social class is a segment of society with all the members of all ages and both the sexes who share the same general status. Maclver says whenever social intercourse is limited by the consideration of social status by distinctions between higher and lower there exists a social class.

DISTINCTION BETWEEN CASTE SYSTEM AND CLASS SYSTEM

Caste system and class system are still prevalent in some countries. Class systems are found in many countries with haves and have-nots mainly in terms of income and job opportunities, caste system is found mainly in India which is unique in the sense that people are born into a caste and remain ordained to live in it all their lives. With India gaining independence and job opportunities increasing for those belonging to lower castes through a system of reservation, the caste system has somewhat diluted. But even today, caste system has a stronghold and the rules of this system apply on all the members of the caste.

One unique feature of caste system, as prevalent in India, is that one has a pre-destined life. If you belong to a scheduled caste, and happen to live in a village instead of a metro, you are almost untouchable and are condemned to move only in your own caste as you will not be allowed to have any truck with people belonging to higher castes. You cannot marry with a person of higher caste, and you die belonging to the caste you were born into.

On the other hand, class system is also in place in many parts in India where those who have either land or property, or money have been asserting their supremacy over those who are poor and deprived of such assets. However, this system is a bit more humane than the rigid caste system as a person can hope to move up the ladder of hierarchy by improving his earnings. Once he is perceived as rich by others, he becomes acceptable to those belonging to higher classes. Thus in a class system, it is possible to improve once social status either through education, or by being able to amass wealth.

In fact this is what is happening in many places in India. As described above, because of the policy of reservation, many lower caste persons got good jobs in government sectors as well as private sectors and are today living a comfortable life. They are now not only acceptable to upper castes (some are even bosses to lots of people belonging to higher castes), they have easily slipped into a higher class also.

In conclusion, it would be fair to say that though caste system is still firmly rooted in India, it is getting diluted by the day and a more humane class system is taking roots in its place which provides more chances to a person to move up in the society depending upon his skills and income earning abilities.

CHARACTERISTICS OF SOCIAL CLASS

A social class is essentially a status group. Class is related to status. Different statuses arise in a society as people do different things, engage in different activities and pursue different vocations. Status in the case of class system is achieved and not ascribed. Birth is not the criterion of status. Achievements of an individual mostly decide his status. Class is almost universal phenomenon. It occurs in all the modern complex societies of the world. Each social class has its own status in the society. Status is associated with prestige. The relative position of the class in the social set up arises from the degree of prestige attached to the status. A social class is relatively a stable group. A social class is distinguished from other classes by its customary modes of behaviour.

This is often referred to as the life-styles of a particular class. It includes mode of dress, kind of living the means of recreation and cultural products one is able to enjoy, the relationship between parent and children. Life-styles reflect the specialty in preferences, tastes and values of a class. Social classes are open-groups. They represent an open social system. An open class system is one in which vertical social mobility is possible. The basis of social classes is mostly economic but they are not mere economic groups or divisions. Subjective criteria such as class—consciousness, class solidarity and class identification on the one hand and the objective criteria such as wealth, property, income, education and occupation on the other hand are equally important in the class system. Class system is associated with class consciousness. It is a sentiment that characterizes the relations of men towards the members of their own and other classes. It consists in the realization of a similarity of attitude and behavior with members of other classes.

Sociologists have given three-fold classification of classes which consists of—upper class, middle class and lower class. *Sorokin* has spoken of three major types of class stratification—they are economic, political and occupational classes. Lloyd Warner shows how class distinctions contribute to social stability. Veblen analyzed the consumption pattern of the rich class by the concept of conspicuous consumption. Warner has classified classes into six types—upper-upper class, upper-middle class, upper-lower class, lower-upper class, the lower middle class and lower class. Anthony Giddens's three class model is the upper, middle and lower (working) class.

FAMILY

Introduction. Meaning of Family: Definition of Family. Functions of the Family: *Economic Functions of a Family.* ***Family History:*** *The Single Family History, Conducting Family History Research, Importance of Family History, Family History Society, Family Tree, Historical Documents.* ***Family Structure and Children's Educational Outcomes:*** *Religious Functions.* ***Variations in Family Structure. Family Structure's Impact on Children's Development. Types and Forms of the Family:*** *On the Basis of Marriage, On the Basis of the Nature of Residence, On the Basis of Ancestry or Descent Family, Nuclear or the Single Unit Family, Disadvantages of Nuclear Family, Myths Behind Single Parent Family, Joint Family or Kutumba or Kula.* ***Successful Joint Family System. Joint Family in India. Joint Family System vs Nuclear Family System:*** *On the Basis of the Nature of Relations Among the Family Members.* ***The Modern Nuclear Family. Domestic violence. Change in Family Pattern. Changing Indian Family and the Patterns in Domestic Violence. Step Families:*** *Meaning, Features of Step Families, Creation of Step Families, Effects of Split Between Partners, Rewards of Step Families, Complexity and Challenge in Step Families, Key Tasks, Legal Status of Step Families, Stepparent Adoption.* ***Gay and Lesbian Marriages. Domestic Violence in Gay and Lesbian Relationships. Divorce. Legal Separation. The Difference Between Legal Separation and Divorce.***

INTRODUCTION

The family unit itself has evolved over many years. In this modern era, it has taken on different meanings to people all over the world. That being said, we tend to take our families for granted, thinking that we'll all be together and have our family around forever. Family should be a place of trust, comfort, and protection. If you think about those little arguments that we have with our sister, brother or another family member, you realize that on a deeper level, none of those things really matter. As a matter of fact, all of our lives are connected in some way, shape, or form.

Family members should depend on each other and occasionally, lean on each other help just like the sister and brother. There are many people out there that do not have any family support, and for whatever reason, these people are by themselves without someone in their lives that they can depend on, just one person. Life can be very difficult at times and we all need to be a part of a family. No matter if it's your biological family or the person that had a hand in raising you over the years.

Parents are the core of the family unit. They are the backbone or the ones we turn to when we need help. Notice the word "parents" is plural. Too many households these days only have one parent at home. Sometimes we must deal with people in our families that we do not get along with or that person we tried to help in some way turns out to be ungrateful or took advantage of the help they were given. There's no question that being part of a family causes some stressful moments. Any relationship that we're involved in will present some ups and downs through the course of time. The key is to come together and support our families. Everyone benefits from the family unit as we can become better human beings.

MEANING OF FAMILY

Family is a word that has a true meaning behind it; there is more than just a definition. The word family means a group of relatives that are bonded together as one. Family is used as a noun; it is more than one person, but it is used as a singular noun. A family does not have to be related either; it can be a group of friends that consider themselves as relatives because of how close they are with each other.

A family can consist of a father, mother, and children. They all live in the same house until they are old enough to leave. Family atmosphere's are rare these days. The kids are into computers, games and into girls and almost the same thing can be said for the girls of the family, but hopefully one day a week, everyone puts everything aside and sits down to a family meal.

DEFINITION OF FAMILY

"A group of organisms, either animal or vegetable, related by certain points of resemblance in structure or development, more comprehensive than a genus, because it is usually based on fewer or less pronounced points of likeness. In zoology a family is less comprehensive than an order; in botany it is often considered the same thing as an order."

The Kapoor Family is a family with a long legend in India's Bollywood cinema.

"The collective body of persons who live in one house, and under one head or manager; a household, including parents, children, servants and as the case may be, lodgers or boarders."

A family of five on a motorbike (India).

"The group comprising a husband and wife and their dependent children, constituting a fundamental unit in the organization of society."

FUNCTIONS OF THE FAMILY

The family is the social unit for bringing the children into the world. All societies—primitive, developing and industrialization's have some from of marriage among men and women. Marriage is the approved setting for bearing children. Children born to the couple are expected to be raised within that family setting. The very basic functions that family perform as an institution are:

(a) Socialization,

(b) Reproductive and sexual functions,

(c) Economic functions,

(d) Identity and social status, and

(e) Emotional security.

One of the primary functions of the family is to produce and reproduce persons, biologically and socially. Thus, one's experience of one's family shifts over time.

From the perspective of children, the family is a family of orientation: the family serves to locate children socially and plays a major role in their enculturation and socialization.

From the point of view of the parent(s), the family is a family of procreation the goal of which is to produce and enculturate and socialize children.

However, producing children is not the only function of the family; in societies with a sexual division of labour, marriage, and the resulting relationship between two people, is necessary for the formation of an economically productive household.

1. To ensure that new babies actually survive to become adult members of that society

Babies are the most immature animals born. Many animals can help themselves survive within hours or weeks of birth; they can run or hide. Even helpless kittens can leave home at six weeks old.

Human children are not socially mature till many years later because the rules for society are so complicated. This is shown by the fact that people are still being trained to do certain jobs until they are in their twenties.

2. To regulate sexual activity

It is usually expected that sexual relations between men and women take place inside some kind of marriage relationship or pairing and that they are regulated by some social rules. Families exist to control sexual behaviour so that the new offspring are as healthy as is possible.

3. To ensure that children are satisfactorily socialised into the norms and values of society

Children are born egocentric. They actually believe themselves to be the centre of everything that takes place around them and have to be taught the rules of their society and their place within it. The process of learning the rules about how to behave is called socialisation and it lasts for all of our lives.

In our society, the rules are so complicated that people are still considered children who have to be protected till they are eighteen years of age. There are people who are specially trained and fairly well-paid to do this job of training children, but the most important trainers are the family members.

4. To provide economic support for other family members

This can take many forms in all societies. In hunting societies, women forage for most of the food and men hunt to provide extra protein foods. In farming societies, all the family members work to help produce food.

5. To satisfy our emotional needs for love and security

People need to feel loved and wanted by other people, particularly when they are very young. They can survive without, but for most people, their family is their strongest emotional bond.

Children who are abused and loathed by their parents, often still love them even if their feelings are horribly confused by the treatment that they have received. It had been found by some psychologists who study human development that children find it difficult to learn how to love other people if they have never been taught how to love by someone else who has loved them.

ECONOMIC FUNCTIONS OF A FAMILY

The family's relationship to the use of development assistance is modelled in different ways for different purposes. Until now, the analysis of intra-household factors has been constrained by the expense of collecting detailed and highly accurate information.

1. Household unified preference function for aggregate policy

The unified preference function, according to which household members e.g., parents are assumed to allocate resources as if they have common preferences, remains useful for determining the effects of price changes on demand for basic commodities, i.e., foods or nutrients. This information is essential to permit governments to use such means as tariffs, support prices, or export prices to modify the price structure in ways that protect poor families. For macro or regional policy purposes, a price subsidy to increase food consumption of a population or a segment of the population can be implemented with the assumption that households will re-allocate this food to their members. This is the least expensive approach because household-level income and consumption data are sufficient.

2. Health reduced-form relation function

The household unified preference function, however, offers little information regarding to what extent changes in food prices affect individual family members; for this purpose, individual food intake or other commodity consumption is needed. Collecting individual food intake data is difficult and costly.

3. Household health production function

While the reduced-form relation permits policy makers to estimate the effects of aggregate policy on individuals, it does not reveal how programme interventions affect household allocations of inputs to family members. Decisions regarding which services are most productive with respect to health, or how food supplementation programmes can improve child nutrition, may require information obtained by using a framework that investigates household allocation among members.

FAMILY HISTORY

Family history is the systematic narrative and research of past events relating to a specific family, or specific families. While genealogy is the convenient label for the field, family history is the over-arching term, since genealogy in the strict sense is only concerned with tracing unified lineages. Other sectors of family history, such as one-name studies, may pay only rudimentary attention to lineages, or may emphasize biography rather than vital data.

Family history needs little justification in communitarian societies, where one's identity is defined as much by one's kin network as by individual achievement, and the question "Who are you?" would be answered by a description of father, mother, and tribe.

Family history plays a part in the practice of some religious belief systems. For example, The Church of Jesus Christ of Latter-day Saints have a doctrine of Baptism for the dead, which necessitates that members of that faith engage in family history research.

Until the late 19th century, family histories were almost exclusively of interest to persons who had obtained their wealth or rank by inheritance. Other people, who had inherited nothing, might, in extreme cases, suppress their family history as a matter of shame.

In societies such as the United States or Australia, there was by the 20th century growing pride in the pioneers and nation-builders. Establishing descent from these was a concern in groups such as the Daughters of the American Revolution, and helped differentiate those descendants from later immigrants with lower status.

In Nazi Germany, family histories were compiled to affirm individuals' affiliation with the "master race" and to adhere to legal requirements for marriage. In Germany today, family history is still often perceived as a threat to privacy rather than as a source of self-esteem. Most 20th-century sources remain unavailable to the public on privacy grounds. Funding of support for family history at archives is limited. German family historians thus tend to emphasize instead how family history can contribute to learning and science.

Modern family history explores new sources of status, such as celebrating the resilience of families that survived generations of poverty or slavery, or the success of families in integrating across racial or national boundaries. Some family histories even emphasize links to celebrity criminals, such as the bushranger Ned Kelly in Australia.

The growing interest in family history in the media coupled with easier access to online records has allowed people with a curiosity to start to investigate their ancestry. This curiosity can be particularly strong due to lost family histories, for example, through adoption or bereavement.

THE SINGLE FAMILY HISTORY

In the narrower sense of the term, a family history is a biography of a single family over several generations, based on a tested genealogy and fleshed out with the fuller story of the family's place in society, the dramas of its achievements or failures and its acquisition or loss of wealth and rank.

Such a study mainly draws on oral history for the recent period and archival records for the period beyond living memory. Where an individual's own story is unknown, much can be inferred from other literature. For example, a single soldier's experiences can be inferred from the history of his military unit, or a migrant's journey can be described from the shipboard diary of a fellow traveler.

CONDUCTING FAMILY HISTORY RESEARCH

Family history can either be in the form of a printed document, electronic document or sound or video recording that preserves this history for future generations. The readers will expect it to describe where the family originated from, name the members of the family and state who they married. Family Histories are often created as a memorial for the deceased and are written to be passed down to future generations. Some records that are used to create family histories are:

- Apprenticeship records
- Baptism or christening records
- Birth certificates
- Cemetery records and tombstones
- Census records
- Coroner's reports
- Death records
- Diaries, personal letters, family Bibles, scrapbooks and ephemera
- Directories — trade directories, street directories, telephone directories
- Earlier family histories
- Marriage records
- Military records
- Newspapers — both news items and advertisements
- Property records and contemporary maps
- Public records — Social Security records (in the U.S.), Poor Law records (in the UK), registers of electors
- Tax records
- Wills and probate records
- Poll Books and Registers of Electors.

Today many people are using these records to recover their family history. But most of these records include only technical details of a person's life, such as their birth date, whom they married, the jobs they did, and so forth, but they contain very little about the person themselves such as their likes, dislikes, hobbies, hopes and dreams. These personal details can only be gleaned by more detailed research, and the use of social history. Some family histories are published and become useful historical records in their own right.

Family history websites and indexes are also useful, and for modern researchers they are often the main source of information. Some offer resources (e.g., censuses or civil registration records) that have previously only been available in microform or as hard copies; some are designed for individual researchers to share their information with others; some exist primarily to link people who share the same ancestors, or the same research interests. Some websites offer useful free resources to family historians in addition to helpful hints and tips.

IMPORTANCE OF FAMILY HISTORY

The benefits of family history projects may vary according to the people who pursue the hobby. Some schools engage students in such projects as a means to reinforce lessons regarding immigration and the history of the nation. Other benefits include family medical histories with families with serious medical conditions that are hereditary.

FAMILY HISTORY SOCIETY

A family history society is a society, often charitable or not-for-profit, that allows member genealogists and family historians to profit from shared knowledge. Large societies often own libraries, sponsor research seminars and foreign trips, and publish journals. Some societies concentrate on a specific niche, such as the family history of a particular geographical area, ethnicity, nationality, or religion. Lineage societies are societies that limit their membership to descendants of a particular person or group of people of historical importance.

FAMILY TREE

A family tree, or pedigree chart, is a chart representing family relationships in a conventional tree structure. The more detailed family trees used in medicine, genealogy, and social work are known as genograms.

Genealogical data can be represented in several formats, for example, as a pedigree or ancestor chart. Family trees are often presented with the oldest generations at the top and the newer generations at the bottom. An ancestry chart, which is a tree showing the ancestors of an individual, will more closely resemble a tree in shape, being wider at the top than the bottom. In some ancestry charts, an individual appears on the left and his or her ancestors appear to the right. A descendancy chart, which depicts all the descendants of an individual will be narrowest at the top.

Family trees can have many themes. One might encompass all direct descendants of a single figure, or all known ancestors of a living person. Another might include all members of a particular surname (e.g. male-line descendants). Yet another approach is to construct a tree including all holders of a certain office, such as kings of Germany. This relies on dynastic marriage to hold together the links between dynasties.

HISTORICAL DOCUMENTS

Historical documents are documents that contain important information about a person, place, or event. Most famous historical documents are either laws, accounts of battles (often given by the victors or persons sharing their viewpoint), and the exploits of the powerful. Though these documents are of historical interest, they do not detail the daily lives of ordinary people, or the way society functioned. Anthropologists, historians and archeologists, generally are more interested in documents that describe the day-to-day lives of ordinary people, indicating what they ate, their interaction with other members of their households and social groups, and their states of mind. It is this information that allows them to try and understand and describe the way society was functioning at any particular time in history.

Many documents that are produced today, such as personal letters, pictures, contracts, newspapers, and medical records, would be considered valuable historical documents in the future to such people. However most of these will be lost in the future since they are either printed on ordinary paper which has a limited lifespan, or stored in digital formats that will become obsolete fairly soon.

Some companies and government entities are attempting to increase the number of documents that will survive the passage of time, by taking into account the preservation issues, and either printing documents in a manner that would increase the likelihood of them surviving indefinitely, or placing selected documents in time capsules or other special storage environments.

FAMILY STRUCTURE AND CHILDREN'S EDUCATIONAL OUTCOMES

A comprehensive review of recent academic research shows that family structure—whether a child's parents are married, divorced, single, remarried, or cohabiting—is a significant influence on children's educational performance. Family structure affects preschool readiness. It affects educational achievement at the elementary, secondary, and college levels. Family structure influences these outcomes in part because family structure affects a range of child behaviours that can bear directly on educational success, such as school misbehaviour, drug and alcohol consumption, sexual activity and teen pregnancy, and psychological distress.

RELIGIOUS FUNCTIONS

A religion is a system of beliefs usually involving the worship of supernatural forces or beings. Religious beliefs provide shape and meaning to one's perception of the universe. In other words, they provide a sense of order in what might otherwise be seen as a chaotic existence. Religions also provide understanding and meaning for inexplicable events such as a loved one being killed in an earthquake or some other unpredictable force of nature.

Sociologists of religion study every aspect of religion from what is believed to how persons act while in worship and while living out their stated convictions. They study the changing role of religion both in the public arena such as: political, economic and media and in intimate interpersonal relationships.

Fairs are generally associated with religious functions in temples.

In Hindu Indian wedding and other religious functions.

Auguste Comte, the founder of Sociology, said that religion has believed a significant social phenomenon for sociology. When *Max Weber* accounted that the capitalism had developed in West only, he regarded the religion as foundation of value-systems that determine social organization. Comte's ideas were not being accepted in society. Comte tried to substitute the sociology for the religion.

The performance of *rituals* is an integral part of all religions. Rituals are stylized and usually repetitive acts that take place at a set time and location. They almost always involve the use of symbolic objects, words, and actions.

Most religious rituals are performed in special places and under special conditions, such as in a dedicated temple or at a sacred spot. This is an intentional separation between the secular and the sacred. By being removed from the ordinary world, the sacred acts are enhanced for the believers. The separation makes the rituals more effective. Only allowing initiated people to participate in religious rituals also can have the same effect.

VARIATIONS IN FAMILY STRUCTURE

Some family types bear special mention because of their unique qualities. In the sub-Himalayan region of Uttar Pradesh, *polygyny* is commonly practiced. There, among Hindus, a simple polygynous family is composed of a man, his two wives, and their unmarried children. Various other family types occur there, including the supplemented subpolygynous household—a woman whose husband lives elsewhere (perhaps with his other wife), her children, plus other adult relatives. Polygyny is also practiced in other parts of India by a tiny minority of the population, especially in families in which the first wife has not been able to bear children.

Among the Buddhist people of the mountainous Ladakh District of Jammu and Kashmir, who have cultural ties to Tibet, fraternal *polyandry* is practiced, and a household may include a set of brothers with their common wife or wives. This family type, in which brothers also share land, is almost certainly linked to the extreme scarcity of cultivable land in the Himalayan region, because it discourages fragmentation of holdings.

The peoples of the northeastern hill areas are known for their *matriliny*, tracing descent and inheritance in the female line rather than the male line. One of the largest of these groups, the Khasis—an ethnic or tribal people in the state of Meghalaya—are divided into matrilineal clans; the youngest daughter receives almost all of the inheritance including the house. A Khasi husband goes to live in his wife's house. Khasis, many of whom have become Christian, have the highest literacy rate in India, and Khasi women maintain notable authority in the family and community.

Perhaps the best known of India's unusual family types is the traditional Nayar taravad, or great house. The Nayars are a cluster of castes in Kerala. High-ranking and prosperous, the Nayars maintained matrilineal households in which sisters and brothers and their children were the permanent residents. After an official prepuberty marriage, each woman received a series of visiting husbands in her room in the taravad at night. Her children were all legitimate members of the taravad. Property, matrilineally inherited, was managed by the eldest brother of the senior woman. This system, the focus of much anthropological interest, has been disintegrating in the twentieth century, and in the 1990s probably fewer than 5 percent of the Nayars live in matrilineal taravads. Like the Khasis, Nayar women are known for being well-educated and powerful within the family.

Malabar rite Christians, an ancient community in Kerala, adopted many practices of their powerful Nayar neighbours, including naming their sons for matrilineal forebears. Their kinship system, however, is patrilineal. Kerala Christians have a very high literacy rate, as do most Indian Christian groups.

FAMILY STRUCTURE'S IMPACT ON CHILDREN'S DEVELOPMENT

The case for marriage education is being based upon research that draws the conclusion that children have better outcomes when growing up in a family of two married biological parents in a nonconflicitual relationship. Today about two-thirds of children are living with two married, biological parents. If the child is living with biological parents in a middle class context in which adequate financial resources are available to support their health and development, that child has the best of all worlds to foster development. However, frequently comparisons are made between children growing up in the ideal of the biological two parent family with other forms of families. To accurately draw conclusions concerning the influence that family structure has upon children's development, appropriate comparisons of groups of children with the same family structure need to be made, such as two-biological married parents versus two-biological parents cohabitating, stepfamilies married versus stepfamilies cohabitating. Not only is the family structure of importance, but also the socioeconomic family context. Poor families face stresses that impact their adult relationship decisions and their children's development that middle class families typically do not.

When accurate comparisons are made it appears that biological parentage rather than marital status is more important in determining child well-being. When the focus of the discussion of the impact of children's well-being shifts to the impact that growing up with one's biological parents has upon their overall development, clearer comparisons can be made. Overall, children growing up with biological parents whether married or cohabiting, fare the same in terms of school achievement and behavior problems. Even in families where both biological parents are present children experience poor outcomes in high conflict family environments. High conflict family contexts lower children's emotional well-being and increase behavior problems.

Of equal importance is the impact that the parent's race and education make upon the outcomes of their children's development. Low income black women embrace marriage less frequently than Hispanic and Caucasian women. Poor women move away from marriage because of affordability, respectability, trust and control. Low-income women define a man's marriage acceptability based upon his employment and economic stability, ability to trust his sexual fidelity and level of responsibility with children as precursors to marriage. For many women cohabitation affords them greater control that they believe they will lose through marriage.

The outcomes for children growing up in single parent families are less positive. Children being raised in single parent families appear to be the most affected by their family structure. Frequently, single parents are poor, have less education than cohabiting and married parents, and less likely to be employed. The outcomes for children raised in a single parent household are: that academic achievement declines, emotional and behavioral problems increase. However, caution needs to be taken to not generalize to the total population of single parent families. Most children in single parent families will not experience these negative outcomes. Many unmarried parents are poorly equipped to support themselves and their children. Lacking the financial resources and parenting skills increases the likelihood that children will experience some difficulty in development.

More and more children are living in stepfamilies. The transition that children experience in moving from one family context and structure to another creates stress and may lead to poor outcomes. In spite of better economic circumstances on average, children in stepfamilies are more likely to have negative behavior, health and educational outcomes. These risk factors increase the poorer a child is and with the increase in the number of transitions to new family situations.

The outcomes for children's development are influenced by the family structure in which they grow up. However, one's family structure does not guarantee negative or positive outcomes. The family's stability may be the most significant determinant. The effect of living with two biological parents in a stable cohabitating family versus a married family seems to indicate that there are many factors beyond those of the parental relationship that come into play to produce positive and negative outcomes for children. However, as cohabitating unions continue to increase more effort needs to be expended to determine ways to support positive development of children no matter what their family structure.

TYPES AND FORMS OF THE FAMILY

ON THE BASIS OF MARRIAGE

On the basis of marriage family has been classified into three major types:

1. Polygamous or Ppolygynous Family

Polygyny is a form of marriage in which a man has two or more wives at the same time. It is distinguished from a relationship where a man who has a sexual partner outside marriage, such as a concubine, casual sexual partner, paramour, or other culturally recognized secondary partner. Polygyny is the most common form of polygamy. The much rarer practice of polyandry is the form of marriage in which one woman has two or more husbands at the same time.

2. Polyandrous Family

Polyandry refers to a form of sexual union, in which a woman is married to two or more husbands at the same time. The form of polyandry in which a woman is married to two or more brothers is known as "fraternal polyandry," and it is believed by many anthropologists to be the most frequently encountered form.

3. Monogamous Family

Monogamous family is a social group, found among lesser apes and other primates, consisting of a single mated pair and their young offspring.

ON THE BASIS OF THE NATURE OF RESIDENCE

On the basis of the nature of residence family can be classified into two main forms:

1. Family of Matrilocal/Matriarchal Residence

Matriarchy or gynecocracy refers to a gynecocentric form of society, in which the leading role is taken by the women and especially by the mothers of a community. There are no known societies that are unambiguously matriarchal, although there are a number of attested matrilinear, matrilocal and avunculocal societies, especially among indigenous peoples of Asia and Africa, such as those of the Basques, Minangkabau, Mosuo, Berbers or Tuareg. Strongly matrilocal societies sometimes are referred to as matrifocal, and there is some debate concerning the terminological delineation between matrifocality and matriarchy.

2. Family of Patrilocal/Patriarchal Residence

The patriarchal family makes much greater demands on human nature. It requires chastity and self-sacrifice on the part of the wife and obedience and discipline on the part of the children, while even the father himself has to assume a heavy burden of responsibility and submit his personal feelings to the interests of the family tradition. But for these very reasons the patriarchal family is a much more efficient organ of cultural life. It is no longer limited to its primary sexual and reproductive functions. It becomes the dynamic principle of society and the source of social continuity. Hence, too, it acquires a distinctively religious character, which was absent in matrilinear societies, and which is now expressed in the worship of the family hearth or the sacred fire and the ceremonies of the ancestral cult. The fundamental idea in marriage is no longer the satisfaction of the sexual appetite, but, as Plato says: "the need that every man feels of clinging to the eternal life of nature by leaving behind him children's children who may minister to the gods in his stead." This religious exaltation of the family profoundly affects men's attitude to marriage and the sexual aspects of life in general.

It is not limited, as is often supposed, to the idealization of the possessive male as father and head of the household; it equally transforms the conception of womanhood. It was the patriarchal family which created those spiritual ideals of motherhood and virginity which have had so deep an influence on the moral development of culture. No doubt the deification of womanhood through the worship of the Mother Goddess had its origin in the ancient matrilinear societies. But the primitive Mother Goddess is a barbaric and formidable deity who embodies the ruthless fecundity of nature, and her rites are usually marked by licentiousness and cruelty.

It was the patriarchal culture which transformed this sinister goddess into the gracious figures of Demeter and Persephone and Aphrodite, and which created those higher types of divine virginity which we see in Athene, the giver of good counsel, and Artemis, the guardian of youth. The patriarchal society was in fact the creator of those moral ideas which have entered so deeply into the texture of civilization that they have become a part of our thought. Not only the names of piety and chastity, honour and modesty, but the values for which they stand are derived from this source, so that even where the patriarchal family has passed away we are still dependent on the moral tradition that it created.

In the classical cultures of the Mediterranean world, however, this was not the case. Here the patriarchal family failed to adapt itself to the urban conditions of the Hellenistic civilization, and consequently the whole culture lost its stability. Conditions of life both in the Greek city state and in the Roman Empire favoured the man without a family who could devote his whole energies to the duties and pleasures of public life. Late marriages and small families became the rule, and men satisfied their sexual instincts by homosexuality or by relations with slaves and prostitutes.

ON THE BASIS OF ANCESTRY OR DESCENT FAMILY

On the basis of ancestry or descent family can be classified into two main types:

1. Matrilineal Family

A matriline is a line of descent from a female ancestor to a descendant (of either sex) in which the individuals in all intervening generations are mothers. In a matrilineal descent system an individual is considered to belong to the same descent group as her or his mother.

2. Patrilineal Family

Patrilineality is a system in which one belongs to one's father's lineage; it generally involves the inheritance of property, names or titles through the male line as well.

A patrilineage (or patriclan) is a consanguineal male and female kin group each of whom is related to the common ancestor through male forebears.

NUCLEAR OR THE SINGLE UNIT FAMILY

A nuclear family is a family group consisting of only a father and mother and their children, who share living quarters. This can be contrasted with an *extended family*. Nuclear families can be of any size, as long as the family can support itself and there are only children and two parents. Nuclear families meet their individual members' basic needs because available resources are divided among only a few individuals or the family would be known as an extended family.

"The nuclear family is a social group characterized by common residence, economic cooperation and reproduction. It contains adults of both sexes, at least two of whom maintain a socially approved sexual relationship, and one or more children, own or adopted, of the sexually cohabiting adults."

For a group to be called a nuclear family there must at some time be a father, mother and at least one child. This type of family structure is found in almost all societies, although the length of time in which the family remains in this form varies even within the same society. The nuclear family was most popular in the 1950's and 60's.

Urban India's nuclear families find ever new forms in the face of rapidly changing realities.

The nuclear family can be a nurturing environment in which to raise children as long as there is love, time spent with children, emotional support, low stress, and a stable economic environment. In nuclear families, both adults are the biological or adoptive parents of their children.

The nuclear family consists of a married couple and their children. The nuclear family is ego-centred, and impermanent, while descent groups are permanent (lasting beyond the life-spans of individual constituents) and reckoned according to a single ancestor. One's family of orientation is the family in which one is born and grows up, while one's family of procreation is formed when one marries and has children. Claims made for the universality of the nuclear family, based upon the universality of marriage, do not hold up—the nuclear family is widespread, but not universal. In societies where the nuclear family is important, this structure acts as a primary arena for sexual, reproductive, economic, and acculturative functions, but it is not the only structure used by societies for these.

DISADVANTAGES OF NUCLEAR FAMILY

A nuclear and opposed to the extended family is a relatively new social norm. Given that people are more likely to migrate in their lifetimes than ever before we now have smaller and more dispersed families. This causes the breakdown of the traditional ties that bound and supported families through out the ages.

A nuclear family is a family on to it's self. A small compact unit that does not offer much support to the parents. With out the involvement of the grandparents and other family members outside of the "Mom, Dad, Kids" element many families fall on to hard times. Stress, money etc.

Humans by nature are a social creature. To reach our fullest potential we must keep the family intact.

An extended family situation is better than a nuclear family, but a nuclear family is far better than a single parent household.

Single-Parent Families

Single-parent families in today's society have their share of daily struggles and long-term disadvantages. The issues of expensive day care, shortage of quality time with children, balance of work and home duties, and economic struggle are among the seemingly endless problems these families must solve.

As many single-parent households are female-headed, their economic burden is much greater than that of a single-father family. This issue results from the fact that single women typically do not earn the same income as a single man; thus, there is a consequent economic struggle not experienced in the single-father household.

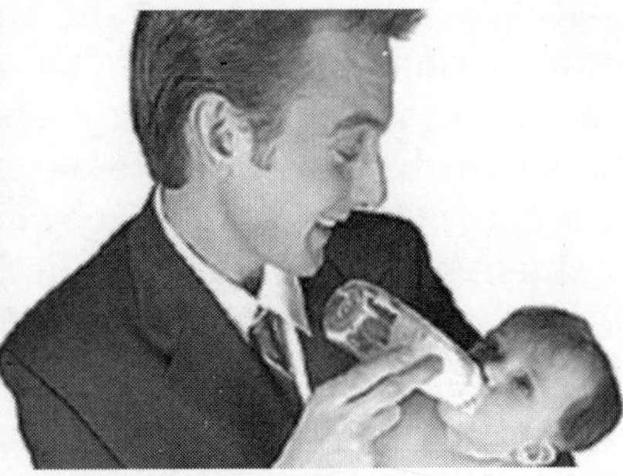

Single parents, are not unfortunate. In Indian society they are looked at with sympathy but it is necessary to see the other side of the coin.

An offshoot of this economic struggle is the balance of work and family duties. Single mothers often must work overtime shifts to compensate for the low salaries, thus taking time away from their children and other domestic chores. This results in a child that is home alone, without adult supervision, or placed in a daycare service for up to 8-10 hours per day.

Two parents are always better than one according to the parental loss perspective.

In a two-earner family, one parent may be able to stay at home with the children. But in a single-parent family, the parent rarely has the option of staying home to care for children full-time. Finding affordable, available childcare is likely to be a challenge.

According to the parental conflict perspective, children suffer from witnessing spousal abuse.

The parental adjustment perspective suggests that children in single parent families suffer because their parents have difficulty adjusting and functioning.

According to the economic hardship perspective, children suffer from lower incomes more common among single-parent families. Children in single-mother households are especially vulnerable because women tend to earn lower pay.

MYTHS BEHIND SINGLE PARENT FAMILY

Single parenthood in India may be the result of many things. In most cases it is an unforseeable tragedy as in the death of one parent, divorce, or abandonment by one parent. On the other hand many independent youngsters choose to become a single parent as in adoption, artificial insemination, surrogate motherhood and extramarital pregnancy. However the sad part for the single parent family is that many single parents and their children often have to face stigma, violence and social problems based on myths, stereotypes, half-truths and prejudices. This text is a cross-examination of such myths and a revelation of actual facts behind those myths.

The traditional society believes that a family with both parents is normal or predominant and the single parent families will be alienated from the normal interactions. The real fact behind this myth is that single parent families are showing a sharp rise. In India itself around 49% children are living in single-parent homes and despite the divorce or remarriages both the parents may actively involved in parenting or offering their children two separate families. Since the single parent norm becomes a common phenomenon, the parents do not feel alienated in the common society.

There is a major scandal against single parent families that they are broken families. This may not be the real factor in all cases. Many of the single parents are avoiding those unwanted quarrels and arguments with their partners. In that aspect they are setting a peaceful and stable ambience for their children. Single parents are often more independent and multi-tasking and their children actually gets the training to handle greater responsibility from their homes itself.

The children in the single parent families are widely believed to have emotional or behavioural problems. Society expects those children to do poorly at schools and possess a low self-esteem. These conclusions are completely false and the living proof for it is Vivian Richard's and Neena Gupta's daughter Masaba. Children in single parents may possess the accused problems as their counterparts in two parent families. The low esteem of children in single parent families mostly related to the low income in the families. However this syndrome can be seen in children from low financial two-parent families also.

The financial crisis is a major area of dread for most of single parent families. One has to learn to be interdependent, give and receive; taking our own responsibilities and asking for support and engaging even professional help, when needed. However, this financial crisis may not be in some of the well-off single parent families and not a common feature of these families.

Single parent families are not shame to the society but a form of gradual variations from a joint family to a nuclear family and now to a single parent family. Single parent families should engage in volunteering within the community so that they learn the balance between nurturing and being nurtured to make each family member mature and independent. Then only the myths and prejudices against this family system will be a farce.

JOINT FAMILY OR KUTUMBA OR KULA

The Hindu social unit consisting of several generations of kindred living together under the same roof or in a joining compound. Traditionally, joint families live in a large single home, but in modern times accommodations are often in individual, nuclear homes within a shared compound. The joint family includes the father and mother, sons, grandsons and great-grandsons with their spouses, as well as the daughters, granddaughters and great-grand-daughters until they are married—thus often comprising several married couples and their children.

The Joint Family System—creating a stable society.

The head of the joint family, called *kutumba mukhya* (also mukhya or kartri), is the father, supported by the mother, and in his absence, the elder son, guided by his mother and supported by his spouse. From an early age, the eldest son is given special training by his father to assume this future responsibility as head of the family. In the event of the father's death, sacred law does allow for the splitting of the family wealth between the sons.

Division of family assets may also be necessary in cases where sons are involved in different professions and live in different towns, when there is an inability for all to get along under one roof, or when the family becomes unmanageably large.

Characteristics of the Joint Family

The main characteristics of the joint family are that its members:

- Share a common residence,
- Partake of food prepared in the same kitchen,
- Hold their property in common and
- Ideally, profess the same religion, sect and sampradaya.

Each individual family of husband, wife and children is under the guidance of the head of the joint family. All work together unselfishly to further the common good. Each joint family extends out from its home to include a second level of connections as an "*extended family* (brihat-kutumba or mahakutumba)."

Benefits

A harmonious joint family set-up can be a boon. It can provide a wonderful support system emotionally and financially. In the ideal sense, one can share both one's triumphs and failures. The joint family is ideal for the woman who wants to work as well as have a family. Working women have someone to leave their children with when they are away at work, rather than leaving their children in a creche or with servants. They can be assured that their children are being looked after by people who care for them almost as much as they do themselves. After all, as they say, "blood is thicker than water."

Everyone knows how difficult family relations are in general. Nuclear families sometimes find it hard to maintain cordial relations. One would probably think that in joint families with so many people and so many vested interests, maintaining family harmony must be an uphill task. Dr. Mehrotra feels that as far as problems are concerned she would definitely not say that there are more problems in joint families and less in nuclear families. Some people have difficulty dealing with other people and such people will face problems wherever they go. For a joint family system to work, the members will have to learn to adjust, to overcome their petty jealousies, to develop mutual respect between the generations, and to learn to give each other space.

A joint family system can become a training ground for the future generation to learn and develop attributes and skills of living in harmony with fellow citizens in a society. If our current family model is reflective of a lifestyle that is based on selfish existence and intolerance to others views then how can we expect the society (of which such a family is a unit) to be any different. A joint family system can help build a society that is more tolerant of personal differences in views and thoughts and where people appreciate and carry forward the value of mutual respect, love and co-operation.

Disadvantage

"Not every family is a happy family. What is most important is the atmosphere in a joint family. If there is a congenial atmosphere in a joint family, it can be a virtue. However, if there is tension and conflict between the members of a joint family and if they are constantly playing games and trying to score over each other, all the advantages of a joint family are lost."

Dowry deaths, property disputes, domestic violence, sexual and mental abuse—while this would be an extreme view, as these are family problems, not necessarily joint family problems, the fact is that the joint family is definitely not all joy and laughter. It would be unrealistic to expect it to be so.

If there are several children in the joint family, there is a tendency for parents to make comparisons. Also, if one child is given something and the other is not, it could lead to the development of unhealthy competition and feelings of envy. Most 'unhealthy' children come from joint families because they live together out of compulsion and not out of choice.

Another problem is that there are too many authority figures in joint families. Sometimes, grandparents undermine the mother's authority because they feel that they have more experience in raising children. They pass adverse remarks to the mother in front of the children like, "You do not know how to handle children" – As a result, the mother feels suppressed, depressed and frustrated. She, in turn, takes her frustration out on her children, which affects the overall development of the child.

In spite of living in a joint family, children don't know how to share. "It is always assumed that children from joint families are more likely to share their things as they interact on a daily basis with so many people. However, if the family atmosphere is hostile, it can have an adverse affect on children. Especially in families where there is a lack of transparency, where many things are left unsaid, and where there is a lack of free expression."

Another problem is that there are too many authority figures in joint families. Sometimes, grandparents undermine the mother's authority because they feel that they have more experience in raising children. They pass adverse remarks to the mother in front of the children like, "You do not know how to handle children." As a result, the mother feels suppressed, depressed and frustrated. She, in turn, takes her frustration out on her children, which affects the overall development of the child.

Generation gap is another important factor to be taken into consideration. The needs and expectations of the younger generation are constantly changing. The fact remains that there are no standards and rules written in stone as far as parenting is concerned. Now, in joint families, members of the older generation, tend to lay down the law in an autocratic fashion. The authority figures need to operate in a democratic fashion and make an attempt to bridge the generation gap. They must try to update their knowledge about the lifestyle of the younger generation and not constantly pass judgement on their activities. They must realize that times change and the way things were done in their time may not work any more. Everything cannot be seen in black and white. If they insist on being rigid, they will just distance themselves from their children and grandchildren. There will be a breakdown in communication and the elders will find that they are slowly becoming marginalized in the family. There should be respect and concern for each other's feelings rather than a constant battle for supremacy and authority.

SUCCESSFUL JOINT FAMILY SYSTEM

If we were to revive and revamp the 'joint family system' model to create a new one we need to think how can we learn from the mistakes that we made in old joint family system and create a new system with the insight gained from the experiences of nuclear and joint family system.

Here are some things that can be done differently from the old system to make the 'joint family system' a success :

1. Mutual Love and Respect

One of the major reasons why my generation was desperate to break out of the joint family was the attitude of the older generation to impose their views and thoughts on us. In some families the father's word would be the final word and nobody could dare say or do anything against it. Such an autocratic style of leading a family leads to repression and suppression giving rise to feelings of discontentment and unhappiness.

If the joint family system is laid on the founding stone of mutual and genuine love and respect for each and every member (including children) then the system is guaranteed to be a success. It helps to keep in mind that love, respect and affection are things that can be only commanded and not demanded. We command these precious things by giving them first. For example, you cannot expect your son or your daughter to have respect for your advice and suggestions if you cannot demonstrate understanding, love and respect to them through your actions and words and by being sensitive to their individual aspirations and ways of thinking.

2. Open and Honest Communication

Family members need to communicate openly and honestly with one another. The elders in the family must encourage and create an environment conducive to open communication. In the absence of such an environment, family members can feel repressed and suppressed that can lead to discontentment. Non-judgmental listening and demonstrating mutual trust are necessary to help family members open up to one another.

One of the things that disintegrated the old joint family system was the constant interference and meddling by elders in the matters of youngsters. Learning from the past mistake, another important aspect of communication is knowing when not to communicate. In other words, it is important to give one another space and respect the boundaries of each other. Living under one roof does not have to be about transgressing the personal space of the members. Personal space is more mental than physical. If a joint family system has to succeed, recognizing and respecting this space is crucial.

3. Realistic Expectations of Members

It is important that members in a joint family system feel accepted for who they are and as they are. The crucial part of acceptance of one another is acceptance of our own weaknesses and limitations and that of others. By doing this, expectations of members of one another become more realistic. Realistic expectations help us to be more tolerant of weaknesses of one another. Having unrealistic expectations of others is often the root cause of disappointments and discontentment with others.

4. Acknowledgement of and Being Grateful for What is

When more than one family live together, it brings together members of different strengths. One of the great advantages of this (when compared to a nuclear family) is that different strengths of different members can be potentially enriching to the family and in turn provide a sense of fulfillment to the members. For a joint family system to be a place where the members feel valued and nurtured, acknowledgement of the strengths and different positive aspects that each member brings to the family and being grateful for the same is useful and even necessary.

JOINT FAMILY IN INDIA

In India the joint family has endured for as long as many records exist. Even about 1000 BC, in the time of the Mahabharata, the joint family existed more or less as it exists today. A joint family is a group of people who generally live under one roof, who eat food cooked in one kitchen, who hold property in common, participate in common family worship and are related to one another as some particular type of kindred.

A joint family has always an ancestral seat or locality. However humble an Indian might be, he will always refer to his ancestral village as his home. As all services were paid for in land in ancient days, every Indian had a small family holding in some village—maybe just a strip of land or for an artisan, just a small house. This connection of a family with a locality lingers even after the family has finally migrated out of its village. Such families keep on worshipping the gods of their former locality or come back time and again to keep certain vows made to these gods.

The 'joint family system' is one such thing that has the potential to ensure sustainability of life and natural resources on this planet. The beauty about the Indian culture lies in its age-long prevailing tradition of the joint family system. It's a system under which even extended members of a family like one's parents, children, the children's spouses and their offspring, etc. live together. The elder-most, usually the male member is the head in the joint Indian family system who makes all important decisions and rules, whereas other family members abide by it dutifully with full respect.

A major factor that keeps all members, big and small, united in love and peace in a joint family system in India is the importance attached to protocol. This feature is very unique to Indian families and very special. Manners like respecting elders, touching their feet as a sign of respect, speaking in a dignified manner, taking elders' advice prior taking important decisions, etc. is something that Indian parents take care to inculcate in their kids from very beginning. The head of the family responds by caring and treating each member of the family the same.

The intention behind the formation of any social unit will fail to serve its purpose if discipline is lacking and the same applies to the joint family system as well. Due to this reason, discipline is another factor given utmost importance in the joint family system in India. As a rule, it's the say of the family head that prevails upon others. In case of any disagreement, the matter is diligently sorted out by taking suggestions from other adult members. One usually also has to follow fixed timings for returning home, eating, etc.

The reason why Indians are proving to emerge as a prosperous lot globally, many researches claim, is because of the significance they attach to the joint family system. All working cohesively to solve a problem faced by any one or more members of the joint family, is what works magic in keeping one tension-free, happy and contended even in today's highly competitive environment. An Indian may be a top corporate honcho or a great sportsperson or a movie actor and so on in a particular professional field, but all these accomplishments relegate to the backseat when at home.

JOINT FAMILY SYSTEM VS NUCLEAR FAMILY SYSTEM

Today we have a generation of people who after having lived in a joint family system have taken the initiative to break out and start a nuclear family. This generation today has come of age and very well appreciates the strengths and weaknesses of both the system. In a sense one represent such a generation and therefore wish to present his personal thoughts on why and how we could revive and make a 'the joint family system' work.

The generation that broke out of the old joint family system did so when individualistic thinking began to gain predominance in the society. It was exciting to explore, experiment and establish a living set up on one's own. The nuclear family gave immense freedom from the traditions and ways of life that the old system was ridden with. Hence whenever and wherever the parents and the grown up adult children could not get along well and when the adult children could afford to build a house to call their own, nuclear families began to be formed. As it happens with most changes in the society, initially the people from the old system did not take this change very well. They were saddened to see the disintegration of family values and system and emergence of individualistic nuclear families. However, gradually when nuclear families became the order of the day, the old generation slowly began to accept the realities and became comfortable with it.

The other factor that gave rise to nuclear families was industrialization. Industrial revolution brought with it increase in job opportunities in and around major industrialized and commercial cities and towns. This forced men and women to move out of their family home and away from the parents. In this case, often the parents who remained emotionally attached to the place where they spent most of their life preferred to continue staying in their family home and accepted with some sadness their children starting out new life away from them.

Today, as a person from the generation that broke out of the system in the hope of immense freedom, one can look behind and ask himself 'what has his generation really and truly gained from the quest for freedom and what has it lost'.

The one and only major gain that anyone see from the 'nuclear family' system is the opportunity it provides us to create an identity of our own—something we as human beings crave for and are born for. On the loss side there are several reasons:

- being physically far removed from the family members and as a result inadvertently getting disconnected from their hearts and minds,
- stresses in bringing up our children only relying on child care centers. In Indian cities and towns, it can be even more difficult where there are not enough facilities available for care of children.
- coping with all problems—big and small on our own as we are unable to afford the privilege of sharing and downloading worries on someone (other than spouse) whom we feel close and connected to. This has led to increase in several problems in the society like depression, suicides and heart disorders due to highly stressed lives.
- missing out on celebrations and festivities that binds us to our culture and gives us a sense of being at home. This is more relevant to those living out of the country.

- having difficulty in passing on the cultural values to our children. Cultural values are learnt and taught by seeing them in action.
- facing great difficulty in even passing on our own language to the next generation. (This is more applicable for those who have moved out of the country.)

ON THE BASIS OF THE NATURE OF RELATIONS AMONG THE FAMILY MEMBERS

On the basis of the nature of relations among the family members the family can be classified into two main types:

1. Conjugal Family

A conjugal family is a nuclear family of adult partners and their children (by birth or adoption) where the family relationship is principally focused inward and ties to extended kin are voluntary and based on emotional bonds, rather than strict duties and obligations. The spouses and their children are considered to be of prime importance, and other more distant relatives less important. The marriage bond is important and stressed.

2. Consanguinity Family

Consanguinity refers to the property of being from the same kinship as another person. In that respect, consanguinity is the quality of being descended from the same ancestor as another person. Consanguinity is an important legal concept in that the laws of many jurisdictions consider consanguinity as a factor in deciding whether two individuals may be married or whether a given person inherits property when a deceased person has not left a will.

THE MODERN NUCLEAR FAMILY

The "nuclear", "isolated", or "restricted" family is not a recent phenomenon, but has existed in many cultures throughout human history. Indeed, the extended family of several generations is found mostly in relatively advanced, stable, and affluent, but not yet industrialized societies. Very primitive and very sophisticated societies seem to prefer the nuclear family model.

However, nuclear families can vary in the degree of their isolation and restrictedness. For example, before the Industrial Revolution the Western nuclear family was often embedded in a larger social unit, such as a farm or estate, an aristocratic court, or a village populated by relatives. Many older city neighborhoods also kept kinship ties strong, and thus even very small families remained open to the community. Family visits might be frequent and extended; children might freely circulate and feel at home in several households.

On the other hand, we have seen that, beginning in the late 17th century, a trend toward "closeness" reduced the size of many larger households and changed the relationships between the remaining family members. They became more concerned about each other. They needed each other more. The idyllic home of the "bourgeois" became an island of serenity in the gathering storm of modernization, a haven secure from the world "out there", from aggressiveness, competition, and class warfare. We have also seen how this home sheltered women and protected the children from sexual and other temptations. Other nasty social realities were also kept safely at bay. The family income was no longer earned inside, but rather outside the house. The division of labour between the sexes became more pronounced as men spent more and more time away from their families as wage earners in factories, shops, and offices. Their wives became almost the only companions of their small children whose care and education was now their main responsibility. (Formerly, these tasks had been divided between mothers, grandmothers, nurses, and servants.) Virtually the only middle-class men who still worked at home were doctors and lawyers in private practice. As a rule, however, the bourgeois family saw its "head" and "breadwinner" only when he returned from his work at night. This work itself remained an abstraction to both his wife and his children.

The removal of productive work from the home into the factories had, of course, important consequences for all family members. It was no longer necessary for any of them to develop strong roots in any particular community or to become attached to a particular house. Instead, they became free to move about, to follow industrial development into new settlements, to "go after the jobs" wherever they might be. Moreover, family connections became less important, as factory work became ever more rationalized and efficient. Nepotism gave way to hiring and promotion on merit alone. By the same token, the new worker, business man, or bureaucrat no longer had to take care of distant relatives. He now worked exclusively for his own small family and this made him more industrious. He could advance faster, since his income had to support only very few people. Thus, the individual husband and father was no longer weighed down by traditions or extensive social obligations. In addition, the education of his children and the care of his aged or sick parents began to be taken over by the state.

In view of these developments, many observers have noted a "fit" between the nuclear family and industrialism. In other words, small, intimate, and mobile families seem best suited to advance the cause of industrialization and conversely, industrialization seems to encourage the formation of small families. After all, in modern industrial societies there is a general trend toward equality and personal independence. This, in turn, allows for the free choice of a marriage partner, place of residence, and occupation. In an extended family these freedoms are always restricted, because a "wrong" choice would affect too many relatives. Thus, people who want to take full advantage of the new possibilities normally marry late and keep their families small. However, this rule also has its exceptions. Sometimes large families are more useful, because they can serve as a "back-up unit" by providing shelter and aid at crucial moments. This may be especially important for lower-class individuals who try to "move up", although the higher classes often also maintain extensive family ties. Thus, even in fully industrialized societies one can find many men and women who appreciate the traditional extended family or at least a large network of relatives.

Still, by and large, the closely-knit nuclear family has been dominant in Western societies for the last several generations, and thus it has shaped the general perception of what a family should be: A man and a woman marry for love, have two or three children, live alone by themselves in a "family home" or apartment, and spend all their free time together. The man leaves for work in the morning, while the woman takes care of the children and the house. She also cooks dinner and ministers to her exhausted husband when he returns at night. Once or twice a year, at Thanksgiving or Christmas, there is a brief, ceremonial get-together with other relatives at "Grandma's house", but otherwise everyone keeps his distance and minds his own business.

Obviously, according to this "ideal" model, the family members are relatively isolated from the larger kindred and, indeed, from the rest of the community. However, they are to be compensated for this isolation by a greater emotional warmth inside the nuclear circle. Father, mother, and children are to be the world for each other. A deep mutual love is supposed to keep them together and boost their morale as they compete economically with other small family units. Unfortunately, as many families have discovered, things do not always work out that way. The lack of wider contacts is often perceived as crippling, too much closeness becomes oppressive, and inescapable familiarity breeds contempt. Therefore, almost from the beginning, the modern nuclear family has also been subject to criticism.

In Victorian times, when the "cult of the home" was at its height, this criticism was expressed mainly by great bourgeois writers, such as Flaubert, Ibsen and Strindberg, who denounced the hypocrisy, shallowness, and dullness of middle-class life, and who exposed the suffering and vicious psychological infighting behind the façade of respectability. The family was further criticised on philosophical and political grounds by Friedrich Engels who tied it to the origin and maintenance of private property. Finally, Sigmund Freud provided perhaps the most serious, if indirect, accusation when he described the "happy" nuclear household as the breeding ground of neurosis and sexual perversion.

At any rate, by the late 19th century the disadvantages of the bourgeois family model had also become evident to many average men and women. The emotional hothouse atmosphere of the home began to seem stifling, and what once had been praised as a sanctuary was more and more often condemned as a prison. In the traditional extended family, children had been able to choose between several male and female adult role models; now they had only their parents. Formerly, their early education had been shaped by a number of different people and a variety of influences; now they depended entirely on their own mother and father. Actually, the latter was not even always available. Since he no longer worked inside the house, his children had no clear conception of his social role. Instead, he became simply an abstract "provider" and disciplinarian, a mysterious and distant authority figure. He was occasionally loved, frequently feared, but rarely understood. At the same time, the wife and mother found herself more restricted than ever before. Her greatly increased maternal duties kept her confined inside her "four walls." She could venture outside only for a visit to church or to go shopping. Her world had shrunk, and her functions were narrowly circumscribed. She had to be feminine, motherly, sensitive, "proper", and in all matters of importance she had to defer to her husband.

Recent decades have seen a continuation of this trend. In many families today both husband and wife work outside the house, while the children spend much of their time in a nursery, daycare center, kindergarten, or school. As a result, the emotional ties between family members have become somewhat less constrictive, and a greater tolerance prevails. The influence of peer groups has grown, not only for the children, but also for their mothers. The traditional male and female roles are being reevaluated. The mass media keep everyone in touch with the larger community and its continued transformation. Still, the family circle as such has not widened. Grandparents are rarely part of the household, but live on their own in "retirement villages", "senior citizen centers", or nursing homes. Unmarried relatives move to a "singles' hotel" or apartment building. Thus, the average American family remains fairly small. Indeed, there are now many "fatherless" families consisting only of a woman and her children.

The one-parent family or "core family" is usually described as an "incomplete" nuclear family, and there is a general assumption that it is socially undesirable. The lack of a "father figure" is seen as detrimental to child development, and hasty generalizations are made about "undue" female influence. In the U.S. these comments sometimes even have racist overtones, as mother-child families are frequently found in the poor black population. However, with the rising divorce rate, this family type has also become increasingly common in the white middle class. Indeed, at the present time about 1 out of 6 children in America lives with only one parent, and the number of such households may well increase in the future. After all, our welfare regulations and other government policies often have the effect of breaking up families that would otherwise stay together. Our legislatures have not yet learned how to test new laws through "family impact studies" which would reveal such unintended consequences in advance. Still, in the meantime it should be remembered that the one-parent family is not necessarily bad. In the years following the two World Wars, millions of women have successfully brought up their children alone, and this impressive example should caution us against superficial judgments. Moreover, upon closer examination, many "core families" are discovered to maintain close connections to wider kinship groups and thus turn out to be more open and viable than might have been supposed. Finally, we know that there are also many father-child families which have not received sufficient critical attention.

It is another question whether the nuclear family itself, even when "complete", is still the best available option. Many people today are convinced that small, single households are uneconomical and wasteful, that they are still emotionally unhealthy, that they perpetuate outmoded sterotypical sex roles, and that they produce competitive, egotistical children in an age when universal cooperation seems the only hope of mankind. It is also argued that the modern family no longer has any other function than to provide love and intimacy, and that this is by no means enough to justify its existence. Indeed, since families have been largely relieved of their economic, educational, and protective functions by the state, sexual attachment has become the nearly exclusive basis of marriage, and this basis is notoriously weak. Frequent divorce and remarriage, however, while perhaps practical for the adults, hardly seem in the best interest of the children. Under the circumstances, it is only fitting that a number of thoughtful men and women should continue to search for more stable, "new and improved" family models.

DOMESTIC VIOLENCE

Domestic violence, also known as domestic abuse, spousal abuse, family violence, and *intimate partner violence* (IPV), can be broadly defined as a pattern of abusive behaviours by one or both partners in an intimate relationship such as marriage, dating, family, friends or cohabitation.

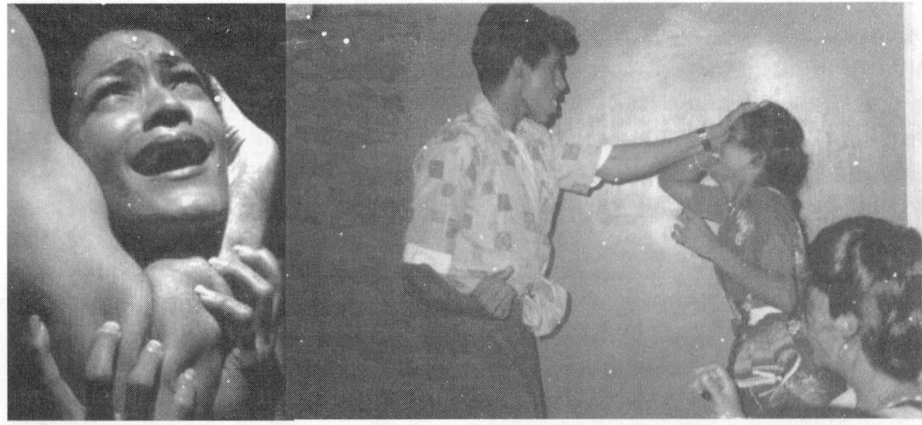

Domestic Violence.

Domestic violence has many forms including physical aggression (hitting, kicking, biting, shoving, restraining, slapping, throwing objects), or threats thereof; sexual abuse; emotional abuse; controlling or domineering; intimidation; stalking; passive/covert abuse (e.g., neglect); and economic deprivation. Alcohol consumption and mental illness can be co-morbid with abuse, and present additional challenges when present alongside patterns of abuse.

Awareness, perception, definition and documentation of domestic violence differs widely from country to country, and from era to era. According to some studies, less that 1 per cent of domestic violence cases are reported to the police. According to the Centers for Disease Control, domestic violence is a serious, preventable public health problem affecting more than 25 million American women.

Family violence is a broader definition, often used to include child abuse, elder abuse, and other violent acts between family members. Wife abuse, wife beating, and battering are descriptive terms that have lost popularity recently for at least two reasons:

- Acknowledgment that many victims are not actually married to the abuser, but rather cohabiting or other arrangement.
- Abuse can take other forms than physical abuse and males are often victims of violence as well. Other forms of abuse may be constantly occurring, while physical abuse happens occasionally.

These other forms of abuse have the potential to lead to mental illness, self-harm, and even attempts at suicide.

All forms of domestic abuse have one purpose: to gain and maintain control over the victim. Abusers use many tactics to exert power over their spouse or partner: dominance, humiliation, isolation, threats, intimidation, denial and blame.

The *form* and *characteristics of domestic violenc*e and abuse may vary in other ways. *Michael P. Johnson* argues for three major types of ***intimate partner violence***. The typology is supported by subsequent research and evaluation by Johnson and his colleagues, as well as independent researchers.

Distinctions need to be made regarding types of violence, motives of perpetrators, and the social and cultural context. Violence by a person against their intimate partner is often done as a way for controlling "their partner", even if this kind of violence is not the most frequent. Other types of intimate partner violence also occur, including violence between gay and lesbian couples, and by women against their male partners.

Distinctions are not based on single incidents, but rather on patterns across numerous incidents and motives of the perpetrator. Types of violence identified by Johnson:

- *Common couple violence* is not connected to general control behaviour, but arises in a single argument where one or both partners physically lash out at the other. Intimate terrorism is one element in a general pattern of control by one partner over the other. Intimate terrorism is more common than common couple violence, more likely to escalate over time, not as likely to be mutual, and more likely to involve serious injury.

- *Intimate terrorism* may also involve emotional and psychological abuse.
- *Violent resistance*, sometimes thought of as "self-defense", is violence perpetrated by victims against their abusive partners.
- *Mutual violent control* is rare type of intimate partner violence occurs when both partners act in a violent manner, battling for control.

Another type is situational couple violence, which arises out of conflicts that escalate to arguments and then to violence. It is not connected to a general pattern of control. Although it occurs less frequently in relationships and is less serious than intimate terrorism, in some cases it can be frequent and/or quite serious, even life-threatening. This is probably the most common type of intimate partner violence and dominates general surveys, student samples, and even marriage counseling samples.

CHANGE IN FAMILY PATTERN

The original Indian family has been described as a "patrilocal joint family" in which a line of brothers, their wives, and children live in a common household compound with the men's fathers as patriarch. It is marked by a frequent coresidence of nuclear families related along filial or fraternal lines, and by a strong patriarchal system with the seclusion of women. The joint/extended family is usually composed of three or more generations, living together in the same house, cooking in the same kitchen, owning property in common, and pooling their incomes for common spending. In India, the family was a corporate unit jointly holding title to land, which was the general marker of wealth. The father was more or less the household head, but it was the brothers who ran the affairs of the family property. The extended family structure is characterized by parental selection of mates, the transmission of property to male members within the family, the rarity of divorce, and the subjugation of women.

The indentured Indians, from their initial entry into Trinidad (1845) up until the 1880s and 1890s, grew up with a different set of family relationships from which their parents had experienced. Most of the Indians during this period were plantation residents and experienced fluid family patterns. Between the 1890s and 1940s, the extended family was more or less the norm in villages and among peasant Indians including the majority of landowning Indo-Trinidadian families. After the 1940s and 1950s there was a steady decline in the extended family form.

The move to Trinidad resulted in a new set of rules by which the structure of relative domination within and among families had to be arranged. First, members of joint/extended families were separated in the estate barracks where the indentured Indians were initially lodged. No provision was made for the behaviour patterns appropriate to the indentured immigrants society of origin and by the very nature of barrack life there was minimal opportunity for exercising traditional customs and practices. Where the family did exist, plantation conditions conflicted with normal Indian family and other behaviour patterns and expectations. The disparity between the numbers of men and women, for example, created conditions conducive to change.

Because men greatly outnumbered women throughout the indenture period, the joint family system could not be maintained and began to fade. The disproportion of the sexes, non-recognition of customary marriages, erosion of traditional restraints and marriage customs, produced conditions that led to the demise of the extended family. As a result of the disparity between the sexes, many of the indentured Indians entered into common-law unions, which could easily be terminated. Indian religious marriage ceremonies were not recognized by civil authorities until well after the indenture period had ended. Islamic marriages, for example, were declared legal in 1936, but Hindu ceremonies remained outside the law until 1946. This legal double standard probably had the effect of weakening the traditional bonds of marriage since a discontented husband could very easily abandon a woman who was not really a "wife" in the eyes of the law.

Similarly, inter-caste marriage and cohabitation were unavoidable because of the scarcity of women. Lack of land and other forms of property, and the independent wage-earning capacity of women and sons, evidently curtailed the authority of Indian males. Consequently, the structure of domestic units was under the direct jurisdiction of the plantation manager rather than under the control of the male household heads. The housing arrangement in the estate barracks also kept people close to each other irrespective of caste backgrounds. Although the majority of indentured Indians came from the lower agricultural castes, many were also members of higher castes such as Brahmins and Kshatriyas (mainly Rajputs). As the indentured Indians settled into villages and attempted to establish themselves, strict caste restrictions were gradually broken down virtually irreparably. Though not as frequent as inter-caste marriage, unions also occurred between Muslims and Hindus.

Therefore, the prevalence of inter-caste interactions as a result of living conditions and the experience of passage may have created the conditions for the initial transformations of one of the fundamental cornerstone of Hinduism, namely, caste arrangements. The crossing of the *kaala pani*, or the conditions arising out of the experience of passage itself, resulted in profound changes to the traditional Indian family system. In India, for example, social relationships were dominated by the patrilineal system. In a single village in India, the people were largely from the same "gotra", and potential marriage partners were sought from outside. In the Caribbean, however, this system gave way to a new system, namely, jahajibhai/jahajibahin or ship brotherhood/sisterhood. Many of the indentured Indians did not come from the same village, and this led to the development of solidarity as experienced in communal life. Thus, it is conceivable that the breakdown of caste barriers, in some ways, radically transformed particular spheres of Indian social and cultural life in the Caribbean. In his research on Indo-Trinidadian social organization, Nevadomsky found that in some areas of community life the cultural content is perhaps traditional (e.g., religion), but the organizational form is "new" (i.e. the erosion of caste and the declining authority of the household head in the extended family. Given the circumstances of indentureship and plantation life, it was difficult for the indentured Indians to maintain the joint/extended family system as was known in India. Although a few specific features of this system remained in tact, mainly in rural areas (e.g., the authority of the father, and a system of extensive kinship), today, however, the extended family has become almost extinct in Trinidad.

The increasing shift from the extended family form to the nuclear family can be attributed to a number of factors operating in Trinidadian society. One such factor is the Indo-Trinidadian bride's growing awareness of her subjugation and exploitation as *bahu* (daughter-in-law). Many Indo-Trinidadian women, as wives and mothers have, historically, been oppressed by their mothers-in-law. In Trinidad, the Indo-Trinidadian bride was property, and thus needed to be abused in order to make clear that her in-laws possessed her completely—a situation aptly referred to as "sexual politics." The Indo-Trinidadian bride's desire to achieve autonomy may indicate her desire to break with traditional patterns of male dominance. Thus, the desire by the Indo-Trinidadian bride for marital stability (i.e. away from the powers of her mother-in-law) and independence may have also contributed to the rise in nuclear family forms.

This emphasis on nuclear families supports Schwartz's assumption that the nuclear family household is the group best adapted to the socio-economic conditions present in Trinidadian society, and only under particular conditions is the extended family household possible as an effective unit. Many Indo-Trinidadians have made increasing use of education as a vehicle for social mobility. People involved in "modern" jobs outside of the sugar industry tend to establish neolocal, nuclear family residences while maintaining ties to the wider family.

Typically, most Indo-Trinidadian families preferred to have their married sons and wives live at home with them. They built extra rooms to accommodate them. However, the current trend is for young couples to live on their own, earning and managing their own family budgets. This movement away from the sharing of residence with parents has resulted in the emergence of nuclear family homes. It is no longer a disgrace for newly-wed couples to find their own home. One possible reason for the adoption of autonomous living (i.e., living in a nuclear family situation involving just parents and children) may have to do with education. Thus, the typical western criteria of status - education, occupation, and income— by and large, now form the basis of the Indo-Trinidadian attitude toward education.

Another factor responsible for the demise of the traditional extended family system in Trinidad can be attributed to widespread industrialization and urbanization. The rapid expansion of the economy produced high rates of urbanization and suburbanization which may have, to some extent, outmoded the traditional extended family system. The emergence of a profitable oil export economy in Trinidad significantly changed the island's economic structure – one that was based on a plantation economy to one based on an export-oriented industrial economy. Research by Angrosino indicates that the most significant concomitant of family styles in Trinidad is socioeconomic. Angrosino's study points to the impact that changes to income had on the changes to the traditional Indo-Trinidadian family structure.

This type of economic development, coupled with the adoption of "creole values", also resulted in attitudinal changes toward divorce. Traditional Hindu thought was definitely against divorce, especially for females. Hinduism advocated that women should not marry more than once even after their marriage partners died. Muslim women, on the other hand, had opportunities for separation since Islam permitted divorce. During the period 1870-1940s, Hindu women in Trinidad had no access to divorce. Today, however, divorce among Indo-Trinidadians is becoming more and more common place.

Structural and cultural factors such as those previously discussed gave rise to other changes in the Indo-Trinidadian family. The gradual decline in arranged marriages among Indo-Trinidadians is a case in point. During the early indenture period arranged marriages were probably the cultural ideal and statistical norm. Increasing educational opportunities and wide scale urbanization undoubtedly led to changes in attitudes towards arranged marriages. From the 1940s, marriages were not parentally arranged, and Indo-Trinidadian women increasingly opted for their own selection of a spouse. By the 1950s, most Indo-Trinidadian parents, including village parents, conceded to personal choice as the best method of mate selection.

First, it was a situation where neither the bride nor the groom saw each other until the day of the wedding. This situation was later modified so that the couple would arrange to meet each other, and would then indicate to their parents if they agreed to marry. Then there arose another modification – one involving a system of arranged courtship. In this situation the prospective bridegroom would visit a few times and shortly after marriage plans would be finalized. Since the 1970s to the present, the situation has become almost entirely courtship. Many Indo-Trinidadian parents try to pass on their religion and culture to succeeding generations, and expect the same from their children's choices in marriage. Today, arranged marriages are usually frowned upon by the younger generation of Indo-Trinidadians. The norm is for individual choice with parental approval.

Particular aspects of marriage customs associated with Indian weddings were also re-adapted in Trinidad. For example, in northern India (where the majority of indentured Indians came from) the payment of dowry was a common practice. However, in nineteen-century Trinidad, the system of dowry has become extinct. The giving of gifts to both the *dulaha* (bridegroom) and *dulahin* (bride) is the accepted practice today.

Changes have also occurred in the area of wedding rituals and practices. No longer is the "*muhurta*" (the time when a Hindu marriage is most propitious) seen as important. It has been replaced by a particular day most suited to merriment i.e. Sundays . Also, the traditional attire worn by Indo-Trinidadian brides has undergone some changes.

For example, it was customary for the Hindu bride to wear a yellow sari, then a red sari followed by a white sari. With increasing westernization, Hindu brides are now wearing both the traditional sari as well as the white wedding gown typical of western/Christian weddings.

But, inspite of these transformations and modifications, Indo-Trinidadian marriages continue to have the full force of moral and social authority behind them. Indeed, the "Indian" character of the wedding ceremony has become one of the principal markers of a distinct Indo-Trinidadian ethnic identity. An Indo-Trinidadian marriage symbolizes participation in Indian culture. As Jha argued: "the importance of the wedding feast by both Hindus and Muslims in Trinidad is critical to an understanding of cultural preservation and pride."

CHANGING INDIAN FAMILY AND THE PATTERNS IN DOMESTIC VIOLENCE

For the past four weeks, India Probe has been devoted to issues of the political variety. Its time to take a break from politics and discuss something more social. The strength and weakness of the family system often determines the cohesion and disintegration of a society. Family is the foundation stone of society. It teaches us to be social. It teaches us to digest the fact that there is a common interest, which may be more important than individual interest. Thus, it may require to be given up in favour of family interest. It modifies individual behaviour and cultivates tolerance, patience, respect for others, love and affection, dedication, care and sacrifice. It checks selfishness and restrains rigidity. In fact, a family is the first institution that cultivates social values and social behaviour among individuals. Social values are basically family values written at large. Had the family been absent, concepts like nationalism could never originate. Traditional Asian societies have survived for thousands of years mainly because there has been a consistent emphasis on enforcing family values. Collapse of the family system simultaneously leads to social breakdown. There is a visible rise in criminal behaviour and violence. The individual looses the ability to tolerate those who differ from him.

The traditional Indian family was a large sized joint family. Vertically, one could find 3-4 generations living together in a single house. Horizontally, many brothers with their families lived jointly in one house. The base of such a joint family was either an agrarian land holding or a traditional business. Women were usually uneducated but they were very well versed in Indian epics such as Ramayana and Mahabharata. These epics are an encyclopaedia of family values, social behaviour and issue clear guidelines regarding what is to be done in particular circumstances confronting a family or a nation. Simultaneously, these women were well versed in stories of legendary heroes specific to every community. The epics combined with a repeated recital of hero stories provided the basic education to every child from where he/she learnt norms of social behaviour. By the time he/she grew up, the child too was well versed in such values. Therefore, generations kept following them. In fact, these norms and values are so comprehensive that it is impossible to find a second instance of such comprehensiveness in modern literature. For example, the Bible provides comprehensive guidelines of social behaviour. Such a family structure entailed collective decision-making on most issues. Whether it is marriage or a business decision.

Globally, violence within the home is universal across culture, religion, class, and ethnicity. Despite this widespread prevalence, however, such violence is not customarily acknowledged and has remained invisible—a problem thought unworthy of legal or political attention. The social construction of the divide between public and private underlies the hidden nature of domestic violence against women. Legal jurisprudence has historically considered the domain of the house to be within the control and unquestionable authority of the male head of household. Thus, acts of violence against members of the household, whether wife or child, were perceived as discipline and essential for maintaining the rule of authority within the family. Available statistics from around the globe indicate that one out of every three women has experienced violence in an intimate relationship at some point in her life. This is only an average based on available national surveys across industrialized and developing countries.

Statistical evidence on the actual prevalence of domestic violence in India is scant however. This is not surprising considering the fact that it is only in the year 1995 that the Government of India officially recognized domestic violence, particularly violence against women as a critical issue in the country report for the Fourth World Conference on women in Beijing. For many decades, the magnitude of the problem has been hidden behind a cultural emphasis on the privacy and sanctity of the family and on self sacrificing womanhood, as well as generally conservative and insensitive judiciary.

Nevertheless, the few studies available on the subject of domestic violence in India indicate that physical abuse of Indian women is quite high, ranging from 22 percent to 60 percent of women surveyed. It may be noted that many of these studies are of qualitative in nature using very small sample size.

Domestic violence is perpetrated by the men and therefore any studies on the pattern of this type of violence involve an understanding of men's role in the family and home. India is a vast country and subsumes within itself a variety of ethnic groups, cultures, values, traditions and ways of living. Interestingly there is a great variation in these attributes of the population across different regions of the country lending itself to a geographical interpretation in the pattern of domestic violence against women which is the main research focus. As is well known, the perceived status and value of womenvaries greatly across different ecological regions of the country. Many authors have observed a north-south difference in the perceived value of women based on cropping pattern that requires substantive female involvement in agriculture in the latter and their marginal involvement in the former. Likewise, the tribal women have always enjoyed a better status due largely to their egalitarian family structure that rarely distinguishes between men and women. The depressed class/caste women have always played an important role in the sustenance of their family under difficult conditions. The hold of patriarchal values that are so crucial in the perpetration of domestic violence too is not uniform across geographical regions. All these variations in ecology and culture have defined the sexual division of labour, the place and importance of women in the family and the role of men. The extent of domestic violence against women is thus related to these dimensions.

However, the Indian society is passing through a difficult phase in history. While modern development is paving the way for the general acceptance of the new values which insist on gender equality and free competition between the sexes in the fields of economy, education, administration and arts, traditional secular and egalitarian values are being sidetracked by a heightened concern for the past which has acquired the character of a "revivalist" movement. The two forces are mutually contradictory and antithetical. Modernization, if properly articulated, will ensure a better deal for women. Cultural revivalism will commit them to their traditional roles hastening the process of female subordination. The revivalist tendencies are greatly responsible in changing the role of men in the family and are in a way responsible for an increased violence against women both at home and outside. It is in this context that the present research assumes nuances of meanings.

STEP FAMILIES

MEANING

Step families are very common now-a-days. Many people enter new relationships as step families with the same expectations they entered their first marriage. They expect that the family will function just like a first marriage family. They expect everyone to get along quickly and the step family to integrate quickly. The reality may be quite different and it pays to understand and deal with the complexities of stepfamilies.

FEATURES OF STEP FAMILIES

Step-familes are unique in several ways:

- The bond between the parent and the biological child existed before the marriage.
- The spouse gets an instant family upon marriage, rather than slowly through childbirth.
- Often one of the child's biological parent lives elsewhere.
- The children may have visitation and move between homes.

Step parents than in families where both parents are still together.

- The ex-spouse will often be involved in co-parenting with one of the spouses in the new relationship.
- Some or even all of the new family members have already experienced loss through divorce or death.

CREATION OF STEP FAMILIES

The creation of the step family is basically depend on the environment. Forming a step family is a unique opportunity to start over, to rebuild a life with a partner and to share the responsibilities of raising children. For some couples things work well but many people find the realities of stepfamily life are hard to manage. The step families are created when one person who has children marries, or cohabits, again. Of course this can happen after a death, but nowadays it's much more common after divorce, or after the breakdown of a live-in relationship.

EFFECTS OF SPLIT BETWEEN PARTNERS

Whenever such type of step families are created, lots of tensions between the partners generally exists. During any split between two co-habiting partners, there is often a lot of trauma and bad feeling. And sometimes the adults concerned are so busy with their own upset and grief, that they do not have much time for their children–or for explaining things to them. Unfortunately, the youngsters in such situations often feel completely bewildered. They have loyalties to both parents, but they are forcibly removed from one of them. They may also hear very strong criticism of each parent by the other, and yet they are expected to 'be a good boy' or to 'be a nice girl' and do not make a fuss. Meanwhile, they often feel they do not know exactly what's going on, but that they hate the changes. They also feel quite strongly that they have not asked for all this upset in their lives. This is a very important point for adults to remember.

No matter how difficult life is for the grown-ups in all of this, they should take on board that it can be absolutely terrifying for the children – and mostly that the kids would give anything for the split not to have happened. This is not true for every child of course, but it does seem to be the feeling of the vast majority of them.

REWARDS OF STEP FAMILIES

As we now that stepfamilies have many rewards. Couples who have children from a previous marriage or relationship do not have a leisurely adjustment to (re-) married life, though. There is no honeymoon period. The first two years are the period of greatest challenge.

COMPLEXITY AND CHALLENGE IN STEP FAMILIES

Relations with the outside parent (former spouse(s), etc.) are complicating. Couples must create a boundary around their marriage relationship and (in neo-traditional stepfamilies) become a real parenting team. There is a continuum of complexity and challenge in stepfamily situations. Among the less complex and less challenging and disruptive stepfamily situations is one where the man is the non-custodial parent of the only stepchildren, so they are present only at certain holiday, vacation and other designated periods. Among the more complex, more challenging situations are those with children—especially adolescent children—from multiple previous relationships. Major challenges for step families include: Resolving complex insider and outsider roles and boundaries. Initially, expect bonds between parents and children to be stronger than those between marriage partners.

KEY TASKS

There are four key tasks for successfully forming a step family which are as follows:

- Creating a satisfying new marriage relationship.
- Gradually integrating the stepparent into the life of the stepchildren.

- Managing change.
- Creating rules for dealing with former spouses.

The stages of stepfamily transition are:

- **Fantasy:** The stepfamily will be just like a biological family, maybe better. Denial is operating. The couple must give this up in order to succeed.
- **Immersion:** The first year or two are challenging with lots of confusion, conflict and feelings of isolation. This is the period when couples need to be very flexible, pragmatic, willing to abandon preconceptions, and persevering - do not give up.
- **Adaptation:** New relationships formed. Members begin to have a sense of belonging, insider-outsider splits are less prominent and gains outweigh losses.
- **Disruption:** Children who reach pre-adolescence (ages 11-16) can disrupt the stepfamily adaptation and conflict will re-emerge with possible regression to another immersion-like stage.
- **Re-adaptation:** Going through the initial immersion stage with adolescent children is much more challenging because their normal developmental needs for separation and independence from the family are in conflict with the need of the stepfamily to form new family bonds and relationships.

There are two basic adaptation models for stepfamilies:

- **Neo-traditional:** Responsibility is shared for parenting. The non-biological parent(s) gradually assume a parental role with all children.
- **Matriarchal:** The woman has children from a previous relationship. She basically takes all responsibility for parental decisions with her children. The man serves as parenting helper but does not attempt to fill the father role and defers to her in parenting matters. The success of this adaptation depends on the woman being interested in being in charge and on the man being willing to accept a secondary role in parenting.

LEGAL STATUS OF STEP FAMILIES

Although, historically, stepfamilies are built through the institution of marriage, and are legally recognized, it is currently unclear if a stepfamily can be both established and recognized by less formal arrangements, such as when a man or woman with children cohabits with another man or woman outside of marriage. This relationship is becoming more common in all Western countries.

Historically and to this day, there appear to be many cultures in which these families are recognized socially as de facto families. However, in modern Western culture it is often unclear as to what, if any, social status and protection they enjoy in law.

The stepparent is a "legal stranger" in most of the U.S. and has no legal right to the minor child no matter how involved in the child's life they are. The biological parents (and, where applicable, adoptive parents) hold that privilege and responsibility. So if the biological parent does not give up his or her parental rights and custody of the child, the other parent's subsequent marriage cannot create a parental relationship without the biological parent's written consent before a "child" reaches adulthood. In most cases, the stepparent can not be ordered to pay child support.

With regard to unmarried couples, one can easily imagine such social and legal recognition, most notably in the case of common law marriage. Unmarried couples today may also find social recognition locally through community consensus.

Still, it is not at all clear what formal parenting roles, rights, responsibilities and social etiquette should exist between "stepparents" and their "stepchildren." This often leaves the parents in unexpected conflicts with each other, their former spouses and the children.

For all the confusion which stepparents may feel, it is often even less clear to the stepchildren what the interpersonal relationships are, or should be, between themselves and their stepsiblings; between themselves and their stepparent; and even between themselves and their birth parents. These relationships can be extremely complex, especially in circumstances where each "stepspouse" may bring children of their own to the home or in households where children are expected to actively participate in each of the newly created families of both birth parents.

Although most stepfamilies can agree on what they do not want to be for one another, they are often hard pressed to agree upon what they do want to be for one another. This makes it difficult for everyone in the family to learn their roles. It is especially difficult for the children, because the roles and expectations of them change as they move between the homes and families of both of their birth parents.

STEPPARENT ADOPTION

Stepparents can become legal parents to their stepchildren through the process of stepparent adoption. Both biological parents, if living, must consent or agree to the adoption. When a stepparent adopts a stepchild, either the non-custodial parent of the child willingly gives up his or her parental rights to the child, or the court terminates the parental rights of a biological parent if there is evidence of abuse or neglect to the child. If a parent is not involved in the child's life, the court can terminate that biological parent's rights on the grounds of abandonment. Grounds for abandonment in most states are no contact between the parent and child for at least one year.

It is important to check with local laws when looking to complete a stepparent adoption. While having the non-custodial parent consent to the adoption is the easiest way to complete a stepparent adoption, it is still possible to have one completed when they either do not consent, or cannot be located.

If the biological parent who is not involved in the child's life cannot be found, a stepparent adoption can still occur. Typically, a public notice must be published in the newspaper for 30–45 days, stating the intention to have the biological parent's rights terminated, and the intent for the stepparent to adopt the child. If the biological parent does not respond to the notice, then the stepparent adoption will continue as though the absent parent consented to the adoption. Stepparent adoption also can occur if the other biological parent is deceased.

GAY AND LESBIAN MARRIAGES

In modern English, gay has come to be used as an adjective and occasionally as a noun, referring to the people, especially to men, and the practices and cultures associated with homosexuality. The term's use as a reference to homosexuality may date as early as the late 19th century, but its use gradually increased in the 20th century.

By the end of the 20th century, the word gay was recommended by major style guides to describe people attracted to members of the same sex. At about the same time, a new, pejorative use became prevalent in some parts of the world.

In these days, Gay marriage is becoming fashionable in every country. Many countries are starting to legalize this union. However, according to a survey, mostly older people are against this same-sex marriage while younger ones are more acceptable towards it.

Same-Sex Marriage.

People supporting the gay marriage are saying that:

- We are solving the world's most serious problem—overpopulation.

- It was practiced from the ancient times. In ancient Greeks, homosexuality was highly respected. They believed that it inspires youth to become worthy members of the community.
- The only thing that should matter in marriage is love.
- It does not hurt society or anyone in particular.

And people who are not supporting this union say that

- The legalization of homosexual marriage will quickly destroy the traditional family.
- It's against the definition of marriage. Also, some groups are changing the term 'marriage' "one man and one woman" to "two persons."
- It may lead to other immoral behaviours.

Many gay and lesbian people are in committed same-sex relationships. These relationships are equivalent to heterosexual relationships in essential psychological respects. Homosexual relationships and acts have been admired, as well as condemned, throughout recorded history, depending on the form they took and the culture in which they occurred. Since the end of the 19th century, there has been a movement towards increased visibility, recognition and legal rights for homosexual people, including the rights to marriage and civil unions, adoption and parenting, employment, military service, and equal access to health care.

Gay and Lesbain marriage is a legally or socially recognized marriage between two persons of the same biological sex or social gender. Since 2001, ten countries and various other jurisdictions have begun legally formalizing same-sex marriages, and the recognition of such marriages is a civil rights, political, social, moral, and religious issue in many nations. The conflicts arise over whether same-sex couples should be allowed to enter into marriage, be required to use a different status (such as a civil union, which either grant equal rights as marriage or limited rights in comparison to marriage), or not have any such rights. A related issue is whether the term marriage should be applied.

One argument in support of same-sex marriage is that denying same-sex couples legal access to marriage and all of its attendant benefits represents discrimination based on sexual orientation; several American scientific bodies agree with this assertion. Another argument in support of same-sex marriage is the assertion that financial, psychological and physical well-being are enhanced by marriage, and that children of same-sex couples benefit from being raised by two parents within a legally recognized union supported by society's institutions. Court documents filed by American scientific associations also state that singling out gay men and women as ineligible for marriage both stigmatizes and invites public discrimination against them. The American Anthropological Association avers that social science research does not support the view that either civilization or viable social orders depend upon not recognizing same-sex marriage. Other arguments for same-sex marriage are based upon what is regarded as a universal human rights issue, mental and physical health concerns, equality before the law, and the goal of normalizing LGBT relationships. Al Sharpton and several other authors attribute opposition to same-sex marriage as coming from homophobia or heterosexism and liken prohibitions on same-sex marriage to past prohibitions on interracial marriage.

One argument against same-sex marriage arises from a rejection of the use of the word "marriage" as applied to same-sex couples, as well as objections about the legal and social status of marriage itself being applied to same-sex partners under any terminology. Other stated arguments include direct and indirect social consequences of same-sex marriages, parenting concerns, religious grounds, and tradition.

Like this, many people around the world are talking about the pros and cons of gay marriage. But what is the status of this marriage in India? We are hearing news only from other countries. Lets understand the India's situation in this issue.

Gay marriages are happening in India. What most Indians are thinking is it is imported from Western part of Asia or from America. You can find the examples of same-sex intercourse in ancient Hindu temple walls and gateways.

Some interesting facts from India:

- In June 2003, about 35 men, many wearing jewelry and lipstick, took part in a rare gay pride march in Kolkata.
- The Internet has given the gay community a relatively safe way to connect. So many gay sites are coming into India like, www.indiangayclub.com, www.gaymarriage.com.
- Telephone gay counseling is now available in major cities, like Delhi.
- The first gay men's conference in the sub-continent was held in India, which was organized by The Humsafar Trust, a support group for gay-marriage.
- Bombay Dost, India's only gay and lesbian publication.
- Aanchal, a helpline and counseling centre for lesbian and bisexual women in Mumbai.
- AMALG India—a dating service operates like a matrimonial for lesbians and gays.

Like many other countries, Gay Marriage is supported by one group and not supported by another one. However, there's not many supporters of gay movement compared to the opponents. In India, homosexuals remain victims of violence in different forms supported by the society.

We all confident that Indian people never ever support this type of marriage. To prove this confident, here are the some points:

- In India, marriage is life's most important event and no family is complete without children.
- In India, homosexual acts are illegal. We are already having a law from 1885 to avoid unnatural sexual activities. India is the only country having this type of laws. An interesting thing on the incident, when Queen Victoria framed this law in 1885. This law makes homosexual acts between men illegal but does not technically cover lesbians. When it was told to extend this law to address female homosexuality as well, she refused to believe that such acts between women were possible.
- The Indian Supreme Court and government told that homosexuality cannot be legalized in India as the society disapproves of such behavior.
- From 1860 to 1992, only 30 cases were there in courts under this homosexual law. Out of the 30 cases, 18 were non-consensual, 4 were consensual of which 3 were before 1940 and 8 were unspecified.
- Many cases are filled against the gay people under public nuisance law.
- When a film 'fire' on Gay Marriage was released in India, it faced a lot of issues. The theatres in which this powerful story of two sisters-in-law who fall in love was screened, faced a serious problems.

A protracted legal battle has finally come to an end. In a landmark ruling, the Delhi High Court scrapped parts of Section 377, a colonial law that criminalised gay sex – and indeed anything other than heterosexual vaginal intercourse – in India. Hence, consensual sex involving two adults of the same sex can no longer be a criminal offence.

The importance of this verdict cannot be understated. This is the first time that an Indian Court has gone on record to say that sexual minorities are not second-class citizens, and that they cannot be discriminated against. Granted, the anti-gay law was seldom used to secure convictions. However, for decades, the police and sometimes society at large used the law as an excuse to persecute gay men and women, who were harassed, blackmailed, detained or raped, unable to seek any protection or justice from the law. In addition, the law was also a significant impediment to fighting HIV/Aids among sexual minorities.

More importantly, the ruling may finally pave the way for sexual minorities to lead open lives, and ultimately to provide them with legal equality. At least, that's the hope.

But is it too soon to be that optimistic? No sooner had the judgment been passed than all the religious groups in India started opposing it. While the law minister has said that the Congress-led government will study the judgment carefully, the main opposition party, the Hindu nationalist Bharatiya Janata Party, is firmly opposed to it. Gay sex is immoral and unnatural and Indian society does not approve of it, they say. The usual pseudo-arguments invoking a nebulous notion of "Indian culture" also abound.

There is a very real worry that in order to appeal to the religious groups, and regional political parties, the government might choose to appeal the decision to the Supreme Court, though preliminary reports suggest otherwise. After all, only a few days ago, after initially conceding that it might consider scrapping the law, the home ministry backtracked the next day when the news made front-page headlines in national newspapers, triggering opposition from religious groups. Even if the government does not, religious groups and opposition parties have indicated that they will challenge the ruling.

DOMESTIC VIOLENCE IN GAY AND LESBIAN RELATIONSHIPS

Domestic violence in lesbian and gay relationships has been an under-researched area. Its importance, however, is beginning to be recognised and investigated. The available research literature includes bodies of knowledge that relate generally to people experiencing violence within same-sex relationships, as well as research that is more specifically focussed on the experiences of either gay men or lesbian women. Same-sex domestic violence also refers to abuse in the context of same gender relationships. Transgender people (who may identify as gay/lesbian, bisexual, hetero-sexual or other sexualities) and bisexual people may experience domestic violence in the context of same-gender or opposite gender relationships. Transgender and bisexual people may experience domestic violence in different ways and have to deal with different challenges when accessing services. However, many of the experiences of abuse and barriers to services would also be relevant for transgender and bisexual people. This overview highlights issues and implications of domestic violence in lesbian relationships and makes reference to general issues and to issues confronting gay men where these are useful.

Domestic Violence in Gay and Lesbian Relationships defined as 'the irrational fear and hatred of homosexuals' and heterosexism as 'the use of heterosexuality as the dominant and institutionalised form of sexual identity' for dominance and privilege. Abusive partners can rely on homophobia or heterosexism as a tool to control their partner. This type of abuse can involve:

- 'Outing' or threatening to out their partner to friends, family, police, church or employer;
- Telling their partner that s/he will lose custody of the children as a result of being 'outed';

- Telling a partner that the police or the justice system will not assist because the legal justice system is homophobic;
- Telling a partner that the abusive behaviour is normal within gay relationships and convincing the abused partner that s/he does not understand lesbian or gay relationships and sexual practices because of heterosexism.

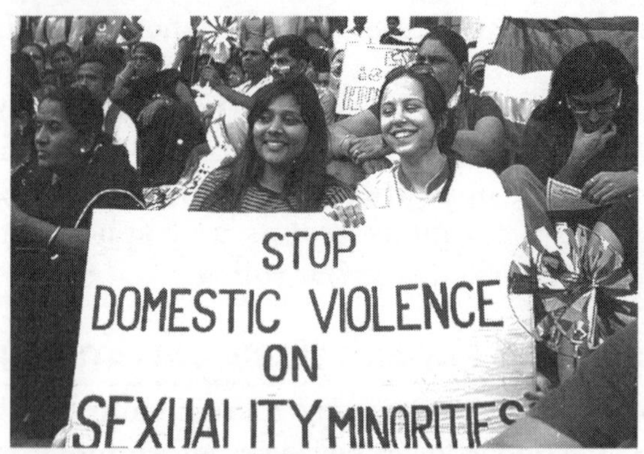

Violence Against Women Act applies with Equal Force in cases when the Victim and perpetrator are of the same sex.

For gay men and some lesbians living with HIV or AIDS, there are related and specific forms of abuse. Although HIV or AIDS can also affect heterosexual people, for gay people, there could be the specific abuse of being threatened to be 'outed' by their abusive partner if they did not wish their sexual identity to be disclosed, thereby impacting on their employment and social relationships, as well as the additional perception or fear of the police or justice system as not being receptive to their needs because of homophobia. Although HIV/AIDS does not cause domestic violence, it can be a factor in abuse; for example, the inability to resist unsafe sex in the context of sexual assault, and threatening to reveal a person's HIV status. HIV status has been shown to influence gay men's decision making about staying in abusive relationships. Victims of same-sex domestic violence who are HIV positive may also feel they have no other support apart from their abusive partner. If the abusive partner is HIV positive, the victim may feel guilty about reporting the abusive partner to the police as this may be perceived as betraying the gay community. Some patients in special care AIDS units have reported that they experienced violence in their relationships only after their HIV status had seroconverted and, in some cases, their abusive partners withheld medication from them. One pilot study involving 81 people, comprising mostly gay men but also including some lesbians and heterosexuals, explored participants' experiences of HIV/AIDS and domestic violence. It revealed that (of those who experienced domestic violence), most lived in a constant state of fear, including the fear of abusers disclosing their HIV status to parents or to employers without their consent.

Merrill highlighted the 4 most common misconceptions about same-sex domestic violence as the following:

1. An outbreak of gay male domestic violence is logical (because all or most men are prone to violence), but lesbian domestic violence does not occur (because women are not prone to violence);
2. Same-sex partner violence is not as severe as when a woman is abused by a man;
3. Because the partners are of the same gender, it is mutual abuse, with each perpetrating and receiving 'equally';
4. The perpetrator must be the 'man' or the 'butch' and the victim must be the 'woman' or the 'femme' in emulation of heterosexual relationships.

Misconceptions such as these, also derivative of homophobic assumptions, can contribute to the isolation of abused gay and lesbian people by masking the realities of domestic violence in same-sex relationships and placing the safety of the abused person at continued risk.

DIVORCE

Divorce (or the dissolution of Marriage) is the final termination of a marital union, canceling the legal duties and responsibilities of marriage and dissolving the bonds of matrimony between the parties. In most countries divorce requires the sanction of a court or other authority in a legal process. The legal process for divorce may also involve issues of spousal support, child custody, child support, distribution of property and division of debt.

Divorce Profoundly Affects Children.

In most Western countries, a divorce does not declare a marriage null and void, as in an annulment, but it does cancel the married status of the parties. Where monogamy is law, this allows each former partner to marry another. Where polygyny is legal, divorce allows the woman to marry another. Divorce laws vary considerably around the world. Divorce is not permitted in some countries, such as in Malta and in the Philippines, though an annulment is permitted. A referendum have been held in Malta 28th May 2011 to determine if the public wishes to make divorce legal.

From 1971 to 1996, four European countries legalised divorce: Spain, Italy, Portugal and the Republic of Ireland.

LEGAL SEPARATION

Legal separation (sometimes "judicial separation," "separate maintenance," "divorce a mensa et thoro", or "divorce from bed-and-board") is a legal process by which a married couple may formalize a de facto separation while remaining legally married. A legal separation is granted in the form of a court order, which can be in the form of a legally binding consent decree. The most common reason for filing legal separation is to make interim financial arrangements, such as deciding who will pay bills, possess property, and whether alimony is appropriate, prior to a divorce. These financial arrangements are actually what the term "separate maintenance" refers to, and "separate maintenance" is not a synonym for "legal separation."

Furthermore, in cases where children are involved, a court order of legal separation often makes temporary arrangements for the care, custody, and financial support of the children (for the time being). Thus, part of the court order is a document in child custody. Some couples obtain a legal separation as an alternative to a divorce, based on moral or religious objections to divorce.

Legal separation does not automatically lead to divorce. The couple might reconcile, in which case they do not have to do anything in order to continue their marriage. If the two do not reconcile, and they wish to proceed with a divorce, they must file for divorce explicitly.

THE DIFFERENCE BETWEEN LEGAL SEPARATION AND DIVORCE

Unlike divorce, a legal separation does not put an end to the marriage. During a legal separation, you have a court order that outlines the rights and responsibilities of each spouse while they are living apart. You remain legally married while choosing to live separate lives. Issues that can be addressed in a separation agreement are division of assets and debts, child custody and child support, visitation schedules and spousal support.

The same issues addressed during the divorce process are also addressed in a legal separation agreement. A legal separation can protect your interests until the decision is made to file for divorce. The separation agreement also sets a precedence for the divorce that may follow. If you divorce after a separation and your case goes to court, a judge is likely to assume that since you were satisfied with the legal separation agreement, the agreement should carry over to the divorce settlement agreement. For that reason, it is important that you come to a separation agreement you can live with long term.

Although a legal separation and divorce have, many things in common there are some advantages to obtaining a legal separation rather than a divorce. Those advantages include:

- It allows couples time apart, away from the conflict of the marriage to decide if divorce is what they truly want.
- It allows for the retention of medical benefits and certain other benefits that divorce would bring to an end.
- If your religious beliefs conflict with the idea of divorce, you are able to live separately and retain your marital status for religious beliefs.
- If you are a military spouse, you may wish to remain married for 10 years so that you can take advantage of benefits set up by the Uniformed Services Former Spouse Protection Act.
- Remaining married for 10 years or more also means being able to take advantage of certain social security benefits for a spouse.
- If the decision to divorce is made, the legal separation agreement can be converted into a divorce settlement agreement.

RELIGION

Introduction to Religion. Totemism and Animism. Pluralistic Religion. Monistic Religion. Judaism, Christianity and Islam: *Judaism, Christianity, Islam.* ***Hinduism, Buddhism, Confucianism, and Taoism:*** *Hinduism, Buddhism, Confucianism and Taoism.* ***Sociological Theories of Religion:*** *Durkheim and Functionalism, Weber and Social Change, Marx: Conflict Theory. The Functions of Religion. Emile Durkheim's View on Religion. Karl Marx's Views on Religion. Marx Webers Views on Religion.* ***Types of Religious Organizations. Social Correlates of Religion. Religious Fundamentalism. Religion and Politics. What is the Role of Religion in Society? Global Trends in Religion. New Religious Movement. Religion and Science. Science and Religion in India:*** *Science and Hinduism, Science and Christianity.* ***Religion and Migration. Organization of Religion. Religion and Magic:*** *Magic is a Special Sense, Conclusion.* ***Religion and Mythology:*** *How Religion and Mythology Relate.* ***The Difference between Religion and Mythology.***

INTRODUCTION TO RELIGION

The variety and number of religious organizations and beliefs around the world is so large that sociologists have a difficult time arriving at a single definition of religion. In Western societies, people usually identify religion with Christianity: the belief in Jesus Christ as the Son of God who promises salvation through faith and life after death. Yet religion as a global phenomenon presents a much more complex picture, because most of the world's religions lack the core concepts of Christianity.

At the simplest level religion is the belief in the power of supernatural. These beliefs are present in all the societies and variations seem endless. A belief in the supernatural almost always incorporates the idea that supernatural forces have some influence or control upon the world. The first indication of a possible belief in the supernatural dates from about 60,000 years ago. Archaeological evidences reveal that Neanderthal man buried his dead with stone tools and jewellery. Religion is often defined as people's organized response to the supernatural although several movements which deny or ignore supernatural concerns have belief and ritual systems which resemble those based on the supernatural. However these theories about the origin of religion can only be based on speculation and debate.

Though religion is a universal phenomenon it is understood differently by different people. On religion, opinions differ from the great religious leader down to an ordinary man. There is no consensus about the nature of religion. Sociologists are yet to find a satisfactory explanation of religion.

Durkheim in his 'The Elementary Forms of the Religious Life' defines religion as a unified system of beliefs and practices relative to sacred things that is to say things set apart and forbidden. James G. Frazer in his 'The Golden Bough' considered religion a belief in powers superior to man which are believed to direct and control the course of nature and of human life. Maclver and Page have defined religion as we understand the term, implies a relationship not merely between man and man but also between man and some higher power. According to Ogburn religion is an attitude towards superhuman powers. Max Muller defines religion as a mental faculty or disposition which enables man to apprehend the infinite.

To avoid thinking about religion from a culturally biased point of view, sociologists first define what religion is not.

- First, religion is not necessarily monotheistic, which is the belief in monotheism, or a single deity. Instead, many religions embrace polytheism, or the belief in multiple deities. Still other religions, such as Confucianism, recognize no gods at all.
- Religion is not necessarily a body of moral rules and demands concerning the behaviour of believers. The notion that deities somehow keep track of how believers behave is foreign to many religions.
- Religion is not necessarily a belief in the supernatural, heaven, hell, or even life after death. Confucianism, again as an example, emphasizes acceptance of the natural harmony of the world, not finding truths that lie beyond it.
- Finally, religion is not necessarily an explanation of the origins of creation. The Christian story of Adam and Eve explains the origins

of humanity. Many religions, but not all, have similar myths of origin.

The Creator of the Universe Brahma and the various Symbols of Different Religions.

Having examined what religion is not, sociologists consider what characteristics do constitute religion. Sociologists generally define religion as a codified set of moral beliefs concerning sacred things and rules governing the behavior of believers who form a spiritual community. All religions share at least some characteristics. Religions use symbols, invoke feelings of awe and reverence, and prescribe rituals for their adherents to practice. Religion differs from magic, which involves superstitious beliefs and behaviors designed to bring about a desired end.

Religion has numerous *rituals* and *ceremonies*, which may include lighting candles, holding processions, kneeling, praying, singing hymns and psalms, chanting, listening to sacred readings, eating certain foods, fasting from other foods on special days, and so forth. These rituals, because of their religious nature, may differ quite a bit from the procedures of ordinary daily life. Religious individuals may practice their rituals and ceremonies alone, at home, or within special spaces: shrines, temples, churches, synagogues, or ceremonial grounds.

In most traditional societies, religion plays a central role in cultural life. People often synthesize religious symbols and rituals into the material and artistic culture of the society: literature, storytelling, painting, music, and dance. The individual culture also determines the understanding of priesthood. A priest offers sacrifices to a deity or deities on behalf of the people. In smaller hunting-and-gathering societies no priesthood exists, although certain individuals specialize in religious (or magical) knowledge. One such specialist is the shaman, who the people believe controls supernatural forces. People may consult the shaman when traditional religion fails.

TOTEMISM AND ANIMISM

Totemism and animism are religious forms common to smaller societies. A totem is any species of plants or animals thought to possess supernatural powers. Each group within the society may have its own totem, including associated ceremonies. Totemic beliefs may not be as foreign to the Western mind as first expected; many Westerners have totems. School mascots, symbols, and emblems all constitute totems.

Animism is the belief that spirits, apparitions, angels, or demons inhabit the earth. Either good or bad, these spirits interact with and/or influence humans in a variety of ways. For example, animists believe that malevolent spirits cause demonic possession, insanity, and disapproved behavior. From the animistic perspective, treating unsanctioned actions and attitudes requires praying to good forces and exorcising evil ones. Animism is not limited to small, simple, pre-industrial societies; various Americans in the 1990s believe in the existence of supernatural entities that influence humans.

Totemism occurs among Pacific Islanders and Australian Aborigines. Most American Indian societies had totems as well.

Animism is the traditional religion in Niger and arrived before Islam.

PLURALISTIC RELIGION

Religious pluralism is the belief that one can overcome religious differences between different religions and denominational conflicts within the same religion. For most religious traditions, religious pluralism is essentially based on a non-literal view of one's religious traditions, hence allowing for respect to be engendered between different traditions on core principles rather than more marginal issues. It is perhaps summarized as an attitude, which rejects focus on immaterial differences, and instead gives respect to those beliefs held in common.

Religion and Ethics in World Politics.

The existence of religious pluralism depends on the existence of freedom of religion. Freedom of religion is when different religions of a particular region possess the same rights of worship and public expression. Freedom of religion is consequently weakened when one religion is given rights or privileges denied to others, as in certain European countries where Roman Catholicism or regional forms of Protestantism have special status. Religious freedom has not existed at all in some communist countries where the state restricts or prevents the public expression of religious belief and may even actively persecute individual religions.

Religious pluralism has existed in the Indian Subcontinent since the rise of Buddhism around 500 BC and has widened in the course of several Muslim settlements (Delhi Sultanate, 1276-1526 AD and the Mughal Empire 1526-1857 AD). In the 8th century, Zoroastrianism established in India as Zoroastrians fled from Persia to India in large numbers, where they were given refuge. The colonial phase ushered in by the British lasted until 1947 and furthered conversions to Christianity among low caste Hindus. The rise of religious pluralism in the modern West is closely associated with the Reformation and the Enlightenment.

Religions like Judaism and Islam had existed alongside Christianity in many parts of Europe, but they were not allowed the same freedoms as the established form of Christianity. Freedom of religion encompasses all religions acting within the law in a particular region, whether or not an individual religion accepts that other religions are legitimate or that freedom of religious choice and religious plurality in general are good things.

MONISTIC RELIGION

Monism is the metaphysical view that all is of one essential essence, substance or energy. Monism is to be distinguished from dualism, which holds that ultimately there are two kinds of substance and from pluralism, which holds that ultimately there are many kinds of substance. Monism is often seen in relation to pantheism, panentheism, and an immanent God. Monism is often seen as partitioned into three different kinds:

1. Physicalism or materialism, which holds that only the physical is real and that the mental can be reduced to the physical.
2. Idealism or phenomenalism, which holds the converse.
3. Neutral monism, which holds that both the mental and the physical can be reduced to some sort of third substance, or energy.

Functionalism, like materialism, holds that the mental can ultimately be reduced to the physical, but also holds that all critical aspects of the mind are also reducible to some substrate-neutral "functional" level. Thus something need not be made out of neurons to have mental states. This is a popular stance in cognitive science and artificial intelligence. Eliminativism, which holds that talk of the mental will eventually be proved as unscientific and completely discarded.

Leading religious luminaries and exponents of the Bhagavata Mahapurana.

Just as we no longer follow the ancient Greeks in saying that all matter is composed of earth, air, water and fire, people of the future will no longer speak of "beliefs," "desires" and other mental states. A subcategory of eliminativism is radical behaviourism, a view held by B.F. Skinner. Anomalous monism, a position proposed by Donald Davidson in the 1970s as a way to resolve the Mind-body problem. It could be considered (by the above definitions) either physicalism or neutral monism.

Davidson holds that here is only physical matter, but that all mental objects and events are perfectly real and are identical with (some) physical matter. But physicalism retains a certain priority, inasmuch as:

1. All mental things are physical, but not all physical things are mental.
2. (As John Haugeland puts it) Once you take away all the atoms, there's nothing left.

This monism was widely considered an advance over previous identity theories of mind and body, because it does not entail that one must be able to provide an actual method for redescribing any particular kind of mental entity in purely physical terms.

For some, monism may also have religious/spiritual implications. Recognizing this, some inveigh against the 'dangers of monism,' asserting that in order to resolve all things to a single substrate, one dissolves God in the process. Others say that the "single substrate is God." Theological arguments can be made for this within Christianity for example the Roman Catholic doctrine of "divine simplicity," as well as in many other religions (Hinduism, Ayyavazhi and Judaism in particular). Historically, monism has been promoted in spiritual terms on several occasions, notably by Ernst Haeckel. To the dismay of most modern observers, Haeckel's various ideas often had components of social darwinism and scientific racism.

JUDAISM, CHRISTIANITY AND ISLAM

As societies become larger and more complex, its people become more likely to join monotheistic religions. The three most influential monotheistic religions in world history are Judaism, Christianity, and Islam, all of which began in the Middle East.

JUDAISM

Judaism dates from about 1200 B.C. The first Hebrews were nomads who settled in the land of Canaan near Egypt. Unlike their polytheistic neighbours, the Jewish patriarchs ("leaders") and prophets ("inspired" teachers) committed themselves to one almighty God. They stressed utter obedience to Yahweh in the form of a strict moral code, or law.

The crux of Judaism is the belief that the Divine Lord, Adonai, whose secret, unutterable Name is YHWH (Yahweh/Jaweh).

Jews call their holy text the Tenakh, which Christians call the "Old Testament." Within the Tenakh lie the five books of the Torah, which begins with the creation of the world by God's word. The Torah primarily tells the story of the early Hebrews and Yawheh's communications to Moses, which established laws on worship and daily life.

The Torah plays a central role in Jewish worship. During services in the synagogue, the rabbi removes the Torah (rolled into a scroll) from the ark (a cupboard). The rabbi then carries the scroll, capped with a silver crown, in procession to a lectern, opens it, and reads from it to the congregation.

CHRISTIANITY

Christians believe that Jesus Christ is the Son of God and the "Messiah" (meaning "Christ" and "Annointed One") who saves the world. This global religion first emerged as a sect of Judaism, and in the beginning embraced many Judaic views and practices. Within decades of Jesus' death, Christians began distinguishing themselves from their Jewish neighbors. Much of Christianity's rapid growth in the early years was due to a Greek-speaking Jew and Roman citizen named Saul of Tarsas. Later known as St. Paul, he preached extensively and planted churches in the Middle East, Turkey and Greece. Because Christians refused to worship the Roman Emperor as divine, Romans severely persecuted Christians until the 4th century. At that time, Emperor Constantine made Christianity the official religion of the Roman State. Today, Christianity has grown into an influential force throughout the world, but especially in the West.

The Bible's (the 66 books of the Judeo-Christian Scriptures) "New Testament" (new covenant) is a collection of 26 books and letters interpreting portions of the Tenakh from a Christian point of view. The New Testament also presents a range of unique teachings, such as the writings of St. Paul, which early Christians sent to newly established churches. The authors of the Gospels, or presentations of Jesus' life and teachings, probably wrote them decades later, though contemporary Biblical scholarship on this topic remains inconclusive.

Christianity represents the largest of the world's religions and is also more evenly spread around the globe than any other religion. Christianity claims more than a billion adherents, though Christians belong to many different denominations (groups with a particular theology and form of organization) that sharply divide the religion. The three largest Christian denominations are Roman Catholicism, Eastern Orthodoxy, and Protestantism (which includes such denominations as Methodist, Presbyterian, Episcopalian, and Baptist).

ISLAM

The second largest religion in today's world is Islam, which originated from the teachings of the 7th century prophet Mohammed. His teachings most directly express the will of Allah, the one God of Islam. Moslems, or followers of the Islamic religion, believe that Allah also spoke through earlier prophets such as Jesus and Moses before enlightening Mohammed.

Moslems have five primary religious duties ("The Pillars of Islam"):

- Reciting the Islamic creed, which states that Allah is the one God and Mohammed is His messenger.
- Taking part in ceremonial washings and reciting formal prayers five times every day. During these prayers, worshippers always face towards the holy city of Mecca in Saudi Arabia.

- Observing of Ramadan—a month of fasting when Moslems may have no food or drink during daylight hours.
- Giving money to the poor.
- Making at least one pilgrimage to Mecca.

Messages that Mohammed received from Allah comprise the Islamic scriptures, called the Koran. ("Koran" derives from the Arabic term meaning "to recite.") Because the prophet could not write or read, he memorized Allah's words and later relayed them to his students. After Mohammed's death, his followers wrote down these revelations. The Koran sets forth standards of daily behavior and the Pillars of Islam.

Islam has grown to more than 600 million adherents throughout the world. Most Moslems live in the Middle East, Pakistan, and parts of Africa.

HINDUISM, BUDDHISM, CONFUCIANISM AND TAOISM

The four major religions of the Far East are Hinduism, Buddhism, Confucianism, and Taoism.

HINDUISM

Hinduism, a polytheistic religion and perhaps the oldest of the great world religions, dates back about 6,000 years. Hinduism comprises so many different beliefs and rituals that some sociologists have suggested thinking of it as a grouping of interrelated religions.

Hinduism teaches the concept of reincarnation—the belief that all living organisms continue eternally in cycles of birth, death, and rebirth. Similarly, Hinduism teaches the caste system, in which a person's previous incarnations determine that person's hierarchical position in this life. Each caste comes with its own set of responsibilities and duties, and how well a person executes these tasks in the current life determines that person's position in the next incarnation.

Hinduism is the Predominant and Indigenous Religious Tradition of the Indian Subcontinent.

Hindus acknowledge the existence of both male and female gods, but they believe that the ultimate divine energy exists beyond these descriptions and categories. The divine soul is present and active in all living things.

More than 600 million Hindus practice the religion worldwide, though most reside in India. Unlike Moslems and Christians, Hindus do not usually proselytize (attempt to convert others to their religion).

BUDDHISM, CONFUCIANISM AND TAOISM

Three other religions of the Far East include Buddhism, Confucianism, and Taoism. These ethical religions have no gods like Yawheh or Allah, but espouse ethical and moral principles designed to improve the believer's relationship with the universe.

Buddhism originates in the teachings of the Buddha, or the "Enlightened One" (Siddhartha Gautama)—a 6th century B.C. Hindu prince of southern Nepal. Humans, according to the Buddha, can escape the cycles of reincarnation by renouncing their earthly desires and seeking a life of meditation and self-discipline. The ultimate objective of Buddhism is to attain Nirvana, which is a state of total spiritual satisfaction. Like Hinduism, Buddhism allows religious divergence. Unlike it, though, Buddhism rejects ritual and the caste system. While a global religion, Buddhism today most commonly lies in such areas of the Far East as China, Japan, Korea, Sri Lanka, Thailand, and Burma. A recognized "denomination" of Buddhism is Zen Buddhism, which attempts to transmit the ideas of Buddhism without requiring acceptance of all of the teachings of Buddha.

Confucius, or K'ung Futzu, lived at the same time as the Buddha. Confucius's followers, like those of Lao-tzu, the founder of Taoism, saw him as a moral teacher and wise man—not a religious god, prophet, or leader. Confucianism's main goal is the attainment of inner harmony with nature. This includes the veneration of ancestors. Early on, the ruling classes of China widely embraced Confucianism. Taoism shares similar principles with Confucianism. The teachings of Lao-tzu stress the importance of meditation and nonviolence as means of reaching higher levels of existence. While some Chinese still practice Confucianism and Taoism, these religions have lost much of their impetus due to resistance from today's Communist government. However, some concepts of Taoism, like reincarnation, have found an expression in modern "New Age" religions.

SOCIOLOGICAL THEORIES OF RELIGION

The ideas of three early sociological theorists continue to strongly influence the sociology of religion: Durkheim, Weber, and Marx.

Even though none of these three men was particularly religious, the power that religion holds over people and societies interested them all.

They believed that religion is essentially an illusion; because culture and location influence religion to such a degree, the idea that religion presents a fundamental truth of existence seemed rather improbable to them. They also speculated that, in time, the appeal and influence of religion on the modern mind would lessen.

DURKHEIM AND FUNCTIONALISM

Emile Durkheim, the founder of functionalism, spent much of his academic career studying religions, especially those of small societies. The totetism, or primitive kinship system of Australian aborigines as an "elementary" form of religion, primarily interested him. This research formed the basis of Durkheim's 1921 book, 'The Elementary Forms of the Religious Life', which is certainly the best-known study on the sociology of religion. Durkheim viewed religion within the context of the entire society and acknowledged its place in influencing the thinking and behaviour of the members of society.

Durkheim found that people tend to separate religious symbols, objects, and rituals, which are sacred, from the daily symbols, objects, and routines of existence referred to as the profane. Sacred objects are often believed to have divine properties that separate them from profane objects. Even in more-advanced cultures, people still view sacred objects with a sense of reverence and awe, even if they do not believe that the objects have some special power.

Durkheim also argued that religion never concerns only belief, but also encompasses regular rituals and ceremonies on the part of a group of believers, who then develop and strengthen a sense of group solidarity. Rituals are necessary to bind together the members of a religious group, and they allow individuals to escape from the mundane aspects of daily life into higher realms of experience. Sacred rituals and ceremonies are especially important for marking occasions such as births, marriages, times of crisis, and deaths.

Durkheim's theory of religion exemplifies how functionalists examine sociological phenomena. According to Durkheim, people see religion as contributing to the health and continuation of society in general. Thus, religion functions to bind society's members by prompting them to affirm their common values and beliefs on a regular basis.

Durkheim predicted that religion's influence would decrease as society modernizes. He believed that scientific thinking would likely replace religious thinking, with people giving only minimal attention to rituals and ceremonies. He also considered the concept of "God" to be on the verge of extinction. Instead, he envisioned society as promoting civil religion, in which, for example, civic celebrations, parades, and patriotism take the place of church services. If traditional religion were to continue, however, he believed it would do so only as a means to preserve social cohesion and order.

WEBER AND SOCIAL CHANGE

Durkheim claimed that his theory applied to religion in general, yet he based his conclusions on a limited set of examples. Max Weber, on the other hand, initiated a large-scale study of religions around the globe. His principal interest was in large, global religions with millions of believers. He conducted in-depth studies of Ancient Judaism, Christianity, Hinduism, Buddhism, and Taoism. In The Protestant Ethic and the Spirit of Capitalism (1904/1958), Weber examined the impact of Christianity on Western thinking and culture.

The fundamental purpose of Weber's research was to discover religion's impact on social change. For example, in Protestantism, especially the "Protestant Work Ethic," Weber saw the roots of capitalism. In the Eastern religions, Weber saw barriers to capitalism. For example, Hinduism stresses attaining higher levels of spirituality by escaping from the toils of the mundane physical world. Such a perspective does not easily lend itself to making and spending money.

To Weber, Christianity was a salvation religion that claims people can be "saved" when they convert to certain beliefs and moral codes. In Christianity, the idea of "sin" and its atonement by God's grace plays a fundamental role. Unlike the Eastern religions' passive approach, salvation religions like Christianity are active, demanding continuous struggles against sin and the negative aspects of society.

MARX: CONFLICT THEORY

Marx's views on the sociology of religion came from 19th century philosophical and theological authors such as Ludwig Feuerbach, who wrote The Essence of Christianity (1841). Feuerbach maintained that people do not understand society, so they project their own culturally based norms and values onto separate entities such as gods, spirits, angels, and demons. According to Feuerbach, after humans realize that they have projected their own values onto religion, they can achieve these values in this world rather than in an afterlife.

Marx once declared that religion is the "opium of the people." He viewed religion as teaching people to accept their current lot in life, no matter how bad, while postponing rewards and happiness to some afterlife. Religion, then, prohibits social change by teaching nonresistance to oppression, diverting people's attention away from worldly injustices, justifying inequalities of power and wealth for the privileged, and emphasizing rewards yet to come.

Although people commonly assume that Marx saw no place for religion, this assumption is not entirely true. Marx held that religion served as a sanctuary from the harshness of everyday life and oppression by the powerful. Still, he predicted that traditional religion would one day pass away.

THE FUNCTIONS OF RELIGION

- Providing solutions for unexplained natural, phenomena.
- Supplying a means for controlling the natural world.
- Religion tends to support the normative structure of the society.
- Furnishing a psychological diversion from unwanted life situations.
- Sustaining the existing class structure.
- Religion serves as an instrument of socialization.
- Religion suppports other social institutions.
- Religin may both promote and retard social change.
- Religion may both reduce and encourage conflict in groups.

EMILE DURKHEIM'S VIEW ON RELIGION

The Elementary Forms of Religious Life (1915)

- Viewed religion as a reflection of society.
- Religion functioned to bring about social cohesion (holding the group together) (folk society).
- Religious beliefs and rituals function to restrain deviant behavior and bring about conformity to existing normative structure (heaven = reward) (hell = punishment).
- Religion functions to provide a vehicle through which cultural traditions and values are transmitted from generation to gereration (religious beliefs make cultural values sacred).

KARL MARX'S VIEWS ON RELIGION

- Viewed religion as a reflection of society.
- Marx felt that primitive religion arose from the ignorance of preliterate peoples of natural processes.
- In complex societies the dominant ideas would tend to legitimize the interests of the ruling class. (The Divine Right of Kings).
- Marx felt religion was used to exploit the masses of people.
- Marx said: "Religion is the sigh of the oppressed creature, the sentiment of a heartless world and the soul of soulless conditions. It is the opium of the people. The abolition of religion and the illusory happiness of men is a demand for thei real happiness."

MARX WEBERS VIEWS ON RELIGION

The Protestant Ethnic and the Spirit of Capitalism (1905)

- Saw a strong connection between religious values and economic value.
- Weber differed from Marx and Durkheim in that he thought that religious values tend to influence and shape the social structure rather than reflect it.

— Weber maintained that the value system of Protestantism formed the framework upon which capitalism was developed.
— "The Protestant Ethnic", work hard, save money, get ahead; "Righteous and good Christians live frugally."

TYPES OF RELIGIOUS ORGANIZATIONS

All religious organizations involve communities of believers. However, these communities come in different forms. The most basic of these today are religious movements, denominations, sects, and cults.

RELIGIOUS MOVEMENTS AND DENOMINATIONS

A form of social movement, religious movements involve groups of people who join together to spread a new religion or to reinterpret an old one. Religious movements are large and typically "open" in their memberships, especially at the beginning of the movement. Examples of religious movements include the early Christian movement, the Lutheran movement that began the Protestant Reformation, the Reformed Jewish movement, and, more recently, the Islamic Fundamentalist movement.

The agendas of many religious movements fade when their leaders lose influence, are replaced, or die. A movement that survives, though, may become a church, or denomination. In other words, the movement may become a formal organization of adherents with established symbols, rituals, and methods of governance.

Millennial movements periodically come on the scene, especially at the turn of centuries and millennia. Popular among some fringe Christian sects and cults, millennialists anticipate large-scale catastrophe, disaster, and social changes—perhaps in fulfillment of Scriptural prophecies. They may also look forward to the collective salvation for a particular group of believers—usually themselves.

Denominations are large and established religious bodies that have a hierarchy of religious leaders operating within a formal, bureaucratic structure. Most denominational members are born into and grow up within the body. Examples of Christian denominations include the Roman Catholic Church, the United Methodist Church, and the Antiochian Orthodox Church.

SECTS AND CULTS

Sects are smaller, less organized religious bodies of committed members. They typically arise in protest to a larger denomination, like the Anglicans originally did to the Roman church in the 1500s. They may have few or no leaders and little formal structure. Convinced that they have "the truth" and that no one else does (especially not the denomination against which they are protesting), sects actively seek new converts. People are more likely to join sects than to be born into them.

As sects grow, they may mellow and become an institutional religious body instead of a protesting group. If a sect survives over an extended period of time, it will probably become a denomination. In contrast to sects, denominations normally recognize each other as legitimate churches (though doctrinally in error) and peacefully coexist.

At first cults may resemble sects, but important differences exist. Cults, the most transient and informal of all religious groups, provide havens for people who reject the norms and values of larger society. Cultists may live separately or together in communes. Additionally, cults normally center around a charismatic leader who focuses on bringing together people of the same turn of mind. The potential for abuse and other problems in such environments has led American society to give much negative press to cults, although not all cults are necessarily abusive.

SOCIAL CORRELATES OF RELIGION

Religious persuasion seems to relate to political persuasion. Jews and Catholics are more likely to be Democrats than are Protestants. Likewise, Jews tend to be more liberal than Catholics, who tend to be more liberal than Protestants. Membership of religious organizations also correlates positively with socioeconomic status. Baptists tend to be comparatively poor, whereas Anglicans, Presbyterians, and Jews tend to be wealthy. And Catholics, on average, have higher income than comparable members of Protestant denominations do. However, these generalizations are just that: general statements. You must interpret statistics with caution. For example, some of the poorest people in the United States belong to the Roman Catholic church, and considerable differences exist among members of the Protestant churches. Some of the wealthiest people now belong to the Church of Jesus Christ of Latter Day Saints (the "Mormons").

Are religion and politics more or less intertwined today than they were four years ago?

The vast majority of Americans—around 95 percent—say they have some form of religious beliefs: in God, heaven, the divine inspiration of Scriptures, and so on. Whereas 70 percent of Americans belong to religious organizations, only about 40 percent claim to attend weekly synagogue or church services. People in upper social groups, on average, attend church more regularly than those in other social groups. Similarly, Catholics, on average, attend church more regularly than Protestants. Members who actually attend services tend to actively participate within their congregations.

RELIGIOUS FUNDAMENTALISM

Fundamentalism refers to "black-and-white" thinking that opposes modernism, or progressive thinking about religion and other social topics. Fundamentalist groups tend to oppose anything that challenges their religious group's interpretations and opinions. For instance, Christian fundamentalists believe in the literal inerrancy of the Bible, and often define themselves as theologically and ritually conservative, or even "not Catholic."

To most Americans the term fundamentalist conjures up images of "Bible-thumping" Protestants, which is far from the case. All denominations and groups—including those of religions like Islam—contain fundamentalist members. These activists usually think that they have a corner on "the truth," and do not tolerate other viewpoints or practices.

The most well-known fundamentalist denominations in the United States are the Assemblies of God, the Southern Baptist Convention, and the Seventh-Day Adventists. Organizations such as these often become politically active, and support the conservative political "right," including groups like the Moral Majority.

RELIGION AND POLITICS

In India, religion plays an quintessential role in the day to day life and is a major influence over the Indian population and culture. Religion covers every aspect of the life of the Indian people. Religion also plays an important role in the politics of India. A political party's acknowledgment of a particular religion decides the support it gets. The main religions of India are Hinduism and Islam and each religion has parties from whom support is given.

An excellent example of this negative action towards religions is the long standing struggle between Hindus and Muslims. Hindus have an extremely keen hatred for Muslims and vice versa. Many believe this is because the religions are not related in any way. The other religions of India are quite similar to that of Hinduism. However, Islam is completely unto itself.

The eighty-percent of the Indian population that supports Hinduism does so because of the mix of traditions and beliefs. The Hindu religion has no specific books of worship like Bible in the case of Christians. The Hindus have many religious books like the Rig-Veda, Upanishads and Bhagwad Gita. There are multiple Gods in the Hindu religion ranging from gods, like Shiva and Vishnu, to plants and animals, to rivers, rocks and planets.

In contrast to the Hindu population, India has the second largest population of Muslims in the world. Only Indonesia has more Islamic followers than India. Initiated by Arabian merchants in the beginning of the eighth century the religion only caught on near the twelfth century.

Differing from other religions such as Buddhism, Jainism, and Sikhism, Islam is not based on Hinduism. Islam's main beliefs are worldwide friendship and absolute belief in Allah, their only god.

Christianity is another prominent religion within the country of India. In 1544 Saint Francis Xavier brought Christianity to India. In the following years Portugal, Denmark, Holland, Germany and Great Britain followed in Xavier's footsteps and came to India to preach the benefits of Christianity. In the eighteenth and nineteenth centuries, Catholics and Protestants began to preach. The churches and preachers built educational facilities.

Currently there are approximately thirty million Christians in India. The way in which the government of India is set up allows for a large amount of control by the political parties. Religion greatly affects these political parties. Often so much so, that what looks like a religious hate crime can be, in actual fact, a complete political occurrence.

The governmental system of India allows for a lot of control by political parties thus, there is heavy competition for power between parties. The government of India is based on a constitution not unlike that of the United States. India is a group of twenty-five sovereign, secular, democratic states and seven Union Territories. A President, Vice-President, Council of Ministers and a Prime Minister make up the executive branch. The country of India is in many facets similar to The United States of America.

The political parties that control these positions are split into two categories, National and State parties. State parties are supported in majority in four or less states however, if more than four states are there then the party becomes a National party with more influence and power in the government of India. The confrontations between parties are caused by the excessive power the parties have within the government. Hate-crimes amongst the three religions of India run rampant. However, only recently have any of these crimes been directed at Christians.

The effect of religion on Indian politics is staggering. The hatred that has for so many years put the country in political strife does not seem to be declining. The feelings between all three religions, especially Hinduism and Islam, are just as strong as ever. The structure of the Indian government sets up for the confrontations between the opposing political parties. These confrontations are the basis for power struggle within the Indian government.

WHAT IS THE ROLE OF RELIGION IN SOCIETY?

Many people believe that religion occurs only in the church, temple, or other spiritual places of gathering. They see religion and society as complete, separate entities. While this view may appear correct on the surface, a closer look at religion and society reveals that the two are not separate at all, but intricately interconnected and codependent. In reality, religion is inherent within many aspects of society, and religious beliefs inevitably affect areas such as politics, economics, and cultural values. This relationship between religion and society can be seen in Islamic religion and Muslim social culture, Christianity and economics, and Buddhism and politics. In each of these religions we can find insight for understanding the society in which it exists, as well as in the comparison of these religions and their relationships with society. There are no known societies that do not have some form of religion, although religious beliefs and practices vary from culture to culture. All religions involve a set of symbols, invoking feelings of reverence, linked to rituals practiced by a community of believers. The three most influential monotheistic religions in world history are Judaism, Christianity, and Islam. Sociological approaches to religion have been most influenced by Marx, Weber, and Durkheim. Churches, sects, cults, and denominations are four main types of religious organizations. Religious movements have played a central part in the development of religion in general and have influenced other aspects of social life. Although the influence of religion has declined, religion is certainly not on the verge of disappearing. Religion may take a variety of forms. Religious beliefs give meaning to life, and the experiences associated with them provide personal gratification as well as a release from the frustrations and anxieties of daily life.

Since the earliest prehistoric times, faith and belief have always been part of the texture of human society: neither in the past nor in the present is it possible to find a society in which religious issues have not been raised. It may even be claimed that human endeavour in the realm of religion and belief has been more strenuous and longer-lasting than his efforts in the area of knowledge and art. In many historical events, religion can be seen to have dominated all relationships. All members of society belong to the church. Churches, sects, denominations and cults are religious organizations. The differences among them lie in their relationship to the social environment. It is possible that in many human societies, unfavorable economic conditions, stagnation and backwardness may coexist with religious belief. But this coexistence does not necessitate any causal relationship; one cannot be presented as the cause of the other. The espousal of a religious doctrine influences the way a person views the world, and when an entire society of people adopt the same religious beliefs, cultural, political, and economic changes are inevitable. Elements of society such as geography, resources, and outside pressure also influence religious doctrines. Although societies and religions differ a great deal from one to the next, the connections between the two are inherently evident and similar in all religions. The power of humans to control events is limited, so religion provides an institutionalized means of adjusting to life's uncertainties and risks. Humans need to feel that the world is comprehensible, that there is a rhyme and reason for the events of their lives.

Religion is generally perceived as fulfilling social functions such as preserving and solidifying society, creating a community of believers, cultivating social change, and providing a means of social control. It also fulfills personal functions such as answering ultimate questions, providing rites of passage, and reconciling people to hardship. In traditional societies, religion was seen as an authority in all areas of social life; few activities remained unaffected. In modern industrial societies, religion is one of many specialized institutions. As a result, religion has been stripped of many of its former functions and must compete with other institutions for authority. To the extent that individuals accept religious teachings and incorporate them in their business, politics, education, or family life, religion has an indirect influence on these spheres. But religious institutions have no direct authority or control.

Today a religious organization may declare that one should give generously to the poor, or that using birth control is a sin, but individuals or society may not take these declarations seriously. Whenever Religion has played its proper role, Society has been able to maintain a relatively peaceful balance and harmony among the generally disruptive and self-interested tendencies of politics and economics. Thus, the original role of Religion prefigures the idea that Civil Society is needed to balance and correct the competing interests of State and Capital in modern societies.

Four roles listed above are crucial for a healthy Civil Society. The proper role of Religion has been:

- — to provide a higher purpose and meaning to human life, one that transcends limited self-interest;
- — to counter-balance the disruptive tendencies of politics and economics with shared values able to hold society together;
- — to provide a moral structure in which human beings act (social ethics);
- — to stand up for and protect the "little ones," those who are marginalized and oppressed within the usual power schemes.

In Christianity, the Catholic Church provides an example of a religion that has been institutionalized and become a powerful economic force. After its excommunication with the Eastern Orthodox Church in the middle Ages, it began to develop independently from the state. Although it remains unclear which change occurred first, society's economic shift or the Catholic Church's own change to capitalism, the fact that they both made the shift to capitalism at the same time suggests a significant relationship between Christianity and the economics of the time frame through the institution of the Catholic Church. Events in an economy—levels and standard of living or governmental market interference—influence such things as church attendance or religious beliefs.

GLOBAL TRENDS IN RELIGION

The Persistence of Religious Persecution

Religious faith and freedom in this century has trod through the valley of the shadow of death, surviving the Soviet gulags, the Nazi death camps and Cambodian killing fields. With the end of the "Cold War" many have thought this persecution, or to be specific, martyrdom, was a thing of the past. But that is not so. Although it has dropped from its yearly rate of 330,000 at the height of the Soviet state, it still averages 160,000 martyrs a year. You can add to that figure of premature death, a ten-fold number of religious people who are harassed, arrested, tortured, imprisoned for their faith each year.

Many of those killed fall under the definition of martyrdom, that is people whose lives are prematurely taken due to their religious faith. Religious persecution, in Africa or Asia is by no means directly solely against Christians. Muslims suffer persecution in Algeria, Bahais lose their lives in Iran. And Shik violence against Hindus continues in Northern India.

Recently, the U.S. Congress has brought the country of Sudan under close scrutiny for the religious persecution it propogates. The government's professed goal of re-Islamization of the country has led to a state of civil war with the mostly Christian or animistic southern regions. The atrocities are numerous, and include aerial bombardment, massacres, slavery, and even reports of crucifixions.

The Attraction of Militant Fundamentalism

As Martin Marty and Scott Applebee note in their five volume Fundamentalism Project, religious fundamentalism is on the rise, not just within Islam or Christianity, but is also being felt among Buddhism and Judaism.

Religious/racial-based states did not pass away with the fall of apartheid in South Africa. The May 1996 elections in Israel showed that religious nationalism is alive and well among Judaism and capable of becoming a "monster double" of Hamas Islamic fundamentalism. For a fascinating look at this trend, I recommend The Revenge of God, by French author Gilles Kepel. He profiles the resurgence of Islam, Christianity and Judaism in the modern world from the mid '70s till now.

A Rising Growth Rate of Islam

The third trend which frames out our century-end context is Islam. Among world religions, Islam ranks as the fastest growing faith. This is demographically driven by higher birth rates in the third world rather than by an increase in conversion growth. Worldwide, the number of Muslims has doubled since 1970 to 1.2 billion adherents.

Religious researchers project the growth of Islam to roughly 2 billion adherents by 2025, Christianity to 3 billion. That is out of a projected world population of 8 billion. It is less likely that Islam will overtake Christianity in sheer numbers in the mid-range future. Yet in long-range statistical scenarios reaching out to the year 2200 and beyond, it is possible that Islam will surpass Christianity in absolute number of adherents.

A Shift to Non-white Christianity

This century has witnessed the shift of Christianity from a white to a majority position of non-white followers. Today more than 60% of all Christians come from non-white races outside Europe and America.

This shift in the center of Christian gravity southward into the Third World has come about from evangelical Protestant church growth in Africa, Asia and Latin America. This produces all kinds of interesting facts, such as the largest Presbyterian church in the world is not found in Scotland, but in Seoul, Korea, or the statistical mean follower of Christ today is under 20 years old, living in Asia, with a per capita income of less than $600 a year.

The Growth of Pentecostal and Non-denominational Christianity

While much has been said about the decline of the mainline in the U.S., the resurgence of Pentecostal Christianity has more than made up for it. Estimates put the number of new non-denominational churches in this country at 100,000 since 1980.

The 20th century will no doubt be remembered as a Pentecostal century, given the birth of the modern Pentecostal/Charismatic movement and its dramatic growth. In less than three generations, this movement in the West, Africa and Asia has grown to an amazing 520 million making it the second largest expression of faith within the Christian movement, second only to Roman Catholics.

Harvey Cox chronicles how Pentecostal spirituality will reshape religious experience in the new century in his 1995 book, Fire from Heaven.

A Decline of Tribal Religions

By 2000, the tribal religions will have shrunk from 6.5% in 1900 to 1.6% of world population. There are still some 5,000 ethno, folk or tribal religions among indigenous people of Africa and Asia number. By mid-century many western religionists thought that these ethno-religionists would disappear by 2000. And despite large numbers converting to Islam or Christianity in Africa, the world's ethno-religions remain stable at about 100 million. But in terms of keeping pace with world population, they have shrunk from 6.5% to 1.6% of world population.

A Level Growth of Nonreligious Persons

While the growth rate of Islam is increasing, the worldwide growth of persons professing no religion, whether agnostics, freethinkers, atheists or non-religious humanists appears to have plateaued since the collapse of communism. Statistically speaking, the non-religious population of the world is holding its own at 15% of the world's population, and will continue so as we enter the 21st century.

An Increase of Pluralism in Society

Another century-end trend which religionists encounter is growing pluralism. This is particularly so within the West. Driven by multiculturalism and internationalization of the West, increasing diversity in society is both an opportunity and a challenge for religions. Increasing cultural diversity and interfaith contact can offer opportunities for mutual understanding, growth and dialogue. On the other hand, the challenge of modernity, with its relativism and individualism continues to undermine traditional beliefs that once informed shaped various common creeds, producing culture wars between traditionalists and progressives.

An Increase of Women in Pastoral Roles

At the turn of the century, except for sectarian groups such as the Salvation Army and various Pentecostal and Holiness groups, women preachers were not common. Barriers to women's ordination in major U.S. denominations began falling in the fifties and sixties.

As a result, we have seen the emergence of women in pastoral roles, from 1% at the turn of the century to more than 5% of all clergy worldwide. In the U.S., women comprise 10% of all clergy. And for every woman in the pastorate, there are 30 others working in ministry roles, whether in religious education or outreach.

Although there is still resistance to women in pastoral roles, the basic trend of women in church and pastoral leadership continues to grow and appears irreversible. Some suggest the impact of increasing numbers of women in the pastorate will bring more emphasis on nurture and growth, with more holistic models of communities and congregations.

The Anticipation of A New Millennium

This tenth trend has been in the making for 30 years, but is intensifying as each month passes. Reaching far beyond human understanding, the attraction of the year 2000 has crossed all fields, from commerce to government, from humanitarian causes to religious work.

From a cultural perspective, the year 2000 or C.E. 2000 is the bimillennium of our global civic calendar. For a religious perspective, A.D. 2000 is the 2,000th anniversary of the birth of Jesus. As we approach the millennial years, 1999 to 2001, a whole constellation of congresses and commemorations are being planned to mark the advent of the third millennium.

Australia is sponsoring the year 2000 Olympics in Sydney. Ten years after reunification, Germany is hosting a World's Fair under the theme, "Humanity, Technology and Nature" for 40 million visitors. England is spending close to 700 million pounds to stage a Millennium Exhibition on Time at Greenwich. Rome is expecting some 25 million visitors for the Holy

Year 2000. And the Holy Land is expecting an increase in tourists for the bimillennium.

Never has humanity had such an opportunity to prepare itself for a more peaceful and spiritual new millennium.

NEW RELIGIOUS MOVEMENT

Of all types of social movements in contemporary India, religious and sectarian movements have, by and large, been predominant. For a long time religious ideas have often been the language of protest, innovation and expression of individuality as well as separate identity. They provide an enormous scope for reinterpretation in order not only to legitimize the aspiration of various sections of the population but also to justify changes in the existing order of social relationships. Clearly, these movements meet the emotional and spiritual needs of those suffering from the destructive impact of colonialism, modernization and globalization in a familiar world. Research on new religious movements, therefore, always has a unique significance in a country like India where religious faith is a dynamic conditioning factor for the vast majority of people. Furthermore, India has long been known for being "a Guru Factory" and these spiritual teachers have played an active role in bringing solace to the masses at the global forum. Consequently, they have an international influence as well.

The term New Religious Movement (NRM) is used by sociologists of religion to classify faith-based communities or groups of relatively recent origin. The NRM can be completely new (even if, like the Church of Scientology, it borrows heavily from other religions), or be an offshoot (sect) of an established religion.

The term new religious movement evolved in part to replace the term cult, which has colloquially taken on many negative connotations. New religious movements need to possess substantial differences from older, more traditional religions. However, the amount of difference required varies from user to user. Some academics attribute the term only to unique religions, while others include movements such as the Church of Latter Day Saints and Jehovah's Witnesses – both of which are non-mainstream denominations within the religion of Christianity.

Even the requisite age of a movement varies from speaker to speaker. The term frequently applies to post-World War II religions, but it also is commonly applied to religions created within that last two hundred years. A few even extend the definition to anything originating since the 17th century. There is agreement that the term does not make sense for religions or denominations dating to before the 17th century. For example, mainstream Protestant denominations are not included among the new religious movements.

Today religion is becoming more and more progressively global. Studies on the ideas and activities of an international Guru and the reason for her/his wealth in the age of globalization is a necessity to understand the real role of a Guru in terms of religious or secular communications and the widespread challenges she/he still faces.

New religious movement (NRM), the generally accepted term for what is sometimes called, often with pejorative connotations, a "cult." The term new religious movement has been applied to all new faiths that have arisen worldwide over the past several centuries.

NRMs are characterized by a number of shared traits. These religions are, by definition, "new"; they offer innovative religious responses to the conditions of the modern world, despite the fact that most NRMs represent themselves as rooted in ancient traditions. NRMs are also usually regarded as "countercultural"; that is, they are perceived (by others and by themselves) to be alternatives to the mainstream religions of Western society, especially Christianity in its normative forms. These movements are often highly eclectic, pluralistic, and syncretistic; they freely combine doctrines and practices from diverse sources within their belief systems. The new movement is usually founded by a charismatic and sometimes highly authoritarian leader who is thought to have extraordinary powers or insights. Many NRMs are tightly organized. In light of their often self-proclaimed "alternative" or "outsider" status, these groups often make great demands on the loyalty and commitment of their followers and sometimes establish themselves as substitutes for the family and other conventional social groupings. NRMs have arisen to address specific needs that many people cannot satisfy through more traditional religious organizations or through modern secularism. They are also products of and responses to modernity, pluralism, and the scientific worldview.

RELIGION AND SCIENCE

The relationship between religion and science has been a focus of the demarcation problem. Somewhat related is the claim that statements about the world made by science and religion may rely on different methodologies. Religion, is often argued to rely on revelation and faith. The methods of science are elaborate and science does not depend on faith. Some scholars say the two are separate, as in John William Draper's conflict thesis and Stephen Jay Gould's non-overlapping magisteria, while others (Thomas Berry, Brian Swimme, Ken Wilber, et al.) propose an interconnection. The Pew Forum has published data on attitudes about religion and science.

SCIENCE AND RELIGION IN INDIA

Are science and religion in India really at war—a battle between provable facts and unprovable myth? Reason against wishful thinking? And how does India approach this apparent conflict? Argument over the Big Bang... The sun at the center of the universe... A round world... Evolution...

These concepts have been used as flails to rail against the reality of a God cause at the center of life and the universe. There is a pretense that science and religion are at war. But this modern invention is just that: a man-made "reality"...or rather a myth of man's making.

SCIENCE AND HINDUISM

Although the Subcontinent has felt the heat of conflict between many of its religions, even to the point of massive bloodshed in instances like Partition, there has not been the same level of enmity between science and religion in India so often found in Western cultures—particularly in places like America.

In India, many Hindus point to the pliability to be found within the breadth of Hinduism. They meld evolution into ancient legends and point to the on-target order of incarnations within the ten avatars of Vishnu, beginning with Matsya the fish and ending with Kalki, the machine man, who is yet to come.

Hindu astronomical texts appear as early as 1200 BC. Astronomy and astrology were intertwined. Indian philosophers and scientists, both Hindu and Buddhist, were aware of atoms and advanced theories regarding their nature.

While certain points they advanced have since been disproven (such as the timeless, durationless nature they proposed for atoms—an error Western science was also party to), it is certain that India did not languish in a state of scienceless unreason before it was colonized.

SCIENCE AND CHRISTIANITY

"Ever since the creation of the world, His invisible nature, namely His eternal power and deity, has been clearly perceived in the things that have been made."

For centuries, faith in God was the greatest motivation for exploring science. It was seen as a way to know God better, through understanding of His creation.

From the earliest times, Christians like Augustine and Thomas Aquinas employed reason as a way of knowing God. Christianity, at its core, has not been about escape from truth and reason...but about embracing it to seek out what is real.

Many of our most ground-breaking scientists have been Christians: Copernicus, Kepler, Galileo, Newton, Lemaitre, Descartes, Ohm, Faraday, Pasteur, Mendel...the list goes on.

Some were monks dedicated to science as a part of their worship for God. Others, like Newton and Boyle, wrote both scientific and theological works. These people were not merely nominal Christians, but people for whom faith was deeply important.

RELIGION AND MIGRATION

Religion has a role at different levels of community life:

— It can be simply a very personal issue of the spiritual life of an individual.

— It may be an aspect of community building, or even the basic reason for community life.

— At states level religion can be an instrument for political and social cohesion or on the opposite a state chooses to leave religious issues completely in the private sphere. It can also become a major cause of conflicts within a state.

All three aspects may play a role for migration processes. There are individual implications, but also community life and the internal cohesion within a country may be influenced by this factor.

RELIGION AND THE INDIVIDUAL

(A) *RELIGION AND PERSONAL IDENTITY*

For many persons religion is a component of their personal identity. A specific creed is part of the life of persons. The teachings, the traditions and the habits of a specific religion will influence these people in their behaviour, their way to approach situations and how they relate to each other. The personal value system will be based on the religion the person belongs to. Religion can be an important part of an individual, and even if such a person will migrate to another country he or she will carry with her these elements of faith. Even if loosing all material possessions this religious capital will stay with this migrant.

It is known that religion can become an important part of the identity of a migrant, even if he had rather little interest in religious matters until leaving his home country. In the new situation, having left behind family and social links and feeling the need to defend his identity, religion becomes an important factor. It depends on what the person will find in the host country if this part of identity will become a positive or negative element for the personal integration process. Will religion become an isolating force or a possibility to find a sense of belonging. Faith and religion may become an instrument and opportunity to experience a transnational identity. The migrant may find a way to define for him a new identity made out of components from both societies. This would not be just a summary of two cultures but something new, which could be important for both societies. Precondition for this is an open and tolerant receiving society, where also the local faith communities practise these values.

(B) *RELIGION MAY PLAY A ROLE IN MANY PARTS OF DAILY LIFE*

Religious convictions and rules influence the life of a believer nearly in all parts of daily life: health and health care are affected. For instance migrant women may find it difficult to access health services because of their religious education.

The education of children depends widely on religious values, so as the whole issue of family life. The well-known conflict between first and second generation in migrant communities is also a consequence of this. Religious laws influence the working conditions, the rhythm of the workday and free time; clothing and food rules may not allow people to work in certain places. The question of equal rights for men and women may create critical situations.

RELIGION AND COMMUNITY LIFE

Often religion is not only a personal conviction; the believer may be requested to participate actively in community life, as non-renounceable part of his faith. If these believers migrate abroad they will put much energy into finding or rebuilding in the host country some kind of faith community where to live their faith.

Religious migrant communities can have a positive or a negative role within the integration process. They may give to the migrant in the first phase of integration, a feeling of home and belonging which will give him or her a sense of security and mutual support, but if these communities are closed and/or marginalised by the host society creating a ghetto like situation this could be contra-productive for the integration process. Parallel societies may rise and communication between the host society and that of the migrants could become difficult.

On the other hand if such a community is an open or even a mixed community with migrant and *autochthonous* members, where a common faith is the binding link this may become a bridge, and allow a smoother integration process.

Finally, the religious community has an important role in directing migration movements. It is known that migrants often choose the country or even the town they aim to because of having religious links in that place. They may know that in a certain city lives a community which professes the same creed and where it will be easier to feel at home and to receive support. In this way religion may even become a pull factor for migration. I'm thinking for instance at the migration of Christians from the Middle East.

RELIGION AND STATE

As long as society was considered homogenous Governments did not consider the question of religion a priority although no society has ever been totally homogeneous. Migration has always existed. Today migration is a structural factor of all states and all must cope with heterogeneous societies, and latest with the events of 11th September in New York the religious question has become an issue in migration politics.

The role of religion within the legal system and the functioning of a state is very different in the various parts of the World. There can be total division between religion and state, or there are other states where religion is a dominant factor for legislation and functioning of all parts of the state. In between these two solutions there is a large spectrum of diverse approaches to the question.

Problems may arise if migrants who come from one system must cope with the opposite situation in the host country. An example could be a person or a whole community which comes from a state with Sharia law and will now have to live in a secularised state of the industrialised World. The religious needs, the strong convictions and values the person is carrying with her may create conflicts with the legislation and the way of life in the host country. Social cohesion may be at risk.

This becomes even more important if religious institutions of the country of origin continue to influence the life of migrant communities in a country of immigration.

As we saw before religion can be important for all parts of daily life and legislation and public administration will have to keep this in mind. The public health system may be affected. Labour legislation needs to consider the issue. In schools and all educational institutions the problem may arise.

Commerce and industry may be influenced by consumer behaviour based on religious rules; the same may be said for cultural and scientific work.

Reassuming these reflections it can be said:

- Migrants need to express and to live their religious creed. This can be a tool for stabilisation, avoiding marginalisation, meanwhile the loss of religious identity will lead to the loss of ethical values and these migrants will be even more disoriented and uprooted in the host society.
- Similar religious communities of the host society and of the migrant communities should promote exchange and sharing, becoming like this a bridging tool for integration, avoiding marginalisation and frustration of migrant faith communities which may lead to radicalisation.
- The religious communities of the host society may be enriched by the contributions of migrant religious communities. Intercultural experiences can be experienced and eventually transferred into other sectors of social life. The so-called social capital, of basic importance for social cohesion, will be incremented if the religious factor of migration movements is governed correctly. All components of the society and governments will have to work together to pursue this aim.

THE ROLE OF CHRISTIAN CHURCHES

(A) WHY SHOULD CHURCHES FEEL THE NEED OR THE WISH TO BECOME ACTIVE IN THIS FIELD?

Churches are faith communities and as such have a religious mandate, which makes them act. The basis of the Christian mandate is a book, the Bible and from this text in a theological process Christians elaborated their code of conduct. As far as migrants are concerned there are precise rules which Churches should respect. Here are some of these, which are as follows:

- Human dignity must be respected in any case and in any situation.
- Christian should love their neighbour and migrants may become neighbours.
- Migrants must be received and protected.
- All human beings are "citizens in the household of God", that means they are equal and have rights and duties like citizens, they are not only guests or "Gastarbeiter."
- Christians are convinced that there is a total truth, but only God is the owner of it. Human beings have only a partial insight of this truth. Therefore Christians must respect the conviction of others, even if these do not correspond to their own.
- The Christian faith has at the same time an universalistic approach, believing in the Universal Church, and on the other hand the individual spirituality is part of a personal faith. Both aspects are part of the Christian identity.

(B) THE ROLE OF CHURCHES CAN BE LOOKED AT FROM TWO POINTS OF VIEW

On the basis of their creed churches may be involved in the field of migration in different ways:

- In order to protect human dignity, rights and freedom churches will become active parts of the society, similar to other social actors.
- Churches will also act as faith communities, which have their creed in common with certain migrant communities.

Churches as active players in the society defending migrants' and refugees' rights

Churches are faith communities and as such feel like responsible parts of the organised civil society. They cannot live in a spiritual ghetto. This responsibility within the state makes them active players as far as social cohesion is concerned. They intend to be involved in advocacy for the respect of Human Rights and the dignity of all human beings. They should do this in the same conditions as other parts of the society and should not claim for a privileged status—this is at least the position of many

Protestant Churches. Working for issues of social and economic justice they will not distinguish between migrants of their own faith and those belonging to other creeds.

They will work in two directions:

- advocacy work on migration and asylum policy and legislation.
- solidarity programmes to support individuals.

Advocacy: As far as migration policy is concerned they will monitor and lobby decision making processes in order to promote a correct migration policy which respects values so as human rights, solidarity, burden sharing, non-discrimination.

Speaking on religious issues churches will also have to lobby and to monitor on religious freedom, not only freedom for their own communities but also for the freedom of other creeds and faith communities. Churches must insist on correct legislation on religious freedom. There must be full respect for religious minorities, also if these are not Christian. In this context the whole debate on common values and on how far faith communities can push their right to promote certain religious rules which may seem not compatible with values which are perceived basic in the host community. A balance must be found between religious freedom of a certain religious community and the basic values and the freedom of all other citizens and communities which the state must protect.

Solidarity and support to individuals: In Europe churches promote their own programmes of mutual support for migrants in order to allow their integration and full access to equal rights in all parts of civil life. They run programmes on housing, education, access to the labour market, counselling for migrants and refugees, legal assistance and empowerment by leadership training and support to migrant associations.

- They promote language schools and courses for vocational training, support refugees who wish to study at university.
- They run homes for refugees and for unaccompanied minors, for mothers with small children and other vulnerable groups.
- They protect women who became victims of trafficking and violence.

ORGANIZATION OF RELIGION

Religion has been around as long as human beings have been around, indeed, the origins of religion and the worship of gods is so far back in human consciousness that a start point cannot be precisely identified. It is known that human beings have been worshiping gods prior to recorded history. Religion has been an attempt to find meaning and value in life, and it also seems to have been something that we have always done. Mythology and ritual helped to evoke a sense of significance to members of monotheistic faiths. When science and rationalism took over at the end of the nineteenth century as the means to provide an explanation of the world and its mysteries.

Christian theology also began to emphasize rational discourse and attempted to replace mysticism, intuition, and liturgy with reason. Christian religions, particularly the Roman Catholic Church, follow a certain structure in the manner in which they set up their organization. The pyramidal structure inherent in the organization was well suited to rational discourse. The pyramid has three main properties:

- Unity of Command
- Span of Responsibility
- Stacking

In *Unity of command*, there is one person at the top, God, or in the case of the Roman Catholic Church, his representative, the Pope. This is the single person ultimately responsible for the performance of the organization. The span of responsibility encompasses the monitors, those who observe the people under them and report to the unity of command. In the Roman Catholic Church, there are several layers of monitors.

Directly under the Pope are the Cardinals; under the Cardinals are the Archbishops, then the Bishops and finally the Priests. Even in the *span of responsibility* there is a hierarchy of subordinates and superiors and a definite structure to their relationship. At the bottom of the pyramid is the stacking. These are the individuals that are controlled by the hierarchy in the pyramid above them. They represent the lay people and worshipers in the Catholic religion. In order to reach the apex of the pyramid, the members of the bottom layer must travel up the hierarchical chain in a structured fashion.

Conversely, the flow of information down the pyramid is not subject to the same delays and interpretations, since the information to be disseminated is not subject to question as is the information originating at the bottom of the pyramid. This is reminiscent of the structure of many organizations in Western society and the cause of conflict when eastern organizations, such as Japanese manufacturing with their more organic structure, attempt to work within Western hierarchical standards.

The Industrial Revolution and the rise of manufacturing in the late eighteenth century called for a new method of management in order to keep control over the vast quantities of people and materials now available. The style that evolved from this complexity was 'scientific management', the proponent of which, Frederic Winslow Taylor attempted to create a form of cheap, passive, interchangeable people that mirrored the cheap, passive, interchangeable machine parts readily available in this new era.

Factory efficiency had been enhanced by standardization of product design, component parts, and tools, and by the widespread use of standard, engine driven machine tools. What remained non-standardized was the labor component.

Scientific management came at the end of an era where the church found itself in competition with science for the hearts and minds of the people. Science was rational, objective, and could prove its hypotheses by reason. Religion relied on faith to prove its point, and when religion attempted to apply scientific principles to theology, it seemed to contradict the literal meaning of the Bible (Armstrong, 2000). Human beings began to focus on the here and now rather than the afterlife, while at the same time responding to the basic ideas of the Protestant Reformation that work is a profound moral obligation, and a path to eternal salvation. The focus is on this world and materialism. The individual's obligation is self-discipline and systematic work.

Discouraged from placing their fate in the hands of religion without scientific proof, people looked for another place to put their faith, while still retaining their underlying need to be a part of a something bigger than themselves. They were trapped in the ritual and myth that was religion.

Since its beginnings, religion has been a psychic prison. Religion had created a reality and structure to the world that people were reluctant to live without. With the perceived failure of religion to keep up with the times, people sought to replace it with another structure that offered the same organization, and rules. People were trapped in the artificially constructed reality of the religious hierarchy, and rather than using the disruption of the Industrial Revolution to transform their thinking, they chose to replace the religious organizational structure with the scientific management structure of an organization. They paired themselves with industry and organizations in hopes that they would be delivered from the uncertainty of religion's place in the modern world.

In doing so, people merely exchanged their place at the bottom of one pyramid for a place at the bottom of another, different pyramid. This is the beginning of the idea of organizations as machines-routine, efficient, reliable, and as cultures, sharing a common societal value. Organizations operated in the same manner as religions, but disguised themselves with the trappings of scientific reasoning. There is structure and order to the organization, and everyone knows their place in the hierarchy and what is expected of them. German sociologist Max Weber identified some of the basic elements of this bureaucratic structure, which have parallels in religious hierarchy. Bureaucratic organizations tend to have:

- Formal rules and behavior bounded by rules (Religions also have formal rules and their behavior is bound by those rules)
- Uniformity of operations continuity despite changes in personnel (The church runs the same, no matter if the Pope dies or if there is a sudden influx of adherents. Everyone has a recognized place in the order)
- Functional division of labor based on functional specialization (The Pope is the ultimate authority on all matters concerning the Catholic

Church. Cardinals, Archbishops, Bishops and Priests all have their areas of responsibility and do not exceed their authority in those areas. A layperson's job is to worship, and the Priest's job is to direct their worship and answer questions pertaining to their worship. Questions outside the Priest's scope of authority are passed up to another specialist, the Bishop)

- Rational allocation of tasks (Priests are responsible for their parishioners, Bishops are responsible for making sure Priests understand their responsibility, and interceding between the Priests and the Archbishops. Priests are not ready for the responsibilities of a Bishop or above, so they are not given information they do not need)
- Membership constitutes a career (Membership constitutes a career, Priests aspire to become Bishops, Cardinals, and even Pope one day)
- Prescribed authority-legally defined (There are definite guidelines for recourse, a rigid structure parallels the pyramid and is defined by the Pope, the Bible, or the Church)
- Specific sphere of competence (Priests are not expected to know as much as Bishops, Bishops do not have the knowledge and decision making power of Archbishops and so on up the chain. They are authorities in their own areas of the world and church structure. The Pope is assumed most competent because of his position. All decisions made by the Pope are to be received as if they came from God)
- Legally based tenure (God given tenure).

This bureaucratic structure also serves as the model for organizations as political systems. Managers and church leaders both talk about authority, power, and superior-subordinate relationships. These are the activities of the ruler and the ruled. The Roman Catholic Church is an authoritarian structure, and this coincides with the hierarchical way it is run. The Pope is an authoritarian manager who wields considerable power as a result of his position in the organization. This power is stable, and clearly defined. There are no challenges to this autocratic system, because not everyone has an equal right to rule the Church. The nature of the pyramidal structure keeps control concentrated under a few individuals, and conflict within the structure minimal, and mostly covert. As a political system, the religious organization is well insulated against change. Failure to adapt to the current political system in the organization results in excommunication (firing). The position and importance of the individual in this type of organizational structure is directly related to his position in the pyramid.

RELIGION AND MAGIC

Since religion represents knowledge, and knowledge is not absolute in itself but occurs in a context of action – there is a source of ritual. Psychologically there is a relation between action-inaction and anxiety: so – the war dance, and bonding, and the healing – medicine – dance. There is a psychic translation: from ritual to consciousness to action or directly from ritual to action; ritual may also catalyze communication between the conscious and the autonomic or animal modes. It is never given that formal knowledge – whether science or religion – results in or induces the "best" action; formal philosophy contains concepts but no final definitions of the nature of "best" actions.

Belief in magic may stem from a desire to reunite symbol-object: this is the expression of "life-as-flow".

Consideration of magic is interesting because it shows the existence of a religious sense. However, it will be seen that this sense is not special or compartmentalized, nor is it born essentially of fear and weakness. The sense can be seen as human essence, and its expression can be occasioned by fear and tragedy but also by beauty and wonder.

Earlier discussion showed religion to be intrinsically connected to symbolic-iconic consciousness and this consciousness to be psycho-biologically based: It is an adaptation that enables a single species, human beings, to be adapted to multiple, previously unknown, mental and physical environments without genetic change. This adaptation, adaptability through symbolic-iconic thought, is orientation to all of existence. It was also noted that the process of symbolic knowledge was:

1. Idea-hypothesis,
2. Test.

Magic identifies symbol with object: And, therefore, symbol manipulation is object control–magical influence.

Belief in magic implies: belief in extraordinary influence: Impossible influence from the skeptical view, and belief that hypothesis formation is reality. Actually, there is "magic" in the idea-test scheme of symbolic-iconic consciousness—power from the inside of substance – atom – grew from ideas, the theories of nuclear physics.

A *hypothesis* – there is power in magic. *Explanations;*

Social power: belief and trust lead to *heightened action;*

Personal power: for the same reason; and

Power over nature and the real: magical thought and magical action may, of course, be "mistaken".

But the alternative–rational thought and action–may be impotent in crucial situations. In these situations magic provides the leap-of-faith: which may sometimes succeed; and this success is enhanced by "magical" intuition.

MAGIC IS A SPECIAL SENSE

An example of magical thinking in twentieth century civilization: institutional science is the answer to the world's problems. This is surely a belief, since the belief has not been shown to be true. That science is not the full answer is not a criticism of science, but may be a criticism of the nature and magnitude of the investment in science

Belief in magic may stem from a desire to reunite symbol-object: this is the expression of "life-as-flow". Despite this psychological interpretation as a possible weakness, if magical thought were essentially and excessively destructive, it would be self-eliminating. Magic is sometimes necessary, "useful" orientation to existence. Myth and ritual create a magical environment.

CONCLUSION

Magic and religion have gone hand-in-hand for centuries. It is impossible to create a distinct line between magic and religion, because they both have relatively the same concept. There are other reasons as well. They both depend on the belief of supernatural powers.

Magic was used in ancient Native American tribes for many purposes. An example of this exercise is blowing powdered tobacco up a patients nose to rid him or her of evil spirits. A well-known practice is the art of *Voodoo.* Voodoo is when you make a doll with a distinct likeness of a person, and inflict pain upon the doll to duplicate the damage on the victim. To do this, a personal item of the victim must be taken, and ceremonies must be performed, specifically for that person.

Magic is used in many ceremonies for many different purposes. These ceremonies are called rites of passage. Some rites are birth, naming, puberty, marriage, illnesses, and death. The ceremonies may include magical objects, words, songs or places. Other ceremonies are performed to pray to the people's gods for help; rain dances, protection against diseases or parasites, preparation for planting season, harvests, hunting and fishing ceremonies, and returns of victorious warriors. Some ceremonies may be a sort of two-in-one deal. For example, ceremonies that heal one person may also protect the entire community.

RELIGION AND MYTHOLOGY

The relationship between religion and mythology is one of continuing debate. While some historians stress that religion and mythology have similar origins, others emphasize the theological divide between them. With the many stories, folklores and legends that have been passed down through generations, the difference between religion and mythology can be, at times, hard to distinguish.

Generally speaking, religion is a set of beliefs and practices held by a group of people. The definition can be extended to include beliefs regarding moral codes, the nature and purpose of the universe and a system of worship. In most cases, religion is institutionalized, and the followers of that faith use its associated stories to recruit new worshippers and remind fellow followers of the religion's tenets.

Mythology, on the other hand, is a body of stories belonging to a particular culture or group. These stories, which usually contain supernatural elements, are about a culture's origin, history, ancestors and heroes. They are intended to be instructional or inspirational without necessarily imparting a system of belief or moral codes.

While some scholars insist that myths are religious and sacred, others maintain that this is not always the case. The real discrepancies occur when attempting to determine whether or not a religious story is a myth.

HOW RELIGION AND MYTHOLOGY RELATE

Religion and mythology are closely linked because they both involve explanations (or stories) of creation, human life and how things came to be. In addition, both often include supernatural elements.

However, this is where the discernible similarities end. Beyond these basic principals, all other creation stories can debatably be classified as either religious or mythological or both.

According to classicist scholar Robert Graves, a religious story is only a myth to those who do not belong to or understand that religion. Alternatively, folklorists (those who study folklore) believe that myths are sacred stories that describe how things came to be. Therefore, any religious story that accomplishes this is a myth.

THE DIFFERENCE BETWEEN RELIGION AND MYTHOLOGY

One concrete difference between religion and mythology is that mythology only refers to a collection of stories or myths, while religion encompasses an entire set of beliefs and practices, stories included.

Another difference is that the word "myth" often connotes that a story is false. Consequently, many are opposed to the categorizing of sacred stories as myths. However, keep in mind that myths aren't necessarily fictional stories. It depends, of course, on how you define a myth.

To further complicate things, individuals' interpretations of religious stories vary. Just as the definition of myth depends on the person, so too does the interpretation of a religious story. As a result, the lines between fact versus fiction in both myths and religious stories are blurred and negotiable, depending on a person's belief system and interpretations.

KINSHIP SYSTEM

Introduction. Kinship Systems. Kin Selection. Structural Principles of Kinship: *Family Systems, Genealogy and Descent, Marriage and Divorce, Dowries, Bridewealth, and Inheritance.* ***Descent — "Hereditary Succession":*** *Descent Group, Rule of Descent, Determinants of Descent Systems.* ***Kinship Usages,*** *Avoidance.* ***Kinship Systems in India:*** *Variations in Family Structure, Large Kinship Groups, Family Authority and Harmony.*

INTRODUCTION

The kinship system is a feature of aboriginal social organisation and family relationships across Central Australia. It is a complex system that determines how people relate to each other and their roles, responsibilities and obligations in relation to one another, ceremonial business and land.

The kinship system determines who marries who, ceremonial relationships, funeral roles and behaviour patterns with other kin. Today the number of 'wrong skin' marriages is increasing, and families are attempting to accommodate the contradictions. However, there are some rules which are adhered to, in particular certain 'avoidance relationships', especially that between a mother-in-law and a son-in-law.

This relationship requires a social distance, such that they may not be able to be in the same room or car. Be sensitive to the signals that alert one to this situation, for example being told that there is 'no room' in a car or a building when there appears to be sufficient 'space'. Aspects of this system of social organisation differ between regions. This is seen in the so-called 'skin system', a method of subdividing the society into named categories which are related to one another through the kinship system.

A *moiety system* (i.e., division into two groups: 'sun side' and 'shade side') exists across the region. Most language groups also use a section or subsection system with either four to eight 'skin names'. An individual gains a 'skin name' upon birth based on the skin names of his or her parents, to indicate the section/subsection that he/she belongs to.

Kinship Care Program Grand parents with Grand daughter.

"A kinship system is the way close relations are organized and usually includes the names that are given for specific kin. There are many different systems and each is indicative of how close relations are considered. In Hawaii, for example, aunts are called mother, uncles father and cousins brother and sister. This is relatively consistent with most polynesian islands. In vietnam each cousin and sibling has a name which indicates whether they are older or younger than the speaker."

'Kinship' is the broad term for all the relationships that people are born into or create later in life that are considered binding in the eyes of society. Every person belongs to a family of orientation (e.g., mother, father, brothers, and sisters); many adults also belong to a family of procreation (which includes a spouse or spouses and children). Familial bonds of descent and marriage may be traced through a genealogy, a written or oral statement of the names of individuals and their kin relations to one another. Inheritance and succession (the transmission of power and position in society) usually follow kinship lines. It is a system of social organization between people who are or are held to be biologically related or who are given the status of relatives by marriage, adoption, or other ritual.

Kinship is one of the most basic principles for organizing individuals into social groups, roles, categories, and genealogy. Family relations can be represented concretely (mother, brother, grandfather) or abstractly after degrees of relationship. A relationship may have relative purchase (e.g., father is one regarding a child), or reflect an absolute (e.g., status difference between a mother and a childless woman). Degrees of relationship are not identical to heirship or legal succession. Many codes of ethics consider the bond of kinship as creating obligations between the related persons stronger than those between strangers, as in Confucian filial piety.

KINSHIP SYSTEMS

There are two basic types of kin recognized by anthropologists:

— *Affinal kin* are those who are related to you by marriage.

— *Consanguineal kin* are those who are related to you by blood.

There are numerous systems that cultures use to classify people. We will only consider five such systems. The terms used to designate these systems were developed by *Lewis Henry Morgan* in 1871, and were named after the first people in which Morgan discovered the system.

ESKIMO

It is found in bilateral descent systems. This is what Americans use. Here biological mother is called mother and biological father is called father.

HAWAIIAN

The simplest system. People only differentiate between gender and generation. These societies tend to be bilateral and live in extended families.

OMAHA

Father and father's brother are both referred to by the same term. Mother and mother's sister are lumped. Female members of my mother's patrilineage of any generation are called the same term. All male members of mother's patrilineage are also called a single term. Associated with patrilineal descent.

CROW

Is the reverse of the Omaha system. That is, mother's side of the equation is differentiated and father's side is lumped. Crow terminology is associated with matrilineal systems of descent.

IROQUOIS

The term father includes father's brother, but not mother's brother. Mother includes mother's sister, but not father's sister. Uncle is used for only for mother's brother; aunt is used only for father's sister. Cross-cousins are called cousins, but parallel cousins are called siblings. This system is associated with bilateral cross-cousin marriage.

KIN SELECTION

Kin selection refers to changes in gene frequency across generations that are driven at least in part by interactions between related individuals, and this forms much of the conceptual basis of the theory of social evolution. Indeed, some cases of evolution by natural selection can only be understood by considering how biological relatives influence one another's fitness. Under natural selection, a gene encoding a trait that enhances the fitness of each individual carrying it should increase in frequency within the population; and conversely, a gene that lowers the individual fitness of its carriers should be eliminated. However, a gene that prompts behaviour which enhances the fitness of relatives but lowers that of the individual displaying the behaviour, may nonetheless increase in frequency, because relatives often carry the same gene; this is the fundamental principle behind the theory of kin selection. According to the theory, the enhanced fitness of relatives can at times more than compensate for the fitness loss incurred by the individuals displaying the behaviour.

STRUCTURAL PRINCIPLES OF KINSHIP

"Kinship" is an abstraction relating to the network of relationships based upon birth (either real or fictive) and marriage, and it forms one of the four foundational social domains which social scientists analyse. While families are a universal phenomenon, they are configured in a multitude of ways, are controlled by different mechanisms, and serve different functions. Because humans universally construct relationships with those to whom they are related by birth or marriage, "family" is perhaps the easiest set of relationships to misconstrue when observing another culture; it is the easiest place to ethnocentrically confuse biology and culture.

The social spheres or domains addressed by social scientists (politics, economics, religion and kinship) are never discrete entities that operate in isolation from one another—they are interactive in every society. But beyond interaction, one sphere may be embedded in another. By this, it means that its definition, structures, and authority are dictated by another sphere.

The social domain of kinship covers a broad range of institutions: *genealogy* and *descent*, *marriage* and *divorce*, and *dowry-systems* and *inheritance*. Because kinship in the ancient Mediterranean impacted virtually every part of life and every other social domain, it is fundamental for readers of the Bible to have a solid grasp of how kinship functioned in these cultures. While one might assume that "family" is a straightforward concept determined by biology, it is, in fact, a social construction.

Williams draws our attention to *three* different aspects of kinship analysis.

"*Kinship structure*" is the overall term referring to the full range of kinship norms and organization.

The "*family system*" deals with the configuration of the basic kinship unit, for example: polygamous or monogamous; patrilocal, matrilocal, or neolocal; patriarchal or matriarchal.

And "*family groups*" refer to actual manifestation of kinship practices in particular forms and permutations.

At the most general level, kinship has *two basic social functions*—group formation and inheritance. But group formation has a variety of dimensions: production (work and food), reproduction and childrearing, protection, worship, sociality/belonging, patronage, and play. Neither should inheritance be construed too narrowly as receiving money from dead relatives. One of the most important aspects of ancient Mediterranean culture is that status in the form of ascribed honour derives from one's family.

Another factor to consider is that for peasants, the primary issue of inheritance was land, not money. At the most basic level of kinship is the household.

FAMILY SYSTEMS

A universal hypothesis is possible: the ideological system is everywhere the intellectual embodiment of family structure, a transposition into social relations of the fundamental values which govern elementary human relations . . . One ideological category and only one, corresponds to each family type.

Todd's hypothesis of a one-to-one correspondence between family form and ideology, his typology of family forms is useful to analyse large, cross-cultural patterns. He employs the variables of spousal choice (determined by custom, parents, or individual choice), spousal relationship (exogamy or endogamy), division of inheritance (equality or unequal shares), and cohabitation of married sons with their parents. His typology yields seven basic family forms:

(i) **Exogamous Community Family:** equal distribution of inheritance; cohabitation of sons with parents; and exogamous, e.g., ancient Roman, China, and Russia.

(ii) **Authoritarian Family:** unequal distribution of inheritance—one son inherits; cohabitation of the married heir with parents; and exogamous, e.g., Germany, Japan and Korea.

(iii) **Egalitarian Nuclear Family:** equal inheritance delineated by rules; no cohabitation of married children with parents; and exogamous, e.g., northern France, northern Italy and Greece.

(iv) **Absolute Nuclear Family:** no definite inheritance rules; no cohabitation of married children with parents; and exogamous, e.g., U.S., the United Kingdom, and the Netherlands.

(v) **Endogamous Community Family:** equal inheritance delineated by rules; cohabitation of married sons with parents; and endogamous, e.g., ancient Israelites, and the traditionally Muslim countries of the Middle East.

(vi) **Asymmetrical Community Family:** equal inheritance rules; cohabitation of married sons with parents; and restricted endogamy—matrilateral cross-cousins (155-70)—primarily southern India.

(vii) **Anomic Family:** uncertainty about brothers' equality—inheritance rules egalitarian in theory, flexible in practice; cohabitation of married children with parents rejected in theory, but accepted in practice; and the possibility of endogamy, e.g., Indonesia, Philippines, and native South Americans.

One should keep three factors in mind when employing *Todd's typology—First*, these are dominant forms in a given society, not necessarily practised by every single family. *Second*, the typology is significant for historical studies because family forms are relatively constant over time; this is especially true in peasant societies. And *third*, Todd has not fully taken into account the role dowry systems play in inheritance practices.

GENEALOGY AND DESCENT

Genealogy

"Genealogy" is a particular sub-genre of the genre "list" (note also in the Bible: king list, administrative list, booty list, itinerary). They are lists of relatives arranged by generation, but may skip any number of generations for a variety of reasons. Genealogies may be oral or literary in origin, and organize relatives (literal or fictive) into their appropriate relationships by generation and parentage.

Wilson has analysed the biblical genealogies in terms of their social functions and uses in traditional cultures. He provides a cross-cultural comparison of the biblical genealogies to those of other traditional peoples. Wilson's work is significant, not only for the specifics of his analysis, but also for leading the way among biblical scholars in employing cross-cultural analysis.

Segmented genealogies (those which identify more than one member per generation) seldom extend beyond four or five generations, even in written form. They can serve a number of different functions, separately or simultaneously. They are important in traditional cultures to defend a claim to honour, identify social roles and obligations, establish inheritance rights, identify eligible endogamous marriage partners or actual exogamous partners, and within the family to indicate birth order, honour order, or motherhood (important in polygynous families).

Linear genealogies (those tracing only one member per generation) are not as diverse in their interests. Wilson argues that they have one function: "to ground a claim to power, status, rank, office, or inheritance in an earlier ancestor. Such genealogies are often used by rulers to justify their right to rule and by office-holders of all types to support their claims". Wilson also identifies several metaphorical uses of genealogies: *political* relationships, *economic* status, and *geographical* location.

Genealogy.

It is fundamental to note, however, that genealogies are always social constructs, not objective reflections of reality. That is to say, a variety of factors affect genealogy construction: how many generations one covers, whom one includes (all known kin, only males, only the narratively significant), excludes (females, embarrassing relatives, the narratively insignificant), puts first and last (the current generation or apical ancestor), and whether they are patriarchal, matriarchal or cognatic—all of these issues are choices in composing genealogies and say something about the interests of those who compose or repeat them. How one composes a genealogy reflects one's social values, perspective, and specific goals. As Wilson says: "All of them are accurate when their differing functions are taken into consideration". But one must add to Wilson's caveat that they are all "accurate" given their particular construction of reality and cultural matrix. This comports with another of Wilson's conclusions: "All genealogies, whether oral or written, are characterized by fluidity", although writing tends to limit this fluidity.

Descent

Descent is the series of links which connects the members of a kin-group to a common ancestor; it defines who constitutes a family intergenerationally. But Sahlins broadens our perspective here:

Descent in major residential groups is a political ideology and not a mere rule of personal affiliation. It is a way of phrasing political alignments and making political differentiations. It is a charter of group rights and an expression of group solidarity. And quite beyond relating man to man [sic] within the group, the descent ideology makes connections at a higher level: it stipulates the group's relation, or lack of relation, to other groups.

But societies are interested in different sets of ancestors. The different principles of descent exemplified throughout the world have attracted the attention of anthropologists; indeed the overviews of kinship spend a great deal of space on analysing the possibilities.

The *primary types* are patrilineal, matrilineal, and cognatic. "*Patrilineal descent*" traces the kinship associations through the father's ancestors, "*matrilineal descent*" through the females, and "*cognatic descent*" through a combination of male and female ancestors.

MARRIAGE AND DIVORCE

In traditional societies, the marriage of a male and female is seldom (if ever) an arrangement between individuals. It is a social contract negotiated between families, with economic, religious, and (occasionally) political implications beyond the interests of sexuality, relationship, and reproduction.

"Arranging marriages is a highly serious matter, like waging war or making big business deals" (Geertz). The three primary strategies for choosing a spouse are: custom (e.g., preference for close kin), the choice of the parents, and the choice of the marrying individuals. But even where custom is a heavy determinant, the parents or other relatives may play a key role in the precise choice.

DOWRIES, BRIDEWEALTH, AND INHERITANCE

"Dowry" is the property that a bride's family provides the bride or couple (usually under the control of her husband) at the time of marriage. This might be movable property (such as bedding, cooking utensils, jewellery, animals), immovable property (land and buildings), cash, or a combination of these.

Three cross-cultural studies of pre-industrial societies have appeared which inform our understanding of dowry. Goody was the first to demonstrate that dowry has broader implications than just as one aspect of a marriage transaction. It is, in fact, a payment of a daughter's share of the family inheritance (full or partial) given to the daughter at the time of marriage.

Women in traditional, patriarchal societies shift from being "embedded in" (under the authority, legal responsibility, and care of) their fathers to their husband. Thus the groom was given the woman's property to administer (the legal term is "usufruct"); but it nonetheless belonged to her and was passed to her children, as distinct from the personal property of the husband, or his kin-group, or his children from other marriages. This is nowhere made clearer than in the *Code of Hammurabi*, where the laws of inheritance, dowry, indirect dowry, and bridewealth are all interconnected.

"Bridewealth" is a term that covers a wide range of transfers of goods and services from the groom's kin to the bride's kin. And, as Goody makes clear, these diverse transactions have very different implications for social structure. "Indirect dowry" is property and/or cash given by the groom's kin either directly to the bride or indirectly through her kin; it may be all or part of the bridewealth. Dowries and indirect dowries, as already noted, originate in opposite families. On the other hand, they have the same (or similar) economic result by bestowing property on the new couple. This gives each family a vested interest in the new couple. Bridewealth that is not handed over to the bride is utilized in some societies to secure wives for the bride's brothers, if she has any: "Indeed it involves a kind of rationing system. What goes out for a bride has to come in for a sister."

DESCENT — "HEREDITARY SUCCESSION"

Descent, like family systems, is one of the major concepts of anthropology. Cultures worldwide possess a wide range of systems of tracing kinship and descent. Anthropologists break these down into simple concepts about what is thought to be common among many different cultures.

DESCENT GROUP

A descent group is a social group whose members claim common ancestry. A unilineal society is one in which the descent of an individual is reckoned either from the mother's or the father's line of descent.

In a society which reckons descent *bilaterally* (bilineal), descent is reckoned through both father and mother, without unilineal descent groups. Societies with the *Eskimo kinship system*, like the Eskimo proper, are typically bilateral. The egocentrid kindred group is also typical of bilateral societies.

Some societies reckon descent patrilineally for some purposes, and matrilineally for others. This arrangement is sometimes called double descent. For instance, certain property and titles may be inherited through the male line, and others through the female line.

1. Patrilineal, or Agnatic, Descent

Patrilineal or agnatic, descent is established by tracing descent exclusively through males from a founding male ancestor. The individuals indicated in blue constitute the patrilineal descendants of a common ancestor. Both men and women are included in the patrilineage formed but only male links are utilized to include successive generations.

With patrilineal descent, individuals belong to their father's descent group. Societies with the Iroquois kinship system, are typically uniliineal, while the Iroquois proper are specifically matrilineal.

2. Matriline Descent

A matriline is a line of descent from a female ancestor to a descendant (of either sex) in which the individuals in all intervening generations are female. In a matrilineal descent system (uterine descent), an individual is considered to belong to the same descent group as his or her mother. With matrilineal descent individuals belong to their mother's descent group. Matrilineal descent includes the mother's brother, who in some societies may pass along inheritance to the sister's children or succession to a sister's son.

3. Bilateral Descent

Bilateral descent is a system of family lineage in which the relatives on the mother's side and father's side are equally important for emotional ties or for transfer of property or wealth. It is a family arrangement where descent and inheritance are passed equally through both parents. Families who use this system trace descent through both parents simultaneously and recognize multiple ancestors, but unlike with cognatic descent it is not used to form descent groups.

4. Unilineal Descent

Unilineal kinship institutions occur at over twice the incidence of cognatic ones among the world's cultures. In many societies, unilineal descent groups assume important corporate functions such as land ownership, political representation and mutual aid and support.

LINEAGE

A lineage is a descent group that can demonstrate their common descent from a known apical ancestor. Unilineal lineages can be matrilineal or patrilineal, depending on whether they are traced through mothers or fathers, respectively. Whether matrilineal or patrilineal descent is considered most significant differs from culture to culture.

CLAN

A clan is a descent group that claims common descent from an apical ancestor (but often cannot demonstrate it, or "stipulated descent"). If a clan's apical ancestor is nonhuman, it is called a *totem*. Examples of clans are found in the Chechen, Chinese, Irish, Japanese, Polish, Scottish, Tlingit, and Somali societies. In the case of the Polish clan, any notion of common ancestry was lost long ago.

PHRATRY

A phratry is a descent group containing at least two clans which have a supposed common ancestor.

MOIETY

If a society is divided into exactly two descent groups, each is called a moiety, after the French word for half. If the two halves are each obliged to marry out, and into the other, these are called matrimonial moieties. *Houseman and White* have discovered numerous societies where kinship network analysis shows that two halves marry one another, similar to a matrimonial moieties, except that the two halves—which they call *matrimonial sides* — are neither named nor descent groups, although the egocentric kinship terms may be consistent with the pattern of sidedness, whereas the sidedness is culturally evident but imperfect.

DEME

The word deme is used to describe an endogamous local population that does not have unilineal descent. Thus, a deme is a local endogamous community without internal segmentation into clans.

RULE OF DESCENT

Descent is the title, whereby a person, upon the death of his ancestor, acquires the estate of the latter, as his heir at law: This manner of acquiring title is directly opposed to that of purchase. It will be proper to consider: (i) What kind of property descends and, (ii) The general rules of descent. All real estate, and all freehold of inheritance in land, descend to the heir. And, as being accessory to the land and making a part of the inheritance, fixtures, and emblements, and all things annexed to, or connected with the land, descend with it to the heir. Terms for years, and other estates less than freehold, pass to the executor, and are not subjects of descent. It is a rule at common law that no one can inherit read estate unless he was heir to the person last seised.

The General Rules of the Law of Descent

It is a general rule in the law of inheritance, that if a person owning real estate, dies seised, or as owner, without devising the same, the estate shall descend to his descendants in the direct line of lineal descent, and if there be but one person, then to him or her alone; and if more than one person, and all of equal degree of consanguinity to the ancestor, then the inheritance shall descend to the several persons as tenants in common in equal parts, however remote from the intestate the common degree of consanguinity may be. This rule is in favour of the equal claims of descending line, in the same degree, without distinction of sex, and to the exclusion of all other claimants.

When the intestate dies leaving no lineal descendants, nor parents, brothers, sisters or any of their descendants, nor grand parents, as a general rule it is presumed the inheritance descends to the brothers and sisters of both the intestate's parents, and to their descendants, equally. When they all stand in equal degree to the intestate, they take per capita, and when in unequal degree, per stirpes. To this general rule, however, there are slight variations in some of the states.

When the inheritance came to the intestate on the part of the father, then the brothers and sisters of the father and their descendant's shall have the preference and, in default of them, the estate shall descend to the brothers and sisters of the mother, and their descendants and where the inheritance comes to the intestate on the part of his mother, then her brothers and sisters and their descendants, have a preference, and in default of them, the brothers and sisters on the side of the father and their descendants, inherit.

When there is a failure of heirs under the preceding rules, the inheritance descends to the remaining next of kin of the intestate, according to the rules in the statute of distribution of the personal estate, subject to the doctrine in the preceding rules in the different states as to the half blood, to ancestral estates, and to the equality of distribution. This rule prevails in several states, subject to some peculiarities in the local laws of descent, which extend to this rule.

DETERMINANTS OF DESCENT SYSTEMS

- Bilateral and Ambilineal descent systems are found in 60% of all foragers, and are almost universal in modern societies.
- Patrilineal descent is found in 75% of all pastoral groups.
- Matrilineal descent seems to occur with high levels of intragroup fighting where men are leaving for extended periods of time.

KINSHIP USAGES

Kinship usages or the rules of kinship are significant in understanding kinship system. They serve two main purposes:

- They create groups or special groupings or kin. For example—family extended family, clan etc.
- Kinship rules govern the role of relationships among the kins.

Kinship usage provides guidelines for interaction among persons in these social groupings. It defines proper and acceptable role relationships. Thus it acts as a regulator of social life. Some of these relationships are: avoidance, teknonymy, avunculate, amitate, couvades and joking relationship.

AVOIDANCE

It means that two kins normally of opposite sex should avoid each other. In almost all societies avoidance rules prescribe that men and women must maintain certain amount of modesty in speech, dress and gesture in a mixed company. Thus a father-in-law should avoid daughter-in-law. The purdah system in Hindu family in the north illustrates the usage of avoidance.

In Western societies the archetypical instance is mother-in-law avoidance. These relationships are, to a differing degree in different societies, subject to strain—either because of the potential for (threatening) sexual relations or because of lack of a specified role content for incumbents. Typically, strain is avoided by physical avoidance; by codifying the relationship so that it is subject to minute regulation of correct behaviour and precise requirements; or by 'personalization', whereby the parties involved are expected to create a working relationship, merely on the basis of their own goodwill and personalities.

Teknonymy

According to the usage of this usage a kin is not referred directly but is referred to through another kin. In a traditional Hindu family wife does not directly utter the name of her husband but refers to her husband as the father of so and so.

Avunculate

It refers to the special relationship that persists in some societies between a man and his mother's brother. This usage is found in a matriarchal system in which prominence is given to the maternal uncle in the life of his nephews and nieces.

Amitate

The usage of amitate gives special role to the father's sister. Here father's sister is given more respect than the mother. Among Todas the child gets the name not through its parents but through the father's sister. Naming the child is her privilege.

Couvade

The usage of couvades prevalent among the Khasi and the Todas tribes makes the husband to lead the life of an invalid along with his wife whenever she gives birth to a child. He refrains from the active work, takes diet and observes some taboos which are observed by his wife. According to Malinowski the usage of couvade contributes to a strong marital bond between the husband and wife.

Joking Relationship

A joking relationship involves a particular combination of friendliness and antagonism between individuals and groups in certain social situations. In these situations one individual or group is allowed to mock or ridicule the other without offence being taken. The usage of the joking relationship permits to tease and make fun of the other.

It is clearly defined relationships of reciprocal, ritual, mildly abusive behaviour, between persons who are not only permitted but expected to behave in ways that would be offensive or insulting to persons not so related. These relationships express a form of friendliness by a show of mild hostility. Joking relatives are expected not to take offence but to respond in kind.

KINSHIP SYSTEMS IN INDIA

In India, people learn the essential themes of cultural life within the bosom of a family. In most of the country, the basic units of society are the patrilineal family unit and wider kinship groupings. The most widely desired residential unit is the joint family, ideally consisting of three or four patrilineally related generations, all living under one roof, working, eating, worshiping, and cooperating together in mutually beneficial social and economic activities. Patrilineal joint families include men related through the male line, along with their wives and children. Most young women expect to live with their husband's relatives after marriage, but they retain important bonds with their natal families.

Despite the continuous and growing impact of urbanization, secularization, and Westernization, the traditional joint household, both in ideal and in practice, remains the primary social force in the lives of most Indians. Loyalty to family is a deeply held ideal for almost everyone.

Large families tend to be flexible and well-suited to modern Indian life, especially for the 67 percent of Indians who are farmers or agricultural workers or work in related activities. As in most primarily agricultural societies, few individuals can hope to achieve economic security without being part of a cooperating group of kinsmen. The joint family is also common in cities, where kinship ties can be crucial to obtaining scarce jobs or financial assistance. Numerous prominent Indian families, such as the Ambanis, Tatas, Birlas, and Sarabhais, retain joint family arrangements even as they work together to control some of the country's largest financial empires.

Cultural or Genealogical Grounds...and Middle Eastern Kinship System.

The joint family is an ancient Indian institution, but it has undergone some change in the late twentieth century. Although several generations living together is the ideal, actual living arrangements vary widely depending on region, social status, and economic circumstance. Many Indians live in joint families that deviate in various ways from the ideal, and many live in nuclear families—a couple with their unmarried children—as is the most common pattern in the West. However, even where the ideal joint family is seldom found (as, for example, in certain regions and among impoverished agricultural laborers and urban squatters), there are often strong networks of kinship ties through which economic assistance and other benefits are obtained. Not infrequently, clusters of relatives live very near each other, easily available to respond to the give and take of kinship obligations. Even when relatives cannot actually live in close proximity, they typically maintain strong bonds of kinship and attempt to provide each other with economic help, emotional support, and other benefits.

As joint families grow ever larger, they inevitably divide into smaller units, passing through a predictable cycle over time. The breakup of a joint family into smaller units does not necessarily represent the rejection of the joint family ideal. Rather, it is usually a response to a variety of conditions, including the need for some members to move from village to city, or from one city to another to take advantage of employment opportunities. Splitting of the family is often blamed on quarrelling women—typically, the wives of coresident brothers. Although women's disputes may, in fact, lead to family division, men's disagreements do so as well. Despite cultural ideals of brotherly harmony, adult brothers frequently quarrel over land and other matters, leading them to decide to live under separate roofs and divide their property. Frequently, a large joint family divides after the demise of elderly parents, when there is no longer a single authority figure to hold the family factions together. After division, each new residential unit, in its turn, usually becomes joint when sons of the family marry and bring their wives to live in the family home.

VARIATIONS IN FAMILY STRUCTURE

Some family types bear special mention because of their unique qualities. In the sub-Himalayan region of Uttar Pradesh, polygyny is commonly practiced. There, among Hindus, a simple polygynous family is composed of a man, his two wives, and their unmarried children. Various other family types occur there, including the supplemented subpolygynous household—a woman whose husband lives elsewhere (perhaps with his other wife), her children, plus other adult relatives. Polygyny is also practiced in other parts of India by a tiny minority of the population, especially in families in which the first wife has not been able to bear children.

Among the Buddhist people of the mountainous Ladakh District of Jammu and Kashmir, who have cultural ties to Tibet, fraternal polyandry is practiced, and a household may include a set of brothers with their common wife or wives. This family type, in which brothers also share land, is almost certainly linked to the extreme scarcity of cultivable land in the Himalayan region, because it discourages fragmentation of holdings.

The peoples of the northeastern hill areas are known for their matriliny, tracing descent and inheritance in the female line rather than the male line. One of the largest of these groups, the Khasis—an ethnic or tribal people in the state of Meghalaya—are divided into matrilineal clans; the youngest daughter receives almost all of the inheritance including the house. A Khasi husband goes to live in his wife's house. Khasis, many of whom have become Christian, have the highest literacy rate in India, and Khasi women maintain notable authority in the family and community.

Perhaps the best known of India's unusual family types is the traditional Nayar taravad, or great house. The Nayars are a cluster of castes in Kerala. High-ranking and prosperous, the Nayars maintained matrilineal households in which sisters and brothers and their children were the permanent residents. After an official prepuberty marriage, each woman received a series of visiting husbands in her room in the taravad** at night. Her children were all legitimate members of the taravad. Property, matrilineally inherited, was managed by the eldest brother of the senior woman. This system, the focus of much anthropological interest, has been disintegrating in the twentieth century, and in the 1990s probably fewer than 5 percent of the Nayars live in matrilineal taravads. Like the Khasis, Nayar women are known for being well-educated and powerful within the family.

Malabar rite Christians, an ancient community in Kerala, adopted many practices of their powerful Nayar neighbours, including naming their sons for matrilineal forebears. Their kinship system, however, is patrilineal. Kerala Christians have a very high literacy rate, as do most Indian Christian groups.

LARGE KINSHIP GROUPS

In most of Hindu India, people belong not only to coresident family groups but to larger aggregates of kin as well. Subsuming the family is the patrilineage (known in northern and central India as the *khandan*, *kutumb*, or *kul*), a locally based set of males who trace their ancestry to a common progenitor a few generations back, plus their wives and unmarried daughters. Larger than the patrilineage is the clan, commonly known as the gotra or got, a much larger group of patrilineally related males and their wives and daughters, who often trace common ancestry to a mythological figure. In some regions, particularly among the high-ranking Rajputs of western India, clans are hierarchically ordered. Some people also claim membership in larger, more amorphous groupings known as vansh and sakha.

Hindu lineages and clans are strictly exogamous—that is, a person may not marry or have a sexual alliance with a member of his own lineage or clan; such an arrangement would be considered incestuous. In North India, rules further prohibit marriage between a person and his mother's lineage members as well. Among some high-ranking castes of the north, exogamy is also extended to the mother's, father's mother's, and mother's mother's clans. In contrast, in South India, marriage to a member of the mother's kin group is often encouraged.

Muslims also recognize kinship groupings larger than the family. These include the khandan, or patrilineage, and the azizdar, or kindred. The azizdar group differs slightly for each individual and includes all relatives linked to a person by blood or marriage. Muslims throughout India encourage marriage within the lineage and kindred, and marriages between the children of siblings are common.

Within a village or urban neighborhood, members of a lineage recognize their kinship in a variety of ways. Mutual assistance in daily work, in emergencies, and in factional struggles is expected. For Hindus, cooperation in specific annual rituals helps define the kin group. For example, in many areas, at the worship of the goddess deemed responsible for the welfare of the lineage, patrilineally related males and their wives join in the rites and consume specially consecrated fried breads or other foods. Unmarried daughters of the lineage are only spectators at the rites and do not share in the special foods. Upon marriage, a woman becomes a member of her husband's lineage and then participates regularly in the worship of her husband's lineage goddess. Lineage bonds are also evident at life-cycle observances, when kin join together in celebrating births, marriages, and religious initiations. Upon the death of a lineage member, other lineage members observe ritual death pollution rules for a prescribed number of days and carry out appropriate funeral rites and feasts.

For some castes, especially in the north, careful records of lineage ties are kept by a professional genealogist, a member of a caste whose traditional task is maintaining genealogical tomes. These itinerant bards make their rounds from village to village over the course of a year or more, recording births, deaths, and glorious accomplishments of the patrilineal descent group. These genealogical services have been especially crucial among Rajputs, Jats and similar groups whose lineages own land and where power can depend on fine calculations of pedigree and inheritance rights.

Some important kinship linkages are not traced through men but through women. These linkages involve those related to an individual by blood and marriage through a mother, married sisters, or married daughters, and for a man, through his wife. Anthropologist David Mandelbaum has termed these "feminal kin." Key relationships are those between a brother and sister, parents and daughters, and a person and his or her mother's brother. Through bonds with these close kin, a person has links with several households and lineages in many settlements. Throughout most of India, there are continuous visits—some of which may last for months and include the exchange of gifts at visits, life-cycle rites, and holidays, and many other key interactions between such relatives. These relationships are often characterized by deep affection and willingly offered support.

These ties cut across the countryside, linking each person with kin in villages and towns near and far. Almost everywhere a villager goes—especially in the north, where marriage networks cover wide distances—he can find some kind of relative. Moral support, a place to stay, economic assistance, and political backing are all available through these kinship networks.

The multitude of kinship ties is further extended through the device of fictive kinship. Residents of a single village usually use kinship terms for one another, and especially strong ties of fictive kinship can be ceremonially created with fellow religious initiates or fellow pilgrims of one's village or neighborhood. In the villages and cities of the north, on the festival of Raksha Bandhan (the Tying of the Protective Thread, during which sisters tie sacred threads on their brothers' wrists to symbolize the continuing bond between them), a female may tie a thread on the wrist of an otherwise unrelated male and "make him her brother." Fictive kinship bonds cut across caste and class lines and involve obligations of hospitality, gift-giving, and variable levels of cooperation and assistance.

Neighbours and friends may also create fictive kinship ties by informal agreement. Actually, any strong friendship between otherwise unrelated people is typically imbued with kinship-like qualities. In such friendships, kinship terms are adopted for address, and the give and take of kinship may develop. Such bonds commonly evolve between neighbors in urban apartment buildings, between special friends at school, and between close associates at work. The use of kinship terms enhances affection in the relationship. In Gujarat, personal names usually include the word for "sister" and "brother," so that the use of someone's personal name automatically sounds affectionate and caring.

FAMILY AUTHORITY AND HARMONY

In the Indian household, lines of hierarchy and authority are clearly drawn, shaping structurally and psychologically complex family relationships. Ideals of conduct are aimed at creating and maintaining family harmony.

All family members are socialized to accept the authority of those ranked above them in the hierarchy. In general, elders rank above juniors, and among people of similar age, males outrank females. Daughters of a family command the formal respect of their brothers' wives, and the mother of a household is in charge of her daughters-in-law. Among adults in a joint family, a newly arrived daughter-in-law has the least authority. Males learn to command others within the household but expect to accept the direction of senior males. Ideally, even a mature adult man living in his father's household acknowledges his father's authority on both minor and major matters. Women are especially strongly socialized to accept a position subservient to males, to control their sexual impulses, and to subordinate their personal preferences to the needs of the family and kin group.

Reciprocally, those in authority accept responsibility for meeting the needs of others in the family group.

There is tremendous emphasis on the unity of the family grouping, especially as differentiated from persons outside the kinship circle. Internally, efforts are made to deemphasize ties between spouses and between parents and their own children in order to enhance a wider sense of harmony within the entire household. Husbands and wives are discouraged from openly displaying affection for one another, and in strictly traditional households, they may not even properly speak to one another in the presence of anyone else, even their own children. Young parents are inhibited by "shame" from ostentatiously dandling their own young children but are encouraged to play with the children of siblings.

Psychologically, family members feel an intense emotional interdependence with each other and the family as an almost organic unit. Ego boundaries are permeable to others in the family, and any notion of a separate self is often dominated by a sense of what psychoanalyst Alan Roland has termed a more inclusive "familial self." Interpersonal empathy, closeness, loyalty, and interdependency are all crucial to life within the family.

Family resources, particularly land or businesses, have traditionally been controlled by family males, especially in high-status groups. Customarily, according to traditional schools of Hindu law, women did not inherit land or buildings and were thus beholden to their male kin who controlled these vital resources. Under Muslim customary law, women are entitled to inherit real estate and often do so, but their shares have typically been smaller than those of similarly situated males. Under modern law, all Indian women can inherit land.

MARRIAGE

What is Marriage?: *Meaning and Definitions of Marriage.* ***Features of Wedding:*** *Arranged cum Love Marriage, Arranged Marriages, Inter Caste and Inter Religion Marriages, Love vs. Arranged Marrige, Love Marriage, Marriage Rituals and Customs, Marriages in Metros, Marriages in Indian Villages, Changing Trends in Indian Marriages.* ***Type and Functions of Marriage:*** *Marriage — Western World, Marriage — Eastern World, Marriage — Traditional Cultures.* ***Forms of Marriages:*** *Polygyny, Monogamy, Bilateral Cross Cousin Marriage, Matrilateral Cross Cousin Marriage, Patrilateral Cross Cousin Marriage, Parallel Cousin Marriage.* ***Polyandry:*** *Fraternal Polyandry, Non-Fraternal Polyandry, Polygynandry, Line Marriage, Levirate and Sororate, Group Marriage.* ***Other Types of Marriages:*** *Hypergyny, Hypogyny, Endogamy, Exogamy.* ***Marriage Rules Across the Cultures in India.***

WHAT IS MARRIAGE?

It is said that marriages are made in heaven and celebrated on earth. The popular belief is true to many extent, because it is a special bond shared between two souls, who tie the wedding knot after promising to be companions for a lifetime. It is the physical, mental and spiritual unison of two souls. It brings significant stability and substance to human relationships, which is otherwise incomplete. It plays a crucial role in transferring the culture and civilization from one generation to the other, so that the human race is prospered. The institution of marriage is beneficial to the society as a whole, because it is the foundation of the family, which in turn is the fundamental building block of the society.

While the concept of marriage remains the same across the globe, the way of solemnizing it differs extensively. Different laws have been formulated to legalize the ceremony, which proves to be an important turning point in one's life. Apart from the laws of marriages, the rituals following during the ceremony are in total contrast to each other. Something that is seen in the western countries cannot be witnessed in other nations in the developing world, primarily due to the contrast in the lifestyle and religious beliefs. One of the prime reasons for the paramount status of marriage is that it is the license for two individuals to live together in a society, without much limitations.

Coming to the subcontinent of India, marriage encompasses a number of meanings, apart from being a legalized way of uniting two people. It bears a lot of social significance. This is primarily because in India, marriage has been considered a way to bring the families of two individuals closer. Since the ancient times, marriages have been celebrated as ceremonious occasions, just like the religious festivals, wherein a number of rituals and customs are followed. A number of ceremonies are observed before, during and after wedding.

In the ordinary sense of the term, marriage is a social institution which may be defined as a relation of one or more men to one or more women that is recognised by custom or law, and involves certain rights and duties both in the case of the parties entering the union and in the case of the children born of it. These rights and duties vary among different peoples and cannot, therefore, all be included in a general definition; but there must, of course, be something that they have in common. Marriage always implies the right of sexual intercourse: society holds such intercourse allowable in the case of husband and wife, and, generally speaking, regards it as their duty to gratify in some measure the other partner's desire. But the right to sexual inter-course is not necessarily exclusive: there are polyandrous, polygynous, and group-marriages, and even where monogamy is the only legal form of marriage, adultery committed by the husband is not always recognised as a ground for dissolving the union.

The key to successful marriage is love, understanding, mutual respect, trust, commitment and togetherness. While many couples are able to find all the key ingredients in their marital relationships, others find one element or more lacking in their bond. This gives rise to consequences that are not always expected, or desired. This is a reason why a number of couples face adverse consequences, like divorce. One of the visible reasons why married couples find marriage as an intimidating bond is that they face a number of problems, while being in the relationship. Lack of trust, mutual respect, love and understanding contribute to the deterioration of the bond.

MEANING AND DEFINITIONS OF MARRIAGE

Marriage is a legal, social, and religious relationship between individuals which has formed the foundation of the family for most societies. Historically, marriage has been a social contract between a man (husband) and a woman (wife). Polygamy has been a common variation in some cultures, usually in the form of polygyny (a man taking several wives) but occasionally in the form of polyandry (a woman taking several husbands). In some western societies today, same-sex marriage is recognized as a variant.

Marriage is that it is a Social Contract between two Individuals that Unites their Lives Legally, Economically and Emotionally.

The definition of marriage depends on not only the historical period, but also on the geographical location and the cultural traditions of the individuals involved in the marriage relationship.

A general definition of marriage is that it is a social contract between two individuals that unites their lives legally, economically and emotionally.

Historically, the definition of marriage is a relationship between a male, a female and their families whose primary purpose is to raise offspring. Today many people use the word to describe a committed, loving relationship with or without children. Specifically speaking, the definition of marriage is an interpersonal relationship with governmental, social, or religious recognition, usually intimate and sexual, and often created as a contract. The most frequently occurring form of marriage unites a man and a woman as husband and wife. What is more, marriage is society's largest institutions—Religion and Government—often codify the practices of the society into Law, either religious law or secular law.

The next definition of marriage tells us that a marriage provides a secure, stable place for married people to pursue their innate desire for inner peace, tranquility, and happiness. The marriage covenant requires protecting, helping, and nurturing any children who are part of the family whether they be a product of that marriage or any other union.

There are some definitions with conflicting opinions. Compared with the above mentioned one, here is another definition of marriage: marriage is not about sex, love, or happiness. Marriage is the basic building block of society in that it creates stability for its members and that of the future generations, and therefore society as a whole. Maintaining love in marriage by the avoidance of harm and the meeting of needs is the mortar that holds the commitment to that union together. Loss of love is not reason for dissolution of the marriage but a call to explore.

The institution of marriage is found in all societies. In the United States, marriage means stabilized patterns of norms and roles associated with the mutual relationship between husband and wife. It joins together a man (or men) and a woman (or women) in a special kind of social and legal arrangement that serves several purposes for a society. While this definition fits what is meant by marriage in the United States and other Western nations, it is not broad enough to encompass the essential features of marriage across all cultures. However, because marriage as an institution may differ in structure, function, dynamics, and meaning from one culture to another, no all-encompassing definition of marriage is possible (Kottak 1991). In almost all societies, it entails a legal contract (written or verbal), and this contract varies in the degree to which it can be broken.

FEATURES OF WEDDING

In India, marriage has a special significance, since it is believed to bring together not only two people, but two families as well. It involves a lot of customs and rituals, all having deep meanings behind them. Be it in the modern metros or the traditional villages, the significance of a marriage in India remains the same. There was a time when love marriages were frowned upon in the country and the union of two people, without prior consent of their parents, was simply unheard of. However, all that has changed with the passing time. Today, love marriage is as much a part of Indian culture as an arranged marriage. In this section, we have covered the various features of a wedding, in context of India as well as otherwise. Go through them and know more about weddings, a sacred ceremony that brings about a union of two souls.

ARRANGED CUM LOVE MARRIAGE

Along with time, the Indian society has witnessed substantial changes in the social and marital set up. Though most of the parents still remain staunch about their kind of arrange marriage, a wave of change have been brought by few parents who whole heartedly welcome the choice of their kids in their family.

Love Marriages or even 'Love-cum-arranged' Marriages.

ARRANGED MARRIAGES

The concept of arranged marriage may sound impractical to the Western world, but in India, it is a usual norm. No matter how westernized India may have become, arranged marriages are still viewed as the most preferred choice in the Indian families.

INTER CASTE AND INTER RELIGION MARRIAGES

Caste systems and racial discriminations act as a bane for progressive India. For years, the different societies of India, especially Hindu society have been divided on the basis of caste system and religion. The problem of caste system was so deep rooted that it took years for the Indians to come out of that idea.

LOVE VS. ARRANGED MARRIAGE

Whenever we talk of Indian wedding we try to equate it with arrange marriages. In India the social structure is such that we associate Indian marriages mainly with arrange marriages. Most of us have the feelings that arrange marriage is the concept of Indian society.

LOVE MARRiAGE

Have you ever tried defining the relationship between love and marriage? If yes, then you would have realized that both are synonymous to each other. Love is a dream and marriage is just an extension of this dream to reality.

MARRIAGE RITUALS AND CUSTOMS

India is a land of diverse culture and religion. Every region of the country has its own unique way of celebrating their marriage. Be it east, west, north and south all the four regions have its own wedding customs and rituals. Marriages in India are not just coming together of two individuals and exchange of vows and rings.

MARRIAGES IN METROS

Wedding is the most important celebration in one's life, as it marks the transition of a man from boyhood to manhood and a woman from girlhood to womanhood. In India, marriage is not just a social or religious obligation, but an institution, which teaches much about life and living.

MARRIAGES IN INDIAN VILLAGES

India is a land of diverse culture and ethnicity, wherein the important occasions are celebrated in myriad ways. Throughout the length and breadth of the country, you will see that wedding is given a paramount importance in people's social life.

CHANGING TRENDS IN INDIAN MARRIAGES

The concept of Indian wedding has seen drastic changes, over the last few years. In the yesteryears, the ceremony was a brief affair, confined to an economical budget, even though the guest list was long.

TYPE AND FUNCTIONS OF MARRIAGE

The type and functions of marriage vary from culture to culture. In the Americas and Europe, in the 21st century, legally sanctioned marriages are monogamous (although some pockets of society still sanction polygamy socially, if not legally) and divorce is relatively simple and socially sanctioned. The type and functions of marriage vary from culture to culture.

MARRIAGE — WESTERN WORLD

In the Americas and Europe, in the 21st century, legally sanctioned marriages are monogamous (although some pockets of society still sanction polygamy socially, if not legally) and divorce is relatively simple and socially sanctioned. In the West, the prevailing view toward marriage today is that it is based on a legal covenant recognising emotional attachment between the partners and entered into voluntarily.

MARRIAGE — EASTERN WORLD

Some societies permit polygamy, in which a man could have multiple wives; even in such societies however, most men have only one. In such societies, having multiple wives is generally considered a sign of wealth and power. The status of multiple wives has varied from one society to another. In the Muslim world, marriage is sanctioned between a man and a woman, but there are verses in *chapter 4 of the Qur'an* which state that in certain conditions a man is allowed up to four wives. In Muslim societies, the different wives are considered equal and must be treated as such. In Indonesia, the largest Muslim majority state, marriage is allowed between a man and a woman who profess the same faith, while atheists are not allowed to marry.

In Imperial China, formal marriage was sanctioned only between a man and a woman, although among the upper classes, the primary wife was an arranged marriage with an elaborate formal ceremony while concubines could be taken on later with minimal ceremony. Only the children from the official union were considered legitimate. To better control population growth after the rise of Communism, only strictly monogamous marital relationships are permitted, although divorce is a relatively simple process.

MARRIAGE — TRADITIONAL CULTURES

Some traditional cultures still practice marriage by abduction, a form of forced marriage in which a woman who is kidnapped and raped by a man is regarded as his wife. This practice is limited to a few traditional cultures in a small number of countries and is generally regarded as abhorrent by other cultures.

FORMS OF MARRIAGES

Monogamy, polygamy and polyandry are some of the marriage contracts used throughout the world. The version of marriage allowed in a society traditionally on the geographical location, religious make-up of the society, availability of males and females and economic status of the society.

POLYGYNY

Polygyny is the type of marriage where a man has more than one wife at the same time. A variety of biological, economic and sociological reasons explain why polygyny has been accepted in 80%+ of cultures around the world. Some say it reflects a basic biological need for numerous sex partners, particularly in cultures where childbirth and childrearing require lengthy abstinence. It may have helped societies with a surplus of women where men were often killed in warfare, though it has also been popular in societies with an even ratio of men and women. Polygyny tends to be accepted in cultures where the head of a large household has more prestige, and may even the distribution of work throughout a family. For moral reason, some say it gives more respect and honor to women and discourages the dishonesty of having a mistress or frequenting prostitutes. Islamic proponents also point out that women can stipulate their husband not take subsequent wives in prenuptial contracts.

Polygyny Marriage.

It has been very popular since bible times and, the record breaker had to be King Solomon who had hundreds of wives. However, with the onset of the New Testament, Christians are now restricted and can only marry one wife. In Islam, they have very liberal rules in this regard and, a man can marry up to 4 wives. Therefore, religion and polygamy are so closely knit and many do not divorce themselves from this fact. In traditional African societies, polygamy was the order of the day.

Polygamous marriages had many advantages and, it was a sign of wealth. The more the wives and the children, the more a man became of substance and importance. Polygamy is still common place in Africa and, it is something that has been passed down from generations.

Despite those cited advantages and worldwide recognition, polygyny has declined in developing countries (including Muslim countries). Low income and difficult economic reasons make the lower classes unable to afford more than one wife. Polygyny in the wealthier Muslim societies may be declining due to influence from the Western culture. It is also acknowledged that many polygynous unions suffer from sexual jealousy.

The Muslim countries of the Middle East, Asia and North Africa can have polygamous marriages where men who are wealthy enough can afford more than one wife. Muslim men are allowed by the Koran to have up to four wives, though many take pains to note that Islam merely "permits" polygyny and does not in fact "promote" it.

(i) Sororal Polygyny

Sororal polygyny is a type of marriage in which two or more sisters share a husband. It has been suggested that in a polygynous structure, jealousy between co-wives over perceived unequal attention from or access to their shared husband is common. It is further suggested that this is often avoided, or at least reduced, if each wife has a separate house and a ranked status. The first wife is usually considered the senior or honoured wife. Rivalry is also reduced by sororal polygyny, with sisters marrying the same man. The assumption is that sisters will be more likely to amicably share a husband. The most disruptive rivalry in a polygynous family is often between the children, especially if there is something important to inherit, such as a royal title or wealth. This also results in rivalry between the mothers. The typical way of avoiding this situation is to formally define the eldest son or daughter of the senior wife as the heir apparent.

(ii) Non-sororal Polygyny

It is a type of marriage in which the wives are not related as sisters.

MONOGAMY

Monogamy, while globally accepted, is relatively rare in both animals and people. It is thought that only 1-2% of animal species form monogamous pairings. More interestingly, of nearly 850 human societies studied only 16% were monogamous and 83% polygamous.

Monogamy is generally divided into two different types; *strict monogamy* where a person is allowed only one spouse per lifetime and *serial monogamy* where people can be married to more than one person — just not at the same time. There are also several specialized types of monogamous marriages that involve cousins; *bilateral*, *matrilateral*, *patrilateral* and *parallel cousin marriage*.

(i) Strict Monogamy

The only universally recognized form of marriage that is acceptable in all societies is strict monogamy — marriage between two people. Only 20% of the world's societies are considered strictly monogamous, in which a person is married once in his or her life. This type of system does not allow for a widow or widower to re-marry. The Catholic church is primarily responsible for encouraging strict monogamy.

(ii) Serial Monogamy

The United States is not a strictly monogamous society. Our society has serial monogamy, in which a person may marry more than one person, so long as the person has only one spouse at a time. In most cases people remarry after divorce or the death of a spouse. Serial monogamy is in contrast to strict monogamy where a person is allowed only one spouse per lifetime. Critics of serial monogamy sometimes call divorce "legalized adultery" and refuse to recognize it as a valid reason for remarriage.

A Serial monogamy.

BILATERAL CROSS COUSIN MARRIAGE

Bilateral cross cousin marriage occurs when two men marry each other's sisters. This entwines families very closely, and some societies continue it over several generations.

MATRILATERAL CROSS COUSIN MARRIAGE

Matrilateral cross cousin marriage occurs when a man is expected to marry his mother's brother's daughter. Continued over a number of generations, this eventually forms a circle where everyone is connected to each other.

PATRILATERAL CROSS COUSIN MARRIAGE

Patrilateral cross cousin marriage occurs when a man is expected to marry his father's sister's daughter. Continued over a number of generations, this eventually forms a circle where everyone is connected to each other.

PARALLEL COUSIN MARRIAGE

Parallel Cousin Marriage is an interesting form of marriage encouraged in some societies between the children of two brothers. This helps keep inheritance and property concentrated within the family line. It is associated with both Arab and Israeli societies. The Bible specifically describes this situation with Isaac, Jacob and Esau and especially recommends it for men who have only daughters. This type of marriage allows, for example, herds of animals to stay within the family rather than dispersed to other families.

POLYANDRY

Polyandry is where a woman can have more than one husband at the same time and is generally divided into fraternal polyandry (where the husbands are brothers) and non-fraternal polyandry (where the husbands are not related). Polyandry in general is described as a woman with multiple husbands at the same time. Different types of polyandry are also described; fraternal polyandry that involves marriage to multiple brothers, and non-fraternal polyandry where the husbands are not related. This practice has been rare throughout history and today generally occurs in harsh climates of India and Asia where there is economic hardship and too few women. Areas that abandon girls at birth are thought to compensate later for the shortage of women with polyandry. While this marriage practice is not widely practiced today, in 2000 an Indian-born city councilor in Sweden made headlines by calling for the legalization of both polyandry and polygyny in Sweden.

In Southern India, the Toda are a pastoral tribe. During the wife's pregnancy, it is decided who the father is. He gives her a toy as a symbolic acceptance of responsibility.

In many countries polyandry is discouraged, illegal and sometimes carries considerable punishment. While Islamic law allows polygyny it forbids polyandry, citing concerns that a child's father would be unknown and cloud the recognition of lineage. In other religions, certain interpretations of the Christian Bible lead some to insist that polyandry is actually adultery and similarly forbid it.

While polyandry is rare in human societies, it is slightly more common in fish and bird mating behaviors. But it's not much more common—only 2% of birds species (more waders and shorebirds) exhibit polyandry where the female has multiple mates during a breeding season and the assorted males help raise the offspring.

Urfi marriages can cause particular difficulty for women and polyandry. An Urfi marriage is an Islamic marriage contract performed in front of a Muslim cleric by repeating the pledge "We got married" and signing a document in front of 2 witnesses. However, it is not officially recorded, usually kept secret and can be ended easily by destroying the paper. It is frequently used as a loophole around the Muslim ban against premarital sex, or by the poor who cannot afford to get married. Complications arise in the recognition of this marriage. The Egyptian government started recognizing the relationships in 2000 and also recognizes the divorces. Since the marriage is not officially recognized it has no financial binding on the man if he dissolves it, and if a woman seeks divorce she cannot receive alimony or child support.

FRATERNAL POLYANDRY

Fraternal polyandry is a type of marriage where a woman is married to a group of brothers. This type of marriage usually occurs in the Himalayan areas of Nepal, Sri Lanka and Tibet. Brothers live in a common area and share a common wife. This arrangement also lets family property stay within the family for generations and distributes work within the family.

Tibet is traditionally the main source of fraternal polyandry, though it was outlawed in 1982 and Chinese officials have tried to stamp the practice out. As on 1994 there were still reports the practice continued, citing a village Tibet where 37 women had 2 husbands and 3 women had 3 husbands. Men from the village quoted on the topic said their arrangements were happy and it made tending livestock easier by keeping the men's work within the family. When children are born into the arrangement, they call the oldest brother "father" and the other brothers "uncle" regardless of who the biological father is. On the other hand, others from the area complained that the practice made it more difficult for some women to find husbands and increased the number of births out of wedlock.

NON-FRATERNAL POLYANDRY

Non-fraternal polyandry is a type of marriage where a woman has multiple husbands who are not related to each other. This is said to exist in India within the Nair people, who allow women to marry men who are on the same or superior social rank.

POLYGYNANDRY

Polygynandry— or "group marriage"— is where several men are married to several women at the same time and all members take responsibility for the children. The theory that it was once common in ancient times has been abandoned. It is thought to have been rare and not reported as a dominant form of marriage anywhere. The Caingang of Brazil are said to have practiced this infrequently. Interestingly, it is thought to appear only in areas that practice polyandry, with benefits cited as better economic distribution in times of hardship. In the animal kingdom this has been described for elephants and rheas.

LINE MARRIAGE

Line marriage is a type of group marriage where spouses are added over time to continue the marriage and presumably ensure more economic and parental stability. This type of marriage is generally associated with the fiction books Robert Heinlein that describe centuries-long line marriages.

LEVIRATE AND SORORATE

Levirate is a specialized version of polygamy where a man marries the widow of his dead brother. It comes from the Latin word "levir" that means "husband's brother". This practice helped maintain and reinforce family connections and alliances created by marriages.

Levirate was described extensively in the Christian Bible and used mostly by ancient Hebrews. In both Hebrew society children born from the levirate marriage were considered descendants of the first (usually older) brother. This was important for first born son inheritance.

In Southern Sudan, their custom is called "ghost marriage". If a man dies without a male heir his widow may be married to his brother. Children from this marriage are considered descendants of the first brother.

Sororate allows a widower to marry one of his wife's sisters. This still occurs in the world today and is generally used due to the first wife's death or inability to bear children. This has been practiced by the Maricopa Indians of Arizona where they replaced the deceased wife with one of her sisters.

GROUP MARRIAGE

It means the marriage of two or more women with two or more men. Here the husbands are common husbands and wives are common wives. Children are regarded as the children of the entire group as a whole.

OTHER TYPES OF MARRIAGES

HYPERGYNY

Hypergyny is when a woman is married into a family of higher social status or rank. It tends to be more common or even expected in societies with dowry rituals where the woman's family pays the groom's family. It is often paired with a society's preference for sons.

HYPOGYNY

Hypogyny is when a woman is married to a husband of lower social status, rank or age.

ENDOGAMY

Endogamy is the practice of marrying within a specific ethnic group, class or social group, rejecting others on such bases as being unsuitable for marriage or other close personal relationships. A Danish endogamist, for example, would require that a marriage be only with another Dane.

Endogamy is common in many cultures and ethnic groups, but globalization tends to counteract this tendency by exposing isolated ethnic groups to a wider variety of people and cultures. Several ethnic religious groups are notably endogamous, although with the added dimension of requiring marital religious conversion, permitting an ostensibly endogamous marriage to be performed, as the convert has accepted the partner's culture. Certain groups such as Orthodox Ashkenazi Jews have practiced endogamy strictly as an inherent part of their religious beliefs and traditions.

Endogamy, proponents say, encourages group affiliation and bonding. It is a common practice among displanted cultures attempting to make roots in new countries as it encourages group solidarity and ensures greater control over group resources (which may be important to preserve when a group is attempting to establish itself within an alien culture). Endogamy helps minorities survive over a long time in societies with other practices and beliefs.

Famous examples of strictly endogamous religious groups have been the Assyrians, Jews, Yazidi in Northern Iraq (under Islamic majority), Turkmens and Armenians in Iran, Old Order Amish, Jehovah's Witnesses, Mormons and the Parsi of India (a non-Hindu minority in India). Through the 1940-1950s in the United States, the Roman Catholic Church was successful at keeping its people marrying within the Catholic community. Since the 1960s, that has been changing as well. The caste system in India is based on an order of (predominantly) endogamous groups. Its formation has been suggested to have originated from the social organization of these groups.

EXOGAMY

Exogamous marriage or exogamy is the custom of marrying outside a specified group of people to which a person belongs. In addition to blood relatives, marriage to members of a specific totem, clan(s) or other group(s) may be forbidden.

In narrow sense, exogamy is a practice used to control the relations between the sexes and the selection of marital partners. In general, exogamy can be divided into two types—(i) family and (ii) society.

Family exogamy is usually defined by degrees. For instance, saying that one can marry anyone outside of the second degree of a blood-line relationship is a type of exogamy. Family exogamy is characteristic of nonindustrial societies, and is usually based on ties of kinship or moiety rather than on political or territorial lines. Exogamous rules usually characterize unilineal descendent groups, in which descent is reckoned either patrillineally or matrillineally. The marriage prohibition will apply only to one side of the family. Thus, some blood relations will inevitably be available for marriage in this instance.

Society exogamy is practiced by groups that want their members to marry people from outside their culture, village, religion, or/and social class. Sometimes, groups even specify the group they want its members to marry in to.

MARRIAGE RULES ACROSS THE CULTURES IN INDIA

Marriage across the cultures in India is considered to be a sacred union since the ancient times. Though there had been a considerable change in the sense and presentation with time, the significance has continued to remain even in the modern days. Due to social and political changes, a lot of harmful and anti social activities started getting involved into the practices of marriage. Customs like *Sati*, *Dowry* and *child marriage* started occupying a major part of marriage deals. Social reformers tried to remove these wrong doings from the society, fought against cleaning these mal customs from the blessed knot. Though these customs sure were gone from the society, there came the need for making rules and applying some legal acts to diminish them completely. While making these laws Indian customs, traditions and beliefs were taken into consideration to have it apply more wide range. Certain validations are common through out the India under a common Family Act like a legal age for a man is 21 years of his age and a woman 18 years of her age for marriage.

Marriages in India

Introduction. Ceremonies for An Indian Wedding: *Hindu Weddings, The Seven Holy Steps.* ***Traditional Hindu Marriage—A Sacrament. Aims of Hindu Marriage. Important Rites Assoicated with Hindu Marriage:*** *Vagdana or Oral Agreement and Lagna-Patra, Kanya Daan, Panigrahana Hathlewa, Gathabandhan, Mangalsutra, Saptapadi, Vidaai.* ***Recent Trends in Hindu Marriages:*** *The Concept of Arranged and Love Marriage, Inter-Caste and Inter-Religion Marriage, Wedding Attire, Planning.* ***Hindu Marriage Act:*** *Basic Provisions of Hindu Marriage Act.* ***Muslim Wedding:*** *Mangni or Engagement Ceremony, The Manjha Ceremony, The Wedding Day, The Wedding Attire, The Wedding Ceremony or Nikaah, Rukhsat (or Farewell), Chauthi, Valeema or the Reception.* ***Essential Pre-conditions for Muslim Marriage. Marriage Among Muslim in India:*** *Basic Interpretations of Muslim Marriage Act.* ***Valid and Invalid Marriages:*** *Applicability, Conditions of a Hindu Marriage, Essential Ceremonies, Registration, Voidable Marriages.* ***Divorce among Muslim:*** *Divorce by Husband (Shariah Act, 1937), Divorce by Wife (Muslim Marriage Act, 1939), Divorce by Mutual Consent.* ***Importance of Iddat in Muslim Divorce:*** *The Purpose of the Iddat, Different Types of Iddat.* ***Influences of Legislation on Marriages:*** *Prevention of Sati Act, 1829, Civil Marriages Act,* ***Difference Between Hindu and Muslim Marriages:*** *Hindus, Muslim.*

INTRODUCTION

Marriage is deemed essential for virtually everyone in India. It has been said that two people marry not only themselves but two families get married to each other. In India there is no greater event in a family than a wedding, dramatically evoking every possible social obligation, kinship bond, traditional value, impassioned sentiment, and economic resource. In the arranging and conducting of weddings, the complex permutations of Indian social systems best display themselves. For the individual, marriage is the great watershed in life, marking the transition to adulthood. Generally, this transition, like everything else in India, depends little upon individual volition but instead occurs as a result of the efforts of many people. Even as one is born into a particular family without the exercise of any personal choice, so is one given a spouse without any personal preference involved.

Arranging a marriage is a critical responsibility for parents and other relatives of both bride and groom. Marriage alliances entail some redistribution of wealth as well as building and restructuring social realignments, and, of course, result in the biological reproduction of families. Some parents begin marriage arrangements on the birth of a child, but most wait until later.

Many marriages are, still to this day, arranged within the religion and preferably in the same community. Traditionally, either the boy's parents or the girl's parents initiate the proposal. A 'pundit' matches the proposed couple's 'kundlis'. After the 'kundlis' are matched, both the families come to a mutual agreement and the girl and boy are meet. The 'pundit' informs the families about the auspicious days for the wedding ceremony.

Everywhere in the world, there is no greater event in a family than a wedding.

In the past, the age of marriage was quite young, and in a few small groups, especially in Rajasthan, children under the age of five are still united in marriage. In rural communities, prepuberty marriage for girls traditionally was the rule.

In the late twentieth century, the age of marriage is rising in villages, almost to the levels that obtain in cities. Legislation mandating minimum marriage ages has been passed in various forms over the past decades, but such laws have little effect on actual marriage practices.

Essentially, India is divided into two large regions with regard to Hindu kinship and marriage practices, the north and the south. Additionally, various ethnic and tribal groups of the central, mountainous north, and eastern regions follow a variety of other practices. These variations have been extensively described and analyzed by anthropologists, especially Irawati Karve, David G. Mandelbaum, and Clarence Maloney.

Broadly, in the *Indo-Aryan*-speaking north, a family seeks marriage alliances with people to whom it is not already linked by ties of blood. Marriage arrangements often involve looking far afield. In the Dravidian-speaking south, a family seeks to strengthen existing kin ties through marriage, preferably with blood relatives. Kinship terminology reflects this basic pattern. In the north, every kinship term clearly indicates whether the person referred to is a blood relation or an affinal relation; all blood relatives are forbidden as marriage mates to a person or a person's children. In the south, there is no clear-cut distinction between the family of birth and the family of marriage. Because marriage in the south commonly involves a continuing exchange of daughters among a few families, for the married couple all relatives are ultimately blood kin. Dravidian terminology stresses the principle of relative age: all relatives are arranged according to whether they are older or younger than each other without reference to generation.

On the *Indo-Gangetic Plain*, marriages are contracted outside the village, sometimes even outside of large groups of villages, with members of the same caste beyond any traceable consanguineal ties. In much of the area, daughters should not be given into villages where daughters of the family or even of the natal village have previously been given. In most of the region, brother-sister exchange marriages (marriages linking a brother and sister of one household with the sister and brother of another) are shunned. The entire emphasis is on casting the marriage net ever-wider, creating new alliances. The residents of a single village may have in-laws in hundreds of other villages.

In most of *North India*, the Hindu bride goes to live with strangers in a home she has never visited. There she is sequestered and veiled, an outsider who must learn to conform to new ways. Her natal family is often geographically distant, and her ties with her consanguineal kin undergo attenuation to varying degrees.

In *Central India*, the basic North Indian pattern prevails, with some modifications. For example, in Madhya Pradesh, village exogamy is preferred, but marriages within a village are not uncommon. Marriages between caste-fellows in neighboring villages are frequent. Brother-sister exchange marriages are sometimes arranged, and daughters are often given in marriage to lineages where other daughters of their lineage or village have previously been wed.

In *South India*, in sharp contrast, marriages are preferred between cousins (especially cross-cousins, that is, the children of a brother and sister) and even between uncles and nieces (especially a man and his elder sister's daughter). The principle involved is that of return—the family that gives a daughter expects one in return, if not now, then in the next generation. The effect of such marriages is to bind people together in relatively small, tight-knit kin groups. A bride moves to her in-laws' home—the home of her grandmother or aunt—and is often comfortable among these familiar faces. Her husband may well be the cousin she has known all her life that she would marry.

Many South Indian marriages are contracted outside of such close kin groups when no suitable mates exist among close relatives, or when other options appear more advantageous. Some sophisticated South Indians, for example, consider cousin marriage and uncle-niece marriage outmoded.

Rules for the remarriage of widows differ from one group to another. Generally, lower-ranking groups allow widow remarriage, particularly if the woman is relatively young, but the highest-ranking castes discourage or forbid such remarriage. The most strict adherents to the nonremarriage of widows are Brahmans. Almost all groups allow widowers to remarry. Many groups encourage a widower to marry his deceased wife's younger sister (but never her older sister).

Among *Muslims* of both the north and the south, marriage between cousins is encouraged, both cross-cousins (the children of a brother and sister) and parallel cousins (the children of two same-sex siblings). In the north, such cousins grow up calling each other "brother" and "sister," yet they may marry. Even when cousin marriage does not occur, spouses can often trace between them other kinship linkages.

Some *tribal* people of Central India practice an interesting permutation of the southern pattern. Among the Murias of Bastar in southeastern Madhya Pradesh, as described by anthropologist Verrier Elwin, teenagers live together in a dormitory (ghotul), sharing life and love with one another for several blissful years. Ultimately, their parents arrange their marriages, usually with cross-cousins and the delights of teenage romance are replaced with the serious responsibilities of adulthood. In his survey of some 2,000 marriages, Elwin found only seventy-seven cases of ghotul partners eloping together and very few cases of divorce. Among the Muria and Gond tribal groups, cross-cousin marriage is called "bringing back the milk," alluding to the gift of a girl in one generation being returned by the gift of a girl in the next.

Finding the perfect partner for one's child can be a challenging task. People use their social networks to locate potential brides and grooms of appropriate social and economic status. Increasingly, urban dwellers use classified matrimonial advertisements in newspapers. The advertisements usually announce religion, caste, and educational qualifications, stress female beauty and male (and in the contemporary era, sometimes female) earning capacity, and may hint at dowry size.

In *rural areas,* matches between strangers are usually arranged without the couple meeting each other. Rather, parents and other relatives come to an agreement on behalf of the couple. In cities, however, especially among the educated classes, photographs are exchanged, and sometimes the couple are allowed to meet under heavily chaperoned circumstances, such as going out for tea with a group of people or meeting in the parlor of the girl's home, with her relatives standing by. Young professional men and their families may receive inquiries and photographs from representatives of several girls' families. They may send their relatives to meet the most promising candidates and then go on tour themselves to meet the young women and make a final choice. In the early 1990s, increasing numbers of marriages arranged in this way link brides and grooms from India with spouses of Indian parentage resident in Europe, North America, and the Middle East.

Almost all Indian children are raised with the expectation that their parents will arrange their marriages, but an increasing number of young people, especially among the college-educated, are finding their own spouses. So-called love marriages are deemed a slightly scandalous alternative to properly arranged marriages. Some young people convince their parents to "arrange" their marriages to people with whom they have fallen in love. This process has long been possible for Indians from the south and for Muslims who want to marry a particular cousin of the appropriate marriageable category. In the upper classes, these semi-arranged love marriages increasingly occur between young people who are from castes of slightly different rank but who are educationally or professionally equal. If there are vast differences to overcome, such as is the case with love marriages between Hindus and Muslims or between Hindus of very different caste status, parents are usually much less agreeable, and serious family disruptions can result.

In much of India, especially in the north, a marriage establishes a structural opposition between the kin groups of the bride and groom—bride-givers and bride-takers. Within this relationship, bride-givers are considered inferior to bride-takers and are forever expected to give gifts to the bride-takers. The one-way flow of gifts begins at engagement and continues for a generation or two. The most dramatic aspect of this asymmetrical relationship is the giving of dowry.

In many communities throughout India, a dowry has traditionally been given by a bride's kin at the time of her marriage. In ancient times, the dowry was considered a woman's wealth—property due a beloved daughter who had no claim on her natal family's real estate—and typically included portable valuables such as jewelry and household goods that a bride could control throughout her life. However, over time, the larger proportion of the dowry has come to consist of goods and cash payments that go straight into the hands of the groom's family. In the late twentieth century, throughout much of India, dowry payments have escalated, and a groom's parents sometimes insist on compensation for their son's higher education and even for his future earnings, to which the bride will presumably have access. Some of the dowries demanded are quite oppressive, amounting to several years' salary in cash as well as items such as motorcycles, air conditioners, and fancy cars. Among some lower-status groups, large dowries are currently replacing traditional bride-price payments. Even among Muslims, previously not given to demanding large dowries, reports of exorbitant dowries are increasing.

The dowry is becoming an increasingly onerous burden for the bride's family. Antidowry laws exist but are largely ignored and a bride's treatment in her marital home is often affected by the value of her dowry. Increasingly frequent are horrible incidents, particularly in urban areas, where a groom's family makes excessive demands on the bride's family—even after marriage—and when the demands are not met, murder the bride, typically by setting her clothes on fire in a cooking "accident." The groom is then free to remarry and collect another sumptuous dowry. The male and female in-laws implicated in these murders have seldom been punished.

Such dowry deaths have been the subject of numerous media reports in India and other countries and have mobilized feminist groups to action. In some of the worst areas, such as the National Capital Territory of Delhi, where hundreds of such deaths are reported annually and the numbers are increasing yearly, the law now requires that all suspicious deaths of new brides be investigated. Official government figures report 1,786 registered dowry deaths nationwide in 1987; there is also an estimate of some 5,000 dowry deaths in 1991. Women's groups sometimes picket the homes of the in-laws of burned brides. Some analysts have related the growth of this phenomenon to the growth of consumerism in Indian society.

Fears of impoverishing their parents have led some urban middle-class young women, married and unmarried, to commit suicide. However, through the giving of large dowries, the newly wealthy are often able to marry their treasured daughters up the status hierarchy so reified in Indian society.

After marriage arrangements are completed, a rich panoply of wedding rituals begins. Each religious group, region, and caste has a slightly different set of rites. Generally, all weddings involve as many kin and associates of the bride and groom as possible. The bride's family usually hosts most of the ceremonies and pays for all the arrangements for large numbers of guests for several days, including accommodation, feasting, decorations and gifts for the groom's party. These arrangements are often extremely elaborate and expensive and are intended to enhance the status of the bride's family. The groom's party usually hires a band and brings fine gifts for the bride, such as jewelry and clothing, but these are typically far outweighed in value by the presents received from the bride's side.

After the bride and groom are united in sacred rites attended by colorful ceremony, the new bride may be carried away to her in-laws' home, or, if she is very young, she may remain with her parents until they deem her old enough to depart. A prepubescent bride usually stays in her natal home until puberty, after which a separate consummation ceremony is held to mark her departure for her conjugal home and married life. The poignancy of the bride's weeping departure for her new home is prominent in personal memory, folklore, literature, song, and drama throughout India.

CEREMONIES FOR AN INDIAN WEDDING

There are a number of ceremonies for an Indian wedding. The main functions are the engagement, the 'mehndi' party, pre-dinner parties, the wedding and the reception. Besides these functions, there are numerous small functions like the boy's family inviting specific close relatives from the girl's family over for lunch or dinner, vice versa, small specific ceremonies relating to specific religions followed by either of the families and close relatives inviting the wedding families over.

COMMON TERMS RELATED TO INDIAN MARRIAGES

- *Kundli*—is a horoscope made when a child is born.
- *Pundit*—is a religious person who carries out the prayers for the marriage ceremonies.
- *Mehndi*—a paste made out of dried and crushed Henna leaves and applied on the hands and feet in a decorative manner. This is also known and popularized here in the US as "temporary tatoos".
- *Mehndi-wallis*—women who apply mehndi on a professional basis.
- *Saree*—a traditional outfit for women, which is a 6 feet long cloth tied in a traditional manner around the waist and worn with a figure-hugging blouse.
- *Puja*—ceremony or prayer.
- *Puja samaan*—religious items used for the ceremony.
- *Shlokas*—religious sayings.

The **shehnai** is a North Indian oboe. Although it is referred to as a double-reeded instrument it is actually a quadruple-reed instrument. This is because it has two upper reeds and two lower reeds. The instrument has a wooden body with a brass bell. The reed is attached to a brass tube which is wrapped in string. The shehnai has eight holes.

HINDU WEDDINGS

Traditional Hindu wedding ceremonies can last for days and involve much ritual in Sanskrit which may be understood only by the priest conducting the service.

Hindu weddings are supposed to take place outside, on the earth, under a canopy known as a mandap.

A Hindu Wedding is not simply an exchange of vows and rings. It includes a number of religious rites before and during the nuptials, which are performed in the presence of family deities. These represent the importance of the bond between a husband and wife. A Hindu marriage or "Vivaha" is incomplete without the blessings of God.

The Seven Holy Steps.

THE SEVEN HOLY STEPS

Hindu marriage ceremonies involve many elaborate rituals, one of the most important being the "Saat Pheere" or 7 circles around the holy fire. Also known as "Saptapadi" – "Sapta" means "seven" and "padi" means "steps". This ritual involves the bride and groom circumam-bulating around the sacred fire seven times while the priest chants the holy mantras. With every step, the couple invokes the Gods to shower their blessings on them.

TRADITIONAL HINDU MARRIAGE—A SACRAMENT

Traditional Hindu marriage was strictly based on absolute trust, mutual affection, capacity to adjust and sharing the responsibilities equally. At every stage of the wedding ceremony when the incantations (Mantras) from the Vedas were uttered, prayers were offered to ensure a smooth life. The duties were demarcated and freedom given to both. The union being sacred, the vow did not give room for separation.

The character of the bridegroom was first assessed and his qualifications were taken into consideration. Both husband and wife should be loyal to each other and contrary to the mistaken belief that the wife was not treated on par with her husband she had full charge of the household while he was to assist her in maintaining the family. Wealth accumulated by him should be used for the family insisting that it should not be frittered away.

A Traditional Hindu Marriage.

The process of marriage commenced when the parents felt that their son was mature enough to shoulder responsibility. Unlike the prevailing custom now, in olden times the eligible boy's father used to go in search of a girl from a noble family and seek her parent's approval.

A verse refers to the expectations regarding the factors governing compatibility: the bride yearning for a spouse with charm; her mother, a wealthy boy; the father, a boy of character and high educational qualifications and the relatives, about the family tradition. For the bridegroom, she must be a companion, an adviser and one who enthuses him in all his tasks.

Sri A. Sivaramakrishna Sastrigal in a discourse explained the significance of the mantras recited during the marriage ceremony. The solemn assurance of upholding the spirit of unity was made before the Lord of Fire (Agni) serving as witness. The "*Paanigrahanam*" was an important step.

The significance of taking seven steps was that the couple should never give scope for differences of opinion and should an occasion arise, both should respect the sentiments of the other, thereby ensuring that no confrontation takes place.

As one who was in charge of the household, she should stand like a rock. Whether a fine image is carved out of it or rain pours on it or made to bear heat, the stone is impervious. Another statement records that the father of the bride felt extremely happy and relieved that the interests of his daughter have been entrusted to a capable person. From then on, he concentrated on his personal work. The sanctity attached to the marriage has been clearly brought out in the Ramayana by the manner in which the Divine couple conducted themselves, both in prosperity and in adversity.

AIMS OF HINDU MARRIAGE

The aims of Hindu marriage are said to be *dharma*, *praja* (progeny) and *rati* (pleasure). Through sex is one of the function of marriage it is given third place, indicating there by that it is least desirable aim of the marriage. To stress the lower role of sex in marriage, the marriage of a *Sudra* is said to be for pleasure only. The Sudra is considered to be a contemptible fellow who has no high purpose in life. Because the Sudra is despised, relations with a Sudra woman are viewed unfavorable through they can't be stopped. Consequently the brahmanic legislators enjoined that a sudra wife would be taken only for pleasure. This association of Sudra wife with sex is another way of indicating the proper place of sex in marriage. The institution of Hindu marriage occupies a prominent place in the social Institution of the civilized world. Hindu marriage can be defined as religions sacrament in which a man and woman are bound in permanent relationship for physical, social and spiritual purpose of dharma, procreation and sexual pleasure.

The Hindu marriage is not really a social contract but a religious sacrament. It results in a more or less permanent relationship between a man and woman. Their aim is not nearly physical pleasure but spiritual advancement. It is not merely an individual function but has a serial enjoyment of sexual pleasure. It exhibits unintegral approach to this serial institution. The main aim of Hindu marriage can be summarized as follows:

(i) *Fulfillment of dharma or religions duties:* According to the Hindu scriptures marriage is a basic of all religion activities. In the words of K.M Kapadia "marriage is primarily for the fulfillment of duties; the basic aim of marriage was dharma".

(ii) *Procreation:* In Hindu families the child is given a very important place. According to Riga Veda, the husband accepts the palm of wife in order to get a high breed progeny. According to Manu, the chief aim of marriage is procreation Mahabarat has also maintained the same view.

(iii) *Sexual pleasure:* The Hindu scriptures have compared the sexual pleasure with the relation of divine bliss. According to vatsyanyan sexual pleasure is the chief in aim marriage.

As marriage is said to be sacred it is irrevocable, other parties to the marriage can't dissolve it at will. Each is bound to the other until the death of either of them and the wife is supposed to be bound to her husband even after his death.

Marriage was a serious duty towards the family and the community and there was little idea of individual interest. The social background provided by the authoritarian joint family, and caste with its dominion small spheres of life, afforded no scope for the recognition of any personal factor, individual, interest or aspiration, in the relations between husband and wife.

Dharma, Artha, Kama and even *Moksha* are some of the guiding factors of Hindu marriage. Attainment of lines is also the main object of a married life. A man is only half of a whole unless he is not married. Marriage is also essential according to Hindu scriptures because only by entering a matrimonial alliance with opposite sex, a man can enter into grahs thaskram, and it is only this asharma where he is allowed to practice dharma, artha, kama and mokhsa.

IMPORTANT RITES ASSOICATED WITH HINDU MARRIAGE

VAGDANA OR ORAL AGREEMENT AND LAGNA-PATRA

The pre-wedding ceremonies include engagement (involving vagdana or oral agreement and lagna-patra written declaration) and arrival of the groom's party at the bride's residence, often in the form of a formal procession. The post-wedding ceremonies involve welcoming the bride to her new home.

KANYA DAAN

Kanya Daan, which means the giving away of one's daughter, has been derived from the Sanskrit words Kanya which means girl and Daan which means donation. Kanya Daan is a very significant ritual performed by the father of the bride in presence of a large gathering that is invited to witness the wedding. The father pours out libation of sacred water symbolizing the giving away of his daughter to the bride groom. The groom recites Vedic hymns to Kama, the God of love, for pure love and blessings.

As a condition for offering his daughter for marriage, the father of the bride requests a promise from the groom for assisting the bride in realizing the three ends:

- Dharma,
- Artha, and
- Kama.

The groom makes the promise by repeating three times that he will not fail the bride in realizing dharma, artha and kama.

Ideally, the parents of the bride place the right hand of the bride over the right hand of the groom and place their own left hands at the bottom and the right hands (the two of them) on top, securing the Conch with gold, betel nut, flowers and a little fruit (in it) placed in bride's hand. It is at this point that the purpose of the Kanyadaan is clearly stated per scripture and the names of the parents and forefathers are stated from both sides.

In Indian Wedding Kanyadaan is the most important ritual of wedding.

PANIGRAHANA HATHLEWA

After being led to the wedding mandup, the bride and groom have their hands tied together. The priest does a puja to Lord Ganesh and then puts a coin and mehendi on the bride's right hand where the round empty spot is (where no mehendi was put) and ties his hand with the brides. This puja is done schedule in advance based on an auspicious time and date.

GATHABANDHAN

In this ritual priest tying a knot using the ends of the clothing worn by the bride and groom. The priest ties the end of the groom's dhoti or the kurta; whichever he is wearing, with that of the bride's saree, the knot signifying the sacred wedlock.

MANGALSUTRA

A mangalsutra (also mangala sutra or mangalasutra) is an Indian symbol of Hindu marriage, consisting of a gold ornament strung from a yellow thread, a string of black beads or a gold chain. Mangalya dharanam (literally "wearing the mangalya") is the most important part of a Hindu marriage ceremony. The mangalya is strung on a yellow thread prepared by using Turmeric paste. It is tied around the bride's neck with three knots. In some families, the groom ties the first and his sisters tie the rest.

According to Hindu culture, there are five signs of marital status of women. They are mangalsutra, Toe rings, Kumkum, bangles and a nose ring. Mangalsutra is the most important among them.

SAPTAPADI

A Hindu bride shortly after the saptapdi ceremony. The Saptapadi or the *saat pheras* is perhaps the most important component of Vedic Hindu weddings. The couple conduct seven circuits of the Holy Fire (Agni), which is considered a witness to the vows they make each other.

VIDAAI

A bride bids her family farewell at the end of the wedding ceremony. Also called rukhsati in North India. This is considered to be the most emotional ritual, when the bride leaves her parents' home and makes her way to her husband's. Family and friends, who also shower her with blessings and gifts, give her a tearful farewell. The male members of the bride's family bid farewell to the groom by applying the traditional 'tilak' (vermilion) on his forehead and shower him with gifts.

Vidaai.

RECENT TRENDS IN HINDU MARRIAGES

The concept of Hindu wedding has seen drastic changes, over the last few years. In the present time, the occasion is generally celebrated in an elaborated way, with number of rituals that are conducted before, during and after it. A long guest list, colourful and extravagant venue, lavish feast and a series of rituals are the key ingredients of the 'big fat Hindu wedding' that we see today. In the following lines, we have discussed about the changing trends in Hidu marriages.

THE CONCEPT OF ARRANGED AND LOVE MARRIAGE

The custom of arranged marriages has been a part of Indian culture since the fourth century. The practice was begun primarily to maintain and pass on the family traditions from one generation to the other. It is still prevalent in both rural and urban parts of India, former being more inclined towards the system. In fact, arranged marriages are in majority, because not all people have accepted the concept of love marriage. However, with the changing time, people in India have accepted the concept of love marriage, which is otherwise considered against the Indian culture. People in the rural India are now more liberal, when it comes to love marriages. Therefore, both arranged and love marriage find equal importance in the wedding scenario of India.

INTER-CASTE AND INTER-RELIGION MARRIAGE

Until some time back, marrying a person belonging to some other caste or religions was strictly not permitted by the families. With the modernization of the Indian society and social awareness of the people, inter-caste and inter-religion marriages have become a common sight. This is primarily due to the acceptance of the concept of love marriage. Nonetheless, people with an orthodox or conservative outlook of life are still firm about marrying within the same caste, community and religion. Contrary to this thought, people in the present time do believe in solemnizing weddings of two different individuals belonging to different family background and culture. The recent trend in Indian marriages is the acceptance of the concept of homosexual marriage.

WEDDING ATTIRE

The wedding attire has also seen a drastic change, over the passing years. Initially, the bride and the groom used to wear traditional dress, of their respective religions, regions or community. Today, although they still wear their traditional dress during the important wedding ceremonies, they resort to the outfit that is different from the traditional ones for other rituals. With the changing fashion trend, the way of getting dressed for a wedding has also been changing. People, especially in the elite class, are now hiring fashion designers to choose the wedding attire for the bride and the groom. Inspired by the high-profile weddings of business tycoons and Bollywood stars, people now want to look like a celebrity, on their 'important day'. Hence, the attire chosen for the wedding ceremony is often a reflection of the hot trend.

PLANNING

People's perception of planning the wedding has also changed over the passing years. Few years back, wedding and engagement were the sole responsibility of the bride's family. People within the family took efforts in decorating the venues chosen for conducting different ceremonies. Moreover, the wedding expenses were also borne by the bride's parents. Today, although the bride's parents still finance for the wedding ceremony (except the reception party, which is thrown by the groom's family), people are now resorting to professionals to make arrangements for their weddings, right from the menu to the decorations. They hire wedding planners for the purpose. This is especially prevalent in the urban upper-middle class of India, where they want their wedding to be a trendsetter and the talk of the town for a long time.

HINDU MARRIAGE ACT

Unlike West, marriage in India is regarded more as a religious and social affair than a legal affair. Despite a very detailed chapter on the Indian marriages in the Indian constitution, most of the people in the country are unaware of the laws associated with marriages. In a cosmopolitan culture like India where umpteen numbers of cultures and religion prevail under the same canopy, it is very difficult to regulate all the customs by same kind of regulation especially of the matter is related with sensitive issues like marriage and hierarchy. Therefore, different kinds of Marriage Acts have been defined for different religions in the country. The Hindu marriage is governed by, 'The Hindu Marriage Act', which came into existence on 18 May 1955.

BASIC PROVISIONS OF HINDU MARRIAGE ACT

- The provision under the Act is that it applies to any person who is Hindu by religion and it is also applicable to Buddhists, Jains, and Sikhsas well as and the person who is not a Muslim, Christian, Parsi or Jew, and who is not governed by any other law.
- It extends to the entire India except the State of Jammu and Kashmir, and it is applicable to Hindus domiciled in the territories to which this Act extends who are outside the said territories.
- Under this law the bridegroom should be of 21 years of age and the bride should be of 18 years of age. They both should be Hindu by origin and should not be within the degree of prohibited relationship. Neither party should have a spouse living nor any party should be subject to recurrent attacks of insanity or epilepsy, either of them

should not be suffering from mental disorders or should not be unfit for marriage and procreation of children and both should be of sound mind and capable of giving valuable consent.

- Bigamy or Polygamy is now prohibited and as per law it is treated as an offence under the Indian Penal code.
- Just like marriages the law also governs divorces. Under the law divorce can be obtained on the grounds of adultery, cruelty, desertion for two years, conversion in religion, unsound mind, etc.
- The Hindu Marriage law has also described certain prohibited relationships whose marriage is not legalized. Like father and daughter, son and mother, brother and sister and many more.
- The Hindu Marriage act also does not set any prescribe or particular ceremonial for marriage. It states that a Hindu marriage may be formalized in accordance with the customary rites and ceremonies of either party. Where rituals include the saptapadi (seven steps by the bridegroom and the bride jointly before the sacred fire), the marriage is said to be solemnized once the seventh step is taken.
- It has now become mandatory to register a Hindu Marriage.

MUSLIM WEDDING

Muslim weddings have a place of their own when it comes to uniqueness and traditionalism. Among Muslims, it is the family of the groom-to-be which searches for a suitable bride.

A Muslim Weddings Ceremony.

MANGNI OR ENGAGEMENT CEREMONY

In this ceremony, the exchange of rings takes place between the boy and the girl. The outfit worn by the girl is provided by the boy's family. The actual ring ceremony takes place with the serving of sweetmeats like peda to celebrate the auspicious occasion.

THE MANJHA CEREMONY

In this ceremony, the girl is anointed with turmeric paste. The haldi lapetan ceremony takes place at the girl's house one or two days before the wedding day. The haldi and chameli oil are provided by the boy's family. Only unmarried girls apply haldi on the bride-to-be. A symbolic token in the form of a spot of the heena is put on the groom too by the girl's cousins.

The *girl's attire*: The girl limits herself to yellow clothes, the colour of turmeric, and does not wear any jewellery. After this ceremony, she does not move out of her house or change her clothes till the wedding day.

The *musical night* (at the girl's place): This festivity takes place one night before the wedding. There is natural gaiety and rejoicing accompanied by traditional songs sung to the beat of the dholak.

THE WEDDING DAY

The *baraat* (or the procession of friends and relatives accompanying the groom) starts from the groom's place and moves towards the wedding venue, with the groom seated on a horse or in a car. A *shamiana* is pitched if no concrete covered area is available for conducting the wedding ceremonies. The arrival of the groom is accompanied by the beating of drums playing of musical instruments. Dancing rhythmically to add to the gaiety around.

On arrival, the groom and the brother of the bride exchange a glass of sharbet (or juice) and money. The *saalis* (or the sisters of the bride) welcome the guests by playfully hitting them with a *phoolon ki chadi* or a stick wrapped around with flowers.

THE WEDDING ATTIRE

It is customary for the boy's family to send the wedding attire, jewellery and cosmetics for the girl. She usually wears the outfit as per the norms of the state she hails from; for instance, a *gharara* or a *zari sari* or *salwar kameez*. The groom normally wears a *sherwani* or an *achkan*. Both the bride and the groom put on a *sehra* or a veil of flowers around their foreheads.

THE WEDDING CEREMONY OR NIKAAH

Traditionally, the men and women have to be seated in separate rooms or have a *purdah* (or curtain) separating them. The amount of *meher* or gift is decided upon by the elders of the two families. (The *meher* is the compulsory amount of money given to the bride's family by the groom's family.) It is either fixed at an affordable price for the boy or fixed according to traditions in their gharana or family.

Next, the *Uakeel* or an eminent person with two male persons as witnesses and the *Maulvi* or the officiating priest ask the girl personally if she is happy with the arrangement and whether she agrees to marry the groom. The boy asked the same question. In case of assent from boy, the Maulvi then makes the boy read a selected piece of the Quran, the holy book of the Muslims.

The *Nikaahnama*: This is a documents wherein the marriage is registered. First, the groom and the two witnesses sign and later the bride does so.

THE ACCOMPANYING CEREMONIES

(a) After the nikaah the groom is taken to the *zenana* (ladies' section). At the threshold, he gives money and gifts to the sisters of the bride. The groom receives the blessings of the elder women and offers them his *salaam* or salutations.

(b) Dinner is served separately to the ladies and the gentleman. The family of the boy is given a feast separately.

(c) After dinner for the first time, the groom and the bride are seated together and a *dupatta* is used to cover their heads while the Maulvi makes them read some prayers.

(d) *Aarsimashaf*: The Holy Quran is kept in between the newly weds and they are allowed to see each other only through reflection by mirrors.

(e) *Misri*, dried dates and *batasha* are distributed to the guests. The dried dates have a religious significance.

(f) A half-eaten *laddoo* (a sweetmeat) is given to the girl by her cousins.

(g) The groom stays overnight in a separate room at the girl's house with a younger brother. In the morning, he is given clothes, money and gifts by the bride's parents.

(h) The relatives of the boy come to accompany the bridal couple to their home in the afternoon.

RUKHSAT (OR FAREWELL)

The father of the bride gives her hand to her husband and asks him to protect her always. The last farewells are said and the bride departs for her husband's house by car or *palki* (palanquin).

The bride's first entrance.

The bride first enters her new home under the cover of the Quran held by her mother-in-law and the groom follows.

CHAUTHI

The bride is taken back to her parents' place on the fourth day after the wedding.

VALEEMA OR THE RECEPTION

The husband brings back his wife and her family to attend the reception hosted by his family. Thus, the two families unite to become one.

ESSENTIAL PRE-CONDITIONS FOR MUSLIM MARRIAGE

Muslim marriages are social contracts between a woman and man on the following terms:

1. There shall be a proposal and its acceptance. The proposal of marriage are tied to agreements on a dowry (a gift by the family of the groom to the family of the bride) and a mahr (a marriage gift by the groom to the bride), etc.
2. Competence of parties. Any Muslim who is sound mind and who has attained age of puberty may enter into contract of marriage.
3. No legal disability. There can be no restriction on any valid Islamic grounds that would preventing the couple to marry.
4. There shall be free consent of both parties to the marriage.
5. There shall be two male witnesses (or one male and two female witnesses). These witnesses shall be sane, adult and Muslim.

MARRIAGE AMONG MUSLIM IN INDIA

India is land of diverse culture and religions. People of many religions live here with peace and harmony. Though similar constitutional rights and duties are assigned to all the citizens of the country, they are free to abide by their own social and religious belief. The marriage acts of different religions are framed in the Indian constitution in accordance with their social and religious set up, as the Hindu Marriages are framed according to the Hindu cultural beliefs and customs, the Muslim Marriage Act has been framed keeping in mind the social, religious and cultural traditions of the Muslims.

BASIC INTERPRETATIONS OF MUSLIM MARRIAGE ACT

- Under the law, Nikah or marriage is a civil contract and may be permanent or temporary and no religious ceremony or ritual is necessary. It states that to have a valid Nikah or marriage under the Muslim law, presence of a Qazi or priest is not necessary. Merely a proposal in the presence and hearing of two normal males or one normal Muslim male and two normal Muslim female adults, and acceptance of the said proposals at the same time constitute a legal wedding under the Muslim Personal Law.
- The Muslim Marriage law permits a man four wives if he treats all of them equally.

- It is assumed that on completion of 15 years of age, a person attains puberty. If a person is of sound mind, normal and has attained puberty his or her marriage cannot be performed without his or her consent.
- To have a legal and valid marriage following conditions are to be satisfied like both should be of sound mind or the guardian in marriage should act on behalf of the person of unsound mind in arranging the marriage contract. Either the parties should have attained the age of puberty or the guardian in marriage on behalf of the party concerned should enter into the marriage contract.
- In case of divorce a husband can leave his wife without any reasons merely by pronouncing the word "Talak" thrice. However for a Muslim woman to obtain divorce certain conditions are necessary. The husband and the wife with mutual agreement can also put an end to the marriage.
- There are certain prohibited relationships, whose marriage is considered void. Like mother and son, grandmother and grandson, uncle and niece, brother and sister and nephew and aunt.
- There is a slight variation in the laws that govern the Sunni and Shia Marraiges. However, the basic elements are same in both of the cases.

VALID AND INVALID MARRIAGES

The Hindu Marriage Act, which came into power on 18th May 1955, governs all the Hindu marriages. The Act has reformed the Hindu law of marriage and covers entire India except the state of Jammu and Kashmir.

APPLICABILITY

Only if both the parties are Hindus can the marriage take place under the Hindu Marriage Act.

The Act applies to:

- Any person who is Hindu, Buddhist, Jain or Sikh by religion.
- Any person who is born to Hindu parents.
- Any person who is not a Muslim, Christian, Parsi or Jew and who is not governed by any other law.

The Act does not apply:

- To persons who are Muslims, Christians, Parsis or Jews by religion.
- To members of the scheduled tribes coming within the meaning of clause (25) of Article 366 of the Constitution of India unless the Central Government by notice otherwise directs.

CONDITIONS OF A HINDU MARRIAGE

A marriage to be valid has to fulfill the following conditions:

1. Neither party should have a spouse living at the time of marriage. The spouse does not include a divorced husband/wife.
2. At the time of marriage, the parties should be capable of giving a valid consent to the marriage. A person who is of a sound mind shall be considered to be a person capable to give a valid consent. Neither party, though capable of giving a valid consent should be suffering from mental disorder of such a kind or to such an extent as to be unfit for marriage and procreation of children. Neither party should be suffering from recurrent attacks of insanity or epilepsy.
3. The bridegroom should have attained the age of 21 years and the bride should have attained the age of 18 years at the time of marriage.
4. The parties should not be within the degrees of prohibited relationships, unless the customs or usage, permits such a marriage.

Two persons are said to be within the degrees of prohibited relationships

1. If one is a lineal ascendant of the other. For example, a Daughter can not marry her father and grandfather. Similarly, a mother can not marry her son or grandson.
2. If one was the wife or husband of a lineal ascendant or descendant of the other. For example, a son can not marry his stepmother. Similarly, a person can not marry his Daughter-in-law or son-in-law.
3. If one was the wife of the brother or of the father's or mother's brother or the grandfather's or grandmother's brother of the other.
4. If the two are brother and sister; uncle and niece; Aunt and Nephew or children of brother and sister of two brothers or two sisters. It must have been noticed in some communities the marriage with the wife of the brother and mother's brother and the first cousins are solemnized, those marriages, in the absence of a custom in the community are not valid marriages.
5. A person can not marry upto his second cousin from the mother's side and upto his fourth cousin from the side of the father. It is also necessary the parties should not be sapindas of each other from either side.

In case, either party has a spouse living at the time of marriage, within the degree of prohibited relationship and are sapindas of each other, the marriage between the parties shall be null and void.

ESSENTIAL CEREMONIES

A Hindu marriage can take place according to the customary rites and ceremonies.

The ceremony of saptapadi and kanyadana are important ceremonies prevalent among vast majority of Hindus and the ceremony of saptapadi before the sacred fire has been held essential for a valid Hindu Marriage.

REGISTRATION

The marriages solemnized, may be registered under the Special Marriage Act with office of the registrar, in the Hindu Marriage Register.

Registration is not compulsory and in no way effects the validity of the marriage. It is entirely upto the parties to have the marriage registered.

No marriage can be registered unless the following conditions are fulfilled:

- A ceremony of marriage has been performed between the parties and they have been living together as husband and wife.
- Neither party has at the time of registration more than one spouse living.
- Neither party is an idiot or lunatic at the time of registration.
- The parties have completed the age of twenty one years at the time of registration.
- The parties are not within the degrees of prohibited relationship.
- The parties have been residing within the district of the Marriage Officer for a period of not less than thirty days immediately preceding the date on which the application is made to him for registration.
- On receiving the application signed by both the parties the Marriage Officer shall give public notice and after allowing 30 days for objections and on being satisfied that all the conditions are fulfilled he shall enter a certificate in the marriage certificate book, which shall be signed by the parties and three witnesses.

VOIDABLE MARRIAGES

Voidable marriages are those which are void at the option of the aggrieved party. Such marriages can be annulled by a decree of nullity on any of the following grounds :

- That the marriage has not been consummated owing to the impotence of the Respondent.
- That the marriage is been performed with a person of unsound mind or having a mental disorder or suffering from recurrent attacks of epilepsy.
- That the consent of the Petitioner or its Guardian was obtained by force or by fraud as to the nature of the ceremony or as to any material fact or circumstances concerning the Respondent.

— To succeed on this ground, it is necessary that the Petition must be presented in the Court within one year after the force has ceased to operate or the fraud has been discovered. It is also necessary that after the force has ceased or fraud discovered, the Petitioner has not, with consent, lived with the other side.

— That the Respondent was at the time of marriage pregnant by some person other than the Petitioner.

DIVORCE AMONG MUSLIM

Muslim Divorce a husband can leave his wife without any reasons merely by pronouncing the word "*Talak*" thrice. However for a Muslim woman to obtain divorce certain conditions are necessary.

India is a land of many culture and religion and there is personal law for every religion. Indian law give a big relief to the Muslim women, their husbands would not be able to get rid of their wives in future by simply reciting talaaq, talaaq, talaaq.

The All-India Muslim Personal Law Board is set to ban this practice. They are drafting a new *talaqnama*, the separating couples would be given a minimum of three months to reconcile, instead of *shauhar* (husband) just firing talaaqs to separate without giving any chance to his *begum* (wife). The draft of the new talaqnama was already approved in Board's at Patna meeting in October 2003, it was awaiting a final nod from the 41-member working committee, Board's highest-decision making body.

DIVORCE BY HUSBAND (SHARIAH ACT, 1937)

— *Talaq*: which is release from the marriage tie immediately or eventually.

— *Ila:* where a husband of sound mind takes a vow that he will abstain from all relationship from his wife.

— *Zihar*: where husband sane and adult compares his wife to his mother or any other female within the prohibited degrees.

DIVORCE BY WIFE (MUSLIM MARRIAGE ACT, 1939)

- That the whereabouts of the husband have not been known for a period of 4 years.
- That the husband has neglected or has failed to provide for her maintenance for a period of 2 years.
- That the husband has been sentenced to imprisonment for a period of 7 years or upwards.
- That the husband has failed to fulfill his marital obligation for a period of 3 years.

- That the husband has been insane for two years or is suffering from leprosy or a virulent form of venereal disease.
- That the husband was impotent at the time of marriage and continues to be so.

DIVORCE BY MUTUAL CONSENT

- Both should be of sound mind or the guardian in marriage should act on behalf of the person of unsound mind in arranging the marriage contract.
- The parties should have attained the age of puberty or the guardian in marriage on behalf of the party concerned should enter into the marriage contract. There are certain prohibited relationships, whose marriage is considered void. Like mother and son, grandmother and grandson, uncle and niece, brother and sister and nephew and aunt.
- There are even differences in marriage rules among the Sunni and Shias.

IMPORTANCE OF IDDAT IN MUSLIM DIVORCE

Iddat (also pronounced IDDAH) is a period of waiting that Islam has imposed upon a woman who has been divorced or whose husband has died, after which a new marriage is permissible.

Iddat is established from The Holy Quran and the Hadith of Rasoolullah (sallallahu alaihi wasallam). We cite the relevant verses in this regard: In Surah Baqarah Almighty Allah states:

"And those women who are divorced, should keep themselves in waiting for three periods."

This verse establishes the iddat for a woman who is divorced, such iddat being a period of three haidh according to the hanafi mazh-hab. In another verse in Surah Baqarah, Allah Ta'ala says:

"And those among you who expire and leave behind wives, they (the wives) shall keep themselves in waiting for four months and ten days."

THE PURPOSE OF THE IDDAT

There are several reasons why the iddat has been ordained. As regards the iddat that is calculated according to the cycle of menstruation, the purpose is, firstly, to establish the state of the womb, i.e., to ascertain whether there has been conception prior to divorce or not. When menstruation has been fixed as the basis for iddat, it will be a mere formality to establish this, for when the blood of haidh flows it is a sure sign that the womb is empty of a fetus. However, one period of menses is insufficient to provide definite evidence of the 'emptiness' of the womb, so the Shariah prescribes the elapse of another period for added confirmation. After this second haidh it will be conclusively proven that the womb is indeed free of pregnancy. Now that the womb has been certified as free of burden, the third haidh or menstruation period is merely a mark of respect for the bond of nikah and to prolong the termination of the nikah thus increasing the chances of reconciliation The result of all this is an iddat consisting of three haidh periods. As for those ladies who do not experience haidh for reasons already outlined, the straightforward three-month iddat prescribed for them will serve the same purpose as expounded above, beyond any shadow of doubt. Furthermore, the three-month iddat is to differentiate between the iddat of the free woman and the woman in bondage, whose iddat the Shariah has set at two months, or two menstruation periods.

INFLUENCES OF LEGISLATION ON MARRIAGES

India is a country with diverse socio-cultural communities. The country has various laws to safeguard the interest of its inhabitants. Owing to this, the country has number of laws to regulate the marriage and divorce related matters. Needless to say, there are a number of marriage laws in India like; Hindu Marriage Act, Muslim Marriage Act and special marriage acts in addition to others.

PREVENTION OF SATI ACT, 1829

Sati was a religious funeral practise among some Hindu communities in which a recently widowed. Hindu woman either voluntarily or by use of force or coercion would have immolated herself on her funeral pyre. The practice is rare and has been outlawed in India since 1829. Sati was supposed to be voluntary but is known that it is often been forced. Setting aside the issue of social pressure, many account exist of woman being physically forced to death. For instance Maharani Raj Rajeshwari Devi of Napal after her husband's assassination by his own brother was forced to commit Sati. Raja Ram Mohan Roy is the one of many who played the pivoted role in abolition of Sati. He is known as the Maker of Modern India. He was the founder of Brahma Samaj, one of the first Indian social religious reform movements. He was a great scholar and an independent thinker. He was against Idol Worship and Orthodox Hindu rituals.

CIVIL MARRIAGES ACT

THE SPECIAL MARRIAGE ACT, 1954

The first law of civil marriages in India was the Special Marriage Act 1872 enacted during the British rule on the recommendation of the first Law Commission of pre-independence era. It was an optional law initially made available only to those who did not profess any of the various faith traditions of India. The Hindus, Muslims, Christians, Sikhs, Buddhists, Jains and Parsis were all outside its ambit. So, those belonging to any of these communities but wanting to marry under this Act had to renounce whatever religion they were following. The main purpose of the Act was to facilitate inter-religious marriages. The Special Marriage Act 1872 contained no provision for dissolution or nullification of marriage. For these matrimonial remedies it only made the Indian Divorce Act 1869 applicable to the marriages governed by it. In 1922 the Special Marriage Act 1872 was amended to make it available to Hindus, Sikhs, Buddhists and Jains for marrying within these four communities without renouncing their religion. As so amended, the Act remained in force until after independence.

THE FOREIGN MARRIAGE ACT, 1969

In 1954 the first Special Marriage Act of 1872 was repealed by and replaced with a new law bearing the same title. This is an optional law, an alternative to each of the various personal laws, available to all citizens in all those areas where it is in force. Religion of the parties to an intended marriage is immaterial under this Act; one can marry under its provisions both within and outside one's community. The Special Marriage Act does not by itself or automatically apply to any marriage; it can be voluntarily opted for by the parties to an intended marriage in preference to their personal laws. It contains its own elaborate provisions on divorce, nullity and other matrimonial causes and, unlike the first Special Marriage Act of 1872, does not make the Divorce Act 1869 applicable to marriages governed by its provisions.

For the Hindus, Buddhists, Jains and Sikhs marrying within these four communities the Special Marriage Act 1954 is an alternative to the Hindu Marriage Act 1955. The Muslims marrying a Muslim have a choice between their uncodified personal law and the Special Marriage Act.

The Indian Christian Marriage Act 1872, however, says that all Christian marriages shall be solemnized under its own provisions [Section 4]. The issue of availability of the Special Marriage Act for a marriage both parties to which are Christians thus remains unresolved.

INTER-RELIGIOUS CIVIL MARRIAGES

The Special Marriage Act is available also for inter-religious marriages and does not exempt any community from its provisions in this respect. The Hindu Marriage Act 1955 applicable to the Hindus, Buddhists, Jains and Sikhs does not allow them to marry outside these four communities. So, if any member of these communities wishes to marry a person not belonging to these communities, the only choice available would be the Special Marriage Act 1954.

The Muslim law allows certain inter-religious marriages to be governed by its own provisions. Under this law a man can marry a woman of the communities believed by it to be Ahl-e-Kitab (People of Book) – an expression which includes Christians and Jews and may include followers of any other monotheistic faith. Since Muslim law only permits an inter-religious marriage and does not require that such a marriage must take place under its own provisions, it does not come in conflict with the Special Marriage Act 1954.

The Indian Christian Marriage Act 1872 says that apart from Christian-Christian marriages the marriage of a Christian with a non-Christian must also be solemnized under this Act (Section 4). The Special Marriage Act on the other hand says that any two persons (whatever be their religion) can marry in accordance with its provisions. There is, thus, a conflict-of-law situation in respect of marriage of a Christian with a non-Christian.

THE HINDU WIDOWS' REMARRIAGE ACT

A Hindu widow is expected to live a life of prayers and noble endeavors by the society she lives in. The expectation does not extend to Hindu widowers. Interestingly, a man who loses his wife is usually pressurized to marry for the sake of 'companionship' and so on.

Hindu Widows' Remarriage .

The obvious gender discrimination begins from within the society and percolates to the people who are a part of it. Those who question it are disapproved of or alienated tacitly and those who abide by these social norms are labeled as respectable.

Times are changing and so have many such prejudices. However, in a majority of Hindu families, the concept of widow remarriage is still not fully acceptable. While changing the outlook of family members about remarriage may be an insurmountable task, the Hindu laws support the same to emancipate such aggrieved women and help them lead a fulfilled life.

THE CHILD MARRIAGE RESTRAINT ACT, 1929

Child Marriage Restraint Act 1929 popularly kwown as the Sarda Act after its sponsor Rai Sahib Harbilas Sarda to the British India Legislature in India was passed on 28 September 1929 fixed the age of marriage for girls at 14 years and boys at 18 years. It came into effect six months later on April 1, 1930 and it applies to all of British India, not just to Hindus. It was a result of social reform movement in India. The legislation was passed by the British Indian Government.

Child Marriage.

THE HINDU MARRIAGE ACT, 1955

The Hindu Marriage Act was established in 1955 as part of the Hindu Code Bills. Three other important acts were also created during this time and they include the Hindu Succession Act (1956), the Hindu Minority and Guardianship Act (1956), and the Hindu Adoptions and Maintenance Act (1956). All of these acts were put forth under the leadership of Jawaharlal Nehru, and were meant to modernize the then current Hindu legal tradition.

DOWRY PROHIBITION ACT, 1961

Though the legislation, the Dowery Prohibition Act, 1961, aptly prohibits the giving or taking of dowry, it was felt that the present law has been totally ineffective to curb this social evil. The convention, which was attended by chairpersons of various State Commissions for Women, members of NGOs', Civil Servants as well as retired and working police officers from various states, felt that there was a dire need to make the requisite amendments to the Act so as to make it effective.

DIFFERENCE BETWEEN HINDU AND MUSLIM MARRIAGES

HINDUS

- Hinduism is polytheistic.
- Hindus tend to take a more passive role to taking more people on board.
- According to Hindu Sastra there are four stages of life, of which Grahastha Ashram or married life signifies the second stage. It begins, when a man and a woman come together and marry. In India, marriage is treated as an institution, which teaches the actual values of life.

Hindu Marriages.

- Hindu marriages are decorative.
- In a hindu marriage the groom puts on a thali around the bride's neck.

- In Hindu marriage, only one marriage is allowed.
- Hindu marriage laws are more inclusive than their Muslim counterparts.
- Hindu religious texts do not prohibit inter-religious marriages.
- Hindus follow the Vedic customs of marriage and thereby give primacy to the Vedic yajna or the fire-sacrifice. Hinduism views marriage as sacramental.

MUSLIM

- Islam is monotheistic.
- Muslims seem a lot more keen to convert people.
- Muslim wedding is divided into pre-wedding, wedding and post-wedding rituals. Pre-wedding rituals largely involve the exchange of sweets, fruits and visits to the bride and groom's houses. The pre-wedding rituals increase the level of excitement among the families of the bride and groom, who keenly look forward to the wedding day. The wedding is organized in an elegant and charming way, while the culmination of the entire ceremony, known as post wedding rituals, is special in its own terms. If you are keen about knowing more about Muslim wedding, then go through our section, where we have provided detailed information on the rituals of Muslim wedding.

Muslim Marriages.

- In Muslim marriage, divorce through only word Talak.
- In muslim marriages they exhange rings.
- Islam texts does prohibit inter-religious marriages.
- Muslims abide by the rules laid down by Sharia law.
- Islamic Nikaah (marriage) is a contract to obey Allah.

FOLKWAYS AND MORES

Concept and Meaning of Folkways. Characteristics of Folkways. Folkway Versus Custom. Meaning of Mores. Functions of Mores.

CONCEPT AND MEANING OF FOLKWAYS

The concept of folkways is associated with the name of William Sumner who made one of the clarifying analyses of culture and its implications. In his sociological classic folkways he has made a notable contribution to the understanding of individual behavior. Sumner conceived of culture in terms of folkways and mores and used the terms folkways in a very comprehensive sense. According to him: They are like products of natural forces which men unconsciously set in operation or they are like the instinctive ways of animals which are developed out of experience which reach a final form of maximum adaptation to an interest which are handed down by tradition and admit of no exception or variation yet change to meet new conditions still within the same limited methods and without rational reflection or purpose. From this it results that all the life of human beings in all ages and stages of culture is primarily controlled by a vast mass of folkways handed down from the earliest existence of the race having the nature of the ways of other animals only the top-most layers of which are subject to change and control and have been somewhat modified by human philosophy, ethics and religion or by other acts of intelligent reflection.

Folkways are recognized ways of behavior in a society which arise automatically within a group to meet the problems of social living. Social life is full of problems and man seems to have tried every possible way of dealing with such problems. Different societies have found different workable patterns. A group through trial and error, sheer accident or some unknown influence may arrive at one of the possibilities, repeats it and accepts it as the normal way of behavior. It is passed on the succeeding generations and becomes one of the ways of the group of the folk hence a folkway. According to Sumner men inherited from their beast ancestor's psycho-physical traits, instincts and dexterities or at least predispositions which give them aid in solving the problem of food supply, sex, commerce and vanity. The result is mass phenomena: currents of similarity, concurrence and mutual contribution and these produce folkways. The folkways are thus the product of frequent repetition of petty acts, often by great numbers acting in concert or at least acting in the same way when face to face with the same needs.

Folkways of the Achang People.

Folkways are the patterns of conventional behavior in a society, norms that apply to everyday matters. They are the conventions and habits learned from childhood. In western culture, folkways include wearing gender-appropriate clothing, respecting the privacy of strangers, and eating food with the proper utensil.

According to Lundberg, folkways designate those uniformities in the behavior of a group which develop relatively spontaneously and even unconsciously in adapting to common life conditions and which become established through repetition and general occurance. Thus they are those unconscious collective modes of behavior that are believed to ensure the survival and growth of the group. They include the innumerable ways of behavior men have evolved about the business of social living. They are the customs and usages which have been passed from old generations and to which new elements are added according to the changing needs of times. They represent man's unique means of adapting himself to his environment. No member of the group ever questions a folkway nor is anyone needed to enforce a folkway.

CHARACTERISTICS OF FOLKWAYS

Spontaneous Origin: Folkways arise spontaneously. They are not deliberately planned or designed. They are developed out of experience. They are unplanned and uncharted.

Approved Behavior: Folkways are the recognized ways of behavior. The group accords recognition to certain way while rejects others. Only such ways of behavior are folkways as have been approved by the group to which they relate.

Distinctiveness: There is numerous folkways in different societies, the folkways become related to a particular group. There is considerable variation in the folkways between groups.

Hereditary: Folkways are passed on from one generation to another. An individual receives folkways from his ancestors.

FOLKWAY VERSUS CUSTOM

Custom is often referred to as a folkway. But there is a difference between the two that the folkways are of more general and wider character than the customs and cover all those modes of behavior or spontaneous usages which are not included in the term customs. Thus for example—shaking hands, eating meals etc. are folkways rather than of customs. Customs are related to the survival and growth of the group but folkways are not necessarily so related. They are not made obligatory by the group. They are sanctioned informally.

MEANING OF MORES

Sumner applied the term mores to those folkways which are considered by the group to be of great significance and therefore rather indispensible to its welfare. He writes I mean by mores the popular usages and traditions when they include a judgment that they are conducive to social welfare and when they exert coercion on the individual to conform to them although they are not coordinated by any authority.

The term mores is derived from the Latin word 'mos' which stands for customs and just as customs cannot be violated by any individual so mores also cannot be violated without incurring severe punishment. The mores relate to the fundamental needs of society more directly than do the folkways. They express the group sense of what is fitting, right and conducive to social welfare. Sumner has written the Latin word mores seems to be on the whole more practically convenient and available than any other for our purpose as a name for the folkways with the connotations of right and truth in respect to welfare embodied in them.

FUNCTIONS OF MORES

According to Maclver following are the functions of mores:

They both compel behavior and forbid it. They are forever molding and restraining the tendency of every individual. In other words they are the instruments of control. In society there are innumerable mores like monogamy, anti-slavery, democracy and prohibition conformity to which is regarded as necessary.

By conforming to the mores the individual gains identification with his fellows and maintains those social bonds which are essential for satisfactory living.

This four-piece S'mores nativity set includes S'more Mary wearing a blue head piece with her arms outstretched welcoming the new S'more King lying in the manager. Joseph stands back observing the scene before him traditionally dressed in a green head piece and holding his staff.

The mores hold the members of the groups together. The members of the group though characterized by the consciousness of the kind are also competing with one another by the good things of this life and status. They are held in line by the constraints of mores. There is a sense of unreflecting solidarity among people who share the same mores because their sentiments are alike. It also implies that there is a sense of resistance and antagonism towards anyone with different mores. There are mores for each sex for all classes and for all groups whose function is to maintain the solidarity of the group.

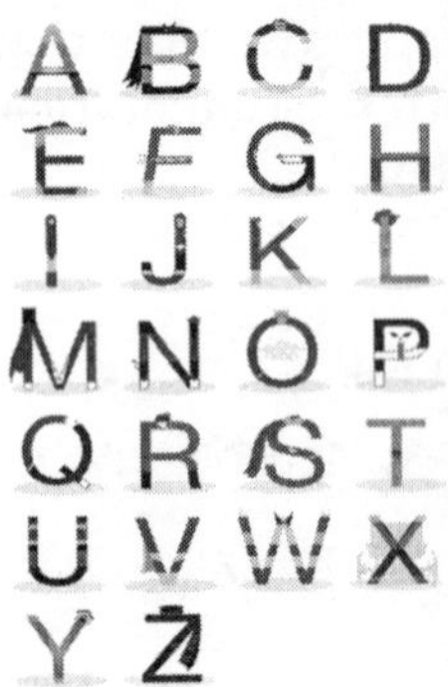

EDUCATION

Concept and Meaning of Education: *Definition of Education,* ***Significance of Education in Society. Education as a Social Process. Education as Growth. Social Functions of Education:*** *Knowledge and Skills Transfer, Socialization, Child Care and Supervision, Social Placement, Social Change, Strategic Value of Education, Research and Development, Entertainment.* ***Education and Social Change. Education and Culture. Equality of Educational Opportunity. Problems Concerning Equality of Opportunities in Education. Education and Modernization. Education and Social Control. Social Mobility. Social Inequality or Stratification:*** *Conflict Theories, Functionalist Theories.*

CONCEPT AND MEANING OF EDUCATION

The definition of education is living life. We are constantly being educated, regardless of age or race. There are two types of education: formal and informal.

Formal education is what a person receives from the age of five in structured classrooms, be it public or private, through college. The quality of this formal education solely depends on where one may live, or how much money one's parents may have. There is not a national standard, so schools across our country are completely different. A child, therefore, gets a formal education, through schools, but not necessarily one of excellence.

The second type of education is ***informal education***. People of all ages receive this type of education throughout their lives. Let's begin from birth.

Babies are taught from birth, first how to suckle. They are taught how to eat, talk, and walk, usually by family. Each year of life brings about different types of informal education. Do not doubt there are not things being learned on the playground in play groups. In every sports arena coaches are dispersing wisdom. Sunday school classes across the nation are guiding children through the doctrine of their particular faith.

Technology is a leader in informal education. Television is probably at the top of this list still. No one escapes the stretch of this educator. Humans are obsessed with T.V. Age is not relevant. Computers come closely behind, gaining importance in our family lifestyles everyday. The learning curve on the computer is limitless. Teachers cannot compete with the entertainment industry. Lessons are being learned everyday through the media. And then, living, itself, is an informal education. We feel emotions; love, hate, happiness, sadness and disappointment. We experiment, sometimes we succeed and grow. Sometimes we fall and fail. How we respond to all of these things is a learning experience. When a person is no longer learning, he is no longer living. Because everyday is a learning experience!

Worlds of Education.

Once one gets beyond a dictionary definition— a meaning that is often of little practical value—the *meaning* we assign to a word is a *belief*, not an absolute fact. Here are a couple of examples.

"The central task of education is to implant a will and facility for learning; it should produce not learned but learning people. The truly human society is a learning society, *where grandparents, parents, and children are students together.*" *—Eric Hoffer*

"No one has yet realized the wealth of sympathy, the kindness and generosity hidden in the soul of a child. The effort of every true education should be to unlock that treasure." *—Emma Goldman*

"The only purpose of education is to teach a student how to live his life-by developing his mind and equipping him to deal with reality. The training he needs is theoretical, i.e., conceptual. He has to be taught to think, to understand, to integrate, to prove. He has to be taught the essentials of the knowledge discovered in the past—and he has to be *equipped to acquire further knowledge by his own effort.*" *—Ayn Rand*

"The aim of education should be to teach us rather how to think, than what to think—rather to improve our minds, so as to enable us to think for ourselves, than to load the *memory with the thoughts of other men."*

—Bill Beattie

"The one real object of education is to leave a man in the condition of continually asking *questions."* *—Bishop Creighton*

"The central job of schools is to maximize the capacity of each student."

—Carol Ann Tomlinson

These quotations demonstrate the diversity of beliefs about the purpose of education.

DEFINITION OF EDUCATION

The definition of education is an act or process of imparting or acquiring general knowledge, developing the powers of reasoning and judgment, and generally of preparing oneself or others intellectually for mature life. It could be a certain degree, level or kind of schooling. It is a training imply a discipline and development by means of the special and general abilities of the mind or a training by which people learn to develop and use their mental, moral, and physical power or skill. It is a gaining experience, either improving or regressing. Education means to learn in every means in order to reach into a certain goals.

Education is very essential in everyday to be able to cope and survive whatever the difficulties and complication may experience. Without education, life can be so hard and frustrating in every aspect. Education will help to attain a certain ambition or dreams in life and to be successful.

The instances of education can be from school, society or home, Internet, or anywhere. It is necessary that everyone needs to go to school, to learn academically and socially. It helps build up the confidence in every person, it gives a high self-esteem as well. Also, we need to educate ourself in the society, so that we are aware in catastrophic situation. To know what's going on around us, it is an advantage to be prepared. Other than that, we need to educate ourself in the Internet, it is one of the biggest technology that revolve around the world, from researching or communicating. It is a big help to explore and educate ourself to the world of technology. Education requires discipline, patient, time, hard-work and effort. With these important behavioural qualities, it will be easier to deal with life. Education does not require a perfect physical appearance but it requires attention and focus.

Having the knowledge in everything, it refer to a high intellect power, a power that ready for anything. The skills to educate ourself is something that we could not share to anyone but we could extend it in some ways.

Technically, education is really important and it is a necessity for us, to have a better life and a better future. We need to get the best of education that we want to, it is worth it to have the knowledge, intellect, the capacity to participate in the world and it can change our life tremendously.

SIGNIFICANCE OF EDUCATION IN SOCIETY

Education is very important for an individual's success in life. Education provides pupils teaching skills that prepare them physically, mentally and socially for the world of work in later life. Education is generally seen as the foundation of society which brings economic wealth, social prosperity and political stability. Higher education helps in maintaining a healthy society which prepares health care professionals, educated health care consumers and maintaining healthy population. Education is major aspect of development of any modern society since if there is a deficit of educated people then society will stops its further progress. Government should pay serious attention to education and support it economically and morally all over the country.

Education is the best investment for the people because well educated people have more opportunities to get a job which gives them satisfaction. Educated individuals enjoy respect among their colleagues and they can effectively contribute to the development of their country and society by inventing new devices and discoveries. Today's ever growing numbers of people mostly are not satisfied with their basic education and try to get secondary or tertiary education in order to meet the demands of contemporary society. Some of them enter higher educational institutions and some search additional information on the internet. Good People sacrifices their time and money and sometimes even their health to raise educational level because they realize that education is their passport to the future and for tomorrow.

Education plays vital role in building up a good society where people can help each other.

Main purpose of education is to educate individuals within society, to prepare and qualify them for work in economy as well as to integrate people into society and teach them values and morals of society. Role of education is means of socializing individuals and to keep society smoothing and remain stable. Education in society prepares youngsters for adulthood so that they may form the next generation of leaders. It will yield strong families and strong communities. Indeed, parents taking an active role in their child education produce a willingness in children to learn. Education and society provides a forum where teachers and scholars all over the world are able to evaluate problems in education and society from a balanced and comparative social and economic perspective.

Education is an important aspect of the work of society and it will raise the countryside issues and promote knowledge and understanding of rural communities. One of the education essential tasks is to enable people to understand themselves. Students must be equipped with knowledge and skills which are needed to participate effectively as member of society and contribute towards the development of shared values and common identity. Education has a vital role to play in assisting students to understand their cultural identity. Education acts as the distribution mechanism of the cultural values such as it more layered the society and participate in society that carries the culture.

Education and society provides a forum where teachers and scholars all over the world are able to evaluate problems in education and society from a balanced and comparative social and economic perspective. Education is an important aspect of the work of society and it will raise the countryside issues and promote knowledge and understanding of rural communities. One of the education essential tasks is to enable people to understand themselves. Students must be equipped with knowledge and skills which are needed to participate effectively as member of society and contribute towards the development of shared values and common identity.

Education has a vital role to play in assisting students to understand their cultural identity. Education acts as the distribution mechanism of the cultural values such as it more layered the society and participate in society that carries the culture. In our culture today, there is a great emphasis on higher education. In a society, more educated you are, better off you are. Every society has specialized individuals that require extended education to fulfil certain main positions. These persons are normally known as professors, priests, doctors, mechanics or artists. Education has been a higher part of every culture on earth and education is a systemic project. Whole society should care for and support the education patriotism, cause and socialism among the young people.

Everyone must do work hard to cultivate moral conduct. Education mainly begins at home; one does not acquire knowledge from a teacher, one can learn and get knowledge from a parent or a family member. In almost all societies, receiving education and attending school is very necessary is one wants to achieve success. Education is the key to move in the world, seek better jobs and ultimately succeed in life. Schools play a vital role in preparing our children and young people for effective participation and responsible citizenship in society. The development of education and educational opportunities is built on creativity tempered by knowledge and wisdom gain through the experience of learning.

Investment in human capital, life long learning and quality education help in the development of society. Teachers are the most important factors for an innovative society because teachers' knowledge and skills not only enhance the quality and efficiency of education, but also improve the prerequisites of research and innovation. Many members of our society are not provided with a safe and secure environment in which children can develop, child abuse, violence against women and interpersonal violence cause a cancer on our society. Society play a key role in the realization of life long learning. The improvement of social education facilities such as libraries and the learning opportunities are implemented by the local governments. Students today are exposed to loads of technology and information at everywhere.

EDUCATION AS A SOCIAL PROCESS

Social process is a process involved in the formation of groups of persons. Social environment forms the mental and emotional disposition of behaviour in individuals by engaging them in activities that arouse and strengthen certain impulses, that have certain purposes and entail certain consequences. The development within the young of the attitudes and dispositions necessary to the continuous and progressive life of a society cannot take place by direct conveyance of beliefs, emotions and knowledge. It takes place through the intermediary of the environment. The environment consists of the sum total of conditions which are concerned in the execution of the activity characteristic of a living being. The social environment consists of all the activities of fellow beings that are bound

Education spreads awareness in society about
how we can be a good social being and help others in our daily life.

up in the carrying on of the activities of any one of its members. It is truly educative in its effect in the degree in which an individual shares or participates in some conjoint activity. By doing his share in the associated activity, the individual appropriates the purpose which actuates it, becomes familiar with its methods and subject matters, acquires needed skill, and is saturated with its emotional spirit.

The deeper and more intimate educative formation of disposition comes, without conscious intent, as the young gradually partake of the activities of the various groups to which they may belong. As a society becomes more complex, however, it is found necessary to provide a special social environment which shall especially look after nurturing the capacities of the immature. Three of the more important functions of this special environment are: simplifying and ordering the factors of the disposition it is wished to develop; purifying and idealizing the existing social customs; creating a wider and better balanced environment than that by which the young would be likely, if left to themselves, to be influenced.

Some kinds of participation in the life of those with whom the individual is connected are inevitable; with respect to them, the social environment exercises an educative or formative influence unconsciously and apart from any set purpose.

EDUCATION AS GROWTH

In directing the activities of the young, society determines its own future in determining that of the young. Since the young at a given time will at some later date compose the society of that period, the latter's nature will largely turn upon the direction children's activities were given at an earlier period. This cumulative movement of action toward a later result is what is meant by growth.

The primary condition of growth is immaturity. This may seem to be a mere truism—saying that a being can develop only in some point in which he is undeveloped. But the prefix "im" of the word immaturity means something positive, not a mere void or lack. It is noteworthy that the terms "capacity" and "potentiality" have a double meaning, one sense being negative, the other positive. Capacity may denote mere receptivity, like the capacity of a quart measure. We may mean by potentiality a merely dormant or quiescent state — a capacity to become something different under external influences. But we also mean by capacity an ability, a power; and by potentiality potency, force. Now when we say that immaturity means the possibility of growth, we are not referring to absence of powers which may exist at a later time; we express a force positively present — the ability to develop.

Children, if they could express themselves articulately and sincerely, would tell a different tale; and there is excellent adult authority for the conviction that for certain moral and intellectual purposes adults must become as little children. The seriousness of the assumption of the negative quality of the possibilities of immaturity is apparent when we reflect that it sets up as an ideal and standard a static end. The fulfilment of growing is taken to mean an accomplished growth: that is to say, an ungrowth, something which is no longer growing. The futility of the assumption is seen in the fact that every adult resents the imputation of having no further possibilities of growth; and so far as he finds that they are closed to him mourns the fact as evidence of loss, instead of falling back on the achieved as adequate manifestation of power. Why an unequal measure for child and man?

Taken absolutely, instead of comparatively, immaturity designates a positive force or ability—the pouter to grow. We do not have to draw out or reduce positive activities from a child, as some educational doctrines would have it. Where there is life, there are already eager and impassioned activities. Growth is not something done to them; it is something they do. The positive and constructive aspect of possibility gives the key to understanding the two chief traits of immaturity, dependence and plasticity.

1. It sounds absurd to hear dependence spoken of as something positive, still more absurd as a power. Yet if helplessness were all there were in dependence, no development could ever take place. A merely impotent being has to be carried, forever, by others. The fact that dependence is accompanied by growth in ability, not by an ever increasing lapse into parasitism, suggests that it is already something constructive. Being merely sheltered by others would not promote growth.
2. It would only build a wall around impotence. With reference to the physical world, the child is helpless. He lacks at birth and for a long time thereafter power to make his way physically, to make his own living. If he had to do that by himself, he would hardly survive an hour. On this side his helplessness is almost complete. The young of the brutes are immeasurably his superiors. He is physically weak and not able to turn the strength which he possesses to coping with the physical environment.

The importance for human life of the two facts of dependence and variable control has been summed up in the doctrine of the significance of prolonged infancy. This prolongation is significant from the standpoint of the adult members of the group as well as from that of the young. The presence of dependent and learning beings is a stimulus to nurture and affection. The need for constant continued care was probably a chief means in transforming temporary cohabitations into permanent unions. It certainly was a chief influence in forming habits of affectionate and sympathetic watchfulness; that constructive interest in the well-being of others which is essential to associated life. Intellectually, this moral development meant the introduction of many new objects of attention; it stimulated foresight and planning for the future. Thus there is a reciprocal influence. Increasing complexity of social life requires a longer period of infancy in which to acquire the needed powers; this prolongation of dependence means prolongation of plasticity, or power of acquiring variable and novel modes of control. Hence it provides a further push to social progress.

SOCIAL FUNCTIONS OF EDUCATION

KNOWLEDGE AND SKILLS TRANSFER

- Society needs transfer its accumulated knowledge and skills from one generation to the next.
- Fundamental of social evolution and progress and foundation of economic prosperity.
- Our society.
- Knowledge — technical, scientific, information (facts), civic and cultural values.
- Skills — reading, writing, computation, scientific reasoning, arts, skilled crafts.
- Our postindustrial, knowledge economy depends on highly trained, knowledgeable work force and workers with high level of cognitive skills and flexibility.
- Beyond capacities of the family – requires specialized institution dedicated to the goal.
- Complexity of knowledge beyond parental abilities or on-the-job apprenticeships.
- Specialized knowledge requires specialist teachers.
- Family members working so cannot devote adequate time to the task.

SOCIALIZATION

- Society needs to pass symbolic constructions from one generation to the next and socialize everyone into the same core cultural values and norms.
- Beyond capacities of the family – requires specialized institution dedicated to the goal.
- Complexity and specialized nature of our symbolic constructions.
- Requires specialized teachers – parents lack the credentials.
- Requires hours of learning and practice – family does not have the time.
- Education important for social integration.
- Integration = social order based upon general consensus about general values/norms and acceptance of the legitimacy of the culture.
- Everyone using with same cultural values and norms; consensus on how things should be:

  Integration = voluntary conformity based on acceptance of the social order's rightness.

- In a diverse society like ours, integration also requires exposure to people from all parts of the community (ethnic, social class, etc.) and comfort with and an acceptance of diversity. Three major components:
    1. Transmission of cultural values and norms + specialized occupational values and norms
    2. Hidden curriculum (attitudes, behavior traits) of obedience to authority, standardized rules and policies, group cooperation, etc.
    3. Group interaction and decision-making; competing with peers for finite rewards and working with peers in achieving collective goals.

CHILD CARE AND SUPERVISION

- Once work separated from family, society needs ways of supervising and controlling children and youth populations.
- Latest phenomenon — day care and before/after school care.
- Schools set up to process and control large populations of young people.
- Children – physical protection and security.
- Teens – discourage deviant behaviour.

SOCIAL PLACEMENT

- Class-based society (like ours) needs system for categorizing people according to abilities (brains, motivation, etc.), customizing education to ability and motivating performance with appropriate rewards.
- Screening and selecting mechanism.
- Screen individuals according to abilities; sift population into levels according to ability.
- Select by qualifications; channel people by qualifications into different slots in the stratification system.
- Link between screening/selecting and economic success.
- Educational attainment extremely important predictor of occupation, income, and mobility.
- Educational screening huge impact on individual's fate in life.
- Cultural values require equal opportunity in screening/selecting.
- No discrimination; screening should be based upon individual abilities (achieved status) and not any ascribed status (gender, race, religion, etc.).
- Modern society – credentialing based upon grades and level of schooling achieved.
- Link between education credentials and labor market.

SOCIAL CHANGE

- A "hot society" like ours needs institutional leverages for implementing and controlling social change.
- "Hot society" = rapid, constant social change.
- Emphasis on "progress" and rational control.
- Acceptance of change in values, norms, and institutions; seen as inevitable and desirable.
- Ideology of planned social change.
- Change can be engineered by design; designers = specialized experts (professionals).
- Socialization function of education makes school an especially strategic lever in planned social change.

STRATEGIC VALUE OF EDUCATION

- Children and youth not "set in their ways"; can be changed; still open to new ways.
- Children and youth = the future; if change them, then change the future
- Strategic value of school.
- Bureaucratic control; change can be implemented as organizational policy.
- Daily control of child/youth population (child care and supervision function) allows constant exposure to change messages.
- Link change messages to reward system built into social placement function.
- Examples of using schools for social change.
- Racial integration/Sex education/Computer skills/Driver's education/ Smoking and drugs.

RESEARCH AND DEVELOPMENT

- A scientifically-based society (like ours) needs an organized way of producing new knowledge.
- Cadre of highly trained, specialized professionals + Sophisticated research technology + Funding processes.
- Source of progress, innovation, and new technology.
- Institutional setting where the open processes of science (investigation, debate, scrutiny and testing, and credentialing) can occur, without the daily pressures of market competition.
- School setting, especially higher education, provides such an institutional setting.
- Faculty motivated by science and rewarded for scientific pursuits.

- Low paid (or unpaid) student labor.
- Sacrifices wages in exchange for mentoring and apprenticeship.
- Libraries, laboratory facilities, information services, and other technology oriented to research purposes.
- Economic sphere largely outside of market processes.
- Allows the "leisurely pace" and "disinterested nature" of scientific research.

ENTERTAINMENT

- Society needs to provide outlets for human creativity and play.
- Schools tend to be center of three types of entertainment—Sports, Social activities (dances, parties, volunteer activities, etc.) and Culture (arts, museums, theatre, music, etc.).

EDUCATION AND SOCIAL CHANGE

The role of education as an agent or instrument of social change and social development is widely recognized today. Social change may take place – when humans need change. When the existing social system or network of social institutions fails to meet the existing human needs and when new materials suggest better ways of meeting human needs. According to *MacIver* social change takes place as a response to many types of changes that take place in the social and nonsocial environment.

Education can initiate social changes by bringing about a change in outlook and attitude of man. It can bring about a change in the pattern of social relationships and thereby it may cause social changes. Earlier educational institutions and teachers used to show a specific way of life to the students and education was more a means of social control than an instrument of social change. Modern educational institutions do not place much emphasis upon transmitting a way of life to the students.

The traditional education was meant for an unchanging static society not marked by any change. But today education aims at imparting knowledge. Education was associated with religion. It has become secular today. It is an independent institution now. Education has been chiefly instrumental in preparing the way for the development of science and technology. Education has brought about phenomenal changes in every aspect of men's life. Francis J. Brown remarks that education is a process which brings about changes in the behaviour of society. It is a process which enables every individual to effectively participate in the activities of society and to make positive contribution to the progress of society.

EDUCATION AND CULTURE

Education encompasses teaching and learning specific skills and also something less tangible but more profound: the imparting of knowledge good judgement and wisdom. Durkheim sees education as the socialization of the younger generation. It is a continuous effort to impose on the child ways of seeing, feeling and acting which he could not have arrived at spontaneously.

Education has as one of its fundamental goals the imparting of culture from generation to generation. Culture is a growing whole. There can be no break in the continuity of culture. The cultural elements are passed on through the agents like family, school and other associations. All societies maintain themselves through their culture. Culture here refers to a set of beliefs, skills, art, literature, philosophy, religion, music etc. which must be learned. This social heritage must be transmitted through social organizations.

Education has this function of cultural transmission in all societies. The curriculum of a school, its extracurricular activities and the informal relationships among students and teachers communicate social skills and values. Through various activities school imparts values such as co-operation, teamspirit, obedience, discipline etc. Education acts an integrative force in the society by communicating values that unites different sections of society. The school teach skills to the children which help them later to integrate within the culture of the society. Education in its formal or informal pattern has been performing this role since time immemorial. Education can be looked upon as process from this point of view also. Education has brought phenomenal changes in every aspect of man's life.

EQUALITY OF EDUCATIONAL OPPORTUNITY

The equalization of educational opportunities is essentially linked with the equality notions in the social system. The social system which intends to provide equal opportunities for the advancement of all has to make provisions for equal educational opportunities also. In modern industrial society education has become the main agency for socializing new born into law abiding citizens and productive members of the society. Formal education has become almost indispensable because to participate in economic production one needs to learn specialized skills which cannot be acquired through family or any other agency. Due to the indispensability of formal education in advanced industrial societies education is provided by the state as a matter of right for all its citizens. Formal institutions – schools, colleges and universities are organized for this purpose.

In most societies today legislation exist guaranteeing equality of the right of education. In fact to realize this ideal of equality of educational opportunities special efforts are made by the welfare states in industrial societies to provide compulsory education to the socially deprived.

In developing countries like India state has assumed the responsibility to provide universal free education at the school level. Special policy measures have been developed to spread modern scientific secular education to rural areas and policy of protective discriminating has been adopted to encourage the traditionally deprived section like SC and ST to take to modern education. However in spite of the creation of a legal framework in most societies to ensure quality of educational opportunity such an ideal continues to be elusive in reality even in the industrially advanced societies. Raymond Bourdon has investigated the problem of equality of educational opportunities. Bourdon has tried to analyse the relationship between social structure and educational attainment. Bourdon maintain that even if there were no subcultural difference between classes the very fact that people start at different positions in the class system will produce inequality of educational opportunity.

For example, the costs involved and the benefits to be gained for a working class boy and an upper middle class boy in choosing the same educational course are very different simply because their starting positions in the class-system are different. Bourdon also relates the costs and benefits of course selection to family and peer group solidarity. His work has important implications for practical solutions to the problem of inequality of education opportunity. Even if positive discrimination worked and schools were able to compensate for the primary effects of stratification considerable inequality of educational opportunity would remain.

Bourdon argues that there are two ways of removing the secondary effects of stratification. The first involves the educational system. If it provides a single compulsory curriculum for all students the element of choice in the selection of course and duration of stay in the system would be removed. The individual would no longer be influenced by his courses and remain in full time education for the same period of time. He argues that more the branching points there are in the educational system point at which the student can leave or choose between alternative courses the more likely working class students are to leave or choose lower level courses. The gradual raising of the school leaving age in all advanced industrial societies has reduced inequality of educational opportunity but the present trend indicate that his reduction will at best proceed at a much slower rate. Bourdon's second solution to the problem of inequality of educational opportunity is the abolition of social stratification. He sees moves in the direction of economic equality as the most effective way of reducing inequality or educational opportunity. As a result he argues that the key to equality of opportunity lies outside rather than inside the schools. Bourdon concludes: for inequality or educational opportunity to be eliminated either a society must be unstratified or its school system must be completely undifferentiated.

PROBLEMS CONCERNING EQUALITY OF OPPORTUNITIES IN EDUCATION

Education helps in establishing equality and ensuring social justice but the system of education itself can add to the existing inequalities or at least perpetuate the same. Inequalities of educational opportunities arise due to

- Poverty as the poor cannot afford to meet the expenses of education.
- Children studying in the rural schools have to compete with the children in urban areas where there are well-equipped schools.
- In the places where no primary, secondary or collegiate educational institutions exist children do not get the same opportunity as those who have all these in their neighbourhood.
- Wide inequalities also arise from differences in home environments. A child from a rural household or slum does not have the same opportunity as a child from an upper class home with educated parents.
- There is wide sex disparity in India. Here girl's education is not given the same encouragement as boys.
- Education of backward classes including SC and ST and economically backward sections is not at par with that of other communities or classes.

EDUCATION AND MODERNIZATION

Modernization is a process of sociocultural transformation. It is a thorough going process of change involving values, norms, institutions and structures. Political dimensions of modernization involves creation of a modern nation state and the development of key institutions – political parties, bureaucratic structures, legislative bodies and a system of elections based on universal franchise and secret ballot. Cultural modernization involves adherence to nationalistic ideology, belief in equality, freedom and humanism, a rational and scientific outlook. Economic modernization involves industrialization accompanied with monetization of economy, increasing division of labour, use of management techniques and improved technology and the expansion of service sector. Social modernization involves universalistic values, achievement motivation, increasing mobility both social and geographic increasing literacy and urbanization and the decline of traditional authority.

The secular and scientific education act as an important means of modernization. It helps in the diffusion of modern values of equality, freedom and humanism. The modern school system can inculcate achievement motivation. These values can form the basis of new relations in the society and growth of rationality can enable the development of administrative system. Diffusion of values of equality, freedom and humanism can lay the foundations of a democratic political system. The spread of modern education in the second half of the 19th century led to the emergence of modern political elite in India who provided leadership in the freedom struggle. The diffusion of scientific and technical knowledge by modern educational institutions can help in the creation of skilled manpower to play the occupational roles demanded by the industrial economy. Other values like individualism and universalistic ethics etc. can also be inculcated through education. Thus education can be an important means of modernization. The importance of education can be realized from the fact that all modernizing societies tend to emphasize on universalization of education and the modernized societies have already attained it.

EDUCATION AND SOCIAL CONTROL

Helvetius referring to education in 18th century France observed that men are born ignorant not stupid; they are made stupid by education. This is not the modern view. There may be still be societies in which men's minds are stupefied by dogmatic instruction which inclines them to accept uncritically the views of political or religious authorities but the general character of formal education has been profoundly changed by modern science and technology. The great difference between primitive and early societies and modern industrial societies is that in the former education is largely concerned with transmitting a way of life while in the latter because of the mass of available knowledge the application of science to production and the elaborate division of labour formal education not only preponderates in the process of education as a whole but is largely devoted to the communication of empirical knowledge.

One aspect of this change is indicated by the observation that in modern societies the content of education is less literary and more scientific. A second major difference is that whereas in earlier societies a relatively unchanging way of life and sum of knowledge were transmitted the scientific knowledge communicated by modern education is expected to change moreover education is increasingly required to prepare individuals for a changing rather than a static world.

Formal education in modern societies communicate independently ideas which play a part in regulating behaviour. Malinowski rightly mentioned this feature in its rudimentary form in primitive societies when he included the rules of craftmanship as an element in social control. Modern science and technology are not only the basis of infinitely more complex rules of craftmenship but also of a general rational approach to nature and social life which has an increasingly important role in establishing and maintaining social cooperation. The scientific thought implicitly or explicitly criticized the ideas propounded in religious and moral doctrines and has largely been responsible for the changes which the latter have undergone. The whole rationalization of the modern world with which Max Weber was pre-occupied is connected with the development of science. Since the chief vehicle of this development has been the educational system we can speak of formal education as a type of social control.

Education has contributed to the regulation of conduct that is the early socialization of the child. The work of educational reformers such as Montessori and Froebel has brought about great changes in the education of young children. So far the reforms were connected with scientific studies of the development of children such as those of Piaget they arose from the development of the social sciences. Moreover being based upon this observation and analysis of the actual development of children's activities, needs and problems they can be regarded as having arisen very largely within the educational sphere itself as independent discoveries.

The changes in the formal education system have themselves brought about changes in the family socialization aided by the spread of social science knowledge. In this sense, the formal education of children has originated new forms of regulation of behaviour. Education in a broad sense from infancy to adulthood is thus a vital means of social control and its significance has been greatly enhanced in recent years by the rapid expansion of education at all levels in the developing countries and by the equally rapid growth of secondary and higher education in the industrial countries.

Through education new generations learn the social norms and the penalties for infringing them; they are instructed also in their station and its duties within the system of social differentiation and stratification. In modern societies where formal education becomes predominant and where an important occupational group of teachers comes into existence, education is also a major type of social control as the source of scientific knowledge which is in competition and sometimes in conflict with other types of control. This conflict may become particularly acute with the extension of higher education to a much larger proportion of the population. As the experience of Europe and USA show and the educational system may increasingly provide one of the main sources of change and innovation in the social norms.

SOCIAL MOBILITY

Individuals are recognized in society through the statuses they occupy and the roles they enact. The society as well as individuals is dynamic. Men are normally engaged in endless endeavour to enhance their statuses in society, move from lower position to higher position, secure superior job from an inferior one. For various reasons people of the higher status and position may be forced to come down to a lower status and position. Thus people in society continue to move up and down the status scale. This movement is called social mobility.

Social inequality is rising at a time when the escalators of social mobility.

According to *Wallace* and *Wallace* social mobility is the movement of a person or persons from one social status to another. W.P Scott has defined sociology as the movement of an individual or group from one social class or social stratum to another. The study of social mobility is an important aspect of social stratification. Infact it is an inseparable aspect of social stratification system because the nature, form, range and degree of social mobility depends on the very nature of stratification system. Stratification system refers to the process of placing individuals in different layers or strata.

SOCIAL INEQUALITY OR STRATIFICATION

Social inequality is a universal phenomenon in all societies. It can exist either in form of a hierarchy of groups or individuals or it may exist without the creation of a hierarchy. In the former case it is called social hierarchy. While in the latter case it is known as social differentiation for in almost all societies men and women are treated unequally. If social inequality manifests itself in the form of a hierarchy involving ranking of groups then it is known as social stratification, thus social stratification is a particular case of the social inequality. Social stratification is essentially a group phenomena. According to Ogburn and Nimkoff the process by which individuals and groups are ranked in a more or less enduring hierarchy of status is known as stratification. Melvin Tumin defines social stratification as an arrangement of any social group or society into a hierarchy of positions that are unequal with regard to power, property, social evaluation and psychic gratification. According to Lundberg a stratified society is one marked by inequality by differences among people that are evaluated by them as being lower and higher.

India has one of the fastest widening of social inequalities, where rich are getting richer and poor are getting poorer. India is becoming rich land with poor people.

There are two approaches to the study of stratification:

CONFLICT THEORIES

According to Karl Marx in all stratified societies there are two major social groups: a ruling class and a subject class. The ruling class derives its power from its ownership and control of the forces of production. The ruling class exploits and oppresses the subject class. As a result there is a basic conflict of interest between the two classes. The various institutions of society such as the legal and political system are instruments of ruling class domination and serve to further its interests. Marx believed that western society developed through four main epochs—primitive communism, ancient society, feudal society and capitalist society.

Primitive communism is represented by the societies of pre-history and provides the only example of the classless society. From then all societies are divided into two major classes—master and slaves in ancient society, lords and serfs in feudal society and capitalist and wage labourers in capitalist society. Weber sees class in economic terms. He argues that classes develop in market economies in which individuals compete for economic gain. He defines a class as a group of individuals who share a similar position in market economy and by virtue of that fact receive similar economic rewards. Thus a person's class situation is basically his market situation. Those who share a similar class situation also share similar life chances. Their economic position will directly affect their chances of obtaining those things defined as desirable in their society.

FUNCTIONALIST THEORIES

Talcott Parsons believe that order, stability and cooperation in society are based on value consensus that is a general agreement by members of society concerning what is good and worthwhile. Stratification system derives from common values it follows from the existence of values that individuals will be evaluated and therefore placed in some form of rank order. Stratification is the ranking of units in a social system in accordance with the common value system. Those who perform successfully in terms of society's values will be ranked highly and they will be likely to receive a variety of rewards and will be accorded high prestige since they exemplify and personify common values. According to Kingsley Davis and Moore stratification exists in every known human society.

All social system shares certain functional prerequisites which must be met if the system is to survive and operate efficiently. One such prerequisite is role allocation and performance. This means that all roles must be filled. They will be filled by those best able to perform them. The necessary training for them is undertaken and that the roles are performed conscientiously. Davis and Moore argue that all societies need some mechanism for insuring effective role allocation and performance. This mechanism is social stratification which they see as a system which attaches unequal rewards and privileges to the positions in society. They concluded that social stratification is a device by which societies insure that the most important positions are conscientiously filled by the most qualified persons.

VALUES AND NORMS

Introduction. The Origin of Values and Norms. Concept of Value. Concept of Norm. The Structure of Values and Norms. Characteristic of Values and Norms. The Basis of Evaluation Criteria. Dimensions of Importance: *Strength, Centrality, Range, Conditionality, Intent.* ***Interrelationships:*** *Conceptual Domain, Dimensions of Importance, Behavioural Context, Interdependence.* ***The Social Origin of Personal Values and Norms. Sources of Change in Social Values and Norms. The Role of Values and Norms in Explaining Behavior.***

INTRODUCTION

Values and norms are evaluative beliefs that synthesize affective and cognitive elements to orient people to the world in which they live. Their evaluative element makes them unlike existential beliefs, which focus primarily on matters of truth or falsehood, correctness or incorrectness. Their cognitive element makes them unlike motives that can derive from emotions or psychological drives. Values and norms involve cognitive beliefs of approval or disapproval. Although they tend to persist through time and therefore faster continuity in society and human personality, they also are susceptible to change.

The evaluative criteria represented in values and norms influence the behavior of subject units at multiple levels (e.g., individuals, organizations, and societies) as well as judgments about the behavior of others, which also can influence behaviour. For example, values and norms affect the evaluation of individuals as suitable marriage partners and in that way influence marital behavior. Values and norms also affect evaluation of the governing policies and practices of societies and thus have an impact on diplomatic relations and the policies of one society's government toward other societies.

THE ORIGIN OF VALUES AND NORMS

Multiple values and norms are organized and linked in the cultures of human social systems, which are linked when they are internalized by human actors or institutionalized by corporate actors. Social values and norms, in contrast to personal, or internalized, values and norms refer to the values and norms of a social unit that encompasses more than one person. These may refer to the officially stated or otherwise institutionalized values and norms of an organization or society, or to the collective, or shared, values and norms of the individuals who constitute a social unit such as an informal reference group, a formal organization, a society, or a societal subgroup defined by a shared characteristic. When a social value or norm refers to a collective property of the members of a social unit, it may be held with varying degrees of consensus by those who constitute that unit (Rossi and Berk 1985). An important difference between formal organizations and informal social groups or geographically defined social units is that formal organizations usually come into being for a specific purpose and are dedicated to particular types of activity and to achieving particular ends. As a result, their objectives are both narrower and more varied than those of other social units.

CONCEPT OF VALUE

A value is a belief about the desirability of a mode, means, or end of action. It indicates the degree to which something is regarded as good versus bad. A value tends to be general rather than specific, transcending particular types of action and situations. As a general evaluative criterion, it is used to assess specific behaviours in specific situations.

The evaluative criteria represented by values derive from conceptions of morality, aesthetics and achievement. That is, a mode, means, or end of action can be regarded as good or bad for moral, aesthetic, or cognitive reasons and often for a combination of those reasons. For example, being considerate of others may be valued positively (i.e., be viewed as desirable or good) for moral reasons, neatness may be valued positively for aesthetic reasons, and intelligence may be valued positively for cognitive reasons. Since the distinguishing characteristic of a value is evaluation as good or bad, a value that has a cognitive basis is a function of cognitive appraisal based on competency and achievement rather than on scientific or utilitarian grounds. For example, the choice of steel rather than iron to construct a building is a decision based on scientific or utilitarian criteria rather than on values.

The concept of a value must be differentiated from other concepts that appear to be similar. One of those concepts is a preference. A value may be thought of as a type of preference, but not all preferences are values. The distinctive characteristic of a value is that it is based on a belief about what is desirable rather than on mere liking. A preference for an equitable rather than inequitable distribution of rewards is a value, but a preference for vanilla rather than chocolate ice cream is not.

The concept of a value also bears some similarity to the concept of an attitude. Some analysts have suggested that a value is a type of attitude, but there are differences between the two concepts. An attitude refers to an organization of several beliefs around a specific object or situation, whereas a value refers to a single belief of a specific kind: a belief about desirability that is based in conceptions of morality, aesthetics, or achievement and transcends specific behaviors and situations. Because of its generality, a value occupies a more central and hierarchically important place in human personality and cognitive structure than does an attitude. It is a determinant of attitudes as well as behaviour. Thus, evaluations of numerous attitude objects and situations are based on a relatively small number of values. Not all attitudes, however, derive from values. For example, an attitude toward skiing may be based on the extent to which that sport is found to be enjoyable rather than on a value. The concept of a value also differs from the concept of an interest in much the same way that it differs from the concept of an attitude, since an interest is a type of attitude that results in the directing of one's attention and action toward a focal object or situation. As is true of attitudes more broadly, some interests derive from values but others do not.

The concept of a value also can be distinguished from the related concept of a motive. The basic property of a motive is the ability to induce valences (incentives) that may be positive or negative. A value has a motive property, involving a predisposition to act in a certain way, because it affects the evaluation of the expected consequences of an action and therefore the choice among possible alternatives; however, it is a less person-centered concept than a motive, which also encompasses emotions and drives. A value is a particular type of motive involving a belief about the desirability of an action that derives from an evaluation of that action's expected consequences in a situation. A value is a distinctively human motive, unlike motives that operate at both the human and the infrahuman levels.

A value also *differs* from a need. Although both function as motives because of their ability to induce valences, a need is distinctive in being a requirement for the continued performance of an activity and the attainment of other valued outcomes. Some needs have a biological basis; others are psychological, often deriving from the persistent frustration of important goals. Although a value may arise from a need, becoming a cognitive transformation of that need, not all needs are transformed into values and not all values derive from needs. Needs also may derive from the structure of a situation, having a social or economic basis rather than a personcentered biological or psychological basis. For example, a need for income may cause an actor to behave in ways that conflict with his or her values. A need differs from a value in that the continued functioning of the actor and the acquisitions of other valued outcomes are contingent on its being met. A need also differs from a value in that it implies a deficit that imposes a requirement, whereas a value implies motivation that is based on a belief about desirability.

Finally, a value can be differentiated from a goal. A value sometimes is thought of as a goal because goals are selected on the basis of values. However, some values focus on modes of action that are personal attributes, such as intelligence, rather than ends of action, or goals. Values are not goals of behavior. They are evaluative criteria that are used to select goals and appraise the implications of action.

CONCEPT OF NORM

Like a value, a norm is an evaluative belief. Whereas a value is a belief about the desirability of behavior, a norm is a belief about the acceptability of behavior (Gibbs 1965; Marini 1984). A norm indicates the degree to which a behavior is regarded as right versus wrong, allowable versus unallowable. It is an evaluative criterion that specifies a rule of behavior, indicating what a behavior ought to be or ought not to be. A prescriptive norm indicates what should be done, and a proscriptive norm indicates what should not be done. Because a norm is a behavioral rule, it produces a feeling of obligation. A value, in contrast, produces a feeling of desirability, of attraction or repulsion.

A norm also *differs* from a value in its degree of specificity. A norm is less general than a value because it indicates what should or should not be done in particular behavioral contexts. Whereas a value is a general evaluative criterion that transcends particular types of action and situations, a norm is linked directly to particular types of action and situations. For example, there may be a norm prescribing the killing of other human beings that is generally applicable except in situations such as war, self-defense, capital punishment and euthanasia. Situational variability of this type sometimes is referred to as the conditionality of a norm. A norm, like a value, is generally applicable to the types of action and situations on which it focuses, but it is less general than a value because it is less likely to transcend particular types of action and situations.

Because norms often derive from values, they have their basis in conceptions of morality, aesthetics, and achievement and often in a combination of those conceptions. The basis of a norm tends to affect its strength, or the importance attached to it. For example, a norm based in morality that differentiates right from wrong is likely to be considered more important than a norm based in aesthetics that differentiates the appropriate from the inappropriate, for example, in matters of dress or etiquette. A norm, however, differs from a custom in much the same way that a value differs from a preference. A norm involves an evaluation of what an actor should do, whereas a custom involves an expectation of what an actor will do. It may be expected, for example, that people will drink coffee, but it is usually a matter of indifference whether they do. Drinking coffee is therefore a custom, not a norm; it is not based on a belief about what people ought to do.

THE STRUCTURE OF VALUES AND NORMS

Multiple values and norms are organized and linked in the cultures of human social systems and also are linked when they are internalized by individuals. Cultural "value orientations" organize and link values and norms to existential beliefs in general views that also might be called worldviews or ideologies. They are sets of linked propositions embracing evaluative and existential elements that describe preferred or obligatory states. Values and norms are linked to and buttressed by existential beliefs about human nature, the human condition, interpersonal relations, the functioning of social organizations and societies, and the nature of the world. Since existential beliefs focus on what is true versus untrue, they are to some degree empirically based and verifiable.

In most of the early conceptual and theoretical work on values, values and norms were not differentiated clearly. Later, particularly as attempts to measure values and norms were made, the two concepts were routinely considered distinct, and studies focusing on them have been carried out separately since that time. As a result, the relationship between values and norms rarely has been analyzed theoretically or empirically.

Values and norms are *closely* related because values usually provide the justification for norms. As beliefs about what is desirable and undesirable, values often are associated with normative beliefs that require or preclude certain behavior, establishing boundaries to indicate what is acceptable versus unacceptable. For example, the positive value attached to human safety and security is supported by norms that proscribe doing harm to other persons and their property. Not all values are supported by norms, however. Displaying personal competence in a variety of ways is positively valued, but norms do not always require it. Similarly, not all norms support values. For example, norms in regard to dress and etiquette can be quite arbitrary. Their existence may support values, but the specific rules of behavior they establish may not.

Many cultural value orientations organize and link the values and norms that operate as evaluative criteria in human social systems. These orientations are learned and internalized by individuals in unique ways that vary with an individual's personal characteristics and social history and the interaction between the two. Cultural value orientations and internalized individual value orientations are more comprehensive systems of values and norms than those activated as influences on particular types of behavior. The latent structure of values and norms that characterizes a social system or an individual can be thought of as a map or blueprint. Only a portion of the map or blueprint that is immediately relevant to the behavioural choices being made is consulted, and the rest is ignored temporarily. Different subsets of values and norms that make up different portions of the map or blueprint are activated when different types of behavioural choices are made. For example, the values and norms relevant in choosing a mate differ from those relevant in deciding how to allocate one's time among various activities.

CHARACTERISTIC OF VALUES AND NORMS

A characteristic of values and norms that is important for understanding their structure is the type of object unit to which they pertain, such as an individual, an organization, or a society. Values and norms establish what is desirable or acceptable for particular types of object units. For example, physical and psychological health are positively valued ends of action for individuals, and norms that proscribe or prescribe action to maintain or promote health govern individual action. Democracy, distributive justice, and world peace are positively valued ends of action for societies, and norms, usually in the form of laws, proscribe and prescribe certain actions on the part of a society's institutions in support of those values. Individuals may value democracy, justice and peace, but these are societal values, not individual values, since they pertain to the characteristics of societies, not to those of individuals. Differentiating values by their object units is important in conceptualizing and measuring values relevant to the explanation of behaviour because correspondence between the actor, or subject unit, and the object unit determines the extent to which behavior by the actor is relevant to achieving a particular end. Individuals differentiate between personal and societal values because they do not have direct influence over social values, thus distinguishing their beliefs on the basis of whether they think those beliefs will lead to action.

THE BASIS OF EVALUATION CRITERIA

As evaluative criteria, values and norms have the ability to induce valences (incentives). They affect evaluation of the behavior of others and involve a predisposition to act in a certain way because they affect the evaluation of the expected consequences of action. The evaluation that occurs on the basis of values and norms derives from two structural properties: the polarity, or directionality, of the value or norm and the standard of comparison that is used.

Polarity: The polarity of a value or norm is the direction of its valence, or motive force, which may be positive or negative. In the case of a value, something that is evaluated as desirable will have a positive valence, whereas something that is evaluated as undesirable will have a negative valence. In the case of a norm, something that should be done will have a positive valence, whereas something that should not be done will have a negative valence.

Standard of Comparison: A value or norm also is characterized by a standard, or level, of aspiration or expectation. This evaluative standard is a reference point with respect to which a behavior and its consequences are evaluated. A subject unit's own action and that of others, as well as the ends that result or may result from action, are evaluated on the basis of whether they are above or below an evaluative standard.

In the case of a value, the evaluative standard determines the neutral point on the value scale at or above which a behavior or its consequences will be evaluated as desirable and below which a behavior or its consequences will be evaluated as undesirable. In both economics and psychology, it has been recognized that there is a utility, or value, function that should be considered nonlinear provides a discussion of these developments, and there is empirical evidence that it generally is appropriate to assume the existence of a reference point on a utility, or value, scale. This reference point plays a critical role in producing a nonlinear relationship between the value scale and the objective continuum of behavior and its consequences. It has been observed that value functions change significantly at a certain point, which is often, although not always, zero.

In the *prospect theory of Kahneman and Tversky*, outcomes are expressed as positive or negative deviations from a neutral reference outcome that is assigned a value of zero. Kahneman and Tversky propose an S-shaped value function that is concave above the reference point and convex below it but less steep above than below. This function specifies that the effect of a marginal change decreases with the distance from the reference point in either direction but that the response to outcomes below the reference point is more extreme than is the response to outcomes above it. The asymmetry of the value function suggests a stronger aversion to what is evaluated as undesirable, an asymmetry that is consistent with an empirically observed aversion to loss.

In the case of a norm, the evaluative standard is set by what is defined to be acceptable versus unacceptable. It is a level of expectation that is determined by the specific behaviors that are regarded as right versus wrong, appropriate versus inappropriate. An important difference between a value and a norm is that whereas there is a continuous, nonlinear relationship between a value scale and the objective continuum of behavior or its consequences above the neutral point set by the evaluative standard, this relationship is not expected between the scale of evaluation based on a normative criterion and the objective continuum of behavior. Because a normative standard establishes a boundary of acceptability or requirement that applies to all those covered by the norm, compliance with a normative expectation is not evaluated as a continuous variable on the basis of variation in behavior above the reference point set by the normative expectation. However, violation of a normative standard is evaluated as a continuous variable on the basis of variation in behaviour below the reference point set by the standard. Negative deviations from the standard are likely to be evaluated in much the same way as are negative evaluations from the reference point on a value scale, which is convex below the reference point. Because of the strong aversion to what is evaluated as being below the reference standard, behavior that violates a normative standard is likely to be eliminated from consideration as an option.

The level of aspiration or expectation that operates as an evaluative standard for an actor is socially determined to a large degree. It is a "comparison level" learned from others whom the actor takes as referents. As a result of variation in the characteristics of actors, the social environments to which they are exposed, and the interaction between those two factors, the evaluative standards associated with values and norms vary across actors. Even among actors in the same social environment, the evaluative standard is specific to the actor, although there may be a high degree of consensus about it in a social group.

The evaluative standards associated with values and norms are *subject to change in an individual actor*. An important source of change is experience that affects the level of ability, knowledge, or accomplishment of an actor. For example, the evaluative standard for achievement values is affected by an actor's level of achievement. There is evidence that people tend to raise their value standards with success and lower them with failure. Thus, as a worker learns a job, that worker's ability to perform the job increases, as does the worker's evaluative standard. A level of ability that once was aspired to and evaluated as "extremely good" may, after increases in the worker's ability, come to be viewed as "mediocre" and below the worker's current evaluative standard for expected performance. Experience also may affect the evaluative standard for norms. For example, there is evidence that the experience of divorce changes normative beliefs about divorce in the direction of increasing its acceptability. Another source of change in the evaluative standards associated with the values and norms of an actor is an increase in knowledge of the world that alters the existential beliefs connected with values and norms.

The evaluative standards associated with values and norms *vary not only among actors and over time for the same actor but also with the characteristics of other actors whose behaviour is the object of evaluation.* These characteristics may differentiate among actors or among the circumstances of the same actor at different times. For example, the value standard used by an adult to evaluate a child's knowledge will vary for children who have completed different amounts of schooling, such as an elementary school student, a high school student, or a college student: The amount of knowledge evaluated as "very good" for an elementary school student will differ from that evaluated as "very good" for a student at a more advanced stage of schooling. Different value standards will be applied to different students and to the same student at different stages of schooling. Similarly, in a work organization, the value standard used to evaluate performance may vary for different categories of workers. Those with more experience may be evaluated according to a higher standard. Again, these different standards may be applied to different workers who are in different categories or to the same worker as he or she progresses from one category to another.

Like a value standard, a normative standard may vary with the characteristics of other actors whose behaviour is an object of evaluation. However, there is a difference between a value and a norm in this regard. Because a value is a continuous variable, variation in the value standard with the characteristics of the other actors whose behaviour is being evaluated need not have implications for whether the value applies to those actors. In contrast, because a norm is a discrete variable that differentiates what is acceptable from what is unacceptable, variation in the evaluative standard of a norm with the characteristics of other actors whose behavior is being evaluated determines whether the norm applies to other actors with particular characteristics. This variability—that is, variability in whether a value or norm applies based on the characteristics of the actors being evaluated—is a dimension of the importance of a value or norm and is labeled its conditionality.

DIMENSIONS OF IMPORTANCE

It is commonly recognized that values and norms differ in their priority, or importance, and that those differences are another aspect of the structure of values and norms. Differences in priority produce a structure that is to some degree hierarchical. Recognition that not all values are of equal importance has led to the use of ranking procedures to measure values. These procedures have been criticized for forcing respondents to represent their values in a ranked order that does not allow for the possibility that some values may be of equal importance. Although there is a hierarchy among values, there may be sets of values that occupy the same position in the hierarchy. The priority of a value or norm not only has implications for its influence on behavior but also may have implications for the probability that it will change, since values and norms of high priority have been argued to be less likely to change than are those of low priority. The priority, or importance, of a value or norm can be assessed on a number of dimensions:

1. strength, or intensity,
2. centrality,

3. range,
4. conditionally, and
5. intent.

Although these dimensions are conceptually different, they are likely to overlap empirically to a considerable degree. The extent to which and ways in which they overlap in reflecting the importance of a value or norm are not known.

1. STRENGTH

The strength of a value or norm can be defined as the maximum strength of the force field it can induce. The strength of the valence reflects its hierarchical position in the latent map or blueprint that characterizes the structure of values and norms for a social system or an individual. Although the strength of a value or norm is likely to display considerable stability, it is also subject to change. At the level of the social system, it may change as a result of long-term changes in social organization and aspects of culture as well as precipitating events. As the social system changes, socializing influences on individuals change. Changes in the values and norms of individuals occur both over the life course and as a result of differences between those who are born and move through life in different historical periods. The motivational force of a value at a particular time, however, is not necessarily the maximum strength of its latent force field, because attaining a valued outcome may reduce the subjective utility of additional units of that outcome as a result of diminishing marginal utility, or satiation. In the case of either a value or a norm, whether one attains an outcome also may alter the maximum strength of its latent force field. For example, if attainment is problematic, the importance of a value or norm may decline as a way of reducing cognitive dissonance.

2. CENTRALITY

The centrality of a value or norm can be defined as the number and variety of behaviors or ends to which it applies. Because a central value or norm contributes more than does a peripheral one to the coherent organization and functioning of the total system, the disappearance of a central value or norm would make a greater difference to the total system than would the disappearance of a peripheral value or norm. A central value or norm is more resistant to change than is a peripheral value or norm; however, if change occurs, the more central the value or norm changed, the more widespread its repercussions.

For individuals and even for social groups, concern and responsibility for the well-being of others is a central value that pertains to a large number and variety of specific behaviors and ends. It is supported by a central proscriptive norm that one should not harm others and a central prescriptive norm that one should help others, particularly if they are in need. These norms pertain to a large number and variety of specific behaviours. In contrast, excitement and adventure are more peripheral values, affecting a smaller number and variety of specific behaviours and ends. In connection with these values, peripheral norms govern the carrying out of specific types of activities that may be sources of excitement and adventure, such as the rules governing sports and potentially dangerous recreational activities.

For individuals, life values that pertain to the overall ends, or goals, of life along with the norms that support them tend to be more central than are the values and norms that pertain to particular life domains or social roles. Part of the reason for this is that life values affect whether particular life domains or social roles are entered into and the amounts of time and energy a person spends in different domains and roles. They also affect an individual's domain- and role-specific values and norms. For example, life values include things such as attaining a high material standard of living, having meaningful family relationships and friendships, making the world a better place, and having a good time. Life values of this type are among the factors that influence entry into various life domains and roles, the activities in those domains and roles, and how much investment is made in each one (e.g., marriage, parenthood, employment, friendships, leisure activities and hobbies, community activities, religion). Values and norms pertaining to each of the domains and roles are to some degree a function of overall life values. For example, if an individual places a higher priority on making the world a better place than on material well-being, that individual's employment values will place a higher priority on the possible influence and significance of the work performed than on the earnings derived from the work. Similarly, if an individual places a higher priority on meaningful relationships than on material wellbeing, marital values will place a higher priority on love and mutual respect than on the shared material standard of living.

3. RANGE

The range of a value or norm can be defined as the number and variety of actors of a particular type of object unit (e.g., individuals, organizations, and societies) to which it applies. Whereas the dimension of centrality focuses on the characteristics of action and its ends (i.e., the number and variety of behaviors or ends to which a value or norm applies), the dimension of range focuses on the characteristics of actors (i.e., the number and variety of individuals or larger social units to which a value or norm applies). The characteristics of actors used to define the range of a value or norm tend to be ascriptive or groupdefining characteristics of individuals or larger social units. In the case of individuals, these are characteristics such as age, sex, nationality, race, and ethnicity. A value or norm with a broad range applies to all actors of a particular type of object unit, whereas a value or norm with a narrow range applies to a very restricted category of actors of that type. For example, concern about and responsibility for the well-being of others is a value with a broad range that applies universally to individuals throughout the world. In contrast, wisdom is a value with a narrower range because although it applies throughout the world, it applies primarily to people of older ages. Similarly, the norm against incest has a broad range because it applies universally to individuals throughout the world. In contrast, the norm prescribing paid employment has a narrower range because it applies primarily to men in particular age categories.

4. CONDITIONALITY

The conditionality of a value or norm can be defined as the number and variety of situations to which it applies. Whereas the dimension of centrality focuses on the characteristics of action or its ends and the dimension of range focuses on the characteristics of actors, the dimension of conditionality focuses on the characteristics of situations, including a situation's actors. When conditionality pertains to the characteristics of a situation's actors, it usually refers to emergent or potentially changing characteristics of actors that define the situation rather than to ascriptive characteristics that define membership in social groups. Although values are less tied to specific types of situations than norms are, both values and norms vary in the degree to which they are conditioned on the characteristics of situations. For example, some values pertaining to modes of conduct, such as courtesy, cleanliness, and honesty, are applicable across most situations. Others are applicable in many fewer situations or may even be bipolar, with the polarity of the value being conditional on the situation. For example, aggressiveness is positively valued in some types of competitive situations, such as warfare and sports, but negatively valued in some types of cooperative situations, such as conversation and child rearing.

The conditionality of a value or norm is evident when a given subject actor who is evaluating a given type of action or end of action makes different evaluations in different types of situations, that is, when the evaluation varies with the characteristics of the situation. For example, friendliness is valued positively, but it is a value characterized by some conditionality, since it is valued negatively when exhibited toward strangers in dangerous environments. Killing other human beings is normatively proscribed in almost all situations, but the norm has some conditionality because killing is not proscribed in warfare, self-defense, capital punishment, and euthanasia. In capital punishment and some types of warfare, killing actually is prescribed. Abortion is believed by some people to be normatively proscribed, and whether it is normatively proscribed often depends on the characteristics of the situation, including how conception occurred, whether the mother's health is in danger, and whether the mother can care for the child. Opposition to abortion is therefore a norm of higher conditionality than is the proscription against killing other human beings. The conditionality of a value or norm is defined by the number and variety of situations to which it applies consistently, that is, with the same polarity. A value or norm that has the same polarity across many and varied types of situations is a value or norm of low conditionality and therefore of high priority. A value or norm that has the same polarity in only a few similar types of situations is a value or norm of high conditionality and low priority.

5. INTENT

Whether a value applies to a mode, means, or end of action has been labeled its intent. Mode values pertain to the manner or style in which an action is carried out and refer to both the action and the actor. They pertain to qualities manifested in the act, and if such qualities are observed consistently over time for a type of action or for an actor, they are applied not just to a single instance of action but to a type of action or to an actor more generally. Adjectives such as "intelligent," "independent," "creative," "responsible," "kind," and "generous" describe mode values. Instrumental values focus on necessary means to other ends. They refer to action that constitutes the means or from which the means are derived. For example, a job and the earnings it provides may be viewed as means to other ends such as acquiring the material resources necessary to sustain life. Goal values, in contrast, pertain to self-sufficient, or autonomous, ends of action. They are not subordinate to other values and are what an actor values most. Some analysts have argued that they can be defined as what an actor desires without limit. They focus on sources of intrinsic satisfaction or happiness but are distinguished from pleasures, which, except when elevated to become goal values, are satisfactions that are enjoyed incidentally and along the way. Pleasures are not necessarily based on beliefs about desirability, since they can be based on mere liking.

A norm may apply to a mode or means of action but not to an end of action. By requiring or prohibiting a way of acting or a type of action, norms limit the modes and means used in accomplishing ends. For example, the values of honesty and fairness govern modes and means of accomplishing ends, and associated with these values are norms that require honest and fair action.

Values and norms cannot always be identified as falling into a single category of intent. For some types of action, mode values and norms and instrumental or goal values and norms overlap; choosing an action as a means or to directly achieve an end actually defines the mode of action. For example, accomplishing a task by a means that shows concern for others defines a mode of acting that is kind, considerate, polite, and caring. Choosing to accomplish a task by honest means defines a mode of acting honestly. Acting to achieve an end that benefits others defines a mode of acting that is caring, giving, and generous. Mode values and norms and instrumental or goal values and norms do not always overlap, however. A given mode may be applied to a variety of means and ends, and choosing a means or acting to achieve an end does not necessarily imply or define a mode. For example, for modes that reflect ability or competence, as described by adjectives such as "intelligent", "creative," "efficient," "courageous," "organized," and "self-reliant," there may be no necessary connection or only a limited one between the values reflected in the mode and the values reflected in the acts undertaken as means or ends.

Differentiating between instrumental values and goal values is difficult because the two types are interdependent. Their relationship is not just one of sequence, since achieving particular ends may require the use of certain means. Differentiating between instrumental values and goal values also requires reflection by the actor. An important concern of moral philosophy has been identifying the end or ends of action that ultimately bring satisfaction to human beings, that is, that have genuine, intrinsic value. The focus has been on identifying important goal values and distinguishing them from less important instrumental values. This means—end distinction is not as well developed in the category systems of all cultures as it is in Western culture, and even among persons exposed to Western culture, it is not developed equally or similarly in all actors. Not all actors make the distinction or make it in the same way. What are instrumental values to some actors are goal values to others.

When mode, instrumental, and goal values are separable, they can all affect behavior. Sometimes they point to identical actions, and sometimes they do not. Similarly, when mode and instrumental norms are separable, both can affect behavior. Among values that can pertain to either means or ends, the distinction between instrumental and goal values is a dimension of importance, with goal values being of higher priority than instrumental values. However, values that can pertain only to a mode or means are not necessarily of lower priority than are values that can pertain to ends.

INTERRELATIONSHIPS

Because social structure, as defined both organizationally and culturally, links sets of values and norms, there are patterned relationships among the sets of values and norms held by actors. These relationships can be seen as being influenced by conceptual domain, dimensions of importance, behavioral context, and interdependence.

CONCEPTUAL DOMAIN

Values and norms that are conceptually similar are thought of as falling within the same conceptual domain, and a conceptual domain is identified by the observation of strong empirical relationships among sets of values or norms. Domains that are conceptually distinct also can have relationships to one another. Compatible domains are positively related, and contradictory domains are negatively related. Empirical research provides some evidence of the existence of conceptual domains of values and norms and the relationships among them. For example, in Western societies, a value domain emphasizing pleasure, comfort, and enjoyment has a negative relationship to a prosocial value domain that emphasizes concern and responsibility for others. Similarly, a value domain emphasizing the extrinsic attainment of power, money, and position has a negative relationship to the prosocial value domain. Values appear to be organized along at least three broad dimensions:

1. emphasis on the self versus others,
2. emphasis on achievement versus pleasure, and
3. emphasis on the external versus the internal.

Although there has been less research on the pattern of interrelationships among norms, evidence indicates that norms fall into conceptual domains. Norms pertaining to honesty, for example, are conceptually separable from norms pertaining to personal freedom in family matters, sexuality, and mortality.

DIMENSIONS OF IMPORTANCE

Interrelationships among values and norms also are affected by dimensions of importance, since these dimensions affect their application across object units, social institutions, social roles, and behavioral contexts. Dimensions of importance such as centrality, range, and conditionality are linked to variability in application across object units, social institutions, and social roles. Values and norms that have high importance because they are broadly applicable are more likely to be interrelated than are values and norms that have low importance, which apply more narrowly. Values and norms that apply narrowly are related to each other and to values and norms that apply more broadly only under the conditions in which they apply.

BEHAVIOURAL CONTEXT

Interrelationships among values and norms are influenced not only by conceptual domains and dimensions of importance but also by the behavioural contexts to which they apply. Values and norms that are relevant to the same or related behavioral contexts tend to be interrelated. For example, the values and norms that play a role in interpersonal relationships differ in some respects from those which play a role in educational and occupational performance. The value of concern for others and the norms that support it are of high priority in interpersonal relationships but can be of low priority in the performance of educational and occupational tasks.

INTERDEPENDENCE

Socially structured or otherwise necessary links among modes, means, and ends of action are a source of interdependence among values and norms. Mode values and norms and instrumental or goal values and norms can overlap, and instrumental and goal values are interdependent when achieving particular ends requires the use of certain means. This interdependence constrains the extent to which the relative priority of values can affect action. For example, attaining a less highly valued means cannot be forgone to attain a more highly valued end if the end cannot be attained without the means.

THE SOCIAL ORIGIN OF PERSONAL VALUES AND NORMS

The values and norms of individual persons derive from the social environments to which they are exposed. Through socialization, individuals become aware of and internalize social values and norms, which then become important internal determinants of action. An individual's internalized values and norms reflect the values and norms of the society and the various subgroups and organizations within that society to which that individual is exposed, particularly, although not exclusively, in the early stages of the life course. Once social values and norms are internalized, they can direct the behavior of individuals irrespective of external influences. Internalized values and norms are a source of self-expectations and a basis of self-evaluation, with the subjective response to an outcome ensuing from the self-concept. Adherence to self-expectations enhances self-esteem, producing a sense of pride and other favorable self-evaluations. Violation of self-expectations reduces self-esteem, producing guilt, self-depreciation, and other negative self-evaluations. To preserve a sense of self-worth and avoid negative self-evaluations, individuals try to behave in accordance with their internalized values and norms. Sociologists tend to see internalized values and norms as an important influence on human behaviour, and this makes them see the social values and norms of society as governing and constraining the choices individuals make. Social values and norms also affect behaviour because they are internalized by significant others and thus affect an actor's perception of other people's expectations. To the extent that actors are motivated to comply with what they perceive the views of others to be, social values and norms become a source of external pressure that exerts an influence that is independent of an individual's internalized values and norms.

Although change in personal values and norms occurs over the life course, there is some evidence that levels of stability are relatively high. It has been argued that values and norms that are more closely tied to the self-concept and considered more important are more resistant to change. Those values and norms may undergo less change because they are internalized through conditioning-like processes that begin early in life and are strongly linked to existential beliefs. They tend to be tied to shared mental models that are used to construct reality and become embedded central elements of cognitive organization with a strong affective basis. Some types of values, norms, and attitudes (for example, political attitudes) are quite malleable into early adulthood and then become relatively stable. After this "impressionable," or "formative," period when change is greatest, they are relatively stable in midlife, and this stability either persists or declines in the later years. The pattern of life-course change and stability described above has been argued to be due to a number of influences. One is the process of biological and psychological maturation with age, which is most rapid in the early stages of life. As functional capacity develops, influences at that time have the advantage of primacy, and when they are consistent over a period of years, affective "mass" is built up. Nevertheless, some types of values, norms, and attitudes remain malleable into early adulthood, and strong pressure to change or weak earlier socialization can lead to resocialization in late adolescence or early adulthood. It is likely that change declines after early adulthood in part because individuals tend to act on previously formed values, norms, and attitudes as they seek new information and experiences. This selective structuring of new inputs enhances consistency over time, since new inputs tend to reinforce rather than call into question earlier ones.

Another influence on life-course change and stability in values and norms is change in social experiences and roles over the life course. These changes are extensive during the transitional years of early adulthood and may increase after retirement. They represent opportunities for change because they bring the individual into contact with new individuals, reference groups, and situations, and change in values and norms is likely to occur through both interaction with others and adaptation to situations. Role change can produce change as a role occupant engages in new behaviors, is exposed to new circumstances and information, and learns the norms governing role behavior. After early adulthood, a decline in the number of changes in social experiences and roles leads to greater stability in values and norms.

SOURCES OF CHANGE IN SOCIAL VALUES AND NORMS

Change in social values and norms occurs through a variety of processes. One influence is historical change in the conditions of life that occurs through technological innovation, alterations in economic and social organization, and change in cultural ideas and forms. Historical change by definition involves "period effects," but because those effects tend to be experienced differently by different birth cohorts (i.e., those at different ages when a historical change occurs), the influence of historical change on social values and norms occurs to some degree through a process of cohort succession.

Change in social values and norms also occurs through change in the social values and norms of subgroups of social units. This change can be of several types. First, change in the presence and size of subgroups with different values and norms produces change in the collective values and norms of the group. For example, the presence of new immigrant groups with different values and norms or a change in the relative size of groups with different values and norms affects the values and norms of the collective unit. Second, change in the degree of similarity or difference in the values and norms of subgroups can produce change in overall values and norms. On the one hand, acculturation through intergroup contact and similar experiences will reduce the distinctiveness of subcultural groups; on the other hand, segregation and increasing divergence in the life experiences of subgroups will widen their cultural distinctiveness. Third, some subcultural groups may be more subject to particular period influences than others are, and this differential responsiveness can increase or decrease differences in values and norms among subgroups.

Another source of change in social values and norms is change in exposure to social organizations that exert distinct socializing influences. For example, exposure to religious, educational, or work organizations may produce differences in values and norms between those with such exposure and those without it. The extent to which exposure to different organizational environments is likely to affect personal values and norms depends on the distinctiveness of those environments, which also is subject to change. Thus, social values and norms are affected by both changes in the exposure of the population to different organizations and changes in what is socialized by those organizations.

THE ROLE OF VALUES AND NORMS IN EXPLAINING BEHAVIOUR

The ways in which values and norms influence behavior must be understood in a larger explanatory framework, and models of purposive action in all the social sciences provide that framework. These models rest on the assumption that actors are purposive, acting in ways that tend to produce beneficial results. Although the models of purposive action that have emerged in various social sciences differ in the nature of the assumptions made about purposive action, they share the basic proposition that people are motivated to achieve pleasure and avoid pain and that this motivation leads them to act in ways that, at least within the limits of the information they possess and their ability to predict the future, can be expected to yield greater reward than cost. If reward and cost are defined subjectively and individuals are assumed to act in the service of subjective goals, this proposition links subjective utility, or value, to action. In sociology, a model of purposive action assumes the existence of actors who may be either persons or corporate actors. The usefulness of these models in sociology hinges on making appropriate connections between the characteristics of social systems and the behaviour of actors (the macro-micro connection) and between the behaviour of actors and the systemic outcomes that emerge from the combined actions of multiple actors (the micro-macro connection).

In a model of purposive action, an individual actor (person or corporate actor) is assumed to make choices among alternative actions structured by the social system. Choices among those actions are based on the outcomes expected to ensue from those actions, to which the actor attaches some utility, or value, and which the actor expects with some probability. The choices of the actor are governed by beliefs of three types:

— the perceived alternatives for action available,

— the perceived consequences expected to result from each alternative, and

— the perceived probabilities with which those consequences are expected to result.

The choices of the actor also are governed by the actor's preferences, or the subjective utility (rewards and costs) of the consequences expected to result from each alternative. Values and norms are among the preferences of an actor that influence action. As evaluative beliefs that synthesize affective and cognitive elements, they affect the utility of the outcomes expected to ensue from an action. Action often results not from a conscious weighing of the expected future benefits of alternatives but from a less deliberate response to internalized or institutionalized values and norms (Emerson 1987). The actor's finite resources—the human, cultural, social, and material capital available to the actor that enables or precludes action—operate as influences on the choices made by the actor.

The component of a model of purposive action that makes the macro-micro connection links the characteristics of the social system to the behavior of actors and models the effects of social structure (both organizational and cultural) on the beliefs and preferences of actors as well as on the available alternatives for action and actors' resources. In this component of the model, characteristics of the micro model are taken as problematic and to be explained. These characteristics include:

— the beliefs and preferences on the basis of which an actor makes choices,

— the alternatives available to an actor, and

— the resources available to an actor.

A third component of a model of purposive action makes the micro–macro connection, linking the behavior of individual actors to the systemic outcomes that emerge from the combined actions of multiple actors. This link may occur through a simple mechanism such as aggregation, but it is more likely that outcomes emerge through a complex interaction in which the whole is not just the sum of its parts. The action, or behavior, of the system is usually an emergent consequence of the interdependent actions of the actors that compose it.

19

CHAPTER

SOCIAL DIFFERENTIATION AND SOCIAL CHANGE

Social Inequality: *Social Inequality and Tribal, Social Inequality and the Disabled, Social Inequality and Gender.* ***Social Differentiation. Types of Social Differentiation. Social Differentiation as Decomposition or Emergence. Causes of Social Differentiation. Consequences of Social Differentiation. Social Change. Causes of Social Change:*** *Culture and Change, Conflict and Change, Ideas and Change, Demographic Change, Environmental Changes.*

SOCIAL INEQUALITY

Social inequality is a universal phenomenon in all societies. It can exist either in form of a hierarchy of groups or individuals or it may exist without the creation of a hierarchy. In the former case it is called *social hierarchy*. While in the latter case it is known as *social differentiation* for in almost all societies men and women are treated unequally. If social inequality manifests itself in the form of a hierarchy involving ranking of groups then it is known as *social stratification*, thus social stratification is a particular case of the social inequality.

Social Inequality.

In every society some people have a greater share of valued resources—money, property, education, health and power than others. These social resources can be divided into three forms of capital-economic capital in the form of material assets and income; cultural capital such as educational qualifications and status; and social capital in the form of networks of contacts and social associations. Often these three forms of capital overlap and one can be converted into the other. For example, a person from a well-off family can afford expensive higher education and so can acquire cultural or educational capital. Patterns of unequal access to social resources are commonly called social inequality. Social inequality reflects innate differences between individuals for example their varying abilities and efforts. Someone may be endowed with exceptional intelligence or talent or may have worked very hard to achieve their wealth and status. However by and large social inequality is not the outcome of innate or natural differences between people but is produced by the society in which they live.

SOCIAL INEQUALITY AND TRIBAL

The Social Tribes are social groups recognized by the Indian Constitution as specially marked by poverty, powerlessness and social stigma. The jana or tribes were believed to be people of the forest whose distinctive habitat in the hill and forest areas shaped their economic, social and political attributes. Tribal groups have had long and close association with Hindu society and culture making the boundaries between tribe and caste quite porous.

The Independence of India in 1947 should have made life easier for adivasis but this is not the case. Firstly, the Government monopoly over forests continued leading to acceleration in exploitation of forests. Secondly, the policy of capital intensive industrialization adopted by the Indian Government required mineral resources and power generation capacities which were concentrated in Adivasi lands. Adivasi lands were rapidly acquired for new mining and dam projects. In the process millions of Adivasis were displaced without any appropriate compensation or rehabilitation. Justified in the name of national development and economic growth these policies were also a form of internal colonialism, subjugating adivasis and alienating the resources upon which they depended. Projects such as Sardar Sarovar Dam on the river Narmada in western India and the Polavaram dam on the river Godavari in AP will displace hundred and thousands of adivasis driving them to greater destitution. These processes continue to prevail and have become even more powerful since the 1990s when economic liberalization policies were officially adopted by the Indian Government.

The term Adivasi connotes political awareness and the assertion of rights. Literally meaning original inhabitants the term was coined in the 1930s as part of the struggle against the intrusion by the colonial government and outside settlers and moneylenders. Being adivasi is about shared experiences of the loss of forests, the alienation of land, repeated displacements since Independence in the name of development projects and much more.

Inspite of the heavy odds against them and in the face of their marginalization many tribal groups have been wagging struggles against outsiders and the state. In post independence India, the most significant achievements of Adivasi movements include the attainment of statehood for Jharkhand and Chattisgarh which were originally part of Bihar and Madhya Pradesh.

SOCIAL INEQUALITY AND THE DISABLED

The differently abled are not disabled only because they are physically or mentally impaired but also because society is built in a manner that does not cater to their needs. In contrast to the struggles over Dalit, adivasi or women's rights the rights of the disabled have been recognized only very recently. Yet in all historical periods, in all societies there have been people who are disabled.

In India labels such as disability, handicap, crippled, blind and deaf are used synonymously. Often these terms are hurled at people as insults. In culture that looks up to bodily perfection all deviations from the perfect body signify abnormality, defect and distortion. Labels such as bechara accentuate the victim status for the disabled person. The roots of such attitudes lie in the cultural conception that views an impaired body as a result of fate. Destiny is seen as the culprit and disabled people are the victims. The common perception views disability as retribution for past karma from which there can be no reprieve. The dominant cultural construction in India therefore looks at disability as essentially a characteristic of the individual. The popular images in mythology portray the disabled in an extremely negative fashion.

The term disabled challenges each of these assumptions. Terms such as mentally challenged, visually impaired and physically impaired came to replace the more negative terms such as retarded, crippled or lame. The disabled are rendered disabled not because they are biologically disabled but because society renders them so. The social construction of disability has yet another dimension. There is a close relationship between disability and poverty. Malnutrition, mothers weakened by frequent childbirth, inadequate immunization programmes, and accidents in overcrowded homes all contribute to an incidence of disability among poor people that is higher than among people living in easier circumstances. Furthermore disability creates and exacerbates poverty by increasing isolation and economic strain not just for the individual but for the family there is little doubt that disabled people are among the poorest in poor countries. It is only recently with the efforts of the disabled themselves that some awareness is building in society on the need to rethink disability. Recognition of disability is absent from the wider educational discourse. This is evident from the historical practices within the educational system that continue to marginalize the issue of disability by maintaining two separate streams—one for disabled students and one for everyone else.

SOCIAL INEQUALITY AND GENDER

Because of the obvious biological and physical differences between men and women, gender inequality is often treated as natural. However despite appearances, scholars have shown that the inequalities between men and women are social rather than natural. There are no biological reasons that can explain why so few women are found in position of public power. Nor can nature explain why women generally receive a smaller or no share in family property in most societies. But the strongest argument comes from the societies that were different from the normal or common pattern. If women were biologically unfit to be inheritors and head of families how did matrilineal societies work for centuries? How have women managed to be successful farmers and traders in so many African societies? There is nothing biological about the inequalities that mark the relations between men and women. Gender is thus also format of social inequality and exclusion like caste and class but with its own specific features.

SOCIAL DIFFERENTIATION

Social differentiation is an important attribute of society, especially modern society. The concept of differentiation spread within sociology since Herbert Spencer's evolutionary theory of societal development from incoherent homogeneity to coherent heterogeneity. Later on, *Emile Durkheim*, *George Simmel*, *Talcott Parsons*, and *Niklas Luhmann* were important proponents of the concept. Other social thinkers, such as *Karl Marx* and *Max Weber*, who did not use the term differentiation prominently nevertheless contributed to a proper understanding of the social structures and dynamics it designates. At the start of the twenty-first century, the theoretical and, more and more, empirical debate about social differentiation is continued, especially by American

Social Differentiation.

'neo-functionalists' in their discussion of Parsons' legacy, and some German sociologists who keep up the critical debate about Luhmann's theory of society.

Social differentiation means both a *process* and a *structure*. In structural terms, it refers to the fact that a unit of analysis, such as a society, consists of a number of distinct parts. These parts may be of the same kind, such as families as the basic components of tribal societies. Or the parts may be different, such as the subsystems economy, politics, mass media, etc. making up modern society. As a process, social differentiation is the dynamic that brings about and changes a given structure of differentiation.

Two fundamentally diverging views of the social differentiation of modern society have been put forward in sociological thought. These views do not strictly contradict, but balance each other in important respects. In the following, the partly opposing but mostly complementary relationship between both views will be sketched, with respect to the features, causes and consequences of social differentiation. The focus of attention will be put on the differentiation of modern society.

TYPES OF SOCIAL DIFFERENTIATION

Intragroup and intergroup differentiation are two basic types of social differentiation.

Intragroup differentiation represents a division of the group into subgroups that perform different functions in the group without being superior or inferior to each other. Division of a government into legislative, executive and judicial branches, or of a university into various departments, exemplifies intragroup differentiation. Another example is the division of labor in a family between husband and wife. When such subgroups become ranked, factually or formally, as "superior" and "inferior," then intragroup differentiation becomes intragroup stratification.

Intergroup differentiation, on the other hand, is represented by the millions of various organized,

SOCIAL DIFFERENTIATION AS DECOMPOSITION OR EMERGENCE

For Durkheim and Parsons as the most important representatives of the first view of social differentiation, it is a process of decomposition of a functionally diffuse unit a role, or an institution into several, functionally more specific units. This idea is modeled after the division of labor in work organizations, a process which fascinated nineteenth-century thinkers. Durkheim's major illustration is the widespread specialization of occupations in industrial society. In Parsons' more abstract analysis, the theoretical and structural-functional analytical framework of society is composed of four principal subsystems (economy, polity, societal community, and fiduciary system) each of which fulfills one of the four fundamental functional prerequisites of societal reproduction. Social differentiation as a process of social change tends towards a successive decomposition of each of these subsystems into four second-level subsystems. Parsons called this 'functional differentiation,' a term that is still used to describe the type of differentiation of modern society. His analytical perspective, Parsons suggests, is validated empirically over time by the concrete differentiation of social roles and institutions.

In structural terms, the decomposition perspective on social differentiation highlights the advantages of specialization for society, which are basically the same as on the organizational level. Specialization greatly improves performance. For instance, if formal education in schools is differentiated from the family, where education was previously concentrated, both sides profit in terms of functional efficiency and effectiveness teachers can rely on primary socialization accomplished by parents and are able to focus on secondary socialization, and vice versa.

In contrast to this perspective of social differentiation as a fruitful division of labor, Weber portrayed the birth and composition of modern society as the emergence of a number of autonomous 'value-spheres.' One after another, science, law, art, politics, economics, sexuality, and others freed themselves from their former domination by religious ideas. These value-spheres became societal domains of their own which cultivate their particular central value without concern for the value orientations of other domains. Science, for instance, does not care about economic profits, aesthetic beauty, legality, or the conformity of its truths with religious doctrine. Weber (1919, pp. 27-8) speaks graphically about the 'polytheism' of value-spheres in modern society.

Luhmann formulates this second perspective on social differentiation even more to the point. To him, society consists of about a dozen subsystems in each of which communication is guided by a specific binary code. For example, the science systems binary code is true/untrue, the legal systems legal/illegal. The binary code of each subsystem establishes a highly selective searchlight onto the social world, illuminating certain corners of it and leaving the rest in the dark.

The binary codes generate self-referentially closed universes of communication. Thus, a societal subsystem consists of chains of communications each of which refers to other communications of the same kind. For this fundamental feature, Luhmann picks up the concept of 'autopoiesis' from biological thinking. To illustrate, in the social system of science assertions of truth are the specific kind of communication. These assertions, usually made in scientific publications, lead to other such assertions, and within science not to political declarations or declarations of love. Any scientific publication, if it provokes any reactions at all, is either affirmed or rejected by later publications. Which of these two eventualities happen does not matter with respect to the reproduction of science as a societal subsystem. In both instances science continues as an open-ended sequence of publications.

Luhmann's conceptualization is better suited than Weber's to grasp the basic dynamics of continual reproduction of a societal subsystem or value-sphere. For both, each subsystem can take only its own code-determined perspective on social events. In science, nothing but its own concerns are important, and the same holds true for all other subsystems. The overall result is an effective multiplication of society with respect to the communicative meanings of events. An event, such as a train accident, looks totally different from the point of view of the economy, compared to the point of view of science, compared to the point of view of the health care system, compared to the point of view of the mass media, and so on. Borrowing a term from philosopher Gotthard Guenther, Luhmann (1997) calls this the 'polycontexturality' of modern society.

Although all subsystems have, in this sense, no 'window' to the social world outside, this basic autonomy goes along with an openness to their societal environment with respect to resources and functional performance. The science subsystem, for instance, needs financial resources among other things, and gets them from the political subsystem, or the economy. In the other direction, science provides these and other societal subsystems with knowledge. Since all societal subsystems make essential contributions to the reproduction of many others and none of them can substitute any other one, each is a functional prerequisite of modern society. Modern society would break down without economy, but also without mass media, or without a health care system, and the latter could not be replaced, for example, by politics or education.

Despite these manifold mutual dependencies, Luhmann insists that it makes no sense to understand the ensemble of societal subsystems as a division of labor. In a division of labor, the subsystems as parts are Ideologically oriented towards the performance and maintenance of the whole society. Thus, the whole comes first, historically and logically, and decomposes itself for its own benefit. By contrast, Weber and Luhmann emphasize that social differentiation consists of a simultaneous birth and liberation of the parts. They emerge and become autonomous from each other and from the whole. Even more, the whole vanishes in the sense that it becomes nothing more than the often tension-ridden and antagonistic interrelationship of the parts.

CAUSES OF SOCIAL DIFFERENTIATION

Both analytical perspectives identify different driving forces of social differentiation. Four kinds of causal factors can be distinguished, improvements of performance, evolution, cultural ideas and interests of actors.

The first causal factor, improvements of performance by specialization, was especially emphasized by Parsons and structural-functionalist studies of social differentiation. Such specialization is initiated either by performance deficits of existing structures of differentiation, or by opportunities to improve a satisfactory level of performance. An example of the problem-driven dynamic is the previously mentioned differentiation of the education system. Schools, and a duty of all children to attend them, were established because other societal subsystems, especially the economy, needed a general level of cognitive skills and social discipline within the population that could no longer be provided by the family alone. A differentiation dynamic driven by opportunities was the spur for differentiation of the radio and television sector within the mass media. Entirely new possibilities of public communication opened up by the technological innovations of radio and television, rather than any perceived performance deficits of newspapers, caused the sectoral differentiation of roles and organizations within mass media.

By contrast to a planned division of labor within organizations, on the societal level performance improvements by differentiation occur often as unintended results of actions motivated by quite different reasons. In this sense, Parsons already relied on evolution as the mechanism that brings about performance improvements. In contrast, Luhmann gives up all connotations of evolution with progress. Adopting neo Darwinian evolutionary thinking from biology, he conceives of evolution as an interplay of three mechanisms, variation, selection, and retention. Each societal subsystem has its own specific evolutionary mechanisms. For instance, in the science subsystem most publications are variations of the existing body of knowledge. Selection happens whenever one of these publications is cited affirmatively. Retention occurs when this new knowledge is incorporated into overview and review articles and into textbooks for students. As in biological evolution, most variations are not selected, and most of those selected do not reach the stage of retention. This evolutionary cognitive growth and differentiation goes along with a social differentiation of scientific specialties.

Luhmann does not deny that this evolution of the science system may bring about performance improvements usually called 'scientific progress.' But for him, this is no necessary outcome of evolutionary differentiation. Evolution may also lead to dysfunctional differentiation. For instance, the growing quest for interdisciplinary research indicates an over-specialization in more and more scientific fields. An understanding of evolutionary differentiation as progress becomes even more dubious in other societal subsystems, such as art, politics, or the mass media. But even if evolutionary differentiation on the level of each subsystem would result in performance improvements of all of them, the overall result for society would not add up to progress but only to an increase of societal complexity which manifests itself particularly in a growing destabilization of society. Each evolutionary change within one subsystem is also a change of the societal environment of all other subsystems. For them, often adaptive changes become necessary each of which again changes the societal environment, with new adaptive pressures arising. Thus, social differentiation becomes permanently autodynamic. Until now, these dynamics often brought about increasing differentiation. But Parsons' statement that this is a linear and unlimited social process is clearly wrong as not only Luhmann's theoretical reflections point out but also empirical cases presented especially by the 'neofunctionalists' demonstrate.

A third driving force of social differentiation was already mentioned with respect to Weber: an autodynamic rationalization of cultural ideas. In pre-modern societies the values that today constitute the guiding principles of the various societal subsystems were closely interwoven with each other and, moreover, integrated into an encompassing order of religious values. The differentiation of the principal subsystems of modern society is understood by Weber as a gradual but irresistible separation of economic, political, scientific, aesthetic, legal, erotic, and other values, first, from the religious context, and second, from each other. This dynamic is triggered and sustained by the compelling intellectual urge to contemplate extensively the implications and consequences of each value for everyday life. When this rationalization reaches the point where each value is rigorously reflected in its own terms, without regard to others, soon a self-referential closure of value-spheres occurs, giving way to a corresponding differentiation of roles, organizations, and subsystems.

The fourth driving force of social differentiation is the general interests of individual, collective, or corporate actors who are involved in constellations with each other. One explanation of an ongoing division of labor mentioned by Durkheim is growing 'social density' resulting in an intensification of competition among actors. This constellation evokes an interest to preserve one's own domain of action, be it an occupation for an individual or a market position for a firm. This interest, in turn, leads many of the respective actors to find new niches for themselves where they are relieved from high competitive pressure. The aggregate effect of such domain-preserving activities is social differentiation on the level of roles and organizations.

Other general interests of actors that often stimulate dynamics of social differentiation are the preservation or extension of one's autonomy, of one's control of other actors, and of one's resource base. Some professions, especially those guided by such interests were strong carriers of the differentiation of certain societal subsystems including science, law, education, and health care. Sometimes, a particular kind of social differentiation is the explicit goal of certain groups of actors who believe that this will serve their interests best. In other cases, social differentiation is an unnoticed, unforeseen, or unwanted effect of actors' pursuit of their interests. Outcomes often diverge markedly from intentions because usually the relevant constellation consists of actors in quite different positions: catalyzers and promoters of the respective process of change;

followers who join in when a 'critical mass' has been mobilized; defenders of the status quo who resist any change; more open-minded defenders with whom compromises are possible; and those who are indifferent or indecisive at the beginning and whom the promoters of change as well as the defenders of the status quo try to recruit as allies.

Each of these four kinds of driving-forces is causally relevant in the dynamics of social differentiation, although the combination varies greatly from one case to another. Often these factors are interrelated. Thus, what actors understand as their interests are framed by cultural ideas. Cultural ideas as well as actors' interests are explicit or implicit criteria to judge the performance of a given differentiation structure; and vice versa, performance deficits provoke actors' interests. Finally, the evolution of societal subsystems creates new challenges, restrictions, and opportunities for the pursuit of interests and the spelling out of cultural ideas.

CONSEQUENCES OF SOCIAL DIFFERENTIATION

The differentiation of modern society became a central theme not just of sociological thought but also of public discourse in the nineteenth century, and still is today. This is because social differentiation has far-reaching consequences for society at large, as well as for each individual member of it. These consequences are neither totally positive nor totally negative but a mixed blessing.

To begin with, the modern individual profits from role differentiation and an enormous increase of options in every sphere of life, from economic markets for goods and services to opportunities of political participation, sports activities, lifelong education, and cultural life. The abundance of options is the result of performance improvements in all societal subsystems and of an inclusion of all members of society into the status of customers, clients, and public of the subsystems. In connection with the polycontexturality of modern society, role differentiation and the growth of options allow each person to become an individual in the proper sense of the word: a person who creates a unique biography for himself or herself. However, options are only one side of a person's 'life chances' (Dahrendorf, 1979). The other side includes 'ligatures,' meaningful attachments which tie a person to certain institutions, cultural worlds, social groups or communities. In this respect, the functional differentiation of modern society seems to neglect important psychic needs of persons. Ligatures are eroded by 'polycon texturality' and individualization. As a consequence, anomy, alienation, and other experiences of mean-inglessness are present in modern society, not just as individual misfortunes and temporary phenomena, but as structurally produced permanent vulnerabilities of everyone.

Looking at society at large, social differentiation exhibits the same kind of ambivalence. First, it is obvious that functional differentiation is evolutionary highly successful. All kinds of premodern, traditional societies were overrun by those national societies from Europe and North America that converted to functional differentiation since the sixteenth century. Worldwide, there was no alternative to the adoption of functional differentiation. As shown by the socialist experience, those countries that tried to stop halfway failed. Countries where the political system attempted to control all other subsystems were beaten by the fully developed functional differentiation of Western countries, as Parsons, among others, had anticipated in the 1960s.

However, global supremacy of a fully-fledged functional differentiation implies serious problems. Their common denominator is an endangering of the integration of modern society. More precisely, systems integration, social integration, and ecological integration must be distinguished.

Systems integration seems to be the least problematic aspect. Coordination and cooperation among different subsystems of modern society is obviously possible, despite the fact that each of them is governed by its own self-referential binary code. But there are manifold interrelationships by which subsystems adapt to each other in a decentralized way. Where this does not suffice, representatives of subsystems, such as the respective interest groups, meet and bargain for common solutions in the political arena. Finally, political guidance may support or promote intersystems adaptation and bargaining among subsystems. Thus, problems of systems integration remain fragmented and manageable for modern society.

With social integration, it is different. The integration of individual members into modern society may be precarious as a result of the already mentioned erosion of ligatures. More important could be the fact that the increase in individual options might put excessive demands on all subsystems' abilities in the long run. In this respect, social inequality and the subsystems' unlimited drive to improve their performance work hand in hand. In conflicts among those who, as individuals, profit more and those who profit less from a particular subsystem's performance, the former will try to avoid redistribution. One way to achieve this is a growth of the subsystem's performance so that those whose claims were not satisfied can be served somewhat better without those who were better of giving up anything. For instance, children from the lower classes have got access to higher education. But this has been no zero-sum conflict in which the higher classes have lost some of their educational opportunities but a positive—sum constellation because the higher education sector has been extended which has fitted also the interests of the respective groups of teachers and professors and has been reinforced by the cultural imperative of 'progress.' Such dynamics, driven by complementary interests and backed by powerful cultural ideas could go on forever, were there no limits to subsystems' growth. But because these limits exist, for example with respect to resources, continuing inequalities contain a potential for serious social conflict to which functional differentiation has no ready answer.

Finally, the functional differentiation of modern society is a major cause of the growing problems of ecological integration. Modern society's path away from a 'sustainable' relationship with its natural environment has occurred as a result of two basic characteristics of all societal subsystems, their growth tendencies, and the neglect of ecological aspects by their binary codes. The modern economy is the most obvious example, but the same is true of the family, the subsystem primarily responsible for population growth. No societal subsystem exists now that takes care of the ecology, only social movements address their protest to the political system. But this subsystem, following its binary code of maintaining and increasing power, must listen to many other demands from society and so often disregards ecological concerns.

Thus, the functional differentiation of modern 'world society' is a high-risk outcome of social evolution. No alternative to this type of social differentiation is apparent as an option for the future. But whether modern society can survive in this way or will ruin itself sooner or later is an open question that sociological theories of social differentiation cannot answer. Theorists can only observe what has happened previously and infer warnings from this.

SOCIAL CHANGE

Change is difference between two points in time. What was at time one and what it is at time two. The difference between two points in time can be called as *change*.

Present Time – Past Time = Difference, i.e., change

Social change means the changes in the social structure and social relationships. At macro level we can look at social change at the societal level just like the changes in the population structure of the country. One could look at age structure of the population.

Educational distribution of people is another angle of population structure; there is lot of shifting from rural to urban areas. One could also look at changing birth rate as an aspect of social change. At the micro level one could also look at the changes taking place in the structure of families in terms of size, authority structure, age at marriage, number of children per woman.

There can be change in the relationships of people. For example, there is decline in the neighborliness, there are changes in the employer and

Social Change.

employee relationships, there is change in the men and women relationships (women empowerment), and so on. Similar to social change there is another concept of cultural change, which means changes in the culture of society. This change could be seen in the patterns of behavior of people (norm), in the laws of society, in the technology of the society. Social change and cultural change overlap and sometimes it become difficult to make a distinction between social change and cultural change. Therefore to overcome such an ambiguous situation the two concepts are combined and called as *socio-cultural change.*

Social change usually does not appear suddenly unless there is some natural catastrophe. It is usually a continuous process. The process of social change has four major characteristics. Social change happens all the time. Nothing is constant and change is inevitable. The process of change may be slow at one time than another time. One society may be changing faster than the other. Hunting and food gathering societies have been changing quite slowly; members of today's high income societies on the other hand, experience significant change within a single lifetime.

Some elements of culture change faster than the others. The gap between the two has been referred as cultural lag. The concept of cultural lag was given by W.F. Ogburn. This concept may be defined as: when two interrelated parts of culture change at different rate so that one moves faster than the other whereby one is left behind, the gap between the two is called cultural lag. Within the culture, material culture usually changes faster than the non-material culture (ideas, attitudes).

Social change is sometimes intentional but often unplanned

Industrial societies actively encourage many kinds of change. For example, scientists seek more efficient forms of energy, and advertisers try to convince us that life is incomplete without this or that new gadget. So market researchers find out new ways of convincing people to use the new product. Yet rarely one can envision all the consequences of the changes that are set in motion. Automobile has been introduced for mobility and transportation. At the same time there have appeared many unintended consequences like pollution, accidents, and the same autos being used for robbery and other unlawful activities.

Social change is controversial

Social change brings both good and bad consequences. Capitalists welcomed the industrial revolution because new technology increased productivity and increased profits. However, the workers feared that the machines would make their skills outdated and resisted the push for progress.

Look at women empowerment; for some it could be a sign of progress while others may consider it as a sign of decline.

Some changes matter more than others. Some changes (such as clothing fads) have only passing significance, whereas others (like computers) last a long time and may change the entire world. Information technology may revolutionize the whole world just like the industrial revolution.

CAUSES OF SOCIAL CHANGE

Social change has many causes. Also in a world linked by sophisticated communication and transportation technology, change in one place often begets change elsewhere. Some of the causes of social change are being discussed here.

CULTURE AND CHANGE

There are three important sources of cultural change: invention, discovery, and diffusion.

Invention is the combination of existing elements of culture into something new. Inventions produce new objects, ideas, and social patterns. Invention of ideas, objects and social patterns bring social change.

Discovery occurs when people take note of existing elements of the world. Medical advances, for example, offer a growing understanding of the human body. Human body has been there but perhaps in the olden times humans did not know much about its functioning and dis-functioning. Discoveries about the functioning of human body have added to the scientific knowledge. Beyond the direct effects on human health, medical discoveries have stretched life expectancy. Increase in life expectancy is change in society.

Diffusion is the transference of cultural traits from place and/or group to another. Diffusion creates change as products, people, and information spread from one culture to another. Many of the familiar elements of culture may have come from other cultures. For purposes of diffusion to take place, it is necessary to have contact between two cultures. In the past contact used to be physical contact through whatever means, i.e., exchange of visits of people belonging to different cultures; one way visit of travelers, traders; conquerors who may invade, plunder and leave with booty; other invaders who conquer and stay as rulers; colonizers who rule their colonies. All these situations demonstrate diffusion situations where the establishment of contact leads to borrowing of cultural traits from each other. The invaders and colonizers may bring their own culture and impose it on the local people. Nevertheless, these very rulers may have picked up some elements from the local culture. In the present times, for purposes of diffusion, the two different societies do not have to have a physical contact with each other. Presently mass media of communication has demolished the physical boundaries for contacting other cultures. Now perhaps you have to have a control over the "mouse" and reach anywhere in the world, know about its culture, understand it and if like may borrow its cultural traits. Look at borrowing of fashions from outside, mixing of cultures, and exchange of communication across the cultures.

World is becoming a global village where information spreads instantaneously and becomes a source of change. Diffusion is the most important factor of bringing change in the culture of society. Inventions, discoveries, and diffusion, all bring change in culture which in turn bring change in the social structure and the relationships of people.

CONFLICT AND CHANGE

Tension and conflict in a society also produce change. Karl Marx saw class conflict as the engine that drives societies from one historical era to another. Social class has been considered by Marx as a means to social change. The two classes identified were the capitalists and the workers. Both these classes are based on inequality. Social classes are located in the different relationships of people to the means of production. The relationships become important if a group becomes conscious and organized for action. Out of these two groups capitalists oppose social change, whereas the workers want to change the society. According to Marx the conflict between the two classes is a means to social change. The two classes cannot remain in conflict for all the time. The conflicting situation has to be resolved, and what ever the 'give and take' for resolving the conflict, the new situation will be different from the previous one ... a social change ... new relationships.

In more than a century since Marx' death this model has proven simplistic. Yet Marx correctly foresaw that social conflict arising from inequality (involving not just class but also race and gender) would force changes in every society.

IDEAS AND CHANGE

For Karl Marx the most important aspect of human beings social life is the material basis of that life. In this approach society where private property is the source of material production there exists a basis of social conflict — which in turn will lead to social change.

Max Weber considered Marx's view just one perspective. There could be other explanations of social change. So instead of economic determinism, according to Weber, ideas could also determine economic structure. Weber traced the roots of social change to ideas. For example, people with charisma can carry a message that sometimes changes the world. Look at the prophets who have changed the societies with new ideas. The religious ideas turned into movements which changed the societies. Changes brought by Islam and its ideas brought drastic changes in the structure of society and relationships among the people.

Weber also highlighted the importance of ideas by showing how the religious beliefs of early Protestants set the stage for the spread of industrial capitalism. The fact that industrial capitalism developed primarily in areas of Western Europe where Protestant *work ethic* was strong proved to Weber the power of ideas to bring about change.

Ideas also generate social movements. For example, we come across movements for bringing change in the ideas of people like social movements against "big dams" as part of environmentalism. There are movements for improving the lives of poor. There are movements for the rights of women.

DEMOGRAPHIC CHANGE

Population patterns also play a part in social change. There could be change in the structure of population with respect of age, education, occupation, etc. Pakistani population is experiencing all these changes. Migration within and among societies is a demographic factor that promotes change. In Pakistan there is a lot of migration from rural to urban areas. The urban population has increased from 20 percent in 1947 to 33 percent in 1998. The size of the urban settlements has increased putting pressure on the local resources, and other relationships. With the change in education of women, female participation in the labor force is on the increase which has implications for the institution of family.

ENVIRONMENTAL CHANGES

Environmental change can bring changes in the structure of societies and relationship of people. Degradation of the environment may force people to migrate to new places. Water logging and salinity of agricultural land makes people to migrate simply because they have lost their means of livelihood. Similarly people leave their settlements due to drought.

Environmental changes brought about by "development projects" can also be a factor for social change. For the construction of water reservoirs, motor ways, and industrial zones may necessitate the displacement of populations. The same populations may get training for new jobs and follow new occupations. It may change the life styles of the whole communities. Similarly the natural calamities can destroy the human settlements as well as their means of livelihood, and thereby could be a factor of social change. People may change their occupations, develop new settlements, migrate to new areas; all these situations are situations of social changes.

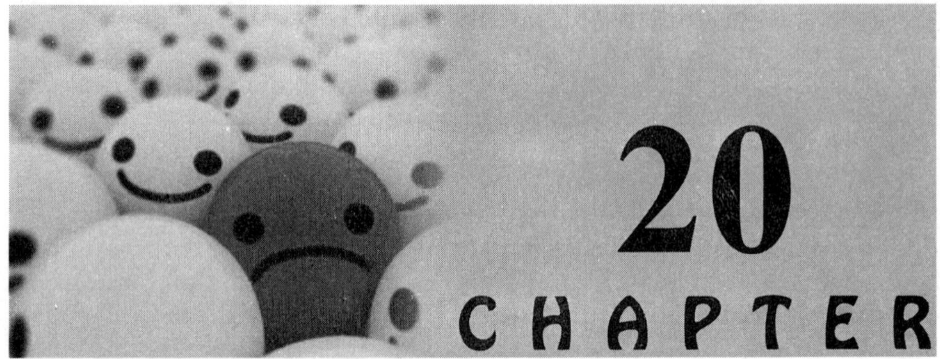

SOCIAL DISORGANIZATION AND SOCIAL PROBLEMS

Meaning of Social Disorganization. Social Disorganization in the Modern Society. Relationship Between Social Organization, Social Disorganisation, Social Problem. Nature of Social Disorganization. Causes of Social Disorganization. Social Disorganization Theory. Causes of Juvenile Delinquency. Conditions for the Formation of Delinquent Trajectories. Prevention From Juvenile Delinquency. Population Problem. The Causes and Effects of Rapid Global Population Growth. Problems Caused by Population Growth. World Population Trends. Effects of Population Growth. Problems with Rapid Population Growth. Demographic Population Trends in India. National Population Policy of India. Poverty. Causes of Poverty in India. Reasons for Rural Poverty. Poverty in India. Urban Poverty in India. Measuring Poverty. Anti-poverty Programmes in India. Unemployment. Types of Unemployment. Causes of Unemployment. Adverse Effects of Unemployment. Problem of Unemployment. Suggestions of Unemployment. Problems of the Under-priviliged: Scheduled Caste and Scheduled Tribes. Scheduled Castes ("SC"S) and Scheduled Tribes ("ST"S). What is "Untouchability"?. Corruption. Black Money.

MEANING OF SOCIAL DISORGANIZATION

Some condition of order and system pervades all forms of physical, biological and social existence. The sociologists have at least accepted a starting point that some order and organisation exist in social life. The very essence of the group, culture pattern, and social personality implies an arrangement of parts into an integrated whole. But side by side social organisation and social order have their concomitants in social disorder.

Social organisation and social disorganisation are two relative terms, because neither there is any society totally organised not only disorganised. There is social disorganisation when the equilibrium of social factors is disrupted. As observed by Ogburn and Nimkoff, "Society is a going concern of an organisation. The organization consists of habits and institutions among which there is a fair degree of equilibrium. This equilibrium is often shaken by social changes. We begin therefore, by considering how the balance achieved in a stationary contract with the condition of changing society".

Similarly, according to Elliott and Merrill, "Social disorganization occurs when there is a change in the equilibrium of forces, breakdown of social structure, so that former patterns no longer apply and the accepted forms of social control no longer function effectively. The dynamic nature of society involves a constant rearrangement of the constituent element.

DEFINITION OF SOCIAL DISORGANIZATION

- *According to Mowerer:* "Social disorganization is the process of by which the relationship between members of a group are broken".
- *As per Ogburn and Nimkoff:* "Social disorganization imply some break in cultural contact, some disturbance in the equilibrium among the various aspects of the culture pattern".

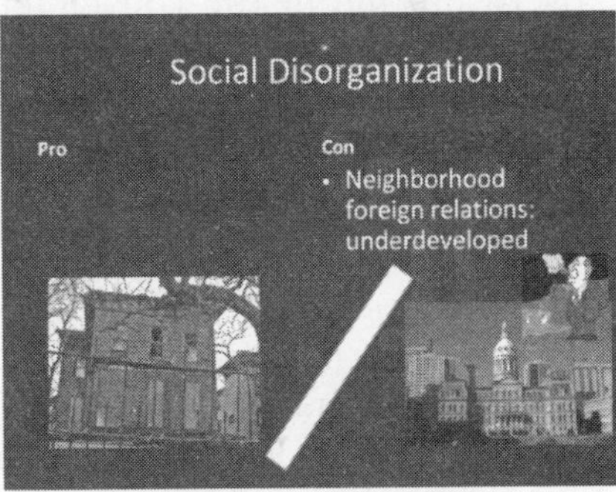

Social Disorganization.

- *According to Fairies:*
  - (a) "Social disorganization refers to the disruption of the function of some social unit such as group, in institution or community".
  - (b) "Social disorganization is a disturbance in the patterns and mechanisms of human relation".

- *According to Fairs Robert E.L:* "Social disorganization is the disruption of the functional relations among persons to a degree that interferes with the performance of the accepted task of the group".
- *According to Ellict and Francis:* "Social disorganization is the process by which the relationship between members of a group are broken or dissolved".
- *According to Josep B. Glittler:* "When affairs deviate either from the existent order of from the desired order, the inference is that there is social disorder. It is the deviation that is referred to as social disorganization. It consists of the relative decline and breakdown of those factors that have made and do mark for the effective patterning of collective living".

Social disorganization is not the negation of the harmonious relationship in a given society, it is indicative of serious breakdown of those relationships. Strike by factory workers or by sanitary workers results in the dislocation and paralysis of normal function of the society, besides it involves a direct conflict between the employer and the employee. Social disorganization is therefore a product of clash of interests of groups. Conflicts between the interests of individuals, if not organised as group conflict, have little bearing on social disorganization.

SOCIAL DISORGANIZATION IN THE MODERN SOCIETY

In our own times, the process of social disorganization has assumed in universal dimension. The developed as well as the underdeveloped societies, both are almost equal suffers. The society of the old world was comparatively peaceful partly due to stronghold of customs and traditions over the social conduct of man. Modernization of human society is mainly the result of industrials revolution of the consequent breakdown of old social relationships, first at the economic place and later on at cultural level. The man himself was swayed by the tides of industrial revolution which crushed the old order with ruthless velocity but the establishing some substitute values. Old society was not divided into sharp economical classes with mutually-conflicting interests.

In the old world order, societies cultures and communities were isolated from each other by distinct geographical barriers. Modern means of communication and transport have pushed the barriers of space and time into background. But the old attitudes and concepts die a hard way. Culture is regarded as he distinguishing feature of a community or people. Preferences are given to one's own culture and others are looked down as inferior. The West has its own ways and East follows the suit. Culture is still regarded completely synonymous with group, community or class interest when in fact the speed of modern life and means of communication have accelerated greatly cultural diffusion. Culture by itself does not stand in clashing position in modern world but it is the class interests which push them into the forefront of conflict. When cultures clash, social disorganization affected by cultural conflicts work from within. Cultural clash has become more frequent with the increasing urbanization of country's population.

According to Maclver and Page, "The situations we have just been describing, especially those in which the resistance is to an imported technology, serve also to illustrate the phenomenon of culture clash. We have used this expression to denote the conflict of opposing value scheme, creeds or ways of life when these are brought into contact inside the same community. The feat of an alien technology is not simply a fear that it will disturb the old values; it is also a fear that with it will be introduced alien values different goals. We do not include under culture clash the conflict of creeds and ideologies, so frequent in every modern society. We refer only to conflicts between two entire culture patterns each of which embraces a whole way of life. Such clashes arise permanently from the coming together within a single community of groups that have been bred in separation before they become thus conjured. Usually one of the cultures concerned is an imported culture while the other indigenous or at least has long been established in its present home. The two are brought rather abruptly into contact and out of those conditions one of them appears to be a threat to the very existence of the other especially if the former is associated with a dominant group."

Cultural clashes cause social disorganization but this fact has also to be kept in mind that industrial civilization has disrupted the overall pattern of human culture. Old cultural patterns themselves have undergone the process of disorganization resulting further breakdown of those elements of solidarity in our society which were directly based on cultural patterns. Social disorganization is thus happening in every sphere of modern life, from all sides directly or indirectly. The outcome has yet to crystallize before any prediction may be made about the nature of the new social set up that is bound to replace in the old one.

RELATIONSHIP BETWEEN SOCIAL ORGANIZATION, SOCIAL DISORGANISATION AND SOCIAL PROBLEM

Social organization of a group includes how people interact, the kinship systems they use, marriage residency patterns, how they divide up the various tasks that need to be completed, who has access to specific goods and knowledge, what ranking strategy is being used.

Archaeologists look for clues to the social organization of the people who occupied a site by looking for concentrations of artifacts in a site, a comparison of grave goods, and other considerations.

The people in a society considered as a system organized by a characteristic pattern of relationships; "the social organization of England

and America is very different;" "sociologists have studied the changing structure of the family".

Disruption or breakdown of the structure of social relations and values resulting in the loss of social controls over individual and group behavior, the development of social isolation and conflict, and a sense of estrangement or alienation from the mainstream of one's culture; the condition or state of anomie.

Social disorganization is the normal consequence of social change as well as the natural condition to social change. The terms *social problems* and *social disorganization* are closely related. When social problems arise to the extent that the smooth functioning of the society is threatened, social disorganization is in existence.

According to Elliott and Merrill *social disorganization* represents a breakdown in the equilibrium of forces, decay in the social structure so that old habits and forms of social control no longer function effectively. Whereas *social organization* consists of the coordination of individual responses as a consequence of the operation of conventionalized patterns of consensus and control and change in the cultural context which impedes or destroys the functioning of the patterns of coordination which constitute the social order represents social disorganization.

NATURE OF SOCIAL DISORGANIZATION

In order to understand the full implications of a study of social disorganization, we must keep in mind the complex nature of all social phenomena. Out of man's fruitless search for unique causes has come a recognition of the multiple factors which account for such characteristics of modern society as the decline in the acceptance of revealed religion, the changing structure of the family, the increasing importance of the central government, the lowering standards of morality, or other equally patent indices of a dynamic society. These factors have all been regarded as singly responsible for social disruptions and social disorganization. Like the alchemists of old, reformers and would-be scientists have zealously sought for some simple solution to the problems of human welfare.

Even today in the present world crisis, for example, there are some persons who believe that all the disorganization of a dynamic society has its beginning in original sin. Other earnest souls ascribe the existence of such varied manifestations as crime, immorality, political corruption, unemployment, and divorce to the decline of the traditional controls of orthodox Christianity. Others would rely upon a reconstruction of the fundamental economic institutions to bring about the millennium. Still another group insists that the basis of all human woes lies in the biological field. If we would only eliminate the physically and mentally unfit, cry the eugenists, the social organism would automatically undergo a complete and rapid rejuvenation.

CAUSES OF SOCIAL DISORGANIZATION

According to Maclver and Page five main factors such as psychological, biological, physical, technological and culture bring about social change. When the changes brought about these factors in the social structure are so disturbing that the present institution and other means of social control are no longer able to control them by adjusting themselves to the new situations there arise social disorganization. Factors of social disorganization at a particular period are so interrelated that it is difficult to find which factor is predominant.

Elliott and Merrill observe that in order to understand the full implications of a study of social disorganization we must keep in mind the complex nature of all social phenomena. Out of man's fruitless search for unique causes has come recognition of the multiple factors which account for such characteristics of modern society as the decline in the acceptance of revealed religion the changing structure of the family, the increasing importance of the central government, and the lowering standards of morality. Others would rely on a reconstructuction of the fundamental economic institutions to bring about the changes. Still another group insists that the basis of all human woe lies in the biological field. Each of these groups however ignore the selective nature of the interpretation while on the other hand any realistic social understanding must consider all the factors related to the particular manifestation of social disorganization which is under investigation.

SOCIAL DISORGANIZATION THEORY

The social disorganization theory is a key component in the study of criminology. Theories under the umbrella of social disorganization seek to identify and predict trends in criminal or deviant behavior among groups within a social network. The effort is designed to address criminal activity and the variables that might predict undesired behavior within a community.

The social disorganization theory attributes crime and delinquency to communities where failing communal institutions, such as family, church, local government and schools, are found. According to this theory, communal relationships reinforce positive behavior, a sense of community responsibility and concern for the social network within a close area. When these communal relationships are faulty or nonexistent, that social network loses a sense of organization and social responsibility, which can potentially lead to negative or even criminal behavior spreading through that neighborhood.

Social disorganization theory began its focus on urban plight. The theory development began with a group of professors from the Department of Sociology at the University of Chicago beginning in 1920. This team formed key assumptions used to further shape and define most social disorganization theories. These assumptions indicate crime and delinquency are results of social issues and should be based more on fieldwork as opposed to crime and environment statistics. The Chicago School felt that social structure was unstable, particularly among lower classes. Because of their focus on lower classes, they felt cities with their tight urban centers were natural laboratories to explore these theories.

URBAN CRIME

Many theories offer field work linking high crime rates to densely populated urban areas. They focus on immediate social environment variables, including the family, peer group and schools in the urban environment. Study in urban areas reinforces a link between criminal behavior and high occurrences of family disruption, frequent migratory household environments and poor resources and skills offered from weakened school systems, all prevalent in urban communal systems. According to this theory, these factors prohibit the development of strong social responsibility within a community as the community fails to exhibit social control during an individual's formative years.

Some 60 per cent of urban residents in developing countries have been victims of crime.

SUBURBAN CRIME

In a study focused on crime rates in suburban communities published in the Western Criminology Review, sociologists found that a lack of positive communal networks combined with variables like economics are not exclusive to an urban environment. Results demonstrated that smaller communities within larger suburban areas experienced higher levels of disorganization or broken resources and family structures reflecting similar crime patterns previously linked to urban environment. These predominately non-white pockets within suburbia mirror urban environment crime rates, single parent households rates, lower economic status and the absence of civil services typically considered organizational strengths in the suburban community.

Suburban Crime.

GANG VIOLENCE

A team of University of Chicago sociologists formed the model, a theory that ties gang violence to a lack of social opportunities and disorganization within poor urban environments. The model studied local enforcement and social agencies in 65 cities to produce several strategies to combat gang activity in urban areas. This model sought to involve local citizens in the creation of programs with social agencies to connect with troubled youth, provide training and employment programs in an attempt to rebuild broken social institutions, monitor and correct negative behaviors through schools, churches and grassroots organizations and provide ongoing resources to assist communities in connecting with their deviant youth.

Gang violence.

MEANING AND DEFINITION OF JUVENILE DELINQUENCY

Juvenile delinquency, in social science, refers primarily to social acts of juveniles that are defined and evaluated as deviant or antisocial by legal or social norms and that are usually socially learned. The precise legal definition of a "juvenile delinquent" or "young offender" is someone between 12 and 17 years of age who through the due process of law has been found to have violated criminal legislation and is therefore subject to punishments determined by a youth court. Children under the age of 12 who commit what would otherwise be criminal offences can only be dealt with under child protection legislation

As juvenile delinquency affects the society greatly, it is important for people to know about what is it exactly, and how to control it.

Children often test the limits and boundaries set by their parents and other authority figures. Among adolescents, some rebelliousness and experimentation is common. However, a few children consistently participate in problematic behaviors that negatively affect their family, academic, social, and personal functioning. These children present great concern to parents and the community at large. The prevention of delinquency requires identifying at-risk individuals and their environments before delinquent activity and behavior occur, and then removing such risk factors or strengthening resistance to the risk factors already present. The most logical starting place for prevention efforts is the family.

The prevention of delinquency requires identifying at-risk individuals and their environments before delinquent activity and behavior occur, and then removing such risk factors or strengthening resistance to the risk factors already present. The most logical starting place for prevention efforts is the family.

MEANING

Crime is always a serious problem when it occurs in a culture, but when the perpetrators are children, it becomes even more difficult to address. Most states have specific laws to guide the way that the courts and legal system handle juvenile delinquents because it is widely assumed that minors do not exercise a mature approach to decision making. Therefore, they may not have been able to appropriately judge what the consequences of their criminal actions would be.

DEFINITION

It refers to the antisocial or criminal activity of the child below 18 years of age and which violates the law. In true context, that same activity would have been a crime if it was committed by the adult. Such activities are definitely tried in juvenile court and is sentenced a bit differently that that of an adult.

A juvenile delinquent is a person who is less than 18 years old who commits a crime. Although these children do have to take responsibility for their actions, go before a judge and serve a sentence, most states do not allow them to be sentenced as an adult. There are courts, parole officers and juvenile detention centers that are specially equipped to provide juvenile delinquents with the services they need while they serve their sentences.

CAUSES OF JUVENILE DELINQUENCY

Understanding the causes of juvenile delinquency is an integral part of preventing a young person from involvement in inappropriate, harmful and illegal conduct. Four primary risk factors can identify young people inclined to delinquent activities: individual, family, mental health and substance abuse. Often, a juvenile is exposed to risk factors in more than one of these classifications.

INDIVIDUAL RISK FACTORS

Several risk factors are identified with juvenile delinquency. A minor who has a lower intelligence and who does not receive a proper education is more prone to become involved in delinquent conduct. Other risk factors include impulsive behavior, uncontrolled aggression and an inability to delay gratification. In many instances, multiple individual risk factors can be identified as contributing to a juvenile's involvement in harmful, destructive and illegal activities.

FAMILY RISK FACTORS

A consistent pattern of family risk factors are associated with the development of delinquent behavior in young people. These family risk factors include a lack of proper parental supervision, ongoing parental conflict, neglect and abuse (emotional, psychological or physical). Parents who demonstrate a lack of respect for the law and social norms are likely to have children who think similarly. Finally, those children that display the weakest attachment to their parents and families are precisely the same juveniles who engage in inappropriate activities, including delinquent conduct.

MENTAL HEALTH RISK FACTORS

Several mental health factors are also seen as contributing to juvenile delinquency. It is important to keep in mind, however, that a diagnosis of certain types of mental health conditions—primarily personality disorders—cannot be made in regard to child. However, there are precursors of these conditions that can be exhibited in childhood that tend to end up being displayed through delinquent behavior. A common one is conduct disorder. Conduct disorder is defined as "a lack of empathy and disregard for societal norms."

SUBSTANCE ABUSE RISK FACTORS

Substance abuse is found in a majority of cases of juvenile delinquency, Two trends are identified in regard to substance abuse and minors. First, juveniles are using more powerful drugs today than was the case as recently as 10 years ago. Second, the age at which some juveniles begin using drugs is younger. Children in elementary schools are found to be using powerful illegal drugs. The use of these illegal substances or the use of legal substances illegally motivates young people to commit crimes to obtain money for drugs. Additionally, juveniles are far more likely to engage in destructive, harmful and illegal activities when using drugs and alcohol.

CONDITIONS FOR THE FORMATION OF DELINQUENT TRAJECTORIES

The intensity and severity of juvenile offences are generally determined by the social, economic and cultural conditions prevailing in a country. There is evidence of a universal increase in juvenile crime taking place concurrently with economic decline, especially in the poor districts of large cities. In many cases street children later become young offenders, having already encountered violence in their immediate social environment as either witnesses or victims of violent acts. The educational attainments of this group are rather low as a rule, basic social experience acquired in the family is too often insufficient, and the socio-economic environment is determined by poverty and under- or unemployment.

The causes of and conditions for juvenile crime are usually found at each level of the social structure, including society as a whole, social institutions, social groups and organizations, and interpersonal relations. Juveniles' choice of delinquent careers and the consequent perpetuation of delinquency are fostered by a wide range of factors, the most important of which are described below:

ECONOMIC AND SOCIAL FACTORS

Juvenile delinquency is driven by the negative consequences of social and economic development, in particular economic crises, political instability, and the weakening of major institutions (including the State, systems of public education and public assistance, and the family). Socio-economic instability is often linked to persistent unemployment and low incomes among the young, which can increase the likelihood of their involvement in criminal activity.

CULTURAL FACTORS

Delinquent behaviour often occurs in social settings in which the norms for acceptable behaviour have broken down. Under such circumstances many of the common rules that deter people from committing socially unacceptable acts may lose their relevance for some members of society. They respond to the traumatizing and destructive changes in the social reality by engaging in rebellious, deviant or even criminal activities. An example of such a setting would be the modernization of traditional societies and the accompanying changes wrought by the application of new technologies; shifts of this magnitude affect the types and organization of labour activity, social characteristics, lifestyles and living arrangements, and these changes, in turn, affect authority structures, forms of obedience, and modes of political participation—even going so far as to influence perceptions of reality.

In both developed and developing countries, consumer standards created by the media are considerably beyond the capacity of most families to achieve. Nevertheless, these ideals become a virtual reality for many young people, some of whom will go to great lengths to maintain a lifestyle they cannot afford. Because not all population groups have access to the necessary resources, including education, professional training, satisfactory employment and income, health services, and adequate housing, there are those who are unable to achieve their goals by legal means. The contradiction between idealized and socially approved goals and the sometimes limited real-life opportunities to achieve them legally creates a sense of frustration in many young people. A criminal career becomes one form of addressing this contradiction. One of the reasons for delinquent behaviour is therefore an excessive focus on proposed goals (achieving success) coupled with insufficient means to achieve them.

The likelihood of deviant acts occurring in this context depends in many respects not only on the unavailability of legal opportunities but also on the level of access to illegal opportunities. Some juveniles, cognizant of the limitations imposed by legal behaviour, come under the influence of adult criminals. Many young people retreat into the confines of their own groups and resort to drug use for psychological or emotional escape. The use of alcohol and illegal drugs by juveniles is one cause of delinquency, as they are often compelled to commit crimes (usually theft) to obtain the cash needed to support their substance use.

PREVENTION FROM JUVENILE DELINQUENCY

Juvenile delinquency is a complex problem that exacts a substantial and continuing toll on our society. After being stable for more than 10 years, juvenile violent crime rates soared between 1988 and 1994. If this trend continues they will double by the year 2010. Social indicators suggest that recent declines in the proportion of teenagers in the population may soon reverse as children of the "baby boomers" come of age. Emerging trends in family demographics also reveal that more children than ever are growing up homeless, in poverty, and in single parent homes, while funding for social programs is decreasing.

While the exact mechanisms and likely strength of the relationships between these conditions and juvenile crime remain ambiguous, these trends suggest that the press to find adequate intervention methods for juvenile delinquents will only increase. Primary and secondary prevention of delinquency rest on the principle of identifying individuals and environments at risk for delinquent activity before the behavior has occurred and then either removing risk factors or strengthening resistance to the risk factors. The impact of this approach depends upon the process of identifying risk factors and the choice of when and where to direct the intervention.

FAMILY-BASED PREVENTIVE INTERVENTIONS

The family is one of the most logical starting places for prevention efforts. Because of the weight of recent empirical evidence relating family functioning to various forms of adolescent antisocial behavior, and alarm at the rapidly changing demographics of U.S. families, early family intervention has received wide endorsement as a locus for preventive intervention.

Early family interventions, however, may be perceived as an invasion of privacy. They may also stigmatize or inappropriately label youth and families as problems, and may have unanticipated negative long-term effects. These barriers to primary prevention may prohibit well-intentioned interventions from being adequately implemented. To provide both widely acceptable services and targeted programs for those who need it most, preventive efforts have generally been of two types: (a) those that focus on training parents in family management techniques and (b) those that provide an array of supportive services such as child care and/or medical and social services to socially disadvantaged families.

PARENT TRAINING

Parent training interventions developed during the 1960's when behavioral-oriented child therapists recognized the importance of involving parents in child behavior management in the home. Unfortunately, although several studies have supported the efficacy of parent training for reducing problem behaviors of conduct disordered youth, scant evidence exists concerning its effectiveness as a primary prevention strategy. Because parent training is typically a component of community based or school-based interventions, it is impossible to separate its effects from the other aspects of the interventions. One interesting finding, however, was that siblings of behavior-disordered youths were less likely to exhibit problem behaviors and delinquency following intervention than siblings of comparison youth.

SCHOOL-BASED PREVENTIVE INTERVENTIONS

The second major social system historically charged with responsibility for socializing youth is the school. A large body of research has shown that low IQ, learning disability, poor attitudes toward school, and school failure are related to and often precede official and self-reports of delinquent behavior. While schools traditionally have provided a number of individual-focused prevention services such as free lunches, health screening, counseling, and remedial and special education, system-level preventive interventions have only recently been tried. These interventions have been encouraged by research showing that school processes and climate are related to academic achievement and rates of delinquent behaviour. However, individual-focused interventions are still far more common than system-level interventions.

EDUCATION

Model programs have assisted families and children by providing them with information. Some programs inform parents on how to raise healthy children; some teach children about the effects of drugs, gangs, sex, and weapons; and others aim to express to youth the innate worth they and all others have. All of these programs provide youths with the awareness that their actions have consequences. This is particularly important in an era where youth are barraged with sexual and violent images. Educational programs have the underlying intent of encouraging hope and opening up opportunities for young people.

RECREATION

One of the immediate benefits of recreational activities is that they fill unsupervised after-school hours. The Department of Education has reported that youths are most likely to commit crimes between 2 p.m. and 8 p.m., with crime rates peaking at 3 p.m. Recreation programs allow youths to connect with other adults and children in the community. Such positive friendships may assist children in later years. Youth programs are designed to fit the personalities and skills of different children and may include sports, dancing, music, rock climbing, drama, karate, bowling, art, and other activities.

POPULATION PROBLEM

People are to be equipped to achieve progress in social and economic fields. For this, all countries give special significance on human resource development. The quality and size of population are two factors that are emphasised in the development of human resource. Rapid growth in population will create many obstacles to economic progress.

WHAT IS POPULATION?

Total number of people living in a country at a given time is called its *population*. The significance of population in the production-consumption sector of an economy is very great. The demand for consumer goods depends mainly on the size of population, sex ratio, population-density, age-structure of the people, income, preferences etc. Since there is day-to-day variation in the population of a country, it is difficult to calculate the exact population.

SIGNIFICANCE OF THE STUDY OF POPULATION

We know that family includes parents and children. We need better food, clothing, shelter, health, education and other facilities. Think how these are related to the number of members of the family. In addition to the number of members, age difference, number of males and females, their preferences and income also play an important role in estimating the quantity of essential commodities and services required for the family. Features of population in selected countries. The study of population of a country can be made use of for the following purposes.

India is facing number of problems due to its vast population.

- To assess the availability of human resource needed for production.
- To estimate the required basic infrastructure.
- To estimate the requirements of products and services.
- To understand the social and cultural structure of a population.
- To compare with the population of other countries.
- To assess the quality of standard of living.

IS INDIA OVERPOPULATED?

Overpopulation is a condition where an organism's numbers exceed the carrying capacity of its habitat. The term often refers to the relationship between the human population and its environment. The world's population has significantly increased in the last 50 years, mainly due to medical advancements and substantial increases in agricultural productivity.

The recent rapid increase in human population over the past two centuries has raised concerns that humans are beginning to overpopulate the Earth, and that the planet may not be able to sustain present or larger numbers of inhabitants. The population has been growing continuously since the end of the Black Death, around the year 1400; at the beginning of the 19th century, it had reached roughly 1,000,000,000 (1 billion). Increases in life expectancy and resource availability during the industrial and green revolutions led to rapid population growth on a worldwide level. By 1960, the world population had reached 3 billion; it doubled to 6 billion over the next four decades. As of 2009, the estimated annual growth rate was 1.10%, down from a peak of 2.2% in 1963, and the world population stood at roughly 6.7 billion. Current projections show a steady decline in the population growth rate, with the population expected to reach between 8 and 10.5 billion between the year 2040 and 2050.

The scientific consensus is that the current population expansion and accompanying increase in usage of resources is linked to threats to the ecosystem. The InterAcademy Panel Statement on Population Growth, which was ratified by 58 member national academies in 1994, called the growth in human numbers "unprecedented", and stated that many environmental problems, such as rising levels of atmospheric carbon dioxide, global warming, and pollution, were aggravated by the population expansion. At the time, the world population stood at 5.5 billion, and optimistic scenarios predicted a peak of 7.8 billion by 2050, a number that current estimates show will be reached around 2022.

Overpopulation does not depend only on the size or density of the population, but on the ratio of population to available sustainable resources. It also depends on the way resources are used and distributed throughout the population. Overpopulation can result from an increase in births, a decline in mortality rates due to medical advances, from an increase in immigration, or from an unsustainable biome and depletion of resources. It is possible for very sparsely populated areas to be overpopulated, as the area in question may have a meager or non-existent capability to sustain human life (e.g., a desert).

The resources to be considered when evaluating whether an ecological niche is overpopulated include clean water, clean air, food, shelter, warmth, and other resources necessary to sustain life. If the quality of human life is addressed, there may be additional resources considered, such as medical care, education, proper sewage treatment and waste disposal. Overpopulation places competitive stress on the basic life sustaining resources, leading to a diminished quality of life.

THE CAUSES AND EFFECTS OF RAPID GLOBAL POPULATION GROWTH

Population growth is now a growing problem in countries around the world. Population growth is when the population grows very quickly in certain places of the world. The world's population has been steadily growing over the years, and soon there would not be enough resources for everyone.

In most places in the world, the population rate has been growing, especially the poorer countries where the survival rate is lower, this can be because of, for instance in Africa, the lack of birth controls, and also because a woman will want to have more children if she knows that the chances of them dying are much higher than them living. Family planning aids are also much less. This may also contribute to why many people live in poverty. For poor families who live on farms, they may not be able afford labourers, so the children are born to provide these labouring needs. These families may also find that they need children to care for the parents to care for them when they are old.

PROBLEMS CAUSED BY POPULATION GROWTH

At this present time, we are already short of jobs, and desperately need them to support our families. When people cannot work, they take money from the government under a "Job Seekers Fund." This is paid with money from people who work, and have a job.

In the poorer countries of the world, there will be large shortages of food, and many people will go hungry. Already in many places in the world there are large shortages of food, and water.

Water is a main problem in many places. We have so much water wrapped up in places that are hard to reach. For instance, none of us want the glaciers to melt, yet there must be hundreds of tonnes of water in them, this could help to provide water for others. As all of us know, water is made of a compound containing hydrogen, and oxygen. If we found a source of hydrogen, then it would be incredibly easy to make water.

Indian women fill their containers with drinking water from the mobile water tankers in local city. India's huge and growing population is putting a severe strain on all of the country's natural resources.

If we have so many people in the world, then there are more people to add to global warming, more people breathing carbon dioxide, more people driving cars, and more people needing resources that make the factories thrive. The more people on the earth, the more water and resources are needed, and soon there will be wars fought. If World War three is ever fought, many people are sure that it will be over the different resources.

WORLD POPULATION TRENDS

PROJECTIONS OF POPULATION GROWTH

According to projections, the world population will continue to grow until at least 2050, with the population reaching 9 billion in 2040, and some predictions putting the population in 2050 as high as 11 billion. According to the United Nations' World Population Prospects report:

- The world population is currently growing by approximately 74 million people per year. Current United Nations predictions estimate that the world population will reach 9.0 billion around 2050, assuming a decrease in average fertility rate from 2.5 down to 2.0.
- Almost all growth will take place in the less developed regions, where today's 5.3 billion population of underdeveloped countries is expected to increase to 7.8 billion in 2050. By contrast, the population of the more developed regions will remain mostly unchanged, at 1.2 billion. An exception is the United States population, which is expected to increase 44% from 305 million in 2008 to 439 million in 2050.
- In 2000-2005, the average world fertility was 2.65 children per woman, about half the level in 1950-1955 (5 children per woman). In the medium variant, global fertility is projected to decline further to 2.05 children per woman.

- During 2005-2050, nine countries are expected to account for half of the world's projected population increase: India, Pakistan, Nigeria, Democratic Republic of the Congo, Bangladesh, Uganda, United States, Ethiopia, and China, listed according to the size of their contribution to population growth. China would be higher still in this list were it not for its One Child Policy.
- Global life expectancy at birth, which is estimated to have risen from 46 years in 1950-1955 to 65 years in 2000-2005, is expected to keep rising to reach 75 years in 2045-2050. In the more developed regions, the projected increase is from 75 years today to 82 years by mid-century. Among the least developed countries, where life expectancy today is just under 50 years, it is expected to be 66 years in 2045-2050.
- The population of 51 countries or areas, including Germany, Italy, Japan and most of the successor States of the former Soviet Union, is expected to be lower in 2050 than in 2005.
- During 2005-2050, the net number of international migrants to more developed regions is projected to be 98 million. Because deaths are projected to exceed births in the more developed regions by 73 million during 2005-2050, population growth in those regions will largely be due to international migration.
- In 2000-2005, net migration in 28 countries either prevented population decline or doubled at least the contribution of natural increase (births minus deaths) to population growth. These countries include Austria, Canada, Croatia, Denmark, Germany, Italy, Portugal, Qatar, Singapore, Spain, Sweden, United Arab Emirates and United Kingdom.
- Birth rates are now falling in a small percentage of developing countries, while the actual populations in many developed countries would fall without immigration.
- By 2050 (Medium variant), India will have 1.6 billion people, China 1.4 billion, United States 439 million, Pakistan 309 million, Indonesia 280 million, Nigeria 259 million, Bangladesh 258 million, Brazil 245 million, Democratic Republic of the Congo 189 million, Ethiopia 185 million, Philippines 141 million, Mexico 132 million, Egypt 125 million, Vietnam 120 million, Russia 109 million, Japan 103 million, Iran 100 million, Turkey 99 million, Uganda 93 million, Tanzania 85 million, Kenya 85 million and United Kingdom 80 million.

EFFECTS OF POPULATION GROWTH

The increase in the average length of a human life affected the amount of children they could reproduce during their reproductive years. In addition, improvements in basic health meant that many, if not all, of the offspring would survive until they too could have children. Whereas many babies used to die as infants, modern medicine coupled with better nutrition during pregnancy made it possible for a mother to give birth to many healthy children. It became common to see multi-generational families, with grandparent and great grandparent surviving to see their descendants. The population growth occurred quite rapidly because people had more children and survival until old age became common. However, as Western nations were just beginning to realize it was time to have fewer children, less developed countries began to pick up on many of these advances, and their populations exploded in growth as well.

PROBLEMS WITH RAPID POPULATION GROWTH

As human beings have evolved to a stage of scientific advancement and plenty, the population of the Earth has also expanded rapidly. In less developed times, more people died earlier due to disease. These days, due to medical advances, people are living longer, which is one reason why the world population is growing. This sort of growth has brought about some problems. Among the most notable are the demands made on the Earth's resources and overcrowding.

USE OF RESOURCES

The higher the number of people on the Earth, the bigger the need for resources. The U.S. Census Bureau projects that the world's population, which in 2010 is close to 7 billion, will be closer to 9.5 billion by 2050. The availability of food and energy for this growing population are major issues. Population growth in developed countries has put a greater strain on the Earth's resources than growth in developing countries because developed countries consume more of the Earth's resources.

SOIL EROSION

In areas of high population, the need for food leads to an extensive cultivation of the land, leading to tree cutting and the use of techniques such as crop rotation. When cleared ground is left bare, the valuable topsoil erodes. Without sturdy root systems to anchor the soil, water events become much more serious, possibly leading to severe flooding and mudslides.

OVERCROWDING

As the world population expands, there will be overcrowding on the Earth as more people fill the world. Some major world cities in developing countries are already experiencing this problem. For instance, according to demographia.com, the population density of Kowloon, a part of Hong Kong, was at more than a million people per square kilometer in 1990. This figure compares with a population density of 138 people per square kilometer for Oshkosh, a county in Wisconsin. As the world gets overcrowded, it may be more difficult to find any wide open spaces.

DEMOGRAPHIC POPULATION TRENDS IN INDIA

With (1.20 billion) people, India is currently the world's second largest country. India crossed the one billion mark in the year 2000, one year after the world's population crossed the six billion threshold. Demographers expect India's population to surpass the population of China, currently the most populous country in the world, by 2036. At that time, India is expected to have a population of more than 1.53 billion while China's population is forecast to be at its peak of 1.46 billion (and will begin to drop in subsequent years).

India is currently home to about 1.15 billion people, representing a full 17% of the earth's population. When India gained independence from the United Kingdom sixty years ago, the country's population was a mere 350 million. Since 1947, the population of India has more than tripled.

In 1950, India's total fertility rate was approximately 6 (children per woman). Nonetheless, since 1952 India has worked to control its population growth. In 1983, the goal of the country's National Health Policy was to have a replacement value total fertility rate of 2.1 by the year 2000. That did not occur.

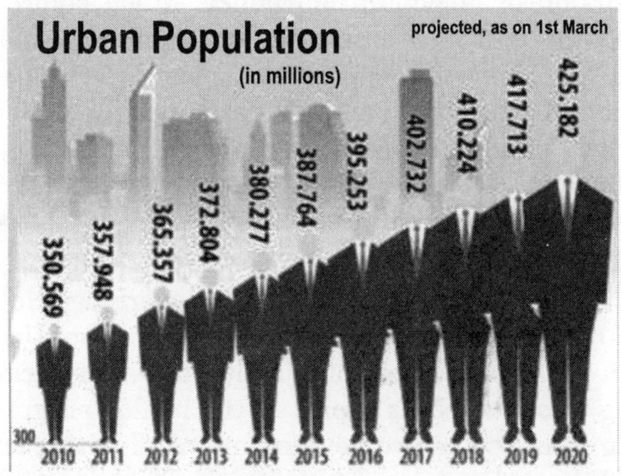

India's population: Demographic dividend or explosion.

In 2000, the country established a new National Population Policy to stem the growth of the country's population. One of the primary goals of the policy was to reduce the total fertility rate to 2.1 by 2010. One of the steps along the path toward the goal in 2010 was a total fertility rate of 2.6 by 2002.

As the total fertility rate in India remains at the high number of 2.8, that goal was not achieved so it is highly unlikely that the total fertility rate will be 2.1 by 2010. Thus, India's population will continue to grow at a rapid rate. The U.S. Census Bureau does predict a near-replacement total fertility rate of 2.2 to be achieved in India in the year 2050.

India's high population growth results in increasingly impoverished and sub-standard conditions for growing segments of the Indian population. As of 2007, India ranked 126th on the United Nations' Human Development Index, which takes into account social, health, and educational conditions in a country.

Population projections for India anticipate that the country's population will reach 1.5 to 1.8 billion by 2050. While only the Population Reference Bureau has published projections out to 2100, they expect India's population at the close of the twenty-first century to reach 1.853 to 2.181 billion. Thus, India is expected to become the first and only county on the planet that will ever reach a population of more than 2 billion (recall that China's population is likely to drop after reaching a peak of about 1.46 billion in 2030 and the U.S. is not likely to see a billion).

Although India has created several impressive goals to reduce its population growth rates, the India and the rest of the world has a long way to go to achieve meaningful population controls in this country with a growth rate of 1.6%, representing a doubling time of under 44 years.

NATIONAL POPULATION POLICY OF INDIA

It was long before procuring our Independence even that several discussion benches saw the onset of population policy. Much before Independence; in the year 1938 only a Sub Committee on population was set up by the National Planning Committee appointed by the Interim Government. The National Planning Committee passed a resolution in 1940 that stated the need for the state to adopt family planning and welfare policies in order to bring about a harmonious order of social economy. The resolution also stressed the need of limitation of children.

April, 1951 recorded further enhancements in this policy formulation as the First Five Year Plan labeled for an overt population policy and adjudged family planning as a pragmatic and essential step towards improvement in health of mothers and children. It was because in the plan, family planning was treated as a part of the health program and received a 100% funding from the centre government. And with each passing year, the amount of these funds has increased. The success of this family planning agenda was so dear to the heart of the government that even a separate department coined as Department of Family Planning was carved out in the Ministry of Health in the year 1966. This was done with an objective to reinforce the population control program.

INDIAN POPULATION POLICY

This National Population Policy was further modified and reannounced in 1977. In this new policy, what was reinforced was education and health. The latter component of the reformulated policy included the general as well as maternal and child health both. A voluntary family planning was also introduced here on. This also saw the change of the phrase from Family Planning to Family Welfare program that is maintained till date.

FAMILY PLANNING

The National Family Welfare Programme in India has traditionally sought 'to promote responsible and planned parenthood through voluntary and free choice of family planning methods best suited to individual acceptors' (Ministry of Health and Family Welfare, 1998). In April 1996, the programme was renamed the Reproductive and Child Health Programme and given a new orientation to meet the health needs of women and children more completely. The programme now aims to cover all aspects of women's reproductive health throughout their lives.

In case of this family, there is need to be Planning i.e., Family Planning.

With regard to family planning, the new approach emphasizes the target-free promotion of contraceptive use among eligible couples, the provision to couples of a choice of contraceptive methods (including condoms, oral pills, IUDs, and male and female sterilization), and the assurance of high-quality care. An important component of the programme is the encouragement of adequate spacing of births, with at least three years between births.

The new National Population Policy, 2000, adopted by the Government of India has set as its immediate objective the task of addressing unmet need for contraception in order to achieve the medium-term objective of bringing the total fertility rate down to replacement level by the year 2010. One of the 14 national socio-demographic goals identified for this purpose is to achieve universal access to information/counselling and services for fertility regulation and contraception with a wide range of choices.

ACHIEVEMENTS

Over five decades of work in social development has helped millions of people living in urban and rural areas in fulfilling their aspirations for a better quality of life.

Every decade was marked by pioneering work:

- `50s family planning started.
- `60s population education introduced in Universities.

Painting a mural for family planning.

- `70s sexuality education programs initiated.
- `80s community mobilisation and women's empowerment special projects implemented.
- `90s inclusion of all aspects of sexual and reproductive health integrated into Family Planning activities.
- `00s integration of HIV/AIDS into sexual and reproductive health core services.

POVERTY

Poverty is one of the main issues, attracting the attention of sociologists and economists. It indicates a condition in which a person fails to maintain a living standard adequate for a comfortable lifestyle.

Though India boasts of a high economic growth, it is shameful that there is still large scale poverty in India. Poverty in India can be defined as a situation when a certain section of people are unable to fulfill their basic needs. India has the world's largest number of poor people living in a single country. Out of its total population of more than 1 billion, 350 to 400 million people are living below the poverty line. Nearly 75% of the poor people are in rural areas, most of them are daily wagers, landless laborers and self employed house holders. There are a number of reasons for poverty in India. Poverty in India can be classified into two categories namely rural poverty and urban poverty.

CAUSES OF POVERTY IN INDIA

- High level of dependence on primitive methods of agriculture.
- High population growth rate.
- High illiteracy (about 35% of adult population).
- Regional inequalities.
- Protectionist policies pursued till 1991 that prevented high foreign investment.

Government has introduced a number of antipoverty programs since independence to alleviate poverty. These include various employment guarantee programmes such as National Rural Employment Programme, Rural Landless Employment Guarantee Programme etc. Recently, Government has initiated National Rural Employment Guarantee Program (NREGP). As per NREGP, the government will provide 100 days of employment per year to whosoever is willing to work. NREGP is considered as a landmark program in poverty alleviation measures.

One of the major problems with poverty alleviation programs is their implementation. Rajiv Gandhi once said that out of 100 paisa allocated for poor only 14 paisa reaches them. But in spite of their weaknesses, poverty alleviated program can be credited for their success in alleviating poverty to an extent. Greater public-private partnership and committed and efficient bureaucratic machinery is required to tackle poverty.

STRUCTURAL ADJUSTMENT

Cutbacks in health, education and other vital social services around the world have resulted from structural adjustment policies prescribed by the International Monetary Fund (IMF) and the World Bank as conditions for loans and repayment. In addition, developing nation governments are required to open their economies to compete with each other and with more powerful and established industrialized nations. To attract investment, poor countries enter a spiraling race to the bottom to see who can provide lower standards, reduced wages and cheaper resources. This has increased poverty and inequality for most people. It also forms a backbone to what we today call globalization. As a result, it maintains the historic unequal rules of trade.

HUNGER ARE RELATED TO POVERTY

There are many inter-related issues causing hunger, which are related to economics and other factors that cause poverty. They include land rights

The main causes of poverty are illiteracy, a population growth rate by far exceeding the economic growth rate for the better part of the past 50 years.

and ownership, diversion of land use to non-productive use, increasing emphasis on export-oriented agriculture, inefficient agricultural practices, war, famine, drought, over-fishing, poor crop yields, etc. This section introduces some of these issues.

CORRUPTION

We often hear leaders from rich countries telling poor countries that aid and loans will only be given when they show they are stamping out corruption. While that definitely needs to happen, the rich countries themselves are often active in the largest forms of corruption in those poor countries, and many economic policies they prescribe have exacerbated the problem. Corruption in developing countries definitely must be high on the priority lists, but so too must it be on the priority lists of rich countries.

No cash? No problem - I take credit cards!

Rare case of Corruption—Policeman taking bribe by credit card.

FOOD AND AGRICULTURE ISSUES

Food and agriculture goes to the heart of our civilizations. Religions, cultures and even modern civilization have food and agriculture at their core. For an issue that goes to the heart of humanity it also has its ugly side. This issue explores topics ranging from the global food crisis of 2008, to issues of food aid, world hunger, food dumping and wasteful agriculture such as growing tobacco, sugar, beef, and more.

FOOD DUMPING [AID] MAINTAINS POVERTY

Food aid (when not for emergency relief) can actually be very destructive on the economy of the recipient nation and contribute to more hunger and poverty in the long term. Free, subsidized, or cheap food, below market prices undercuts local farmers, who cannot compete and are driven out of jobs and into poverty, further slanting the market share of the larger producers such as those from the US and Europe. Many poor nations are dependent on farming, and so such food "aid" amounts to food dumping. In the past few decades, more powerful nations have used this as a foreign policy tool for dominance rather than for real aid.

REASONS FOR RURAL POVERTY

Some of the basic reasons of rural poverty in India are:

- Unequal distribution of income.
- High population growth.
- Large families.
- Illiteracy.
- Caste system.

PROBLEMS OF RURAL POVERTY

- Presence of malnutrition, illiteracy, diseases and long term health problems.
- Unhygienic living conditions, lack of proper housing, high infant mortality rate, injustice to women and social ill-treatment of certain sections of society.

STEPS TAKEN BY GOVERNMENT TO REDUCE RURAL POVERTY

The government of India has been trying its best to remove poverty. Some of the measures which the government has taken to remove rural poverty are:

- Small Farmer's Development Programme.
- Drought Area Development Programme.
- Minimum Needs Programme.
- National Rural Employment Programme.
- Assurance on Employment.

CAUSES FOR URBAN POVERTY

The causes of urban poverty in India are:

- Improper training.
- Slow job growth.
- Failure of PDS system.

PROBLEMS OF URBAN POVERTY

- Restricted access to employment opportunities and income.
- Lack of proper housing facilities.
- Unhygienic environments.
- No social security schemes.
- Lack of opportunity to quality health and educational services.

POVERTY IN INDIA

Poverty in India is still rampant despite an impressive economic growth. An estimated 250 million people are below the poverty line and approximately 75 per cent of them are in the rural areas.

In general, poverty can be defined as a situation when people are unable to satisfy the basic needs of life. The definition and methods of measuring poverty differs from country to country. According to the definition by Planning Commission of India, poverty line is drawn with an intake of 2400 calories in rural areas and 2100 calories in urban areas. If a person is unable to get that much minimum level of calories, then he/she is considered as being below poverty line.

Though India boasts of a high economic growth, it is shameful that there is still large scale poverty in India. Poverty in India can be defined as a situation when a certain section of people are unable to fulfill their basic needs. India has the world's largest number of poor people living in a single country. Out of its total population of more than 1 billion, 350 to 400 million people are living below the poverty line. Nearly 75% of the poor people are in rural areas, most of them are daily wagers, landless laborers and self employed house holders. There are a number of reasons for poverty in India. Poverty in India can be classified into two categories namely rural poverty and urban poverty.

Since India's independence, the subject of poverty in India has remained a major concern. According to the common definition of poverty, when a person can no longer meet the required levels to maintain specified standard of living, they are considered poor. This means that in India alone there are almost 220.1 million people living below the poverty line. This adds up to almost 25% of India's population which is a truly staggering amount.

The division of resources, as well as wealth, is very uneven in India – this disparity creates different poverty ratios for different states. For instance, states such as Delhi and Punjab have very low poverty ratios. On the other hand, nearly half of the populations in Bihar and Orissa live below the poverty line and the figures get worse for Kolkata and Maharashtra.

RURAL POVERTY IN INDIA

A number of factors are responsible for poverty in the rural areas of India. Rural populations primarily depend on agriculture as their livelihoods, which in turn, is highly dependant on rain patterns and monsoons. Inadequate rain and improper irrigation facilities can obviously cause low, or in some cases, zero production of crops followed by the obvious but sometimes catastrophic repercussions that often follows.

An Indian family unit can be often very large, which can exacerbate the effects of poverty. Also, the caste system which is still found a lot in India (although it is getting less) is a major reason for rural poverty for it keeps people locked in the endless cycle with less facilities and opportunities for the lower castes. The government has planned and implemented poverty eradication programs, but the benefits of all these programs have yet to reach the core of the country.

URBAN POVERTY IN INDIA

The phenomenal increase in the city populations is one of the main reasons for poverty in the urban areas of India. The massive and relatively recent increase is a result of major migration of rural families to cities. This migration is mainly caused by poor employment opportunities in villages and is exacerbated by the fact that there are few job opportunities in the cities as well.

MEASURING POVERTY

ABSOLUTE POVERTY

Absolute poverty measures the number of people living below a certain income threshold or the number of households unable to afford certain basic goods and services.

RELATIVE POVERTY

Relative poverty measures the extent to which a household's financial resources falls below an average income threshold for the economy. Although living standards and real incomes have grown because of higher employment and sustained economic growth over recent years, the gains in income and wealth have been unevenly distributed across the population.

There is little doubt that Britain has become a more unequal society over the last 20-25 years. Indeed a report published in July 2001 found that inequality had continued to grow during the first four years of the Labour Government, with as many as one children in six in Britain living in poverty.

ANTI-POVERTY PROGRAMMES IN INDIA

ANTI-POVERTY AND EMPLOYMENT GENERATION PROGRAMS

SWARNAJAYANTI GRAM SWAROZGAR YOJANA (SGSY)

This programme was started on April 1, 1999. It has replaced the following programs:

- Integrated Rural Development Programme (IRDP) : Started in 1978-1979.
- Development of Women and Children in Rural Areas (DWCRA) : Started in 1978-1979.
- Ganga Kalyan Yojana (GKY) : Started in 1997.
- Million Wells Scheme (MWS) : Started in 1989.
- Supply of Improved Tool—kits to Rural Artisans (SITRA) : Started in 1992.
- The Yojana takes into account all the strengths and weaknesses of the earlier self-employment programs.

- It aims at establishing a large number of micro–enterprises in the rural areas.
- Every assisted family will be brought above the poverty line. It is proposed to cover 30% of the rural poor in each block.
- To target at least 50% Scheduled Castes and Scheduled Tribes, 40% Women and 3% disabled.
- Shared 75 : 25 by Centre and States.

PRADHAN MANTRI GRAMODAYA YOJANA (PMGY)

- It was introduced in 2000—2001 with the objective of focusing on village level development in five critical areas, i.e., Primary Health, Primary Education, Housing, Rural Roads and Drinking Water and Nutrition with the overall objective of improving the quality of life of people in rural areas. Rural electrification was added as an additional component from 2001—2002.

It has the following components:

PRADHAN MANTRI GRAM SADAK YOJANA (PMGSY)

- It was launched on December 25, 2000 with the objective of providing road connectivity through good all weather roads to all rural habitations with a population of more than 1000 persons by the Year 2003 and those with a population of more than 500 persons by the Year 2007.

PRADHAN MANTRI GRAMODAYA YOJANA (GRAMIN AWAS)

- It was launched on April 1, 2000. Based on the pattern of Indira Awas Yojana, the scheme is being implemented in the rural areas throughout the country with the objective of sustainable habitat development.
- Pradhan Mantri Gramodaya Yojana (Rural Drinking Water Project).

NATIONAL RURAL EMPLOYMENT GUARANTEE SCHEME (NREGS)

It was launched on February 2, 2006. The on–going programs of Sampoorna Grameen Rozgar Yojana (SGRY) and National Food for Work Programme (NFWP) were subsumed within the NREGS in the 200 districts identified in the initial stage. All the districts in the country are covered under the scheme now. The features of the scheme are :

- State Government to provide at least 100 days of guaranteed wage employment in every financial year to every household whose adult members volunteer to do unskilled manual work.
- Until such time as a wage rate is fixed by the Central Government, the minimum wage for agricultural laborers shall be applicable for the scheme.
- An applicant not provided employment within fifteen days, to be entitled to a daily unemployment allowance as specified by the State

Government subject to its economic capacity, provided such rate is not less than quarter of the wage rate for the first thirty days during the financial year and not less than a half of the wage rate for the remaining period of the financial Year.

SAMPOORNA GRAMIN ROZGAR YOJANA (SGRY)

- It was started on September 25, 2001, with the mergence of the Employment Assurance Scheme (EAS) and the Jawahar Gram Samriddhi Yojana (JGSY). Earlier Jawahar Rozgar Yojana, which started in 1989, was merged with Jawahar Gram Samriddhi Yojana.
- This scheme has been subsumed in National Rural Employment Guarantee Scheme.

BHARAT NIRMAN YOJNA

- Accepting the policy 'a step towards village', Union Government launched a new scheme, named 'Bharat Nirman Yojana' on December 16, 2005. This scheme aims at developing rural infrastructure. The duration of implementing this scheme has been determined for four years with the expected expenditure of Rupee 1,74,000 crore. The major six sectors and their targets for next four years are :
- *Irrigation* : To ensure irrigation for additional one crore hectare of land by 2009.
- *Roads* : To link all villages of 1,000 populations with roads and also to link all ST and hilly villages up to 500 populations with roads.
- *Housing* : Construction of 60 lakh additional houses for the poor.
- *Water Supply* : To ensure drinking water to all remaining 74,000 villages.
- *Electrification* : To supply electricity to all remaining 1,25,000 villages and to provide electricity connection to 2.3 crore houses.
- *Rural Communication* : To provide telephone facility to all remaining 66,822 villages.

SWARNAJAYANTI SHAHARI ROZGAR YOJANA (SJSRY)

- The SJSRY came into operation in December 1997, through a restructuring and streamlining of the earlier urban poverty alleviation programs, the Nehru Rozgar Yojana (NRY), the Urban Basic Services for the Poor (UBSP) and the Prime Ministers Integrated Urban Poverty Alleviation Programme (PMIUPEP).
- It seeks to provide employment to the urban employed or underemployed living below poverty line and educate up to IX standard through encouraging the setting up of self-employment ventures or provision of wage employment.
- It is funded by the Centre and States on 75 : 25 bases.

ANTYODAYA ANNA YOJANA

- Launched on December 25, 2000, the scheme aims at providing food security to poor families.
- The Scheme contemplates identification of 10 million poorest of the poor families and providing them with 25 kg. of food grains per family per month at a low price of Rupee 2 per kg of wheat and Rupee 3 per kg for rice.

ANNAPURNA YOJANA

- Inaugurated on March 19, 1999.
- Initially the scheme provided 10 kg food grains to senior citizens who were eligible for old age pension but could not get it due to one reason or the other. Later on, it was extended to cover those people also who get old age pensions.
- Food grains are provided to the beneficiaries at subsidized rates of Rupee 2 per kg of wheat and Rupee 3 per kg of rice.

PRIME MINISTER'S ROZGAR YOJANA (PMRY)

- The scheme was launched on October 2, 1993 and initially was in operation in Urban areas from April 1, 1994, the scheme is being implemented throughout the country.
- Under this scheme every selected educated unemployed youth in the age group of 18-35 years and having family income below Rupee 40,000 is provided a loan of up to Rupee 1 lakh for opening his own enterprise and Rupee 2 lakhs for other activities.
- Projects involving two or more than two partners may be given a loan up to Rupee 10 lakhs. Under this scheme, 15% of the total project cost (maximum Rupee 15,000) is given to the beneficiary as subsidy. 5% of equity is to be invested by the beneficiary himself and the remaining cost of the project is financed by the concerned bank.
- The entrepreneurs of these tiny units are provided adequate training and also given assistance of raw material and marketing, if required.
- Micro-enterprises from commercial sector should not comprise more than 30 percent. This scheme is being administered by Union Industry Ministry. SC/ST and other backward classes have been given reservation of 22.5% and 27% respectively.

SARVA SHIKSHA ABHIYAN

The Scheme of Sarva Shiksha Abhiyan (SSA) was launched in 2001. The goals of SSA are as follows:

- All 6-14 age children in School/Education Guarantee Scheme Centre/ bridge course by 2003.
- All 6-14 age children complete five year primary education by 2007.

- All 6-14 age children complete eight years of schooling by 2010.
- Focus on elementary education of satisfactory quality with emphasis on education for life.
- Bridge all gender and social category gaps at primary stage by 2007 and at elementary education level by 2010.
- Universal retention by 2010.

The assistance under the program of SSA was on a 85:15 sharing arrangement during the Ninth Plan, 75:25 sharing arrangement during the Tenth Plan, and 50:50 sharing thereafter between the Central Government and State Government.

RURAL HOUSING—INDIRA AWAAS YOJANA (IAY)

Housing constitutes a very basic requirement for human survival. It assumes great significance for the rural poor in that it lays the foundation for a life of dignity for them by dispelling the gloom of shelterlessness and conferring a distinct, secure identity. Addressing housing shortage is thus an important strategy of poverty alleviation in India. The 2001 Census places the rural housing shortage figure in India at 148 lakhs. The Bharat Nirman Programme has recognised and accorded due priority to the need to end shelterlessness and it is envisaged to construct 60 lakh houses over the next four years across the country, starting from 2005-06.

The rural housing programme is implemented by the Ministry of Rural Development through the Indira Awaas Yojana scheme, which is a centrally sponsored scheme where the cost is shared between the Centre and the States on a 75:25 basis. The criteria adopted for allocation of financial resources between the States/UTs gives greater emphasis to the states with higher incidence of shelterlessness. 75% weightage is given to housing shortage and 25% weightage to the poverty ratios prescribed by the Planning Commission for State-level allocations. For district-level allocations, 75 % weightage is given again to housing shortage and 25% to SC/ST component of the population. Grant assistance is provided to the extent of Rs. 25,000 per house for normal areas and Rs. 27,500 for hilly areas. Funds are released to the DRDAs in two installments.

The implementation guidelines of the scheme specifically target the rural below poverty line (BPL) households. The selection of beneficiaries is done by the respective Gram Sabha from the BPL list and no higher approval is required. The guidelines also clearly specify that the house allotment should be in the name of the female member of the family as a first priority. While seeking to empower the rural women, the scheme also provides a quota for physically and mentally challenged persons, ex-servicemen, widows and freed bonded labourers. An important requirement in the implementation is that at least 60% of the beneficiaries should belong to the SC/ST communities. The objective of alleviating the lot of the underprivileged members of society is built into the scheme guidelines. The IAY scheme also lays emphasis on individual sanitation and health by incorporating the cost of a sanitary latrine and smokeless chulha into the grant.

Various state governments have responded to the housing programme by placing it at the top end of their development priorities, thereby imparting great vigour to the implementation process. While the implementation lies with the DRDAs, the houses are constructed by the individual beneficiaries themselves, with absolute freedom of choice over the design. The scheme is closely monitored by an extensive network at the district, state and national level to ensure right selection and effectiveness in the implementation mechanism.

NATIONAL FOOD FOR WORK PROGRAMME

The Planning Commission has identified 150 most backward districts of the country on the basis of prevalence of poverty indicated by SC/ST population, agricultural productivity per worker and agricultural wage rate. Most of them happen to be tribal districts. There is a need for substantial additional investment in these districts to convert their surplus labour into required capital formation solving livelihood issues.

The new Food for Work Programme is such an attempt. Substantial resources in the form of cash and food grains are being provided under the programme to generate additional supplementary wage employment and to create productive assets in these 150 identified districts. Through the programme, an attempt will be made to coordinate among different on going schemes which have wage employment potential, so that the focused approach provides a solid base for the districts to take off on their own. The success of the programme will depend on the vision with which it is implemented.

The new Food for Work Programme is also a move towards wage employment guarantee. It is an experiment, which if successfully carried out, will give the government the necessary confidence to take responsibility for providing wage employment guarantee, initially in these 150 identified districts and later, gradually in the remaining districts of the country.

VALMIKI AMBEDKAR AWAS YOJANA (VAMBAY)

The VAMBAY was launched in December 2001 to ameliorate the conditions of the urban slum dwellers living below the poverty line without adequate shelter.

The scheme has the primary objective of facilitating the construction and up-gradation of dwelling units for slum dwellers and providing a healthy and enabling urban environment through community toilets under Nirmal Bharat Abhiyan, a component of the scheme.

The Central Government provides a subsidy of 50 per cent, the balance 50 per cent being arranged by the State Government.

There are prescribed ceilings on costs both for dwelling units and community toilets. During 2003-04, Central subsidy to the extent of Rs. 239 crore has been released. Since inception up to May 2004, Rs. 522 crore have been released as Government of India subsidy for the construction/ upgradation of 2,46,035 dwelling units and 29,263 toilet seats under the scheme.

UNEMPLOYMENT

India as a nation is faced with massive problem of unemployment. Unemployment can be defined as a state of worklessness for a man fit and willing to work. It is a condition of involuntary and not voluntary idleness. Some features of unemployment have been identified as follows:

- The incidence of unemployment is much higher in urban areas than in rural areas.
- Unemployment rates for women are higher than those for men.

Activists of the All-India Youth Federation take a pledge to root out the unemployment problem from the country.

- The incidence of unemployment among the educated is much higher than the overall unemployment.
- There is greater unemployment in agricultural sector than in industrial and other major sectors.

TYPES OF UNEMPLOYMENT

Economists and social thinkers have classified unemployment into various types. Generally unemployment can be classified in two types:

(1) Voluntary Unemployment

In this type of unemployment a person is out of job of his own desire does not work on the prevalent or prescribed wages. Either he wants higher wages or does not want to work at all. It is in fact social problem leading to social disorganization. Social problems and forces such as a revolution, a social upheaval, a class struggle, a financial or economic crisis a war between nations, mental illness, political corruption mounting unemployment and crime etc. threaten the smooth working of society. Social values are often regarded as the sustaining forces of society. They contribute to the strength and stability of social order. But due to rapid social change new values come up and some of the old values decline. At the same time, people are not is a position to reject the old completely and accept the new altogether. Here, conflict between the old and the new is the inevitable result which leads to the social disorganization in imposed situation. In economic terminology this situation is voluntary unemployment.

(2) Involuntary Unemployment

In this type of situation the person who is unemployed has no say in the matter. It means that a person is separated from remunerative work and devoid of wages although he is capable of earning his wages and is also anxious to earn them. Forms and types of unemployment according to Hock are:

(i) ***Cyclical unemployment*:** This is the result of the trade cycle which is a part of the capitalist system. In such a system, there is greater unemployment and when there is depression a large number of people are rendered unemployed. Since such an economic crisis is the result of trade cycle, the unemployment is a part of it.

(ii) ***Sudden unemployment*:** When at the place where workers have been employed there is some change, a large number of persons are unemployed. It all happens in the industries, trades and business where people are employed for a job and suddenly when the job has ended they are asked to go.

CAUSES OF UNEMPLOYMENT

(i) ***Unemployment caused by failure of industries*:** In many cases, a business a factory or an industry has to close down. There may be various factors responsible for it there may be dispute amongst the partners, the business may give huge loss or the business may not turn out to be useful and so on.

(ii) ***Unemployment caused by deterioration in industry and business*:** In various industries, trades or business, sometimes, there is deterioration. This deterioration may be due to various factors. In efficiency of the employers, keen competitions less profit etc. are some of the factors responsible for deterioration in the industry and the business.

(iii) ***Seasonal unemployment*:** Certain industries and traders engage workers for a particular season. When the season has ended the workers are rendered unemployed. Sugar industry is an example of this type of seasonal unemployment.

ADVERSE EFFECTS OF UNEMPLOYMENT

The adverse effects of unemployment in a capitalistic society. What drives the machine of capitalism? It is a demand for goods and services and a return on investment, is not it? If people are unemployed, production of goods and provision of services falls off, and simultaneously, the people who are unemployed lack the wherewithal to purchase goods and services. People who still have money, investors, are reluctant to invest any money in the production of goods or the provision of services because when production and consumption are down, there is no opportunity to get a return on the investment.

Effects of unemployment are social, too, not just economic. Frequently, crime rates rise as people are unable to meet their needs through work. Divorce rates often rise because people cannot solve their financial problems. The rate of homelessness rises, as do the rates for mental and physical illness. Homes are foreclosed upon or abandoned, and neighborhoods deteriorate as a result.

The ability of government to provide for people is also seriously compromised. When there is high unemployment, people pay less in income taxes and also pay less in sales taxes because they purchase fewer goods and services. This leads to less in the way of public services, which includes everything from police and fire protection to the staffing for the municipal swimming pool and rubbish pickup.

PROBLEM OF UNEMPLOYMENT

The problem of unemployment has becoming a colossal. Various problems have caused this problem. There are individual factors like age, vocational unfitness and physical disabilities which restrict the people. External factors include technological and economic factors. There is enormous increase in the population. Every year India adds to her population afresh. More than this every year about 5 million people become eligible for securing jobs. Business field is subject to ups and downs of trade cycle and globalization. Economic depression or sick industries are often close down compelling their employees to become unemployed. Technological advancement contributes to economic development. But unplanned and uncontrolled growth of technology is causing havoc on job opportunities.

There are millions of young men and women waiting and waiting for job opportunities. This chronic problem of unemployment is not confirmed to any particular class, segment or society. It is all pervading. There is massive unemployment among educated, well-trained and skilled people, and it is also there among semi-skilled and unskilled laborers, small and marginal farmers and workers. Then there is underemployment. The jobs being created have miserably failed to keep pace with the ever increasing number of job-seekers. It is a problem which presents a great challenge to leaders, thinkers, planners, economists, industrialists and educationists.

The computerization and automation has led to technological unemployment. Strikes and lockouts have become inseparable aspect of the industrial world today. Due to these industries often face economic loses and production comes down. Since workers do not get any salary or wages during the strike period they suffer from economic hardships. They become permanently or temporarily unemployed.

Today young people are not ready to take jobs which are considered to be socially degrading or lowly. Our educational system has its own irreparable defects and its contribution to the unemployment is an open truth. Our education does not prepare the minds of young generation to become self-employed on the contrary it makes them dependent on government vacancies which are hard to come. Our State right from the beginning of Five Year Plans has introduced several employment generating schemes and programmes over the years but in the absence of proper implementation and monitoring have failed to achieve the required targets.

Recently UPA Government has come up with Rural Employment Guarantee Program which aims to provide minimum days of employment to people living in the villages. This is a laudable programme if implemented sincerely because it will provide employment to people during natural calamities like drought, floods etc. The remedial measures for reducing unemployment may lay greater emphasis on creation of opportunities for self-employment, augmentation of productivity and income levels of the working poor, shift in emphasis from creation of relief type of employment to the building up of durable productive assets in the rural areas and instead of attempting to revert somewhat to protectionist policies the pace of privatization may be accelerated.

SUGGESTIONS OF UNEMPLOYMENT

Unemployment can have a devastating effect on morale and self-confidence. The stress of joblessness can impact sleeping schedules, appetite, mood and even your ability to function effectively. The endless rounds of fruitless applications and interviews can lead to a sort of jobless despair—the belief that you will never work again, or that if you do it will be in a job far beneath your skill level. The depressing reality of unemployment is that you do not really know what to do with yourself. If you were independently wealthy and had no work you would travel or golf or buy a sailboat. Because you need a job, you have free time but no sense of freedom. This is why joblessness is so debilitating. So how do you counter the negative effects of unemployment?

Believe it or not, structuring your time can go a long way towards easing the negative physical and emotional responses to joblessness. Set your alarm and get up each day, shower and dress just as you would if you were going to work. By getting to your desk at a set time each day you will maintain the rhythm of employment and therefore feel a similar sense of accomplishment. Spend a set amount of time each day in the job search. Whether you decide that 2 hours or 6 hours is the right amount, stick to that routine 5 days each week. Always keep in mind that your transition back into the workforce will be easier if you have maintained the same “work hours” as in an actual work day.

Once you have completed your pre-set time applying for jobs the rest of the day is yours to use as you will. Clean the house, complete projects that are long overdue, work on that novel you always wanted to write, take an online training course or take an extended workout. Fill the hours that remain in your day until your normal day's end. Then walk away from your 'work' and enjoy the evening with family or friends.

By structuring your day into a normal work pattern you will feel more motivated and secure. Not only will you sleep better and be more responsive but you will come across stronger in interviews as well which can speed hiring. Keeping active in a structured way, and observing normal 'off time' patterns is the key to coming through a period of unemployment with a minimum of disruption. Taking a training course while you are unemployed can be a great way of showing prospective employers that you are motivated and ready to get 'back in the game'.

PROBLEMS OF THE UNDER-PRIVILIGED: SCHEDULED CASTE AND SCHEDULED TRIBES

SCHEDULED CASTE

Scheduled caste are *Dalit*, also called *Harijan*, is a self-designation for a group of people traditionally regarded as of lower class and unsuitable for making personal relationships. Dalits are a mixed population of numerous caste groups all over South Asia, and speak various languages. While the caste system has been abolished under the Indian constitution, there is still discrimination and prejudice against Dalits in South Asia. Since Indian independence, significant steps have been taken to provide opportunities in jobs and education. Many social organizations have encouraged proactive provisions to better the conditions of Dalits through improved education, health and employment.

Scheduled Castes (SC) are communities accorded with special facilities provided by Indian constitution viewing their long history of being oppressed, excluded and denied from the mainstream Hindu population, and accorded with the most polluted occupations like manual scavenging and leather works.

Indian after independence has faced a lot of trouble in identifying and labeling population as SCs because of politico-economical reasons. The exact documentation has not been done as they show state wise as well as regional variation. The 2001 census shows they constitute about 16 percent of India's population.

NATURE OF THEIR PROBLEMS

Traditionally SCs constitute a bulk of Indian population who had to lie outside the vernacular system and had no chance of entry to the upper caste through change processes described by M.N. Srinivas. This resulted in denial of access to resources, public service and decision making. The census shows that about 19 percent of them live in Urban centres and most of them are still engaged in inhuman and vulnerable profession. They have highest fertility and low level of literacy.

CONSTITUTIONAL PROVISIONS FOR PROTECTION AND DEVELOPMENT OF SCHEDULED CASTES

The National Commission for Scheduled Caste (NCSC) classifies different safeguards in the following broadheads:

1. Social Safeguards

Articles 17, 23, 24 and 25(2)(b) of the Constitution enjoins the State to provide social safeguards to Scheduled Castes.

Article 17 relates to abolition of untouchability being practiced in society. The Parliament enacted the Protection of Civil Rights Act, 1955 and the Scheduled Castes and Scheduled Tribes (Prevention of Atrocities) Act, 1989 to tackle the problem of untouchability, which is being practiced against Scheduled Castes.

Article 23 prohibits traffic in human beings and 'begar' and other similar forms of forced labour and provides that any contravention of this provision shall be an offence punishable in accordance with law. Although there is no specific mentions about the SCs in this Article but majority of the bonded labours comes from SCs. Thus, this Article has a special significance for them. The Parliament enacted Bonded Labour system (Abolition) Act, 1976 for identification, liberation and rehabilitation of bonded labourers.

Article 24 provides that no child below the age of 14 years shall be employed to work in any factory or mine or engaged in any other hazardous employment. Even in this Article, there is no specific mention about the SCs but substantial portion of child labour engaged in hazardous employment belong to SCs.

Article 25(2)(b) provides that Hindu religious institutions of a public character shall be opened to all classes and sections of Hindus. The term Hindu includes persons professing Sikh, Jain and Buddhist religion.

2. Economic Safeguards

Articles 23, 24 and 46 form part of the economic safeguards for the Scheduled Castes and Scheduled Tribes. The provisions of Articles 23 and 24 have already been discussed in earlier paragraphs.

Article 46 provides, "The States shall promote with special care the educational and economic interests of the weaker sections of the people, and in particular, of the Scheduled Castes and the Scheduled Tribes, and shall protect them from social injustice and all forms of exploitation."

3. Educational and Cultural Safeguards

Articles 15(4) empowers the State to make special provisions for the advancement of any socially and educationally backward classes of citizens and for SCs. This provision has enabled the State to reserve seats for SCs in educational institutions in general and professional courses etc.

4. Political Safeguards

Reservation of seats for SCs/STs in the local bodies of the States/UTs, Legislative Assemblies of the State and in Parliament is in practice.

Article 243D assures the reservation of seats for Scheduled Castes and Scheduled Tribes in every Panchayat according to the proportion of population. Such seats may be allotted by rotation to different constituencies in a Panchayat. No less than one-third of reserved seats should be allotted to women.

Article 243T assures the reservation of seats in Municipality area. The rule is same.

Article 330 assures reservation of seats for SCs and STs in the House of the People. The allotment of seats is based on the number of the seats and proportion of SCs and STs in the state or Union Territories.

Article 332 assures reservation of seats in the state legislative assembly. The allotment of seats is based on the number of the seats and proportion of SCs and STs in the state or Union Territories.

5. Service Safeguards

The allotment of seats is based on the number of the seats and proportion of SCs and STs in the state or Union Territories. The effect of this amendment is that the SCs/STs promoted earlier than their counterpart in general category by virtue of reservation policy shall be senior to general category in the promoted scale/post.

SCHEDULED TRIBES

Scheduled Tribes (ST) represent substantive indigenous minority population of India which are recognised by fifth schedule of Indian Constitution on the basis of their 'primitive' technology, relative geogra-phical isolation, distinctive culture and relative shyness of contact with larger communities.

According to 2001 census they represent roughly 8 percent of Indian population mostly living in less accessible places of the country. Today they represent second largest landless population. The geographic distribution shows two concentric zone of their habitation. First, at the central belt of the mainland India, second, at the north eastern region.

CRITERIA FOR LABELING

Criteria for labeling a population as ST have been a source of debate. The labeling of a population as ST has political and electoral importance. Furthermore the criteria are themselves problematic. The criteria are primarily based on traits like language, social organisation, identity, economic and technological achievements, and cultural distinctiveness. However, these features also characterises other communities. Traits like language and identity are also volatile, since, many groups have lost their primary language and identity. The economic criteria like egalitarianism, reciprocity and self-sufficiency no longer holds to be true. Yet with these debates, Government of India is determined to provide special incentives to these special groups. At present with 698 ST groups of India represent world's largest population of STs.

NATURE OF PROBLEMS

At a global level, the indigenous population faces two major problems identified by United Nations, (a) Poverty and (b) social discrimination. World Health Organisation focuses on the fact that these people suffer from higher rate of infant mortality, under and mal nutrition and lower life expectancy.

INDIA'S AFFIRMATIVE MEASURES

India has taken a number of affirmative measures for the upliftment of tribal people. It is important to see initiatives taken by India in her several five years plans for the benefit of her weaker section.

Five Year Plans and development initiatives for Scheduled Tribes are as follows:

An analysis of five year plans show that the schemes under tribal development programmes have ranged from infrastructure building to empowerment. The schemes range from collective welfare to family and beneficiary oriented programmes. Though the thrust areas have undergone change from one plan to another, some of the important issues like providing food security and nutrition, improving health services and checking morbidity, and education have been given priority during all the planning periods.

The first plan (1951-56) emphasised the equitable distribution of development inputs. It emphasises the importance of providing special provision for weaker section of Indian population.

The second plan(1956-61) emphasises on reducing economic inequalities between Tribals and others. It showed the sensitivity to their cultural and mental life. Multipurpose tribal blocks were set up. Later these blocks were termed as Tribal Development Blocks (TDB).

The third plan (1961-66) continued with the same principle of reducing economic and other inequalities. The number of TDB increased to 489, each of which covered 25000 people.

The fourth plan (1969-1974) focused on the rapid increase in the standard of Tribal people's living. Six pilot projects were set up in Andhra Pradesh, Bihar, Madhya Pradesh and Orissa for the benefit of tribals.

The fifth plan (1974-78) launched the concept of Tribal Sub Plans (TSP) which is aimed at providing direct development incentives additional to overall state and/or central budget. TSP took two strategies, first, promotion of development initiative to raise their standard of living and second, protection of tribal interest through legal and administrative support.

The sixth plan (1980-85) seen high degree of devolution of funds to help tribals crossing the poverty line.

The Seventh plan (1985-90) showed substantial increase in the flow of funds for the development of STs through infrastructure facilities and enlargement of coverage. Tribal Cooperative Marketing Development Federation (TRIFED) to provide credit and marketing facilities to the Tribals is set up. National Scheduled Castes and Scheduled Tribes Finance and Development Corporation (NSFDC) is set for employment generation activities.

The eighth plan (1992-97) efforts to minimise the gap between levels of development between Tribals and Non-tribals.

The ninth plan (1997-2002) emphasises the issues of empowerment. It recognises the importance of creating and environment where STs can lead a life of self reliance and dignity. It puts emphasis on three vital components, viz. (i) Social Empowerment, (ii) Economic Empowerment, (iii) Social Justice.

The tenth plan and eleventh plan largely follow the same procedures with an emphasis on tackling unresolved issues. The eleventh plan has created a working group which will look into the empowerment issues.

SCHEDULED CASTES ("SC"S) AND SCHEDULED TRIBES ("ST"S)

Scheduled Castes ("SC"s) and Scheduled Tribes ("ST"s) are Indian population groupings that are explicitly recognized by the Constitution of India, previously called the "depressed classes" by the British. SCs/STs together comprise over 24% of India's population, with SC at over 16% and ST over 7.50% as per the 2001 Census. The proportion of Scheduled Castes and Scheduled Tribes in the population of India has steadily risen since independence in 1947.

The Constitution (Scheduled Castes) Order 1950 lists 1,108 castes across 25 states in its First Schedule. The Constitution (Scheduled Tribes) Order 1950 lists 744 tribes across 22 states in its First Schedule.

Post Independence Scheduled Castes have been benefited by Reservation policy. The policy was made an integral part of Constitution by the efforts of Dr. Ambedkar who was the leader of the Depressed classes and participated in Round Table Conferences and fought for the rights of Depressed classes. The Constitution lays down general principles for the policy of affirmative action for the SCs and STs.

According to the Central Government policy these three categories are entitled for positive discrimination. Sometimes these three categories are defined together as Backward Classes. 15% of India's population are Scheduled Castes. According to Central Government policy 15% of the government jobs and 15% of the students admitted to universities must be from Scheduled Castes. For the Scheduled Tribes about 7.5% places are reserved which is their proportion in Indian population. The Other Backwards Classes are about 50% of India's population, but only 27% of government jobs are reserved for them.

Along with the Central Government, the State Governments of India also follow a positive discrimination policy. Different states have different figures of communities entitled for positive discrimination based on the population of each state. Different State Governments have different lists of communities entitled for positive discrimination. Sometimes a specific community is entitled for rights in a particular state but not in another state of India.

In modern India new tensions were created because of these positive discrimination policies. The high caste communities feel discriminated by the government policy to reserve positions for the Backward Classes. In many cases a large number of high caste members compete for a few places reserved for them. While the Backward Classes members do not have to compete at all because of the large number of reserved places for them compared to the candidates. Sometimes in order to fill the quota, candidates from the lower classes are accepted even though they are not suitable. Sometimes some reserved positions remain unmanned because there were few candidates from the lower classes causing more tension between the castes. Between the lower castes there are also tensions over reservation.

In the order of priority for a reserved place of the Backward Classes, candidate from the Scheduled castes is preferred over a candidate from the Scheduled Tribes who is preferred over a candidate from the other Backward Classes. As stated earlier Other Backward Classes are about 50% of India's population but only 27% of the Other Backward Classes are entitled for positive discrimination according to Central Government policy. Some Other Backward Classes communities are organizing politically to be recognized as Backward Classes entitled for positive discrimination.

The Scheduled Tribes who are seen as the aborigins of India got ownership and certain rights over Indian land. Many communities in India claim also to be aborigins of India and they are claiming the same rights as the Scheduled Tribes.

The caste identity has become a subject of political, social and legal interpretation. Communities who get listed as entitled for positive discrimination do not get out of this list even if their social and political conditions get better. In many cases the legal system is involved to decide if a certain person is entitled for positive discrimination.

But with all this positive discrimination policy, most of the communities who were low in the caste hierarchy remain low in the social order even today. And communities who were high in the social hierarchy remain even today high in the social hierarchy. Most of the degrading jobs are even today done by the Dalits, while the Brahmans remain at the top of the hierarchy by being the doctors, engineers and lawyers of India.

In 2010: Some of the sub-castes of scheduled castes have become relatively better economically. As a benefit of Reservation they have acquired technical and management education as well.

Many of them are working in the Government sector, again because of a certain percentage of seats specifically reserved for them in the Government sector. However, the prevailing condition of SCs/STs can not be ascertained in the private sector because of absence of reservation in private sector and due to the absence of any data on the community wise break up of work force in private sector.

WHAT IS "UNTOUCHABILITY"?

Untouchability is a direct product of the caste system. It is not merely the inability to touch a human being of a certain caste or sub-caste. It is an attitude on the part of a whole group of people that relates to a deeper psychological process of thought and belief, invisible to the naked eye, translated into various physical acts and behaviours, norms and practices.

Untouchability is prompted by the spirit of social aggression and the belief in purity and pollution that characterises casteism. It is generally taken for granted that Dalits are considered polluted people at the lowest end of the caste order. The jobs considered polluting and impure are reserved for Dalits, and in many cases Dalits are prevented from engaging in any other work. These jobs include removing human waste (known as "manual scavenging"), dragging away and skinning animal carcasses, tanning leather, making and fixing shoes, and washing clothes. They are supposed to reside outside the village so that their physical presence does not pollute the "real" village. Not only are they restricted in terms of space, but their houses are also supposed to be inferior in quality and devoid of any facilities like water and electricity.

Untouchability — A social evil.

Untouchability is present in nearly every sphere of life and practiced in an infinite number of forms. At the village level Dalits are barred from using wells used by non-Dalits, forbidden from going to the barber shop and entering temples, while at the level of job recruitment and employment Dalits are systematically paid less, ordered to do the most menial work, and rarely promoted. Even at school, Dalit children may be asked to clean toilets and to eat separately.

As an instrument of casteism, Untouchability also serves to instill caste status to Dalit children from the moment they are born. Kachro (filth), Melo (dirty), Dhudiyo (dusty), Gandy (mad), Ghelo (stupid), Punjo (waste) are just some of the names given to Dalit boys in Gujarat. Of course, names with similar meanings are given to Dalit girls too. This shows the debilitating effect of Untouchability, as it becomes a conscious act of cooperation between two individuals of distinct caste or sub-caste identity. The person treated as untouchable submits himself or herself to untouchability practices because of a generational integrated belief that it is right, justified, religious and natural. Untouchability is in this sense a corollary of the caste system, and the only way to get rid of it seems to be to get rid of the caste system itself. Focusing on Untouchability ignores the root cause of the problem, all the more so as Article 17 of the Indian Constitution, which bans Untouchability, confines its definition to individual discrimination against certain classes of persons not easily identifiable.

The 1950 national constitution of India legally abolishes the practice of "untouchability," and there are constitutional reservations in both educational institutions and public services for Dalits. Unfortunately, these measures have not changed the reality of daily life for most Dalits, as the Indian Government frequently tolerates oppression and open discrimination aimed at this group. As the former Indian President K.R. Narayanan, himself a Dalit, noted in his public address to the nation on the eve of Republic Day, January 25, 2000, "these [Constitutional] provisions remain unfulfilled through bureaucratic and administrative deformation or by narrow interpretations of these special provisions." Dalits usually live in separate areas away from the caste Hindu communities, and they are often forbidden to access public wells. In many areas, when Dalits eat in public restaurants or patronize street vendors, they must use a special glass for drinking tea or coffee to prevent sharing between Dalits and caste Hindus. Dalits in different parts of India cannot enter Hindu temples or Christian churches, and many religious and caste leaders forbid inter-caste marriages.

Should a Dalit break one of these rules, frequently the entire Dalit community will be punished for the perceived individual transgression. Punishment often takes the form of denial of access to land or employment, physical attacks on Dalit women, and the burning down of Dalit homes. Despite a clear record of violence against the Dalits, there are numerous reports that police officials have refused to register complaints about violations of the law or to prosecute those responsible for the abuses. With little knowledge of their rights, limited access to attorneys, and no money for hearings or bail, Dalits are easy targets for human rights violations.

ERADICATION OF UNTOUCHABILITY

Hindutva BVelongs Equally to Caste Hindus and Untouchables

...Asking suicidal questions such as "Tell us if Hinduism belongs to us or not" and then giving shameless answers such as "or else we shall forsake Hindutva" is destructive both in principle and practice. It is shameful even to use this threat as a ploy. It is as shameful as threatening your wicked brother that you will disown your father even if that threat happens to be only an empty one. To spit at the age-old Hindu tradition followed by your ancestors merely to threaten the caste Hindus is condemnable and insulting to the sanctity of your soul.

Pledge that you shall become a caste Hindu while remaining a Hindu. Hindu dharma, Hindu sanskriti (culture) and Hindutva are not the monopoly of caste Hindus. It is the common heritage of both caste Hindus and untouchables. Why are you asking the caste Hindus if you should forsake it? Are they its owners and you mere upstarts? And those sinful and stone-hearted caste Hindus who refuse to eradicate untouchability even when you convert in your thousands are hardly likely to have a change of heart if a few thousand of you leave (the Hindu fold). I fervently appeal to my untouchable brethren not to commit the sin of entertaining this ill-conceived notion (of conversion) as it is not only shameful to them but also self-defeating in the long run.

You shower abuses on Hinduism but do you have the guts to point out defects in Christianity and Islam?

Possessed by hatred for Hinduism, Dr. Ambedkar has been selectively showering abuses on Hinduism day in and day out. He claims that Buddhism is rational, free of defects and superior to other religions. While condemning what he terms as superstitions and evil practices in Hinduism, he should be equally forthright in condemning similar practices in the followers of Christianity and Islam. For example, the exponents of both these religions have given sanction in their religious scriptures to the practice of slavery and condemning slaves to a status worse than animals. But his (Dr. Ambedkar's) pen or tongue generally dare not express a murmur of criticism against Christianity and Islam for these heinous practices. There it suddenly gets paralyzed. The reason is obvious—fear (of physical assault)!.

Buddhist religious practice has also become replete with superstitions and hypocrisy

Ambedkarites mock at Hindus by quoting the myth that Karna was born of Kunti's ear. But why do they hide the fact that the Buddhist texts give the following account of the Buddha's birth? "The Buddha's mother conceived at the age of forty-five without male contact, delivered without labour pains and the numerous miracles associated with his birth"...such superstitious tales are taken to be true by Buddhists too. Will the Ambedkarites characterize Buddhism as one big fable?...if the Muslim atrocity—yes, I call it an atrocity—of burning Buddhist texts is not a pious act to be glorified, then Ambedkar's action of burning the Manusmriti (code of Manu, the Hindu law-giver) is no pious act either; he will have to admit that he committed an atrocity.

Ambedkar tells our Mahar brethren that they should embrace Buddhism because there is no place for God, soul, reincarnation and the like in Buddhism. But fact is that millions and millions of Mahayanist Buddhists from Manchuria to Indo-China not only believe in gods but have elevated the Buddha to the status of a God. They believe in the Hindu gods such as Indra, Varuna, Lakshmi, Saraswati as well as yakshas and kinnars (yakshas and kinnars are supposed to be celestial beings) with the Buddha as the presiding deity of all of them. Today the Buddhist world is engaged in daily worship of the Buddha. Why are Ambedkarites suppressing this truth?

The Buddha himself believed in reincarnation. This is evident from the fact that he has himself spoken of his previous births not only in human but also in animal and bird forms.

The Buddha himself preached that no one should indulge in animal slaughter. But if some one else kills fish, fowl and animals and offers their cooked meat it is alright not only for a lay Buddhist but also for a monk to partake of the same!

The contention of the Ambedkarites that under the influence of the Buddha's teachings, no large-scale yagnas (ritual animal sacrifices) took place after his death is pure falsehood...It is a historical fact that for around 1000 years after the Buddha right up to the seventh century, several Kshatriya heroes such as Yashovarman who defeated the Huns used to perform Ashvamedha (horse-sacrifice) and several such yagnas.

Whilst criticizing the practice of giving alms to the Brahmins, (let it not be forgotten that) the burden imposed by the Buddhists on society through sustenance of thousands of good-for-nothing and beggarly monks and the resultant deceit of society was a hundred times more.

You (Buddhists) mock at the Hindus for doing tree-worship but what about your reverence for the Bodhi tree (the tree under which Siddhartha Gautam attained enlightenment and became the Buddha)?

BUDDHISM AND UNTOUCHABILITY

Even in the days of the Buddhist emperor Harsha, the Buddhists used to consider the Chandalas as untouchables. They had to live outside the village boundary and they were obliged to announce their arrival in the village with bells and walk on the sides of the road taking care not to touch any one else. Even today, Buddhists in a Buddhist country like Ceylon (now Sri Lanka) practise untouchability in some form or the other in the villages.

Dr. Ambedkar who contends that Buddhism is the best religion was about to embrace Christianity and Islam!

Nowadays, Dr. Ambedkar is constantly saying in his newspapers and speeches that Buddhism is the best amongst all the world religions. But was it not the same gentleman who not long ago praised Islam and announced his firm intention of embracing that 'great religion'? Did he not once announce with fanfare that he was going to embrace 'the great religion of Christianity'? After that, had he not raised dust by saying that he was going to embrace Sikhism? At that time, Dr. Ambedkar was not an immature school boy. Then too, he was flaunting a doctorate. Did he not realize then that Buddhism is the best amongst all the world religions? And if he had not realized this at that time, is it not obvious that his slogans in those days were not due to any deep study of different religions but a result of either immature intellect or simple deception?

The acceptance of Buddhism by some untouchables is not a change of religion but a change of sect

So long as Ambedkar remains an Indian Buddhist, his fatherland and holyland inevitably remain Bharat that extends from the Sindhu (Indus river) to the seas and as such he will be inevitably included in the ambit of Hindutva. At least so long as Ambedkar remains a Buddhist, it is not possible for him to violate the borders of Hindutva...All that has happened due to Ambedkar's embracing of Buddhism is that he renounced the Vedic sect of Hinduism and entered a non-Vedic sect or religion (if that is what you want to call it) within the ambit of Hindutva.

Do not praise Ambedkar's conversion blindly

Had not the Congress initially embraced Barrister Jinnah as a nationalist Muslim? When the Pakistan Plan was first mooted, was it not Nehru who termed it 'fantastic nonsense.' From the beginning, we should be alert about any separatist movement such as this conversion so that we may not repeat the same naïve and blind mistakes. We should but oppose it as a potential calamity. Especially when some foreign statesmen come here and dig out the Buddha's remains and raise Ambedkar on a pedestal, we need to analyze this increasing glorification of the Buddha from the religious and national angle. We need to re-read and understand the history of the Buddhist period that they themselves have opened up before us. We need to remember that right from the days of the Yavan (Greek), Shaka, Kushana, Hun and other foreign aggressors to the time of the Muslim invasions, treacherous individuals like Jaychand or Indian Buddhists as a group have allied with those alien forces not for personal gain but as a matter of collective religious duty. By consolidating these alien rulers in Bharat, they (Indian Buddhists) performed this betrayal to the Hindu state and the Hindu nation time and again. It was these sins that ignited Indian fury and claimed the glorification of the Buddha as its victim in the past. Buddhism was once eclipsed from this country as a result.

Though it does not seem definitely probable that history will repeat itself, it is better to be eternally vigilant against this Buddhist revolt by those working against the interests of the Hindu nation. Rather than test this poison, it is better not to swallow it in the first place! When Muhammad bin Qasim invaded Sind in 712 CE, Buddhists welcomed him with open arms. They rejoiced at his victory over the Hindu king Dahir. Of course, as they were still infidels in the eyes of Muhammad bin Qasim, he mercilessly massacred them.

The people's representatives of independent Bharat have announced this decision independently, voluntarily and unanimously. This is not a reluctant surrender but a spontaneous penance on the part of caste Hindus!

The caste Hindu member representatives of the Constituent Assembly were drawn from all the four varnas, different sub-castes and all provinces.

At least in this announcement of the demise of untouchability, the so-called caste Hindu representatives had the nationwide support of enlightened, prominent and distinguished caste Hindus.

Like the caste Hindus, the untouchable Hindus also spontaneously undertook penance for their sins!...Their sin being that those castes who were styled as 'untouchable' by the caste Hindus, believed themselves to be superior to other 'lower' castes and considered them 'untouchable' !

This social revolution is greater compared to those in other countries.

This social revolution is much greater compared to those in other countries. No civil war was fought. No blood was shed. Even an apparently developed country like America had to fight a civil war to eradicate slavery.

When will untouchability eradication become a reality?

The true majesty of this announcement (of eradication of untouchability by the Constituent Assembly) lies in its implementation. This slogan will become meaningful only when untouchability is uprooted completely from the length and breadth of this vast Bharatiya nation within the coming ten years. All wise, learned and nationalist minded workers drawn from both caste Hindus and untouchables alike should resolve and draw up a consensual programme appealing to the humanism, good intentions and nationalism present in every heart not to observe birth-based untouchability, creating a moral force in every individual and in society at large but if adamant prejudice persists, they should not occasionally hesitate to get the judiciary or the executive to enforce this law.

CORRUPTION

Corruption not only has become a pervasive aspect of Indian politics but also has become an increasingly important factor in Indian elections. The extensive role of the Indian state in providing services and promoting economic development has always created the opportunity for using public resources for private benefit. As government regulation of business was extended in the 1960s and corporate donations were banned in 1969, trading economic favors for under-the-table contributions to political parties became an increasingly widespread political practice. During the 1980s and 1990s, corruption became associated with the occupants of the highest echelons of India's political system. Rajiv Gandhi's Government was rocked by scandals, as was the government of P.V. Narasimha Rao. Politicians have become so closely identified with corruption in the public eye that a Times of India poll of 1,554 adults in six metropolitan cities found that 98 percent of the public is convinced that politicians and ministers are corrupt, with 85 percent observing that corruption is on the increase.

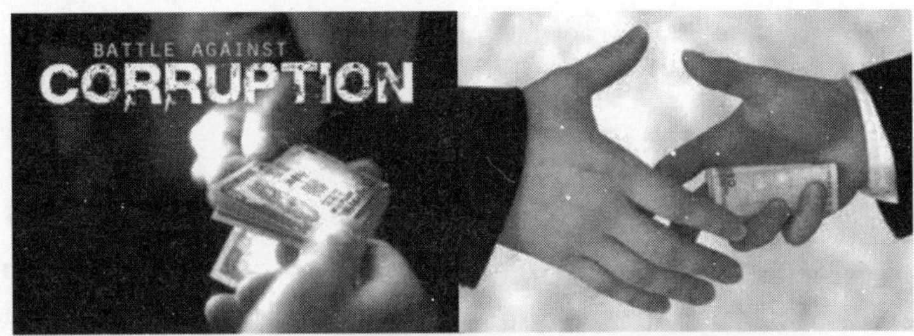

The crime of corruption is easily forgotten, the law offers easy way back into the mainstream and acceptance by the society.

The prominence of political corruption in India in the 1990s is hardly unique to India. Other countries also have experienced corruption that has rocked their political systems. What is remarkable about India is the persistent anti-incumbent sentiment among its electorate. Since Indira's victory in her 1971 "*Garibi Hatao*" election, only one ruling party has been reelected to power in the central government. In an important sense, the exception proves the rule because the Congress (I) won reelection in 1984 in no small measure because the electorate saw in Rajiv Gandhi a "Mr. Clean" who would lead a new generation of politicians in cleansing the political system. Anti-incumbent sentiment is just as strong at the state level, where the ruling parties of all political persuasions in India's major states lost eleven of thirteen legislative assembly elections held from 1991 through spring 1995.

From small time clerks to the high profile politicians, commissioners, police inspectors, traffic police, stock exchange brokers, military establishments, recruiters, sportsmen, judiciary and most of the government employees, corruption is seen and felt in every transaction from bottom of the chain till the top. In the recent times the private Indian companies captured the top spot in encouraging corruption when dealing with international clients in order to grab lucrative contracts.

Greater solutions may include population control to improve the quality than the quantity, Controlling population will bring up the quality of life and thus lesser competition and effective control of people and government processes. However feasible solutions are to impart moral principles in schools, and introduction of stringent audits, accountability, effective tracking of corrupt individuals through citizen cards or tax id's.

Computerization of processes, privatization of public sectors, eliminating the chain of corruption by not just punishing the first level but also higher levels involved.

Corruption is not limited to atheists, even the most corrupts are highly religious and have close family ties, in other words corruption has no boundaries. Religion and religious congregations can support and promote anti-corruption drives.

Corruption is NOT a luxury tax. Whoever described corruption is a luxury tax probably said it out of frustration, the religion of corruption, the corruption of politics, the dishonest souls and perversion of integrity is unpardonable.

CORRUPTION CAUSES AND FORMS

Determining the causes and forms of corruption could stand as a preliminary step in future fighting against corruption actions. In order to achieve the desired outcomes in the fight against corruption, it is important that after identifying favorable environments for acts of corruption, to have established the factors that generate the corrupt behavior as well as the forms it takes. The following questions need answers: Which?, What?, and How does it manifest itself?

What are the Institutions Most Affected by Corruption?

The answer is provided by many institutes researching corruption, at a national, regional or international level. According to the results of the Transparency International Barometer (the barometer evaluates the degree to which corruption affects the lives of ordinary people, with questions on public attitudes towards corruption, the degree to which people consider public institutions to be corrupt, their experiences on the small scale corruption and their opinions on the future of the fight against corruption) on Corruption in Romania, should there be a top of the most affected institutions, the first place would be shared by political parties and the parliament, the second by the legislative/juridical system, and the third by medical services.

Also vulnerable to corruption are the economic-financial and banking system, the privatization process, capital and patrimony transfers, the field of industry and material resources, especially the oil sector, the food and the alcohol industry, the customs and frontier field and the public administration system. The fact that people consider first place institutions as corrupted, can be explained in terms of population's dissatisfaction with the effects of economic, educational and medical reforms, with the amplification of acts of violence and the discretionary application of law. Results are furthermore alarming as the most affected institutions are those that draft laws and see to their application: *the Parliament*, *the political parties*, *the police*, and *the justice system*.

What are the Factors that Favour Corruption? Sources of Corruption

As the social system was replaced by the market economy conditions, risk factors multiplied and corruption became a structured phenomenon, well-specialized and professional. By means of informal organizational networks it can influence decision-makers of the political, legislative, administration, justice, and even security fields.

Exerting power discretionarily and the very often monopolist market position of public companies, stand as prerequisites for corruption, whereas political, bureaucratic and economic interests' convergence provides it with a favorable environment.

Specific activities determine specific risks and vulnerabilities to corruption, some of them shared by all public institutions, while others generated by the very specificity of the activity performed. Among these, some of the most common will be mentioned, the ones occurring within high risk institutions. Within the Ministry of the Interior, for instance, corruption appeared and evolved as a consequence of: laws, institutional relationships, and the great volume of activities to be performed in a given amount of time, organizational culture, wage levels, logistics and individual structure.

Quite often, the causes generating corruption include: the recruitment and promotion system in local or national public administration, based on who you know instead of what you know, relations with public decentralized services and governmental organizations (long term contracts, high and certain incomes), nepotism and services provided to people for economic or political benefits, vague objectives and superficial control and audit (both internal and external ones), and shallow organizational culture. A high demand for a type of service could also result in corruption if the possibility that authorities have for supplying it are limited. When demand is higher than the offer, under these circumstances, the result is not the same as on the free market. The price of the desired good or service is not necessarily higher, but the cost for purchasing it is increased by the price paid in order to gain access to it.

Education is of utmost importance in the fight against corruption in terms of increasing resistance to its benefits. There are some of the risk factors in graduate and under-graduate education. These are as follows:

(i) Legislative instability (lack of correlation between the laws on education);

(ii) Inefficiency and lack of involvement of some national and local institutions;

(iii) Low level of competitiveness between institutions;

(iv) Low professional motivation (determined by career prospects, working-place and wage conditions, the adverse selection, evaluation and promotion systems;

(v) Procedures applied in evaluating students (objectivity and transparency).

Corruption is an instrument of economic criminality that is used in order to avoid indictment of criminals, to facilitate tax evasion, intellectual property-related crimes, to sign contracts in the public/private sector and win contracts by firms that act as cover for organized crime groups or networks. According to some authors, there are no criminal organizations beyond corruption, these structures being formed by professionals in crime and corruption.

How Does Corruption Go Off?

The range and implications of corruption differ from one country to the other, from a region to another as it appears under different forms. An act of corruption, under Romanian law is considered to be accepting and giving bribery, accepting undue advantage, using influence or paying for it, abusing power, forgery in documents drafted to acquire European funds, as well as malversation of these funds even if they were legally obtained. Corruption's escalation at all levels, from public servants at the basis of the public organizational system (small corruption), to higher political ranks (the large corruption), has harmful implications on the society and the business environment. According to studies, depending on the fields it affects, corruption can be grouped into: political corruption, administrative corruption and kleptocracy.

The Global Corruption Report defines political corruption as the politicians' abuse of power for personal advantage. Politicians' integrity is mostly affected by the conflict between public and personal interests. Corruption in political finance can appear under various forms, from vote buying to use of illicit funding for candidate position selling and the misuse of state funds and public administrative resources. Administrative corruption appears in the area of laws and rules' application, at the public administration level, mostly under the form of small corruption.

Kleptocracy is a political corruption subcategory and it mostly appears in the countries that have juridical systems less structured and where public and private activity transparency is limited. It includes the highest level officials that systematically use public funds, directly or indirectly, for their own enrichment.

In kleptocrat economies, economic and social problems are ignored, there is little respect for the law, and moral values are forgotten. Kleptocrats are concerned with taking-over state assets, no matter if we are talking about natural resources (oil, diamonds etc.), state budget, companies or estates. Unlike administrative corruption, kleptocracy influences the laws and regulations, which are especially drafted to favour it.

According to Michael Johnston, the difference of influence exerted by corruption (and the other way around) on wealth and power exchanges, state institutions and societies, leads to the emergence of four corruption categories, as follows: influence markets, elite cartels, oligarchs and official mogul clans. The author's statement, according to which identifying major corruption syndromes and their implications helps understand the main underlying variations of the ways that wealth and power are gained and used in personal interests, can be complemented by other interests, such as that of transnationals', political parties' etc.

Corruption Levels and Consequences

The analyses on corruption highlight the fact that it has become "a global issue involving global reactions". A lack of action can result into state capture by private interest groups, with harmful effects on the state, its economy and society, because the "rules of the game" can be "fundamentally distorted for good", in the favour of some privileged individuals".

Developing market economies are perceived as being a constant source of corruption, a fact that discourages investment as entrepreneurs are aware that some part of their investment could be claimed by corrupt officials. In this environment corruption prospers, as in transition periods frail political and administrative structures lack the legitimacy and the institutionalized power. Some studies argue that lack of security around corrupt transactions is amplified by three characteristics: corruption does not allow legal resources; it has to be hidden from the public; mutual exposure threats are everpresent as partners in corruption are bound even after the exchange is final.

Corruption and poor governing can affect reforms, economic efficiency and tax revenue implicitly, public expenditure and the fiscal deficit. Hence, an empiric study on corruption's impact on tax structure shows an increase in the corruption index by 1% reduces the collected taxes level by 2.7% of the GDP.

Corruption interferes with economic growth, generates inequities and erodes government credibility and the efficient functioning of state institutions. As it becomes generalized and perpetuates, corruption becomes a major threat to stability and democracy, eroding the fundamentals of the state. Consequences of corruption that are acknowledged as well include: low quality services, public resource embezzlement, increase in the degree of population poverty and suffering, high social costs, abuse spreading, property impairment, decrease in public income, inefficient allotment and faulty public resources management.

Because of the fact that corruption affects public projects, that it determines significant loss to education, health and poverty prevention budgets, in both underdeveloped and developed countries, corruption is considered to be an important obstacle in the way of sustainable development [...] Transparency International estimates that the loss in public purchases caused by corruption amounts to at least 400 billion dollars each year, all over the world.

The Corruption Perceptions Index 2004 performed by Transparency International underlines the poisonous connection between poverty, malfunctioning institutions and corruption. "For the poorest countries, the level of corruption can draw the line between life and death, when money for hospitals and drinkable water is at stake". The Global Corruption Report performed by Transparency International in 2008 evaluates corruption costs to 50 billion USD (35 billion Euros), sum that represents half of the annual assistance expenditure, of the costs of water and sewage systems.

BLACK MONEY

The black money scam, sometimes also known as the 'wash wash scam', is a scam where con artists attempt to fraudulently obtain money from a victim by persuading him or her that piles of banknote-sized paper in a trunk or a safe is really money which has been dyed black (e.g., to avoid detection by customs). The victim is persuaded to pay for chemicals to wash the "money" with a promise that he will share in the proceeds. The black money scam first appeared around the year 2000. It is yet another variation of what is known as advance fee fraud.

Well the Govt. till date has taken some measure to curb out the black money.

All countries, to a greater or smaller percentage, have what is known as a parallel, or cash, economy that operates outside the legitimate loop. But India's parallel economy is unparalleled, in that by many guesstimates it is not only as big as the legit economy but in fact a couple of times bigger. And we have a unique name for it.

Black money is not a synonym for the cash economy. For instance, there are several transactions which have to be carried out in cash: Municipal tax, passport fees, purchase of government stamp paper, opening a bank account. Is the money that you perforce have to use in such dealings, which often involve the sarkar, black money? God forbid. Or, better still, Chidambaram forbid.

REASONS OF BLACK MONEY

Black money is generated due to the following reasons:

- The people do not pay their taxes. Even if they pay taxes, they are not in correct proportions to their incomes. The tax evasions by corporate and industrial houses are to the tune of billions of rupees. These firms are able to make clever usage of the income tax rules and hence, they save taxes. This tax evasion leads to the generation of black money.
- The black money is earned by gifts, hawala transactions and illegal foreign exchange deals. These deals are not scrutinized by the government simply because these are without any documentary evidences.
- The procedures of over billing or under billing and exaggeration of expenses lead to the generation of black money. The sale and purchase of assets also lead to the generation of black money. The value of the property is shown to be very low in the documents whereas it has a very high value in the actual transaction. The businesses are conducted in other sectors of economy in the same manner and non-billed amounts are retained by the individuals and the firms as black money.
- Black money is harming our national economy and we have achieved an economic growth rate of five percent per annum whereas the economy should have grown at the rate of eight percent in order to make up for the rising population pressures and infrastructural development requirements. Black money is the chief inhibiting factor in the process of national economic development.
- The menace of black money has also increased the rich poor divide. The poor families are unable to afford even the square meals whereas the rich and the neo-rich are enjoying the luxuries of life. The Indian society has become poorer. Only the few sections of the society, which account for fifteen percent of the total population, have been able to enjoy the highest standards of living in this subcontinent. Therefore, the real poverty has increased and not decreased over a period of fifty years. The black money menace started during the seventies and it is now at its peak and the masses have suffered due to rising prices, inflation in business, poor exports and industrial recession.

The rich few, however, have not felt the heat and continue to lead luxurious lives at the cost of their poor countrymen. It has connotation for which you have to exercise care and caution by utilizing your brain for converting a portion of black money or the entire money by converting into white money on a piece meal basis. In this form, you will be able to avoid the rigors of economic measures including taxation.

- Black money could be curbed only through the strict efforts of the state and this is for the benefit of the masses as well. We should disclose our real incomes and must pay taxes regularly. We should avoid unhealthy means of making money. The nation must get out of the evil net of black money. Only the honest Indians could save the nation.

PROBLEMS OF BLACK MONEY

Even after 60 years of independence, our country is faced with poverty and numerous economic ills. Even though socialistic pattern of society has been accepted in the constitution, our country is far away from socialism and her economy is in the grip of private enterprises. In fact, India has unlicensed economy which has given birth to corruption, inflation and black money. The concept of mixed economy has been harmful to both private and public enterprises. It has jeopardized our economy and hit the common man below the belt. The poor man has been becoming poorer and rich richer just because of the economic ills like inflation and black money. Black money which runs a parallel currency in wealth which is made overnight in violation of the rules and provisions stipulated by the state and a collusion with the state officials does not go unchecked. This kind of money is earned setting aside all human and moral values.

SOURCES OF BLACK MONEY

There are many sources of black money. Chief among these areas follows:

- Import licenses.
- Selling of cement licenses, steel and iron.
- Transactions in heavy industries.
- Transaction in public sector.
- Release of industrial licenses.
- Government and commercial transactions.
- Forged and face currency.

Today the making of black money has become factor in our society because palatial houses, and cars, and in arranging cocktail parties and recreations in big hotels. Moreover, it helps a person getting everything done in time and to his best satisfaction.

CAUSES OF CONVERTING GENUINE PROFIT INTO BLACK MONEY

There are many causes of converting genuine profit into black money. The chief among them are:

- Inflation.
- General and mid-term election.
- Tax evasion.

The government itself is responsible for the creation of black money. The exorbitant rates of taxation on income, sales, wealth production and revenue inevitably lead to tax-evasion. The taxes on income and wealth are so high that an honest person will be left with little after he pays his due taxes. Many taxes on income and wealth are so high that an honest person will be left are encouraged by the government's taxation policy to look for loopholes in order to refrain from reporting their income. Thus, the money earned as profit remains unaccounted for an unreported and is converted into white money by investing it in big houses, luxury items, gold ornaments, and showy marriages. The government has full knowledge about the quantum of black money which is pumped into our economy every year, but the government measures to check the growth and increase of unaccounted wealth has been ineffective. The missing element has been the will to strike at the root of the evil. That has been the sad story all these years. The customary ritual of declaring war on tax evasion at conferences of income-tax commissioners is faithfully performed every year. The public is told as usual that black money will be unearthed and evaders duly punished. Some operations of the income-tax department get wide popularity. The income-tax officials put themselves on news when the flat of a film star is auctioned or legal action taken against an industrial tycoon. But the problem of black money cannot be solved in this manner.

The political system itself breeds black money. The democratic system which means unlicensed freedom is largely responsible for the growth of corruption and black money. When political parties accept unaccounted money for election campaigns they not only heap generate black money but also protect the hoarders of ill-gotten wealth. It will be a major blow against the parallel economy, if it is made mandatory to audit the books of political parties. Such financing of elections could be also considered. The drive against the parallel economy will never be effective unless the nexus between politics and black money is broken.

The inflationary pressure also threatens our economy and gives birth to black money, which plays a decisive role in inflation and price responsible for inflation and black money. The inflation rate at present is above fifty percent of what has already taken place since twenty years back. In other words, we have become high cost economy with prices averaging fifty percent above what they had been in the country and the lowering of the common man. Unless some strict measures are taken to counter inflation and check high cost economy, the problem of black money cannot be solved. Black money, however, should be dealt with strict application of penal provisions and devaluation of our currency.

Thus, black money is growing unabated and it has become almost a parallel economy. People hoarding black money are trying to convert it into white money and thus causing inflationary pressure and high cost economy. One school of thought is of the view that the parallel economy has come to stay and it need not be disturbed because it plays a useful role. Condemnation of what is illegal goes against the grain of good administration and no government will be justified in pampering black marketers and tax evaders.

MEASURES TO CHECK BLACK MONEY

Since inflation is a phenomenon where income or purchasing power is rising faster than the real goods and services, the measures to check inflation should either be of a check on the increase in money incomes or making available more of real goods and services. The various measures which can be taken to establishment a better balance between aggregate supply and demand for money can be studied under three main heads—monetary and fiscal measures, control over investment and other measures.

(i) Monetary Measures: Monetary measures aim at reducing money incomes.

- *Credit control:* One of the important monetary measures is monetary policy. The central bank of the country adopts a number of methods to control the quantity and quality of credit. For this purpose, it raises the bank rates, sells securities in the open market, raises the reserved ratio, and adopts a number of selective credit control measure, such as raising margin requirements and regulating consumer credit. Monetary policy may not be effective in controlling inflation, if inflation is due to cost-push factors. Monetary policy can only be helpful in controlling inflation due to demand-pull-factors.
- *Demonetization of currency:* However, one of the monetary measures is to demonetize currency of higher denominations. Such a measure is usually adopted when there is abundance of black money in the country.
- *Issue of new currency:* The most extreme monetary measure is the issue of new currency in place of the old currency. Under this system, one new note is exchanged for a number of notes of the old currency. The value of bank deposits is also fixed accordingly. Such a measure is adopted when there is an excessive issue of notes and there is hyperinflation in the country. It is a very effective measure. But is inequitable for it hurts the small depositors the most.

(ii) Fiscal Measures: Monetary policy alone is incapable of controlling inflation. It should, therefore, be supplemented by fiscal measures. Fiscal measure are highly effective for controlling government expenditure, personal consumption expenditure, and private and public investment. The Principal fiscal measures are the followings:

- *Reduction in unnecessary expenditure :* The government should reduce unnecessary expenditure on non-development activities in order to curb inflation. This will also but a check on private expenditure which is dependent upon government demand for goods and services.
- *Increase in taxed:* To cut personal consumption expenditure, the rates of personal, corporate and commodity taxes should be raised and even new taxes should be levied, but the rates of taxes should not be as high as to discourage saving, investment and production.
- *Increase in savings:* Another measure is to increase saving on the part of the people. This will tend to reduce disposable income with the people, and hence personal consumption expenditure.
- *Surplus budgets:* An important measure is to adopt anti-inflation- ary budgetary policy. For this purpose, the government should give up deficit financing and instead have surplus budgets. It means collecting more in revenues and spending less.
- *Public debt:* At the same time, it should stop repayment of public debt and postpone it to some future date till inflationary pressures are controlled within the economy. Instead, the government should borrow more to reduce money supply with the public.

(iii) Other Measures: The other types of measures are those which aim at increasing aggregate supply and reducing aggregate demand directly.

- *To increase production:* The followings measure should be adopted to increase production:
  - One of the foremost measure to control inflation is to increase the production of essential consumer goods like food, clothing, kerosene oil, sugar, vegetable oils, etc.
  - If there is need, raw materials for such products may be imported on preferential basis to increase the production of essential commodities.
  - Efforts should also be made to increase productivity. For this purpose, industrial peace should be maintained through agreements with trade unions, binding them not to resort to strikes for some time.
  - The policy of rationalization of industries should be adopted as a long-term measure. Rationalization increase produc-

tivity and production of industries through the use of brain, brawn and bullion.

  - All possible help in the form of latest technology, raw materials, financial help, subsidies, etc. should be provided to different consumer goods sectors to increase production.

- *Rational wage policy*: Another important measure is to adopt a rational wage and income policy, Under hyperinflation, there is a wage-price spiral. To control this, the government should freeze wages, incomes, profits, dividends, bonus, etc. But such a drastic measure can only be adopted for a short period and by antagonizing both workers and industrialists. Therefore, the best course is to link increase in wages to increase in productivity.
- *Price Control*: Price control and rationing is another measure of direct control to check inflation. Price control means fixing an upper limit for the prices of essential consumer goods. They are the maximum prices fixed by law and anybody charging more than these prices is punished by law. But it is difficult to administer price control.
- *Rationing*: Rationing aims at distributing consumption of scarce goods so as to make them available to a large number of consumers. It is applied to essential consumer goods such as wheat, rice, sugar, kerosene oil, etc. it is meant to stabilize the prices of necessaries and assure distributive justice.

SOCIAL CONTROL

Introduction. Meaning of Social Control: *Definitions of Social Control.* ***Social Control Theory. Purposes of Social Control. Types of Social Control:*** *Formal Social Control, Informal Social Control.* ***Social Control as an Independent Variable. Social Control as a Dependent Variable. Propaganda Model Theory of Social Control. Education and Social Control. Control by Customs. Control by Law. Social Control by Sanction. Social Control by Religion. Social Control by Coercion. Need for Social Control.***

INTRODUCTION

The study of social control has been an integral part of sociology since its inception. Originally, the concept was defined as any structure, process, relationship, or act that contributes to the social order. Social control is consequently a pervasive feature of society, of interest to a broad range of sociologists having differing theoretical persuasions and substantive interests, and not just to sociologists of deviance. The sociological issue is not the existence of social control, but determining its precise nature, and identifying the mechanisms at work in particular social contexts. By whom is control exercised? What techniques of control are employed? How far can and do individuals or groups resist processes of social control? In whose interests does control operate? The answers to such questions vary greatly. Normative functionalists tend to suggest that social control is of value to society as a whole, since it is essential to the maintenance of social order; others point to the sectional interests that are served in the process of social control, emphasizing the lack of normative consensus, the differences in power that are involved, and the close linkage between power and control.

MEANING OF SOCIAL CONTROL

Social control has the primary aim of bringing about an idealised social order. This social order is maintained, through the various established institutions and influential mediums such as Politics, Education, Religion, the Media, Family, the Legal system etc.

The means by which individuals are induced or compelled to conform to the usages and life values of the group are so numerous and varied that a classification is not possible. E.A. Ross has described a number of means that have been used by social groups throughout the human history to keep individuals under control. The important among them are public opinion, law, custom, religion, morality, personality, folkways and mores. E.C. Hayes distinguished between control by sanctions and control by suggestion and imitation. According to him, education is the most effective means of control and the family is the most significant agency.

The *family* as a social institute is our first port of call, as it is here, that each of us were taught the norms and values deemed acceptable by the standards of wider society. Straight from the off we are immediately bombarded with social control, with the aim of making us act in a certain way, to view certain things as good, right, acceptable, to be encouraged, to be awarded, and to see other things as wrong, Immoral, Evil, unnatural, different, to be shunned, to be avoided, to be curbed and ultimately be eliminated for the greater good. This is the very backbone of Social control. Our thoughts, and our sense of what is right and what is wrong, what is good and what is bad is established here.

Let us move on to the role *education* plays in moulding us into model citizens, with good jobs and sturdy moral compasses. Our knowledge is regulated by what is taught to us in a set curriculum which is set out by the Government. And in this way, any and all lessons taught, have the primary aim of socialising children into an acceptance of the idealism of the ruling class. Not to get too overly Marxist in my article but certain things within the education system can be interpreted as being in place distinctly to benefit a capitalist ruling society, Such as Sports Day, which sounds ridiculous, but Sports Day could socialise children into an acceptance of competition as being the Norm. The way schools are run, can also affect our ideology, as schools have a hierarchal system, a chain of command leading down to the pupil, which socialises people into an acceptance of a hierarchal society. The role of Education acts to churn out conformists who follow social order without question.

Religion is a potential Gold mine of Social Control, possibly the most water tight institution which could bring order out of chaos. Religion uses fear and consequence to keep the masses in check, regulating behaviour towards a specific desired end.

The problem with religion is that there is no scientific basis to refute it with, as we are told that we have to go off blind faith, hence Religion has a sociological and psychological control over us, as we surrender our life to a higher power, and thus give ourselves meaning and purpose in the process, which doesn't exactly sound like a bad thing, unless you look again a little more closely to uncover the lie behind the lie. To quote Marx: Religion is the opiate of the people.

Religion socialises us into an acceptance of inequality, it keeps the poor resigned to their fate, and if I can return to Marx turns our chains into daisies. Religion is the ultimate form of social control as it gives both meaning and a need to follow order and structure. Religion also helps us deal with earthly injustices such as murder, as we are told that they will eventually be punished in the after life'. The legal system was put in place to specifically maintain the social structure, and reinforce social control through punishment of none conformists to the system. Such punishments are supposed to act as a deterrent to anyone else thinking of going against the established ways of the society. Since the legal system has just been explained above, now we will move on to the next topic, i.e., media.

The *media* is one of the Top Dog's in the way of social control. It is unlike education for example as education only has a grip on us for so long before we leave for the world of work, but the media is a constant medium and flow of information, propaganda, disinformation, ideology etc all with the intended aim of keeping audiences living, breathing eating, sleeping and thinking in a certain way. All these different mediums of thought are entering your eyes, and being processed by your brain at the speed of light. This leaves no time to actually think about what you are seeing, as this control works on a more subliminal level.

Having taken a look at the various means of social control and how it helps to mould us and conform us all, I have concluded that there is no escaping Social control, as it has an infinite number of platforms in which to work, and we have but two way to receive it: Through our eyes and through our minds. The only possible way to release ourselves from the clutches of this control is to be none conformist and reject social order, which is almost as sinister as social control itself.

DEFINITION OF SOCIAL CONTROL

Mannheim defines social control as the sum of those methods by which a society tries to influence human behaviour to maintain a given order. To Ogbuand an established rule is social control.

Ogburn and *Nimkoff* the patterns of pressure which a society exerts to maintain order E Ross defines it the system of devices whereby society brings its members into conformity with the accepted standards of behaviour.

According to *Lapiere* social control is a corrective for inadequate socialization.

Social Control

G.A. Lundberg has defined social control as designating those social behaviours which influence individuals or groups towards conformity to established or desired norms.

Kimball Young defines social control as the use of coercion, force, restraint, suggestion or persuasion of one group over another or of a group over its members or of persons over others to enforce the prescribed rules of the game. These rules may be set down by the members themselves as in a professional code of ethics or they may be those laid down by a larger, more inclusive group for the regulation of other smaller groups.

Social control may thus be defined as:

Social control is an influence where influence may be exerted through public opinion, coercion, social suggestion, religion or any other method. The influence is exerted by the society which means that group is better able to exercise influence over the individual than a single individual. This group may be the family, the church, the state or the trade union etc. The effectiveness of the influence however depends on variable factors. Sometimes family may exercise more effective influence than the state or vice-versa.

SOCIAL CONTROL THEORY

Travis Hirschi propounded a "Theory of Social Control" that emphasizes on the role of society in the control of criminal behaviour. It specifies the fact that no society can afford to denounce criminal activity without duly accepting its responsibility towards the same. Theory of Social Control stresses on the fact that most delinquent behaviour is the result of unmonitored 'Social Control' by the authorities and primarily, the family. The theory is indicative of the fact that relationships and commitments with respect to set norms and a belief structure encourage or discourage individuals and groups to break the law.

The theory spotlights the internalization of values and timely guidance and monitoring of behaviour as the factors responsible for an 'ideal' society. It is highlighted that it is only when an individual or a group has a major stake in the immediate, surrounding community, that the urge to behave in a deviant manner is suppressed willingly. The theory mentions ways by which the likelihood of criminality can be reduced. Some of the ways mentioned include:

- Presence of a wide range of activities.
- Scope for exploring the accepted processes of socialization and ethics.
- Availability of unbiased choices within social contracts.
- Generating a sense of responsibility within the immediate society.
- Predetermining 'costs and consequences' to various choices made available.
- Inner containment of a tendency towards delinquent behaviour and social anxiety through the development of self-image, within the family.
- Harmonious living conditions.
- Reduced family conflicts and aggressiveness and development of healthy family relationships.
- Timely obscuration of delinquent peers and subcultures, via dedicated social networking.

PURPOSES OF SOCIAL CONTROL

The study of social control is an important aspect of sociology. It is a significant field of study. It is a unifying factor in the study of human behaviour. According to Kimball Young the aims of social control are to bring about conformity, solidarity and continuity of particular group or society. These aims are good but most individuals who endeavour to control their fellow men show little perspective in their efforts. They want that others should accept the modes of conduct which they themselves prefer. This preference may be based on any fact-or-experience derived in life, desire to exploit others for one's own gain, political, personal or economic.

Some reformers and leaders try to conceal their motives by good reasons in the form of altruistic rationalization. A newspaper advertisement that offer discount to those who make purchases by a particular date is an example of such rationalizations. It is difficult to know and classify the motives of the agents of social control.

The classification of the motives or purposes of the agents of social control:

1. Exploitative, motivated by self interest.
2. Regulative based upon habit and the desire for behaviour of the customary types.
3. Creative or constructive based on social benefit.

The results of social control are not always beneficial to society or to the individual. Even social control for constructive purposes may confuse the public and end in inactivity. Efforts to regulate behaviour in accordance to custom may cause cultural lag, mental conflict and emotional instability.

TYPES OF SOCIAL CONTROL

Theory of Social Control proposes social learning with the help of 'social control'. This is believed to not only build on and motivate individual and group self-control, but also reduce even the most remote inclination towards antisocial behaviour. Types of social control derived from various functionalist theories include:

- Direct social control via punitive action for wrongful behaviour, by family and state authority.
- Indirect social control via timely identification of wrong influences on behaviour, by family and state authority.
- Internal social control via conscience questioning.
- Control via satisfaction of all basic human needs.

FORMAL SOCIAL CONTROL

Formal social control is expressed through law as statutes, rules, and regulations against deviant behaviour. Government and organizations using law enforcement mechanisms and other formal sanctions such as fines and imprisonment conduct it. In democratic societies the goals and mechanisms of formal social control are determined through legislation by elected representatives and thus enjoy a measure of support from the population and voluntary compl-iance.

Formal Social Control.

INFORMAL SOCIAL CONTROL

Informal social control denominates customs, traditions, norms and other social values inherited by the individual. It is exercised by a society without explicitly stating these rules and is expressed through customs, norms, and mores. Informal sanctions may include ridicule, sarcasm, criticism and disapproval. In extreme cases sanctions may include social discrimination and exclusion. This implied social control usually has more effect on individuals because they become internalized and thus an aspect of personality. Traditional society uses mostly informal social control embedded in its customary culture relying on the socialization of its members to establish social order. More rigidly structured societies may place increased reliance on formal mechanisms.

As with formal controls, informal controls reward or punish acceptable or unacceptable behaviour (i.e., deviance). Informal controls are varied and differ from individual to individual, group to group and society to society. For example, at a women's institute meeting, a disapproving look might convey the message that it is inappropriate to flirt with the minister. In a criminal gang, on the other hand, a stronger sanction would be applied in the case of someone threatening to inform to the police.

Informal Social Control.

SOCIAL CONTROL AS AN INDEPENDENT VARIABLE

Social-control theories assume that norm violations can frequently be so pleasurable and profitable that many, if not most, people are motivated to violate them. Thus, it is not necessary to study deviant motives; rather it is necessary to study what constrains or controls most people from acting on their deviance motives most of the time. Studies of social control as an independent variable focus on the relative effectiveness of social relationships and arrangements in constraining behaviour to social norms and laws. Three general areas have developed. One examines the effectiveness of social ties (bonds, relationships, attachments) to conventional institutions in constraining people from acting on deviant motives. The second examines the effectiveness of macro structures and processes in providing the foundation for these ties. The third examines the effectiveness of the criminal justice system in constraining people from violating the law.

Drawing on a long tradition of work, Hirschi (1969) published an influential formulation of micro social-control theory. He states that the relationship between people and conventional society consists of four bonds: belief, attachment, commitment, and involvement. Belief refers to the extent to which conventional norms are internalized (another term for internal control). Commitment refers to the extent to which people's social rewards are tied to conformity; the more people have to lose upon being socially identified as norm violators, the lower their likelihood of violating the social norms. Attachment refers to people's sensitivity to the opinions of others; the more people are concerned with the respect and status afforded them by others, the more they are subject to social control. Involvement refers to the amount of time people spend on conventional activities; the more people are involved in conventional activities, the less time they have left for deviant activities.

This theory has inspired considerable research on juvenile delinquency. Studies from the 1960s to the 1980s (e.g., Kornhauser 1978; and Matsueda 1982) show that, as attachment to parents and school increase, delinquency decreases. These studies, however, do not show the casual order underlying the relationship between social attachment and delinquency. The theory assumes that low attachment leads to high delinquency; yet high delinquency could very well lead to low attachment. Trying to unravel these causal processes, Liska and Reed (1985) show that low parent attachment leads to high delinquency and that high delinquency leads to low school attachment.

From the 1920s onward, sociologists at the University of Chicago have been interested in the ecological distribution of deviance. Their studies of delinquency, mental illness, and suicide, for example, show that deviance tends to centre in cities, particularly in the area where residential and business activity intermesh. They argued that the ecological conditions that disrupt traditional social-control processes are accentuated in these areas, and, when social-control processes weaken, deviance occurs. Industrialization creates a need for the concentration of labour, thereby increasing population size and density through migration and immigration. Both industrialization and urbanization lead to value and norm conflicts, social mobility, cultural change, and weak primary ties. These social conditions, in turn, disrupt internal and external processes of social control. The internal process is weakened because people are unlikely to accept normative standards as right and proper when they experience value and norm conflicts and social change. The external process is weakened because people are unlikely to constrain their behaviour to conventional norms when social support for unconventional behaviour is readily visible and primary ties to family and conventional friends are weak. In small towns, for example, people may conform even though they may not accept the moral standard because their deviance is easily visible to family and conventional friends.

Perhaps the major problem with this line of research was the failure to measure the disruptive processes directly and the tendency to infer them from either remote causes such as industrialization and urbanization or more immediate causes such as the social, racial, and class composition of areas. Unable to solve this problem, the theory withered from the 1950s through the 1970s.

During the 1980s a group of young sociologists reexamined the theory to understand the renewed disorder of cities. Directly addressing the problem of measuring the processes that disrupt social control, Sampson and Groves (1989) show how community structural characteristics (such as racial, class, and ethnic composition; residential mobility; and divorce rate) affect crime by weakening ties to conventional institutions. Contrary to the early Chicagoans, Bursik (1986) shows that the ecological distribution of crime is no longer stable over time, that crime rates actually influence community characteristics, and that changes in these structures influence social deviance.

A third body of research examines the effectiveness of the criminal justice system in controlling crime. The underlying theory (deterrence) ignores inner controls and emphasizes punishment as the means of social control, particularly state-administered punishment. It assumes that people are rational and that crime is the result of calculating the costs and benefits of law violations; therefore, it assumes that, the higher the costs of crime, the lower the level of crime. As state-administered punishment is a significant cost of crime, it follows that the higher the level of such punishment, the lower the level of crime.

Two types of deterrence processes have been studied: general and specific. General refers to a process by which the punishment of some law violators provides information about the costs of crime to those unpunished (the general public), thereby reducing their law violations. Specific refers to a process by which punishment reduces the future law violations of those punished. Research focuses on three dimensions of punishment: severity, certainty, and celerity. Severity refers to the harshness of punishment, such as the length of incarceration; certainty refers to the probability of punishment, such as the likelihood of being arrested; and celerity refers to the swiftness of punishment. In sum, deterrence theory predicts that crime is lowest when punishment is severe, certain, and swift.

The political climate of the 1980s stimulated considerable interest in this theory, leading to hundreds of studies (Cook 1980). Yet, after all this research, it is still difficult to find any firm evidence for either specific or general deterrence. Regarding general deterrence, which has generated the bulk of the research, there is little consistent evidence of a severity effect. There is somewhat more evidence for a certainty effect, although its strength and duration remain unclear. For example, some studies suggest that, as certainty of punishment increases, crime rates decrease but that the decrease does not occur until certainty reaches about 30 percent, which is infrequently reached (Tittle and Rowe 1974). Some studies suggest that the certainty effect only occurs for crimes about which people have the opportunity to think and calculate, like property crimes, but not for violent crimes. And some studies of drunken driving suggest that the certainty effect occurs only if high certainty is well publicized, and even this effect is short lived (Ross 1984).

In sum, assuming that people are generally motivated to deviate, researchers have tried to understand how people are constrained from acting on their motives. Contemporary studies of social control focus on three areas: the interpersonal relationships that constrain people from acting on their motives, the macro structures and processes that provide the social foundation for these relationships, and the criminal justice system as a source of legal constraints.

SOCIAL CONTROL AS A DEPENDENT VARIABLE

During the 1960s sociologists began to question the assumption of normative consensus and stability and, thus, by implication the viability of the theories built on them. Without clear and stable references points from which to judge behaviour, deviance is difficult to define. Many sociologists came to define it in terms of visible social efforts to control it. Deviance is thus defined as that behaviour that society controls, and deviants are defined as those people whom society controls. Research shifts from studying social control as a cause of deviance to studying the causes of social control.

Micro-level studies examine the social processes by which acts and people are defined, labelled, and treated as deviants by family, friends, the public, and formal agencies of social control such as the criminal justice and mental health systems. Drawing on labelling and conflict theories, many sociologists argue that social control is directed against those who are least able to resist (the disadvantaged and the unfortunate) and that social-control agencies are used by the powerful to control the behaviour of others.

During the 1960s, research reported that resources and power (as indicated by class, ethnicity, and race) significantly affect defining, treating, and controlling people as criminals (Black and Reiss 1970), such as arresting, prosecuting, and sentencing them. Unfortunately, these studies do not adjust for the effects of legal considerations, such as seriousness and frequency of offense, which are related to social resources. Without examining the effects of both legal and social resource variables in the same analysis it is difficult to isolate the effects of one from those of the other.

During the 1970s studies addressed this issue. The results are inconsistent, some studies showing race and class effects and some showing no such effects (Cohen and Kleugel 1978).

During the 1980s research tried to resolve these inconsistencies. One group of researchers tried to show that the effect of resources depends on the stage of the criminal justice process (e.g., arrest, prosecution) and the characteristics of the local community. Some stages may be more sensitive to social status and social power than are others, and some communities may be more sensitive to status and power than are others. Dannefer and Schutt (1982) report more racial discrimination at the arrest stage than at other stages, arguing that police have more discretion than do other decision makers, and they report more racial discrimination when the percentage of nonwhites is high, arguing that a high percentage of nonwhites is threatening to authorities.

Macro studies of social control examine the level and the form of social control across such units as cities, states, regions, and countries. They study why one form of control (physical pain) occurs at one time and place and another form (incarceration) occurs at another time and place.

Since the 1970s, conflict theory has provided the major stimulus for this research. It assumes that social control is more likely when the ruling class or the authorities perceive their interests to be threatened. Threat is thought to be associated with the presence of disruptive acts (crime, civil disorders, social movements) and problematic people (the unemployed, minorities, the urban lower class). The theory assumes that, as disruptive acts and problematic people increase, authorities expand the capacity for social-control bureaucracies and pressure existing bureaucracies to expand the level of control.

Research has focused on the expansion and contraction of three such bureaucracies: the criminal justice system, the mental health system, and the welfare system. It generally suggests that the expansion of the criminal justice system is not necessarily a response to crime, that the expansion of the mental health system is not necessarily a response to mental health, and that the expansion of the welfare system is not necessarily a response to economic need. Rather the expansion and contraction of all three are responses by authorities to the acts and people deemed threatening to their interests.

Studies of the criminal justice system have examined the expansion of the police force in the late 1960s and 1970s, as an indicator of the potential for social control, and the expansion of the prison population in the 1980s, as an indicator of the actual level of control. Liska, Lawrence, and Benson (1981) report that, while the size of the police force is sensitive to the crime rate, it may be even more sensitive to the level of civil disorders, the relative size and segregation of the minority population, and the level of economic inequality. Studies of the prison population and admission rates show that, while these rates, too, are sensitive to the crime rate, they are equally sensitive to the size of problematic or threatening populations such as the unemployed. Studies in England, Canada, and the United States show a substantial relationship between the prison admission rate and the unemployment rate, adjusting for the crime rate (Berk et al. 1981; Inverarity and McCarthy 1988).

Some historical studies (Foucault 1965) assert that mental asylums emerged in the seventeenth century as another social mechanism for controlling the poor urban masses. During the twentieth century the population of mental asylums in the United States continually increased, reaching about 550,000 by the mid-1950s, while the prison population, in comparison, was less than 200,000 at the time. The mental health system seemed to be taking over the role of the criminal justice system in controlling problematic populations. However, since that time the trends for both bureaucracies have reversed. The mental asylum population has decreased from 500,000 to 150,000 and the prison population has increased from 200,000 to 300,000. These trend reversals have stimulated research to examine the extent to which the two bureaucracies are functional alternatives for controlling threatening or problematic populations and acts. Some research (Steadman 1979) studies how various threatening populations that in the past might have been admitted directly into asylums are now first processed in the criminal justice system. Then some of them remain in local jails and others, through various mechanisms such as pleas of Incompetent to Stand Trial and Not Guilty by Reason of Insanity are channeled into asylums.

Welfare is frequently conceptualized as a form of social control. Piven and Cloward (1971) have stimulated considerable controversy by arguing that the welfare expansion in the United States during the mid- and late-1960s was a response to the urban riots of that period, an attempt to control an economically deprived and threatening population. Various studies provide some support for this thesis. Schram and Turbett (1983) report that the riots affected welfare in two stages. Riots during the mid-1960s prodded the federal government to liberalize welfare policies generally; these policies were then more likely to be implemented in the late 1960s by those states experiencing the most rioting.

In sum, the 1970s and 1980s evidenced a research effort to explain the expansion and contraction of bureaucracies of social control, not so much as responses to crime, mental illness, or economic need, but as responses by authorities to control acts and populations deemed threatening to their interests.

The study of social control has come a long way since its inception at the birth of sociology, at which time it was vaguely defined and not distinguishable from the concept social order. Contemporary usage distinguishes the sources of social order from the order itself. The concept socialization has come to refer to internal sources of control, and the concept social control has come to refer to external sources of control, the processes whereby people conform to social norms because they are rewarded when they do and punished when they do not. Studying social control as an independent variable, a body of research examines the relative effects of interpersonal relations, social institutions, and formal agencies in constraining social behaviour. Studying social control as a dependent variable, another body of research examines how social resources influence social control and how the aggregate amount and form of control varies over time and place.

PROPAGANDA MODEL THEORY OF SOCIAL CONTROL

According to the propaganda model theory, the leaders of modern, corporate-dominated societies employ indoctrination as a means of social control. Theorists such as Noam Chomsky have argued that systemic bias exists in the modern media. The marketing, advertising, and public relations industries have thus been said to utilize mass communications to aid the interests of certain business elites. Powerful economic and religious lobbyists have often used school systems and centralised electronic communications to influence public opinion. Democracy is restricted as the majority is not given the information necessary to make rational decisions about ethical, social, environmental, or economic issues.

To maintain control and regulate their subjects, authoritarian organizations and governments promulgate rules and issue decrees. However, due to a lack of popular support for enforcement, these entities may rely more on force and other severe sanctions such as censorship, expulsion and limits on political freedom. Some totalitarian governments, such as the late Soviet Union or the current North Korea, rely on the mechanisms of the police state.

Sociologists consider informal means of social control vital in maintaining public order, but also recognize the necessity of formal means as societies become more complex and for responding to emergencies. The study of social control falls primarily within the academic disciplines of anthropology, political science, and sociology.

The continual application of low-level fear, as in mass surveillance or an electronic police state also exerts a powerful coercive force upon a populace.

EDUCATION AND SOCIAL CONTROL

Helvetius referring to education in 18th century France observed that men are born ignorant not stupid; they are made stupid by education. This is not the modern view. There may be still be societies in which men's minds are stupefied by dogmatic instruction which inclines them to accept uncritically the views of political or religious authorities but the general character of formal education has been profoundly changed by modern science and technology. The great difference between primitive and early societies and modern industrial societies is that in the former education is largely concerned with transmitting a way of life while in the latter because of the mass of available knowledge the application of science to production and the elaborate division of labour formal education not only preponderates in the process of education as a whole but is largely devoted to the communication of empirical knowledge.

One aspect of this change is indicated by the observation that in modern societies the content of education is less literary and more scientific. A second major difference is that whereas in earlier societies a relatively unchanging way of life and sum of knowledge were transmitted the scientific knowledge communicated by modern education is expected to change moreover education is increasingly required to prepare individuals for a changing rather than a static world.

Formal education in modern societies communicate independently ideas which play a part in regulating behaviour. Malinowski rightly mentioned this feature in its rudimentary form in primitive societies when he included the rules of craftmanship as an element in social control. Modern science and technology are not only the basis of infinitely more complex rules of craftmenship but also of a general rational approach to nature and social life which has an increasingly important role in establishing and maintaining social cooperation. The scientific thought implicitly or explicitly criticized the ideas propounded in religious and moral doctrines and has largely been responsible for the changes which the latter have undergone. The whole rationalization of the modern world with which Max Weber was pre-occupied is connected with the development of science. Since the chief vehicle of this development has been the educational system we can speak of formal education as a type of social control.

Education has contributed to the regulation of conduct that is the early socialization of the child. The work of educational reformers such as Montessori and Froebel has brought about great changes in the education of young children.So far the reforms were connected with scientific studies of the development of children such as those of Piaget they arose from the development of the social sciences. Moreover being based upon this observation and analysis of the actual development of children's activities, needs and problems they can be regarded as having arisen very largely within the educational sphere itself as independent discoveries.

The changes in the formal education system have themselves brought about changes in the family socialization aided by the spread of social science knowledge. In this sense the formal education of children has originated new forms of regulation of behaviour. Education in a broad sense from infancy to adulthood is thus a vital means of social control and its significance has been greatly enhanced in recent years by the rapid expansion of education at all levels in the developing countries and by the equally rapid growth of secondary and higher education in the industrial countries.

Through education new generations learn the social norms and the penalties for infringing them; they are instructed also in their station and its duties within the system of social differentiation and stratification. In modern societies where formal education becomes predominant and where an important occupational group of teachers comes into existence, education is also a major type of social control as the source of scientific knowledge which is in competition and sometimes in conflict with other types of control. This conflict may become particularly acute with the extension of higher education to a much larger proportion of the population, as the experience of Europe and USA show and the educational system may increasingly provide one of the main sources of change and innovation in the social norms.

CONTROL BY CUSTOMS

Once a habit is established, it becomes a role or norm of action. Customs often involve binding reciprocal obligations. Also, custom supports law, without which it becomes meaningless. In the words of MacIver and Page, custom establishes a social order of its own so that conflict arising between custom and law is not a conflict between law and lawlessness, but between the orders of reflection (law) and the order of spontaneity (custom).

In general, customs regulate the whole social life of man. Law itself cannot cover the whole gamut of social behaviour. It is the customary practices that contribute to the harmonious social interactions in a society which normal times of peace and tranquility. The influence of custom, at times, extends beyond one's own community. In certain communities custom determines the relations between two communities at war. The Bedouins of the African desert will never destroy a water-well of the enemy.

Some of the customs do not play any role in social control. They just exist because of their ancient nature just as all people bathing in an unhygienic tank or a lake just because of an established religious custom. Even the custom of performing Shradha in India has no meaning if people do not know how to respect what the past has given us as well as accept our moral obligation to the future generations. However, in most of the traditional societies the customary practices are all emptied of their meaning.

CONTROL BY LAW

In our times state is the sole upholder of social control and conformity, and the principal means at its disposal is law. Since law is enforced by State, force is present. Roscoe Pound explains law as social control through systematic application of the force of a politically organized society. In a lighter vein Bertrand Russell remarks that the good behaviour of even the most exemplary citizen owes much to the existence of a police force. Much earlier, Durkheim was the first sociologist to show that law is the means to enforce the collective conscience or collectivity which makes society an entity by itself, almost God.

Law is closely associated with morality and religion. Legislation always rests on social doctrines and ideals which have been derived from religion and morality, and judicial decisions always rely on the fundamental moral ideas of society expressed as reason, natural law, natural justice, and equality and, in more recent times, as public policy or public interest litigation as in India. Law, therefore, rests upon moral sentiments derived from religion and is influenced by institutional arrangements of society; and it brings about, by its precision and sanction, such a degree of certainty in human behaviour that cannot be attained through other types of social control. On occasions, law enforces social attitudes and contracts which initially were those of a small minority of reformers. In Russia, law has established new morals of behaviour which were originally the aspirations of small group of revolutionaries. In democratic societies, too, social reformers played an important part in influencing social behaviour, later on approved by law.

One more characteristic of law is the changed outlook towards punishment. As societies are becoming more confident of their powers to maintain order as a result of rising material standards, declining class differences and spread of education and extension of rights, more and more stress is being laid on the willing cooperation of people with state and its law. This development has been further augmented by studies in sociology and psychology which have shown that crimes are projection of society rather than the results of individual violation. That is why the new discipline, called criminology, has developed as an applied branch of sociology.

Lastly, law as it is today, does not primarily deal with individuals alone. Very often it regulates conflicts between individuals and groups as well as between individuals and large organisations whether public or private. The role of property in social life has been modified by the changes that have accrued in the relations between the employer and the worker through the abolition of the crime of conspiracy, the recognition of collective bargaining, social security and direct limitations on the use of private property, all through legislation.

The law as it exists today partly contributes to social change. As already remarked above, the change in the role of property has led to a great social change in man's social behaviour. Secondly, individual initiative is no longer on the premium in modern societies. Mammoth organizations and corporations undertake the vast socio-economic activities of modern times. Taking into account these changes, American sociologists have introduced expressions such as the 'Other-directed man' and the organization man. As the social complex of modern communities is transforming itself, law, too, is keeping pace with them in making the interaction between the other direct man and the mammoth organizations or the corporations to be smooth and efficient.

In developing societies the role of law in contributing to social change is much more. In all countries there is a continuous rationalization of the existing law by modification, introduction of foreign codes, and systematic legislation in relation to customary and traditional law. The Indian Constitution is an embodiment of such monumental change. The philosophy governing social changes, implied as well as explicitly stated in the Constitution, is governed by the principles stated in the Preamble which are entirely secular and which bear the imprint of the leading minds of the world like the 18th century French philosophers, liberal thinkers of the 19th century, the Fabian socialists of the 20th century, and individual thinkers like Thoreau, Tolstoy and Mahatma Gandhi.

Although law has an important role in maintaining social order or conformity, there are a few weaknesses in the existing law. It no longer has charismatic qualities which it earlier had, although our courts resound with expressions like the Majesty and the sanctity of law, your Lordships and so on. Second, people do not feel collectively and directly involved when any law is violated. It is more in the form of keeping each individual in his limits. Lastly, law does not enable the criminal to be finally reconciled to society. Modern Law, as it has developed, is increasingly being separated from custom and religion. It is only when legislation and litigation, the two processes concerned with law, are harmonized that they take their appropriate place in social control.

SOCIAL CONTROL BY SANCTION

In sociology, the term most commonly refers to forms of punishment for deviant behaviour. Sociologists often distinguish between informal sanctions—the casual expressions of disapproval or pressures for conformity that occur in many aspects of daily life—and formal sanctions, which imply official, institutional procedures for assuring compliance. Sanctions can be either positive or negative. Positive sanctions can consist of informal rewards for conformity (such as a thumbs up or similarly casual sign of approval) or formal rewards (such as titles, prizes, awards, and other forms of official approval). Negative sanctions involve informal punishments for failing to conform, including ridicule, verbal or emotional abuse, and ostracism, as well as formal penalties based on written laws or rules.

Many studies of social control focus on the use of sanctions as a means of maintaining order and punishing nonconforming behaviour. Sociologists often distinguish between informal sanctions (the casual expressions of disapproval or pressures for conformity that occur in many aspects of daily life) and formal sanctions (those that imply official, institutional procedures for assuring compliance). Sociologists and criminologists draw a strong connection between the absence of effective means of socialization and the incidence of deviant behaviour.

SOCIAL CONTROL BY RELIGION

Marx developed his ideas of sociology from Hegel and Feuerbach. Hegel argued that society would evolve towards perfection in Christianity, whilst Marx argued that society would evolve, but away from religion as Feuerbach postulated.

Marx argued that society could be divided into two groups–the working class or proletariat and the ruling class or bourgeoisie. The bourgeoisie own the means of production and exploit the proletariat by paying them little. Marx described this as dehumanising and argued that it leads to a sense of disenfranchisement. This all be resolved in a social revolution in which the thesis of capitalism is challenged by the anti-thesis of anti-capitalism to produce synthesis–socialism.

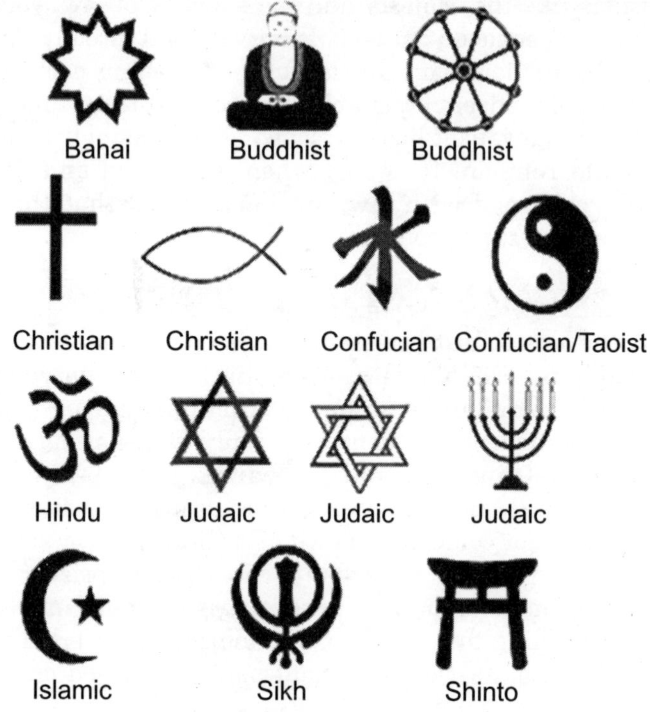

Social Control by Religion.

Marx defined religion as the "opium of the people," a form of social control that dulls the pain of oppression for the proletariat whilst preventing them from seeing what needs to be done to stop their exploitation. Religion uses its ethical systems to govern the way people behave and then reinforces this behaviour with the threat/promise of the afterlife:

"People can not really be happy until the abolition of the illusion of religion."

Marx had a utopian vision of the future in which there would be no need for religion because there would be no class system to exploit. His authority for morality thus comes from the communist ideal.

SOCIAL CONTROL BY COERCION

Coercion is the use of force to achieve a desired end. It may be physical or non-violent. It is the ultimate means of social control when all other means fail. Physical coercion may take the form of bodily injury, imprisonment and death penalty. Physical coercion is without doubt the lowest form of social control. Societies would least desire to use it. If a society has to depend on external force it shows its weakness rather than strength in social control.

Nonviolent coercion consists of strike; boycott and non-cooperation. The students may go on strike to ensure better hostel facilities. Boycott is the withholding of social or economic interaction with others to express disapproval and to force acceptance of demands. Non co-operation is refusal to cooperate. The teachers may refuse to cooperate with the management over the payment of salaries. Non-violent coercion can be a successful way of effecting social control.

NEED FOR SOCIAL CONTROL

Social solidarity is essential for the existence of society. No two persons is alike in their nature, ideas, attitudes and interests. Every individual is a separate personality. There are cultural differences among the individuals. As a matter of fact society is a heterogeneous organization. If every individual is allowed unrestricted freedom to act and behave, it may create social disorder. For an orderly social life social control is necessary. The aims of social control are to bring out conformity, solidarity and continuity of a particular group or society.

Social control is necessary for maintaining order in the society. It is necessary for every society or group to maintain its social order and this is possible only when its members behave in accordance with that social order. An important objective of social control is to maintain the old order. Although enforcement of the old order in a changing society may hinder social progress, yet it is necessary to maintain continuity and uniformity in society.

Without social control social unity would be a mere dream. Social control regulates behaviour in accordance with established norms which brings uniformity of behaviour and leads to unity among the individuals. The family maintains its unity because its members behave in a similar manner in accordance with family norms.

No two men are alike in their attitudes, ideas, interests and habits. Even the children of same parents do not have the same attitudes, habits or interests. Men believe in different religions, dress, eat differently and have different ideologies. There are so many differences in the ways of living of the people that at every moment there is the possibility of clash between them. In modern times this possibility has all the more increased because man has become too self-centred. Social control is necessary to protect social interests and satisfy common needs. If social control is removed and every individual is left to behave freely society would be reduced to a state of lawlessness.

Social control provides social sanction to the social ways of behaviour. There are numerous folkways, modes and customs prevalent in society. Every individual has to follow them. If an individual violates the social norm; he is compelled through social control to observe them. Thus social control provides sanction to social norms.

SOCIAL MOBILITY

Social Mobility: *Origin.* ***Types of Social Mobility. Determinants of Social Mobility:*** *Father's Occupation, Educational Level, Intelligence and Mobility, Discrimination, Other Social Handicaps, A Neglected Source of Downward Mobility.* ***Factors that Affect Mobility. Importance of Social Mobility. Mobility by Gender. Social Mobility and Social Structure. The Sociological Concept of Sanskritization in India. The Sociological Concept of Westernization in India:*** *Characteristics of Westernisation.* ***Modernization of Indian Tradition:*** *Modernization is a Composite Concept.* ***Education and Social Mobility.***

SOCIAL MOBILITY

Individuals are recognized in society through the statuses they occupy and the roles they enact. The society as well as individuals is dynamic. Men are normally engaged in endless endeavour to enhance their statuses in society, move from lower position to higher position, secure superior job from an inferior one. For various reasons people of the higher status and position may be forced to come down to a lower status and position. Thus people in society continue to move up and down the status scale. This movement is called *social mobility*. The study of social mobility is an important aspect of social stratification. Infact it is an inseparable aspect of social stratification system because the nature, form, range and degree of social mobility depends on the very nature of stratification system. Stratification system refers to the process of placing individuals in different layers or strata.

Social mobility is the movement of individuals, families and groups from one social position to another. The theory of social mobility attempts to explain the frequency of these movements, and the ways people became distributed into various social positions (social selection).

According to *Wallace* and *Wallace* social mobility is the movement of a person or persons from one social status to another.

W.P. Scott has defined sociology as the movement of an individual or group from one social class or social stratum to another.

Social mobility is an act of moving from one social class to another. The amount of movement up and down the class structure would indicate the extent of social mobility prevalent in the society.

The social mobility is greatly influenced by the level of openness of the society. Open society is the one where people attain their status primarily by their own efforts. In fact the extent of mobility may be taken as an index of openness of a society indicating how far talented individuals born into lower strata can move up the socioeconomic ladder. In this respect, social mobility is an important political issue, particularly in countries committed to liberal vision of equality of opportunity to all citizens. In this perspective industrial societies are mostly open societies portraying high social mobility. Compared with them, pre-industrial societies have mostly been found to be closed societies where there has been low social mobility. People in such societies have been confined to their ancestral occupations and their social status has mostly been ascribed.

ORIGIN

Scholars were first attracted to the study of social mobility by the regularity with which people end up in roughly the same social position as their parents. Despite some intergenerational movement up and down the social ladder, people born into wealthy and important families are likely to live their lives as wealthy and important people, while those born into the poverty are not. In our society, this regularity is the result of inherited wealth, useful social contacts and education—not superior intelligence and judgement, as some thought originally. Societies have been characterized as "open" or "closed" according to the degree to which the fortune of children depends on that of the parents.

Late 18th- and 19th-century writers, in criticizing their societies, were concerned with the institutional factors affecting mobility. They advocated a society in which merit and talent were rewarded and opportunities for developing them were freely available. Unfortunately, contemporary writers have been more inclined to substitute summary statistical measures of mobility for critical analysis of the entire society.

TYPES OF SOCIAL MOBILITY

Several patterns of social mobility are possible, these are as follows:

Horizontal Mobility

Involves moving within the same status category. An example of this is a nurse who leaves one hospital to take a position as a nurse at another hospital. The movement of individuals and groups in similar socioeconomic positions, which may be in different work situations. This may involve change in occupation or remaining in the same occupation but in a different organization, or may be in the same organization but at a different location.

Vertical Mobility

The movement of *individuals* and *groups* up or down the socioeconomic scale. Those who gain in property, income, status, and position are said to be upwardly mobile, while those who move in the opposite direction are downwardly mobile. A promotion in rank in the Army is an example of **upward mobility**, while a demotion in rank is **downward mobility**.

Individual Mobility

The vertical mobility can take place in two ways —*individuals* and *groups* may improve their position in the hierarchy by moving upwards or their position might worsen and they may fall down the hierarchy. When individuals get into seats of political position; acquire money and exert influence over others because of their new status they are said to have achieved individual mobility. Like individuals even groups also attain high social mobility. When a dalit from a village becomes an important official it is a case of upward mobility.

Intragenerational Mobility

Intragenerational mobility, also termed career mobility, refers to a change in an individual's social standing, especially in the workforce, such as occurs when an individual works his way up the corporate ladder. Mobility taking place in personal terms within the lifespan of the same person is called *intra-generational mobility*. It refers to the advancement in one's social level during the course of one's lifetime. It may also be understood as a change in social status which occurs within a person's adult career. For example, a person working as a supervisor in a factory becoming its assistant manager after getting promotion.

Intergenerational Mobility

Time factor is an important element in social mobility. On the basis of the time factor involved in social mobility there is another type of inter-generational mobility. It is a change in status from that which a child began within the parents, household to that of the child upon reaching adulthood. It refers to a change in the status of family members from one generation to the next. For example, a farmer's son becoming an officer. It is important because the amount of this mobility in a society tells us to what extent inequalities are passed on from one generation to the next. If there is very little inter-generational mobility, inequality is clearly deeply built into the society for people' life chances are being determined at the moment of birth. When there is a mobility people are clearly able to achieve new statuses through their own efforts, regardless of the circumstances of their birth.

Structural Mobility

Structural mobility is a kind of vertical mobility. Structural mobility refers to mobility which is brought about by changes in stratification hierarchy itself. It is a vertical movement of a specific group, class or occupation relative to others in the stratification system. It is a type of ***forced mobility*** for it takes place because of the structural changes and not because of individual attempts. For example, historical circumstances or labour market changes may lead to the rise of decline of an occupational group within the social hierarchy. An influx of immigrants may also alter class alignments — especially if the new arrivals are disproportionately highly skilled or unskilled.

Open and Closed Systems of Mobility

A closed system of mobility is that where norms prescribe mobility. Thus the closed system emphasizes the associative character of the hierarchy. It justifies the inequality in the distribution of means of production status symbols and power positions and discourages any attempt to change them. Any attempt to bring about changes in such a system or to promote mobility is permanently suppressed. In such a system individuals are assigned their place in the social structure on the basis of ascriptive criteria like age, birth, sex. Considerations of functional suitability or ideological notions of equality of opportunity are irrelevant in deciding the positions of individuals to different statuses. However no system in reality is perfectly close. Even in the most rigid systems of stratification limited degree of mobility exists. Traditional caste system in India is an example of closed system.

In the open system the norms prescribed and encourage mobility. There are independent principles of ranking like status, class and power. In and open system individuals are assigned to different positions in the social structure on the basis of their merit or achievement. Open systems mobility is generally characterized with occupational diversity, a flexible hierarchy, differentiated social structure and rapidity of change. In such systems the hold of ascription based corporate groups like caste, kinship or extended family etc. declines. The dominant values in such a system emphasize on equality and freedom of the individual and on change and innovation.

Absolute and Relative Mobility

Absolute mobility means that living standards are increasing in absolute terms: You are better off than your parents, and your children will be better off than you. Structural changes, such as changes in occupational structure rates, means that there is more room at the top, which leads to high absolute mobility rates. For example, suppose a person begins his working career with an income of $32,000. If a decade later his income is $36,000 (adjusting for inflation), he has experienced upward absolute income mobility.

Relative mobility refers to the degree to which individuals move up or down compared to others in their cohort. In other words, relative mobility means that if your family is poor, you have a decent chance of moving up the relative income ladder. That is, the rank order of people in society is malleable. Relative mobility relates to the openness or fluidity of society and is insensitive to the impact of structural changes. For example, suppose a person's income increases from $32,000 at the start of his working career to $36,000 a decade later, but most people who began their work life around the same time experience a larger increase. The person has experienced upward absolute mobility but downward relative mobility.

Because relative mobility depends on one's place in the distribution, it is a zero-sum phenomenon. In other words, if one person moves up in relative terms, another by definition must have moved down. In contrast, absolute mobility is not zero-sum.

Although both absolute and relative mobility are both forms of intragenerational mobility, these two have very little to do with each other. High absolute mobility rates can co-exist with highly unequal relative mobility chances. Thus, you can have an economy with a lot of absolute mobility, and little relative mobility or an economy with a lot of relative mobility, and little absolute mobility. Social mobility is an act of moving from one social class to another. The amount of movement up and down the class structure would indicate the extent of social mobility prevalent in the society. The social mobility is greatly influenced by the level of openness of the society. Open society is the one where people attain their status primarily by their own efforts. In fact the extent of mobility may be taken as an index of openness of a society indicating how far talented individuals born into lower strata can move up the socioeconomic ladder. In this respect, social mobility is an important political issue, particularly in countries committed to liberal vision of equality of opportunity to all citizens. In this perspective industrial societies are mostly open societies portraying high social mobility. Compared with them, pre-industrial societies have mostly been found to be closed societies where there has been low social mobility.

Lateral Mobility

It is a geographical movement between neighbourhoods, towns or regions. In modern societies there is a great deal of geographical mobility. Lateral mobility is often combined with vertical as well as horizontal mobility. The movement of people up or down the social hierarchy can be looked at either within one generation called intra-generational mobility or between generations labelled as inter-generational mobility. Intra-generational mobility consists of movement up and down the stratification system by members of a single generation (the social class in which you began life compared with your social class at the end of your life). Inter-generational mobility consists of movement up and down the stratification system by members of successive generations of a family (your social class location compared with that of your parents, for example). Comparison is usually made between social class status of son and father. Mobility is functional. Open societies provide opportunities to its members for the development of their talents and working toward their individual fulfilment. At the same time a person can select the best person for doing a particular job.

Collective Mobility

Collective mobility has been an effective means of equalizing opportunity. Increasingly, groups of people with a common goal, e.g., unions or associations of professionals, have co-operated to advance themselves. But other, less obvious groups have also mobilized collectively, including ethnic groups such as the Toronto Italian community, language groups such as Canadian Francophones, regional or provincial groups, and networks comprising personal acquaintances, friends or family. In many instances collective mobilization has advanced both group and individual interests. Yet the collective mobilization of everyone would ensure a new stalemate — an indirect, inefficient way of eliminating social inequality.

DETERMINANTS OF SOCIAL MOBILITY

Although the mobility table has been the principal product of many mobility studies, it leaves unanswered many questions central to the theory of social selection and social mobility. The "variable" parental occupation or status embraces, or rather conceals, a host of more specific influences. Research on social mobility is now increasingly directed toward untangling the roles of these more specific variables and shows a corresponding decrease of interest in simply adding new mobility tables to those already available. Further, with respect to the question of how people get sorted into different occupations or status levels, the mobility table can provide at best only a very partial answer, that is, an answer in terms of the statistical dependence of filial status on parental status. But there are clearly many other factors that determine occupational and status selection.

FATHER'S OCCUPATION

Parental occupation or status is related to the probability of filial entry into an occupation in two principal ways: (a) the father's occupational status may be correlated with a variety of filial attributes, such as education, intelligence, and race, that affect the son's occupational locus; (b) the parental occupational status may affect filial occupational locus more directly: the father's occupational experience may influence his son's occupational interests and may provide him with special knowledge, experience, incentives, and opportunities for access to it or other occupations.

EDUCATIONAL LEVEL

Educational level is, of course, in considerable measure dependent upon the status level of parents. This dependence is lessened by increases in the society's investment in educational facilities and the degree to which these make educational opportunities available without respect to social origin. To the extent that this occurs, the relation of education to status achievement is freed from an intermediate dependence on parental status. Sons of similar parental status show variations in educational levels, and the effect of these variations on status certainly cannot be ascribed to parental status. However, the extension of educational opportunities may at the same time reduce the correlation between status achievement and education. The more widespread a certain level of education becomes (for example, primary or secondary education), the less will variations in status, especially in the lower reaches of the status hierarchy, depend on variations in educational level provided, of course, that increased access to education does not change the status significance of the occupational groups.

INTELLIGENCE AND MOBILITY

Part of the effect of education on status achievement is due to the correlation of education with intelligence. In the process of status selection, variations in intelligence operate to influence the achieved level of social status, both by leading to variations in educational level and (for persons of similar educational level) by facilitating the advancement of those of greater intelligence. Certain educational attainments have, however, become such decisive prerequisites for entry into many occupational positions that high intelligence without the added attainment of a corresponding education is unable to produce its full potential effect. Even were educational opportunities commensurate with intellectual capabilities, the correlation of intelligence with status achievement would be limited by the dependence of achievement on motivational and other personality characteristics. An equally important limitation is the fact that, except in a certain gross sense, intelligence is not an overriding criterion in occupational selection and advancement.

Intelligence as customarily measured depends in part, in its turn, on environmental circumstances. But the present state of investigation also leads one to conclude that, even as currently measured, intelligence has a major genetic component. Consequently, part of the dependence of filial on parental status is due to two sources of correlation between parental and filial intelligence social and genetic.

Recent studies have been effective in demonstrating the existence of complex interactions between parental status, education, and intelligence and in establishing that each of these variables plays a significant role in determining filial status, both independently and by mediating the influence of the others. But tested models do not now exist that enable one to state quantitatively the probable change in status ensuing from an increment in one of the variables (occurring at a specified stage of an individual's life), given the values of the other variables. The introduction of a genetic component of intelligence complicates the task of building such a model but at the same time appears indispensable if such models are to be used to derive a picture of the evolution of the mobility or social-selection system over time.

DISCRIMINATION

In some societies the existence of sizable racial or other groups subject to various modes of discrimination increases the dependence of filial status on parental status. The common obstacle shared by father and son tends to show up as a correlation between their status positions. Since status position as defined by mobility studies does not usually include the criterion of race, this necessarily inflates the degree of dependence of filial status on paternal status.

OTHER SOCIAL HANDICAPS

Relatively little attention has been paid in mobility studies to the role of special deficits that are not severe enough to exclude persons from the labour force and yet act as powerful handicaps to occupational achievement. High-grade mental deficiency, physical disabilities, chronic disease, mental disorders, alcoholism, etc., taken together, have a sufficiently high incidence and a sufficiently decided effect on occupational achievement to influence mobility tables. It is possible that a substantial part of the cases of extreme downward mobility can be accounted for in this way.

A NEGLECTED SOURCE OF DOWNWARD MOBILITY

A further source of downward mobility may be viewed either as the result of a bias in the design of mobility studies or as an intrinsic feature of the parent-son status relationship. Mobility studies generally draw a sample of the gainfully occupied within the age range chosen for the investigation. The sample usually includes unmarried subjects and married subjects with and without children. The father sample, arrived at through the son sample, will, however, necessarily include only persons of the preceding generation who have at least one son and are therefore (in most cases) married. Since marriage and sometimes fertility are associated with greater occupational stability, mental and physical health, and general achievement, the fathers of the subjects will represent a special sample of their generation. If this is viewed as a bias in comparing the status of fathers and sons, it could be overcome by choosing the subject (son) sample only from those in the labour force who are married and have at least one child. Since, however, all sons must come from the special (father) sample of the preceding generation, it is more useful to view the differential character of the father and son groups as one source of downward mobility. Given the biological and social significance of marriage and, perhaps, fertility, fathers are, other things being equal, superior as a group to an un-selected sample of their sons. Consequently, one should expect that for this reason a number of the sons will arrive at status positions inferior to those of their fathers.

FACTORS THAT AFFECT MOBILITY

The main factors that affect mobility are as follows:

Structural Factors

Structural factors are the ones, which determine the relative proportion of high-status positions to be filled and the ease of getting them. Societies differ in the relative proportion of high- and low-status positions to be filled. A society with a primarily agricultural economy will have many low-status and few high-status positions, and mobility will be low. The rate of mobility rises with the degree of industrialization of the economy. In an industrial society there is expected to be an increase in the number of occupations as well as in the number of jobs in each occupation. An increase in the division of labour is expected and along with it there is increasing specialization, hence the jobs multiply.

As the societies move from agricultural to industrial and to post industrial societies, there is a change in the nature of jobs, e.g., decline in manufacturing jobs and an increase in service jobs. Such a change provides new opportunities for employment, which the people avail and thereby the whole process becomes instrumental to social mobility. Even in a relatively open society, upward mobility is not open equally to everyone. Middle class children typically have learning experiences which are more helpful in gaining upward mobility than the experiences of lower-class children. Nevertheless, mobility may further depend upon the prevalent policies, laws and other factors that may discriminate between groups and individuals on the basis of factors like race, gender, religion, age, and ethnicity.

Individual Factors

While structural factors may determine the proportion of high-status, well-paid positions in a society, individual factors greatly affect which persons get them. It means that one has to look into the procedures of access and entry to the available positions. There could be the possession of the entry based qualifications by the individuals and there could be number of individual factors that influence the possession of necessary qualifications.

The individuals may have differences in their "mobility oriented behaviours". There is much which persons can do to increase their prospects for upward mobility by improving their educational qualifications. The work habits learned in early childhood are very important for making efforts in improving one's position. Of course hard work carries no guarantee of upward mobility, but not many achieve upward mobility without it.

Then there is the often referred "principle of deferred gratification." This consists of postponing immediate satisfaction in order to gain some later goal. Saving one's money to go for higher studies or to start a business is an example. At the moment you are studying sociology rather than using the same time for having fun somewhere else. You are postponing 'having fun' over studying the subject of sociology. In this way you are practising "deferred-gratification" pattern of behaviour. The parents may spend the money on the education of their child and postpone the celebration of his marriage. Mobility oriented people are likely to demonstrate such pattern of behaviour. It is usually assumed that the "deferred gratification" principle is followed by the middle class people. Gender differential may be another factor as part of individual differences. It is generally observed that there are greater opportunities for males than for females.

IMPORTANCE OF SOCIAL MOBILITY

Social mobility is the movement of individuals, families, and groups from one social position to another. The theory of social mobility attempts to account for the frequencies with which these movements occur.

The study of social mobility relates a present to a past social position. It thus forms part of the more general study of social selection, i.e., of how people get distributed into different social positions. It is, however, hardly possible to study effectively the influence of past social position except in the context of other influences that determine the individual's present social status. In practice, it has become increasingly difficult to separate the fields of social mobility and social selection. No rigorous separation has been attempted in the following discussion.

Studies of intergenerational mobility compare the social positions of parent and offspring; studies of career mobility compare the social positions of the same individual at different times. Group mobility is concerned with changes in the social position of groups possessing a relatively homogeneous status (for example, castes, intellectuals, artisans).

In the context of mobility studies, social position, or social status, signifies a certain rank with respect to the possession of goods (values) esteemed and desired by most members of a society. The changes in social position that interest the theory of social mobility are primarily variations in occupation, prestige, income, wealth, power, and social class. A high or low rank in one of these values is often associated with a roughly corresponding rank in most of the other values; consequently, position with respect to one of these values, and more especially a constellation of them, provides a measure of what in many societies is viewed as success in life. Studies in social mobility do not usually concern themselves with the possession of aesthetic, moral, and spiritual values. This is presumably due to the supposition, correct for most societies, that these goods do not measure "success in life." Nor does their possession seem to lead, except in a limited number of societies, to the attainment of those material goods whose pursuit is more evident in human behaviour and whose possession tends to limit the amount possessed by others and to provide opportunities for or at least the illusion of control over one's own and others' destinies.

MOBILITY BY GENDER

The most interesting research on social mobility today is being done on the mobility of women. Recent research by Creese, Guppy and Meissner suggests a continuing importance of gender in status attainment, alongside declining importance in ethnicity and language group. The mobility of women is documented in a variety of studies using varied data. Some research has paid attention to economic theories of labour-market segmentation and to effects on women of the introduction of new technologies. Unlike the traditional mass survey studies that focused on occupational mobility, recent research has examined major structural changes in the incidence of service sector work. Of particular interest have been changes in part-time work and changed patterning of careers by married women.

Studying the lives of Canadian women, Jones, Marsden and Tepperman, have concluded that increasingly women are experiencing varied patterns of horizontal and vertical mobility. Women's lives have become marked by great variety, fluidity and idiosyncrasy compared with the lives of their mothers, fathers, brothers or husbands. What's more, their lives are even unlike one another's: in a word, their patterns of educational, domestic and work mobility are "individualized."

Future research on social mobility is likely to continue focusing on the issues raised here, especially on the varying kinds and rates of social mobility experienced across the life cycle. We are far from fully understanding race- or gender-based differences in social mobility, or the reasons group differences in social mobility increase during periods of economic difficulty like the 1990s.

SOCIAL MOBILITY AND SOCIAL STRUCTURE

Finally, at least a brief word must be said about the relation of social selection and social mobility to the principal institutional structures of society. The research to which we owe the many mobility tables now available has been mostly pursued in Western industrialized societies with large urban sectors. This has made it easier to disregard the role of major institutional differences in the formation of social-selection systems. Current studies have tended to confine their attention more particularly to demographic and technological changes and to the role of educational institutions and the practices which affect access to them. Although there is a considerable literature on employment procedures, the study of social mobility has not adequately taken account of the fact that the occupational distribution process is a dual process, in which two sets of preferences and decisions, those of the employee and those of the employer or manager, confront each other, and that the distributive outcome is affected by the supply and demand of various qualities.

There are other major institutional features that, because of their relative stability, best reveal their relation to social mobility when it is studied over quite long time spans. Even the most stable political, juridical, and economic institutions of a society are of capital importance for the mobility process. Thus, the occupational selection process in Western society is decisively influenced by the nature of the labour contract, by laws relating to freedom of movement, and, ultimately, by the distribution of political power, together with the political and social sentiments associated with this distribution. As increasingly complex models of the social-selection process are developed, it will become necessary to specify more explicitly and exactly the institutional environment to which the model has application. Perhaps, too, it will become possible to relate parameter values to changes in the institutional environment and thus to unify the interests of quantitative research and comparative historical inquiry.

THE SOCIOLOGICAL CONCEPT OF SANSKRITIZATION IN INDIA

Prof. M.N. Srinivas introduced the term sanskritization to Indian Sociology. The term refers to a process whereby people of lower castes collectively try to adopt upper caste practices and beliefs to acquire higher status. It indicates a process of cultural mobility that is taking place in the traditional social system of India. M.N. Srinivas in his study of the Coorg in Karnataka found that lower castes in order to raise their position in the caste hierarchy adopted some customs and practices of the Brahmins and gave up some of their own which were considered to be impure by the higher castes.

For example they gave up meat eating, drinking liquor and animal sacrifice to their deities. They imitiated Brahmins in matters of dress, food and rituals. By this they could claim higher positions in the hierarchy of castes within a generation. The reference group in this process is not always Brahmins but may be the dominant caste of the locality. Sanskritization has occurred usually in groups who have enjoyed political and economic power but were not ranked high in ritual ranking. According to Yogendra Singh the process of sanskritization is an endogenous source of social change. Mackim Marriot observes that sanskritic rites are often added on to non-sanskritic rites without replacing them. Harold Gould writes, often the motive force behind sanskritisation is not of cultural imitation per se but an expression of challenge and revolt against the socioeconomic deprivations.

In explaining the meaning of Sanskritisation, M.N. Srinivas pointed out that Sanskritization was not always due to Brahmans; generally Sanskritisation qualifies as caste for a higher status. In the dynastic system, Sanskritisation emphasised the status of dynasty.

According to Srinivas, Sanskritization spread during the British Rule with the development of means of communication, the impact of Sanskritisation was felt in the remote corners of the century. With the spread of education and literacy it percolated to the lowest castes. The western terminology radio, press, rail etc. generally facilitated the process of Sanskritisation. The mobility associated with Sanskritisation results only in positional changes in the system and does not lead to any structural change. In other words, the spectrum itself doesn't change. He also notes how the tribal groups such as Bhils of western India, the Gonds and Oraon of central India claim to be a caste through the process of Sanskritisation and thus claim a place in the caste hierarchy. It is well known that there is no conversion process in the traditional Hindu system. While Srinivas took Sanskritisation to mean some kind of Brahminisation, other investigators showed that Sanskritisation could be based on Kshatriya or Vaisya or Sudra morals. As Srinivas himself points out the varna hierarchy is clear and immutable. It is evident; therefore, that Sanskritisation reinforces and consolidates the 'immutable varna hierarchy' rather than dislodges it or modify it. Thus, Sanskritisation is not a process by which structural change in the Hindu society can become possible. It is certainly not a means by which any social change in India can be brought about.

THE SOCIOLOGICAL CONCEPT OF WESTERNIZATION IN INDIA

M.N. Srinivas pioneer of sociology in India has used the term 'westernisation' to indicate the change, which took place in India during the British rule in the nineteenth and early twentieth centuries. Westernisation implies changes in dress, style of eating, manners etc. The change in the medium of instruction. Westernisation started having its impact on the elite because they studied secular subjects with English as medium of instruction. The Brahmins and other castes with tradition of learning and traditions of science in the courts readily took to secular education with English as a medium of education. Another big change introduced in the Indian society by the new system of education is that the schools were thrown open all types in contrast to the traditional schools which were restricted to upper-caste children and which transmitted mostly traditional knowledge. In as much as modernisation in India has come about due to westernisation, therefore, the above-mentioned changes of Modernisation can be taken to be result of westernisation.

CHARACTERISTICS OF WESTERNISATION

The following are the characteristics of westernisation:

(1) *Morally neutral:* Modernisation is generally considered to be good but this is not so with westernisation. Westernisation has been for good as well as evil. In fact westernisation in normally neutral.

(2) *Limits of Westernisation:* A distinction has to be drawn between westernisation and western culture. All the elements of the western culture did not originate in the west for example, Christianity originated in Asia, the decimals system originated in India and via Arabia reached west. Gun powder, printing press and paper were invented in China. All these constitute the important elements of western culture though these did not originate in the west. The manner in which westernisation operates in India is mainly the result of British influence. The culture of Germany, France and Russia etc. is quite different from the British culture.

(3) *Wide, complex and multi level concept:* It substances all changes which are consequent upon western technology and modern science. Secondly it has had varying impact upon the different aspect of the culture, hence it is a complex concept. Thirdly westernisations have affected society at different levels. For example in olden days people used to eating it in thalis or banana leaves in squatting position but now they are using dining table with all its accessaries. While westernisation has had very wide impact, there has been resistance to it in some sequences. Thus westernisation has had variable impact on the Indian society.

(4) *Conscious unconscious process:* Westernisation has not been incorporated willingly everywhere in India at some places the copying of British manners and customs was deliberate at other places it was a subconscious process.

MODERNIZATION OF INDIAN TRADITION

Modernization is process of social change initiated by industrialization in the mid 18th century. As a result of modernization:

- There is decline of small and traditional communities. In the traditional societies there is lot of cohesiveness, strong sense of belongingness, strong neighbourhood relations but all these undergo change as the communities become complex in an industrial society. The structure and relations in the families also undergo change in the modern society.
- There is an expansion of personal choice in the modern society. Personal choices increase for getting education, for choosing an occupation, for a place to live, for choosing a spouse, and even for adopting a lifestyle. There are series of options provided by the modern society and one could choose. Such options were not available in the traditional society.
- There is an increasing diversity in the society. In the urban areas one could see the diversity of people, diversity of occupations, diversity of religions, diversity of races, diversity of ethnic groups, diversity of lifestyles, diversity of economic systems, diversity of political lines, and so on. Such diversities provide rich resources for interactions and changes in society.
- There is future orientation and growing awareness of time. People in the modern societies think more about the future. Being optimistic they try to improve their lives by adopting innovations rather than having emotional attachment with traditions. These people are time conscious and organize their daily routines down to the very minute.

MODERNIZATION IS A COMPOSITE CONCEPT

It is also an ideological concept. The models of modernization co-vary with the choice of ideologies. The composite nature of this concept renders it pervasive in the vocabulary of social sciences and evokes its kinship with concepts like development, growth, evolution and progress. In the book on Essays on Modernization in India Yogendra Singh has analysed the varied and complex processes involved in the modernization in India, the forces released by it and their bearing on the stability, creativity and development in India as a dynamic nation and composite civilization.

India has the distinction of evolving one of the longest continuing civilization in the world, which is constantly adapted itself to the changing political and socio-economic contents and specific watershed events in her history. Her family system has proved to be a remarkable stable unit of society which has shown great flexibility and adaptability in the phase of rapid social changes.

Like China and unlike Japan, India resisted changes in its ancient beliefs about the way the world works (and should work) which modernization entails. Instead, like many Islamic countries today, India wrongly believed Gandhi's doctrine that modernization necessarily means Westernization. Fitfully, and under the influence of the British Raj, parts of the economy and society were modernized during the second half of the 19th century of laissez-faire and free trade. Some of the traditional literary castes also embraced Westernization.

British policy turned India into a pioneer of Third World industrialization, with an economy increasingly based on domestic capital and entrepreneurship combined with imported technology. But modernization stalled when protectionist pressures from Lancashire and the exigencies of Imperial finance led the British to abandon free trade and laissez faire. At the same time, Westernization fuelled the rise of a nationalist movement.

The emphasis on historicity in preference to universality defining the context of modernization the pre-eminence of structural changes in society to render the adaptive process of modernization successful in the developing countries particularly India and the eclectic nature of cultural and ideological response of India to the challenges of modernization represent some of the unifying principles. Singh portrays the challenges and contradictions that India encounters in the course of its modernization.

EDUCATION AND SOCIAL MOBILITY

Migration has been a key channel for mobility – an opportunity to earn money, see a new place, experience new cultures, gain skills and accumulate consumption goods. The decision to migrate however involves a range of trade-offs in terms of allocation of household funds, sale of assets, child work (and/or withdrawal from school) etc., which need detailed analysis from the perspective of net gains in terms of socio-economic mobility. The choices made are both gendered and contextual, and reflect differences in aspirations, opportunities and outcomes.

Education is commonly regarded as an unproblematically beneficial force, and is seen by policy makers as one of the best routes out of poverty. Using oral testimonies from three Norwich social housing estates, the paper explored different educational experiences of residents and the impact they have had on their identities. The experience of education is as intimately tied up with spatial mobility as with class mobility. Schooling based on the estates (primary and secondary, modern/comprehensive) kept the educational experience within an individual's home territory, and if remembered at all, was generally remembered in unproblematic terms. In such cases education typically served to confirm future socio-spatial patterns of housing and employment, while also feeding in more broadly to an individual's established 'working class' identity.

In contrast, those whose educational experiences were found, even in part, out of the boundaries of the estates, tended to have a much more complex relationship both with education and their own identities. In all cases the experience of schooling elsewhere led to the enlargement of spatial boundaries — the entering into 'unknown' and often more privileged parts of the city — as well as social boundaries. Memories of participants often revealed the unsettling and ambiguous impact of 'outside' schooling – shame of poverty revealed to fellow pupils at grammar school, the difficulty of mediating relationships with confident classmates who treated privileged secondary and tertiary education as a given, and a growing feeling that their home life might not be 'normal'.

Education promotes social mobility.

Education in India is seen as one of the ways to upward social mobility. Good education is seen as a stepping stone to a high flying career. Education System in India currently represents a great paradox. On the one hand we have IIMs and IITs that rank among the best institutes in the world and on the other hand there are number of schools in the country that do not even have the basic infrastructure. Even after more than 50 years after independence we are far away from the goal of universal literacy. But on a positive note, Indian professionals are considered among the best in the world are in great demand. This signifies the inherent strength of Indian education system.

The Educational structure in India which operates at all conceivable levels from pre-school to post doctoral is of monumental proportions. According to a World Bank report there are more than 7,40,000 formal schools; more than 3.6 million teachers are working on full time basis; there are more than 175 Universities offering under graduate and post graduate courses and about 6000 colleges affiliated to these universities.

The educational structure in India is generally referred to as the Ten + Two + Three (10+2+3) pattern. The first ten years provide undifferentiated general education for all students. The +2 stage, also known as the higher secondary or senior secondary, provides for differentiation into academic and vocational streams and marks the end of school education. In +3 stage, which involves college education, the student goes for higher studies in his chosen field of subject. This is a comprehensive website on education in India. It gives detailed information on education and career options in India.

23

CHAPTER

SOCIAL CHANGE AND MOVEMENTS

Introduction. Models of Social Change: *Evolutionary Theory, Functionalist Theory, Conflict Theory.* ***Factors of Social Change:*** *Physical Environment, Population Changes, Isolation and Contact, Social Structure, Attitudes and Values, Technological Factors.* ***Impact of Technology Change:*** *Industrialization, Urbanization, Modernization, Development of The Means of Transport and Communication, Transformation in the Economy and the Evolution of the New Social Classes, Unemployment, Technology and War, Changes in Social Institutions, Cultural Lag.* ***Social Movements:*** *Relative Deprivation, Resource Mobilization.* ***Characteristics of Social Movement:*** *Collective Action, Oriented Towards Social Change.* ***Social Movement Theories:*** *Functionalist Perspectives, Value-added Theory (SMELSER), Conflict Theory Perspectives, Resource Mobilization Theory, Mobilization Process, Political Process Theory, New Movement Theory.* ***Types of Social Movements:*** *Reform Movements, Revolutionary Movements, Reactionary or Revivalist Movement, Resistance Movement, Utopian Movement, Peasant Movement, Women's Movement, Backward Caste Movement, Dalit Movement.* ***New Social Movement.***

INTRODUCTION

The term social change is used to indicate the changes that take place in human interactions and interrelations. Society is a web of social relationships and hence social change means change in the system of social relationships. These are understood in terms of social processes and social interactions and social organization. Auguste Comte the father of Sociology has posed two problems — the question of social statics and the question of social dynamics, what is and how it changes. The sociologists not only outline the structure of the society but also seek to know its causes also. According to Morris Ginsberg social change is a change in the social structure.

Social change refers to any significant alteration over time in behavior patterns and cultural values and norms. By "significant" alteration, sociologists mean changes yielding profound social consequences. Examples of significant social changes having long-term effects include the industrial revolution, the abolition of slavery, and the feminist movement.

Today's sociologists readily acknowledge the vital role that social movements play in inspiring discontented members of a society to bring about social change. Efforts to understand the nature of long-term social change, including looking for patterns and causes, has led sociologists to propose the evolutionary, functionalist, and conflict theories of change. All theories of social change also admit the likelihood of resistance to change, especially when people with vested interests feel unsettled and threatened by potential changes.

Become a Social Change Agent—Develop a Diversity Achievement Ideology.

MODELS OF SOCIAL CHANGE

In their search to explain social change, sociologists sometimes examine historical data to better understand current changes and movements. They also rely on three basic theories of social change: evolutionary, functionalist, and conflict theories.

EVOLUTIONARY THEORY

Sociologists in the 19th century applied Charles Darwin's (1809–1882) work in biological evolution to theories of social change. According to evolutionary theory, society moves in specific directions. Therefore, early social evolutionists saw society as progressing to higher and higher levels. As a result, they concluded that their own cultural attitudes and behaviors were more advanced than those of earlier societies.

Identified as the "father of sociology," Auguste Comte subscribed to social evolution. He saw human societies as progressing into using scientific methods. Likewise, Emile Durkheim, one of the founders of functionalism, saw societies as moving from simple to complex social structures. Herbert Spencer compared society to a living organism with interrelated parts moving toward a common end. In short, Comte, Durkheim, and Spencer proposed unilinear evolutionary theories, which maintain that all societies pass through the same sequence of stages of evolution to reach the same destiny.

Contemporary social evolutionists like Gerhard Lenski, Jr., however, view social change as multilinear rather than unilinear. Multilinear evolutionary theory holds that change can occur in several ways and does not inevitably lead in the same direction. Multilinear theorists observe that human societies have evolved along differing lines.

FUNCTIONALIST THEORY

Functionalist sociologists emphasize what maintains society, not what changes it. Although functionalists may at first appear to have little to say about social change, sociologist Talcott Parsons holds otherwise. Parsons (1902–1979), a leading functionalist, saw society in its natural state as being stable and balanced. That is, society naturally moves toward a state of homeostasis. To Parsons, significant social problems, such as union strikes, represent nothing but temporary rifts in the social order. According to his equilibrium theory, changes in one aspect of society require adjustments in other aspects. When these adjustments do not occur, equilibrium disappears, threatening social order. Parsons' equilibrium theory incorporates the evolutionary concept of continuing progress, but the predominant theme is stability and balance.

Critics argue that functionalists minimize the effects of change because all aspects of society contribute in some way to society's overall health. They also argue that functionalists ignore the use of force by society's powerful to maintain an illusion of stability and integration.

CONFLICT THEORY

Conflict theorists maintain that, because a society's wealthy and powerful ensure the status quo in which social practices and institutions favorable to them continue, change plays a vital role in remedying social inequalities and injustices.

Although Karl Marx accepted the evolutionary argument that societies develop along a specific direction, he did not agree that each successive stage presents an improvement over the previous stage. Marx noted that history proceeds in stages in which the rich always exploit the poor and weak as a class of people. Slaves in ancient Rome and the working classes of today share the same basic exploitation. Only by socialist revolution led by the proletariat (working class), explained Marx in his 1867 Das Kapital, will any society move into its final stage of development: a free, classless, and communist society.

Marx's view of social change is proactive; it does not rely on people remaining passive in response to exploitation or other problems in material culture. Instead, it presents tools for individuals wishing to take control and regain their freedom. Unlike functionalism and its emphasis on stability, Marx holds that conflict is desirable and needed to initiate social change and rid society of inequality. Critics of Marx note that conflict theorists do not always realize that social upheaval does not inevitably lead to positive or expected outcomes.

FACTORS OF SOCIAL CHANGE

PHYSICAL ENVIRONMENT

Major changes in the physical environment are very compelling when they happen. The desert wastes of North Africa were once green and well populated. Climates change, soil erodes and lakes gradually turn into swamps and finally plains. A culture is greatly affected by such changes although sometimes they come about so slowly that they are largely unnoticed. Human misuse can bring very rapid changes in physical environment which in turn change the social and cultural life of a people. Deforestation brings land erosion and reduces rainfall. Much of the wasteland and desert land of the world is a testament to human ignorance and misuse. Environmental destruction has been at least a contributing factor in the fall of most great civilization. Many human groups throughout history have changed their physical environment through migration. In the primitive societies whose members are very directly dependent upon their physical environment migration to a different environment brings major changes in the culture. Civilization makes it easy to transport a culture and practice it in a new and different environment.

POPULATION CHANGES

A population change is itself a social change but also becomes a casual factor in further social and cultural changes. When a thinly settled frontier fills up with people the hospitality pattern fades away, secondary group relations multiply, institutional structures grow more elaborate and many other changes follow. A stable population may be able to resist change but a rapidly growing population must migrate, improve its productivity or starve. Great historic migrations and conquests of the Huns, Vikings and many others have arisen from the pressure of a growing population upon limited resources. Migration encourages further change for it brings a group into a new environment subjects it to new social contacts and confronts it with new problems. No major population change leaves the culture unchanged.

ISOLATION AND CONTACT

Societies located at world crossroads have always been centers of change. Since most new traits come through diffusion, those societies in closest contact with other societies are likely to change most rapidly. In ancient times of overland transport, the land bridge connecting Asia, Africa and Europe was the centre of civilizing change. Later sailing vessels shifted the centre to the fringes of the Mediterranean Sea and still later to the north-west coast of Europe. Areas of greatest intercultural contact are the centers of change. War and trade have always brought intercultural contact and today tourism is adding to the contacts between cultures says Greenwood. Conversely isolated areas are centers of stability, conservatism and resistance to change. The most primitive tribes have been those who were the most isolated like the polar Eskimos or the Aranda of Central Australia.

SOCIAL STRUCTURE

The structure of a society affects its rate of change in subtle and not immediately apparent ways. A society which vests great authority in the very old people as classical China did for centuries is likely to be conservative and stable. According to Ottenberg a society which stresses conformity and trains the individual to be highly responsive to the group such as the Zunis is less receptive to the change than a society like the Ileo who are highly individualistic and tolerate considerable cultural variability. A highly centralized bureaucracy is very favorable to the promotion and diffusion of change although bureaucracy has sometimes been used in an attempt to suppress change usually with no more than temporary success. When a culture is very highly integrated so that each element is rightly interwoven with all the others in a mutually interdependent system change is difficult and costly. But when the culture is less highly integrated so that work, play, family, religion and other activities are less dependent upon one another change is easier and more frequent. A tightly structured society wherein every person's roles, duties, privileges and obligations are precisely and rigidly defined is less given to changes than a more loosely structured society wherein roles, lines of authority, privileges and obligations are more open to individual rearrangement.

ATTITUDES AND VALUES

To people in developed nations and societies change is normal. Children there are socialized to anticipate and appreciate change. By contrast the Trobriand Islanders off the coast of New Guinea had no concept of change and did not even have any words in their language to express or describe change. Societies differ greatly in their general attitude toward change. People who revere the past and preoccupied with traditions and rituals will change slowly and unwillingly. When a culture has been relatively static for a long time the people are likely to assume that it should remain so indefinitely. They are intensely and unconsciously ethnocentric; they assume that their customs and techniques are correct and everlasting. A possible change is unlikely even to be seriously considered. Any change in such a society is likely to be too gradual to be noticed. A rapidly changing society has a different attitude toward change and this attitude is both cause and effect of the changes already taking place. Rapidly changing societies are aware of the social change. They are somewhat skeptical and critical of some parts of their traditional culture and will consider and experiment with innovations. Such attitudes powerfully stimulate the proposal and acceptance of changes by individuals within the society. Different groups within a locality or a society may show differing receptivity to change. Every changing society has its liberals and its conservatives. Literate and educated people tend to accept changes more readily than the illiterate and uneducated. Attitudes and values affect both the amount and the direction of social change. The ancient Greeks made great contributions to art and learning but contributed little to technology. No society has been equally dynamic in all aspects and its values determine in which area—art, music, warfare, technology, philosophy or religion it will be innovative.

Cultural factor influences the direction and character of technological change. Culture not only influences our social relationships, it also influences the direction and character of technological change. It is not only our beliefs and social institutions must correspond to the changes in technology but our beliefs and social institutions determine the use to which the technological inventions will be put. The tools and techniques of technology are indifferent to the use we make of them. For example, the atomic energy can be used for the production of deadly war weapons or for the production of economic goods that satisfy the basic needs of man. The factories can produce the armaments or necessaries of life. Steel and iron can be used for building warships or tractors. It is a culture that decides the purpose to which a technical invention must be put. Although technology has advanced geometrically in the recent past, technology alone does not cause social change. It does not by itself even cause further advances in technology. Social values play a dominant role here. It is the complex combination of technology and social values which produces conditions that encourage further technological change. For example, the belief or the idea that human life must not be sacrificed for wants of medical treatment, contributed to the advancement in medical technology. Max Weber in his The Protestant Ethic and the spirit of Capitalism has made a classical attempt to establish a correlation between the changes in the religious outlook, beliefs and practices of the people on the one hand and their economic behavior on the other. He has observed capitalism could grow in the western societies to very great extent and not in the eastern countries like India and China. He has concluded that Protestantism with its practical ethics encouraged capitalism to grow in the west and hence industrial and economic advancement took place there. In the East, Hinduism, Buddhism, Judaism and Islam on the other hand did not encourage capitalism. Thus cultural factors play a positive as well as negative role in bringing about technological change. Cultural factors such as habits, customs, traditions, conservatism, traditional values etc. may resist the technological inventions. On the other hand, factors such as breakdown in the unity of social values, the diversification of social institutions craving for the new thoughts, values etc. may contribute to technological inventions. Technological changes do not take place on their own. They are engineered by men only. Technology is the creation of man. Men are always moved by ideas, thoughts, values, beliefs, morals and philosophies etc. These are the elements of culture. These sometimes decide or influence the direction in which technology undergoes change. Men are becoming more and more materialistic in their attitude. This change in the attitude and outlook is reflected in the technological field. Thus in order to lead a comfortable life and to minimize the manual labor man started inventing new techniques, machines, instruments and devices.

TECHNOLOGICAL FACTORS

The technological factors represent the conditions created by man which have a profound influence on his life. In the attempt to satisfy his wants, fulfill his needs and to make his life more comfortable man creates civilization. Technology is a byproduct of civilization. When the scientific knowledge is applied to the problems in life it becomes technology. Technology is a systematic knowledge which is put into practice that is to use tools and run machines to serve human purpose. Science and technology go together. In utilizing the products of technology man brings social change. The social effects of technology are far-reaching. According to Karl Marx even the formation of social relations and mental conceptions and attitudes are dependent upon technology. He has regarded technology as a sole explanation of social change. W.F. Ogburn says technology changes society by changing our environment to which we in turn adapt. These changes are usually in the material environment and the adjustment that we make with these changes often modifies customs and social institutions. A single invention may have innumerable social effects. Radio for example has one of the most extreme expressions of the concern over the independence of technology is found in Jacques Ellul's 'the technological society'. Ellul claims that in modern industrial societies technologism has engulfed every aspect of social existence in much the same way Catholicism did in the middle ages. The loss of human freedom and the large-scale destruction of human beings are due to the increasing use of certain types of technology which has begun to threaten the life support systems of the earth as a whole.

IMPACT OF TECHNOLOGY CHANGE

INDUSTRIALIZATION

Technology has contributed to the growth of industries or to the process of industrialization. Industrialization is a term covering in general terms the growth in a society hitherto mainly agrarian of modern industry with all its circumstances and problems, economic and social. It describes in general term the growth of a society in which a major role is played by manufacturing industry. The industry is characterized by heavy, fixed capital investment in plant and building by the application of science to industrial techniques and by mainly large-scale standardized production. The Industrial Revolution of 18th century led to the unprecedented growth of industries. Industrialization is associated with the factory system of production. The family has lost its economic importance. The factories have brought down the prices of commodities, improved their quality and maximized their output. The whole process of production is mechanized. Consequently the traditional skills have declined and good number of artisans has lost their work. Huge factories could provide employment opportunities to thousands of people. Hence men have become workers in a very large number. The process of industrialization has affected the nature, character and the growth of economy. It has contributed to the growth of cities or to the process of urbanization.

URBANIZATION

In many countries the growth of industries has contributed to the growth of cities. Urbanization denotes a diffusion of the influence of urban centers to a rural hinterland. Urbanization can be described as a process of becoming urban moving to cities changing from agriculture to other pursuits common to cities and corresponding change of behaviour patterns. Hence only when a large proportion of inhabitants in an area come to cities urbanization is said to occur. Urbanization has become a world phenomenon today. An unprecedented growth has taken place not only in the number of great cities but also in their size. As a result of industrialization people have started moving towards the industrial areas in search of employment. Due to this the industrial areas developed into towns and cities.

MODERNIZATION

Modernization is a process which indicates the adoption of the modern ways of life and values. It refers to an attempt on the part of the people particularly those who are custom-bound to adapt themselves to the present-time, conditions, needs, styles and ways in general. It indicates a change in people's food habits, dress habits, speaking styles, tastes, choices, preferences, ideas, values, recreational activities and so on. People in the process of getting themselves modernized give more importance to science and technology. The scientific and technological inventions have modernized societies in various countries. They have brought about remarkable changes in the whole system of social relationship and installed new ideologies in the place of traditional ones.

DEVELOPMENT OF THE MEANS OF TRANSPORT AND COMMUNICATION

Development of transport and communication has led to the national and international trade on a large scale. The road transport, the train service, the ships and the aero planes have eased the movement of men and material goods. Post and telegraph, radio and television, newspapers and magazines, telephone and wireless and the like have developed a great deal. The space research and the launching of the satellites for communication purposes have further added to these developments. They have helped the people belonging to different corners of the nation or the world to have regular contacts.

TRANSFORMATION IN THE ECONOMY AND THE EVOLUTION OF THE NEW SOCIAL CLASSES

The introduction of the factory system of production has turned the agricultural economy into industrial economy. The industrial or the capitalist economy has divided the social organization into two predominant classes—the capitalist class and the working class. These two classes are always at conflict due to mutually opposite interest. In the course of time an intermediary class called the middle class has evolved.

UNEMPLOYMENT

The problem of unemployment is a concomitant feature of the rapid technological advancement. Machines not only provide employment opportunities for men but they also take away the jobs of men through labour- saving devices. This results in technological unemployment.

TECHNOLOGY AND WAR

The dangerous effect of technology is evident through the modern mode of warfare. The weaponry has brought fears and anxieties to the mankind. They can easily destroy the entire human race reveal how technology could be misused. Thus greater the technological advancement the more risk for the mankind.

CHANGES IN SOCIAL INSTITUTIONS

Technology has profoundly altered our modes of life. Technology has not spared the social institutions of its effects. The institutions of family, religion, morality, marriage, state, property have been altered. Modern technology in taking away industry from the household has radically changed the family organization. Many functions of the family have been taken away by other agencies. Marriage is losing its sanctity. It is treated as a civil contract than a sacred bond. Marriages are becoming more and more unstable. Instances of divorce, desertion and separation are increasing. Technology has elevated the status of women but it has also contributed to the stresses and strains in the relations between men and women at home. Religion is losing hold over the members. People are becoming more secular, rational and scientific but less religious in their outlook. Inventions and discoveries in science have shaken the foundations of religion. The function of the state or the field of state activity has been widened. Modern technology have made the states to perform such functions as—the protection of the aged, the weaker section and the minorities making provision for education, health care etc.Transportation and communication inventions are leading to a shift of functions from local government to the central government of the whole state. The modern inventions have also strengthened nationalism. The modern governments which rule through the bureaucracy have further impersonalized the human relations.

CULTURAL LAG

To provide a law of social change comparable to the laws of physics and biology that William F. Ogburn in 1922 advanced his theory of social lag. Ogburn pointed out that social changes always originate in the invention by some individual of a new way of doing something new to do. So far he was following in the tradition established by Gabriel Tarde; but Ogburn then began to wander in the tracks of Marx, Historically, he argued, inventions occur most often in the field of material technology, if only because the advantages of an improvement in technology are self-evident. With each development in technology there comes, however, some disturbance to the effective working of the existing social order. A strain or stress is set up between the new technique and various organizational aspects of the social system, changes in which come slowly if at all; the result, disequilibrium between new technology and old social organization, is social lag. The core of Ogburn's theory is the idea that change first occurs in the material technology.

SOCIAL MOVEMENTS

While technology, population, environment factors, and racial inequality can prompt social change, only when members of a society organize into social movements does true social change occur. The phrase social movements refers to collective activities designed to bring about or resist primary changes in an existing society or group.

Wherever they occur, social movements can dramatically shape the direction of society. When individuals and groups of people—civil rights activists and other visionaries, for instance—transcend traditional bounds, they may bring about major shifts in social policy and structures. Even when they prove initially unsuccessful, social movements do affect public opinion.

Social scientists interest themselves in why social movements emerge. Do feelings of discontent, desires for a "change of pace," or even yearnings for "change for the sake of change" cause these shifts? Sociologists use two theories to explain why people mobilize for change: relative deprivation and resource mobilization.

RELATIVE DEPRIVATION

When members of a society become dissatisfied or frustrated with their social, economic, and political situation, they yearn for changes. Social scientists have long noted that the actual conditions that people live under may not be at fault, but people's perceptions of their conditions are. Relative deprivation refers to the negative perception that differences exist between wants and actualities. In other words, people may not actually be deprived when they believe they are. A relatively deprived group is disgruntled because they feel less entitled or privileged than a particular reference group. For example, a middle-class family may feel relatively deprived when they compare their house to that of their upper-class physician.

Social Movements, i.e., demonstrating, petitioning, striking, lobbying.

For social discontent to translate into social movement, members of the society must feel that they deserve, or have a right to, more wealth, power, or status than they have. The dissatisfied group must also conclude that it cannot attain its goals via conventional methods, whether or not this is the case. The group will organize into a social movement only if it feels that collective action will help its cause.

The relative-deprivation theory takes criticism from a couple of different angles. First, some sociologists note that feelings of deprivation do not necessarily prompt people into acting. Nor must people feel deprived before acting. Moreover, this theory does not address why perceptions of personal or group deprivation cause some people to reform society, and why other perceptions do not.

RESOURCE MOBILIZATION

Resource mobilization deals with how social movements mobilize resources: political pull, mass media, personnel, money, and so forth. A particular movement's effectiveness and success largely depends on how well it uses its resources.

Members of a social movement normally follow a charismatic leader, who mobilizes people for a cause. Charisma can fade, and many social movements collapse when this happens. Other movements, such as bureaucratic ones, manage to last, however, usually because they are highly organized.

Norms of behaviour develop as people become part of a social movement. The movement may require its members to dress in special ways, boycott certain products, pay dues, attend marches or rallies, recruit new members, and use new language. Concerning the latter, recent social movements have given rise to new terms like Hispanic American, African American, feminists, and psychiatrically disabled.

For a social movement to succeed, leaders must heighten their followers' awareness of oppression. To stimulate their social movement in the 1960s and 1970s, feminists convinced women that they were being discriminated against in various arenas, including work, school, and home.

Unlike the relative-deprivation theory, the resource-mobilization theory emphasizes the strategic problems faced by social movements. Specifically, any movement designed to stimulate fundamental changes will surely face resistance to its activities. Critics feel the theory does not adequately discuss the issue of how opposition influences the actions and direction of social movements.

CHARACTERISTICS OF SOCIAL MOVEMENT

Characteristics of Social Movement is one of the major forms of collective behaviour.We hear of various kinds of social movements launched for one or the other purpose. A social movement can be defined as collectively acing with some continuity to promote or resist change in the society or group of which it is a part. Horton and Hunt have defined it as a collective effort to promote or resist change.Smelser defines it as organized group effort to generate or resist social change. According to M.S.A Rao social movement includes two characteristics.

COLLECTIVE ACTION

Social Movement involves collective action. However it takes the form of a movement only when it is sustained for a long time. This collective action need not be formally organized. But it should be able to create an interest and awakening in relatively large number of people.

ORIENTED TOWARDS SOCIAL CHANGE

A social movement is generally oriented towards bringing social change. This change could either be partial or total. Though the movement is aimed at bringing about a change in the values, norms, ideologies of the existing system, efforts are also made by some other forces to resist the changes and to maintain the status quo. The counter attempts are normally defensive and restorative rather than innovative and initiating change. They are normally the organized efforts of an already established order to maintain itself.

According to Yogendra Singh social movement is a collective mobilization of people in a society in an organized manner under an individual or collective leadership in order to realize an ideologically defined social purpose. Social movements are characterized by a specific goal which has a collective significance ideological interpretation of the collective goal a rank of committed worker and strong leadership. Social movements have a life-cycle of their own origin, maturity and culmination. T.K Oomen observe that a study of social movements implies a study of social structure as movements originate from the contradictions which in turn emanate from social structure. He states that all social movements centre around three factors—Locality, Issues and social categories. Anthony Wallace view social movement as an attempt by local population to change the image or models they have of how their culture operates.

An important component of social movement that distinguishes it from the general category of collective mobilization is the presence of an ideology. A student strike involves collective mobilization and is oriented towards change. But in the absence of an ideology a student strike becomes an isolated event and not a movement. A social movement requires a minimum of organizational framework to achieve success or at least to maintain the tempo of the movement. To make the distinction clear between the leaders and followers to make clear the purposes of the movement to persuade people to take part in it or to support it, to adopt different techniques to achieve the goals—a social movement must have some amount of organizational frame-work. A social movement may adopt its own technique or method to achieve its goal. It may follow peaceful or conflicting, violent or non-violent, compulsive or persuasive, democratic or undemocratic means or methods to reach its goal.

SOCIAL MOVEMENT THEORIES

FUNCTIONALIST PERSPECTIVES

- In 1950s view was that SM were outgrowth of particular type of social behaviour, known as collective behaviour.

- These arise out of a breakdown of traditional order with some underlying shared source of excitement or stress or anxiety or frustration.
- Breakdown of traditional patterns of order and social control produce then elementary forms of collective behaviour which if they persist then may lead to SM and then may evolve into integrated structures and new established norms (follows very much the functionalist view of order and change – gradual).
- SM were adaptive responses to strains in transition from traditional to modern mass societies.
- SM emerge out of spontaneous and amorphous mass discontent.
- SM contribute to formation of public opinion; training ground for leaders of political establishment.

VALUE-ADDED THEORY (SMELSER)

- Emphasized ongoing interaction between movement and society, identified 6 conditions necessary for development of SM, in no sequence but each necessary and each added on to the other.
- Organization of society can facilitate the emergence of conflicting interests.
- Conduciveness of social structure to potential conflict gives way to a perception that conflicting interests do in fact exist.
- Growth of a generalized belief system: ideology, a shared view of reality that redefines social action and serves to guide behaviour.
- Triggering events, found within or outside social structure.
- Mobilization of participants.
- Response of others in society, e.g., counter movements or governmental authorities, latter could either open channel of communication or influence, i.e., co-optation, or alter underlying structural conditions that gave rise to SM, or suppress movement (prevent, delay or interrupt).
- Causal links between six factors unclear, what kinds of structures, what kinds of strains, so more descriptive than explanatory.

CONFLICT THEORY PERSPECTIVES

SM are special sorts of interest-group collectivities that attempt to :

- Gain benefits for individuals.
- Produce social reforms.
- Gain entry into the established structures of society.

RESOURCE MOBILIZATION THEORY

Focuses on role of power and power struggles:

- Assumes a liberal pluralistic political structure where there is continual political realignment, i.e. assumes that there will always be grounds for protest in modern societies, de-emphasizes role of mass discontent which is a constant.
- Society now possesses the resources (money, political influence, access to media and workers) to mobilize variety of change efforts that have appearance of mass based movements.
- Emphasizes ongoing transformation of movements through interaction of competing SMO's in broader political environment.
- Requires an organizational base and continuity of leadership.
- Views participants as rational decision-makers who have weighed costs and benefits of collective action and have decided that goals of protest are worth time and effort.

MOBILIZATION PROCESS

- creating a potential base of support in the population.
- forming recruitment networks to tap potential members.
- arousing motivation among targeted individuals through framing issues.
- removing barriers to participation.
- once activated, commitment is maintained by building a collective identity and continuing to nurture interpersonal relationships.

POLITICAL PROCESS THEORY

- Concurs with resource mobilization theory in emphasizing existence of resources.
- Emphasizes more the existence of favorable structures of political opportunity.
- Addresses the issue of timing of emergence and success of SM, explains why SM often are in waves or cycles and why some SM are unsuccessful for long periods of time and then suddenly appear to grow and succeed.

Political opportunity structures refers to the receptivity or vulnerability of the political system to organized protest by challenging groups, when such structures expand there is intense movement mobilization, can take many forms:

- Growth of political pluralism or decline in effectiveness of repression.
- Elite disunity: Power of political elite is undermined by internal fragmentation, disunity translates into net gain in political opportunity, could lead to crisis of regime/legitimacy and thus revolutionary movements.
- Broadening of access to institutional participation in political process, broadening base of political input.

- Political elites support and facilitation: Elites give popular support by encouraging movements to organize by providing public legitimation and legal or administrative support, support from the top in order to get electoral support.
- **Criticisms:** Too narrow a focus on structural factors, ignoring role of culture and ideas

NEW MOVEMENT THEORY

- Emphasizes the consciousness and culture, ideology, generalized beliefs, values, and focus on modern societies.
- Developed by European scholars: movements emerged in short time span in different Western nations all having different cultural traditions and national structures of political opportunity.
- Developed as reactions to modernizing process in advanced industrial capitalist societies, reactions to erosion of traditional ways of family and work life post WWII.
- Overriding issue is one of "lifespace" and the struggle to regain control of private spheres of life from state bureaucratic regulation (same as postmodernism which comes from literary critics of modernity); promotes autonomy and self-determination as well as improvements in quality of life.
- Have complex agendas that go beyond single issue.
- Do not view government as an ally, inclined to not accept established political or scientific authority.
- Moral crusades, the politics of righteousness, agents of cultural renovation, goals are more cultural rather than political, to change moral climate of nation, frame issues in absolute terms with little room for compromise.
- Differences from SM of previous decades:
  - Ideological contexts are different: framed by concerns about individual and cultural rights, articulating claims about fundamental economic justice or human or political rights, an ideology shaped by values about self-actualization, community and personal satisfaction
  - Preferred action forms are different: distrustful of politics, favoring small scale and decentralized organizations, anti-hierarchical, advocating direct democracy
  - Associated not with grievances of lower status and economic groups but with rise of new middle class of educated professionals whose expertise is cultural or social rather than technocratic, thus have insight into threat posed by pursuit of nonmaterial goals by material conditions of production and institutional framework of welfare state.

Criticisms: Limited by types of movements it tries to explain, those of contemporary welfare states, such movements are more diverse than this theory purports, e.g., many movements are for group rights or for basic human rights.

TYPES OF SOCIAL MOVEMENTS

REFORM MOVEMENTS

Reform movements are organized to carry out reforms in some specific areas. The reformers endeavor to change elements of the system for better. For example: Civil Rights Movement, Women's Liberation Movement, Arya Samaj Movement, Brahmo Samaj Movement etc.

REVOLUTIONARY MOVEMENTS

The revolutionary movements deny that the system will even work. These movements are deeply dissatisfied with the social order and work for radical change. They advocate replacing the entire existing structure. Their objective is the reorganization of society in accordance with their own ideological blueprint. Revolutionary movements generally become violent as they progress. For example: The Protestant Reformation Movement, the Socialist Movement, the Communist Revolution of China.

REACTIONARY OR REVIVALIST MOVEMENT

Some movements are known as reactionary or regressive movements. These aims to reverse the social change. They highlight the importance and greatness of traditional values, ideologies and institutional arrangements. They strongly criticize the fast moving changes of the present.

RESISTANCE MOVEMENT

These movements are formed to resist a change that is already taking place in society. These can be directed against social and cultural changes which are already happening in the country.

UTOPIAN MOVEMENT

These are attempts to take the society or a section of it towards a state of perfection. These are loosely structured collectivities that envision a radically changed and blissful state, either on a large scale at some time in the future or on a smaller scale in the present. The Utopian ideal and the means of it are often vague, but many utopian movements have quite specific programmes for social change. The Hare Krishna Movement of the seventies, the movement towards the establishment of Ram Rajya and the Sangh Parivar, the Communists and Socialists pronouncement of a movement towards the classless, casteless society free from all kinds of exploitation etc.

PEASANT MOVEMENT

Peasant movement is defined by Kathleen Gough as an attempt of a group to effect change in the face of resistance and the peasant are people who are engaged in an agricultural or related production with primitive means who surrender part of their or its equivalent to landlords or to agents of change. The history of peasant movements can be traced to colonial period when repressive economic policies, the new land revenue system, the colonial administrative and judicial system and the ruin of handicrafts leading to the overcrowding of land transformed the agrarian structure and impoverished the peasantry. In the zamindari system peasants were left to the mercies of the Zamindars who exploited them in form of illegal dues. The British government levied heavy land revenue in the Ryotwari areas. Peasants were forced to borrow money from the moneylenders and they were reduced to the status of tenants at will, share croppers and landless laborers while their lands, crops and cattle passed into the hands to landlords, trader moneylenders and such peasants. When the peasants could take it no longer they resisted against the oppression and exploitation through uprisings. Peasant Movements occupy an important place in the history of social unrest in India though the aims and objectives of these movements differ in nature and degree from region to region. It is in this sense that these movements also aimed at the unification of the peasants of a region, development of leadership, ideology and a peasant elite. Through these movements emerged a new power structure and peasant alliance. The genesis of peasant movements rest in the relationship patterns of different social categories existing within the framework of feudal and semi feudal structure of our society. In the post Independence period the nature and objectives of the peasant movement have changed to getting remunerative prices for agricultural produce, to increase agricultural production, to establish parity between prices of agricultural produce and industrial goods and to get minimum wages for the agricultural labourers.

Some of the important peasant uprising:

1770	—	Sanyasi rebellion
1831	—	Wahabi uprising
1855	—	Santhal uprising
1859	—	Indigo revolt
1890-1900	—	Punjab Kisan struggle
1917-18	—	Champaran satyagraha
1921	—	Moplah rebellion
1928	—	Bardoli satyagarya
1946	—	Telangana movement
1957	—	Naxalbadi movement

WOMEN'S MOVEMENT

The women's movement in India is a rich and vibrant movement which has taken different forms in different parts of the country. Fifty years ago when India became independent, it was widely acknowledged that the battle for freedom had been fought as much by women as by men. One of the methods M. K. Gandhi chose to undermine the authority of the British was for Indians to defy the law which made it illegal for them to make salt. At the time, salt-making was a monopoly and earned considerable revenues for the British. Gandhi began his campaign by going on a march—the salt march—through many villages, leading finally to the sea, where he and others broke the law by making salt. No woman had been included by Gandhi in his chosen number of marchers. But nationalist women protested, and they forced him to allow them to participate. The first to join was Sarojini Naidu, who went on to become the first woman President of the Indian National Congress in 1925. Her presence was a signal for hundreds of other women to join, and eventually the salt protest was made successful by the many women who not only made salt, but also sat openly in marketplaces selling, and indeed, buying it. The trajectory of this movement is usually traced from the social reform movements of the 19th century when campaigns for the betterment of the conditions of women's lives were taken up, initially by men. By the end of the century women had begun to organize themselves and gradually they took up a number of causes such as education, the conditions of women's work and so on. It was in the early part of the 20th century that women's organizations were set up, and many of the women who were active in these later became involved in the freedom movement. Independence brought many promises and dreams for women in India—the dream of an egalitarian, just, democratic society in which both men and women would have a voice. The reality was, however, somewhat different. For all that had happened was that, despite some improvements in the status of women, patriarchy had simply taken on new and different forms. By the 1960s it was clear that many of the promises of Independence were still unfulfilled. It was thus that the 1960s and 1970s saw a spate of movements in which women took part: campaigns against rising prices, movements for land rights, peasant movements. Women from different parts of the country came together to form groups both inside and outside political parties. Everywhere, in the different movements that were sweeping the country, women participated in large numbers. Everywhere, their participation resulted in transforming the movements from within. One of the first issues to receive countrywide attention from women's groups was violence against women, specifically in the form of rape, and 'dowry deaths'. This was also the beginning of a process of learning for women: most protests were directed at the State. Because women were able to mobilize support, the State responded, seemingly positively, by changing the law on rape and dowry, making both more stringent. In the early campaigns, groups learnt from day to day that targeting the State was not enough and that victims also needed support. So a further level of work was needed: awareness raising so that violence against women could be prevented, rather than only dealt with after it had happened. Legal aid and counseling centres were set up, and attempts were made to establish women's shelters. Knowledge was also recognized as an important need. The women's activity was geared towards improving the conditions of women's lives. In recent years, the euphoria of the 1970s and early 1980s, symbolized by street-level protests, campaigns in which groups mobilized at a national level, has been replaced by a more considered and complex response to issues. In many parts of India, women are no longer to be seen out on the streets protesting about this or that form of injustice. This apparent lack of a visible movement has led to the accusation that the women's movement is dead or dying. While the participation of urban, middle class women is undeniable, it is not they who make up the backbone of the movement, or of the many, different campaigns that are generally seen as comprising the movement. The anti-alcohol agitation in Andhra Pradesh and similar campaigns in other parts of India were started and sustained by poor, low-caste, often working-class women. The movement to protect the environment was begun by poor women in a village called Reni in the northern hill regions of India, and only after that did it spread to other parts of the country. One of the biggest challenges women have had to face in recent years is the growing influence of the religious right in India. Right-wing groups have built much of their support on the involvement of women: offering to help them with domestic problems, enabling them to enter the public space in a limited way, and all the while ensuring that the overall ideology within which they operate remains firmly patriarchal. For activists too, this has posed major problems. It has forced them to confront the fact that they cannot assume solidarity as women that cuts across class, religion, caste, ethnic difference. It is important to recognize that for a country of India's magnitude, change in male-female relations and the kinds of issues the women's movement is focusing on will not come easy. For every step the movement takes forward, there will be a possible backlash, a possible regression. And it is this that makes for the contradictions, this that makes it possible for there to be women who can aspire to, and attain, the highest political office in the country, and for women to continue to have to confront patriarchy within the home, in the workplace, throughout their lives.

BACKWARD CASTE MOVEMENT

The Backward castes have been deprived of many social, economic, political and religious privileges. These people provided manual labor and the untouchables occupied the lowest position among the caste hierarchy. They were subjected to extreme form of exploitation. The colonial power accentuated the disparities in the distribution of economic power. The atrocities united the lower castes against the upper castes. Some of the important backward caste movement which came up was Satyashodak Samaj and Nadar Movement which consolidated the masses along the castelines. E.V Ramaswamy started Self-Respect movement against the Brahmins in South India. The SNDP movement in Kerala was more of a reformist movement. In 1950s there was a widespread desire among the non-Brahmin castes to be categorized as Backward. Subsequently Backward Class commission was set up to look into the conditions and requirements of these classes. Mandal Commission submitted its report in 1980 recommending reservations for backward castes in educational institutions and government offices. However this move resulted in anti-Mandal Commission movement which resulted in large scale violence and many students lost their lives.

DALIT MOVEMENT

Dalits are the suppressed people at the lost rung of the cast-based hierarchy. Their inferior occupations and low levels of ascriptive status make them vulnerable for attacks at the hands of upper-caste people. The organizational efforts made by Dalit leadership for uplifting their status are known as Dalit movement. It is a protest against untouchability, casteism and discrimination faced by the dalits. Dalit movement indicates some trends of protest ideologies which entail the following -withdrawal and self organization, high varna status and extolling of non-Aryan culture's virtues, abandoning of Hinduism and embracing other religions like Buddhism and Islam. Mahatma Gandhi in 1923 founded the All India Harijan Sevak Sangh to start education and schools for the dalits.Another most important dalit leader Dr. Ambedkar struggled to secure the basic human dignity to the dalits.The Mahad Satyagarh for the right of water led by him was one of the outstanding movements of the dalits to win equal social rights. The role of All India Depressed Classes Association and All India Depressed Classes Federation were the principal organizations which initiated a movement to improve the conditions of the dalits.These organizations aimed at improving their miserable conditions and to spread education among them. They worked to secure rights of admission to school, drawing water from the public wells, entering the temples and to use the roads.

NEW SOCIAL MOVEMENT

The term new social movements (NSMs) is a theory of social movements that attempts to explain the plethora of new movements that have come up in various western societies roughly since the mid-1960s (i.e., in a post-industrial economy) which are claimed to depart significantly from the conventional social movement paradigm.

There are two central claims of the NSM theory. First, that the rise of the post-industrial economy is responsible for a new wave of social movement and second, that those movements are significantly different from previous social movements of the industrial economy. The primary difference is in their goals, as the new movements focus not on issues of materialistic qualities such as economic wellbeing, but on issues related to human rights (such as gay rights or pacifism). Thinkers have related these movements with the postmaterialism hypothesis as put forth by Ronald Inglehart.

Numerous social movements from mid-1960s differed from their precursors, such as the labor movement, which had previously been seen as focused on economic concerns. The new movements instead of pushing for specific changes in public policy emphasize social changes in identity, lifestyle and culture.

Thus the social aspect is seen by the NSM as more important than the economic or political aspects. Some NSM theorists, like F. Parkin (Middle Class Radicalism, 1968), argue that the key actors in these movements are different as well, as they are more likely to come from the "new middle class" rather than the lower classes. Unlike pressure groups that have a formal organisation and 'members', NSMs consist of an informal, loosely organised social network of 'supporters' rather than members. Paul Byrne described New Social Movements as 'relatively disorganised'.

Protest groups tend to be single issue based and are often local in terms of the scope of change they wish to effect. In contrast, NSMs last longer than single issue campaigns and wish to see change on an (international level on various issues in relation to their set of beliefs and ideals). A NSM may, however adopt the tactic of a protest campaign as part of its strategy for achieving wider-ranging change.

Examples of those new movements include the women's movement, the ecology movement, gay rights movement and various peace movements, among others.

Most well known movements in the country are Chipko movement, Save Silent Valley, Narmada Bachao Andolan, Koel Karo, Chhattisgarh Mukti Morcha, Jhola Aandolan (fighting polythene). These movements largely distanced themselves from political parties, or tried to cut across the ideologies of the political parties. Yet many of them rooted themselves or drew from ideologies of the Mahatma Gandhi, various shades environmentalisms or gender politics, or socialism. Some of the popular leaders of such movements are Sunderlal Bahuguna, Medha Patkar, Baba Amte, Vandana Shiva, Vijaypal Baghel, etc.

24

CHAPTER

SOCIAL ORDER

Introduction. ***Modern Social Order:*** *The Social Division of Labour, Modern Occupations: Professions, Social Complexity, Social Solidarity, Modern Sources of the Self, Modern Beliefs, Modern Risks, Modern Thought.* ***Global Modernity. De-Traditionalisation. Bureaucracy and Modern Social Order:*** *Rationalisation, The Irrationality of Rationalisation.* ***Problem of Social Order.***

INTRODUCTION

The issue of social order, how and why it is that social orders exists at all, is historically central to sociology. Thomas Hobbes is recognized as the first to clearly formulate the problem, to answer which he conceived the notion of a social contract. Social theorists (such as Karl Marx, Émile Durkheim, Talcott Parsons, and Jürgen Habermas) have proposed different explanations for what a social order consists of, and what its real basis is. For Marx, it is the relations of production or economic structure which is the basis of a social order. For Durkheim, it is a set of shared social norms. For Parsons, it is a set of social institutions regulating pattern of action-orientations, which again are based on a frame of cultural values. For Habermas, it is all of these, as well as communicative action.

In Russian, the term "*social order*" is often used synonymously with socioeconomic formation. A system of social and state organization characterized by specific production and social relations and a specific political structure. Important examples are the capitalist and the socialist structures. A "social order" is a relatively persistent system of institutions, patterns of interactions and customs, capable of continually reproducing at least those conditions essential for its own existence. The concept refers to all those facts of society which remain relatively constant over time. These conditions could include both property, exchange and power relations, but also cultural forms, communication relations and ideological systems of values.

Imam of Grand Mosque in Mecca: Need for Islamic Social Order.

MODERN SOCIAL ORDER

Sociology is the study of modern societies. Modern societies have a typical structure (organisation):

- industrial capitalist economies,
- democratic political organisation, division into economic classes,
- secular culture.

This contrasts with the typical structure of pre-modern societies:

- agricultural economy,
- aristocratic/monarchical rule,
- family/clan based divisions,
- religious culture.

Sociology developed out of the direct experience of how these far-reaching changes in social structure affected everyday life.

Under the Constitution's terms, the age-old practice of 'untouchability', that had helped create and sustain a hierarchical social order with religious sanction, was officially drawn to a close.

THE SOCIAL DIVISION OF LABOUR

Modern societies are more complex than traditional societies. Social complexity is the process through which social institutions, *established ways of organising collective life*, increase in number and become more specialised in what they do; the social division of labour.

Two key features of the enormous success of ants and other social insects (e.g., termites or honey bees) are the ability to cooperate and to perform efficient division of labour.

For instance, the *family* becomes concerned exclusively with childcare, *religion* with organising relationships with the supernatural. New institutions develop, e.g., *mass media*. Institutions tend to be distinct from each other. In being both more complex and more fragmented than preceding societies modern societies may be more fragile.

MODERN OCCUPATIONS: PROFESSIONS

Professions are middle class, knowledge-based occupational groups, e.g., doctors, lawyers, architects. The number of professions is constantly expanding. Typically, professionals claim expertise the right to practise in particular areas that are barred to the laity, non-experts. Professions are established by powerful institutions, e.g. the state. This confers on professionals the right to define public reality in areas of their expertise.

SOCIAL COMPLEXITY

Social complexity is the study of social phenomenon through the lens of complex systems. This often includes building computational models of social behavior, some of which are related to computer science topics such as: cellular automaton, genetic algorithms, or neural networks. Social network analysis is also related to social complexity as it is used to quantify relationships, roles, and organization amongst agents. Some important properties of social complexity are:

- **Understanding of Differences :** The understanding of differences among description levels in a social system; at the minimum the distinguishment of macro-level (e.g., collective or aggregate phenomena), meso-level (e.g., social interaction among social agents), and micro-level (e.g., the belief systems of individual social agents). In this case, there is a tendency to see a social system as a multi-agent system.

- **Macro-micro Linkages between Description Levels:** There are macro-micro linkages between description levels. The macro levels emerged from the micro levels and in return there is a causality relationship between the macro properties and the micro. This aspect is reminiscent of the concept of emergence in a complex adaptive system. In return, the interplay between macro and micro levels are commonly modelled as non-linear phenomena.
- **Tendency to Use Formal Approaches in Social Complexity Studies:** There is a tendency to use formal approaches in social complexity studies, e.g., *game theory*, *cellular automaton*, *evolutionary programming*, *neural network modeling in many aspects*, *dynamical system modeling*, *computer simulation*, etc.

SOCIAL SOLIDARITY

Solidarity is the integration, and degree and type of integration, shown by a society or group with people and their neighbours. It refers to the ties in a society — social relations — that bind people to one another. The term is generally employed in sociology and the other social sciences.

A key concern of Sociology is the problem of social order that is, what holds society together. Why does it not fragment into anarchy based on self-interest?

A common argument, deriving in particular from Durkheim, is that social order is maintained by normative consensus – *a system of rules and standards that define appropriate behaviour in a given social situation.*

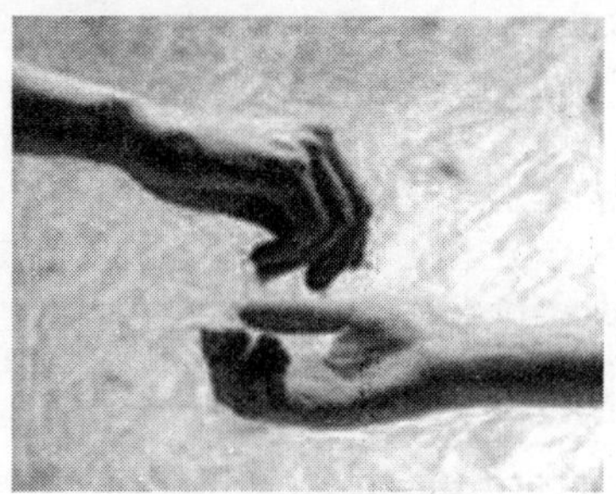

Social Solidarity.

The social fragmentation that comes with the extended division of labour typically weakens normative solidarity by reducing shared interests and experiences.

According to *Émile Durkheim*, the types of social solidarity correlate with types of society. Durkheim introduced the terms "mechanical" and "organic solidarity" as part of his theory of the development of societies in 'The Division of Labour in Society'. In a society exhibiting mechanical solidarity, its cohesion and integration comes from the homogeneity of individuals—people feel connected through similar work, educational and religious training, and lifestyle. Mechanical solidarity normally operates in "traditional" and small scale societies. In simpler societies (e.g., tribal), solidarity is usually based on kinship ties of familial networks. Organic solidarity comes from the interdependence that arises from specialization of work and the complementarities between people—a development which occurs in "modern" and "industrial" societies.

Definition: It is social cohesion based upon the dependence individuals have on each other in more advanced societies. Although individuals perform different tasks and often have different values and interest, the order and very solidarity of society depends on their reliance on each other to perform their specified tasks. Organic here is referring to the interdependence of the component parts. Thus, social solidarity is maintained in more complex societies through the interdependence of its component parts (e.g., farmers produce the food to feed the factory workers who produce the tractors that allow the farmer to produce the food).

MODERN SOURCES OF THE SELF

The extended division of labour and fragmentation of experience tends to encourage the sense that people are distinctive persons: individuals. This supports the plausibility of Individualism: beliefs that celebrate the autonomy of the individual human being in social action and affairs. Individualism encourages the separation between private and public life. Perhaps even more important it tends to hide social reality from us.

MODERN BELIEFS

The relative absence of normative consensus leads to the exclusion of values and beliefs from public life. Secularisation the process in which religious thinking, practise and institutions lose social significance is part of this process through which private beliefs are separated from our public roles.

According to Weber this leads to a distinctive feature of modernity. The dominance of public decision making by value-free, rational decision-making. That is, decisions based on calculation of whether outcomes of action are efficient and effective. Berger and Luckman referred to this distinctively modern way of thinking as technological consciousness.

MODERN RISKS

According to A. Giddens (British; no Beard; as well as can be expected) this process has an unexpected outcome. Rational planning integrates large numbers of people, organisations and decision-making processes. This means that if something goes wrong it is likely to have major knock-on effects. Hence, modern societies are risk societies, they generate a diversity of possible dangers, hazards and futures, e.g., *environmental degradation, warfare, pollution.*

U. Beck (German, no Beard, old but alive) argues that risk societies are therefore focussed on the distribution of bads or dangers, e.g., job uncertainty.

This also affects private life and the dangers of intimacy in a society of strangers.

MODERN THOUGHT

The social structure of modernity affects the way we think. According to Marx modern society is divided into classes, groups that differed from other groups in their relationship to the ownership and control of capital; the proletariat (workers) and bourgeoisie (owners). Each class produces ways of thinking, ideologies, systems of ideas which justifies or legitimates their particular interests, e.g., the legitimacy of collective organisation versus rights of private property.

Later thinkers such as Gramsci and Habermas have extended this to the study of how the mass media reflects dominant class interests. It can be argued that individualism (a major theme of this course) deflects responsibility for the production of social 'bads' from social processes and institutions to persons.

GLOBAL MODERNITY

Rational planning requires the extension of systems of control. This is a major aspect of globalisation the process through which the world becomes a single place.

Consequently, risks and uncertainties are globally produced and distributed e.g. investment decisions relocate work and unemployment from one part of the world to another.

The consequences of actions and decisions can have unanticipated, wide-ranging consequences. We are affected in our daily lives by processes of which we have no knowledge.

This indicates the necessity of the sociological perspective i.e. the global social system is real and has consequences.

DE-TRADITIONALISATION

Globalisation can be seen as transforming how members of modern societies experience space. The experience of time is also transformed. Members of pre-modern societies typically look to the past, their traditions, as guides for action. Members of modern societies typically embrace a progressive way of thinking. The past is no guide to the future which comes to be seen as open and uncertain i.e. 'risky'. According to Giddens this leads to detradi-tionalisation the process through which traditions lose their authority and become objects of nostalgia.

BUREAUCRACY AND MODERN SOCIAL ORDER

The typical modern social organization is the bureaucracy. According to Weber bureaucratic decision making is based on instrumental rationality, the selection of the most efficient means to reach a given end. It, therefore, embodies the principles of rational organisation and planning.

Bureaucratic organisation is also depersonalised. It is based on impersonal written rules and a hierarchy of offices; there is a clear distinction between 'the office' and its incumbent. Official positions are filled on the basis of formal qualifications not interpersonal connections.

The public world (education, politics, economy, media etc.) is typically bureaucratically organised.

RATIONALISATION

A key concept in the sociology of Weber: the increasing tendency to base decision making on considerations of efficiency, predictability, calculability and the use of non-human technologies to control people.

This raises the question of whether in modern societies the creation of a stable social order is dependant on the impersonal control of human activity and the restriction of personal freedom to the private sphere of e.g. family life, hobbies, leisure etc.

THE IRRATIONALITY OF RATIONALISATION

However, it has been argued that rationalisation produces irrational outcomes. We have referred previously to the production of risks. Bauman identifies the destructive potential of rationalisation, e.g., modern warfare. In particular Bauman points out how the holocaust was the product of rational planning.

Rationalisation can also have irrational consequences for everyday life. Cohen and Taylor, show how bureaucratic rationality restricts human freedom to the point that apparently 'free' areas of private life, e.g. holidays, hobbies, leisure are subject to bureaucratic control and regulation.

PROBLEM OF SOCIAL ORDER

Social order is a core theoretical issue in the social sciences. The problem arises because human beings are both individual and social. If we were each living alone on a private planet, we could do what ever we wanted and would never have to worry about anyone else. Or, if each of us were attached to one group mind, we would have no individual impulses and urges. But we are both. Every individual inhabits a separate physical body and thus each has his or her own experiences, information, feelings, and ambitions. Yet we are not completely independent. Stories of people living in isolation—neglected children, prisoners in solitary confinement—tell us that we need social contact to be physically and emotionally healthy and simply to stay alive.

For social order to arise and be maintained, two separate problems must be overcome. People must be able to coordinate their actions and they must cooperate to attain common goals.

Coordination requires that people develop stable expectations about others' behaviour. When driving, for example, it is helpful to know whether others are likely to approach you on the right or the left side of the road.

If you and I agree to a date Friday at 8:00 p.m., we presume that we are referring to the same time zone and calendar and that we will each be at the same place at the specified time. If you and I agree to a phone call Monday at 12:00 and you're in London and I'm in Los Angeles, coordination is more difficult. If you call at noon London time but I'm expecting a call at noon Los Angeles time, then I will likely miss you. I will be asleep.

We can have stable expectations and still not much social order, however. Contemporary Afghanistan, for example, is a society visited by frequent interethnic violence, highly unequal relations between the genders and age grades, and a meager standard of living. Yet Afghan society also exhibits high predictability. Because most Afghanis expect to be living under these conditions, they act according to their expectations and therefore are able to carry on. But life is hard. It is predictable but not what we would call orderly. Something else is required for social order to be maintained. If people are to live together, they must not only be able to coordinate their activities but also to interact productively—to do things that help rather than hurt others. Thus highly ordered societies have a remarkable capacity to sustain cooperation.

Cooperation entails people working together for the same end. Talent aside, a basketball team with high average assists and rebounds will be more successful than one in which players concentrate their efforts on individual scoring. People who care most about their own personal statistics and making the pros are unlikely to be good team players. As a result, the team will be less successful than it could be.

The challenge is that behaving cooperatively may impose costs on the individual. Everyone thinks it's a good idea to spend money on education, but nobody wants to pay more property taxes. We appreciate National Public Radio, but many of us change stations when it's fund- raising time. In many situations, then, the interests of the individual and the group are at odds. Sometimes individuals fail to contribute to the group—they do not volunteer at the local school, do not donate money to National Public Radio, and do not give to people when help is needed. They hope that others will work to improve the community but would prefer to enjoy the benefits without having to make too much effort themselves. At other times, people may do things that impose harm on the group—take others' property, pollute, or cheat. They do what they want regardless of the effects of their actions on others. If order is to be maintained, these tendencies must be overcome.

SOCIAL STRATIFICATION AND CLASS

Introduction. Social Stratification. Divisions of Social Stratification. Basic Principles of Stratification. Approaches to Social Stratification. Types of Social Stratification. Social Class: *Definition.* ***Measuring Social Class. Functions of Social Class. Theories of Class and Stratification:*** *Stratification and Conflict, Karl Marx: Class and Conflict, Max Weber.* ***Social Class as Subculture. Social Class and Health. Social Class and Gender. Race, Ethnicity, and Class. Social Class and Domestic Violence. Social Class and Religion. Social Class and Unemployment. Social Class and Lifestyle.***

INTRODUCTION

Social strata are levels of social statuses. Members of a society who possess similar amount of wealth, power, and privileges occupy each social stratum. We can see layers of social statuses occupied by members of society. Organized systems of such strata are conceptualized as social stratification system.

SOCIAL STRATIFICATION

The concept of social stratification is a key concept in sociology and the unit should begin with definitions of the concept, such as it being a socially constructed concept and based on structured inequality. The inequality may be in the form of income and wealth, an individual's biological or ethnic make-up, or may be as a result of age or disability. Simple reference can be made to contrasting sociological theories that seek to explain social stratification and resultant social inequality, which would help provide candidates with appropriate introduction to what is meant by social stratification. Examples of common sense explanations can be drawn from candidates' everyday lives to help illustrate the extent of social stratification.

Social stratification refers to a system by which a society ranks categories of people in a hierarchy.

Social stratification refers to the social and economic categorization of individuals within a societal framework – it not only makes reference to traditional wealth and influence but also to treatment of an individual with regards to their sex, race, religion, and even appearance.

Social Stratification.

Social stratification is essentially a group phenomena.According to Ogburn and Nimkoff the process by which individuals and groups are ranked in a more or less enduring hierarchy of status is known as stratification. Melvin Tumin defines social stratification as an arrangement of any social group or society into a hierarchy of positions that are unequal with regard to power, property, social evaluation and psychic gratification. According to Lundberg a stratified society is one marked by inequality by differences among people that are evaluated by them as being lower and higher.

DIVISIONS OF SOCIAL STRATIFICATION

Social Stratification

The division and hierarchical ranking of people into layers associated with different degrees of command over material resources, power, and prestige. Divisions upon which stratification may be based include:

- *Income and wealth:* Closely related to occupational and educational status.
- *Race and ethnicity:* Many sociologists believe that racial categories are false and refer to ethnic differences instead. Race is a socially constructed set of distinctions that categorize people on the basis of biological characteristics. Ethnicity is a way of categorizing people on the basis of their shared cultural, linguistic, or national identities.
- *Gender*: The set of socially constructed meanings, practices, norms, skills, and other characteristics ascribed to people on the basis of biological sex.
- *Age*: In many societies, power, prestige, rights, and obligations are assigned to people on the basis of their age.

BASIC PRINCIPLES OF STRATIFICATION

Four basic principles of stratification:

1. Social stratification is characteristic of society, not simply a reflection of individual differences. Children born into wealth families are more likely than born into poverty to enjoy good health, achieve academically, succeed in their life's work, and live well into old age. Neither rich nor poor people are responsible for creating social stratification, yet this system shapes the lives of them all.
2. Social stratification persists over generations. In all societies parents pass their social position along to their children, so that patterns of inequality stay much the same from generation to generation. Some individual experience change in their position in the social hierarchy. For most people, social standing remains much the same over a lifetime.
3. Social stratification is universal but variable. Social stratification is found everywhere. At the same time, what is unequal and how unequal people are vary from one society to another.
4. Social stratification involves not just inequality but beliefs. Any system of inequality not only gives some people more resources than others but also defines certain arrangements as fair. Just as what is unequal differs from society to society, then so does the explanation of why people should be unequal. People with the greatest social privileges express the strongest support for their society's social stratification, while those with social resources are more likely to seek change.

Closed social system: A system of stratification where the status of person is determined by birth. There is a rigid social hierarchy. Social stratification is based on ascription and there is little social mobility. Such a system is supported by its culture. (Traditional Indian caste system).

Open social system: A social system based largely on individual achievement; therefore it permits considerable social mobility. Here strata are called as social classes. Social class is a stratum of people of similar social standing. They have their own way of life.

APPROACHES TO SOCIAL STRATIFICATION

There are two approaches to the study of stratification:

(i) Conflict Approach

According to *Karl Marx* in all stratified societies there are two major social groups: a ruling class and a subject class. The ruling class derives its power from its ownership and control of the forces of production. The ruling class exploits and oppresses the subject class. As a result there is a basic conflict of interest between the two classes. The various institutions of society such as the legal and political system are instruments of ruling class domination and serve to further its interests. Marx believed that western society developed through four main epochs-primitive communism, ancient society, feudal society and capitalist society.

Primitive communism is represented by the societies of pre-history and provides the only example of the classless society. From then all societies are divided into two major classes – master and slaves in ancient society, lords and serfs in feudal society and capitalist and wage labourers in capitalist society. Weber sees class in economic terms. He argues that classes develop in market economies in which individuals compete for economic gain. He defines a class as a group of individuals who share a similar position in market economy and by virtue of that fact receive similar economic rewards. Thus a person's class situation is basically his market situation. Those who share a similar class situation also share similar life chances. Their economic position will directly affect their chances of obtaining those things defined as desirable in their society. Weber argues that the major class division is between those who own the forces of production and those who do not. He distinguished the following class grouping in capitalist society:

- The propertied upper class
- The property less white collar workers
- The petty bourgeoisie
- The manual working class.

(ii) Functionalist Approach

Talcott Parsons believe that order, stability and cooperation in society are based on value consensus that is a general agreement by members of society concerning what is good and worthwhile. Stratification system derives from common values it follows from the existence of values that individuals will be evaluated and therefore placed in some form of rank order. Stratification is the ranking of units in a social system in accordance with the common value system. Those who perform successfully in terms of society's values will be ranked highly and they will be likely to receive a variety of rewards and will be accorded high prestige since they exemplify and personify common values. According to Kingsley Davis and Moore stratification exists in every known human society.

All social system shares certain functional prerequisites which must be met if the system is to survive and operate efficiently. One such prerequisite is role allocation and performance. This means that all roles must be filled. They will be filled by those best able to perform them. The necessary training for them is undertaken and that the roles are performed conscientiously. Davis and Moore argue that all societies need some mechanism for insuring effective role allocation and performance. This mechanism is social stratification which they see as a system which attaches unequal rewards and privileges to the positions in society. They concluded that social stratification is a device by which societies insure that the most important positions are conscientiously filled by the most qualified persons.

TYPES OF SOCIAL STRATIFICATION

Social stratification can be classified into four forms – slavery, estates, caste and class.

The Slavery System

The slavery system has existed sporadically at many times and places but there are two major examples of slavery – societies of the ancient world based upon slavery (Greek and Roman) and southern states of USA in the 18th and 19th centuries. It is an extreme form of inequality in which some individuals are owned by others as their property. The slave owner has full control including using violence over the slave.

Slavery System.

According to *H.J. Nieboer* the basis of slavery is always economic because with it emerged a kind of aristocracy which lived upon slave labour. L.T. Hobhouse defined slave as a man whom law and custom regard as the property of another. In extreme cases he is wholly without rights. He is in lower condition as compared with freemen. The slaves have no political rights he does not choose his government, he does not attend the public councils. Socially he is despised. He is compelled to work.

The Estate System

The estate system is synonymous with Feudalism. The feudal estates had three important characteristics. In the first place they were legally defined; each estate had a status with legal rights and duties, privileges and obligations. Secondly the estates represented a broad division of labor and were regarded as having definite functions. The nobility were ordained to defend all, the clergy to pray for all and the commons to provide food for all. Thirdly the feudal estates were political groups. An assembly of estates possessed political power. From this point of view the serfs did not constitute an estate until 12th century. This period saw the emergence of third estate-burghers who were a distinctive group within the system. Thus the three estates-clergy, nobility and commoners functioned like three political groups.

Gods and Heroes releases Estate System Screens.

The Caste System

The term caste is derived from the Spanish word caste meaning breed or lineage. The word caste also signifies race or kind. The Sanskrit word for caste is varna which means colour. The caste stratification of the Indian society had its origin in the chaturvarna system. According to this doctrine the Hindu society was divided into four main varnas—*Brahmins, Kashtriyas, Vaishyas* and *Shudras*.The Varna system prevalent during the Vedic period was mainly based on division of labour and occupation. The caste system owns its origin to the Varna system. Ghurye says any attempt to define caste is bound to fail because of the complexity of the phenomenon. Caste is closely connected with the Hindu philosophy and religion, custom and tradition. It is believed to have had a divine origin and sanction. It is deeply rooted social institution in India. There are more than 2800 castes and sub-castes with all their peculiarities.

According to *Risely* caste is a collection of families bearing a common name claiming a common descent from a mythical ancestor professing to follow the same hereditary calling and regarded by those who are competent to give an opinion as forming a single homogeneous community. According to *MacIver* and *Page* when status is wholly predetermined so that men are born to their lot without any hope of changing it, then the class takes the extreme form of caste. *Cooley* says that when a class is somewhat strictly hereditary we may call it caste.

Caste System.

M.N Srinivas sees caste as a segmentary system. Every caste for him divided into sub castes which are the units of endogamy whose members follow a common occupation, social and ritual life and common culture and whose members are governed by the same authoritative body viz the panchayat.According to *Bailey* caste groups are united into a system through two principles of segregation and hierarchy. For *Dumont* caste is not a form of stratification but as a special form of inequality. The major attributes of caste are the hierarchy, the separation and the division of labour.*Weber* sees caste as the enhancement and transformation of social distance into religious or strictly a magical principle. For *Adrian Mayer* caste hierarchy is not just determined by economic and political factors although these are important.

SOCIAL CLASS

Class is a complex term, in use since the late eighteenth century, and employed in many different ways. In our context classes are the more or less distinct social groupings which at any given historical period, taken as a whole, constituted British Society. Different social classes can be (and were by the classes themselves) distinguished by inequalities in such areas as power, authority, wealth, working and living conditions, life-styles, life-span, education, religion, and culture.

Early in the nineteenth century the labels “working classes” and “middle classes” were already coming into common usage. The old hereditary aristocracy, reinforced by the new gentry who owed their success to commerce, industry, and the professions, evolved into an “upper class” (its consciousness formed in large part by the Public Schools and Universities) which tenaciously maintained control over the political system, depriving not only the working classes but the middle classes of a voice in the political process. The increasingly powerful (and class conscious) middle classes, however, undertook organized agitation to remedy this situation: the passage of the Reform Act of 1832 and the abolition of the Corn Laws in 1846 were intimations of the extent to which they would ultimately be successful.

The effects of social class can be felt anywhere. Almost every aspect of society is influenced in some manner by social class.

The working classes, however, remained shut out from the political process, and became increasingly hostile not only to the aristocracy but to the middle classes as well. As the Industrial Revolution progressed there was further social stratification. Capitalists, for example, employed industrial workers who were one component of the working classes (each class included a wide range of occupations of varying status and income; there was a large gap, for example, between skilled and unskilled labor), but beneath the industrial workers was a submerged "under class" — contemporaries referred to them as the "sunken people" — which lived in poverty. In mid-century skilled workers had acquired enough power to enable them to establish Trade Unions (Socialism became an increasingly important political force) which they used to further improve their status, while unskilled workers and the underclass beneath them remained much more susceptible to exploitation, and were therefore exploited.

This basic hierarchical structure (presented here in highly oversimplified form), comprising the "upper classes," the "middle classes", the "Working Classes" (with skilled laborers at one extreme and unskilled at the other), and the impoverished "Under Class," remained relatively stable despite periodic (and frequently violent) upheavals, and despite the Marxist view of the inevitability of class conflict, at least until the outbreak of World War I. A modified class structure clearly remains in existence today.

DEFINITION

A status hierarchy in which individuals and groups are classified on the basis of esteem and prestige acquired mainly through economic success and accumulation of wealth. Social class may also refer to any particular level in such a hierarchy. Four common social classes informally recognized in many societies are: (1) Upper class, (2) Middle class, (3) Working class, and the (4) Lower class.

MEASURING SOCIAL CLASS

Subjective Method

Ask people what their social class is.

This approach has limitations. For example there may be just denial of social class. Similarly people may classify themselves by aspiration. But the most commonly observed situation is where everybody belongs to middle class. Is this method useful?

Reputational Method

We ask the informants to classify others. They do it by using their own criteria.

Objective Method

Develop some objective criteria so that the others know exactly what measurements were made. If others like to verify they could do so. The components of these criteria could be the income, education, occupation (prestige), and other wealth related items.

FUNCTIONS OF SOCIAL CLASS

Social class determines the life chances of an individual: It implies that the social class determines the probabilities concerning the fate we can expect in life. From before one is born until one is dead, opportunities and rewards are affected by class position. Poor nutrition for the mother may affect the health and vigor of the fetus before birth, while poverty thereafter continues to handicap the poor. The lower class person is not only likely to die prematurely but will also endure more days of illness during a lifetime. Even the poor are more exposed to accidents.

Social class influences physical and mental health: Underlying the differential death rates is unequal access to medical care and nutrition. Medical care is expensive, and even with government-funded plans for the poor; the higher classes receive better treatment.

Social class also affects mental health: Lower class experiences stress from unemployment, dirty and dangerous work, the threat of eviction, expenses of life, and so on. People higher up the social class ladder also experience stress in daily life, but their stress is generally less and their coping resources greater. Their class position gives them greater control over their lives, a key to good mental health.

Social class and family life: Social class influences the mate selection, age at marriage, number of children, child rearing patterns, women empowerment, educational aspirations and achievements. Lower class children supposed to be obedient at home and at work, whereas middle class children are trained to be creative, independent, and tolerant. The vision of children about future varies by social class.

Social class and education/employment opportunities: Education increases as one goes up the social class ladder. It is not just the amount of education but also the type of education. Public schools are for the poor and private schools are for the rich. In private schools the children are trained to take commanding role in society. With better qualifications from prestigious institutions children from affluent families have better employment opportunities.

Social class and crime and the criminal justice system: The upper and lower classes have different styles of crime. The treatment by the judiciary and by the police also varies by social class.

Social class and lifestyles: Social class determines the lifestyle of the people. In the current age 'symbols' and markers related to consumption are playing an ever-greater role in daily life. Individual identities are structured to a greater extent around lifestyle choices – such as how to dress, what to eat, how to care one's body, and where to relax. One is distinguished on the basis of cultural tastes and leisure pursuits. They are aided in process by the proliferation of 'need merchants' (advertisers, marketers, fashion designers, style consultants, interior designers, web-page designers) involved in influencing cultural tastes and promoting lifestyle choices among the ever-increasing community of consumers. Therefore class divisions can be linked to distinctive lifestyle and consumption patterns. Although in the modern societies have become consumer societies. Consumer society is a mass society where class differences are overridden. All watch the same programs; all shop at the same plazas, yet class differences become intensified through variations in lifestyles and taste.

THEORIES OF CLASS AND STRATIFICATION

The ideas developed by Karl Marx and Max Weber forms the basis of most sociological analysis of class and stratification. Broadly theories have been divided into conflict and functionalist perspectives and these two will be the focus of our discussion.

STRATIFICATION AND CONFLICT

Social conflict perspective argues that, rather than benefiting society as a whole, social stratification benefits some people at the expense of others. This analysis draws heavily on the ideas of Karl Marx, with contributions from Max Weber.

KARL MARX: CLASS AND CONFLICT

Marx (1818-1883) argued that the distinctions people often make between themselves – such as clothing, speech, education, or relative slavery – are superficial matters that camouflage the only real significant dividing line: people either (the bourgeoisie) own the means of production or they (the proletariat) work for those who do. This is the only distinction that counts, for these two classes make up modern society.

Means of production refer to the sources by which people gain their livelihood. Hence people's relationship to means of production determines their social class. Before the rise of modern industry, the means of production consisted primarily of land and the instruments used to tend crops or pastoral animals. In such societies the two main classes were those who owned the land (aristocrats, gentry or slave-holders) and those actively engaged in producing from it (serfs, slaves and free peasantry).

In modern industrial societies, factories, offices, machinery and the wealth or capital needed to buy them have become more important. The two main classes are those who own these new means of production – the industrialists or capitalists called as Bourgeoisie (boorzhwahze) – and those who earn their living by selling their labor to them – the property-less working class called as proletariat.

According to Marx in Das Kapital three great classes exist in modern societies: The owners of mere labor power, the owners of capital, and the landlords, whose respective sources of income are wages, profit, and ground-rent.

The relationship between classes is an exploitative one. In feudal societies, exploitation often took the form of the direct transfer of produce from the peasantry to the aristocracy. Serfs were compelled to give a certain proportion of their production to their aristocratic masters, or had to work for certain number of days in the lord's fields to produce crops consumed by the lord.

In modern industrial societies, the source of exploitation is less obvious, and Marx devoted much attention to trying to clarify its nature. In the course of the working day workers produce much more than is actually needed by employers to repay the cost of hiring them. (Value of product of labor – value of labor = the surplus value) This surplus value is the source of profit, which capitalists are able to put to their own use. The labor becomes a commodity. Wealth is produced on a scale far beyond anything seen before, but workers have little access to the wealth their labor creates.

The capitalist becomes richer while the proletariat gets poorer. Marx used the term pauperization to describe the process by which the working class grows increasingly impoverished in relation to the capitalist class. Even if the workers become more affluent in absolute terms, the gap separating them from the capitalist class continues to stretch ever wider. These inequalities between the capitalist and working class were not strictly economic in nature. Work itself becomes dull and oppressive in the modern factories resulting in dehumanizing the work environment.

The capitalist class draws its strength from more than the operation of the economy. Through the family, opportunity and wealth are passed down from generation to generation. Moreover, the legal system defends this practice through the law of inheritance. Similarly the exclusive schools bring children of the elite together, encouraging informal social ties that will benefit them throughout their lives. In this way capitalist society reproduces the class structure in each new generation.

Marx saw great disparities in wealth and power arising from this productive system, which made class conflict inevitable. Over time, Marx believed, oppression and misery would drive the working majority (labor class) to organize, challenge the system, and ultimately overthrow the capitalist system. Such a class struggle has been part of the history of societies. According to Marx; through this revolution the capitalist system is replaced by socialist system resulting in a classless society. In such a society, humans will be able to live in a world where they are not prevented from realizing their full potential by the constraints of class societies. In a classless society the principle of "from each according to his ability, to each according to his need" comes into operation.

MAX WEBER

Max Weber (1864-1920) built his approach to stratification on the analysis developed by Marx, but he modified and elaborated it. Like Marx, Weber regarded society as characterized by conflicts over power and resources. Yet where Marx saw polarized class relations and economic issues at the heart of all conflict, Weber developed a more complex, multidimensional view of society.

Social stratification is not simply a matter of class, according to Weber, but is also shaped by two other aspects: *status* and *power*. These three overlapping elements of stratification produce an enormous number of possible positions (inequality) within society, rather than the rigid bipolar model, which Marx proposed. According to Weber class divisions derive not only from control or lack of control of the means of production, but from economic differences, which have nothing directly to do with property. Such resources include especially the skills and credentials, or qualifications, which affect the types of job people, are able to obtain.

Weber believed that an individual's *market position* strongly influences his or her 'life chances'. The market positions (capacities) people have in terms of the skills they bring to the labor market as employees, explains the rewards they will receive. Where people have good market capacity they will have very good *life chances:* these chances include income, perks, and pensions together with less tangible benefits such as security of job, pleasant working environment and considerable autonomy at work.

Those in managerial or professional occupations earn more, and have more favorable conditions of work, for example, than people in blue-collar jobs. The qualifications they possess, such as degrees, diplomas and the skills they have acquired, make them more 'marketable' than others without such qualifications.

Managers of corporations *control* the means of production although they do not *own* them. If managers can control property for their own benefit – awarding themselves huge bonuses and magnificent perks – it makes no practical difference that they do not own the property that they so generously use for their own benefit.

Status in Weber's theory refers to differences between social groups in the social honor or prestige they are accorded by others. Presently status is being expressed through people's *styles of life.* Markers and symbols of status—such as housing, dress, manner of speech, occupation – all help to shape an individual's social standing in the eyes of others. People sharing the same status form a community in which there is a sense of shared identity.

While Marx believed that status distinctions are the result of class divisions in society, Weber argued that status often varies independently of class divisions. Possession of wealth normally tends to confer high status, but there are many exceptions. Olympic gold medalists, for example, may not own property, yet they may have very high prestige. Property and prestige is not one way street: although property can bring prestige, prestige can also bring property.

Power, the third element of social class, is the ability to control others, even against their wishes. Weber agreed with Marx that property is a major source of power, but he added that it is not the only source. With time, industrial societies witness the growth of the bureaucratic state. This expansion of government and other types of formal organizations means that power gains importance in the stratification system.

Party formation is an important aspect of power, and can influence stratification independently of class and status. Party defines a group of individuals who work together because they have common backgrounds, aims or interests. Party can be influenced by class but can also influence the economic circumstance of party members and thereby their class. Party membership cuts across class differences. There are parties based on religious affiliations and nationalist ideals and may include the 'haves' and 'have-nots'.

Weber anticipated the proliferation of classes, with a new class of white-collar employees, administrators, technicians and civil servants, who are growing in number and importance.

Property relations are important (Marx) but the market position and marketability is decisive in determining an individual's class position.

Weber rejected Marx's view that the workers (or employees) have nothing but their labor to sell to the highest bidder. The reality is that:

- Workers possess skills.
- The distribution of skills can be controlled (keep it scarce).
- Increase skill marketability.

SOCIAL CLASS AS SUBCULTURE

"The language, beliefs, values, norms, behaviors, and the material objects that are possessed by people and are passed on from one generation to the next" is the usual definition of culture. Within the broad culture we also come across subcultures where a group displays distinct patterns of behavior and the related values, norms, beliefs, and material possessions. These subcultures may relate to an ethnic group, an occupational group, an age group, and even to a social class. Therefore, it can be assumed that each social class has a subculture with a system of behavior, a set of values, and a way of life.

The subculture of a social class serves to adapt people to the life style they lead and to prepare their children to assume their class status. The passing of sub-cultural patterns of behaviour and the related values and norms to the next generation takes place through the process of socialization.

Notwithstanding with some overlapping and some exceptions, it remains true that the average middle class child has socialization very different from that of the average lower class child. Let us take just one aspect of socialization – those experiences that shape ambition, education, and work habits – and see how they differ between the two social class worlds.

Typical upper middle class children live in a class subculture where they are surrounded by educated persons who are ambitious, who go to work even when they do not feel like it, and who struggle to attain success. They are acquainted with the achievements of their ancestors, relatives, and friends. It is normal for them to assume that they too are going to accomplish something in the world.

When they go to school they find its culture close to their family culture. The teacher speaks similar language, the material in the books is reflective of their culture, and there are many other aspects of the environment that are familiar to the child.

"Study hard so you can do well and become a success some day," the advice given by the teachers makes sense. Their parents echo the same words; meanwhile they see people like themselves (brothers, sisters, relatives, acquaintances) who are actually completing educations and moving on into promising careers. For most of the middle class children, to grow up means to complete an advanced education and launch a career.

Lower class children grow up in a class subculture where scarcely any one is educated, and has a steady job for long. In their world meals are haphazard and irregular. They marry early in age and usually have large number of children. Many people sleep three or four in a bed. These children are often not in school and if they do go to school, they often go unwashed and unfed. In school they are likely to be disoriented by coming across people coming from middle class families (the students and the teachers). Very soon they conclude that the school is a prison. They learn little. The school often abandons any serious effort to teach them by branding them as "discipline problems." They receive little reinforcement for paying attention to studies. Even in the environment many children may be out of school, either doing nothing or engaged in some work. For them school may not be a stepping-stone to a career. Since school does not motivate them to study so they drop out early. The horizon of ambitions seldom extends the next week.

The children in varying social classes grow up in a different human capital as well as cultural capital. From growing up in a culture of poverty, the poor, in general, learn to accept their poverty. The poor expect failure, just as people born to affluence expect success. The expectation of failure can deprive the impoverished individuals of the confidence they need to spend their human capital. The expectation of success encourages affluent individuals to maximize their human capital.

As part of the socialization process, social class penetrates our consciousness, shaping our ideas of life and our proper place in society. When the rich look around, they sense superiority and control over destiny. In contrast, the poor see defeat, and a buffeting by unpredictable forces. People tend to see the effects of social class on their lives.

One consequence of facing emergency after emergency and not having enough resources to meet them – and seeing the future as more of the same – is the lack of deferred gratification, giving up things in the present for the sake of greater gains in the future. It is difficult to practice this middle class virtue if one does not have the surplus it requires. Any savings are gobbled up by the emergencies faced by the poor, so any saving for future was fruitless. The only thing that made sense from this perspective was to enjoy what they could at the moment. Immediate gratification was not the cause of their poverty, but its consequence. Cause and consequence loop together, for their immediate gratification, in turn, helped perpetuate their poverty.

Culture of poverty (concept given by Oscar Lewis in mid sixties) assumes that the values and behaviors of the poor make them fundamentally different from other people that these factors largely are responsible for their poverty, and that parents perpetuate poverty across generations by passing these characteristics to their children. Poor form a subculture in which, as a result of their common experiences, they have developed certain attitudes and behavior patterns which have been transmitted from parent to child.

Critics of culture of poverty argue that the "expecting to fail" argument amount to blaming the victim. By blaming the poor for their own poverty, culture of poverty theories divert attention from the social, structural and cultural conditions that are ultimately responsible for poverty. Critics claim that the poor, in general tend to be as success-oriented as the affluent, if not for themselves then for their children. The difference between the poor and the affluent, therefore, lies mainly in their relative access to educational and occupational opportunities to demonstrate their human capital.

SOCIAL CLASS AND HEALTH

Social class is a complex issue that may involve status, wealth, culture, background and employment. The relationship between class and ill health is not simple. There are a number of different influences on health, some of which include social class. This is demonstrated by multilevel analysis (a method of assessing health inequalities using several different factors) which shows health inequalities even between households living in the same street. In 1943, Sigerist, following the line of Virchow, wrote, "The task of medicine is to promote health, to prevent disease, to treat the sick when prevention is broken down and to rehabilitate the people after they have been cured. These are highly social functions and we must look at medicine as basically a social science."

There has always been an association between health and social class and, despite the welfare state and the improvement in health in all sections of societies over the years, this discrepancy remains. It applies to all aspects of health, including expectation of life, infant and maternal mortality and general level of health. Whilst the failure to close the social gap is a disgrace to some, others would claim that so long as these parameters are improving in all levels of society there is no cause for concern. Despite 62 years of 'The National Health Service', there remain marked differences in all parameters of health across the social classes. Women continue to live longer than men but the gap is closing. Based on 2007-2009 mortality rates, a man aged 65 could expect to live another 17.6 years and a woman aged 65 another 20.2 years.

The greatest influences on the improvement in health with longer expectancy of life, lower infant mortality, etc. have been not so much medical discoveries as improved social conditions. One study in America found that, despite improvements in cancer detection and treatment, disparities in cancer mortality rates are chiefly related to race and social class.

SOCIAL CLASS AND GENDER

Gender identity is the gender a person self-identifies as. The concept of being a woman is considered to have more challenges, due to society not only viewing women as a social category but also as a felt sense of self, a culturally conditioned or constructed subjective identity.

Social identity refers to the common identification with a collectivity or social category which creates a common culture among participants concerned. According to social identity theory, an important component of the self-concept is derived from memberships in social groups and categories; this is demonstrated by group processes and how inter-group relationships impact significantly on individuals' self perception and behaviors. The groups to which people belong will therefore provide their members with the definition of who they are and how they should behave in the social sphere.

Categorizing males and females into social roles creates binaries in which individuals feel they have to be at one end of a linear spectrum and must identify themselves as man or woman. Globally, communities interpret biological differences between men and women to create a set of social expectations that define the behaviors that are "appropriate" for men and women and determine women's and men's different access to rights, resources, power in society and even health behaviors. Although the specific nature and degree of these differences vary from one society to the next, they typically favor men, creating an imbalance in power and gender inequalities in all countries.

The World Health Organization defines gender as the result of socially constructed ideas about the behavior, actions, and roles a particular sex performs. The beliefs, values and attitude taken up and exhibited by them is as per the agreeable norms of the society and the personal opinions of the person is not taken into the primary consideration of assignment of gender and imposition of gender roles as per the assigned gender. Intersections and crossing of the prescribed boundaries have no place in the arena of the social construct of the term "gender."

The assignment of gender involves taking into account the physiological and biological attributes assigned by nature followed by the imposition of the socially constructed conduct. The social label of being classified into one or the other sex is obligatory to the medical stamp on the birth certificate. The cultural traits typically coupled to a particular sex finalize the assignment of gender and the biological differences which play a role in classifying either sex is interchangeable with the definition of gender within the social context.

In this context, the socially constructed rules are at a cross road with the assignment of a particular gender to a person. Gender ambiguity deals with having the freedom to choose, manipulate and create a personal niche within any defined socially constructed code of conduct while gender fluidity is outlawing all the rules of cultural gender assignment. It does not accept the prevalence of two rigidly defined genders "Female and Male" and believes in freedom to choose any kind of gender with no rules, no defined boundaries and no fulfilling of expectations associated with any particular gender.

RACE, ETHNICITY AND CLASS

Race, ethnicity and class intrude not only in political and social considerations, but also in economic concerns. Often the terms are disguised by ingenuously constructed euphemisms such as "quotas" or "set asides" or "minority affairs" or "affirmative action" or "diversity" or "multi-cultural."

Race and other large-scale groupings can also influence class standing. The association of particular ethnic groups with class statuses is common in many societies. As a result of conquest or internal ethnic differentiation, a ruling class is often ethnically homogenous and particular races or ethnic groups in some societies are legally or customarily restricted to occupying particular class positions. Which ethnicities are considered as belonging to high or low classes varies from society to society. In modern societies strict legal links between ethnicity and class have been drawn, such as in apartheid, the caste system in Africa, and in the position of the Burakumin in Japanese society.

Throughout India and Asia ethnic groups are continually challenging the political order, peacefully when they can, and militarily when they must. Prime Minister Rajiv Gandhi's assassination resulted from ethnic Tamil hostility to Indian intervention in Sri Lanka.

According to the *Regional Lifestyle Survey*, of all demographic factors, residents' ethnicity and social class best predict what they choose to do with their leisure time and how much importance they attach to local cultural facilities.

A recent analysis of the Survey by Culture West Midlands has shown that ethnicity is the factor that best predicts the extent to which residents' choose where they live based on proximity to cultural facilities, and their likelihood of visiting the countryside. Respondents who described themselves as 'Asian or British Asian' were 36% less likely than 'White' respondents to have cited cultural facilities as important to residential choice, and 31% less likely than 'White' respondents to regularly visit the countryside.

Overall, ethnicity proved to be the best predictor of non-participation in cultural activities amongst residents. When compared with their white co-respondents, both Asian and Black respondents were found to be over 1.5 times more likely to be non-participants in activities including trips to arts or cultural venues, country parks and leisure and sport centres.

After ethnicity, socio-economic class was found to be the most significant predictor of cultural participation patterns. Compared with socio-economic group A, all other socio-economic groups were found to be significantly more likely to be non-participants.

SOCIAL CLASS AND DOMESTIC VIOLENCE

Domestic violence occurs in all ages, races, genders and social classes. Domestic violence is a learned pattern of physical, verbal, sexual and/or emotional behaviors in which one person in a relationship uses force and intimidation to dominate or control the other person. The partners may be married or not married; heterosexual, gay or lesbian; living together, separated or dating.

It is a critical public health problem that has devastating physical-psychological effects on human beings across all societies and classes in the world. It destroys men-women, children and families all over the earth. Women have been found to be more vulnerable to domestic abuse. They become victims of physical, mental and sexual abuse by their partners and ex partners, their families, acquaintances, lovers and even strangers. This is on account of their lower economic and social status and weakness in terms of physical strength and endurance. They also become very dependent on men due to their children and the patriarchal system of society and submit to abuse quietly.

Indian law now recognizes the legal rights of partners who are into live in relationships. All humans whether men, women or children should be made aware that they are entitled to live their lives in a safe and healthy atmosphere, and that they should conduct the business of their lives without the fear of physical, sexual and emotional abuse. Domestic violence requires to be tackled very seriously as a fact of human life and a severe health hazard to human beings.

Domestic violence can destroy the abuser, the victim, their children and other family members repeatedly on various levels. The destructive effect of this form of abuse takes its toll on human health and productivity in terms of economic, social and psychological well being. Violence can also travel from generation to generation in the form of stress, anxiety and personality disorders. It is the duty of each individual to work on the community level to recognize and counter this menace in his own and other families.

Physical assault, spousal abuse, social humiliation, economic abuse, homicide, elder abuse, child battering, child abuse, partner abuse, woman battering, man battering, date violence, courtship violence, same sex violence, sexual assault, marital rape, acquaintance rape, stranger rape are all deadly manifestations of domestic violence.

SOCIAL CLASS AND RELIGION

Rich and poor express their religion in different ways. The *lower classes* are more likely than affluent groups to pray in private, believe in the doctrines of their faith, and have intense religious experiences (Demerath 1965, Davidson 1977); the *middle* and *upper classes* are more likely to attend worship services and take part in church organizations and activities. Stark (1972) suggests that the poor show greater religiousness in those aspects of faith that serve as a relief for suffering; the middle and upper classes participate in religious activities that help confirm the legitimacy of their claim to high status.

Religious groups can be differentiated according to the socioeconomic standing of their members. The first comprehensive studies of denominational socioeconomic rankings were conducted in the 1940s. These early studies showed that colonial *mainline Protestants*, Jews, and Unitarians were located in the upper socioeconomic ranks; *moderate Protestants* (such as Methodists and Lutherans) were located in the middle;

and Catholics and evangelical Protestants occupied the bottom ranks. With a few exceptions, this relative ranking persists today. Groups representative of the colonial mainline continue to rank at the upper levels in terms of education, income, and occupational prestige, whereas sectarian bodies such as the Churches of God rank much lower on socioeconomic indicators.

However, there has been some change in denominational socioeconomic rankings in the last 50 years. The greatest status change has occurred among Roman Catholics, who moved from the bottom socioeconomic levels to the middle ranks during the post-World War II era. Catholics in the 1940s ranked below Protestants on socioeconomic indicators (Cantril 1943), but by the 1960s Catholic-Protestant socioeconomic differences were negligible. Jews well positioned during the 1940s, have improved their socioeconomic standing during the post-World War II years and now rank at the top in terms of socioeconomic status. Mormons also have experienced social and economic gains. Over the long term, Methodists have shown the most dramatic gains, rising from sectarian origins in the nineteenth century to middle-class status by the twentieth.

SOCIAL CLASS AND UNEMPLOYMENT

In addressing the issue of differential responsiveness, attention was focused on the interaction between unemployment and social class in their impact on psychological distress. While rather weak support for the hypothesis of differential vulnerability was found among women, our examination of the impact of husband's unemployment provided no evidence leading in this direction. Among men unemployment actually had a stronger impact for men in higher social classes. The major factors leading to social class differences in psychological distress are greater exposure to unemployment and economic deprivation.

An economy with high unemployment is not using all of the resources, specifically labour, available to it. Since it is operating below its production possibility frontier, it could have higher output if all the workforce were usefully employed. However, there is a trade-off between economic efficiency and unemployment: if the frictionally unemployed accepted the first job they were offered, they would be likely to be operating at below their skill level, reducing the economy's efficiency.

During a long period of unemployment, workers can lose their skills, causing a loss of human capital. Being unemployed can also reduce the life expectancy of workers by about 7 years.

High unemployment can encourage xenophobia and protectionism as workers fear that foreigners are stealing their jobs. Efforts to preserve existing jobs of domestic and native workers include legal barriers against "outsiders" who want jobs, obstacles to immigration, and/or tariffs and similar trade barriers against foreign competitors.

High unemployment can also cause social problems such as crime; if people do not have as much disposable income as before, then it is very likely that crime levels within the economy will increase.

SOCIAL CLASS AND LIFESTYLE

Lifestyle is a term to describe the way a person lives, which was originally coined by Austrian psychologist *Alfred Adler* in 1929. The current broader sense of the word dates from 1961. A set of behaviors, and the senses of self and belonging which these behaviors represent, are collectively used to define a given lifestyle. The term is defined more broadly when used in politics, marketing, and publishing. It is a characteristic bundle of behaviors that makes sense to both others and oneself in a given time and place, including social relations, consumption, entertainment, and dress. The behaviors and practices within lifestyles are a mixture of habits, conventional ways of doing things, and reasoned actions

A lifestyle typically also reflects an individual's attitudes, values or worldview. Therefore, a lifestyle is a means of forging a sense of self and to create cultural symbols that resonate with personal identity. Not all aspects of a lifestyle are entirely voluntaristic. Surrounding social and technical systems can constrain the lifestyle choices available to the individual and the symbols she/he is able to project to others and the self.

The lines between personal identity and the everyday doings that signal a particular lifestyle become blurred in modern society. For example, "green lifestyle" means holding beliefs and engaging in activities that consume fewer resources and produce less harmful waste (i.e., a smaller carbon footprint), and deriving a sense of self from holding these beliefs and engaging in these activities. Some commentators argue that, in modernity, the cornerstone of lifestyle construction is consumption behavior, which offers the possibility to create and further individualize the self with different products or services that signal different ways of life.

Relationships and attitudes to family, school and peers in middle adolescence at 15–16 years of age are first examined, and distinctive patterns of integration within these contexts are identified. The interconnections between these broader aspects of lifestyle, social class and individual health behaviours are then examined. Mid-adolescent patterns of social integration are found to have a clear structural basis, and most importantly, they anticipate social position in later adolescence at 17–18 years of age. It is also found that such patterns of integration into the family, peer and school contexts are linked to subsequent health related behaviours and to self assessed health in later adolescence, and that these links are independent of the young person's social class background. Thus, we conclude that behavioural-cultural lifestyle factors, when these are located within a broader social context, provide a clear and plausible mechanism for indirect health selection in adolescence.

Socio-Economic Factors in Modern India

Introduction: *The Post-independence Years, Devaluation, Liberalization, Consequences, India Today.* ***Socio-Economic Factors in India and China:*** *China National People's Congress' 12th Five-Year Plan, India – Foreign Investment and Jugaad, Foreign Direct, Investment (FDI) in India, Jugaad in India.* ***Comparison China and India:*** *Economic Growth and Development in China and India, Economic Development Lessons.*

INTRODUCTION

India, a land of rich culture, is the second most populous country of the world. And area wise, it is the seventh largest nation. Our Indian economy has undergone a tremendous change, with the implementation of a series of economic reforms.

These reforms focused attention on deregulating the country and inducing foreign investments. Eventually, it paved way for India occupying a position among the top countries in the fast growing Asia Pacific region. India has the largest democracy in the world and has experienced stability, since its. India's political institutions have encouraged the growth of an open society, where people can express themselves freely. It is truly an example of a free economy.

When the talk is about the economy of India, it can be undoubtedly said that it provides a complete security to its foreign investors. It promotes a transparent environment that includes a free press and a proper legal and accounting system. India has a competitive and dynamic private sector that forms the backbone of India's economic activities. It also accounts for more than 75% of India's Gross Domestic Product. It has a lot of scope for joint ventures and mergers.

India has established itself as one of the most aggressively emerging markets of the world, by harnessing the talent and skills of its managerial and technical manpower. India's abundant workforce provides it a competitive edge in the global market.

The state in its earlier avatar failed to bridge the socio-economic gap between 'modern' and 'traditional' sectors. The duality persists in the current regime of market-led prosperity.

India's economy is vast and varied and consists of traditional village farming, modern agriculture, handicrafts, a wide distinctive range of modern industries, and a large number of support services. Government has become more liberal and has reduced its control on foreign trade and investment and is heading its way towards privatizing the domestic sector.

Since 1990, the economy of India has witnessed a decent growth rate of 6% and has been successful in overcoming poverty by about 10%. The strength of India lies in its vast pool of educated and skilled citizens. But, the weakness of India is the continuing public-sector budget deficit, which is nearly 10% of GDP.

In this time of sluggish growth, India's economy continues to grow at a 6.8 percent clip. The size of the Indian economy is projected to outstrip Germany's by 2025, and if present trends continue, India will be the third largest economy in the world by 2035, lagging only the United States and China. Because of the combination of rapid growth and an expanding population, economists regard India as an emerging economic global superpower.

THE POST-INDEPENDENCE YEARS

The rise of the Indian economy is one of the most important economic developments of our day. To put it in context, one needs to start by considering how India gained independence. The year was 1947, and it was the culmination of a long struggle between the British Government and the Indian independence movement. That movement was led by Gandhi, but his most important lieutenant was Nehru. The two had very different views on a number of questions, and in particular on economic issues. Gandhi believed in a very simple life, while Nehru had absorbed the doctrines of British socialism. The British socialist movement at that time aimed to build up a modern economy as rapidly as possible.

India in 1947 was characterized by very low per capita income. There were a lot of people, so there was always a big GDP, but per capita income was very low. In some ways India had a fully developed capitalist economy, and it had some of the oldest capitalist institutions in Asia, such as the Bombay Stock Exchange, founded in 1875. So there was a modern economy, but it was very thin. There was a manufacturing sector, but it did not cover many industries. There was even a steel industry and a relatively strong textile industry, but these were limited. It was predominantly a subsistence economy. Most of the villages at the time did not even have road connections. They were connected only by tracks to the outside world. They were not part of the market economy.

During the independence struggle in the final days of the war, Nehru was put in jail, along with a number of his Congress colleagues. In a matter of weeks, they drew up a consensus which has been called subsequently the Indian Congress Consensus. At that time the Indian Congress absolutely dominated India, so what the Indian Congress thought went. There was certainly a widespread agreement on the need to develop, to create an industrial revolution, to grow rapidly, and to build a modern economy. This would involve moving agricultural workers to the cities, which it was argued – this was a popular line of thought in the early days of development economics-would not really cost anything, because the marginal products of those agricultural workers was negligible anyway. They really were not contributing in the countryside. In any event, with a little agricultural modernization, it would be possible to increase output.

It was generally agreed that society should be based on collective action, not capitalist acquisitiveness. Basically, the view was that the state ought to seize control of the economy and ought not be run by the capitalist sector. Consequently, for the best part of forty years after independence, growth was slow. But the "License Raj" developed very quickly. Everything needed permission. If you owned a business that officially was in the private sector, in order to expand you needed a license. You could not get foreign exchange to import until you had the industrial license to expand. The government effectively controlled everything through a series of interlocking controls of that type.

Even the banks were nationalized in due course. The banking system was one of the later things to be nationalized, in the late 1960s and early 1970s, but even then this philosophy prevailed. The system was dominated as in many developing countries by the idea of import substitution, the idea that you would get expanding markets for industrial goods essentially by producing at home things that had formerly been imported. That was because you simply could not import most goods.

There was on the other hand continuous macroeconomic discipline. Unlike many developing countries in Latin America, or in Africa, or even in Southeast Asia (such as Indonesia), India never suffered from hyper-inflation. India never went above about 20 percent a year. Instead, where the macroeconomic problems showed up was in balance-of-payment pressures. The fact that one required a license to import just about everything was strangling the economy.

DEVALUATION

Finally, in 1966, a year before the UK's famous devaluation, came India's. An attempt was made to undertake some liberalization of the economy at that time, and India sought U.S. aid. But since India would not support the Vietnam War, President Johnson withheld aid. So the envisaged flow of aid that would help make it possible to liberalize the economy was not there, and India went back to slow growth for another 15-20 years.

Another feature of this period was that the educational system was very skewed. Illiteracy continued, and in particular female illiteracy, which is still quite common in India. But at the same time the elites have a very good educational system, typified by the Indian Institutes of Technology and Management, which were established in this period to cater to the elites. The education they received has been important in the subsequent development of the country's economy. But in the early years, the economy grew rather slowly, at what became known as the Hindu rate of growth, merely 3-4 percent per year. At the time, the Indian population was growing at 2.5 percent per year. If GDP is only going up 3.5 percent a year, that does not give much scope for an improvement in living standards and cutting poverty, the ultimate objectives of economic growth. In fact, there was actually an increase in poverty in India in the middle of that period. After reasonably respectable growth in the immediate post-independence years, by the early 1970s it had really slowed down to about 3 percent.

LIBERALIZATION

Then something changed. Initially we did not realize that it had changed. Dani Rodrik, a well-known growth economist at Harvard, and Arvind Subramanian, an Indian economist at the IMF, continuing a line of work pioneered by American economist Brad Delong, have argued that the acceleration in Indian growth really came long before 1991, which is from when reformers had liked to date it. They claim there is evidence that growth speeded up in the mid-1980s. However, up until then, you can explain away the faster growth rate as a consequence simply of catching up, because there was a severe recession in 1979, due to the second oil shock. In any event, by the mid-1990s one has indisputable evidence that the Indian economy had moved to a faster growth rate, following the first, limited reforms.

One example of liberalization was known as "broad-banding." In the earlier period, if a private-sector entrepreneur was given permission to produce something, he produced exactly that and nothing else. Broad-banding meant that as long as he did not use more raw materials, he was entitled to make something else. What you were entitled to produce was broad-banded, or extended. And that in itself led to an important liberalization of the economy.

Another example is that the trucking industry was deregulated in the mid-1980s, which meant that people who owned trucks, still in the private sector, were allowed to go out to bid in order to take loads from one part of the country to another, at prices they could choose. This was successful in that trucking performance improved and prices were lowered as a result of competition, instead of going up, as those who had opposed liberalization had predicted. Toward the end of the 1980s, even though exports were growing rapidly, balance-of-payment pressures were beginning to rise and the budget deficit was increasing. These two things together led to an important crisis in 1991, at the time of the general election. Despite the debate as to whether there had already been some liberalization, 1991 marks the big liberalization of the Indian economy.

Manmohan Singh happened to be the finance minister at the time. When he was a young man at Cambridge in the 1950s, he had written an article that argued that it was a mistake to rely on import substitution, but despite that he had gone back to India, entered the civil service, and been a loyal civil servant implementing these sorts of policies all those years. But when he became finance minister and was presented with the challenge of finding a way out of the crisis, he set about undertaking a major liberalization of the economy. The macroeconomic part of the package was quite orthodox. After all, if you have a balance-of-payment crisis, if you run out of reserves, you have to fix the balance of payments in a hurry. You really cannot start revaluing the exchange rate or spending more, you have to do orthodox things like cutting expenditures, raising taxes, devaluing the exchange rate, and implementing monetary restriction.

The interesting part of the package was the microeconomic liberalization, which was adamantly against the Indian tradition. There had been the very limited liberalization in the 1980s, but the main Indian ethos had remained very statist, hostile to the market economy, capitalism, and free enterprise. Singh swept away the controls of the License Raj, the requirement that one obtain permission from the Capital Issues Committee to raise new money, and the ban on foreign direct investment. So investment was gradually liberalized, as was trade. The initial moves were to get rid of the quantitative trade restrictions. Tariffs were gradually reduced to the point of normal levels, though India's still a fairly protectionist country. Then there was an effort to modernize the tax system. In 1991 about one-quarter of all the tax revenue came out of trade taxes, which would be lost with trade liberalization. Tax rates between one product and another were equalized, again gradually, over the course of the 1990s.

There was the beginning of divesting the public sector of its ownership of enterprises. India was not adventurous in this respect. It certainly did not do anything like the mass privatization in the former Soviet economies. It pursued disinvestment, which meant selling minority shares in enterprises on the stock market. You do not pay a lot of money if all you think you are going to buy is a minority share in a state-owned enterprise. This is not a good way of raising money or changing management incentives. So India was slow in divesting, but the program was started, and it's gradually built up steam. There has been much more willingness to contemplate private enterprises competing against state-owned enterprises in recent years.

Finally, there was financial reform. Where India used to have one stock exchange, which still operated pretty much like in the nineteenth century, today it has a modern stock exchange running parallel to that one. The Capital Issues Committee was abolished, and companies were allowed to borrow freely. Where the banking system at one stage had to lend over 60 percent of its deposits to the government, and most of the others had to be lent as the government dictated, now it has a large degree of freedom to lend where commercial considerations dictate. Today India has a rather impressive financial system by developing-country standards.

CONSEQUENCES

Growth did not in fact accelerate much from the 1980s average to the 1990s average. But the 1980s ended in a crisis because some factors were clearly unsustainable, and although some of us worry about some features of the present economy, there's no suggestion that the present growth rate is unsustainable. So it may have been only slightly faster, but it was sustainable. The growth translated into a fairly substantial fall in poverty over the course of the 1990s. The 1997 East Asian financial crisis really stopped growth in its tracks in many countries. Those countries, some of them more voluntarily than others, had all liberalized their capital accounts, allowing money to flow in and out fairly liberally. In contrast, in India, if you brought money in, you could take it out again, but domestic Indians were not allowed to take their money out freely, and India in any event had not borrowed a great deal. So it was not vulnerable to the 1997 crisis.

In the second half of the 1990s one also began seeing the rise of the IT sector. Two explanations are given for why that sector became so successful. The first is that the bureaucrats did not notice what was happening until it had already happened, so they could not really interfere and put up a web of regulations and restrictions. That's probably overly harsh. The other is that the government did some things right. Its founding of the Indian Institutes led to a flow of highly qualified manpower, many of whom found vocation in the IT sector. India at long last found its niche in the world economy, which wasn't in exporting manufactures, like the East Asian countries, but instead was in the services sector, and IT in particular.

One important consequence of the 1990s is the sharpening of regional differences within India. The fast-growing states were in the south and west: Maharashtra, Haryana, Delhi, Gujarat, etc. The large states of the Ganghetic plain—Bihar, Uttar Pradesh, Madhya Pradesh, and Orissa—became relatively poorer during the 1990s. Policy, which became more attuned to rewarding success over the 1990s, may have exacerbated these regional differences.

Since there were a whole succession of governments over the 1990s, the Congress lost its monopoly as the party of government. There was a period when the regional parties were dominant in the mid 1990s, then the Bharatiya Janata Party (BJP) entered the government and early in this decade there were even several years when there was a solely BJP government. In Indian politics, there's very little notion of economic ideology. The BJP tended to be a little more pro-market, a little less internationalist than the Congress, but the big difference is whether you are in or out of government. Government will introduce something—to privatize the insurance industry, for example; MPs will vote in favour of it when they are in government, and then three years later when the government has changed and they are in opposition, everyone who previously voted in favor now votes against, and vice versa. So there is no sort of socialist ideology in the way that there was in many European countries. All the governments of the 1990s were effectively reforming governments, even if not as strongly as some of us would have liked. They tried to push the reform agenda, and if they were slow, at least there were no big reversals as in Latin America and elsewhere.

INDIA TODAY

At the moment, the Congress-led government is in alliance with some of the regional parties. The BJP is out of government, having run an election campaign that was altogether too complacent last time around. Manmohan Singh is now prime minister, but Sonia Gandhi, who was born in Italy, leads the National Congress Party. To avoid the complications of having a foreigner be prime minister, she handed over running the government to Singh, who sits as a member of the upper house. The other key reformer is Palaniappan Chidambaram, the finance minister. He is a member of one of the smaller regional parties. While they have not been able to move as fast as they may have liked, they have unquestionably been moving in a reforming direction since coming into power two years ago.

Externally, there is no hint of a balance-of-payments crisis. India has something like $130 billion of reserves. Indeed, there is been some debate as to whether it could not spend some of those reserves to advantage. There is a sense of great optimism in India at last. It is found its place in the world economy as the place to which the multinationals outsource jobs.

The debate is how much faster than 6 percent India should grow. When we were young, we regarded 6 percent as a miracle. It is what Italy did in the late 1950s and early 1960s, when we talked about the Italian miracle. Today, developing countries tend to regard 6 percent as the minimum. In India the debate is how much faster it should be able to grow. But there are still some big challenges.

First of all, there is the fiscal deficit, which is around 8 percent of GNP and has been up toward 10 percent. Now India is growing faster than the U.S., so it can afford a deficit larger than the 3-4 percent U.S. deficit without debt's getting out of control relative to GDP, but it still has one of the highest debt ratios in the world outside of Japan. It's still a 90-100 percent debt to GDP ratio. Sixty percent is supposed to be the limit in Europe, by the Maastricht Treaty; the Latin Americans have decided that they really should not go that high, that 30-40 percent is the maximum prudent rate. And here is India with 90+ percent and still rising. They have not had a crisis yet and seem confident that they are not about to. They do have a high private-sector savings rate, which means that the debt is almost all held at home rather than abroad, which makes life simpler. But at some stage they are going to have to get the deficit down. Otherwise, they shall be spending their tax money on nothing but servicing the debt. There are some signs that they are beginning to get a grip on this, but it is still a major problem. As a Brookings Institution economist put it in the 1980s, "The fiscal deficit is not a case of the wolf at the door, it's termites in the woodwork." It diverts resources away from investment in productive activities into excessive spending by the government.

A second difficulty is one that it's hard for people in most developed countries to believe is a real problem. But a large part of that deficit goes to financing the losses of the electric companies. Two and a half percent of GNP goes into power subsidies; only half the electricity that's generated actually gets paid for. Some of the other half goes in unfortunate (we economists think) programs to give free power to the farmers. Unfortunately, the farmers who qualify for free power are the ones who are rich enough to be able to afford power in the first place. But having gotten free power, they let their neighbors tap into it. That is another portion of the power goes that way. Then there are those who tap the lines. It's dangerous, but people know how to do it. So half the power does not get paid for even while there's a big increase in the fiscal deficit, while one has very expensive power for those who do pay, which includes large industry. What do you do if you are an industrialist with power that costs more to buy than you can generate it for? You buy a generator, which is socially wasteful. A lot of the investment in India is wasted by companies' generating their own power so as to bypass the power system. So while there have been some attempts at privatizing the power sector and at imposing a regulatory system, there are still big problems at the moment.

Third, there is the social situation. Education is still a problem in just the same way as it used to be. There's excellent education for a small minority in the elite, and poor or no education at all for some people at the base of the pyramid, particularly women. India's in the region where there are a hundred million missing women, as Amartya Sen wrote. Even if they get born, they do not get educated properly. Malnutrition is another problem. About half of India's pupils are malnourished. The problem is worse than even Subsaharan Africa. In all the other dimensions, India has now passed Subsaharan Africa easily, but in this one it's still worse.

Finally, India is still a poor country. The average person still earns less than $2 a day. The figure is controversial, but the World Bank reckons that a quarter of the population are poor by its measure of $1/day in 1985 prices—that's a destitution level, rather than a poverty level.

SOCIO-ECONOMIC FACTORS IN INDIA AND CHINA

China and India – the world's two biggest countries, and maybe someday, two largest markets have much in common, and much that sets them apart. China's 12th Five-Year Plan and India's penchant for jugaad are prime examples. Why has China's economic growth and development outstripped India's? What accounts for the differences and what doesn't? In this text, we consider some current, lesser known drivers and obstacles of economic development in each country.

CHINA NATIONAL PEOPLE'S CONGRESS' 12TH FIVE-YEAR PLAN

News about China highlights the expectations going into this weekend's China's National People's Congress (NPC) session. Largely a function of the Communist Party of China (CPC or CCP), the NPC is the highest governing body in China and the country's only legislative house. The key output of the latest NPC session will be China's 12th Five-Year Plan. China's Five-Year Plans have played an important role in identifying key economic and social objectives and successfully shaping the course of China's economic development in a number of areas. The latest, 12th iteration of the Five-Year Plan is seen as particularly noteworthy for its emphasis on addressing key factors in sustaining China's development, including the needs to: boost domestic economic demand; provide social safety nets (potentially involving universal health insurance and pension programs); reduce inequality; and nurture strategic emerging industries, such as alternative energy and new materials.

INDIA – FOREIGN INVESTMENT AND JUGAAD

In sharp contrast to the official order of China's Five-Year Plans, recent New York Times coverage of India has focused on the Hindi concept of jugaad and a significant reduction of foreign direct investment in India.

FOREIGN DIRECT INVESTMENT (FDI) IN INDIA

Contrary to the generally positive uptick in foreign direct investment in other BRIC (Brazil, Russia, India and China) countries and emerging markets in Asia and Latin America in 2010, India saw a sizeable reduction in inflows of foreign investment from 2009 to 2010.

Foreign Direct Investment (FDI) in Selected Asian and L. American Countries in 2009 and 2010

(Units: Billions $)

Country	2009	2010	%Change
Indonesia	$4.9	$12.8	162.7%
Singapore	$16.8	$37.4	122.7%
Hong Kong	$48.4	$62.6	29.2%
Brazil	$25.9	$30.2	16.3%
Thailand	$5.9	$6.8	14.2%
China	$95.0	$101.0	6.3%
India	$34.6	$23.7	–31.5%

Sources: New York Times, UN Conference on Trade and Development.

Whereas FDI (direct physical investment as opposed to portfolio or stock market investments) in China increased by 6.3 percent and other countries benefited from much greater gains, FDI in India declined by 31.5 percent from $34.6 billion to $23.7 billion. The chart on the previous page is a reproduction of one from the New York Times that uses data from the United Nations Conference on Trade and Development.

JUGAAD IN INDIA

Jugaad, a Hindi word referring to a seemingly beneficial trait of resourcefulness when the odds are against you, is part of the problem behind India's FDI and more enduring development issues according to several Indian commentators. In a letter to the New York Times, Indian author and editor Manu Joseph describes jugaad as a product of, "an important Indian character – the uncompromising practicality of the individual, an untamed form of great personal freedom and informality." According to Joseph, the pitfalls of jugaad for development and civil society in India include the pronounced lack of a value structure that would provide valuable, long-term guidance and corrosive, rampant political corruption.

Rather than just jugaad itself though, the issue seems to involve a kind of chicken and egg problem related to the conditions and circumstances that give rise to jugaad in the first place. From social science, we know that human beings have a clear tendency to act in accordance with the incentives and parameters of their environment. In other words, did jugaad lay the groundwork for corruption or does jugaad result from the necessity of finding a way to survive and prosper in a corrupt world? It's likely that the answer lies somewhere in the middle or involves healthy portions of both interpretations.

In either case, the spur-of-the-moment, turn-on-a-dime, improvisational nature of jugaad stands in stark contrast to the highly regimented, methodical, long-term planning of the Five-Year Plans generated by China's National People's Congress.

COMPARISON: CHINA AND INDIA

Despite the yin and yang quality of China's Five-Year Plans and jugaad, China and India still look very similar in many respects when compared to the rest of the world. The population of each country is well over one billion people. The world's next largest country, the U.S., has barely one quarter of India's roughly 1.2 billion people.

In terms of geography, culture and politics, the relative global proximity of China and India in Asia has contributed to a history of religious, cultural and economic exchange and influence between the two countries. While China's total area is about triple India's, both countries' large territories make for an abundance of large, distant provinces and states as well as economic centers (like Shanghai, Hong Kong, Mumbai, Guangzhou and Bangalore) that are physically and mentally far removed from the two countries' political capitals and leadership in Beijing and New Delhi.

ECONOMIC GROWTH AND DEVELOPMENT IN CHINA AND INDIA

Both China and India have also made great strides in economic growth and development in recent years. In each country, rapid economic development has led to widespread improvement in living standards and quality of life and lifted hundreds of millions of people out of poverty.

The UNDP's Human Development Index (HDI) accounts for three fundamental components of development and living standards: income, education and health. Some of the key commonalities and differences between China and India are summarized in the table show on next page.

China and India – Comparison of Key Development Indicators

	China	India
Population (2010)	1.34 billion	1.2 billion
Total Area	3.7 million sq miles; 9.6 million sq km	1.24 million sq miles; 3.2 million sq km
GDP Growth Rate (Annual Avgs.)		
1980-2009	10.0%	6.0%
1990-2009	10.1%	6.3%
2000-2009	10.3%	6.9%
2011-2015 (Forecast)	9.5%	8.2%
GDP Per Head (Intl. $, PPP) (2009)	$6,828	$3,270
Literacy Rate (% of Adult Males)	96.7%	75.2%
Literacy Rate (% of Adult Females)	90.5%	50.8%
Life Expectancy at Birth		
1960	46.6 years	42.4 years
2008	73.1 years	63.7 years
Human Development Index (HDI)		
1980 HDI	0.368	0.32
2010 HDI	0.663	0.519
% Increases 1980-2010	80%	62%

Sources: United Nations, IMF, World Bank

From 1980 to 2010, China's human development index (HDI) rose by 80 percent from 0.368 to 0.663. Over the same period, India's HDI increased by 62 percent from 0.320 to 0.519. In comparison to all other developing countries including fellow BRICs Brazil and Russia, China and India rank 4th and 6th respectively in the list of countries with the largest HDI increases from 1980 to 2010. In addition to large increases in per capita income, China and India have also achieved considerable gains in health and longevity. From 1960 to 2008, life expectancy at birth in China and India increased by 56.8 percent from 46.6 to 73.1 years and by 50.2 percent from 42.4 to 63.7 years, respectively.

ECONOMIC DEVELOPMENT LESSONS

Despite their country's impressive performance, many Indians still look to China's economic development and wonder why India has lagged behind. To be sure, the answer is far more complicated than the distinction between long-term planning and short-term adaptation.

Successful economic and social development depends on the complex interplay of a multitude of factors. Education and training, capital and labor markets, entrepreneurship, government policies and regulations, and other important variables can all have a major impact on the pace of economic growth as well as the magnitude and distribution of increases in living standards.

China has certainly not gotten everything right, nor has India done at all badly for itself either. The same highly centralized system in China that facilitates long-term planning and mobilization can be conducive to excessive regulation and control. India has done well to achieve so much in the face of corruption and other systemic obstacles that are part and parcel of the jugaad response.

Still, the concepts of planning and jugaad seem to shed some light on possible lessons for future development initiatives. India's experience suggests countries that are able to adopt value systems and institutions that limit corruption and inefficient bureaucratic red-tape stand a better chance with economic development. China's overall economic development and more targeted wins in clean energy, rare earths and transportation to name a few speak to the merits of long-term planning that can identify and address important development issues by facilitating the effective allocation of resources, overcoming market failures and supplying essential public goods.

ENVIRONMENTAL POLLUTION

Introduction. Meaning and Definition of Environmental Pollution: *Definitions.* ***Types of Environmental Pollution. Pesticide Pollution. Radiation Pollution. Noise Pollution. Sources of Environmental Pollution. Thermal Pollution. Global Warming. Genetically Modified Organisms. Natural and Man-made Environmental Disasters. Why Environmental Problems are also Social Problems. General Environmental Pollution Effects:*** *Environmental Pollution Effects on Humans, Other Animals and Plants, Environmental Pollution Effects on Humans, Environmental Pollution Effects on Animals, Environmental Pollution Effects on Trees and Plants.* ***How can we control environmental pollution?***

INTRODUCTION

Different relationships between environment and society also reflect different social values and norms, as well as knowledge systems. The values underlying capitalism have supported the commodification of nature, turning it into objects that can be bought and sold for profit. For instance, the multiple cultural meanings of a river—its ecological, utilitarian, spiritual, and aesthetic significance, are stripped down to a single set of calculations about profit and loss from the sale of water for an entrepreneure. Socialist values of equality and justice have led to the seizure of lands from large landlords and their redistribution among landless peasants in a number of countries. Religious values have led some social groups to protect and conserve sacred groves and species and others to believe that they have divine sanction to change the environment to suit their needs.

There are many different perspectives on the environment and its relationship to society. These differences include the 'nature-nurture' debate and whether individual characteristics are innate or are influenced by environmental factors. For instance, are people poor talented or hard-working or because they are born into a situation of disadvantage and lack of opportunity? Theories and data about environment and society are influenced by the social conditions under which they emerge. Thus the notions that women are intrinsically less able than men, and Blacks naturally less able than Whites, were challenged as ideas of equality became more widespread during the 18th century's social and political revolutions. Colonialism generated a great deal of knowledge about environment and society, often systematically compiling it in order to make resources available to the imperial powers. Geology, geography, botany, zoology, forestry and hydraulic engineering were among the many disciplines that were created and institutionalised to facilitate the management of natural resources for colonial purposes.

Environmental management is, however, a very difficult task. Not enough is known about biophysical processes to predict and control them. In addition, human relations with the environment have become increasingly complex. With the spread of industrialisation, resource extraction has expanded and accelerated, affecting ecosystems in unprecedented ways. Complex industrial technologies and modes of organisation require sophisticated management systems which are often fragile and vulnerable to error. We live in risk societies using technologies and products that we do not fully grasp. The occurrence of nuclear disasters like Chernobyl, industrial accidents like Bhopal, and Mad Cow disease in Europe shows the dangers inherent in industrial environments.

MEANING AND DEFINITION OF ENVIRONMENTAL POLLUTION

Although pollution had been known to exist for a very long time (at least since people started using fire thousands of years ago), it had seen the growth of truly global proportions only since the onset of the industrial revolution during the 19th century.

The industrial revolution brought with it technological progress such as discovery of oil and its virtually universal use throughout different industries.

Technological progress facilitated by super efficiency of capitalist business practices (division of labour–cheaper production costs–overproduction–overconsumption–overpollution) had probably become one of the main causes of serious deterioration of natural resources.

At the same time, of course, development of natural sciences led to the better understanding of negative effects produced by pollution on the environment.

Environmental pollution is a problem both in developed and developing countries. Factors such as population growth and urbanization invariably place greater demands on the planet and stretch the use of natural resources to the maximum.

It has been argued that the carrying capacity of Earth is significantly smaller than the demands placed on it by large numbers of human populations. And overuse of natural resources often results in nature's degradation.

Environmental pollution.

DEFINITIONS

ENVIRONMENTAL POLLUTION

Environmental pollution is "the contamination of the physical and biological components of the earth/atmosphere system to such an extent that normal environmental processes are adversely affected".

POLLUTION

"Pollution is the introduction of contaminants into the environment that cause harm or discomfort to humans or other living organisms, or that damage the environment" which can come "in the form of chemical substances, or energy such as noise, heat or light". "Pollutants can be naturally occurring substances or energies, but are considered contaminants when in excess of natural levels."

Pollution is "the addition of any substance or form of energy (e.g., heat, sound, radioactivity) to the environment at a rate faster than the environment can accommodate it by dispersion, breakdown, recycling, or storage in some harmless form".

ENVIRONMENTAL AND POLLUTION

In one word, environmental pollution takes place when the environment cannot process and neutralize harmful by-products of human activities (for example, poisonous gas emissions) in due course without any structural or functional damage to its system.

In fact, "the due course" itself may last many years during which the nature will attempt to decompose the pollutants; in one of the worst cases – that of radioactive pollutants – it may take as long as thousands of years for the decomposition of such pollutants to be completed.

Pollution occurs, on the one hand, because the natural environment does not know how to decompose the unnaturally generated elements (i.e., anthropogenic pollutants), and, on the other, there is a lack of knowledge on the part of humans on how to decompose these pollutants artificially.

TYPES OF ENVIRONMENTAL POLLUTION

There are three major types of environmental pollution:

1. Air pollution
2. Water pollution
3. Soil pollution (contamination).

1. Air Pollution

Some of the most important air pollutants are sulfur dioxide, nitrogen dioxide, carbon monoxide, ozone, volatile organic compounds (VOCs) and airborne particles, with radioactive pollutants probably among the most destructive ones (specifically when produced by nuclear explosions).

Air pollution is considered to be a major environmental problem in urban and rural areas.

Air pollution is considered to be a major environmental problem in urban and rural areas, causing respiratory and other problems which result in serious illness and death. The sources of air pollution include emissions from industries and vehicles, as well as the burning of wood and coal for domestic use. We have all heard of pollution from vehicles and factories, and seen pictures of smoking chimneys and exhaust pipes in cars.

But we often do not realise that indoor pollution from cooking fires is also a serious source of risk. This is particularly true of rural homes where wood fires using green or poorly burning wood, badly designed fireplaces (chulhas), and poor ventilation combine to put village women at serious risk because they do the cooking.

2. Water Pollution

Water pollutants include insecticides and herbicides, food processing waste, pollutants from livestock operations, volatile organic compounds (VOCs), heavy metals, chemical waste and others. Water pollution is also a very serious issue affecting surface as well as groundwater. Major sources include not only domestic sewage and factory effluents but also the runoff from farms where large amounts of synthetic fertilisers and pesticides are used. The pollution of rivers and water bodies is a particularly important problem.

Cities also suffer from noise pollution, which has been the subject of court orders in many cities. Sources include amplified loud speakers used at religious and cultural events, political campaigns, vehicle horns and traffic, and construction work.

Water Pollution.

3. Soil Pollution

Some soil pollutants are: hydrocarbons, solvents and heavy metals.

Soil erosion—a result of poor agricultural practices—removes rich humus topsoil developed over many years through vegetative decay and microbial degradation and thus strips the land of valuable nutrients for crop growth. Strip mining for minerals and coal lays waste thousands of acres of land each year, denuding the Earth and subjecting the mined area to widespread erosion problems. The increases in urbanization due to population pressure presents additional soil-erosion

Soil Pollution.

problems; sediment loads in nearby streams may increase as much as 500 to 1,000 times over that recorded in nearby undeveloped stretches of stream. Soil erosion not only despoils the Earth for farming and other uses, but also increases the suspended-solids load of the waterway. This increase interferes with the ecological habitat and poses silting problems in navigation channels, inhibiting the commercial use of these waters.

Solid Waste: The most common and convenient method of disposing of municipal solid wastes is in the sanitary landfill. The open dump, once a common eyesore in towns across the United States, attracted populations of rodents and other pests and often emitted hideous odors; it is now illegal. Sanitary landfills provide better aesthetic control and should be odor-free. Often, however, industrial wastes of unknown content are commingled with domestic wastes. Groundwater infiltration and contamination of water supplies with toxic chemicals have recently led to more active control of landfills and industrial waste disposal. Careful management of sanitary landfills, such as providing for leachate and runoff treatment as well as daily coverage with topsoil, has alleviated most of the problems of open dumping. In many areas, however, space for landfills is running out and alternatives must be found.

Recycling of materials is practical to some extent for much municipal and some industrial wastes, and a small but growing proportion of solid wastes is being recycled. When wastes are commingled, however, recovery becomes difficult and expensive. New processes of sorting ferrous and nonferrous metals, paper, glass, and plastics have been developed, and many communities with recycling programs now require refuse separation. Crucial issues in recycling are devising better processing methods, inventing new products for the recycled materials, and finding new markets for them.

Incineration is another method for disposing of solid wastes. Advanced incinerators use solid wastes as fuel, burning quantities of refuse and utilizing the resultant heat to make steam for electricity generation. Wastes must be burned at very high temperatures, and incinerator exhausts must be equipped with sophisticated scrubbers and other devices for removing dioxins and other toxic pollutants. Problems remain, however: incinerator ash contains high ratios of heavy metals, becoming a hazardous waste in itself, and high-efficiency incinerators may discourage the use of recycling and other waste-reduction methods.

Composting is increasingly used to treat some agricultural wastes, as well as such municipal wastes as leaves and brush. Composting systems can produce usable soil conditioners, or humus, within a few months.

PESTICIDE POLLUTION

Pesticides are organic and inorganic chemicals originally invented and first used effectively to better the human environment by controlling undesirable life forms such as bacteria, pests, and foraging insects. Their effectiveness, however, has caused considerable pollution. The persistent, or hard, pesticides, which are relatively inert and nondegradable by chemical or biologic activity, are also bioaccumulative; that is, they are retained within the body of the consuming organism and are concentrated with each ensuing level of the biologic food chain. For example, DDT provides an excellent example of cumulative pesticide effects. (Although DDT use has been banned in the United States since 1972, it is still a popular pesticide in much of the rest of the world.) DDT may be applied to an area so that the levels in the surrounding environment are less than one part per billion. As bacteria or other microscopic organisms ingest and retain the pesticide, the concentration may increase several hundred- to a thousandfold. Concentration continues as these organisms are ingested by higher forms of life—algae, fish, shellfish, birds, or humans. The resultant concentration in the higher life forms may reach levels of thousands to millions of parts per billion.

Regulating the treatment and prevention of environmental pollution.

Many pesticides are nondiscriminatory; that is, they are not specific for a particular plant or organism. A dramatic example of this effect is DDE (a product of the breakdown of DDT), which effectively inhibits the ability of birds to provide sufficient calcium deposits for their eggs, producing fragile shells and a high percentage of nested eggs that break prematurely. Another reported side effect of pesticides is their effect on the nervous system of animals and fish; they can cause instability, disorientation, and, in some cases, death. These examples are generally a result of relatively high body residuals producing acute (short-term) readily recordable results.

The long-term (chronic) effects of persistent pesticides are virtually unknown, but many scientists believe they are as much an environmental hazard as are the acute effects. Nonpersistent (readily degradable) pesticides or substitutes, insect sterilization techniques, hormone homologues that check or interfere with maturation stages, and introduction of animals that prey on the pests present a potentially brighter picture for pest control with significantly reduced environmental consequences.

RADIATION POLLUTION

Radiation pollution is any form of ionizing or nonionizing radiation that results from human activities. The most well-known radiation results from the detonation of nuclear devices and the controlled release of energy by nuclear-power generating plants. Other sources of radiation include spent-fuel reprocessing plants, by-products of mining operations, and experimental research laboratories. Increased exposure to medical X-rays and to radiation emissions from microwave ovens and other household appliances, although of considerably less magnitude, all constitute sources of environmental radiation.

Public concern over the release of radiation into the environment greatly increased following the disclosure of possible harmful effects to the public from nuclear weapons testing, the accident (1979) at the Three Mile Island nuclear-power generating plant near Harrisburg and the catastrophic 1986 explosion at Chernobyl, a Soviet nuclear power plant. In the late 1980s, revelations of major pollution problems at U.S. nuclear weapons reactors raised apprehensions even higher.

The environmental effects of exposure to high-level ionizing radiation have been extensively documented through postwar studies on individuals who were exposed to nuclear radiation in Japan. Some forms of cancer show up immediately, but latent maladies of radiation poisoning have been recorded from 10 to 30 years after exposure. The effects of exposure to low-level radiation are not yet known. A major concern about this type of exposure is the potential for genetic damage.

Radioactive nuclear wastes cannot be treated by conventional chemical methods and must be stored in heavily shielded containers in areas remote from biological habitats. The safest of storage sites currently used are impervious deep caves or abandoned salt mines. Most radioactive wastes, however, have half-lives of hundreds to thousands of years, and to date no storage method has been found that is absolutely infallible.

NOISE POLLUTION

Noise pollution has a relatively recent origin. It is a composite of sounds generated by human activities ranging from blasting stereo systems to the roar of supersonic transport jets. Although the frequency (pitch) of noise may be of major importance, most noise sources are measured in terms of intensity, or strength of the sound field. The standard unit, one decibel (dB), is the amount of sound that is just audible to the average human. The decibel scale is somewhat misleading because it is logarithmic rather than linear; for example, a noise source measuring 70 dB is 10 times as loud as a source measuring 60 dB and 100 times as loud as a source reading 50 dB. Noise may be generally associated with industrial society, where heavy machinery, motor vehicles, and aircraft have become everyday items. Noise pollution is more intense in the work environment than in the general environment, although ambient noise increased an average of one dB per year during the 1980s. The average background noise in a typical home today is between 40 and 50 decibels. Some examples of high-level sources in the environment are heavy trucks (90 dB at 15 m/50 ft), freight trains (75 dB at 15 m/50 ft), and air conditioning (60 dB at 6 m/20 ft).

The most readily measurable physiological effect of noise pollution is damage to hearing, which may be either temporary or permanent and may cause disruption of normal activities or just general annoyance. The effect is variable, depending upon individual susceptibility, duration of exposure, nature of noise (loudness), and time distribution of exposure (such as steady or intermittent). On the average an individual will experience a threshold shift (a shift in an individual's upper limit of sound detectability) when exposed to noise levels of 75 to 80 dB for several hours. This shift will last only several hours once the source of noise pollution is removed. A second physiologically important level is the threshold of pain, at which even short-term exposure will cause physical pain (130 to 140 dB). Any noise sustained at this level will cause a permanent threshold shift or permanent partial hearing loss. At the uppermost level of noise (greater than 150 dB), even a single short-term blast may cause traumatic hearing loss and physical damage inside the ear.

SOURCES OF ENVIRONMENTAL POLLUTION

In modern industrialized societies, fossil fuels (oil, gas, coal) transcended virtually all imaginable barriers and firmly established themselves in our everyday lives.

Not only do we use fossil fuels for our obvious everyday needs (such as filling a car), as well as in the power-generating industry, they (specifically oil) are also present in such products as all sorts of plastics, solvents, detergents, asphalt, lubricating oils, a wide range of chemicals for industrial use, etc.

Combustion of fossil fuels produces extremely high levels of air pollution and is widely recognized as one of the most important "target" areas for reduction and control of environmental pollution.

Fossil fuels also contribute to soil contamination and water pollution. For example, when oil is transported from the point of its production to further destinations by pipelines, an oil leak from the pipeline may occur and pollute soil and subsequently groundwater. When oil is transported by tankers by ocean, an oil spill may occur and pollute ocean water.

Of course, there are other natural resources whose exploitation is a cause of serious pollution; for example, the use of uranium for nuclear power generation produces extremely dangerous waste that would take thousands of years to neutralize. But there is no reasonable doubt that fossil fuels are among the most serious sources of environmental pollution.

Power-generating plants and transport are probably the biggest sources of fossil fuel pollution.

Common sources of fossil fuel pollution are:

Industry:

- Power-generating plants
- Petroleum refineries
- Petrochemical plants
- Production and distribution of fossil fuels
- Other manufacturing facilities.

Transport:

- Road transport (motor vehicles)
- Shipping industry
- Aircraft.

Fossil fuel combustion is also a major source of carbon dioxide (CO_2) emissions and perhaps the most important cause of global warming. Learn more about the causes and effects of global warming here.

Other (Non-Fossil Fuel) Sources of Environmental Pollution

Among other pollution sources, agriculture (livestock farming) is worth mentioning as the largest generator of ammonia emissions resulting in air pollution. Chemicals such as pesticides and fertilizers are also widely used in agriculture, which may lead water pollution and soil contamination as well.

Trading Activities May be Another Source of Pollution

For example, it's been recently noted that packaging of products sold in supermarkets and other retail outlets is far too excessive and generates large quantities of solid waste that ends up either in landfills or municipal incinerators leading to soil contamination and air pollution.

Residential sector is another significant source of pollution generating solid municipal waste that may end up in landfills or incinerators leading to soil contamination and air pollution.

THERMAL POLLUTION

Thermal pollution is the discharge of waste heat via energy dissipation into cooling water and subsequently into nearby waterways. The major sources of thermal pollution are fossil-fuel and nuclear electric-power generating facilities and, to a lesser degree, cooling operations associated with industrial manufacturing, such as steel foundries, other primary-metal manufacturers, and chemical and petrochemical producers.

The discharge temperatures from electric-power plants generally range from 5 to 11°C (9 to 20°F) above ambient water temperatures. An estimated 90% of all water consumption, excluding agricultural uses, is for cooling or energy dissipation.

The discharge of heated water into a waterway often causes ecologic imbalance, sometimes resulting in major fish kills near the discharge source. The increased temperature accelerates chemical-biological processes and decreases the ability of the water to hold dissolved oxygen. Thermal changes affect the aquatic system by limiting or changing the type of fish and aquatic biota able to grow or reproduce in the waters. Thus rapid and dramatic changes in biologic communities often occur in the vicinity of heated discharges.

GLOBAL WARMING

The release of particular gases (carbon dioxide, methane and others) creates a 'greenhouse' effect by trapping the sun's heat and not allowing it to dissipate. This has caused a small but significant rise in global temperatures.

The resulting climate change is projected to melt polar ice-fields and raise the sea level, thus submerging low-lying coastal areas, and more important, affecting the ecological balance. Global warming is also likely to result in greater fluctuations and uncertainty in climates across the world. China and India are increasingly significant contributors to world carbon and green house gas emissions.

GENETICALLY MODIFIED ORGANISMS

New techniques of gene-splicing allow scientists to import genes from one species into another, introducing new characteristics. For instance, genes from Bacillus thuringiensis have been introduced into cotton species, making it resistant to the bollworm, a major pest. Genetic modification may also be done to shorten growing time, increase size and the shelf-life of crops. However, little is known about the long term effects of genetic modification on those who eat these foods or on ecological systems. Agricultural companies can also use genetic modification to create sterile seeds, preventing farmers from reusing them, and guaranteeing that seeds remain their profit-yielding property, forcing farmers to be dependent on them.

NATURAL AND MAN-MADE ENVIRONMENTAL DISASTERS

This is a self-explanatory category. The Bhopal disaster of 1984 when a toxic gas leak from the Union Carbide factory there killed about 4000 people, and the tsunami of 2004 are the most recent examples of man-made and natural environmental disasters.

WHY ENVIRONMENTAL PROBLEMS ARE ALSO SOCIAL PROBLEMS

How environmental problems affect different groups is a function of social inequality. Social status and power determine the extent to which people can insulate themselves from environmental crises or overcome it. In some cases, their 'solutions' may actually worsen environmental disparities. In

Kutch, Gujarat, where water is scarce, richer farmers have invested in deep bore tubewells to tap groundwater to irrigate their fields and grow cash crops. When the rains fail, the earthen wells of the poorer villagers run dry and they do not even have water to drink. At such times, the moist green fields of the rich farmers seem to mock them. Certain environmental concerns sometimes appear to be universal concerns, not particular to specific social groups. For instance, reducing air pollution or protecting biodiversity seem to be in the public interest. A sociological analysis shows, however, that how public priorities are set and how they are pursued may not be universally beneficial. Securing the public interest may actually serve the interests of particular politically and economically powerful groups, or hurt the interests of the poor and politically weak. As the debates over large dams and around protected areas show, the environment as a public interest is a hotly contested arena.

The school of social ecology points out that social relations, in particular the organisation of property and production, shape environmental perceptions and practices. Different social groups stand in different relationships to the environment and approach it differently. A Forest Department geared to maximising revenues from supplying large volumes of bamboo to the paper industry will view and use a forest very differently from an artisan who harvests bamboo to make baskets.

Their varied interests and ideologies generate environmental conflicts. In this sense, environmental crises have their roots in social inequality. Addressing environmental problems requires changing environment society relations, and this in turn requires efforts to change relations between different social groups—men and women, urban and rural people, landlords and labourers. Changed social relations will give rise to different knowledge systems and modes of managing the environment.

GENERAL ENVIRONMENTAL POLLUTION EFFECTS

Miguel A. Santos notes that a very important aspect of the effect of pollution is its dose (or concentration) required to cause environmental damage. He defines pollution response as "the change in the effect of a pollutant in response to a change in its concentration". In this respect, he identifies 3 different types of response evoked by the environment to different pollution concentrations:

- Linear effect
- Greater-than-linear effect
- Threshold effect.

In the ***linear effect***, environmental damage increases linearly with pollution concentrations. In other words, "the total damage or risk is directly proportional to the accumulated exposure". This effect occurs with radioactive substances as well as mercury, lead, cadmium and asbestos.

In the ***greater-than-linear effect***, environmental damage increases with an increase in pollution concentrations but at a decreasing rate. This means that, as pollution concentrations continue to increase the environmental damage will continue to decrease.

In the ***threshold effect***, pollution produces no effect until a certain threshold in pollution concentrations is achieved. In other words, "so long as a given threshold is not exceeded, the damage from pollution would be completely repaired as quickly as it is produced".

This effect is found with *biodegradable pollutants*.

It is also important to mention synergistic effects of pollutants on the environment. While interacting with each other, pollutants can produce greater impacts than when acting individually. A good example of that is a synergy between asbestos exposure and smoking in causing lung cancer.

There is no doubt that excessive levels of pollution are causing a lot of damage to human and animal health, plants and trees (including tropical rainforests) as well as the wider environment.

ENVIRONMENTAL POLLUTION EFFECTS ON HUMANS, OTHER ANIMALS AND PLANTS

All types of environmental pollution – air, water and soil pollution – have an impact on the living environment. The effects in living organisms may range from mild discomfort to serious diseases such as cancer to physical deformities (for example, extra or missing limbs in frogs).

Experts admit that environmental pollution effects are quite often underestimated and that more research is needed to understand the connections between pollution and its effects on all life forms.

ENVIRONMENTAL POLLUTION EFFECTS ON HUMANS

We know that pollution causes not only physical disabilities but also psychological and behavioral disorders in people. The following effects of environmental pollution on humans have been reported:

Air Pollution

- Reduced lung functioning.
- Irritation of eyes, nose, mouth and throat.
- Asthma attacks.
- Respiratory symptoms such as coughing and wheezing.
- Increased respiratory disease such as bronchitis.
- Reduced energy levels.
- Headaches and dizziness.
- Disruption of endocrine, reproductive and immune systems.
- Neurobehavioral disorders.
- Cardiovascular problems.

- Cancer.
- Premature death.

Water Pollution

Waterborne diseases caused by polluted drinking water:

- Typhoid.
- Amoebiasis.
- Giardiasis.
- Ascariasis.
- Hookworm.

Waterborne diseases caused by polluted beach water:

- Rashes, ear ache, pink eye.
- Respiratory infections.
- Hepatitis, encephalitis, gastroenteritis, diarrhoea, vomiting, and stomach aches.
- Conditions related to water polluted by chemicals (such as pesticides, hydrocarbons, persistent organic pollutants, heavy metals etc.):
  - Cancer, includes prostate cancer and non-Hodgkin's lymphoma.
  - Hormonal problems that can disrupt reproductive and developmental processes.
  - Damage to the nervous system.
  - Liver and kidney damage.
  - Damage to the DNA.
  - Exposure to mercury (heavy metal):
    - ✓ In *the womb:* may cause neurological problems including slower reflexes, learning deficits, delayed or incomplete mental development, autism and brain damage.
    - ✓ In *adults:* Parkinson's disease, multiple sclerosis, Alzheimer's disease, heart disease, and even death.
- *Other notes:*
  - Water pollution may also result from interactions between water and contaminated soil, as well as from deposition of air contaminants (such as acid rain).
  - Damage to people may be caused by fish foods coming from polluted water (a well known example is high mercury levels in fish).
  - Damage to people may be caused by vegetable crops grown/ washed with polluted water (author's own conclusion).

Soil Contamination

- Causes cancers including leukaemia.
- Lead in soil is especially hazardous for young children causing developmental damage to the brain.

- Mercury can increase the risk of kidney damage; cyclodienes can lead to liver toxicity.
- Causes neuromuscular blockage as well as depression of the central nervous system.
- Also causes headaches, nausea, fatigue, eye irritation and skin rash.
- *Other notes:*
  - Contact with contaminated soil may be direct (from using parks, schools etc.) or indirect (by inhaling soil contaminants which have vaporized).
  - Soil contamination may also result from secondary contamination of water supplies and from deposition of air contaminants (for example, via acid rain).
  - Contamination of crops grown in polluted soil brings up problems with food security.
  - Since it is closely linked to water pollution, many effects of soil contamination appear to be similar to the ones caused by water contamination.

ENVIRONMENTAL POLLUTION EFFECTS ON ANIMALS

Air Pollution

- Acid rain (formed in the air) destroys fish life in lakes and streams.
- Excessive ultraviolet radiation coming from the sun through the ozone layer in the upper atmosphere which is eroded by some air pollutants, may cause skin cancer in wildlife.
- Ozone in the lower atmosphere may damage lung tissues of animals.

Water Pollution

- Nutrient pollution (nitrogen, phosphates etc.) causes overgrowth of toxic algae eaten by other aquatic animals, and may cause death; nutrient pollution can also cause outbreaks of fish diseases.
- Chemical contamination can cause declines in frog biodiversity and tadpole mass.
- Oil pollution (as part of chemical contamination) can negatively affect development of marine organisms, increase susceptibility to disease and affect reproductive processes; can also cause gastrointestinal irritation, liver and kidney damage, and damage to the nervous system.
- Mercury in water can cause abnormal behavior, slower growth and development, reduced reproduction, and death.
- Persistent organic pollutants (POPs) may cause declines, deformities and death of fish life.
- Too much sodium chloride (ordinary salt) in water may kill animals.

Soil Contamination

- Can alter metabolism of microorganisms and arthropods in a given soil environment; this may destroy some layers of the primary food chain, and thus have a negative effect on predator animal species.
- Small life forms may consume harmful chemicals which may then be passed up the food chain to larger animals; this may lead to increased mortality rates and even animal extinction.

ENVIRONMENTAL POLLUTION EFFECTS ON TREES AND PLANTS

Air Pollution

- Acid rain can kill trees, destroy the leaves of plants, can infiltrate soil by making it unsuitable for purposes of nutrition and habitation.
- Ozone holes in the upper atmosphere can allow excessive ultraviolet radiation from the sun to enter the Earth causing damage to trees and plants.
- Ozone in the lower atmosphere can prevent plant respiration by blocking stomata (openings in leaves) and negatively affecting plants' photosynthesis rates which will stunt plant growth; ozone can also decay plant cells directly by entering stomata.

Water Pollution

- May disrupt photosynthesis in aquatic plants and thus affecting ecosystems that depend on these plants.
- Terrestrial and aquatic plants may absorb pollutants from water (as their main nutrient source) and pass them up the food chain to consumer animals and humans.
- Plants may be killed by too much sodium chloride (ordinary salt) in water.
- Plants may be killed by mud from construction sites as well as bits of wood and leaves, clay and other similar materials.
- Plants may be killed by herbicides in water; herbicides are chemicals which are most harmful to plants.

Soil Contamination

- May alter plant metabolism and reduce crop yields.
- Trees and plants may absorb soil contaminants and pass them up the food chain.

ENVIRONMENTAL POLLUTION EFFECTS ON WIDER ENVIRONMENT

Apart from destroying the aquatic life in lakes and streams, acid rain can also corrode metals, damage surfaces of buildings and monuments, and cause soil acidification. Pollution of water may cause oxygen depletion in marine environments and severely affect the health of whole ecosystems.

Environmental pollution is causing a lot of distress not only to humans but also animals, driving many animal species to endangerment and even extinction.

The transboundary nature of environmental pollution makes it even more difficult to manage – you cannot build stone walls along the borders of your country or put customs cabins at every point of entry to regulate its flows into your country.

Everything on our planet is interconnected, and while the nature supplies us with valuable environmental services without which we cannot exist, we all depend on each other's actions and the way we treat natural resources.

It's widely recognised that we are hugely overspending our current budget of natural resources—at the existing rates of its exploitation, there is no way for the environment to recover in good time and continue "performing" well in the future.

Perhaps we should adopt a holistic view of nature – it is not an entity that exists separately from us; the nature is us, we are an inalienable part of it, and we should care for it in the most appropriate manner. Only then can we possibly solve the problem of environmental pollution.

HOW CAN WE CONTROL ENVIRONMENTAL POLLUTION?

It is clear that fossil fuels are among the biggest sources of pollution. We need to find alternative renewable sources of energy which can replace fossil fuels in the future. Green investment provides a great platform to explore and develop new and clean sources of energy such as solar electricity.

Building your own solar panels and using solar energy systems to meet at least part of your home electricity needs is another emerging opportunity for enthusiasts. This can really make a positive difference to the environment and reduce current pollution levels.

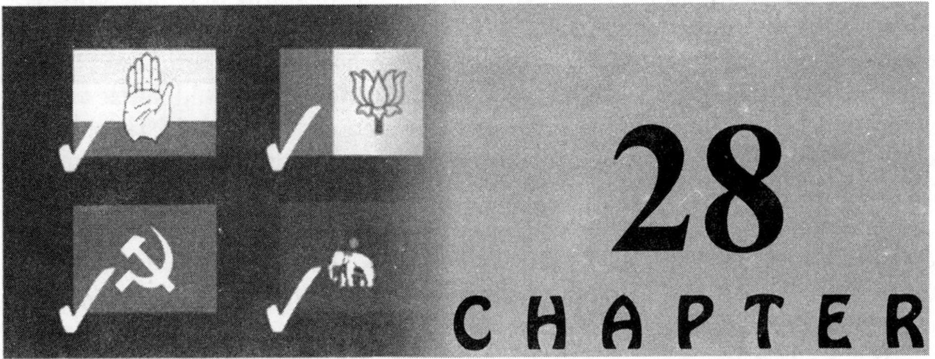

ECONOMIC AND POLITICAL SYSTEM

Overview of Economics: *Economy Defined.* ***Predominant Economic Systems:*** *Capitalism, Socialism.* ***Social Determinants of Economic Development. Democratic Socialism and State Capitalism. Modern Corporations and Multinationals. Alienation at Work. Division of Labour:*** *The Division of Labour in Society.* ***Labour Unions. Politics and Major Political Structure:*** *Totalitarianism, Authoritarianism, Democracy, Principles of Democracy.* ***Elite Theory:*** *Power Elite.* ***Community Power Structure. Political Parties:*** *Functions of a Political Party.* ***Bi-Party System. Political Parties of India. Parties : Classification. National Parties:*** *State Parties.* ***Pressure Groups. Pressure Groups in Different Social Systems. Voting Behaviour:*** *Determinants of Voting Behaviour in India.* ***Democracy and Authoritarian Government. Political Participation. Dictatorship v/s Democracy. Welfare State.***

OVERVIEW OF ECONOMICS

Humans first relied upon hunting and gathering to survive. Social systems of subsistence depended upon the family or small groups for food and did not have a recognizable economy. But through agriculture, specialization, settlement, and trade, an economy did emerge.

With the development of agriculture came pastoral and horticultural societies with more dependable food supplies and surplus. This surplus allowed division of labour, and many in the society took on new roles—specializing in making clothes, tools, or shelter. People could settle in one place and begin producing a surplus of other goods, which in turn led to trade. The primary sector dominated this pre-industrial economy, and cottages or homes produced limited manufacturing. Sociologists studying the transformation from hunting and gathering to pre-industrial society primarily interest themselves in how surplus, trade, and accumulation of possessions led to social inequality (the situation where some people have more possessions and power than others).

Primary sector dominance shifted to the secondary sector in the mid-eighteenth century with the Industrial Revolution. Beginning in England with the invention of steam power, the force of production moved from muscle to machine. The limited manufacturing in cottages or homes of pre-industrial society gave way to centralized, mass production in factories. Workers, now earning wages, became more specialized, doing single repetitive tasks rather than making a product from start to finish.

The secondary sector dominance gave way to tertiary sector dominance in many economies during the mid-twentieth century. Economists call such economies postindustrial because they depend upon service industries and high technology. As the steam engine powered the Industrial Revolution, computers have fuelled the Information Revolution in the twentieth century. In the Information Revolution, information and ideas have replaced manufactured goods as the basis for the economy. Consequently, the economy requires a more literate labour force, which must now communicate through computers rather than simply manipulating machines.

Today, countries may be agricultural (primary sector), industrial (secondary sector), or postindustrial (tertiary sector). The poorest countries are agricultural, while the wealthiest are postindustrial. With the rise of technology, computers, and the Internet, sociologists and economists point to the growing global economy (an economy where product or information development, production, and distribution cross national borders). For example, automobiles, a major production of industrialized nations, were once manufactured and assembled in one country. With the global economy, other countries make many parts for vehicles considered "American," and workers in the United States now assemble vehicles once considered "foreign."

ECONOMY DEFINED

The economy is a social system that produces, distributes, and consumes goods and services in a society. Three sectors make up an economy: primary, secondary, and tertiary.

- The primary sector refers to the part of the economy that produces raw materials, such as crude oil, timber, grain, or cotton.
- The secondary sector, made up of mills and factories, turns the raw materials into manufactured goods, like fuel, lumber, flour, or fabric.
- The tertiary sector refers to services rather than goods, and includes distribution of manufactured goods, food and hospitality services, banking, sales, and professional services like architects, physicians, and attorneys.

PREDOMINANT ECONOMIC SYSTEMS

The two predominant economic systems today are capitalism and socialism. Between these two opposite extremes lies a continuum of variations on the models.

CAPITALISM

Three key principles define the economic system of capitalism:

- Private ownership of production and distribution of goods and services.
- Competition, or the laws of supply and demand directing the economy.
- Profit-seeking, or selling goods and services for more than their cost of production.

Laissez-faire (French for "hands off") capitalism represents a pure form of capitalism not practised by any nation today. The ideology driving today's capitalism says that competition is in the best interest of consumers. Companies in competition for profit will make better products cheaper and faster to gain a larger share of the market. In this system, the market—what people buy and the laws of supply and demand—dictates what companies make, and how much of it they make. Workers are motivated to work harder so they can afford more of the products they want.

Supporters of a capitalist system point to the higher production, greater wealth, and higher standard of living displayed by capitalist countries such as the United States. Critics, however, charge that while the standard of living may be higher, greater social inequity remains. They also denounce greed, exploitation, and high concentration of wealth and power held by a few.

SOCIALISM

Three key principles also define the economic system of socialism:

- State ownership of production and distribution of goods and services.
- Central economy.
- Production without profit.

The ideology of socialism directly rejects the ideology of capitalism. In a socialist economic system, the state determines what to produce and at what price to sell it. Socialism eliminates competition and profit, and focuses upon social equality—supplying people with what they need, whether or not they can pay. The ideals driving socialism come from Karl Marx who saw all profit as money taken away from workers. He reasoned that the labour used to produce a product determined the value of that product. The only way for a company to arrive at profit is to pay workers less than the value of the product. Thus, wherever profit exists, workers are not receiving the true value of their labour.

Just as nations do not adhere to pure capitalism, neither do nations adhere to pure socialism. In pure socialism, all workers would earn exactly the same wage. Most Socialist countries do pay managers and professionals such as doctors a higher wage. But, because the state employs all members of the society, thereby controlling the wages, far less disparity exists between highest and lowest wage earners.

Supporters of socialism, then, point to its success at achieving social equality and full employment. Critics counter that with central planning's gross inefficiency, the economy cannot produce wealth and all people are poorer. They also object to what they see as unnecessary control of personal lives and limited rights—exploitation.

SOCIAL DETERMINANTS OF ECONOMIC DEVELOPMENT

Economic development implies two things—*Economic growth* which leads to increase in production and generation of income and equitable distribution of this income among the population to improve the quality of life. Although economic development does not necessarily imply industrialization there is no historical precedent for substantial increase in per capita income without diversion of both capital and labour from agriculture. Economic development is synonymous with industrialization. *Economic development* is very much influenced by various social factors. Nation states are created with common language and culture. Economic development of any country hinges on the efficient employment of factors of production such as labour, land, capital and organization. There is commercialization of production with monetization of economy. The employment of factors of production is conditioned by cultural and social factors. The people must have the required ability, experience and knowledge to make the best use of the facilities that are made available. There is decline of the proportion of the working population engaged in agriculture. The technology plays very important role when appropriate social conditions are present.

There is trend towards urbanization of society with growth of scientific knowledge. A new value system emerges which emphasis individual initiative and responsibility and enables the individual to function without any control. The exclusiveness of clan, kin or caste breaks down and provides norms of behaviour suited to the secondary group type of relationship characteristic of an industrial society. There is widespread spread of education. The social stratification emerges based on achievement criteria and permitting occupational mobility.

DEMOCRATIC SOCIALISM AND STATE CAPITALISM

Ironically, critics of both capitalism and socialism accuse each system of exploitation. Consequently, some nations have carved out systems more in the middle of the continuum between the two.

One hybrid is democratic socialism, which is an economic system where the government maintains strict economic controls while maintaining personal freedom. Scandinavian nations, Canada, England, and Italy all practice democratic socialism. Sweden provides the most common example in which high taxation provides extensive social programs.

State capitalism is another economic hybrid. In this economic system, large corporations work closely with the government, and the government protects their interests with import restrictions, investment capital, and other assistance. This economic system commonly exists in Asian countries such as Japan and South Korea.

MODERN CORPORATIONS AND MULTINATIONALS

A corporation is a business that is legally independent from its members. Corporations may incur or pay debt, negotiate contracts, sue and be sued. Corporations range in size from local retail stores to Ford Motor Company or General Electric, the nation's largest corporation. These larger corporations sell stocks to shareholders, and the shareholders legally own the company. Management of the company remains separate from, but accountable to, the ownership. The shareholders are organized with a board of directors who hold regular meetings and make decisions on broad policies governing the corporation. Although many Americans own stock, they normally do not participate in regular board meetings or exert significant control over corporate decisions.

Sometimes corporations with closely related business may share board members, which is called an interlocking directorate. In this arrangement a manufacturer, a financial services company, and an insurance company with shared business also share the same board members. These few individuals, then, exert power over multiple companies whose business is interdependent.

A conglomerate is a corporation made up of many smaller companies, or subsidiaries, that may or may not have related business interests. The buying and selling of corporations for profit—rather than for the service or products they provide—form conglomerates. The process of corporate merger often leads to large layoffs because, as companies combine forces, many jobs are duplicated in the other company. For example, a conglomerate may take over a smaller company, including that company's marketing department. The conglomerate will already have a marketing department capable of handling most of the new acquisition's needs. Therefore, as many as half or all of the acquired marketing department employees would lose their jobs. The same situation often occurs when two corporations of a similar size merge.

Other types of corporations include monopolies, oligopolies, and multinationals. Monopolies occur when a single company accounts for all or nearly all sales of a product or service in a market. Monopolies are illegal in the United States because they eliminate competition and can fix prices, which hurts consumers. In other words, monopolies interfere with capitalism. The U.S. government does consider some monopolies legal, however, such as utilities where competition would be difficult to implement without distressing other social systems. But even utility monopolies have seen increased competition in recent years. Telephone companies were the first utility to witness a rise in competition with the breakup of AT&T in the 1980's. Recently electric power companies have seen deregulation and increased competition in some regions as well.

Oligopolies exist when several corporations have a monopoly in a market. The classic example of an oligopoly would be American auto makers until the 1980s. Ford, Chrysler, and General Motors manufactured nearly all vehicles built in America. As globalization has increased, so has competition, and few oligopolies exist today.

Multinationals are corporations that conduct business in many different countries. These corporations produce more goods and wealth than many smaller countries. Their existence, though, remains controversial. They garner success by entering less-developed nations, bringing industry into these markets with cheaper labour, and then exporting those goods to more-developed countries. Business advocates point to the higher standard of living in most countries where multinationals have entered the economy. Critics charge that multinationals exploit poor workers and natural resources, creating environmental havoc.

ALIENATION AT WORK

Alienation at work–feelings of powerlessness, meaninglessness, isolation, and self-estrangement–continues to be an important research issue in sociology and organizational theory because it takes a heavy toll on workers' lives and organizational productivity. The Smithers Institute has collected qualitative data on the work lives of a number of blue collar occupations, including construction workers, autoworkers, mail handlers, nurse's aides, emergency service workers, and store workers. Building on Blauner's social psychological theory of alienation, the Smithers Institute is in the process of completing a book on alienation and blue collar workers in the twenty-first century. In the new globalized economy and its high-commitment organizations, alienation is supposed to be a psychological relic of the past. Our analysis, however, highlights that alienation remains a serious problem for blue-collar workers and their employing organizations and that, under modern theories of managerial control, alienation at work has only become worse.

When, in our highly instrumental society, we find ourselves without natural association and production, we feel alienation.

Normally, living instrumentally does not lead to alienation. After a hard day of instrumental association, one can go home and relax with family and friends—his natural associations. One may even have some friends at work. And, at the end of the week, after all his hard instrumental work, one get his paycheque, which (after taking care of the necessities) brings him some natural pleasures — movies, books, restaurants, hobbies, sports.... And one may even get some natural satisfaction in his work itself.

Unfortunately, in a largely instrumental society, these things are easily undermined. First, we may discover that we lack natural associations — that we are rather lonely people. There may be a fundamental scarcity of natural associations: Our families are very small, we move around a lot, friends and lovers come and go. One death in a modern day "sub-nuclear" family, for example, can be far more devastating than many deaths in a tribal community.

We can also lose faith in people. We teach our kids "never judge a book by its cover," "all that glitters is not gold," "never take candy from a stranger...." We teach them to take people not as they appear to be, but to look for hidden motives, to look for what they are really after — to look at them instrumentally. But what happens, then, when the child decides to put Daddy in the same category he has been taught to use with the used-car salesman? The natural is undermined by the instrumental.

We also discover our lack of natural production — our boredom. Again, the scarcity of natural production is a problem: How many "creative" jobs are there, really? How much of even a good job is actually interesting? How much time and money can we spend on our rather contrived (i.e., instrumental) hobbies and sports?

Further, as with association, instrumental production tends to drive out natural production. Remember Deci's research? Give kids gold stars for what they enjoy doing and, before you know it, they no longer do it unless the gold star is waiting! Paying an artist for creativity or a thinker for inventiveness is like paying someone for sex... the thrill soon evaporates.

But even with little in the way of natural association and production, we can get along quite well. The instrumental life still has its rewards. There has to be something that triggers alienation, that makes us aware of it: This happens when instrumental association and production fail, that is, when we are faced with the fact that all that work actually does not lead to happiness.

The failure of instrumental association and production can happen in two ways. First, it can be a matter of means: If we lose our jobs, to use the obvious example, we cannot pay our bills — and our pleasures are the first things we have to sacrifice. If you flunk out of college, there is no degree, and no fine career, waiting for us.

The failure of the instrumental can also be a matter of ends: Money can provide an opportunity for natural enjoyments, but it cannot buy them. Our inclination, when life begins to bore us, is to throw more money into "entertainment." But when the entertainment fails to entertain, we ask ourselves "is this all there is?"

DIVISION OF LABOUR

Division of labour is the term first used in Adam Smith's the Wealth of Nations to describe the separation of manufacturing process into distinct and simple operations which are then delegated to specific hands or machines to perform. Smith thought that the quality and quantity of work carried out by a workforce organized along the division of labour principle was so superior compared to work done by non-divided labour that he said—The greatest improvement in the productive powers of labour, and the greater part of the skill, dexterity, and judgment with which it is anywhere directed, seem to have been the effects of division of labour.

The Wealth of Nations lies in the concept of economic growth. Growth, according to Smith, is rooted in the increasing division of labour. This idea relates primarily to the specialization of the labour force, essentially the breaking down of large jobs into many tiny components. Under this regime each worker becomes an expert in one isolated area of production, thus increasing his efficiency. The fact that labourers do not have to switch tasks during the day further saves time and money. Of course, this is exactly what allowed Victorian factories to grow throughout the nineteenth century. Assembly line technology made it necessary for a worker to focus his or her attention on one small part of the production process. Surprisingly, Smith recognized the potential problems of this development. He pointed out that forcing individuals to perform mundane and repetitious tasks would lead to an ignorant, dissatisfied work force. For this reason he advanced the revolutionary belief that governments had an obligation to provide education to workers. This sprung from the hope that education could combat the deleterious effects of factory life. Division of labour also implies assigning each worker to the job that suits him best. Productive labour, to Smith, fulfils two important requirements. First, it must "lead to the production of tangible objects." Second, labour must "create a surplus" which can be reinvested into production.

Another main concern for Smith involved tracing the roots of value. He identified two different kinds of value, "use value" and "exchange value." The concept of exchange value interested Smith considerably. The diamond-water paradox, in particular, proved puzzling to him: Why is it that diamonds, which have very little practical use, command a higher price than water which is indispensable to life? By discovering the true source of value Smith hoped to find a benchmark for measuring economic growth. Eventually Smith settled on labour as the source of value: The number of hours labour that a good can be exchanged for constitutes its inherent worth. (Note, this is not the same as saying that a good is worth the number of hours spent in its production.) The value of a good can also be referred to as the "natural price." The natural price need not function as the actual cost of a good in the marketplace. Competition, however, was expected to push the market price towards the natural price.

THE DIVISION OF LABOUR IN SOCIETY

Division of labour is the specialisation of cooperative labour in specific, circumscribed tasks and like roles. Historically an increasingly complex division of labour is closely associated with the growth of total output and trade, the rise of capitalism, and of the complexity of industrialisation processes. Division of labour was also a method used by the Sumerians to categorise different jobs, and divide them to skilled members of a society.

In 'The Division of Labour in Society' Durkheim attempts to determine what is the basis of social solidarity in society and how this has changed over time. This was Durkheim's first major work, so it does not address all the issues that be considered important. However, it does present some of Durkheim's basic views and also illustrates some of the methods he used throughout his life. While this book may seem incomplete or inadequate today, it is a major part of Durkheim's sociological approach.

Durkheim's basic argument is that there are two types of social solidarity, mechanical solidarity and organic solidarity. The former characterizes earlier societies, where the division of labour is relatively limited. The latter characterizes societies with a highly developed division of labour, and it is this division of labour itself which creates organic solidarity. In both types of societies, individuals for the most part "interact in accordance with their obligations to others and to society as a whole." In doing so, each person also receives some recognition of his or her own rights and contributions within the collectivity. Social morality in this sense is 'strictly necessary' for solidarity between people to occur; without morality, "societies cannot exist."

According to Giddens, the main substantive problem for Durkheim stems from "an apparent moral ambiguity concerning the relationship between the individual and society in the contemporary world." On the one hand, with specialization and the highly developed division of labour, individuals develop their own consciousness, and are encouraged in this specialization. On the other hand, there are also moral ideas encouraging people to be well rounded, of service to society as a whole. These two seem contradictory, and Durkheim is concerned with finding the historical and sociological roots of each of these, along with how these two seemingly contradictory moral guidelines are reconciled in modern society.

LABOUR UNIONS

In the face of large corporations, individual workers have typically felt alienated and vulnerable. While corporations may not hear the individual, labourers recognized that they would hear a united voice. This realization led the workers to develop labour unions—organized groups of labourers who advocate improved conditions and benefits for workers. Labour unions remained strong throughout much of the early and mid-twentieth century. In recent years, however, labour unions in the United States have lost numbers and power. With increasing globalization, corporate mergers, and downsizing, many experts expect to see an increase in labour unions again as workers seek stability and a greater share in the benefits of the global economy.

POLITICS AND MAJOR POLITICAL STRUCTURE

Politics is the social structure and methods used to manage a government or state. Just as varying types of economic theories and systems exist, many varying political theories and systems exist as well.

The political system in use depends upon the nation-state. A nation is a people with common customs, origin, history, or language. A state, on the other hand, is a political entity with legitimate claim to monopolize use of force through police, military, and so forth. The term nation-state refers to a political entity with the legitimate claim to monopolize use of force over a people with common customs, origin, history, or language. Sociologists and political scientists prefer the term nation-state to "country" because it is more precise.

While many different political structures have existed throughout history, three major forms exist in modern nation-states: totalitarianism, authoritarianism, and democracy.

Totalitarianism is when the government has complete and total control of economy, market, and all facets of a nation's people's lives.

TOTALITARIANISM

Totalitarianism is a political system that exercises near complete control over its citizens' lives and tolerates no opposition. Information is restricted or denied by complete control of mass media, close monitoring of citizens and visitors, and forbidding the gathering of groups for political purposes opposed to the state. Constant political propaganda, such as signs, posters, and media that focus the populace on the virtues of the government, characterizes these nation states.

Obviously, some totalitarian governments maintain more extreme laws than others do. Totalitarian nation-states include North Korea, Chile, many African and Middle Eastern nations, Vietnam, and others.

AUTHORITARIANISM

Authoritarianism is a political system less controlling than totalitarianism, but still denying citizens the right to participate in government. A dictatorship, in which the primary authority rests in one individual, represents one type of authoritarian government. Dictators rule China, Cuba, Ethiopia, Haiti, and many African nations. In these systems, strong militaries and political parties support the dictators. Another form of authoritarianism is a monarchy, in which the primary authority rests in a family and is passed down through generations. In the past, most monarchies exerted near absolute power—in Saudi Arabia the ruling family still does. Most remaining monarchies today, however, such as those in the Scandinavian nations, Great Britain, Denmark, and the Netherlands, are constitutional monarchies where the royal families serve only as symbolic heads of state. Parliament or some form of democratic electoral process truly governs these nation states.

Militarism and Authoritarianism.

DEMOCRACY

Democracy is a political system where the government is ruled either directly by the people or through elected officials who represent them. Most democracies today rely upon a system of representatives to make decisions. The most common examples of democracies are the United States, Canada, Germany, and many other European nations.

Parliament House of Delhi.

PRINCIPLES OF DEMOCRACY

Democracy is a method of leading a country. The most general explanation of democracy is ruling by the people. This implies, the people approve to the government operating the nation. Citizens are given an opening to select, via their right to vote. They do this in standard, on the house and just elections. Nevertheless, democracy does not conclude there. Democracy also implies that the people who have been elected are liable in multiple ways to the people who voted for them and elected them. They have to function and carry on the pledges they made during elections and they have to be transparent in their duties and actions. Even though gradations are applicable to the world's range of democracies, some principles and strategies differentiate democratic government from other types of government. Democratic principles are thoughts which most citizens believe are vital for a democracy. The most significant principles of democracy are as follows:

(i) **Public Involvement:** Citizens have a right and a responsibility to play a part in government and in social community. Citizens' contribution incorporates contesting for elections, voting for elections, becoming educated and aware, organizing and attending public meetings, being a part of civil and/or political associations, paying taxes, disputing and imploring.

(ii) **Egalitarianism:** All citizens should be deemed uniformly and devoid of prejudice and be given equivalent chances and prospects.

(iii) **Open-Mindedness:** Even as a large amount of people reign in a democracy, the rights of minority sectors are also sheltered. Everybody should be permitted to communicate their views and join the political, holy or civil organizations of their preference. Liability Government must be liable to the citizens for its proceedings, together with the laws that are approved and how these laws are executed.

People's role: The prospects for democracy in India have not shrunk but grown since Independence. This is mainly due to the people and the popular struggles.

(iv) **Lucidity:** Government must be transparent to the citizens about its functions. It must permit the public to give view points before laws are conceded.

(v) **Customary, Liberated and Justified Elections:** Elections must take place in a liberated and fair way, devoid of any pressure, threats, dishonesty and intimidation to the citizens before or during the election. Elections should also be held on a regular basis, every few years.

(vi) **Accepting the Outcome of Elections:** When a political party is defeated in election, its followers must agree with this outcome and not use hostility to modify the results.

(vii) **Financial Liberty:** Citizens in a democracy should be permitted to have some type of personal possession of property and business and they should be permitted to select their own category of work and be a part of labour unions. The government should not completely have power over the economy of a country.

(viii) **Managing Exploitation of Authority:** There should be modes to put off government authorities from misusing their control. The courts should be autonomous and they should have the authority to:

- Function against government representatives or bodies that get involved in an illegitimate or fraudulent act
- Permit for civic contribution and elections
- Keep a check on police misuse of authority

(ix) **Human Rights:** The human rights of persons and groups should be guarded, if possible through a Bill of Rights. A bill of rights consists of a listing of rights and liberties that are assured to all citizens in the nation. All rights and liberties are sheltered if they are harmed.

(x) **Multiple Party Structures:** Over one political party must be permitted to take part in elections and play a task in administration.

(xi) **Rule of Law:** The rule of law implies that nobody and no authority is higher than the law, together with the chief of the country. Everybody must comply with the law and be held answerable if they break the law. The law must also be evenly, reasonably and constantly imposed.

While voting we give the government an authorization to go by and implement laws on our behalf. In formulating laws the government has to pursue what is mentioned in the constitution and it uses the courts additionally just as the police and military to impose the laws.

If the government turns out of favour or does not do what it assured to do then citizens of a nation can vote for another party in the subsequent election and vote the reigning government out of supremacy. This is fundamentally how democracy functions and why it is effectual as a structure of government.

ELITE THEORY

Elite theory developed in part as a reaction to Marxism. It rejected the Marxian idea that a classless society having an egalitarian structure could be realized after class struggle in every society. It regards Marxism as an ideology rather than an objective analysis of social systems. According to Elite theory man can never be liberated from the subjugation of an elite structure. The term Elite refers to those who excel. The classical elite theorists identify the governing elite in terms of superior personal qualities of those who exercise power. However later versions of elite theory places less emphasis on the personal qualities of the powerful and more on the institutional framework of the society.

They argued that the hierarchical organization of social institutions allows a minority to monopolize power. Another criticism of the elite theories against the Marxian view of distribution of power is that the ruling class too large and amorphous a group to be able to effectively wield power. In their view power is always exercised by a small cohesive group of the elite. Elite theory argues that all societies are divided into two main groups a ruling minority and the ruled. This situation is inevitable. If the proletarian revolution occurs it will merely result in the replacement of one ruling elite by another. Classical elite theory was propounded by Pareto and Mosca.

POWER ELITE

C. Wright Mills has presented a new version of the elite theory. Mills limits his analysis to the American society only. He does not believe that elite rule is inevitable. In fact he sees it as fairly recent development. He rejects the view that the members of the elite have superior qualities or psychological characteristics which distinguish them from the rest of the population. Instead he argues that the structure of institutions is such that those at the top of the institutional hierarchy largely monopolized power. Certain institutions can be pivotal positions in societies and the elite comprise those who hold command posts in those institutions. Mills identifies three key institutions: The major corporations, the Military and the Federal Government.

Those who occupy the command posts in those institutions form three elites. In practice however the interest and activities of the elite are sufficiently similar and inter connected to form a single ruling minority which Mills terms the Power Elite. The cohesiveness and unity of the power elite is strengthened by the similarity of the backgrounds of its members and another change and overlapping of personnel between the three elites. Members are largely drawn from the upper strata of the society. They share similar educational backgrounds and mix socially in the high prestige clubs. Within the power elite there is frequent interchange of personnel between the elites. Mills has also rejected the Marxian view that political power automatically follows economic power. He has shown a preference for power elite rather than ruling class.

According to him class is an economic term and rule is a political one. The ruling class in its political connotations does not allow enough autonomy to the political order and its agents and it says nothing about the military. Thus power elite is a more suitable term than ruling class. R.K. Merton has further supported Mills view that the power elite are recruited from the same social class and are educated in similar prestigious colleges and schools and have similar orientation.

COMMUNITY POWER STRUCTURE

Community power structure refers to the distribution of power at the local community level. There are numerous empirical studies to discover the nature of the distribution of power at community level. Among these community studies two categories can be clearly identified one supporting the major contention of the elite thesis and the other refuting the elitist argument and replacing it by what is known as the Pluralist Thesis.

Lloyd Hunter's Community Power Structure based on the study of distribution of power in Atlantic is a prominent study in the elitist tradition. Hunter's study was based on reputational approach. He made a preliminary list of 175 leaders who held formal important positions in politics, business and civic organizations and have reputation for leadership. Then he selected the panel of 14 judges representing religious, business and professional interest and asked them to select those who in their eyes are the top leaders. The result showed that half of these leaders were upper-class businessmen. The empirical study confirms the elitist thesis that a clear defined group of decision makers can be identified who are highly organized and who decisively dominate the public life of the organized and who decisively dominate the public life of the city.

Pluralists led by Robert Dahl have challenged the main elitist contention that a society is marked by the existence of a single centre of political power. They argued that in a society there are multiple centres of political power none of which are completely sovereign. The decision making maybe done by few but then this decision making cannot be understood except within the context of a continuous bargaining process among the elites and also of a general consensus established only through the mass approval which is hard to secure.

Further continuing his criticism of the elite model he argued that the elite theory confuses potential control with actual control. He agrees that it is quite possible that a group in the society has a very high potential for control. But that does not automatically make this group very powerful since the actual power of a group is established not only by a high potential for control but also by a high potential for nuclearity. Next according to Dahl the elite theories disregarded the fact that there may be different scopes of power and that a group having a high degree of influence over one scope may not necessarily have the same degree of influence over another scope within the same system.

Dahl selected three distinct decisions—areas covering urban development, public schools and political nominations. Within each area he studied a number of decisions thus he picks up three categories of political leaders which are political notables, social notables and economic notables and enquires whether each of these groups participate in decision-making only in one or in all of the three issue areas. He takes as the sign of power the ability to successfully initiate or veto the proposals for policies. After examining all the available data Dahl admits that the in The New Haven a tiny group the leaders exert great influence on individuals who are influential in one sector of public activity are found not to be influential in another sector and further leaders exerting influence in different issue areas do not come to be drawn from a single homogenous stratum of the community.

Dahl's pluralist model has been subjected to severe criticisms. Firstly the model wrongly locates power in concrete decisions or in activities having direct bearing on decision making. He ignores the fact that power is also exercised in creating and reinforcing social and political values and institutional practices that limit the scope of the political process to public consideration of only those issues that are comparatively harmless to the interest of the powerful. Thus the powerful groups may never let these issues which affect their vital interests come to the stage of public decision making. Thus Dahl's model fails to differentiate the unimportant issues arising in the political arena.

POLITICAL PARTIES

A political party is essentially a social group having associative type of social relationship activity and inters personal relationship. Membership rests on formally free recruitment. It is a social group because firstly it embodies the system of interdependent activity and inter-personal relationships. Secondly it operates in terms of goal oriented coordinated actions. In so far it demands from its members of rational direction of their behaviour towards commonly acknowledged goal.

The goal of a political party is to secure political power and hold it either singly or in cooperation with the other political parties. A political party is very much a clientele-oriented organization that is a party has always been on gaining as much clientele as possible and hence it tries to remain as open as possible to its potential members. The party is a mutually exploitative relationship as it is joined by those who would use it. Gabriel Almond defined political party as the socialized aggregation structure of modern societies.

Manufacturers of Political Party Banners, Flags and Signs.

FUNCTIONS OF A POLITICAL PARTY

A political party performs a wide range of functions an important one among them is the aggregation of interests. A political party is multi-interested group that represent diverse interests of the society. It tries to harmonize these interests with each other; bridges antagonism between different groups of the society and thereby seeks to produce different groups of the society and thereby seeks to produce a consensus among as many groups as possible. Political parties act as very effective mediator in setting disagreements in society in a peaceful and institutionalized manner.

A political party ensure a two way communication process between the government and the people as it is mainly through the parties that the government is constantly kept informed about the general demands of the society. About the interests and attitudes of the people in relation to the governing process. Similarly it is through the parties organize and articulate public opinion in order to bring this opinion to bear on governmental decisions. They educate and instruct the people on public issues.

These activities of the party are not confined to election time alone but they go on simultaneously. Political recruitment is another function of the political party. In a democracy political elite are recruited mainly through political parties. Leaders of governments are normally leaders of the political parties. The party plays a very significant role in the process of political socialization in a country. Party is a very important instrument for political participation of the people; it is in course of extending the opportunities of this political participation to the people that the party socializes them. The political socialization performed by political parties may however assumes two distinct forms the party may either reinforce the existing political culture or it may try to alter the established political cultural pattern by generating new attitudes and beliefs.

BI-PARTY SYSTEM

The American Government has been controlled by two political parties for many years. The Democratic Party and the Republican Party are the two major political parties. A political party is a group of people with similar political views that want to control government and promote their ideas. Each political party believes that their ways of governing are the best way to lead the country to health and prosperity. The Democrats believe in liberalism and the Republicans believe in conservatism. In the 21st century political parties have become important factors in order to raise money for campaigns, but American citizens have become less loyal to either political party. The political party in power will usually adopt ideas and policy from both sides in order to maintain support from liberals and conservatives. In many ways both political parties use different means to get to the same end. There are many smaller political parties, but most citizens who do not identify with either of the two major parties consider themselves independents. Almost every political campaign has made it a huge priority to gain support of not only their base but to independents as well in order to obtain the majority of the vote.

The Democratic Party was formed in 1792 by Thomas Jefferson as a way to promote the Bill of Rights and oppose the Federalist party. Six years later the "party of the common man" was changed to the Democratic-Republican party. The Republican party started in 1854 and stemmed from the debate on whether or not to expand slavery into the new Western territories.

During the creation of our country and for many years, political party loyalty was a lot more important than it is today. This might be due to politicians being less independent in ideas and policy than they are today. Generally speaking in the past, conservatives running for office would strictly suggest only conservative views and liberals would use only liberal ideas. However, today politicians are given credit and gain more support if they are mavericks and promote whatever policies they believe will accomplish the goal, whether it is a conservative or liberal means of doing so. President Barack Obama has been promoting mostly liberal policies. However, he has issued tax cuts to a majority of Americans and has issued a spending freeze starting in 2011. Tax cuts and spending freezes are both conservative ways to help fix economic problems. Most modern politicians balance liberalism and conservatism in order to fix our nations problems.

Independent voters are a major concern for both political parties. If a politician running for office is promoting policies that are critical to their party, then chances are they have the support of the majority of their party. Having the support from your base is usually not enough to win an election. This is why office seekers must adhere to independent voters. These are people who do not identify with either major party and will support either liberal and conservative policies depending on the issue. Over 19 million independents voted for Barack Obama in 2008.

Many Americans see the two party system as a healthy way to run the country. In order to fix current domestic and national problems, our government will need to take a liberal or conservative approach depending upon the issue. The system that runs our government today is similar to how it was in the beginning in terms of principles and values of the political parties, but we have come a long way from the system that used to be occupied by many parties. Bi-partisanship is an issue that has gotten more popular with American citizens as time goes on. Complete party loyalty is not respected today as much as it used to be and an independent approach is now the goal of many politicians.

POLITICAL PARTIES OF INDIA

Existence of political parties is regarded as an essential requirement of Democracy. In fact, it would not be an exaggeration to say that one cannot exist without the other. It is clear that we have had experience of not only the working of political parties but also of their effective functioning within the legislatures and outside. The existence of political parties and their free functioning is a barometer of the presence or absence of democracy in a country. In short, political parties are essential for democracy. The presence of political parties indicates a mark of political modernization. If we examine the party system in India we notice a strong and well-built party system suited to her conditions.

PARTIES : CLASSIFICATION

The party system being a part of a larger system is related to social, economic, cultural, regional and legal life. It is essentially a sub-system of the political framework and provides the motive force for the political machine.

CHARACTERISTIC FEATURES OF PARTIES

1. All the parties at present can trace their earlier origins to the Indian National Congress.
2. India has Multiple Party system with the dominance of a single political party.
3. The parties are characterized by fragmentation, splits, polarisation, mergers and defections etc.
4. There are no clear-cut ideological differences in the politics and programmes of parties. All parties subscribe to democracy, socialism, secularism and non-alignment.
5. Parties center round personalities rather than ideologies.

THE CONGRESS PARTY

The oldest national party in India is the Indian National Congress (INC). It was established in 1885 as a pro-British Indian organization. The real purpose of the British in establishing this organization was to continue to rule India with the help of liberal and pro-British Indians. Later on this organization became the main voice of India's freedom struggle.

Indian Congress Party workers celebrate their election victory in New Delhi.

Among its founders were Surendranath Benarjee, Dadabhai Naoroji and Justice M.G. Ranade. Before founding of the Congress, Justice M.G. Ranade had established an organization based on the ideas of the Brahmo Samaj with the aim of social and religious reforms in India. One of Ranade's disciples, G.K. Gokhale, became the leader of Indian National Congress till 1915. Gandhijee considered Gokhale as his political guru. Mahatma Gandhi, more than any other Indian, is identified with modern India's creation.

After India's independence, the British passed the administration of India to the leaders of the Indian National Congress. Mahatma Gandhi who was the father figure of the Congress party, suggested to transform the Indian National Congress into a charity organization, because the main cause of the Congress party was achieved. But the other leaders of the Congress did not accept his proposal and the Indian National Congress became a political party with a secular, socialist and democratic tendency.

During its independence, two Congress leaders Jawarharlal Nehru and Vallabbhai Patel wanted to be the first Prime Minister of India. Nehru, who was younger, was secular and socialist oriented, while Patel was more Hindu nationalist oriented. Mahatma Gandhi wanted the young Jawarharlal Nehru to be India's first Prime Minister and therefore Patel withdrew his candidacy.

Before independence the Congress was a roof organization and it included many factions. After independence the Congress leaders changed the structure of the party and established a new political agenda. The different factions in the Congress could either join the new agenda or leave the Congress. Some left the Congress and established other political parties outside the Congress. And so some new political parties were established among them the Socialist Party of India and Forward Bloc .

Until 1950 the Congress was under the influence of these two leaders. After Patel's death in 1950, Congress came under full influence of Jawarharlal Nehru. Nehru died in 1964, without appointing an heir. The party chose Lal Bahadur Shastri as the new leader. In 1966 Shastri arrived in Tashkent, in former Soviet Union to sign a cease-fire agreement with Pakistan. Shastri died in his sleep in Tashkent. After Shastri's death, some Congress leaders competed for the leadership of the party. Surprisingly the inter party election was won by the less favorite candidate, Indira Gandhi. Indira Gandhi was Jawarharlal Nehru's daughter (and had no family relations with Mahatma Gandhi). Some of the veteran members of the Congress did not accept her leadership and they tried to dispose her of. In 1969 the Congress split up into two parties.

The veteran members of the Congress established the Congress (O) Party, while Indian National Congress was recognized as Congress (R). Of these two parties the INC was the larger and dominant party. The Congress (O) was no threat to Indira Gandhi's Congress.

Indira Gandhi was a very centralist leader. She pulled all the strings in the party and was seen as the dictator of her party. She planned to inherit her party to her younger son, Sanjay Gandhi. Between the years 1975-77 Indira Gandhi proclaimed emergency rule. During this period many of Gandhi's political rivals were arrested and put behind the bars. Censorship was enforced on Indian Press. The justice system was restricted and turned into 'puppet show' of the government. The people also suffered a lot from this emergency rule. Under the birth control policy many people were forced to have sterilization. Even so Indira Gandhi was sure that the Indian people supported her because her general intention of making India a better place and so she declared elections in 1977.

Her party lost the 1977 elections to the Janata Party. A few months after the Congress defeat in the elections, another split occured in the Congress party. The party of Indira Gandhi was called Congress (I), because of the initial of her name. During this period many more splits and coalitions occurred within the different Congress Parties. One such party of the Congress during this period was established by former Congress member Sharad Pawar. He even established a government in the state of Maharashtra with this party which later on was known as Congress (S). Another party was established in Uttar Pradesh. Some of these new party members including it establishers like Sharad Pawar returned later on to the Congress (I) Party and the party was renamed Indian National Congress.

But there are others who left the INC at different periods and established parties outside the Congress and have a name Congress in their party name. For example West Bengal Trinamool Congress was established by Mamta Bannerjee in West Bengal before the 1998 elections. Tamil Maanila Congress was established by Moopanar in Tamil Nadu. And there are more other such parties. There were some Congress members who resigned from the Congress and established parties without having the name Congress in their party name. For example Lok Dal which, was established in the 1960s by Charan Singh and Janata Dal which was established by V.P. Singh after resigning from the INC in the late 1980s. Before the 1999 elections some senior members of the INC were forced to resign because they questioned the leadership of Sonia Gandhi. These people have created the National Congress Party to participate in 1999 elections.

Sonia Gandhi who lead the INC in the 1999 elections is the widow of Rajiv Gandhi, the elder son of Indira Gandhi. She was born in Italy to a European Christian family. She met Rajiv Gandhi in England and married him. Indira Gandhi intended to inherit her party to her younger son Sanjay. But Sanjay died in a plane crash in 1980. So Indira Gandhi forced her elder son, who had no interest in politics, to resign from his job as a pilot and join politics. In 1984, Indira Gandhi was assassinated by her Sikh bodyguards. Rajiv Gandhi was proclaimed her heir. He was Prime Minister of India until 1989. In the 1991 election campaign a suicide bomber assassinated him. The Congress appointed Narsimha Rao as its new leader. After losing the 1996 elections Rao resigned. For sometime Sitaram Kesari was the leader, but many Congress members saw in Sonia Gandhi as the new leader and gave her lot of respect. They thought that the Congress needs a 'Gandhi' as its leader to attract votes.

At present, Congress Party is headed by Prime Minister Dr. Mamohan Singh under the U.P.A. Government, which is backed by Mrs. Sonia Gandhi, the Chairperson of the Party.

THE COMMUNIST PARTY OF INDIA

The Communist Party of India is a part of the World Communist Movement. The party existed in the country even during pre-independece days. Though the party has been recognised as a national party its influence is limited to the States of West Bengal, Kerala and Andhra Pradesh. In the World Communist Movement there was ideological schism going on between the Soviet Union and China. This led to a split in the party in 1964. The Communist Party of India is ideologically close to the Soviet Union, while the CPI (M) is a follower of the China camp.

The party organisation is based on its constitution framed in 1958 at the Amritsar Conference. The Constitution was changed to throw away the militant revolutionary ideology and accept Parliamentary Democracy as the method to achieve the party goals. The party structure, in theory is based on democratic centralism wchich rests on two principles (1) Central leadership based on intra-party democracy, and (2) intra-party democracy based on centralised leadership. Intra-party democracy means freedom to debate within the party to check its action.

THE COMMUNIST PARTY OF INDIA (MARXIST)

The Communist Party of India (Marxist) was formed as a result of split in the Communist Party of India in the year 1964. The split was the result of the increasing schism in the Soviet Union-China relations as well as because of the conflicting evaluations by the communists of the economic and political situations within the country. Further, one group favored support to Nehru's government whereas the other demanded tough opposition to the reactionary Congress. These ideological differences reached a point of no return and finally the dissidents held a separate convention at Tenali in July 1964. Thus they got separated from the Dange Group (CPI) under the leadership of Jyoti Basu, E.M.S. Namboodiripad and others. The Communist Party of India (M) was formed in 1964. The CPM has established its stronghold in Kerala, West Bengal, Tripura, Andhra Pradesh and Assam, though its influence has been declining over the years.

Communist Party of India (Marxist).

SOCIALIST PARTIES

The history of the socialist parties is one of splits and merges. The origin of the soclialist party is traced back to the group of socilaist called Congress Socialist within the Congress Party led by Jayapraksash Narayan, M.R. Masani, Ashok Mehta, and others. The party was formed in 1948 and thereafter the history of the Socialist Parties has been one of splits and mergers as well as constant changes in the names of the party, such as Prajas Socialist Party, Socialist Party, Samyukta Socialist Party and again Socialist Party. In 1975 Samyukta Socialist Party and Praja Socialit Party merged and formed the Socialist Party and those who called themselves and lohiaites joined the Bharatheeya Lokdal. The socialist party one of the constituent parties that formed the Janatha Party in 1977.

There was a constant identity in the organizational set up of the Praja Socialist Party and Samyukta Socialist Party. The National Conference was the highest party organ which met once a year. Its function was to elect the Party executive and to lay down the policy and programme for the ensuing year.

ALL INDIA MUSLIM LEAGUE

All India Muslim League was formed in 1906 to protect the interests of the Muslim Community in India. Starting with a request for seperate representation in the Legislatures, the League become vocal in its demand for Pakistan under the leadership of M.A. Jinnah. This demand had to be conceded at the time of the Indian Independence and seperate Pakistan was created in 1947. It is continuing to represent Muslims even after independence.

NATIONAL PARTIES

Abbreviation	Party
BJP	Bharatiya Janata Party
CPI	Communist Party of India
CPI (M)	Communist Party of India (Marxist)
INC	Indian National Congress
JD	Janata Dal
SAP	Samata Party
NDA	National Democratic Alliance

STATE PARTIES

Abbreviation	Party
AC	Arunachal Congress
AIADMK	All India Anna Dravida Munnetra Kazhagam
AGP	Asom Gana Parishad
ASDC	Autonomous State Demanding Committee
AIMIM	All India Majlis-E-Ittehadul Muslimeen
AIRJP	All India Rashtriya Janata Party
BJD	Biju Janata Dal
BSP	Bahujan Samaj Party
DMK	Dravida Munnetra Kazhagam
FBL	All India Forward Bloc (FBL)
FPM	Federal Party of Manipur
HLD(R)	Haryana Lok Dal (Rashtriya)
HVP	Haryana Vikas Party
JDS	Janata Dal (Secular)
JDU	Janata Dal (United)
JKN	Jammu & Kashmir National Conference
JMM	Jharkhand Mukti Morcha

KEC	Kerala Congress
KEC(M)	Kerala Congress (M)
LS	Lok Shakti
MSCP	Manipur State Congress Party
MAG	Maharashtrawadi Gomantak
MDMK	Marumalarchi Dravida Munnetra Kazhagam
MNF	Mizo National Front
MPP	Manipur People's Party
MUL	Muslim League Kerala State Committee
NCP	Nationalist Congress Party
PMK	Pattali Makkal Katchi
PWPI	Peasants and Workers Party of India
RJD	Rashtriya Janata Dal
RPI	Republican Party of India
RSP	Revolutionary Socialist Party
SAD	Shiromani Akali Dal
SDF	Sikkim Democratic Front
SHS	Shiv Sena
SJP	Samajwadi Janata Party
SP	Samajwadi Party
TDP	Telegu Desam Party
UDP	United Democratic Party
UGDP	United Goans Democratic Party
UMFA	United Minorities Front, Assam
WBTC	West Bengal Trinamul Congress

PRESSURE GROUPS

In democratic politics, pressure groups are organisations which attempt to influence the government. The International Encyclopaedia of the Social Sciences describes the groups as representing the interest of the sections into which a society is divided. With advanced specialisation groups will be more numerous and specialised. Such groups represent interest of various sections of society viz., farmers, labourers, government employees, businessmen, professional people and even students. Pressure groups are also known as interest groups.

Pressure groups are organised associations, unions or organisation of people having common interest. Their aim is to seek better conditions for their members through organised efforts. They try to influence the legislature, executive and other decision makers to have decisions made in their favour.

According to V.O. Key, a striking feature of American politics is the extent to which political parties are supplemented by private associations formed to influence public policy. These organisations are commonly called pressure groups. David B. Truman defines an interest group as "a shared attitude group that makes certain claims upon the other groups in the society." One of the major trends in democratic political process is the increasing role of pressure groups. Herman Finer viewed that it is perhaps now an axiom of political science that, where political parties are weak in principles and organisation, the pressure groups will flourish; where pressure groups are strong, political parties will be feeble; and where political parties are strong, pressure groups will be curbed. In the context of the USA, the rigid nature of its constitution, the doctrine of separation of powers, difficulties of conveying the grievances of the people to the government, etc. contribute to the growth of pressure groups in American politics. American pressure groups are not much influenced by the political parties whereas in Britain pressure groups implicitly or explicitly have attachment with political parties. Indian political parties are weak in principles and organisation. Therefore, pressure groups are supposed to be very significant in the functioning of the Indian Political System. In parliamentary system of government, pressure groups exert pressure mainly on the executive with the assumption that legislature is under the control of executive.

PRESSURE GROUPS IN DIFFERENT SOCIAL SYSTEMS

In modern society, pressure groups can be found among the numerous voluntary associations, such as labour unions, trades associations, and reform groups, that have some interest at stake in politics. However, essentially the same phenomenon as the modern pressure-group existed in other times when society was not so mobile and associations not so voluntary.

"Almost every interest in medieval society,"writes Helen Gam "almost every element in its make-up, has left its trace on the legislation of council and parliament." She listed the principal sources of legislative activity as: "The directive or planning urge in the ruler, the need for clarifying and defining experience by the judicature, and the demand from the ruled for redress of grievances. " This last source, "public" demand, meant, especially by the end of the fifteenth century, about what it means today, although the interests have changed somewhat. The medieval pressure-groups were the legal profession, the clergy, the nobility, the landowners, the sheriffs and bailiffs, the merchants, and the leaders of localities. Also, developing continuously as an influence on lawmaking through the late medieval and early modern periods was the notion of the commonwealth, often a mere pretence or rationalization and yet often truly advanced.

Modern pressure-groups have grown in close relation to the various party systems. When there are many parties, a number of such interest groups can be absorbed into the party system. Then the problem of pressure groups becomes almost inextricable from the general study of the political parties. In England, where one kind of two-party system exists, pressure groups play a role different from the role they play in America, where another kind of two-party system exists. In England, until recently, a small group drawn from the same social class had been able to represent dominant landed, religious and commercial interests. Many members of Parliament incarnated the values that might have otherwise prompted strong and numerous pressure groups.

But in America, society has been for a long time relatively classless. The politician has been an individualist, footloose by comparison with his British counterpart, free to bargain and willing to deal with a variety of opposing groups. Furthermore, the American economy is tremendously diversified, the population exceedingly heterogeneous, and the political structure greatly decentralized and unintegrated. The formal structure of the government cannot reflect faithfully any large part of the interests, which must seek informal ways of influencing the government.

An analysis of seventy parliamentary enactments of 1936-37 by Professor W. Ivor Jennings shows that private interests do inspire legislation but also reveals how orderly is the process by which the interests affect the British law. If we abstract, not without some loss of realism, the data furnished by Professor Jennings on the informal sources of law, we find that, of the 70 enactments, the sources of 9 lay in Cabinet policy, of 27 in the departments of the government, of 7 in a combination of departmental and pressure-group interests, of 5 in a combination of departmental and local authorities, of 3 in combinations of individual members and pressure groups, of 3 in pressure groups, of 2 in local authorities, of 2 in combinations of departments, pressure groups, and local authorities, and of 1 each in 10 different elements or combinations of elements.

Thus, if one may take 1936 as a usual year, one may conclude that local authorities and pressure groups are active in the British legislative process. Scrutiny of the many sources reveals, however, that English pressure groups and authorities operate more publicly and with more formality than do pressure groups in American legislatures. Furthermore, British interests appear to be tamed by Cabinet and department to an extent undreamed of in American legislatures. The external interests are operative, but in a consultative and organized fashion. The looseness, informality, and mystery of American lobbying is mainly absent.

VOTING BEHAVIOUR

Elections and voting are an indispensable part of the democratic political system. One of the major tasks of the political parties is to contest elections.

They select such candidates who have greater chances of winning. Candidates who have greater influence on voters and who have greater vote-catching capacity are an asset to any political party.

Voting like a party system is the means to select the representatives of people who perform the functions of a government in a democracy. Through the process of voting an unpopular government can removed from the power by the people. The opposition can also bring down a party in power through a vote of no confidence in the Assembly or Parliament. The voting has its own pattern. Generally educated and educated electorate feels more involved. The rural and illiterate lower classes are somewhat apathetic to it.

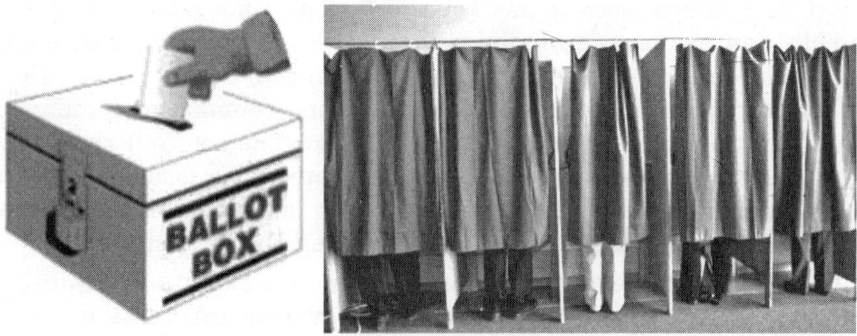

A significant number of voters change their mind about who to vote for when they enter the polling booth.

Some people follow the tradition and vote for the same party. Election system, campaigning and voting depends upon the political culture. Modern democracies have introduced universal adult franchise. The right to vote has been conferred on all the citizens without any kind of discrimination. In India also all the citizens irrespective of their caste, colour, creed, religion, region or sex are given the right to vote. The right to vote is a fundamental right guaranteed by the constitutional law of the country.

DETERMINANTS OF VOTING BEHAVIOUR IN INDIA

In a multilingual, multicultural democratic set up like India, voting behaviour is dictated by a plethora of complex issues. From time and again it has been proved that political parties in India can not rely upon any particular factor to win the trust and confidence of the voters. Such is the complex nature of the voting behaviour that even the best of the psephologists or social scientists or even genius politicians failed to read public psychology on numerous occasions. Below is a summary of the determinants of such perplexing electoral psychology.

Caste has been an important factor in Indian politics. Though recent trends show that its impact is more prominent in the state level politics, it plays a crucial role in shaping up the policy of the governments. Wooing a specific caste has been the principal agenda of many a politicians. This has been a retrogressive character of Indian politics and has so far been playing a divisive role.

Religion is another pull down factor of Indian electoral politics. Rather than uniting people, religion has mostly divided India into many watertight compartments. Fundamentalists have taken political mileage of the situation by wooing people belonging to a specific religion and infused the poison of communalism in the electoral psychology.

Regionalism has been a key determinant of Indian voting behaviour since 1990s. Demanding separate state, promoting region specific interests have been the strategies of politicians to capture the vote bank. This has bred separatism and endangered internal security of the country.

Language is another important factor in this regard. Although its impact is not prominet in state level politics, in the national level it has played a key role. Dividing India into Hindi and non Hindi belts is an unfortunate outcome of this.

Hero worshipping is another popular trend in India psephology. On numerous occasions political parties have tried to capture popular sentiment by using charisma of their leaders. Therefore many political parties of India today are leader based rather than being ideology based.

Ideology has been a key factor in Indian politics. Communism is a glaring example of this and though recent trends show some changes, Bengal, Tripura, Kerala have long been communist strongholds.

Some important or sudden events or incidences can change the voting behaviour as well as political equations. The proclamation of emergency was one such incidence which resulted in the then Congress government being toppled by the Janata Party in 1977.

Development works in the most silent yet the most effective manner in determining the popular mandate in elections in India. Developmental slogans like "Roti, Kapda, Aur Makaan", "Garibi Hathao", "Bijli, Sadak, Aur Pani" have long been used to attract the attention of the people.

Apart from the above mentioned factors, race, anti incumbency factor, terrorism etc have been the other determinants. However it must be noted that many a times a number of factors work in tandem to shape up the popular electoral opinion, thus making it further difficult for the politicians to make use of the existing situation and thereby producing unpredictable results as has happened in the national level in 2004 or in several states in the recent Lok Sabha Election.

DEMOCRACY AND AUTHORITARIAN GOVERNMENT

A democratic society makes a clear distinction between state and society and there is a constitutional limitation on the power of the state. This consists of demarcation of activities as those, which the state is well adapted to perform, and those, which it cannot perform and hence should not interfere, in such activities.

There exist a number of institutions, which keep an eye on the functioning of state to ensure that the state does not overstep its limits. The Fundamental Rights in the Indian Constitution, Judiciary and Press are an example of the limits imposed on the activities of the state. Authoritarian government represents a fusion of state and society an entire social system in which politics profoundly affects the whole range of human activities and associations. Thus an authoritarian government accepts no limitation on the amount or kind of coercion it may use to achieve its ends. It can execute exile or place people in the labour of prison camps without any restraint.

Hence authoritarian power is unlimited in scope. It is all embracing. The government asserts the right to control and regiment every phase of life. In a democratic society power is distributed among plurality of groups. There exist professional associations, trade unions, business organizations and religious institutions like Churches, Mosques and political parties. These institutions keep each other in check thus protecting political freedom. The democratic society encourages competition among political parties and they inhibit monopolies of power. In authoritarian societies there tends to be near total centralization of power in the hands of few.

It does not permit plurality of parties in state. There exists one official political party organization. It plays an important role in strengthening the top leaders. The party is a training ground for future leaders and administrators. The state has an army of volunteers who observe the population and report subversive activities. In democratic societies means of mass communication like T.V., radio and press etc. tend to be independent of government and there exists freedom to criticize. Dissent is permitted. In authoritarian set-up government takes over the entire public communication system and means of media like T.V., radio, cinema and publication of books and magazines. The prohibition of media stifles any opposition. The government filters out anything that might create unfavourable attitudes to their power.

Democratic government is characterized by emphasis on autonomy of individuals and subsystems. There is a greater tolerance for individual and organizational opposition. The right to participate in and to oppose the government is a hallmark of democratic society. Cultural organizations, pressure groups, political parties, trade union actively seek to influence the government. The development of autonomy threatens the authoritarian regime. They try to establish control over organized groups. They do not permit organizations like trade unions, youth clubs and political parties to become powerful. The loyalty to state is above loyalty to family and friends. Government controlled youth leagues; trade unions and other organizations have multiplied under communism and fascism.

They are instituted and controlled from above to mobilize people in courses of action desired by the ruling elite and to prevent the development of independent groups and opinion. An important feature of democratic government is rule of law and equality before law. Thus the leaders and the officials are not permitted to take arbitrary decisions and the law of land equally governs all the individuals irrespective of their status. However authoritarian regime is characterized by arbitrary exercise of powers especially by police and para military forces because authoritarian regimes depend on the extensive use of arbitrary police power. They are often referred to as police state. In a democracy political leaders rely more on persuasion and less on coercion.

The legitimacy of government depends on the popular support. Thus any attempt at coercion would mean antagonizing the public opinion and loss of power in the next elections. However authoritarian regimes rely on coercive methods to root out opposition and dissent. The Nazi concentration camps and Siberian labour camps in Stalin's Russia are classic examples of repressive control in an authoritarian regime. The nature of control in a democracy is reciprocal while the government controls the public through bureaucracy but the government's policies are not unilaterally decided. Often there are discussions, negotiations and bargaining of policy issue between the government and various pressure groups. This is because the survival of the government itself depends on popular control.

In authoritarian regime the control is unilateral and the government relies on techniques of mass indoctrination and wins support among the people. There is hardly any effort towards accommodation of various interest groups. The freedom of speech and expression in expressing the grievances leads to lesser violent conflicts in the democratic set-up. While in authoritarian regimes the absence of legitimate means of expressing dissent leads to violent revolutions and movements.

POLITICAL PARTICIPATION

Political participation is necessary ingredient of every political system. All political systems encouraged political participation through varying degrees. By involving the people in the matters of state, political participation fosters stability and order by reinforcing the legitimacy of political authority. People living in a particular society participate in the political system, which they develop. There are many forms of participation and democracy in the form of government that encourages maximum participation in governmental processes. Participation does not mean more exercise of political rights like franchise, by the people.

It means their active involvement, which in a real manner influences the decision-making activity of the government. Democratic theory considers citizens as rational, independent, and interested political persons capable of expressing their opinion regarding the persons aspiring for holding offices and also competent in electing some persons who deal with the policies of government in a way conducive to the interest of the mass. Perhaps the most pervasive participation is simply living in a democratic community and where all government action and policy are publicized in press, radio, and television. In this situation those in position of authority must conduct themselves in such a fashion as to as appear to the sensible people.

Thus the great public in a democracy serves a sort of sounding board for public policy deliberations and discussion. Thus even a passive participation is a constructive part of democratic process. The most obvious way of political participation in democracy is voting. Other ways include such behaviours as reading or listening or watching the mass media of communications, taking part in political discussions, listening to political speeches, attending party meetings, giving contribution to political parties, writing petitions or letters to public officials or newspaper editors, trying to influence the voters, contesting the election for office etc. Lipset has pointed out that high-level participation cannot always be treated as good for democracy. It may indicate the decline of social cohesion and breakdown of democratic process. A principle problem for a theory of democratic system is under what conditions a society can have sufficient participation to maintain the democratic system without introducing sources of cleavage which will determine cohesion.

Some other political theorists are of the opinion that when majority of the people in a society are contended, participation is small. This should be taken as a favourable rather than unfavourable sign because it indicates stability and consensus within the society and also absence of broad cleavages.

Depending on the intensity and degree of participation Lester Milbraith has categorized political participation in three forms:

- Gladiators represent that small number of party activists, whose active association with political parties keeps them engaged in series of direct party activities like holding party offices, fighting the election as candidates.
- Transitional activities include attending party meetings party spectators or party sympathizers making contributions to the party fund and maintaining contacts with public officials or party personnel.
- Spectator activities on the other hand include voting, influencing others to vote in a particular way, joining political discussions or exposing oneself to the political stimuli.

DICTATORSHIP V/S DEMOCRACY

Dictatorship frames the laws that govern the rights of the people and the economy as well. It also outlines the laws that govern the private property as well. On the other hand, the power to create laws lies with the people in democracy.

In dictatorship if you are unhappy over something then you should continue to be unhappy over it all your life. On the other hand if you are unhappy over something in a democracy there is always a chance to change it and set it right so that it can make you happy finally. This is another important difference between democracy and dictatorship.

It is often felt that dictatorship is efficient in framing new laws to dominate certain sections. On the other hand, in democracy there is no place for creating new laws to dominate certain sections or people or to oppress certain groups of people.

Democracy and Dictatorship are two types of rule over a country. They show differences between them in terms of their methodology and concept. A dictator enjoys an absolute rule over a country or a state. On the other hand in a democracy the choice to create laws is with the people.

One of the biggest differences between democracy and dictatorship is that self indulgence is the keyword in democracy. People would choose what the best is for them. Democracy does not consist in someone else choosing what is good for the people. On the other hand dictatorship consists in someone else choosing what is good for the people.

Personal freedom and personal liberties have to be completely sacrificed in dictatorship. On the contrary there is always respect for personal freedom and personal liberties in democracy. In fact it can be said that democracy encourages and safeguards freedom of expression and freedom of speech and extends them to every single person of the nation.

There is always the probability of innocent people getting convicted often due to lack of proper cross examination in the case of dictatorship. On the other hand justice is done to perfection in a democracy. The accused cannot confront the witness in the case of dictatorship. On the contrary the accused is provided with an opportunity to confront the witness in the case of democracy.

The time taken to implement a decision is fairly fast in the case of dictatorship whereas the process of implementing a decision is slow in the case of democracy.

WELFARE STATE

Welfare State means that the State that take care the Welfare of the State, i.e., State is just not limited to collecting tax and protecting life and property from internal and external threat but also into a look out for the Growth of the People by way of health, education, shelter, food and others. It means that State do care for those who are inequipped and deprived..

As a Welfare State, India is committed to the welfare and development of its people, particularly the vulnerable sections like the scheduled castes (SCs), scheduled tribes (STs), backward classes, minorities and the handicapped. This section of the society constitutes nearly 85% of the population. The Oxford English Dictionary defines "it is a system whereby the

A welfare state is a concept of government where the state plays the primary role in the protection and promotion of the economic and social well-being of its citizens.

state undertakes to protect the health and well-being of its citizens, especially those in need, by means of grants, pensions, and other benefits". The term 'Welfare State' originated during the time of the Second World War to differentiate wartime Britain from the Welfare State of Germany.

It is a concept where government provides the requirements for the welfare or the well being of its citizens completely. India is a country which has accepted the notion of Welfare State by accepting the liability towards securing the public welfare and to sub-serve the interest of all citizens.

The purpose of the welfare state is to create economic equality or to assure equitable standards of living for all. The welfare states provides education, housing, sustenance, healthcare, pensions, unemployment insurance and care for old age people and are available to them as a matter of 'Right'. It also provides for public transportation, childcare, social amenities such as public parks and libraries, as well as many other goods and services.

The study of public policy began in 1922, when Charles Merriam, a political scientist, sought to build a link between political theory and its application to reality. Numerous issues are addressed by public policy, including crime, education, foreign policy, health, and social welfare. In 1993, due to ineffective healthcare policies, the Clinton administration sought to implement a policy that would bring about a national healthcare system.

A fundamental feature of the welfare state is social insurance, a provision common to most advanced industrialized countries. Antipoverty programs and the system of personal taxation may also be regarded as aspects of the welfare state. Personal taxation falls into this category insofar as its progressivity is used to achieve greater justice in income distribution (rather than merely to raise revenue) and also insofar as it used to finance social insurance payments and other benefits not completely financed by compulsory contributions. In socialist countries the welfare state also covers employment and administration of consumer prices. Most advanced nations are not true welfare states, although many provide at least some social services or entitlement programs.

The principal problems in the administration of a welfare state are:

- Determining the desirable level of provision of services by the state,
- Ensuring that the system of personal benefits and contributions meets the needs of individuals and families while at the same time offering sufficient incentives for productive work,
- Ensuring efficiency in the operation of state monopolies and bureaucracies, and
- The equitable provision of resources to finance the services over and above the contributions of direct beneficiaries.

In Indian context, 'Welfare State' denotes establishment of political democracy, provision of social and economic justice and minimizing inequalities in income, status, facilities and opportunities. The concept is embodied in Part IV of the Indian Constitution, Directive Principal of State Policy. According to the Constitution, it is the duty of the government to follow these principles while making laws and thereby set the path towards a welfare State. The uniqueness about the concept in the Indian context is the Directive Principles containing the instructions to the government to establish a welfare State, is non justifiable and citizens cannot claim it as a right. This is because, India being developing and over populated country and it may not possible for welfare activities of the state reach every citizen of our country.

In later part of the 20th century, the wave of privatization and globalization came into existence in many countries. According to the market fundamentalists and Nobel laureates like Friedrich Hayek and Milton Friedman, the welfare state is a source of trouble and an anomaly that should be stopped. However another Noble prize winning economist argues, 'The supremacy of the market which is proclaimed with ideological fervour is a dangerous mistake.`' He considers the role of the state and it's regulating activities to be essential and believes that market mechanisms are unsuitable means for the solution of social problem. It demands some rethinking and reform of various Welfare institutions which is more essential in the developing country like India where disparities exist between different segments of the population and different regions of the country, for shortening these gaps and moving towards a more balanced development of the nation. However the Welfare State is the greatest achievement of the 20th century and should be suitably adapted to the existing global condition as well as the peculiar situation of a particular country in order to lead toward overall prosperity of mankind.

TRIBAL AND RURAL LIFE IN INDIA

Introduction. Characteristics of Tribal Society. Geographical Location of Tribes. Tribes of India. Tribal-Caste Continuum. India's Rribal Belts. Tribal Struggles. Tribal Development Efforts after Independence. Rural/ Village Life In India. Main Features of Rural Society. The Changing Faces of Rural Livelihoods in India. Health Practices and Problems in Rural India.

INTRODUCTION

India is among one of the few countries, where extremes of both modern life and tribal culture exists side by side. Tribals still live in hilly topography of the country where no sign of modern culture can be seen. Hardcore tribal areas are located mostly in north east India, however tribal culture can be seen in almost every part. India is a country of tribes. Roughly saying the tribes make 2–3% of the entire population of India.

For tribals traditions and customs are above everything and they have carried forward age old colourful rituals and ceremonies. Government of India is making special efforts to preserve rich tribal heritage of the country. Tribals are given special status, and their traditions are awarded due respect.

Several research teams from the Government organization, each year do research on these tribes. It is impossible to find the original way of living of these tribes these days. Yet there are tribes, rare of them who still live the way their ancestors lived. To see how they live and what they do, one has to go and live among them with the help of a Guide. For the reason that most of them still speak their own languages and are not very familiar with Hindi or English language. Like the Bodo Tribe, they speak Tibeto – Burmese language, Mundas speak Mundese language. Living in the aboriginal forms, these are still able to sustain their lives with the help of the Government. However there are other tribes which have changed with the time – keeping some of their ancestral values and adapting some of the new ones. Hmars, Dimasa and the Orans are some of them.

MEANING AND DEFINITION OF TRIBAL SOCIETY

A tribe is a human social system existing before the emergence of nation-states, and, in some cases, continuing to exist independent of the state structure. Historically, tribal societies consisted only of a relatively small, local population. The internal social structure of a tribe can vary greatly from case to case, but is often a relatively simple structure, with few (if any) significant social distinctions between individuals. According to Oxford Dictionary, "A tribe is a group of people in a primitive or barbarious stage of development acknowledging the authority of a chief and usually regarding themselves as having a common ancestor".

In Jharkhand, historically tribal society was a collective society residing in the proximity of woods and forest.

D.N. Majumdar defines tribe as a social group with territorial affiliation, endogamous with no specialization of functions ruled by tribal officers hereditary or otherwise, united in language or dialect recognizing social distance with other tribes or castes. According to Ralph Linton tribe is a group of bands occupying a contiguous territory or territories and having a feeling of unity deriving from numerous similarities in a culture, frequent contacts and a certain community of interests.

L.M. Lewis believes that tribal societies are small in scale are restricted in the spatial and temporal range of their social, legal and political relations and possess a morality, a religion and world view of corresponding dimensions. Characteristically too tribal languages are unwritten and hence the extent of communication both in time and space is inevitably narrow. At the same time tribal societies exhibit a remarkable economy of design and have a compactness and self-sufficiency lacking in modern society.

CHARACTERISTICS OF TRIBAL SOCIETY

The tribe inhabits and remains within definite and common topography. The members of a tribe possess a consciousness of mutual unity. The members of a tribe speak a common language. The members generally marry into their own group but now due to increased contact with outsiders there are instances of tribal marring outside as well. The tribes believe in ties of blood relationship between its members. They have faith in their having descended from a common, real or mythical, ancestor and hence believe in blood relationships with other members. Tribes follow their own political organization which maintains harmony. Religion is of great importance in the tribe. The tribal political and social organization is based on religion because they are granted religious sanctity and recognition.

Characteristically too Indian tribal society possess their own set of languages, which are unwritten. Hence the degree of communication both in time and space is predictably narrow. At the same time tribal societies demonstrate an outstanding economy of design and have a compactness and self-sufficiency surprisingly lacking in modern city society. According to Indian aboriginal traditions, the tribal societies inhabit and remain within a definitive and common topography. Members of a tribe possess an awareness of mutual unity. The members of a tribe always speak a common language.

CHARACTERISTICS OF INDIAN TRIBES

Mandelbaum mentions the following characteristics of Indian tribes:

- Kinship as an instrument of social bonds.
- A lack of hierarchy among men and groups.
- Absence of strong, complex, formal organization.
- Communitarian basis of land holding.
- Segmentary character.
- Little value on surplus accumulation on the use of capital and on market trading.
- Lack of distinction between form and substance of religion.
- A distinct psychological bent for enjoying life.

GEOGRAPHICAL LOCATION OF TRIBES

Tribals in India originate from five language families, i.e., Andamanese, Austro-Asiatic, Dravidian, and Tibeto-Burman. It is also important to point out that those tribals who belong to different language families live in distinct geographic settings. For example, in South Orissa there are languages that originate from the Central Dravidian family, Austro-Asiatic (Munda) family and the Indo-Aryan. In the Jharkhand area, languages are from the Indo-Aryan, North Dravidian and Austro-Asiatic.Tribals in India live in the following five territories:

- **The Himalayan Belt:** Assam, Meghalaya, Arunachal Pradesh, Nagaland, Manipur, Mizoram, Tripura, hills of Uttar Pradesh and Himachal Pradesh.
- **Central India:** Bihar, West Bengal, Orissa, and Madhya Pradesh. 55% of the total tribal population of India lives in this belt.
- **Western India:** Rajasthan, Maharashtra, Gujarat, Goa, Dadra and Nagar Haveli.
- **The Dravidian Region:** Karnataka, Andhra Pradesh, Kerala and Tamil Nadu.
- Andaman, Nicobar and Lakshadweep islands.

TRIBES OF INDIA

To be able to live and survive in the coming age, these tribes have taken to odd – jobs for survival – making shoes, doing fishing, making shafts and so on. These jobs make there survival seemingly good, still the survival seems blurred. Still there lies the danger of slow extinction—these tribes need to be protected by us all. A major portion of India lives in its Tribes. These tribes are the living example of how life was in the earlier days. These show what were the difficulties man had to face before the advent of machine and technology.

BODOS — TRIBE OF ASSAM

Bodos are the true ethnic Tribal Community of Assam—the sub branch of the Bodo-Kachari Clan. The Bodos are the largest among the Bodo-Kachari Clan. They are also the most progressive. Bodos reside in the Brahamaputra valley and are considered to be largest ethnic and linguistic group of tribes. The Bodos speak Tibeto-Burmese language. Nowadays the Bodos have accepted the Devnagari Language. Bodos have a language of their own called Deodahi.

Bodos — Tribe of Assam.

Earlier the Bodos were cut off from other parts of the country due to their geographical area and weather conditions. This lead to the their lack in education and economy. This was one of the reasons of the arousal of the Bodoland Movement. The movement took its wings in the late 80's under the leadership of Upendra Nath Brahma who is now regarded as the Father of Bodos. A Bodoland Territorial Council was formed to save the Culture, language and identity of Bodos. It was headed by All Bodo Students Union (ABSU) and an armed militant group called the Bodo Liberation Tigers (BLT). Following the movement a settlement was reached between the Government and the Bodos. A land was given to the Bodos which came to be known as Bodoland. In 2006, the former BLT members, formed an alliance with Indian National Congress under the leadership of Hagrama Mohilary and came into power in Dispur District of Assam. Still in Assam, illegal immigrants occupy tribal belts.

OCCUPATION

The main work of Bodos is tea plantation, silk worm rearing, weaving, pig and poultry farming. They are also good bamboo craftsman.

TEA PLANTATION

One of the major income sources, the Bodos turn to working in tea estates. The women working in Assam tea estates are mostly Bodos.

SERICULTURE

Silk rearing, the Bodos take special interest in this work. Not only it is a source of livelihood, it is also one of the best means to know about the best quality silk.

THE CULTURE OF BODOS

Bodos in their ancient years used to pray their forefathers. Today they have changed significantly—they have accepted Hinduism as their main religion. They practice a Culture known as Bathouism. The plant Siju is taken for the worship as a symbol of Bathou Symbol. For the worship, a clean ground near the home or the courtyard of the home is taken. One pair of Betelnut called Goi betel leaf called pathwi is used as offering. The offering includes rice, milk and sugar. For the Kherai Puja which also happens to be the most important of all Pujas, an altar is placed in the rice field. The Bodos do not practice dowry and caste system as per their rules of Brahma Dharma.

The Culture of Bodos.

The main festivals of Bodos include Kherai—the colourful function which includes, drumming, singing and dancing (Bagurumba) to the rythmn of the drums. Garja, Hapsa Hatarnai, Awnkham Gwrlwi Janai, Bwisagu and Domashi are the other important festivals. The main cuisines of the Bodos include Narzi, Onla and Oma Bedor.

GONDS—THE GODS PEOPLE

Gondvana—the Mighty Kingdom in the olden days still stands with the ruins of the Kingdom in its sand. From the 15th century to the 18th century, this region called Gondwana was the home to the Gonds. The Gondwana Land gave its name to the present day Africa, South America, Australia, India Sub Continent and Antarctica. The Gonds lost their lives in saving their lands from the then upcoming tribe called the Banjaras. Most of the Gonds describe themselves as hill people or as Koi or Koitur.

Gonds who call themselves 'Koytoria' ,the largest tribal group in the state in terms of population.

The inheritors of the Dravidian Culture—the Gonds are the simple tribes with a high thinking of non-egaliriatism. Mainly found in Central India the Gonds preach the Gods path and do agriculture as their main work.

Apart from Madhya Pradesh, Gonds can be found in Chattisgarh, Andhra Pradesh and Orissa. They are the largest Tribe in India, South Asia, and perhaps the world with nine million people (out of which four million resides in India). They speak language related to Telgu and Dravidian language. The spoken languages are generalized as Gondi and Hindi. They practice agriculture growing cereals. Herding cattles is also a part of their livelihood.

GONDS DIFFERENT ASPECTS

Gond Girl

The girl in this photograph looks like any of the modern girls who like traditional dresses. Though not to a large extent but the Gonds have changed themselves with the changing times.

The Home

It looks like any regular house in a small village. The Gonds have begun to live in the wooden houses from quite a time, another big change which is visual in the living ways of the Gonds.

The Culture of Gonds

The main diety of the Gonds is the pantheon—a single temple which bows to all the Gods and Culture of the World. The Gond Clan is known as Persa Pen who protects all Clan Members. They believe in the equality of the human beings without the discrimination of higher and lower society. This transparency can be clearly seen as they themselves have inclusions of Bhils and Santals in their tribes. They also worship the most ancient spirits as Gonds speak the unwritten languages related to Dravidians.

Each village of Gonds a Village Guardian and a Village Mother who are worshipped during all regular festivals. The Spirits both good and bad are supposed to be inhabit hills, villages, lakes and rivers. Sacrifices are made by the Village Priests—Devari—in most of the festivals. Most aspects of the Gond life are filled with animal sacrifices. But then most of the Gonds festivals are related to agriculture.

Most of the Gonds live in a Village with a Headman known as Mahji or Patel. A Village Council is also there which divides the Gonds into Castes called Ahir (Cowherds), Agaria (Blacksmith), Dhuli (Drummers) and Pardhan (bard and singers). A Gond Village has typically several hamlets. Houses made of hatch and mud have a verandah (outer space), living room, kitchen, special room for women, shrine room for Gods and a Guest Room. Gonds welcome visitors with tobacco leaves, fruits or other small gifts.

The Staple Food of Gonds is two millets known as Kodo and Kutki. Vegetables are usually grown in kitchen gardens or collected from forests. Gonds grow tobacco for smoking and make liquor for Mahua tree for celebrations.

For the Celebrations, Gonds have Danderi dancers who retell events from Gond Mythology. Dance, songs, cock fighting are the main attractions of any celebration. During the festive time women wear colored glass bangles and necklaces made of small black beads. Tattooing is also a major charm for Gonds.

Marraiges in Gonds are usually self chosen. However, the tribal council approves the matches. The father of the groom pays a bride price. The newly weds live with the elders of the family till they make a house of their own. The same Council also approves the divorces.

Gonds are educated to a pretty decent level. Around 25 per cent of Gonds in Maharashtra and 15 per cent Gonds of Madhya Pradesh. However the ratio of boys to girls still remain 1:5 per cent.

HMAR—THE CHRISTIAN TRIBE OF INDIA

Hmar also known as Mhar or Mar are the dwellers of the North Eastern parts of India. Hmars can be found in Meghalaya, Mizoram, Cachar, Meghalaya, Chittagong Hill Tracts and Tripura.

Dimasas are supposed to be the aboriginals of the Brahmaputra Valley ascending from the Himalayas with their roots connecting to mainland China. The roots of Hmar find route to the place called Sinlung.

Sinlung is the ancestral home of Zonhna-thlak. However the location of Sinlung is still a controversy but not the roots of Hmar. Hmars eventually left Sinlung which was once a democratic state.

Hmar also known as Mhar or Mar are the dwellers of the North Eastern Part of India.

The Hmars belong to the Chin-Kuki-Mizo group of tribes, and are recognised as Scheduled Tribe under the 6th Scheduled of the Constitution of India. They are medium statured usually 5-5.6 ft in height, sturdy, dark, haried, brown eyed and are known for their bravery. India – Manipur, Mizoram, Assam, Meghalaya, Tripura have the major chunk of Hmar Tribe People.

THE DRESS

The traditional dress of Hmar Tribe is colorful filled with bright and radiant colors. Girls wear short skirts and the men coats and chongas.

THE MODELS

The models have ramped up but these are not the normal ones. These are the gentle ladies of the Hmar Tribe who have changed themselves drastically with the changing time.

THE CULTURE OF HMAR

Hmars speak Hindi, English and Hmas language in their day to day life. They are primarily Baptist and follow Christianity. They are the cultivators as they make their livelihood from farming. These medium statured people beleive in their hands and are known for their bravery. But then with the changing times, one can find pretty educated hmars working in various field and making handicrafts. The handicrafts made by Hmars usually depict scenes of battles, adventure, love, victory and their history. Hmars still believe in their traditional arts including the folk dance and folk songs which they play during their various festivals.

MUNDA — ADIVASIS OF JHARKHAND

Munda —Adivasis of Jharkhand.

Mundas are the Adivasis or the Tribals of the Jharkand. They spread over other states like Bihar, West Bengal, Chhatisgarh, and Orissa. Outside India Mundas can be found in Bangladesh. Today there are around two million Munda People.

The Mundas are highly respected tribals from the time of pre-independence of India. *Birsa Munda*, the Munda who turned into a

Prophet and was a freedom fighter in the Indian Independence Struggle, is the most respected tribal. At a small age of 20 yrs, Birsa Munda was revered by his people as God. His active participation in the freedom fight disturbed the Britishers so much that they finally caught him at the young age of 25. He died in suspicious circumstances in the Jail of Ranchi in 1900. Even today his contribution to the Independence of India is recognised with regard. He has been honoured by the Governent of India.

DIFFERENT ASPECTS OF MUNDAS

Festival of Munda Tribe

Like any other tribes, Mundas also have festivals but here they are a with of difference. Lights, fire games, pomp and show make a big part of their festivals.

God of Jharkhand—Birsa Munda

Birsa Munda, the revolutionary Munda, who fought in the independence freedom fight of India against Britishers, is revered as God in the State of Jharkhand.

CULTURE OF MUNDAS

A one-fourth of the Munda population is Christian. Mundas speak Mundari language. They have a special dance called as Nupur (an anklet) dance. Wearing Nupur in ankles, the Mundas dance in chorus. For the occupation, in the ancient days they used to be the woodcutters, cutting down the forests and then selling the wood. But now they have taken to fishing and earth cutting.

KHASIS—THE HYNNIEW TREP TRIBE

Hynniew Trep, that is how they like to be called - The Khasis Tribe of Meghalaya, a state in the North Eastern Part of India. The Khasis inhabit the Khasi Hills proper, and the Syntengs, or Pnars, the Jaintia Hills. These people whose literal meaning is “Seven Huts” in Khasi Language, cover about 50 percent of the population of Meghalaya. Khasis are the descendants of Mon-Khmer speakers who migrated probably from Yunnan to Meghalaya. They live in the Jaintia Hills in the state of Meghalaya, West Bengal, Mizoram, Maharashtra, Tripura, Tamil Nadu, Arunachal Pradesh, Andaman and Nicobar Islands.

Khasis—The Hynniew Trep Tribe.

The sub-divisions of Khasis, i.e., the Wars, Khynriams, Pnars and Bhois are not only the territorial groups but each of them acquired different socio-cultural traits.

WHAT SETS THE KHASIS?

Apart from other tribes is that in Khasis the descendents are recognised from Mother and not from Father (Matrilineal Society). As per the Khasi Law and tradition the mother inherits the children and property and not the father. In addition to this a Khasi Women is at liberty to take divorce from her husband as per her will. The Khasis have well defined homelands.

THE MODERN AND THE TRADITIONAL KHASIS

Khasi Girls

Khasis have adapted to the changing times to a certain extent. They give equal importance to education as can be seen in the form of these school going khasi girls.

Khasi Knups—Bamboo Hats

The traditional bamboo hats worn by Khasi Men and Women while farming. The bright colors of the bamboo hats match with the lush greenery of the farms giving them the beauty of a bug rather than a hat.

The Culture of Khasis

Khasis are the descendants of Mon-Khmer speakers who migrated probably from Yunnan to Meghalaya, and thus they are of East Asian origin. Khasis are a mix of Presbyterian, Roman Catholic, Hindu castes. Most of the Khasis follow the Presbyterian religion, Anglican, Catholic, or Ka Niam Tynrai—the original Khasi Culture. They are similar in appearance to their Northern Mon-Khmer relatives, most notably the Palaung and Wa.

Khasis have different prayers and functions as per the clan they follow. In most of the festivals Khasi Men wear the traditional Khasi dress called Jymphong (long dress which is sleevless and has thongs in the front). The women however have a colourful dress with several plates of clothing, golden crown with spikes and feathers on it.

Khasis practice shifting cultivation which they call JHUM for their survival. The Kacharis have a peasent based economy. The trend have occupational diversificaiton has also emerged among the Khasis.

GADDIS — THE KHANABADOSH TRIBE

Gaddis are the Tribes of the Himachal Pradesh, residing in the Dauladher Range. The peculiarity of the Gaddis lie in their Khanabadosh Nature—they are Gypsies in true nature as they travel to the higher pastures along their flocks in the summer season and so are transhumance in their traditional practice.

Gaddis — The Khanabadosh Tribe.

In the earlier years the Ancestors of Gaddis left India during their tough times. Later on with the Chauhan Rajputs Brahman Gaddis descended to the place called Chamba in Himachal Pradesh. From those years, Gaddis and their generations have been living in Chamba along with the flocks. Aside from Chamba, they are also found in Kangra district, near Dharamshala, Himachal Pradesh.

MANY FACE OF GADDIS

Gaddis Dance

They go round an round in circles as they dance to the tune of music and drums. The hip hop goes on as the beat of the drum increases, till the feet are dead tired.

Gaddis—The Khanabadosh

Better known as Gypsies, the Gaddis is the nomadic tribe who shifts to upper heights in the summers with their flocks. It has become a tradition followed from generations.

The Culture of Gaddis

Gaddis have a mix of Cultures. Some of them accepted Islam, in fear of Aurangzeb, other remains Hindus. Its a mix culture, which the Gaddis follow, but the most important thing to Gaddis is the 25 yards long strand which they tie around their wrist. It is worn by both men and women as the symbol of the tribe. The strand known as DORA is tied with two coils at a time. The main work of the Gaddis is the rearing of the sheep and making wool. They also sell goat meat for a modest lifestyle.

DIMASA - DIM - FISA—THE TRIBE FROM ASSAM

This tribe from the North Eastern India, is a part of the greater Bodo-Kachari group. Dimasas live in the Jatinga Valley in the North Chhachar Hills of Assam. Dimasas are supposed to be the aboriginals of the Brahmaputra Valley ascending from the Himalayas with their roots connection to the Great Hindu Epic Mahabharata. Dimasas have their seats in the city called Dimapur. Lying on the banks of the river Dhansiri, also known as the Brick City, was the ruling Capital of Kacharis - the prominent and powerful race of those times. Dimapur got its name from the Kachari word Di—meaning water, Ma—meaning big and Pur—meaning City.

The Dimasa Kacharis are distributed in different regions of Assam and Nagaland. The Dimasa Kacharis living in North Chachar Hills appear to have retained much of their traditional tribals more. However, those ones in the in Nagaon district of Assam, the influence of Assamese Culture is very apparent. The Dimasas living in Chachar Hills are highly influenced by the Bengali Culture.

Dimasa- Dim-Fisa—The Tribe from Assam.

DIMASA FESTIVAL

Slow dancing with putting of steps forward and backward covering a half circle, dimasas look pretty happy in their semi-bright dresses. Slow music with thump of drums, are a mark of the Dimasa Festival.

THE HOME OF DIMASA

Its the picture of a typical home of Dimasa. The homes are well groomed though not very large in size. Cleanliness is the main objective of any Dimasa House.

THE CULTURE OF DIMASAS

The Dimasas believe that there is a Supreme Deity in the world called the Banglaraja. The Lord Banglaraja has seven sons who too are worshipped. Out of the seven sons, the eldest Sibrai is the most revered one. Apart from these seven deities, spirits of ill-will and good wills are also worshipped. Sakainjeek—the dreaded female spirits are the most feared ones. Madai—the invisible spirits are also the feared ones. Apart from these the Dimasas believe in Clans. They have both male and female Clans who have their own titulary deities.

Every year Dimasa Kachari family worships its diety before sowing paddy. This small festive is known as Madai Khelimba. For the people who die, Dimasas cremate them. The dead person is bathed with fresh water, draped in new bright clothes and placed inside the house for the last moments. The widow does not tie her hair till the body is cremated near the river side.

CHENCHU—ABORIGINAL TRIBE OF CENTRAL HILLS

Chenchus are the Hindu Tribes—the Aboriginal Tribe—who are found in the Central Hills stations of Andhra Pradesh.

Chenchus are the Aboriginal Tribe who still consider hunting for their livelihood rather then farming. Selling meat is one of their major activity.

Chenchu—Aboriginal Tribe of Central Hills.

Their food consists of gruel made from jowar or maize, and boiled or cooked jungle tubers. They mix tamarind fruit with tamarind. The Caste Hindu which lives with Chenchus take Chenchus land on rent and pay by giving a portion of their harvest to Chenchus. They are the food gathering tribe who mostly speak Telgu.

The Chenchus collect jungle products like roots, fruits, tubers, beedi leaf, mohua flower, honey, gum, tamarind and green leaves and make a mearge income of it by selling these to traders and government cooperatives.

CHENCHU—THE CRAFTSMAN

Self Reliant, the Chenchus have learned various small arts, like craftsmanship, to make their lives more easy. On the other hand, Chenchus prefer to do most of their things on their own.

THE REVERED GOD—HANUMAN

The Chenchus have good faith in various Gods and Goddesses. The Lingamayya, a form of Lord Shiva, a Hindu Deity and the Goddess Maisamma —the Shakti are the most revered ones. Lord Hanuman is also the main God.

THE CULTURE OF CHENCHUS

The Chenchu Village is known as Penta and consists of a few Huts. The Village elder is the one who takes the major decisions and does the Counciling. The marraige of Chenchus is known as Pelli and takes place through negotiation among the elders or by the choice of young couples.

The Chenchus have a strong faith in the Gods and Godesses. They worship their dieties with great devotion. Lord Eshwara among them is known as "Lingamayya", and Shakti as "Maisamma" or "Peddamma". The Gods are prayed with great pomp and show.

BHIL—THE ARCHERS

Bhils—The Archers, are the tribals of Mewar, descandents of original inhabitants of India. The word Bhil is derived from Bil or Vil meaning Bow. The Bhils used to furnish the needs of Prince of Mewar with bowmen, supplies or by guarding their families. Some famous names of Bhils are Bhim, Bhim Singh Maharana, Bhimisi and Bhindar. All of them have special place in the ancient history of India.

Bhils of Rajasthan.

Bhil—The Archers.

Bhils are the tribes of Central India found in Gujarat, Madhya Pradesh, Rajasthan, Mahrashtra and Tripura. Out of India they are found in Bangladesh. In colonial times they were employed by the Rajputs as Shikaris and as Warriors. Today there is a Mewar Bhil Corps—the acclaimed Corps of Mewars. They are supposed to be the best archers and also excellent in geographical knowledge. They are the third largest tribes in India after Gonds and Santhals.

TRADITIONAL DANCE OF BHILS

The Traditional Dance of Bhils known as Ghoomar, involves going round and round at very high speeds without losing balance. It also involves keeping upto ten to twelve water pots on the head and then moving in circles at high speeds.

PLOYGAMY—THE WAY OF LIFE

The Bhils have a strong faith in the ritual called Polygamy. They are at their wish to remarry as many times they wish to. Though polygamy has been a tradition for Bhils, these days some of them restrain from following so.

THE CULTURE OF BHILS

In the olden days the Bhils used to live in hive like huts on isolated hill tops, living there for a few weeks and then constructing a new one. But now, they leave the huts only if a major disease breaks out or if the hut is considered inauspicious. Some of them have also begun to live in bricked houses. For the dresses, men wear turbans, waistcoat and a coat whereas the women wear saris (a five-meter long cloth draped around the body).

They have different ceremonis for birth, death, marriage and divorce. For the various ceremonies they either worship the Lion or the mother nature in the form of wild. The affinity of Bhils to the wild nature attributes to their generations being here for centuries. They have kept with the tradition.

Bhils follow Polygamy. A women is open to marry a man of her choice even after her marriage. They have a 'Paternal Family System' system in which the family considers the joint family as the major force of life. However in Bhils, the women, sons and daughters are free to lead their own lives. There is a tradition of adapting children in this society.

ORANS—THE PROGRESSIVE TRIBE

The Orans or Oraons are the most progressive tribes of all the tribes found in India. They are the ones who are into education and places like Churches. Kartik Oraon, who was the most educated Oraon, an Indian Congress leader and former state communication minister of India, Albert Ekka, the Paramveer Chakra awardees (Highest Award for Bravery in India), The Roman Catholic Archbishop of Ranchi, Cardinal Telesphore Placidus Toppo, are Oraon. People of this community have shown exceptional makes as compared to people of other tribes.

Orans—The Progressive Tribe.

Orans speak the language called Kurukh which belongs to the Dravidian Family and is related to the Pahari language (language of mountains). Kurukh has a special recognition as it is taught in Ranchi University.

The Orans have progressed with the time and have shifted to Indian Metro Cities like Kolkatta, Delhi, Mumbai and other smaller cities like Patna, Buvneshwar, Bhopal, Hyderabad, Allahabad and Lucknow.

THE FAITH

The Oran is a religious tribe. Most of them pray a sacred groove known as Sarna Dharma. Rest of them are the followers of the Christian Religion. However both school of thought live under the same roof called the Orans.

The Culture of Orans

Orans are basically Sarnas (a sacred groove)—Sarna Dharma (Dharmesh the God) which they follow and pray. Rest of the 25 percent are Christians. Orans who are Christians follow the rules guided by the Church. But overall the Orans have a variety of folk dance and music which are played on various ocassions. Both men and women participate in the dance and other festival on equal basis.

Orans have taken to various professions—these include tea estate managment in Assam, West Bengal and Nepal.

TRIBAL-CASTE CONTINUUM

The tribes in India have been influenced by certain traditions of the communities around them. Major neighboring community in all the areas has always been Hindus. As a result from the very period there have been several points of contact between the Hindus of the area and tribal communities living within it. The nature and extent of contact the pattern of mutual participation and characteristics of revitalization movements have been different in different parts of India.

Anthropologists have differed on the question relating to tribe and caste. According to Ghurye tribal people are backward Hindus differing only in degrees from the other segments of Hindu society. Elwin argued for the recognition of separate social and cultural identity of tribal people. Government of India gives tacit recognition to this identity of keeping alive under constitution sanction their lists of Scheduled Tribe.

According to D.N. Majumdar the tribe looks upon Hindu ritualism as foreign and extra-religious even though indulging in it and the in the worship of God and Goddess where as in the caste these are necessary part of the religion.

According to Herbert Risley the convention of endogamy is not rigidly enforced in the tribe where as such is the case in a tribe. But this view is not acceptable since the law of endogamy is enforced with extreme rigidity in some tribes.

Max Weber writes in 'Social Structure' that when an Indian tribe loses its territorial significance it assumes the form of an Indian caste. In this way the tribe is a local group whereas caste is a social group.

According to Andre Beteille there are certain commonly observed differences between tribes and castes. The tribes are relatively isolated as to the castes. They are world within itself having few externalities. Tribes speak a variety of dialects which separates them from non tribes. They follow their own religion and practices which are not common in Hinduism. Language is a criterion of difference as tribes speak their local dialect for example Mundas and Oraons of Chota Nagpur speak different dialects but Bhumij have lost their tribal dialect and speak dominant language of the area.

According to N.K. Bose there are many similarities in customs between tribes and castes and they are interdependent. Marriage within the clan is forbidden both in the tribe as well as in the caste. Both generally do not encourage marriage outside the group.

In caste individuals generally pursue their own definite occupations because functions are divided under the caste system. In the tribe individuals can indulge in whatever profession they prefer as there is no fixed relation between them and occupation.

According to Bailey tribe and caste should be viewed as continuum. He seeks to make distinction not in terms of totality of behavior but in more limited way in relation to the political economic system. Briefly Bailey's argument is that a caste society is hierarchical while a tribal society is segmentary and egalitarian. But in contemporary India both caste and tribe are being merged into a different system which is neither one nor the other.

The ethnographic records establish that the contacts varied from semi-isolation to complete assimilation. The numerous castes among Hindus have emerged out of the tribal stratums. The recent studies of tribes of Himalayan western and middle India have left no doubt that some of the tribes are Hinduized to the extent that they have been assimilated with the different castes at different levels in the caste system.

The study of two major Central Himalayan tribes Tharu and Khasa reveal that though they have a tribal matrix and continue to practice certain distinctive tribal customs they have been accepted as Kshatriya. Their culture have been modeled on the ways of living of the Rajputs and Brahmins of the neighbor plain areas. With their fast adoption of the Hindu names and establishment of social connections with the Rajputs and Brahmins of the plains.

They declare themselves as Rajputs and with Brahmins constitute the apex of the social order. With the long and continuous contacts with the regional Hindu castes the tribals of Kharwars has long been assimilated as Rajput castes. There are numerous other tribes which have undergone selective acculturation and have added selected traits or features of the regional Hindus to their respective traditional cultures. In this practice of acculturation most of them failed to occupy any rank in the castes hierarchy while few of them were integrated into the lower strata of the Hindu social system.

INDIA'S TRIBAL BELTS

The India's tribal belts refer to contiguous areas of indigenous settlement of tribal people of India.

NORTHWEST INDIA

The Tribal Belt of Northwest India includes the states of Rajasthan, Gujarat, Maharashtra, and Karnataka. The tribal people of this region have origins which precede the Vedic Aryan people of the north and the Dravidian people of the south. In fact, the origins of these people are thought to stem back to the Harappan civilisation of the Indus valley, the oldest traceable civilisation of the Indian sub-continent which flourished between 3500 BC and 2500 BC.

The tribes of north-west India were once strong matrilineal societies. The changing fates and fortunes of these people has caused a gradual evolution to a more patriarchal code of living. These days the tribal societies generally follow the rule of patriliny. There are still, however, many strong cases of organised matriarchy in existence today. It is the women who organise matters such as relationships and marriages, the inheritance of land, and the distribution of wealth.

CENTRAL INDIA

The Central India Tribal Belt stretches from Gujarat in the west up to West Bengal in the east across the states of Madhya Pradesh, Chhattisgarh and Jharkhand. It is among the poorest regions of the country. Over 90% of the Belt's tribal population is rural, with primitive agriculture.

TRIBAL STRUGGLES

Numerous uprisings of the tribals have taken place beginning with the one in Bihar in 1772 followed by many revolts in Andhra Pradesh, Andaman and Nicobar Islands, Arunchal Pradesh, Assam, Mizoram and Nagaland. The important tribes involved in revolt in the 19th century were Mizos (1810), Kols (1795 & 1831), Mundas (1889), Daflas (1875), Khasi and Garo (1829), Kacharis (1839), Santhals (1853), Muria Gonds (1886), Nagas (1844 & 1879) and Konds (1817).

After independence the tribal struggle may be classified into three groups:

- Struggles due to exploitation of the outsiders.
- Struggles due to economic deprivations.
- Struggle due to separatist tendencies.

The tribal movements may also be classified on the basis of their orientation into four types:

- Movements seeking political autonomy and formation of separate state.
- Agrarian movement.
- Forest-based movements.
- Socio-religious movements.

Most of the tribal movements were result of oppression and discrimination, neglect and backwardness and apathy of government towards tribal problems.

TANA BHAGAT MOVEMENT

In the Tana Bhagat movement an attempt was made to emulate the way of life of the Hindu higher castes. It emerged among the Oraon of

Chotanagpur; Bihar. It tried to raise the status of its members in the eyes of the surrounding Hindu society and was characterized by a large scale incorporation of Hindu belief-practices into its ideology.

BIRSA MUNDA MOVEMENT

During the second half of the 19th century the whole of Chotanagpur underwent a tremendous change. The old Munda system of Khuntakatti tenure gave way to a new and alien system of exploitation by the landlords known as jagirdar and thikadar. In 1895 Birsa Munda of Chalkad started a movement. In him the Munda found the embodiment of their aspiration. He gave them leadership, a religion and a code of life. He held before them the prospect of Munda Raj in place of foreign rule.

TRIBAL DEVELOPMENT EFFORTS AFTER INDEPENDENCE

The State Governments are required to quantify the funds from State Plan for tribal area development in proportion to percentage of tribal population in the states.

CONSTRUCTION OF THE HOSTELS FOR TRIBAL STUDENTS

Construction and Maintenance expense is to be borne by the State Governments/Union Territories. The rates for construction of the hostels are fixed which are different for the plains and the hills. It has been represented by various States that these rates are not workable any more in view of the escalation of prices of building materials and long distance involved particularly for the hilly areas. It is, therefore, proposed to revise the norms and to adopt the State PWD (Public Works Department) schedule of rates as in the case of construction of Ashram Schools. During 1990-91 to 1992-93, the amount of Rs. 8.64 crores has been released to the States/Union under various stages of completion. The scheme envisages setting up of vocational training institutes in inner tribal areas away from the district headquarters to impart training in various courses relevant to the areas. The tribal youth would be given training in three trades of his or her choice, the course in each trade having duration of four months. The trainee is to be attached at the end of one month training to master craftsman for a period of three months to learn his skills by practical experience. At the end of 15 months, the trainee will emerge as a multi-skilled person who can exploit existing employment potentials to his/her best advantage. This is a Central Sector Scheme where the construction and maintenance costs are fully borne by the Central Government. It is implemented through the State Governments. Proposals are obtained from them along with details of existing infrastructure as well as the employment potentials in the proximity of the proposed location.

Educational complex in low literacy pockets for women in Tribal areas This Scheme provides cent percent financial assistance to NGOs/ Organization established by government as autonomous bodies/educational

& other institutions like Cooperative Societies, to establish educational complexes in 136 identified districts of erstwhile 11 states (now 13) where tribal female literacy is below 10% as per 1991 census. Educational complex is meant for girls studying from class I to V with strength of 30 students in each class. The grants are provided to meet non-recurring as well as recurring expenses on building (hiring or maintenance) teaching, boarding, lodging and to also for medical and health care of students.

GRANT-IN-AID TO STATE TRIBAL DEVELOPMENT COOPERATIVECORPORATION AND OTHERS

This is a Central Sector Scheme, with 100% grant, available to the state Tribal Development Cooperative Corporation (STDCCs) and other similar corporations of State engaged in collection and trading of minor forest produce (MFP) through tribals Grants under the Scheme are provided to strengthen the Share Capital of Corporations, construction of Warehouses, establishment of processing industries of MFPs etc. to ensure high profitability of the corporation so as to enable them to pay remunerative prices for MFPs to the tribals.

PRICE SUPPORT TO TRIFED

The Ministry provides Grants-in-aid to its corporation, TRIFED to set off losses on account of fluctuations in prices of MFPs being marketed by it for ensuring remunerative prices to tribal engaged in collection of MFPs either directly or through STDCCs and other such Cooperative Societies. Investment in Share Capital of Trifed The Ministry is the largest shareholder of TRIFED with over 99% contribution in its Share Capital. Under this Scheme, the Ministry provides funds to TRIFED as its contribution in the Share Capital.

VILLAGE GRAIN BANKS

This Scheme provides Grants for establishment of Village Grain Banks to prevent deaths of STs specially children in remote and backward tribal villages facing or likely to face starvation and also to improve nutritional standards. The Scheme provides funds for building storage facility, procurement of Weights and Measures and for the purchase of initial stock of one quintal of food grain of local variety for each family. A Committee under Chairmanship of village Headman runs the Grain Bank thus established.

GRANT-IN-AID TO VOLUNTARY ORGANIZATIONS

As many as 27 types of projects with focus on tribal education, literacy, medical and health care, vocational training in agriculture, horticulture, craftsmanship etc., are being supported by the Ministry under this Scheme through registered Non-Governmental Organizations.

RESEARCH AND TRAINING

Under the Scheme "Research and Training" the Ministry provides financial assistance under Grants to Tribal Research Institutes on 50:50 sharing basis; for conducting Research & Evaluation Studies, Seminars, and Workshops etc. Award of Research Fellowship to Tribal Students on 100% basis registered in Indian Universities. Supporting projects of All-India or Inter-State nature on 100% basis to NGOs/Universities etc. for conducting research on tribal matters, Travel Grants and for Publication of Books on tribals.

DEVELOPMENT OF PRIMITIVE TRIBAL GROUPS

Under this Scheme cent per-cent assistance is provided to NGOs and other institutions for under-taking projects on development of PTGs on activities mainly focusing on their food security literacy, agriculture technology up gradation, etc.

POST-MATRIC SCHOLARSHIPS, OVERSEAS SCHOLARSHIPS AND BOOK BANKS

The post-matric scholarship scheme provides financial assistance to all ST students for pursuance of post-matric studies in recognized institutions within India. The Scheme provides for 100% assistance from the Ministry to State Governments and UT Administrations implementing the Scheme, over and above their respective committed liabilities. The Ministry also gives financial assistance for setting up Book-Banks in institutions running professional courses like Medicine, Engineering, Law, Agriculture, Veterinary, Chartered Accountancy, Business Management, and Bio-Sciences. Annually, Ministry provides financial assistance to 9 meritorious ST students for Post-graduate, Doctoral and Post-Doctoral studies in foreign universities/institutions of repute.

UPGRADATION OF MERIT AND COACHING

These Schemes provide 100% central assistance to State/UT Administrations. The up gradation of merit Scheme is for arranging coaching classes in reputed colleges for developing competence among ST students for their better performance in competitive examinations conducted by various universities institutes for admission to Medical and Engineering courses while the Scheme for coaching is for conducting Pre-Examination Coaching for tribal students for various examinations conducted by UPSC, SSC, Banking Services Recruitment Boards etc.

TRIBAL ADVISORY COUNCIL (TAC)

Eight states having scheduled areas, namely, Andhra Pradesh, Bihar (now Bihar & Chhatisgarh), Gujarat, Himachal Pradesh, Maharashtra, Madhya Pradesh (now Madhya Pradesh and Chhatisgarh), Orissa and Rajasthan and two non-scheduled area states, namely, Tamil Nadu and West Bengal have constituted TACS. The TAC consists of not more than twenty-five members of whom as many as three-fourth members are scheduled tribe representatives of the state legislative assembly. The governor of the state may refer matters concerning to administration of welfare of tribals to the TAC for recommendations. The ministry issues guidelines for TAC. As per latest guidelines the TAC should meet at least twice a year and discuss the issues concerning tribal interests and making appropriate recommendation for protection of tribal interests.

POINT 11(B) OF 20-POINT PROGRAMME

The point 11(b) of 20-Point Programme is to provide economic assistance to the scheduled tribe families to enable them to rise above poverty line. The ST families are assisted through various schemes implemented by departments of agriculture, rural development, horticulture, animal husbandry, sericulture, forestry, small & cottage industries, etc. The ministry fixes the targets for 22–States/UTs and also monitors the progress of achievements on monthly basis. The officers of the ministry inspected more than 75 projects in the states of Andhra Pradesh, Assam, Manipur, Meghalaya, Orissa, West Bengal, Jharkhand, Maharashtra and Madhya Pradesh.

RURAL/VILLAGE LIFE IN INDIA

Often when we think of Rural life in India — vivid effigies of mud plastered walls, shady trees, green fields, dung cakes, uneven roads, bullock carts and deep dark wells becharms our minds — Ah! And how can one miss hashing out about the sweet and refreshing aroma of the earth when exposed to the very first drop of rain...Indian villages very down to earth and very own always.

Village Life In India.

More than 700 million Indian population live in 600000 villages across rural India. It would not be wrong to say that a true picture of India can be witnessed in its soulful villages. The Government of India is taking commendable steps in promoting the village tourism in India in order to give the visitors a glimpse of "Wonderful Rural India".

Villagers in India manifest a deep loyalty to their village, identifying themselves to strangers as residents of a particular village, harking back to family residence in the village that typically extends into the distant past. A family rooted in a particular village does not easily move to another, and even people who have lived in a city for a generation or two refer to their ancestral village as "our village."

A village that is even a little larger may have pucca houses, or larger living units, usually belonging to the village zamindar family. Consisting of courtyards, and a large cattle enclosure, attached to one side or at the entrance, these are made of a mixture of sun-baked clay bricks covered with a plaster of lime. Floor are made with a mixture of pounded lime, limestone pebbles, and water.

Agriculture life in villages.

Indian villagers share use of common village facilities — the village pond (known in India as a tank), grazing grounds, temples and shrines, cremation grounds, schools, sitting spaces under large shade trees, wells, and wastelands. Perhaps equally important, fellow villagers share knowledge of their common origin in a locale and of each other's secrets, often going back generations. Interdependence in rural life provides a sense of unity among residents of a village.

A great many observances emphasize village unity. Typically, each village recognizes a deity deemed the village protector or protectress, and villagers unite in regular worship of this deity, considered essential to village prosperity. They may cooperate in constructing temples and shrines important to the village as a whole. Hindu festivals such as Holi, Dipavali (Diwali), and Durga Puja bring villagers together. In the north, even Muslims may join in the friendly splashing of coloured water on fellow villagers in Spring Holi rivalries, which involve villagewide singing, dancing, and joking. People of all castes within a village address each other by kinship terms, reflecting the fictive kinship relationships recognized within each settlement. In the north, where village exogamy is important, the concept of a village as a significant unit is clear. When the all-male groom's party arrives from another village, residents of the bride's village in North India treat the visitors with the appropriate behavior due to them as bride-takers—men greet them with ostentatious respect, while women cover their faces and sing bawdy songs at them. A woman born in a village in India is known as a daughter of the village while an in-married bride is considered a daughter-in-law of the village. In her conjugal home in North India, a bride is often known by the name of her natal village; for example, Sanchiwali (woman from Sanchi). A man who chooses to live in his wife's natal village—usually for reasons of land inheritance—is known by the name of his birth village, such as Sankheriwala (man from Sankheri).

Traditionally, villages in India often recognized a headman and listened with respect to the decisions of the panchayat, composed of important men from the village's major castes, who had the power to levy fines and exclude transgressors from village social life. Disputes were decided within the village precincts as much as possible, with infrequent recourse to the police or court system.

In present-day India, the government supports an elective panchayat and headman system, which is distinct from the traditional council and headman, and, in many instances, even includes women and very low-caste members. As older systems of authority are challenged, villagers are less reluctant to take disputes to court.

Farming in villages.

The solidarity of a village is always riven by conflicts, rivalries, and factionalism. Living together in intensely close relationships over generations, struggling to wrest a livelihood from the same limited area of land and water sources, closely watching some grow fat and powerful while others remain weak and dependent, fellow villagers are prone to disputes, strategic contests, and even violence. Most villages of India include what villagers call "big fish," prosperous, powerful people, fed and serviced through the labours of the struggling "little fish." Villagers commonly view gains as possible only at the expense of neighbors. Further, the increased involvement of villagers with the wider economic and political world outside the village via travel, work, education, and television; expanding government influence in rural areas; and increased pressure on land and resources as village populations grow seem to have resulted in increased factionalism and competitiveness in many parts of rural India.

Each village is a multicommunity settlement, the various castes creating a structure of dependence based on the nature of their work. While changes are being wrought in this structure, with ceilings on land holding, and with the young seeking exployment opportunities in towns distant from their villages, the social fabric has still not been rent. At the head of the village settlement are usually the Rajputs, the warrior race whose kings ruled, till recently, over these lands. The Rajputs served their kings, joining their armies, and raising their cavalries, but an attendant pursuit was as agriculturists. Often, they employed labour to work on their extensive fields, and kept cattle for dairy produce: in fact, the cattle density in Rajasthan is very high, and milk from desert settlements is supplied to the large cities close to the state, including Delhi.

The Rajput homes, therefore, came to be the fulcrum around which village life revolved. In their employ were the bards and minstrels who sang their praises in verse and song; tradesment supplied them, and the others in the community, with the goods required for their daily lives, and this was little, since they grew their grains on their own lands; the potters and carpenters were required for their services; and if the village were large enough, there were also ornament makers and cloth dyers and printers. The priests of the Brahmin families cast horoscopes, performed the elaborate rituals of their festive ceremonies, and served at the temples.

In actuality, Indian village life is far from simple. Each village is connected through a variety of crucial horizontal linkages with other villages and with urban areas both near and far. Most villages are characterized by a multiplicity of economic, caste, kinship, occupational, and even religious groups linked vertically within each settlement. Factionalism is a typical feature of village politics. In one of the first of the modern anthropological studies of Indian village life, anthropologist Oscar Lewis called this complexity "rural cosmopolitanism."

Indian village dwellings are built very close to one another in a nucleated settlement, with small lanes for passage of people and sometimes carts. Village fields surround the settlement and are generally within easy walking distance. In hilly tracts of central, eastern, and far northern India, dwellings are more spread out, reflecting the nature of the topography. In the wet states of West Bengal and Kerala, houses are more dispersed;

in some parts of Kerala, they are constructed in continuous lines, with divisions between villages not obvious to visitors.

In northern and central India, neighborhood boundaries can be vague. The houses of Dalits are generally located in separate neighborhoods or on the outskirts of the nucleated settlement, but there are seldom distinct Dalit hamlets. By contrast, in the south, where socioeconomic contrasts and caste pollution observances tend to be stronger than in the north, Brahman homes may be set apart from those of non-Brahmans, and Dalit hamlets are set at a little distance from the homes of other castes.

The number of castes resident in a single village can vary widely, from one to more than forty. Typically, a village is dominated by one or a very few castes that essentially control the village land and on whose patronage members of weaker groups must rely. In the village of about 1,100 population near Delhi studied by Lewis in the 1950s, the Jat caste (the largest cultivating caste in northwestern India) comprised 60 percent of the residents and owned all of the village land, including the house sites. In Nimkhera, Madhya Pradesh, Hindu Thakurs and Brahmans, and Muslim Pathans own substantial land, while lower-ranking Weaver (Koli) and Barber (Khawas) caste members and others own smaller farms. In many areas of the south, Brahmans are major landowners, along with some other relatively high-ranking castes. Generally, land, prosperity, and power go together.

House of Dalits.

In some regions, landowners refrain from using plows themselves but hire tenant farmers and laborers to do this work. In other regions, landowners till the soil with the aid of laborers, usually resident in the same village. Fellow villagers typically include representatives of various service and artisan castes to supply the needs of the villagers—priests, carpenters, blacksmiths, barbers, weavers, potters, oilpressers, leatherworkers, sweepers, waterbearers, toddy-tappers, and so on. Artisanry in pottery, wood, cloth, metal, and leather, although diminishing, continues in many contemporary Indian villages as it did in centuries past. Village religious observances and weddings are occasions for members of various castes to provide customary ritual goods and services in order for the events to proceed according to proper tradition.

Aside from caste-associated occupations, villages often include people who practice nontraditional occupations. For example, Brahmans or Thakurs may be shopkeepers, teachers, truckers, or clerks, in addition to their caste-associated occupations of priest and farmer. In villages near urban areas, an increasing number of people commute to the cities to take up jobs, and many migrate. Some migrants leave their families in the village and go to the cities to work for months at a time. Many people from Kerala, as well as other regions, have temporarily migrated to the Persian Gulf states for employment and send remittances back to their village families, to which they will eventually return.

MAIN FEATURES OF RURAL SOCIETY

VILLAGE IS A COMMUNITY

The village satisfies all their needs in the village. They have a sense of unity and a feeling of amiability towards each other.

VILLAGE IS A INSTITUTION

The development of villages is influenced considerably by the life of the village. In this way village is a primary institution.

RELIGIOSITY

Faith in religion and universal power is found in the life of the villages.

The major occupation is agriculture which involves dependence on nature. Farmers worship forces of nature. The life of the village is the joint family system.

Family has a strict control and administrative powers over the individual. All the members of the family share the burden of the family occupation. In this way of working together the villagers maintain sense of cooperation among themselves. In the life of the villagers group feeling occupies an important place. They respect the judgment and obey the orders of their elders and the panchayats. Society, caste and panchayat have control over the individual.

THE CHANGING FACES OF RURAL LIVELIHOODS IN INDIA

India is witnessing a series of changes since early nineties. Recently, the Sensex crossed 20,000 points and simultaneously India ranked in 94th out of 118 countries in the Global Hunger Index — behind Ethiopia. Unprecedented numbers of farmer suicides, big corporate houses entering into retail business, land allocation for Special Economic Zones, boom in information technology and IT enabled services, zero growth rates in employment, are among many such events that needs introspection.

In recent years the Indian government has made huge investments in development of infrastructure like roads, telecommunication, etc. It has also passed legislation to benefit rural citizens. For example, under universal service obligation, each village should have a village public telephone installed and maintained by the service providers. Also, the "Right To Information Act" passed recently was to make the government system accountable to the citizens. However, civil society organizations are often unaware of such legislation and they fail to leverage the benefits. Corporate houses, private business houses and largely urban citizens are making effective use of the provisions. Thus, the benefits are inequitably distributed between the rural and urban areas. This rural-urban divide in accessing infrastructure services coupled with inability of civil society organizations to utilize the existing provisions has contributed to the slow growth of livelihood opportunities in rural areas.

Initial poverty eradication efforts in India concentrated on supply of agricultural technologies, inputs and services that were often 'production' orientated. However, they were not targeted towards the poor or were largely inappropriate to the needs of the poor and the benefits were mostly captured by the wealthy. Later, the approach changed towards 'capacity-building' in sector organisations to equip people and organisations with the skills and resources to do a better job but, overall little has changed since the new skills are not used. All these approaches tended to be sectoral and supply-driven and the results were not very encouraging. The concept of livelihoods and livelihoods analysis emerged in the mid nineties - closely associated with poverty reduction strategies.

Understanding the livelihood systems of the poor is crucial to effective poverty reduction. Livelihoods of the poor can never be understood in any one-track logic-be it economic, social, technical, cultural or political. The livelihood systems are made up of very diverse elements which—taken together—constitute the physical, economic, social and cultural universe wherein the families live (Hogger). Thus, the livelihood system is more than just a set of physicoeconomic preconditions for continued existence. It also encompasses psychosocial dimensions of experience of living. The livelihoods approach puts households of the poor as its central focus.

It takes holistic consideration of things that the poor might be vulnerable to, assets and resources that help them thrive and survive, policies and institutions that impact their livelihoods, how the poor respond to threats and opportunities and what sort of outcomes the poor aspire to Agriculture and allied activities support livelihoods of nearly 70 percent of India's rural population. In recent years, land based livelihoods of small and marginal farmers are increasingly becoming unsustainable, since their land has not been able to support the family's food requirements and fodder for their cattle. As a result, rural households are forced to look at alternative means for supplementing their livelihoods.

HEALTH PRACTICES AND PROBLEMS IN RURAL INDIA

Rural people in India in general, and tribal populations in particular, have their own beliefs and practices regarding health. Some tribal groups still believe that a disease is always caused by hostile spirits or by the breach of some taboo. They therefore seek remedies through magicoreligious practices. On the other hand, some rural people have continued to follow rich, undocumented, traditional medicine systems, in addition to the recognised cultural systems of medicine such Ayurveda, Unani, Siddha and Naturopathy, to maintain positive health and to prevent disease. However, the socioeconomic, cultural and political onslaughts, arising partly from the erratic exploitation of human and material resources, have endangered the naturally healthy environment (e.g., access to healthy and nutritious food, clean air and water, nutritious vegetation, healthy life styles, and advantageous value systems and community harmony). The basic nature of rural health problems is attributed also to lack of health literature and health consciousness, poor maternal and child health services and occupational hazards.

URBAN LIFE IN INDIA

Introduction. The Concept of Urbanization. Indian Urban Life. Causes of Urbanization. Adverse Effects of Urbanization: *Slums, Environmental Impacts of Urbanization, Benefits of Urbanization.* ***Urban Inequities. Cities as Centers. Urban Transportation. Importance of India's Urban Development. Transport Standards. Urban Infrastructure. E-governance. Future of Urbanization. Urban Governance in India***

INTRODUCTION

Accelerating urbanisation is powerfully affecting the transformation of Indian society. In numerical terms, India's urban population is second largest in the world after China, and is higher than the total urban population of all countries put together barring China, USA and Russia. Urban centres present tremendous opportunities for all people, including the poor. Cities are important vehicles for social and economic transformation in India.

The prominent features of urbanisation in India have been the increase in population, growth of slums, swelling labour force and its marginalisation, and increasing pressure on the urban space and infrastructural services. Congestion noise, traffic jams, air pollution, and major shortages of key necessities characterise urban life. Every major city of India faces the same proliferating problems of grossly inadequate housing, transportation, sewerage, electric power, water supplies, schools, and hospitals.

The present text provides a portrayal of urban life in India. It deals with the means and mechanisms through which people in urban India cope with their lives. The text will be highly informative to anthropologists, sociologists, human geographers and town planners.

THE CONCEPT OF URBANIZATION

Urbanization refers to general increase in population and the amount of industrialization of a settlement. It includes increase in the number and extent of cities. It symbolizes the movement of people from rural to urban areas.

Urbanization happens because of the increase in the extent and density of urban areas. The density of population in urban areas increases because of the migration of people from less industrialized regions to more industrialized areas.

INDIAN URBAN LIFE

Today, India is a curious blend of ancient and modern, epitomised by the *bhajan* blasting from loudspeakers and the *sadhu* with his mobile phone.

More people are moving into towns and cities, and in rural areas the bull is succumbing to the tractor. Industrialisation is taking its toll. Many holy sites are strewn with litter, especially plastic bags, which pose a threat to wildlife.

Extensive deforestation and huge hydro-electric schemes have disrupted the flow of water in India's sacred rivers, causing flash floods after the monsoon and dried-up beds in summer. Some Hindu organisations are voicing their concerns, raising ecological awareness as India runs the path of modernisation. Television and the film industry are having their impact, evident even in the smallest of villages. The younger generation often considers the West its new source of inspiration.

Indian Urban Life.

What is noticeable, though, is that material progress and technology never seem to quite work in India! The recently constructed dual carriageway from Delhi to Agra is more accurately described as "two parallel roads." The driver continuously dodges cows, bicycles and tractors coming towards him on the wrong side of the road. Despite these anomalies – quite shocking to many Westerners – India somehow manages to maintain its sense of spirituality.

Many Hindus living outside India now have quite different lifestyles from their forefathers. Naturally, they tend to get up somewhat later in the day. The extended family is diminishing. Some remain strict about diet, whereas others adopt local eating habits. Unlike in India the temple has become a centre of social activity and an emblem of Hindu identity. Within the UK many multi-million complexes are being constructed in urban areas, replacing the old converted church-halls. Though these temples help Hindus maintain core spiritual practices, there are clear challenges in adjusting to rapidly changing lifestyles, and in applying to the modern context principles largely rooted in rural India .

Every major city of India faces the same proliferating problems of grossly inadequate housing, transportation, sewerage, electric power, water supplies, schools, and hospitals. Slums and jumbles of pavement dwellers' lean-tos constantly multiply.

An increasing number of trucks, buses, cars, three-wheel auto-rickshaws, motorcycles, and motorscooters, all spewing uncontrolled fumes, surge in sometimes haphazard patterns over city streets jammed with jaywalking pedestrians, cattle, and goats. Accident rates are high (India's fatality rate from road accidents, the most common cause of accidental death, is said to be twenty times higher than United States rates), and it is a daily occurrence for a city dweller to witness a crash or the running down of a pedestrian.

In 1984 the citizens of Bhopal suffered the nightmare of India's largest industrial accident, when poisonous gas leaking from a Union Carbide plant killed and injured thousands of city dwellers. Less spectacularly, on a daily basis, uncontrolled pollutants from factories all over India damage the urban environments in which millions live.

CAUSES OF URBANIZATION

Urbanization usually occurs when people move from villages to cities to settle, in hope of a higher standard of living. This usually takes place in developing countries. In rural areas, people become victims of unpredictable weather conditions such as drought and floods, which can adversely affect their livelihood. Consequently many farmers move to cities in search of a better life. This can be seen in Karnataka as well where farmers from Raichur, Gulbarga districts which are drought-stricken areas, migrate to Bangaluru to escape poverty. Cities in contrast, offer opportunities of high living and are known to be places where wealth and money are centralized. Most industries and educational institutions are located in cities whereas there are limited opportunities within rural areas. This further contributes to migration to cities.

ADVERSE EFFECTS OF URBANIZATION

There is increasing competition for facilities due to the high standard of living in urban areas, which has triggered several negative effects. Many people including farmers who move to cities in search of a better life end up as casual laborers as they lack adequate education. This leads to one of the worst problems of urbanization—the growth of slums.

SLUMS

They are urban areas that are heavily populated with substandard housing and very poor living conditions. As a result several problems arise.

- *Land insecurity*—Slums are usually located on land, which are not owned by the slum dwellers. They can be evicted at any time by the landowners.
- *Poor living conditions*—Crowding and lack of sanitation are main problems. This contributes to outbreak of diseases. Utilities such as water, electricity and sewage disposal are also scarce.
- *Unemployment*—Since the number of people competing for jobs is more than jobs available, unemployment is an inevitable problem.
- *Crime*—Slum conditions make maintenance of law and order difficult. Patrolling of slums is not a priority of law enforcing officers. Unemployment and poverty force people into anti-social activities. Slums become a breeding ground for criminal activities.

ENVIRONMENTAL IMPACTS OF URBANIZATION

- *Temperature*—Due to factors such as paving over formerly vegetated land, increasing number of residences and high-rise apartments and industries, temperature increases drastically.
- *Air pollution*—Factories and automobiles are symbols of urbanization. Due to harmful emissions of gases and smoke from factories and vehicles, air pollution occurs. Current research shows high amount of suspended particulate matter in air, particularly in cities, which contributes to allergies and respiratory problems thereby becoming a huge health hazard.
- *Water issues*—When urbanization takes place, water cycle changes as cities have more precipitation than surrounding areas. Due to dumping of sewage from factories in water bodies, water pollution occurs which can lead to outbreaks of epidemics.
- *Destruction of habitats*—To make an area urbanized, a lot of forested areas are destroyed. Usually these areas would have been habitats to many birds and animals.

BENEFITS OF URBANIZATION

Though urbanization has drawbacks, it has its benefits.

- *Efficiency*—Cities are extremely efficient. Less effort is needed to supply basic amenities such as fresh water and electricity. Research and recycling programs are possible only in cities. In most cities flats are in vogue today. Many people can be accommodated within a small land area.
- *Convenience*—Access to education, health, social services and cultural activities is readily available to people in cities than in villages. Life in cities is much more advanced, sophisticated and comfortable, compared to life in villages. Cities have advanced communication and transport networks.
- *Concentration* of *resources*—Since major human settlements were established near natural resources from ancient times, a lot of resources are available in and around cities. A lot of facilities to exploit these resources also exist only in cities.
- *Educational facilities*—Schools, colleges and universities are established in cities to develop human resources. A variety of educational courses and fields are available offering students a wide choice for their future careers.
- *Social integration*—People of many castes and religions live and work together in cities, which creates better understanding and harmony and helps breakdown social and cultural barriers.
- *Improvements in economy*—High-tech industries earn valuable foreign exchange and lot of money for a country in the stock markets.

URBAN INEQUITIES

Major socioeconomic differences are much on display in cities. The fine homes—often a walled compound with a garden, servants' quarters, and garage—and gleaming automobiles of the super wealthy stand in stark contrast to the burlap-covered huts of the barefoot poor. Shops filled with elegant silk saris and air-conditioned restaurants cater to the privileged, while ragged dust-covered children with outstretched hands wait outside in hopes of receiving a few coins. The wealthy and the middle class employ servants and workers of various kinds, but jajmani—like ties are essentially lacking, and the rich and the poor live much more separate lives than in villages. At the same time, casual interaction and physical contact among people of all castes is constant, on public streets and in buses, trains, and movie theaters.

As would-be urbanites stream into the cities, they often seek out people from their village, caste, or region who have gone before them and receive enough hospitality to tide them over until they can settle in themselves. They find accommodation wherever they can, even if only on a quiet corner of a sidewalk, or inside a concrete sewer pipe waiting to be laid. Some are fortunate enough to find shelter in decrepit tenements or in open areas where they can throw up flimsy structures of mud, tin sheeting, or burlap. In such slum settlements, a single outhouse may be shared by literally thousands of people, or, more usually, there are no sanitary facilities at all. Ditches are awash in raw sewage, and byways are strewn with the refuse of people and animals with nowhere else to go.

Despite the exterior appearance of chaos, slum life is highly structured, with many economic, religious, caste, and political interests expressed in daily activity. Living conditions are extremely difficult, and slum dwellers fear the constant threat of having their homes bulldozed in municipal "slum clearance" efforts; nonetheless, slum life is animated by a strong sense of carefree enjoyment of life (*joie de vivre*).

In many sections of Indian cities, scavenging pigs, often owned by Sweepers, along with stray dogs, help to recycle fecal material. Piles of less noxious vegetal and paper garbage are sorted through by the poorest people, who seek usable or salable bits of things. Cattle and goats, owned by entrepreneurial folk, graze on these piles, turning otherwise useless garbage into valuable milk, dung (used for cooking fuel), and meat. These domestic animals roam even in neighborhoods of fine homes, outside the compound walls that protect the privileged and their gardener-tended rose bushes from needy animals and people.

Finding employment in the urban setting can be extremely challenging, and, whenever possible, networks of relatives and friends are used to help seek jobs. Millions of Indians are unemployed or underemployed. Ingenuity and tenacity are the hallmarks of urban workers, who carry out a remarkable multitude of tasks and sell an incredible variety of foods, trinkets, and services, all under difficult conditions. Many of the urban poor are migrant laborers carrying headloads of bricks and earth up rickety bamboo scaffolding at construction sites, while their small children play about at the edge of excavations or huddle on mounds of gravel in the blazing sun. Nursing mothers must take time out periodically to suckle their babies at the edge of construction sites; such "recesses" are considered reason to pay a woman less for a day's work than a man earns (male construction workers earned about US$1 a day in 1994). Moreover, women are seen as physically weaker by some employers and thus not deserving of equal wages with men.

These construction projects are financed by governments and by business enterprises, which are run by cadres of well-educated, healthy, well-dressed men and, increasingly, women, who occupy positions of power and make decisions affecting many people. India's major cities have long been headquarters for the country's highest socioeconomic groups, people with transnational and international connections whose choices are taking India into new realms of economic development and social change. Among these well-placed people, intercaste marriages raise few eyebrows, as long as marital unions link people of similar upper- or upper-middle-class backgrounds. Such marriages, sometimes even across religious lines, help knit India's most powerful people together.

Increasingly conspicuous in India's cities are the growing ranks of the middle class. In carefully laundered clothes, they emerge from modest and semiprosperous homes to ride buses and motorscooters to their jobs in offices, hospitals, courts, and commercial establishments. Their well-tended children are educated in properly organized schools. Family groups go out together to places of worship, social events, snack shops, and to bazaars bustling with consumers eager to buy the necessities of a comfortable life. Members of the middle class cluster around small stock-market outlets in cities all over the country. Even in Kolkata, notorious for slums and street dwellers, the dominant image is of office workers in pressed white garments riding crowded buses—or Kolkata's world-class subway line—to their jobs as office workers and professionals.

For nearly everyone within the highly challenging urban environment, ties to family and kin remain crucial to prosperity. Even in the harshest urban conditions, families show remarkable resilience. Neighborhoods, too, take on importance, and neighbors from various backgrounds develop cooperative ties with one another. Neighbourhood solidarity is expressed at such annual Hindu festivals as Ganesh's Birthday (Ganesh Chaturthi) in Mumbai and Durga Puja in Kolkata, when neighborhood associations create elaborate images of the deities and take them out in grand processions.

CITIES AS CENTERS

Cosmopolitan cities are the great hubs of commerce and government upon which the nation's functioning depends. Mumbai, India's largest city and port, is India's economic powerhouse and locus of the nation's atomic research. The National Capital Territory of Delhi, where a series of seven cities was built over centuries, is the site of the capital—New Delhi—and political nerve center of the world's largest democracy. Kolkata and Chennai fill major roles in the country's economic life, as do high-tech Bangaluru and Ahmadabad (in Gujarat), famous for textiles. Great markets in foods, manufactured goods, and a host of key commodities are centered in urban trading and distribution points. Most eminent institutions of higher learning, cradles of intellectual development and scientific investigation, are situated in cities. The visual arts, music, classical dancing, poetry, and literature all flourish in the urban setting. Critical political and social commentary appears in urban newspapers and periodicals. Creative new trends in architecture and design are conceptualized and brought to reality in cities.

Cities are the source of television broadcasts and those great favorites of the Indian public, movies. Mumbai, sometimes called "Bollywood," and Chennai are major centers of film production, bringing depictions of urban lifestyles before the eyes of small-town dwellers and villagers all over the nation. With the continuing national proliferation of television sets, videocassette recorders, and movie videocassettes, the influence of such productions should not be underestimated.

Social revolutions, too, receive the support of urban visionaries. Among the more important social developments in contemporary India is the growing women's movement, largely led by educated urban women. Seeking to restructure society and gender relations, activists, scholars, and workers in the women's movement have come together in numerous loosely allied and highly diverse organizations focusing on issues of rights and equality, empowerment, and justice for women. Some of these groups exist in rural areas, but most are city based.

The escalating issues of dowry-related murder and suicide are most pressing in New Delhi, where groups such as Saheli (Woman Friend) provide essential support to troubled women. The pathbreaking feminist publication Manushi is published in New Delhi and distributed throughout the country. The overwhelming economic needs of self-employed poor female workers in Ahmadabad inspired Ela Bhatt and her coworkers in the Self-Employed Women's Association, which has been highly successful in helping poor women improve their own lives.

Urban women have initiated protests challenging female feticide, child marriage, child prostitution, domestic violence, polygyny, sati, sexual harassment, police rape of female plaintiffs, and other gender-related injustices. Their efforts have brought new ways of thinking out of elite, educated circles into the broader public arena of India's multilevel society.

In 1994, two attractive urban Indian women won the most prominent international beauty contests, the Miss Universe and the Miss World competitions. Thousands of young Indian women idolized the glamorous beauties and many newspapers gushed about the victories, but women's groups and feminist commentators decried this adulation. They pointed out that the deprivations and injustices experienced by a high proportion of Indian women were being given short shrift. While the beauty contest winners were being paraded about in crowns and white chariots before admiring throngs, almost ignored by the public and the media were the torture-slaying of a village woman accused of theft by a soothsayer and the historic qualification of six women as the Indian air force's first female pilots.

URBAN TRANSPORTATION

Urbanization has been one of the dominant contemporary processes as a growing share of the global population lives in cities. Considering this trend, urban transportation issues are of foremost importance to support the passengers and freight mobility requirements of large urban agglomerations. Transportation in urban areas is highly complex because of the modes involved, the multitude of origins and destinations, and the amount and variety of traffic. Traditionally, the focus of urban transportation has been on passengers as cities were viewed as locations of utmost human interactions with intricate traffic patterns linked to commuting, commercial transactions and leisure/cultural activities. However, cities are also locations of production, consumption and distribution, activities linked to movements of freight. Conceptually, the urban transport system is intricately linked with urban form and spatial structure. Urban transit is an important dimension of mobility, notably in high density areas. To understand the complex relationships between transportation and land use and to help the urban planning process, several models have been developed.

Cities are locations having a high level of accumulation and concentration of economic activities and are complex spatial structures that are supported by transport systems. The most important transport problems are often related to urban areas and take place when transport systems, for a variety of reasons, cannot satisfy the numerous requirements of urban mobility. Urban productivity is highly dependent on the efficiency of its transport system to move labor, consumers and freight between multiple origins and destinations. Additionally, important transport terminals such as ports, airports, and railyards are located within urban areas, contributing to a specific array of problems. Some problems are ancient, like congestion (which plagued cities such as Rome), while others are new like urban freight distribution or environmental impacts.

IMPORTANCE OF INDIA'S URBAN DEVELOPMENT

Our urban development is as important too. We have come a long way since independence in terms of urban economy growth. Urban economy now contributes upto 70% to the nation's GDP, while this figure was 30% in 1960. In the last 50 years, all over the world cities has risen to become hubs of economic activity and certainly future growth is going to come from our cities.

India's urban development.

But unfortunately, the growth and expansion of Indian cities has been unplanned and haphazard. Our cities today face challenges in meeting the demands of infrastructure and resources. The demand for clean water exceeds the supply by about 30%. Waste management systems are almost non-existent, and if they are there, heavily over-stressed with over 40% waste going uncollected. Eco-friendly waste disposal methods are only a dream and even government agencies and engineers are totally unaware about their technicalities. Around 22% of urban population lives in slums and around 25% is below the poverty line. Traffic congestion and pollution has increased like never before.

Clearly, we need to change not only the way our cities are managed, but also how they are planned. Planning for future cities and management of current cities only will result in livable cities which will have decent quality of life and equal opportunities to all citizens. Firstly, we should provide fast and low cost infrastructure for residents like housing, hospitals, schooling, transport and commercial centres. There should also be a provision of how to grow this infrastructure as cities grow in the future.

We must encourage high rise and high density cities to accommodate the continuous migration from villages to cities. While we have seen growth in apartments in cities like Noida, Gurgaon and Bangaluru, most of them are for the upper middle class. There is an urgent need for builders to build affordable low cost housing solutions. The government can help the builders by providing tax rebates as incentives.

TRANSPORT STANDARDS

If we improve our roads and transport standards, our cities can grow horizontally as traveling time will reduce. Transport is like the backbone of a city. Poor transport limits mobility of its people which in turn hamper economic growth. Road capacity must be enhanced but it is not enough in itself. Road transport has to be supplemented by development of mass transit systems like metro rail, mono rail and bus services.

Transport standards in Urban Areas.

Road widening and introducing separate lanes for buses is an important step which is required today in almost every city of India. Other transit systems like metro rail should be integrated with bus services like Hong Kong and Tokyo, as this will reduce travel times and improve efficiency for business and economy.

URBAN INFRASTRUCTURE

Undoubtedly, there is a lot to do to improve urban infrastructure, and huge amounts of money will be required to do this. It is impossible for the government to all of this by itself. It is therefore imperative private sector be involved heavily in infrastructure development activities with the government playing the role of a regulator. In Thailand and Malaysia, even sanitation systems are managed by private operators. Why can't the same model work here? A lot of policy changes will also be required to change how local governments and municipal bodies work. The Mayor of a city is elected by councillors, and is powerless. The mayor should be elected directly by the people and should be given powers to manage and run cities efficiently.

E-GOVERNANCE

To make sure all these systems work in a transparent and efficient manner, we must introduce ratings of municipalities of different cities, and some sort of comparative performance measurement system for officers. All this information should be in the public domain and open to scrutiny by the media and public. E-governance needs to be introduced and systems such as MIS (Management Information Systems) can be used to collate all information and improve efficiency of all services. How we manage our cities today will decide how our country will shape up tomorrow. We need to turn our cities into truly sustainable engines of growth for the whole country.

FUTURE OF URBANIZATION

Urbanization is set to stay for a long time. It may slow but surely does not show any signs of stopping. In 1985, 45% of the world population stayed in cities. Scientists estimate that 60% of the world population will be city-dwellers by 2025.

The main goal of urban planning is to make all amenities and comforts available to the public without imposing many negative effects on society and environment, aptly referred to as "Sustainable growth". The cardinal rule is to plan cities beforehand, rather than let them grow spontaneously and haphazardly. During city planning it should be ensured that adequate infrastructure is available to support the population. Residences should be conveniently located near the civic bodies. This could improve effective provision of the necessary services.

Opportunities can be created within rural areas to reduce stress on cities. This also results in a higher standard of living for the people of the country as a whole. Some of the villages in South Kanara district of Karnataka set a good example for this. They have efficient transport and communication system and electricity. Co-operatives have been set up to provide financial aid to peasants. The rural people have been encouraged to engage in cottage industries and commercial activities such as making pickles, handicrafts, sweets and savories. Through cooperative agencies, marketing of these goods also has become easy. This is an efficient method of curbing urbanization, by creating opportunities for people in villages. This reduces the rate of migration.

Currently, planning cities for sustainable growth, mainly in the third-world societies, is a major challenge for humanity. Restricting the population boom is another major issue of the third millennium.

URBAN GOVERNANCE IN INDIA

Municipal Governance in India exists since 1687 with the formation of Madras Municipal Corporation and then Calcutta and Bombay Municipal Corporation in 1726. In early part of the nineteenth century almost all towns in India had experienced some form of municipal Governance. In 1882 Lord Ripons resolution of local self-government laid the democratic forms of municipal governance in India. In 1919 Government of India act incorporated the need of the resolution and the powers of democratically elected government were formulated. In 1935 Government of India act brought local government under the purview of the state or provincial government and specific powers were given.

In 1992, a major step towards the decentralization and empowerment of local governments in India took place with the enactment of 74th Constitutional Amendment Act. The Amendment calls for greater responsibilities and authorities for local governments by recognizing it as a third tier government. Some of the important aspects include:

- Planning for economic and social development and role of municipal government in implementation of urban poverty alleviation projects.
- Increased responsibility for urban planning at the district and metropolitan levels.
- Greater authority to mobilize and using of resources.

Applied Sociology

Introduction: *A Definition of Applied Sociology.* ***History and Applications of Sociological Practice. The Laboratory of Applied Sociological Researches.*** *Role of Applied Sociology.* ***Roles of the Sociologist in Applied Sociology.*** *Social Policy and Their Contribution.* ***Social Policy in the Indian Development Process. Social Planning:*** *Planning as A 'Learning Process', Planning as a Decision-making Process.* ***Need for Social Planning.***

INTRODUCTION

Applied Sociology is a term that describes practitioners who use sociological theories and methods outside of academic settings with the aim to 'produce positive social change through active intervention'. More specifically, applied sociology might be seen as the translation of sociological theory into practice for specific clients. That is, this term describes the use of sociological knowledge in answering research questions or problems as defined by specific interest groups, rather than the researcher. Applied research is sometimes conducted within a multidisciplinary environment and in collaboration with different organisations, including community services, activist groups and sometimes in partnership with universities. Some applied sociologists may not explicitly use sociological theories or methods in their work, but they may use their sociological training more broadly to inform their work and their thinking. Applied sociologists work in various industries, including private business, government agencies and not-for-profit organisations. The work of applied sociologists is especially concerned with changing the current state of social life for the better. This can include anything from increasing the health and wellbeing of a disadvantaged community group; working with law enforcement organisations to implement a rehabilitation program for criminal offenders; assisting in planning for natural disasters; and enhancing existing government programs and policies.

DEFINITION OF APPLIED SOCIOLOGY

Applied Sociology is a branch of general sociology which at its basis is the scientific study of society as a whole. Sociology looks at society from every angle making observations on how we interact within society, how cultures affect each other and the individual, global issues and more. Sociology is part of the social sciences that aims at answering questions as to why and how we group together to form societies as well as the individual's roles within society.

In a very general sense, sociology can be defined as the study of 'the bases of social membership'. That is, sociology is the study of what it means to be a member of a particular society, and it involves the critical analysis of the different types of social connections and social structures that constitute a society. This includes questions about how and why different groups are formed and the various meanings attached to different modes of social interaction, such as between individuals or social networks; face to face versus online communications; local and global discourses, and so on. Sociology also encompasses the study of the social institutions that shape social action. A social institution is a complex, but distinctive, sub-system of society that regulates human conduct. For example, the media acts as a social institution that can influence the way in which 'facts' are represented and interpreted; the law and politics impact on the ways in which different cultural groups define what is deemed 'right' and 'moral'; the institutions of economy and education affect social status (that is, wealth and inequality among individuals); and the institution of family shapes our ideas about partnership, work, gender, sex, childrearing, and our bodies, as well as various other aspects of our lives.

Sociology can therefore be used to study all the social experiences that human beings are capable of imagining – from practices of childbirth, to the use technologies, to our attitudes and rituals regarding death – and everything else in between. People usually understand their problems in reference to their own personal life story and they are not always aware of the complex links between their own lives and the rest of the world's history. The 'sociological imagination' helps us to make sense of the connections between history, biography and place. Sociology allows us to study individual behaviour in a broader context, to take into consideration how societal forces might impact upon individuals, as well as the ways in which individuals construct the world around them, and how they manage to resist existing power relationships in order to achieve social change. In this light, sociology represents 'a transformation of consciousness'. Sociology questions taken-for-granted assumptions about the world we live in (what we see as 'familiar' and 'normal' within the context of our everyday lives), and it provides a new and more critical perspective of the world, through the use of scientific theories, concepts and empirical evidence.

HISTORY AND APPLICATIONS OF SOCIOLOGICAL PRACTICE

Harry Perlstadt traces the history of applied sociology to 1850, and the work of August Comte, one of sociology's founding figures. Perlstadt writes that Comte divided the discipline of sociology in two parts: social statics, the study of social order, and social dynamics, the study of social progress and development. Perlstadt argues that Comte's theory lends itself to two types of sociologies: 'basic research' and social interventionism. Basic researchers educate and influence public debate, and social interventionists are political activists who are responsible for actively enforcing social change. According to Perlstadt, Comte saw applied researchers as occupying a 'translational role' in-between these two positions. Nevertheless, almost 160 years later, there remains a long-standing divide between the so-called 'pure' and 'practical' research traditions in sociology. While these differences may appear to be artificial, ambivalences persist between academic and applied sociologies, despite the fluidity and intersections between these practices.

Hans Zetterberg argues that 'practical' sociological knowledge might be distinguished into five roles: decision-maker, educator, social critic, researcher for clients, and consultant. First, the sociologist as decision-maker is someone who uses social science in order to shape policy decisions. The sociologist as an educator is a person who teaches sociology to students, typically in a university setting, although sociology is now increasingly taught in high schools and as part of specialist courses. The sociologist as a commentator and social critic is someone who writes for a wider public through books and articles aimed at an educated public, with a view of influencing public opinion. The sociologist as researcher for clients might be someone who works with public or private organisations, such as mental health groups, banks, or some other company that commissions research on very specific topics. Finally, the sociologist who acts as a consultant works to answer a specific and practical problem as defined by a particular client, using their client's language and by making specific reference to their client's problem, rather than a broader social problem or grand social theory. Zetterberg positions applied sociologists as fulfilling the latter two roles: client work and consultancy.

Joseph DeMartini identifies that applied sociology can take on two variations. First, applied researchers might use basic empirical methods in collecting information in order to help shape informed decisions, such as in the creation of social policy. In this meaning, sociologists might be directly working within government agencies, or they might work for private research organisations, or they might be contracted for one or the other. He lists the following activities as examples of this applied methodological approach: 'evaluation research, program evaluation, cost/benefit analysis, systems analysis, community ethnography, public opinion polling, and market analysis'. While these sociologists might employ scientific theories and concepts, their specialisation is actually the application of sociological research techniques in order to gather specific information, rather than the application of sociological theories per se. Second, applied researchers might be employed more specifically for their knowledge of sociological concepts and theories in order to help their clients better understand a narrowly-defined issue. Activities might include assessing the determinants of observed phenomena, such as the causes of crime, explaining demographic changes, and evaluating the shifts in social movements. Alternatively, applied sociologists might propose a course of action in order to achieve targeted change, such as by increasing the economic outcomes of a disadvantaged community, reforming illegal behaviours, or developing a framework in order to prepare a local community in the advent of a natural disaster. To clarify the distinction between these two applied practices, DeMartini uses the example of social policy: in the first case, where methods take primacy, applied sociological research techniques are employed in order to create and inform new social policies; in the second instance, where theories and concepts have greater relevance to the clients, applied sociological knowledge is used to evaluate existing social policies. DeMartini notes, however, that this differentiation is for illustration purposes, and that, in fact, applied practices run along a continuum in between these two practices. Methods and theories cannot be used in isolation, but some jobs might require more emphasis on one than the other.

Howard Freeman and Peter Rossi argue that the application of sociological knowledge is different for academic and applied sociologists. They see that some of the work that academics do might be considered to be 'applied', particularly as universities are seeking more external revenue, and so they encourage academics to carry out contract work. Nevertheless, by and large, Freeman and Rossi see that academic and applied sociologists are distinguished in six ways. First, applied sociologists' careers rely less on publishing in academic journals, and, instead, they focus more on the the utility of their work to a specialised (non-academic) audience. Since, they are hired by external stakeholders, their rewards are judged by their sponsors, on the basis of whether these clients see the work as being useful to them. Academics rely more on peer-evaluations, and there is high prestige in publishing in academic journals. Second, Freeman and Rossi argue that applied sociologists have narrow contraints on their time and the specificity of their work outputs, while academic sociologists are more free to choose their research topic (notwithstanding the politics of grant funding and the publishing potential of certain topics). Third, applied sociologists adhere to 'absolute norms' of rigorous scholarship 'only to the extent necessary to achieve usable results'. There is sometimes a swift turnover expected of the work by applied researchers, while academics generally have a longer timeframe with which to develop their scholarship. Fourth, applied sociologists are more concerned with 'external validity', that is, the extent to which their conclusions speak directly to their specific client's topic area, rather than to some general social problem or broader group. Academics tend to focus more on 'internal validity' — to making a contribution to the academic literature, and the judgements of their peers. Fifth, applied sociologists are driven by the 'practical payoffs' of their activities, such as their client's judgement of the utility of this applied work to the client's situation, while academics are required to defend the merits of their work in relation to their theoretical contribution. In connection, the final difference between applied and academic sociologists is that the former judges the success of their work on their client's adoption of their proposed solutions, and their ability to influence their stakeholders' decision-making, while the conclusions proposed by academics do not always lend themselves to specific actions. Freeman and Rossi's distinctions between the work of academic and applied sociologists are, in reality, not so absolute, but these points do identify some of the broad facets of applied sociology. In summary, applied sociologists work for specific stakeholders, their research topics and time is often constrained by their sponsors' needs and wishes, their work is less concerned with making a contribution to academic scholarship, and they are more interested in practical payoffs that will have a direct influence on their clients.

There are various other sociological practices that fall under the 'applied' rubric. For example, clinical sociology is a term that has been used since the 1930s to describe 'sociologically based interventions', usually in reference to sociological work done across the health sector, in social work, and even in forensic settings. This work includes collaborating with medical practitioners, nurses, psychologists, psychiatrists and nutritionists, as well as advocacy and support in mental health programs, including through counselling, interpersonal therapy, intervention programs with youth, substance abuse services, and group grief counselling. The term social engineering describes the applied research activities that are used in social planning, and it is also used to critique the value judgements made about what constitutes 'pure' and 'applied' research. Jonathan Turner runs with the idea of 'sociological engineering' to describe the type of sociology 'that tries to deal with the real world'. He argues that applied sociological knowledge lends itself to a systems engineering approach. He sees that applied sociology should be used to break abstract theoretical principles into 'rules of thumb' about social structures, in order to identify how societies are built, how to evaluate the problems of a given social structure, and how to break down the structures that are not working well. Whatever we choose to call it, applied sociologists' use of methods and theories has one central goal: to change some specific facet of social life.

One thing that practitioners seem to agree on is that their work needs to be carried out in a way that is both accessible to their clients and devoid of academic jargon. In this connection, applied sociology has some synergy with public sociology, the branch of sociology that aims to engage 'lay' audiences, including neighborhood groups and grassroots organisations, with the aim of stimulating informed public dialogue. Rita Simon argues that communication skills are quintessential in an applied context; sociologists who work in non-academic sectors should therefore be able to express themselves in plain language and not in 'sociologese' (using phrases that only people with a sociology degree might understand). She writes, 'Basically, I think graduate students have to be taught that scientific writing is not a thing apart from ordinary prose; the aim is still to communicate efficiently, effectively, and if possible, aesthetically'.

THE LABORATORY OF APPLIED SOCIOLOGICAL RESEARCHES

The Laboratory of Applied Sociological Researches is one of the main research centers at the Faculty of Sociology. The focus of its studies is rather broad starting with the issues of Armenian higher educational system up to the most urgent social problems in Armenian society. The Laboratory of Applied Sociological Researches supports the development of research potentials and skills of students and professors as well. Thus it reaffirms the crucial traditions of State University, promoting the enlargement and increasing the effectiveness of educational-scientific activities within the faculty.

The research activity of the Laboratory is addressed to such tissues as:

1. Studying and analyzing the issues of self-government of higher educational institutes (HEI);
2. Monitoring and evaluation of the quality of higher education;
3. Testing and evaluation of effectiveness of innovation programs in the State University;

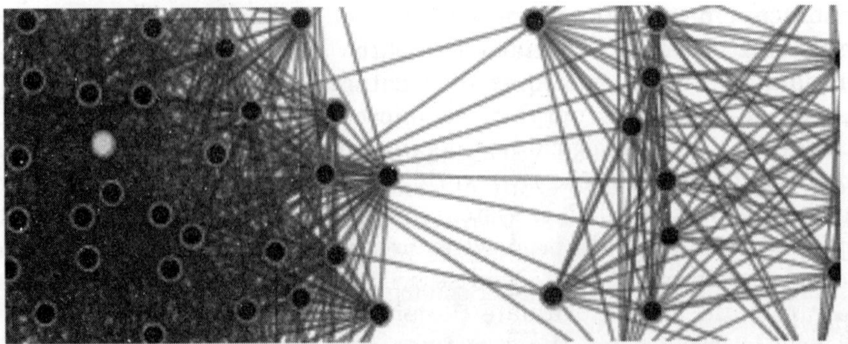

Applied Sociological Researches.

4. Supporting the conduction of researches in the field of Armenian sociological traditions;
5. Organizing the practical courses for the students of the Chair of Sociology;
6. Organizing methodical conferences, summer schools, seminars, etc;
7. Testing of new educational methods;
8. Studying and analyzing the contemporary social problems in Armenian society.

Since 2006 the Laboratory has conducted an amount of projects including:

"Monitoring and Evaluation of the Higher Education System in State University" in 2008. Within this program was implemented the project on "The Elaboration of categories for higher education quality evaluation" that was addressed to designing the criteria system for higher education quality assessment on the basis of local and international experience analysis.

In 2009 the Laboratory is implementing the program on "Elaboration and testing the methodology for higher education quality assesment". In the frameworks of the latter the sociological research in "Participatory evaluation of higher education quality" is implementing which is addressed to the solution of the following issues:

1. To give a comprehensive definitions to the already selected criteria for evaluation of higher education quality;
2. To design research tools and test them;
3. To conduct the field work and analyse the results;
4. To elaborate the preliminary model for higher education evaluation;
5. To test the preliminary model for higher education evaluation;
6. To design the general model for higher education evaluation.

Another project of "Monitoring and Evaluation of the Higher Education System in State University" was addressed to asses the effectiveness of teaching methods in Yerevan State University, Testing and evaluation of effectiveness of innovation programs in the State University. The Laboratory has implemented the project on "Evaluation of Master's program in faculties of social sciences in Yerevan State University" that was addressed to estimate the effectiveness of Master's program functioning and to suggest certain ways of its improvement.

"Studing the image of YSU student". The Laboratory has implemented the research directed to study of sociologist-students social portrait. The objective of the survey was to reveal the features of sociologist-students' self-identification and its dynamics in studying process.

The Laboraoty of Applied Sociological Researches has facilitated the following research programs.

The research works of the Faculty of Sociology. Particularly, Laboratory promoted methodological support for the sociological researches implemented on the frameworks of practical courses at the Faculty of Sociology. The researches that were implemented by the support of Laboratory are the following: within winter practices - "The correspondence between State University's educational system and the demands of Labor market" (2006-07), "The factors effecting the youth migration in Armenia" (2007-08), "The peculiarities of Armenian identity" (2008-09); with summer practices – "The issues of immigration and the transformation of community identity Zhambarak" (2008), "The description of social structure of Vardenik community" (2009).

The creation of sociological literature' database on the basis of the most contemporary research works implemented at the Faculty of Sociology. The Laboratory has designed catalogues of sociological research methodology literature lists on the basis of the modern reseach literature and journals existing in libraries of Yerevan.

ROLE OF APPLIED SOCIOLOGY

Applied sociology is one of the more than a dozen fields within sociology. Applied sociology is what has been deemed the "practical side" of sociology. That's because applied sociology takes sociological theories and research and applies this knowledge to sociological methods which are carried out in order to find solutions to problems within society. This use of sociological theories and methods is called sociological practice.

At one time sociology was not as present in our own culture. In the 20th century sociology saw changes as people began to question the value of the science. Sociology has roots in theory which was regarded as less exact than other sciences and therefore possibly less useful. So, sociologist began using methods of research and applications that were more quantitative to validate their findings. Using these scientific methods is called positivism.

Using qualitative and quantitative research methods led to a resurgence in the science as sociologists began developing new methods for studying society and actual ways to apply the science. As people began to realize its usefulness on local and national levels they found there was an even greater importance for applied sociology.

Due to economic factors as well as increasing forms of communication globalization is now a topic of interest. Applied sociology is now being used to analyze society and its interactions on a global level, which includes online communities. It addresses solutions to questions about political power on a global level, how economics and trade affect societies around the world, how globalization is changing structures of societies and more.

Today applied sociologists play an important role in our country and even the world's development. As societies begin, grow and merge sociologists are reading into every aspect and analyzing where there are problems and applying tested methods to ease those problems. Applied sociologists work in every level of government; local, state and national. These scientists work every day to create a more functional society that serves all the people equally. They also work for community organizations, public administration and even businesses to solve problems of social organizations within smaller environments. Another role of sociologists today is to work with financial companies such as those who issue credit cards and internet companies such as social media websites to understand user behavior and make for a better experience.

ROLES OF THE SOCIOLOGIST IN APPLIED SOCIOLOGY

Sociologists can help to predict the effects of a policy and thus contribute to the selection of policies which achieve the intended purposes. Some sociologists are engaged in planning and conducting community action programmes advising on public relations, employee relations, working on human relations problems etc. Often these sociologists have specialized in social psychology, industrial sociology, urban or rural sociology or the sociology of complex organizations. As a scientist the sociologist's foremost task is to discover and organize knowledge about social life. A number of full time research sociologists are employed by universities, government agencies, foundations or corporations and many sociologists divide their time between teaching and research. Another task of the sociologist as a scientist is to clear away the misinformation and superstition which clutters so much of our social thinking.

Sociologists generally avoided involvement in controversial issues and sought the status of pure social scientists. This view has been challenged in both physical and social science. Many sociologists today believe that sociologists should claim a major role in making decisions about public policy and should involve themselves in the major issues of our society. They feel that not only do sociologists have a duty to say what society might do about problems of race conflict, population growth, birth control, drug addiction, divorce etc. but the sociologists should say what society should do about such problems. Sociologists have helped to clear doubts about hereditary, race, class, sex differences, deviation and nearly every other aspect of behaviour. By helping replace superstition and misinformation with accurate knowledge about human behaviour sociologists are performing their most important role. Sociologists make sociological predictions. Every policy decision is based upon certain assumptions about the present and future state of the society. Most social science prediction consists not of predicting specific developments as the astronomer predicts an eclipse but of forecasting the general pattern of trends and changes which seem most probable. All such predictions or forecasts should be offered with certain humility for no certainty attends them. Instead social scientists offer them as the best most informed guesses available upon which to base our policy decisions and expectations for the future. Sociological prediction can also help to estimate the probable effects of a social policy. Every social policy decision is a prediction. A policy is begun in the hope that it will produce a desired effect. Policies have often failed because they embodied unsound assumptions and predictions.

Sociologist in applied sociology.

The term clinical sociologist has appeared to describe the work of the sociologist as technician. To some extent this is a new name for what sociologists have been doing for a long time but it also includes a considerable broadening of the range of sociologists' efforts to be useful in society. In such positions the sociologist is working as an applied scientist. He or she has been engaged to use scientific knowledge in pursuing certain values—a harmonious and efficient working force an attractive public image of the industry or an effective community action programme.

Teaching is the major career of many sociologists. In addition to the concerns and problems of teaching in any field, the problem of value neutrality versus value commitment is a particularly acute question. The ethics of university teaching have demanded that the teacher refrain from all conscious indoctrination but it is debatable. Scientists seek to discover knowledge but should they tell the society how this knowledge should be used? The basic question is whether science specifically sociology should be value-free. For example sociologists know some things about population growth, race relations, urban development and many other matters involving questions of public policy. Early sociologists gave support to all sorts of public policies they believed in. Between 1920 and 1940 many sociologists shifted to the view that sociology should be a more nearly pure science discovering knowledge but not attempting to decree how it should be used. They sought to build sociology on the model of physics as a value-free science. As such it should be committed to no values except those of free scientific inquiry.

Sociologists have agreed upon some of the propositions: Sociologists should show the relationships between values. If we wish to clean up polluted rivers we must be prepared to spend a lot of tax money in doing so. Sociologists may clarify what value sacrifices must be made if we wish to attain certain other values. A sociologist as an individual may properly make value judgements, support causes and join reform movements like any other citizen. As a scientist the sociologist may not know whether television violence is harmful to children and therefore might not make public recommendations but as a parent will make a decision according to the personal beliefs and values. Beyond this there is no complete agreement among sociologists concerning what role they should assume. Most sociologists have some firm opinions on what policies society should follow and are in considerable agreement with one another upon many of these policies.

SOCIAL POLICY AND THEIR CONTRIBUTION

Social Policy is the study of social services and the welfare state. In general terms, it looks at the idea of social welfare, and its relationship to politics and society. More specifically, it also considers detailed issues in:

- policy and administration of social services, including policies for health, housing, income maintenance, education and social work;
- needs and issues affecting the users of services, including poverty, old age, health, disability, and family policy; and
- the delivery of welfare.

In developing economies this refers to the social contract between capital and labour specifically for the management of the development project. The latter in turn has been defined for much of the past half century, as the project of increasing material welfare for most of the citizenry through economic development, using the agency of the nation state. For many developing countries, including India, this project remains partially or largely unfulfilled although this state of incompletion still has not prevented it from being very nearly abandoned in several instances. At the most basic level, social policies of different types are crucial to the states capacity to manage, modernisation, and along with it the huge economic and social shocks that are necessarily generated.

The second important, and related, role of social policy is of course that of legitimisation, not only of the state, but of the development project itself. This need for legitimisation arises both for the long run process and in terms of short run crisis management. Thus, over the long run, or planning horizon, it is especially important in growth trajectories that rely on high investment and savings rates, thereby suppressing current consumption in favour of high growth for larger future consumption, and which therefore imply sacrifices typically made by workers and peasants. In such a scenario, social policy that is directed towards providing basic needs and social services to those who are otherwise deprived of the gains from economic growth in terms of increased current consumption, would be not just important but even necessary to ensuring social stability and continuity of the process itself.

In so far as the growth process also generates or entails cyclical volatility in growth or incomes, or has a tendency towards periodic crises of whatever sort, social policy can also serve as a cushion for dampening the worst social effects of crisis, which in turn can contribute to the feasibility and sustainability of the entire process. For example, sudden and severe economic contractions causing sharp peaks of unemployment may be socially easier to tolerate if some forms of unemployment compensation or benefit are provided. Even when the shocks stem from natural rather than economic causes (such as earthquakes or cyclones) social policies in the form of say, public insurance schemes or micro credit schemes can cushion the worst effect of such shocks, in addition to direct relief. Such strategies have macroeconomic consequences as well: thus, it is now accepted that economies with a large public sector presence (in terms of share of GDP or employment) have more muted business cycles or tend to suffer less extreme recessions.

The fourth crucial role of social policy is in terms of affecting the conditions of labour such that there is an increase in the aggregate social productivity of labour, rather than simply increases in labour productivity in particular sectors which reflect different technological choices. It is now widely recognised that the universal provision of good education and basic health services is an important condition for raising aggregate labour productivity levels. But even other aspects of social policy, such as working conditions, access to other public services, etc., play important roles in this regard. It is even being accepted that the latter can in turn influence technological choices themselves, and nudge growth trajectories towards high road paths rather than low road strategies which are chiefly dependent upon cheap labour.

In addition to being an integral part of the economic growth process, social policy also evolves with this process, and changes depending upon how the development process impacts upon different classes and groups. In other words, both the economic policy and the social policy patterns, even when they appear to be unchanging in a statutory sense, are actually quite dynamic and intertwined with the political economy configurations, which also constantly evolve. In case this sounds excessively complicated, consider this example: Certain types of industrialisation strategy generate particular types of employment, for example a small scale engineering industry may grow based on supply and demand linkages emanating from a large publicly funded railway expansion programme. Such increases in employment in turn generate demands for certain types of social policy such as provision of housing, health and education facilities for workers, families, and so on.

SOCIAL POLICY IN THE INDIAN DEVELOPMENT PROCESS

Political theorists may be tempted to draw insights from the rather haphazard pattern of social policy implementation in India, finding in its very lack of direction and vision some association with the chaotic democratic polity within which it occurred, and the variegated demands which were sought to be fulfilled at different points of time. Most social policy provisioning has not been universal in terms of actual effects, even when it has been declared as such. Rather, it has been directed to specific (and restricted) target groups. And almost always, these groups included those with sufficient political voice, such as urban organised workers, or increasingly in the 1990s, particular caste groupings. There have also been much trumpeted attempts to include (in however limited a fashion) a small proportion of those who naturally appear to be deserving, such as households under the poverty line, women from lower income groups, and so on. However, because such provisioning, whether in terms of protective legislation or in terms of actual resource transfers, has been extremely limited relative to the scale of requirement, it has meant that social policy has not been a basic instrument of development strategy in the manner outlined in the previous section. Rather, it has emerged essentially in the form of ad hoc responses to particular demands emanating from groups that (at least temporarily) have acquired some degree of political voice.

Nevertheless, it is also true that the overall development strategy, however flawed it was in terms of low social development and lack of fulfilment of basic needs, did at least meet some of the functions of social policy mentioned above. Thus, in very broad terms, the management of at least some of the social effects of modernisation was achieved in that the most destabilising effects were avoided. Similarly, the legitimisation of and indeed the social acceptance of the suppression of current consumption on the part of workers and peasants, was also achieved; however, as pointed out above, the same was not true of the capitalist class and the elites who were unwilling to accept the economic discipline necessary for a sustained path of aggregate development. It is also true that the growing size of the public sector served as a cushion against very sharp fluctuations in aggregate economic activity. However, in a longer term sense the economic regime and associated social policy failed miserably in raising aggregate social labour productivity and reducing the employment slack in the system, or in underwriting labour costs for employers, including exporters.

The more significant forms of social policy in the Indian context have included: agrarian reform; food procurement and distribution; education; employment creation through public works; affirmative action in the form of reservation for public services employment and educational institutions; antipoverty programmes directed towards small asset creation or micro credit; changes in forms and structures of governance through decentralisation and some devolution of resources.

SOCIAL PLANNING

Social Planning is the process of investigating and responding to the needs and aspirations of the people who live or work in a community. Social

Planning is an organised process for investigating and responding to the needs and aspirations of people and communities.

- In practice, it is based on a set of values, techniques and skills that contribute to better communities and quality of life.
- It plays a pivotal role in creating liveable communities, vibrant economies, sustainable places, diverse cultural expression and social cohesion.
- It involves planning for the needs and aspirations of people and communities through strategic policy and action, integrated with urban, regional and other planning activities.
- It is founded on the principles of social justice (equity, access, participation and rights) and aims to enhance community well being and effectiveness.

Social planning is not synonymous to governmental planning because it is a broad term which is relevant for numerous kinds of planning. Almost every form of planning, whether it is education planning, health planning, business planning or science planning, all have clear and definite social characteristics. For this reason, a social planner can have different academic backgrounds: sociologist, economist, business administration, public administration, etc. Planning can be seen as a process in which a definite number of steps in time are undertaken which will result in a strategy necessary to cope with a certain problem. Take, for instance, a housewife who wants to cook her family a nice dinner. She will first decide what sort of meal she will prepare. She will make a list of the necessary ingredients and she will go to the nearest supermarket and buy these ingredients. Back home she will cook the meal which will be ready around dinner time. Her family can enjoy a warm home cooked meal made with fresh ingredients. This is all the result of planning albeit a simple form of planning.

Social Planning.

Unfortunately, the social reality in which we live in is a lot more complex and confusing. So, to solve all those complex problems, the planner has developed numerous techniques and methods of planning. In general, all planners tend to agree that there are two kinds of planning. The first type of planning is called substantial planning. This form of planning is connected with highly specialized planning in a certain sector or area. For instance education planning, spatial planning, business planning, etc. are forms of substantial planning. The second type of planning is procedural planning. This type of planning is concerned with general characteristics of the planning process. The central question of this form of planning is: how can I shape a planning process? This article is about the latter form of planning rather than a specialized method of application of planning. A logical consequence of procedural planning is that planning must be seen as a process. And this process is a process of analysis, anticipation, design, action, and application.

PLANNING AS A 'LEARNING PROCESS'

Planning is not an activity which can be seen as a process which is uncontroversial. The science of planning is still growing and the concept of planning is numerous. Every planner has his own way of looking at planning and this has resulted in a 'jungle' of planning definitions and concepts. Fortunately, this fact has given a strong impulse to the growth of the science of planning. In the beginning, planning was solely a technical and industrial engagement. But recently planners realized that planning should be seen as a social activity. For this reason, sociologists developed a strong interest in the systematic analysis of planning. A significant consequence of this approach of planning is that the learning aspects of planning have been recognized. So, the concept of planning as a 'learning process' can be seen as the most recent approach of planning. This form of planning has integrated certain aspects from the system theories, cybernetics, and the communication and social theories.

Planning as a 'learning process'.

A major characteristic of the system theories is that the social reality is seen as a system which consists of subsystems. If we know that the reality consists of subsystems, then it is possible to make models. Models actually mirror the reality which consists of subsystems. Take, for instance, a mouse who is trying to escape from the claws of a cat. The mouse itself has a dynamic system; it is possible for the mouse to constantly change its system. In order to escape from the cat, the mouse can run into various directions which, in turn, depend on its sight, smell, and hearing capacities. So, the mouse possesses a dynamic system. For planning, however, a dynamic system is not enough because the social reality is also changing constantly. The consequence of the changing social reality is that our analysis of the situation is easily outdated and irrelevant.

There are two strategies to cope with this problem: using forecasting techniques which can be incorporated in the planning process and/or the incorporation of feedback mechanisms in the planning process. The latter strategy is actually an aspect which has been derived from cybernetics. So, it can be stated that planning is a learning process since new ideas, changes in the reality, and experience are all incorporated in the planning system by feed-back mechanisms. It is actually information (the learning aspects of planning) which is incorporated in the planning process; without information we cannot function properly.

There is one final aspect which must be incorporated in the planning system: participation. It is actually an aspect of the communication and social theories. Planning is usually not an individualistic activity, especially when the problem to be solved is complex and when a lot of people are involved. So, participation of others in the planning process is very important since it is essential to make a good and successful plan rather than an unrealistic plan.

PLANNING AS A DECISION-MAKING PROCESS

In most cases, planning is highly related to decision making. Decisions are constantly being made in reality without any difficulties at all. Decisions can be made by simple intuitions, but it can also be made by a deeper analysis of a problem. An example of an intuitive decision: which hand do I use writing a paper or what is the best position for me to get into sleep in bed at night, etc. This kind of decision making happens automatically; there is no need for a deeper analysis. The planner, however, is not a person who believes that all his problems can be solved with intuitions. If this is the case, a dangerous situation might arise for the planner himself or for the people who are affected by his plans. A sensible social planner realizes that the social reality is a complex reality. For this reason, the social planner will base his plans on rational analysis. It must be mentioned that a social planner is also a human being who is not perfect.

Planning is about decision making. In turn, decision making is based on analysis; this means that a certain part of the reality must be subdivided into a certain number of parts. These parts can be analyzed which means that all the consequences of all the problem-solving alternatives must be screened. However, it is impossible to make a complete analysis of the entire reality which is too complex in nature.

NEED FOR SOCIAL PLANNING

The growth of human knowledge and its extending control over the environment made human beings realise the increasing importance of planning in a society. Planning is no more restricted to communist methodology nor associated with totalitarianism and authoritarianism. The old prejudice that planning is unfit for democratic way of living is fast vanishing. Today planning has become popular, the politicians at the highest level plan a policy manning the future of a nation, or seeking the survival of humanity. Every aspect of governmental action is to be planned—objectives, policies, organisation, finances, work methods, incentive systems and public relations. Programmes based on well-reasoned priorities are invaluable for such countries as they cannot afford to waste time, people or material. Drawing up plans, usually in the form of five year programmes for public expenditures, in particular relating to capital formation, has in many developing countries become the accepted practice under which the responsible government agencies must look ahead, determine their long range objectives and agree upon certain priorities in the light of the probable demands of the various sectors of the economy. The programmes of the individual government agencies are usually coordinated by a central planning office in the light of overall available financial resources.

32

CHAPTER

PIONEERS OF INDIAN SOCIOLOGY

Introduction. Ppioneers of Indian Sociology. Govind Sadashiv Ghurye (1893-1983). Dhurjati Prasad Mukerji (1894-1961). Akshay Ramanlal Desai (1915-1994). Mysore Narasimhachar Srinivas (1916-1999): *Contributions by These Great Sociologists, Conclusion.*

INTRODUCTION

The emergence of sociology in India as a formal discipline in the year 1919 coincided with several critical phases of history, both in India and in the West. By 1919 Gandhi had already returned from South Africa. The scars of the First World War (1914-17) were still vivid and were haunting mankind. Post-war reconstruction measures were underway everywhere. Gandhi's presence not only galvanized the freedom movement but also inspired several pioneering sociologists to devote themselves to the cause and study of the common man.

Related to studies of the various aspects of Indian social structure, customs and traditions it was not without ideological biases in the selection of themes and sociological paradigms. The conceptual problems of caste, tribe and village community, reflected in their observations served consciously or unconsciously to exaggerate the elements of segmentary cleavages in Indian society to the exclusion of the principles of organic linkage and societal unity. This bias was rooted in various ideological positions that Western sociologists and scholars held while analyzing Indian social reality.

Now-a-days sociology tends to be taken for granted in India, like most established things. But this was not always so. In the early days, it was not clear at all what an Indian sociology would look like, and indeed, whether India really needed something like sociology. The specificity of the Indian context raised many questions. First of all, if western sociology emerged as an attempt to make sense of modernity, what would its role be in a country like India? India, too, was of course experiencing the changes brought about by modernity but with an important difference — it was a colony. The first experience of modernity in India was closely intertwined with the experience of colonial subjugation. Secondly, if social anthropology in the west arose out of the curiosity felt by European society about primitive cultures, what role could it have in India, which was an ancient and advanced civilisation, but which also had 'primitive' societies within it? Finally, what useful role could sociology have in a sovereign, independent India, a nation about to begin its adventure with planned development and democracy?

The early "pioneers" among Indian sociologists responded skeptically to these ideological formulations of Indian reality by Western scholars. At the same time Indian sociologists responded positively to the Western traditions of the philosophy of rationalism, positivism, and historical materialism. Yet it would be unfair to characterize their thinking as Western-oriented. Their response was dialectical and anchored deeply in nationalist consciousness shaped by the leadership of Indian social reformation. The pioneers of Indian sociology drew their value premises and perspective on studying Indian society from the nationalist reformation leadership of the nineteenth century. It is pertinent here to mention that some of the early pioneers subscribed to an Indological approach, which rested on the assumption that historically, Indian society and culture are unique and that this "contextual" specificity of Indian social realities could be grasped better through "texts." The use of the Indological approach during the early formative years of Indian sociology and social anthropology may well be observed in the works of S.V. Ketkar, B.N. Seal, B.K. Sarkar, and G.S. Ghurye.

The contributions of B.N. Seal, G.S. Ghurye, B.K. Sarkar, Radhakamal Mukherjee, D.P. Mukerji, and K.P. Chattopadhyay during the pre-Independence period are particularly noteworthy. Their intellectual interests, methods of data collection, and their interpretations of the Indian social system and social institutions were strongly influenced by the style and content of the ethnographic works produced by scholar-administrators during the colonial period. Studies on caste, family, marriage and kinship, social stratification, tribal communities, and rural and urban society figured prominently in this period.

PIONEERS OF INDIAN SOCIOLOGY

The reviewers of Indian sociology generally trace its origin to the works of several British civil servants, missionaries, and Western scholars during the eighteenth and nineteenth centuries. British administrators wanted to understand the customs, manners and institutions of the people of India to ensure the smooth running of their administration. Christian missionaries were interested in learning local languages, folklore, and culture to carry out their activities. The origin, development, and functioning of the various customs and traditions, the Hindu systems of caste and joint family, and the economy and polity of the village/tribal community were some of the prominent themes of study by the British administrators and missionaries as well as other British, European, and Indian intellectuals. The first all-India census was conducted in 1871. Several ethnographic surveys, monographs, census documents, and gazetteers produced during this period constitute a wealth of information that is of interest to sociologists even today.

Mukherjee (1979) observes that the works of the civil servants, missionaries, and others during the colonial rule in India "provided the elements from which the British policy for ruling the subcontinent crystallized and also in turn helped to produce the pioneers in Indian sociology". Further, the available studies of Indian society and culture became an important source for testing various theories by scholars such as Marx and Engles, Maine, and Weber.

Although the first universities in India were established in 1857 in Bombay, Calcutta and Madras, formal teaching of sociology began only in the second decade of the twentieth century—at the University of Bombay in 1914, at Calcutta University in 1917 and at Lucknow University in 1921. By this time the observations and impressions of the census commissioners and civil service officials about the caste system, family structure and functions, age at marriage and widowhood, and so forth. It had already begun to be published, along with statistical tables based on the population counts. Prior to India's independence in 1947, only three other universities (Mysore, Osmania, and Poona) were teaching sociology. There was no separate department of sociology; it was joined with the department of economics (Bombay and Lucknow), economics and political science (Calcutta), anthropology (Poona), or philosophy (Mysore). Almost all the pioneers in sociology in the first half of the twentieth century were trained in disciplines other than sociology. Only a limited number of courses in sociology, as fashioned by teachers according to their interest, were taught. Sociology courses included such topics as social biology, social problems (such as crime, prostitution, and beggary), social psychology, civilization, and prehistory. In the case of teaching of Indian social institutions the orientation showed more Indological and philosophical emphasis on the one hand and a concern for the social pathological problems and ethnological description on the other. Strong scientific empirical traditions had not emerged before Independence.

Although many of the pioneers in sociology were educated at Calcutta, substantial impact on Indian sociology during the first half of the twentieth century was made at Bombay University and Lucknow University. Patrick Geddes, the first chairperson of the department of sociology and civics at Bombay University, was a city planner and human geographer. His reports on the city planning of Calcutta, Indore, and the temple cities of south India contain much useful information and demonstrate his keen awareness of the problems of urban disorganization and renewal. G.S. Ghurye succeeded Geddes in 1924. During his thirty-five year teaching career at Bombay University, he guided about eighty research students. Several of his students (e.g., M.N. Srinivas, K.M. Kapadia, I.P. Desai, Y.B. Damle, A.R. Desai, and M.S.A. Rao) later on had a great impact on the development of sociology in India. Trained as a social anthropologist at Cambridge University, he addressed a wide range of themes in his research work and writings: from castes, races, and tribes in India to cities and civilization, from Shakespeare on conscience and justice to Rajput architecture, and from Indian Sadhus to sex habits of a sample of middle-class people of Bombay. He drew attention to several unexplored dimensions of Indian society, culture, and social institutions.

The pioneers of Indian sociology not only had to find their own answers to questions like these, they also had to formulate new questions for themselves. It was only through the experience of 'doing' sociology in an Indian context that the questions took shape—they were not available 'readymade'. As is often the case, in the beginning Indians became sociologists and anthropologists mostly by accident. For example, one of the earliest and best known pioneers of social anthropology in India, *L.K. Ananthakrishna Iyer* (1861-1937), began his career as a clerk, moved on to become a school teacher and later a college teacher in Cochin state in present day Kerala. In 1902, he was asked by the Dewan of Cochin to assist with an ethnographic survey of the state. The British Government wanted similar surveys done in all the princely states as well as the presidency areas directly under its control. Ananthakrishna Iyer did this work on a purely voluntary basis, working as a college teacher in the Maharajah's College at Ernakulam during the week, and functioning as the unpaid Superintendent of Ethnography in the weekends. His work was much appreciated by British anthropologists and administrators of the time, and later he was also invited to help with a similar ethnographic survey in Mysore state.

Ananthakrishna Iyer was probably the first self-taught anthropologist to receive national and international recognition as a scholar and an academician. He was invited to lecture at the University of Madras, and was appointed as Reader at the University of Calcutta, where he helped set up the first post-graduate anthropology department in India. He remained at the University of Calcutta from 1917 to 1932. Though he had no formal qualifications in anthropology, he was elected President of the Ethnology section of the Indian Science Congress. He was awarded an honorary doctorate by a German university during his lecture tour of European universities. He was also conferred the titles of Rao Bahadur and Dewan Bahadur by Cochin state.

The lawyer Sarat Chandra Roy was another 'accidental anthropologist' and pioneer of the discipline in India. Before taking his law degree in Calcutta's Ripon College, Roy had done graduate and postgraduate degrees in English. Soon after he had begun practising law, he decided to go to Ranchi in 1898 to take up a job as an English teacher at a Christian missionary school. This decision was to change his life, for he remained in Ranchi for the next forty-four years and became the leading authority on the culture and society of the tribal peoples of the Chhotanagpur region (present day Jharkhand). Rcy's interest in anthropological matters began when he gave up his school job and began practising law at the Ranchi courts, eventually being appointed as official interpreter in the court. Both Ananthakrishna Iyer and Sarat Chandra Roy were true pioneers. In the early 1900s, they began practising a discipline that did not yet exist in India, and which had no institutions to promote it. Both Iyer and Roy were born, lived and died in an India that was ruled by the British.

GOVIND SADASHIV GHURYE (1893-1983)

No one can dispute the fact that Professor Govind Sadashiv Ghurye is the founding father of Sociology in India. Even in the last decade of his life when he was over eighty years old, he continued to make his intellectual presence felt as an incisive social thinker, highly innovative and equally at ease with Vedic India and contemporary India.

Govind Sadashiv Ghurye

One great advantage that Professor Ghurye had in his studies of India was his thorough grounding in the Sanskrit literature and in the high traditions of Hindu civilization. In 1921, Professor Ghurye was awarded a scholarship by the University of Bombay to study Sociology in England. Ghurye received his sociological training in Cambridge University from where he earned the degree of Ph.D under the guidance of Professor W.H.R. Rivers. For a short time after the untimely death of Rivers in 1922, Ghurye was put under the guidance of Professor A.C. Haddon. Rivers was then considered as a leading intellectual of Britain. He had already become eminent as a psychologist with his own 'school'. He had established his reputation as an anthropologist with his study of the Todas of Nilgris in 1906 which at that point of time was considered as a model of intensive investigation. Professor

Haddon, the other great luminary with whom Ghurye came in close contact in England, was senior to Professor Rivers and had become famous as an Anthropologist with his original works like The Races of Man and The Wanderings of Peoples. This was the kind of academic ethos and milieu in which Professor Ghurye had the privilege of receiving his sociological training

On his return from Cambridge, where he wrote his doctoral dissertation under W.H.R. Rivers and later A.C. Haddon, Ghurye succeeded Sir Patric Geddes as Head of Department of Sociology in the University of Bombay in 1924. He continued to head the Department until his retirement in 1959. After retirement, he was designated the first Emeritus Professor in the University of Bombay. Thus, besides his own outstanding achievements in the field of sociological and anthropological research, Ghurye became internationally known with his clear half a century's record as a post-graduate teacher. With his inspiring leadership and guidance, Professor Ghurye produced a generation of great sociologists some of whom are household names in the field of sociology today, like M.N. Srinivas, I.P. Desai and K.P. Kapadia.

Thus while developing himself as a sociologist, Ghurye was also supremely conscious of his role as a teacher, a 'Guru' in the best of Indian tradition. Kindling the research interests of his colleagues and students was part of his self-chosen and self-imposed duties. Ever conscious of his 'pupil coverage', he attracted brilliant students from different corners of India. He expected them to work like him and gradually created an academic milieu in which writing a paper or a book came to be looked upon as a very natural thing to do for all research students and staff members. In the concluding paragraph of his autobiographical account, Professor Ghurye has written 'So far 80 dissertations have been successfully completed and accepted by the University for appropriate degrees, 25 for the M.A. and 55 for the Ph.D. Of these 38 have been published as books and one is in press'. Very often Ghurye helped his students to find out publishers for their works and this was highly necessary and relevant at a time when sociology had neither substantial government support nor private munificence.

Ghurye's contribution to the development of sociology and anthropology in India was enormous and multi-faceted. A Brilliant scholar in Sanskrit, Indology, Anthropology and History, his invaluable and original contributions to the sociological literature on a wide range of subjects both Indian and foreign, were based on profound scholarship, painstaking research and lucid analysis. A prolific writer, Ghurye wrote 32 books and scores of papers, which cover such wide-ranging themes as kinship and marriage, urbanization, ascetic traditions, tribal life, demography, architecture and literature. He has rightly earned a place with world famous social scientists like Rivers, Morgan and Maine.

Ghurye played a key role in the professionalization of sociology by founding the Indian Sociological Society and its journal 'Sociological Bulletin'. In addition, as noted earlier, he encouraged and trained a large number of talented students who, in turn, advanced the frontiers of sociological and anthropological research in the country. With his own voluminous output and through the researches of his able students Ghurye embarked on an ambitious project of mapping out the ethnographic landscape of India.

Professor Ghurye's greatest work was 'Caste and Race in India' which was published in England as a part of the History of Civilization Series edited by C.K. Ogden in 1932. For 76 years, this has remained a basic work for students of Indian sociology and anthropology, and has been acclaimed by teachers and reviewers as a sociological classic.

The relationship between caste and politics, which he had briefly dealt with in the 1932 edition, was subsequently developed in a more detailed manner in the 1969 edition. In this revised edition, Professor Ghurye came out with a provocative and thorough-going analysis of caste and politics in Tamil Nadu from early times to the present day.

Professor Ghurye gave an incisive analysis of contemporary India and rightly apprehended in 1969 that India will develop into a plural society and not a casteless one, which was a dream of the architects of her Constitution.

Closely linked with the study of Caste was Professor Ghurye's well-known analysis of the Scheduled Tribe problem. His anthropological inclinations naturally brought the tribes close to his heart, and a start was made when one of his pupils studied the tribe of Katkaris in 1930. Other pupils followed it with studies on the Warlis and Agris, all of them on the Western coast, quite close to Bombay. Inspired by the work of his students, Professor Ghurye wrote on the grand theme of 'Integration of Tribals' in 1943 and it was essentially in reply to the 'isolationist' approach of Verrier Elwin, which formed the basis of the British colonial policy. Professor Ghurye viewed that the only solution to the problem was their progressive assimilation with the farmers and peasants of the adjoining districts. He had the vision to conclude that the major problems of the tribals were never different from the problems of poor rural people in general. In the subsequent editions of the book 'The Scheduled Tribes', Professor Ghurye was critical of independent India's government policies which sowed the seeds of disintegration by its internally contradicting steps of laying down the integrationist approach in the Constitution and on the other hand promoting fission by giving importance to the idea of Scheduled Areas. The comprehensive manner in which Ghurye studied the problem 65 years ago led to a methodological contribution as well. In the words of Dr. N. Datta-Majumdar, he raised the study of the tribals from the pure plain of Anthropology to that of Sociology.

Professor Ghurye published a study titled 'The Mahadev Kolis' in 1957 based on field data from three districts of Maharashtra. This was the first major attempt to deal with a problem at the micro level. The kind of attention he paid to even minor details of the life of the Mahadev Kolis brings to life the ethnographer in him but he is not lost in ethnography, for the mould into which he casts his material is sociological. We can easily see the stamp of this approach in other studies done under his guidance: the Coorgs, Thakurs, Newars and Meities at different periods. The study of the Coorgs by M.N. Srinivas, sub-titled 'A socio-ethnic study' became internationally famous.

Ghurye's basic concern with social process, culture and civilization led to his writing three books dealing with some aspects of these themes. The first book, 'Social Process' published in 1938 reviewed the topic in the light of a century of sociology since August Compte christened it so in the fourth volume of his great work, Philosophie Positive, published in 1838. Nature, the well-known scientific journal of London gave an abstract of Ghurye's book in these words: 'Social Process', Ghurye considers, has two aspects: the nature of Cultural Development as reflected in the trend of thought about man as a living entity, and the process by which the individual is assimilating into the cultural flow of the times'. Scientifically, proper planning of a good life must rest on the understanding of life, and the psychological study of the individual and society should precede the study of man as a political and moral being'.

The comparative study of ancient civilization and culture Ghurye thought was a required background for students of sociology, and he instituted a compulsory paper on it at the M.A. level. His own views led to the publication of his second connected work Culture and Society in 1947 in which he discussed the difference between civilization and culture. He said, 'Culture is what we are; it is the individual's participation or cultural endeavour that makes the collective enterprise called civilization possible'. In 1949, he published his third book titled Accidental Civilization.

The birth centenary of Professor Ghurye was celebrated in a befitting manner by the Department of Sociology in the University of Bombay in 1993-94. A national seminar in commemoration of the centenary year was organized by the Department on November 22-23, 1994. In 1997 a landmark book titled Indian Sociology Through Ghurye: A Dictionary was published. It was authored by S. Devadas Pillai. This volume makes an academic 'journey' through the themes and thoughts of Prof. Dr. G.S. Ghurye. This is probably the first time that an Indian thinker has been honoured with a dictionary on the lines of those on Karl Marx, Emerson and others.

Professor Ghurye often spoke of the dignity of learning: 'of the need to keep scholarship pure, to protect it from its three greatest enemies: amateurism, journalistic prostitution, and obsession with doctrine'. Yes. He was a great Sociologist.

DHURJATI PRASAD MUKERJI (1894-1961)

D.P. Mukerji was born on 5 October 1894 in a middle class Bengali brahmin family with a long tradition of involvement in higher education. Undergraduate degree in science and postgraduate degrees in History and Economics from Calcutta University.

D.P. Mukerji—or D.P. as he was generally known—was among the most influential scholars of his generation not only in sociology but in intellectual and public life beyond the academy. His influence and popularity came not so much from his scholarly writings as from his teaching, his speaking at academic events, and his work in the media, including newspaper articles and radio programmes. D.P. came to sociology via history and economics, and retained an active interest in a wide variety of subjects ranging across literature, music, film, western and Indian philosophy, Marxism, political economy, and development planning.

He was strongly influenced by Marxism, though he had more faith in it as a method of social analysis than as a political programme for action. D.P. wrote many books in English and Bengali. His Introduction to Indian Music is a pioneering work, considered a classic in its genre.

AKSHAY RAMANLAL DESAI (1915-1994)

A.R. Desai was born in 1915. A.R. Desai is one of the rare Indian sociologists who was directly involved in politics as a formal member of political parties. Desai was a life-long Marxist and became involved in Marxist politics during his undergraduate days at Baroda, though he later resigned his membership of the Communist Party of India. For most of his career he was associated with various kinds of nonmainstream Marxist political groups.

Desai's father was a middle level civil servant in the Baroda state, but was also a well-known novelist, with sympathy for both socialism and Indian nationalism of the Gandhian variety. Having lost his mother early in life, Desai was brought up by his father and lived a migratory life because of the frequent transfers of his father to different posts in the Baroda state.

After his undergraduate studies in Baroda, Desai eventually joined the Bombay department of sociology to study under Ghurye. He wrote his doctoral dissertation on the social aspects of Indian nationalism and was awarded the degree in 1946. His thesis was published in 1948 as *The* Social Background of Indian *Nationalism*, which is probably his best known work. In this book, Desai offered a Marxist analysis of Indian nationalism, which gave prominence to economic processes and divisions, while taking account of the specific conditions of British colonialism. Although it had its critics, this book proved to be very popular and went through numerous reprints. Among the other themes that Desai worked on were peasant movements and rural sociology, modernisation, urban issues, political sociology, forms of the state and human rights. Because Marxism was not very prominent or influential within Indian sociology, A.R. Desai was perhaps better known outside the discipline than within it. Although he received many honours and was elected President of the Indian Sociological Society, Desai remained a somewhat unusual figure in Indian sociology.

MYSORE NARASIMHACHAR SRINIVAS (1916-1999)

M.N. Srinivas was Born 16 November 1916 in an Iyengar brahmin family in Mysore. It's father was a landowner and worked for the Mysore power and light department. His early education was at Mysore University, and he later went to Bombay to do an MA under G.S. Ghurye 1942: M.A. thesis on Marriage and Family among the Coorgs published as book.

M.N. Srinivas

Probably the best known Indian sociologist of the post-independence era, M.N. Srinivas earned two doctoral degrees, one from Bombay university and one from Oxford. Srinivas was a student of Ghurye's at Bombay. Srinivas' intellectual orientation was transformed by the years he spent at the department of social anthropology in Oxford. British social anthropology was at that time the dominant force in western anthropology, and Srinivas also shared in the excitement of being at the 'centre' of the discipline.

Srinivas' doctoral dissertation was published as Religion and Society among the Coorgs of South India. This book established Srinivas' international reputation with its detailed ethnographic application of the structural — functional perspective dominant in British social anthropology. Srinivas was appointed to a newly created lectureship in Indian sociology at Oxford, but resigned in 1951 to return to India as the head of a newly created department of sociology at the Maharaja Sayajirao University at Baroda. In 1959, he moved to Delhi to set up another department at the Delhi School of Economics, which soon became known as one of the leading centres of sociology in India.

Srinivas often complained that most of his energies were taken up in institution building, leaving him with little time for his own research. Despite these difficulties, Srinivas produced a significant body of work on themes such as caste, modernisation and other processes of social change, village society, and many other issues. Srinivas helped to establish Indian sociology on the world map through his international contacts and associations. He had strong connections in British social anthropology as well as American anthropology, particularly at the University of Chicago, which was then a powerful centre in world anthropology. Like G.S. Ghurye and the Lucknow scholars, Srinivas succeeded in training a new generation of sociologists who were to become leaders of the discipline in the following decades.

CONTRIBUTIONS BY THESE GREAT SOCIOLOGISTS

G.S. Ghurye and D.P. Mukerji were born in the 1890s while A.R. Desai and M.N. Srinivas were about fifteen years younger, having been born in the second decade of the 20th century. Although they were all deeply influenced by western traditions of sociology, they were also able to offer some initial answers to the question that the pioneers could only begin to ask: what shape should a specifically Indian sociology take? G.S. Ghurye can be considered the founder of institutionalised sociology in India. He headed India's very first post-graduate teaching department of Sociology at Bombay University for thirty-five years. He guided a large number of research scholars, many of whom went on to occupy prominent positions in the discipline. He also founded the Indian Sociological Society as well as its journal Sociological Bulletin. His academic writings were not only prolific, but very wide-ranging in the subjects they covered. At a time when financial and institutional support for university research was very limited, Ghurye managed to nurture sociology as an increasingly Indian discipline. Ghurye's Bombay University department was the first to successfully implement two of the features which were later enthusiastically endorsed by his successors in the discipline. These were the active combining of teaching and research within the same institution, and the merger of social anthropology and sociology into a composite discipline. Best known, perhaps, for his writings on caste and race, Ghurye also wrote on a broad range of other themes including tribes; kinship, family and marriage; culture, civilisation and the historic role of cities; religion; and the sociology of conflict and integration.

Among the intellectual and contextual concerns which influenced Ghurye, the most prominent are perhaps diffusionism, Orientalist scholarship on Hindu religion and thought, nationalism, and the cultural aspects of Hindu identity.

Between the 1920s and the 1950s, sociology in India was equated with the two major departments at Bombay and Lucknow. Both began as combined departments of sociology and economics. While the Bombay department in this period was led by G.S. Ghurye, the Lucknow department had three major figures, the famous 'trinity' of Radhakamal Mukerjee (the founder), D.P. Mukerji, and D.N. Majumdar. Although all three were well known and widely respected, D.P. Mukerji was perhaps the most popular.

According to Srinivas, *Sanskritization* spread during the British Rule with the development of means of communication, the impact of Sanskritisation was felt in the remote corners of the century. With the spread of education and literacy it percolated to the lowest castes. The western terminology radio, press, rail etc. generally facilitated the process of Sanskritisation. The mobility associated with Sanskritisation results only in positional changes in the system and does not lead to any structural change. In other words, the spectrum itself does not change. He also notes how the tribal groups such as Bhils of western India, the Gonds and Oraon of central India claim to be a caste through the process of Sanskritisation and thus claim a place in the caste hierarchy. It is well known that there is no conversion process in the traditional Hindu system. While Srinivas took Sanskritisation to mean some kind of Brahminisation, other investigators showed that Sanskritisation could be based on Kshatriya or Vaisya or Sudra' morals. As Srinivas himself points out the varna hierarchy is clear and immutable. It is evident; therefore, that Sanskritisation reinforces and consolidates the 'immutable varna hierarchy' rather than dislodges it or modify it. Thus, Sanskritisation is not a process by which structural change in the Hindu society can become possible. It is certainly not a means by which any social change in India can be brought about.

CONCLUSION

These four Indian sociologists helped to give a distinctive character to the discipline in the context of a newly independent modernising country. They are offered here as examples of the diverse ways in which sociology was 'Indianised'. Thus, Ghurye began with the questions defined by western anthropologists, but brought to them his intimate knowledge of classical texts and his sense of educated Indian opinion. Coming from a very different background, a thoroughly westernised modern intellectual like D.P. Mukerji rediscovered the importance of Indian tradition without being blind to its shortcomings. Like Mukerji, A.R. Desai was also strongly influenced by Marxism and offered a critical view of the Indian state at a time when such criticism was rare. Trained in the dominant centres of western social anthropology, M.N. Srinivas adapted his training to the Indian context and helped design a new agenda for sociology in the late 20th century. It is a sign of the health and strength of a discipline when succeeding generations when succeeding generations learn from and eventually go beyond their predecessors. This has also been happening in Indian sociology. Succeeding generations have subjected the work of these pioneers to constructive criticism in order to take the discipline further. The signs of this process of learning and critique are visible not only in this book but all over Indian sociology.

SOCIAL THOUGHT

Introduction: *European Social Thought, French Social Thought, British Social Thought, German Social Thought, Italian Sociology, Chicago School.* ***The Development of Social Thought. Theories of Sociological Thought:*** *Positivism, Critical Theory, Marxism Theory, Other Perspectives.* ***The Greats in Sociological Thought:*** *Auguste Comte, Herbert Spencer, Emile Durkheim, Karl Marx, Max Weber, Harriet Martineau, IBN Khaldun (1332-1395 C.E.).*

INTRODUCTION

Social thought provides general theories to explain actions and behavior of society as a whole, encompassing sociological, political, and philosophical ideas. Social theory is used to make distinctions and generalizations among different types of societies, and to analyze modernity as it has emerged in the past few centuries. Classical social theory has generally been presented from a perspective of Western philosophy, and often regarded as Eurocentric.

EUROPEAN SOCIAL THOUGHT

Adam Ferguson, Montesquieu, and John Millar, among others, were the first to study society as distinct from political institutions and processes. In the nineteenth century, the scientific method was introduced into study of society, which was a significant advance leading to development of sociology as a discipline.

At the time of the Enlightenment, European societies were still largely rural, with minimal involvement of government in everyday life of citizens. With industrialization and urbanization, societies were significantly transformed, and new ways of thinking about society arose.

In the 19th century, questions involving social order gained importance. The French Revolution freed French society of control by the monarchy, with no effective means of maintaining social order until Napoleon came to power.

FRENCH SOCIAL THOUGHT

- Claude Henri Saint-Simon
- Auguste Comte
- Émile Durkheim

BRITISH SOCIAL THOUGHT

British social thought, with thinkers such as Herbert Spencer, addressed questions and ideas relating to political economy and social evolution. The political ideals of John Ruskin were a precursor of social economy.

GERMAN SOCIAL THOUGHT

Important German philosophers and social thinkers included Immanuel Kant, Georg Wilhelm Friedrich Hegel, Karl Marx, Max Weber, and Georg Simmel.

ITALIAN SOCIOLOGY

Important Italian social scientists include Antonio Gramsci, Gaetano Mosca, and Umberto Eco.

CHICAGO SCHOOL

The Chicago school developed in the 1920s, through the work of Albion Woodbury Small, W.I. Thomas, Ernest W. Burgess, Robert E. Park, Ellsworth Faris, and other sociologists at the University of Chicago. The Chicago school included focus on patterns and arrangement of social phenomenon across time and place, and within context of other social variables. George Herbert Mead, a member of the Philosophy department at the University of Chicago, was also influential.

THE DEVELOPMENT OF SOCIAL THOUGHT

It was during the eighteenth century that a number of different thinkers began to investigate the social world more systematically. Social, cultural and political arrangements began to be thought of as the result of complex processes that were not immediately obvious from casual observation. Neither could they be explained through the study of what ancient authors had to say. This was partly as a consequence of the profound changes that were at work in the European societies of the eighteenth century.

The sociologist Karl Polanyi described these changes as 'the great transformation' and argued that they were part of a fundamental transformation of social, economic and political life which gave birth to the 'modern' world. Polanyi argued that this transformation was well underway by the middle of the eighteenth century. The period of the Enlightenment can therefore be seen as one of transition from 'traditional' to 'modern' forms of society. The new preoccupation with developing forms of explanation ('theories') for how and why societies work in the ways that they do can be seen as a response to these unprecedented changes.

Awareness of these changes led to a desire to understand and to account for them. We have already seen that older forms of explanation began to be considered inadequate to this task. One of the consequences of this was that the study of societies and their development became more closely related to the scientific study of the natural world and to draw on similar methodologies. The scientific revolution of the seventeenth century had, in the work of Isaac Newton, for example, revolutionised the understanding of the natural world and science was held in very high esteem. It is unsurprising therefore that the methods that natural scientists had developed should be put to use to explore aspects of the social world.

The natural sciences were thought to provide a model for disinterested inquiry. They pointed to the possibility of a rational and empirically based method for creating a form of knowledge that was not conditioned by religious dogma or tradition (Hamilton).

The use of methods and ideas derived from the natural sciences is extremely important but it also raises problems that continue within social scientific work. As we have seen, the Enlightenment was to a large extent based on humanitarian principles and a desire to change and to improve social institutions. Social institutions were felt to have been dominated by attitudes based on religious dogma and unthinking forms of tradition. Change and improvement were to be achieved firstly by applying critical and rational methods of inquiry to these institutions, thereby exposing their foundational basis in oppressive or irrational modes of thought.

This is an important point as it opens up a very interesting problem. The use of methods of inquiry based on the natural sciences was intended to produce objective forms of knowledge. However, the Enlightenment itself was based in a moral imperative to improve society. In other words this moral dimension of Enlightenment thought was rooted in a particular set of values. In this sense, the Enlightenment can be seen as a normative project. Scientific inquiry on the other hand regarded itself as a disinterested and value-free pursuit that was interested solely in the discovery of facts in the form of objective 'laws'. One of the blind spots of Enlightenment thought was its inability to recognise that the type of scientific inquiry that it espoused was incapable of providing an objective basis for its moral and ethical values.

THEORIES OF SOCIOLOGICAL THOUGHT

POSITIVISM

Auguste Comte, Herbert Spencer, Émile Durkheim, and Vilfredo Pareto were aligned with the positivist perspective, which favored use of rigorous scientific methodology in developing and testing theories. This approach incorporated determinism and empiricism in formulating theories.

CRITICAL THEORY

Critical theorists including Hegel and Marx and rejected the "objective", scientific approach. They sought to frame theories within ideologies of human freedom.

MARXISM THEORY

Karl Marx wrote and theorized about the importance of political economy on society, and focused on the "material conditions" of life.

OTHER PERSPECTIVES

Other theories include:

- Social constructionist theory
- Rational choice theory
- Structural functionalism – influenced by Spencer and Durkheim
- Action theory – influenced by Weber and Pareto
- Conflict theory – influenced by Marx, Simmel
- Symbolic interaction – influenced by George Herbert Mead

THE GREATS IN SOCIOLOGICAL THOUGHT

Sociology and anthropology share many ideas in common. Both disciplines are based on the work of philosophers and scientists of the nineteenth century. The theories of the early sociological thinkers had great effects on anthropology that last until today. Among sociologists, Emile Durkheim, who is credited as the founder of modern sociology, had a tremendous influence on anthropology.

Durkheim's influence permeates a wide range of anthropological studies, such as analysis of social system, anthropological approaches to religion, and questions about the origins and evolutions of societies. For example, Durkheim's theory of social integration is passed down to functionalism, which examines the arrangement and interrelation of basic social segments. Another example of Durkheim's influence is seen in the analysis of socially created systems of classification. He believed that these systems were essentially dualistic in nature. His emphasis on systems of classification and binary opposition would have enormous effect on structuralism, ethnoscience, and cognitive anthropology.

AUGUSTE COMTE

Auguste Comte was born in 1798 and had a significant part in the formation of sociology. Comte was the founder of French positivism. Comte can also be given credit for inventing or coining the term sociology.

Comte was born a Catholic, but somewhere around the age of fourteen, he apparently stopped believing in God. At the same time, he left the ideals of his royalist family behind and became a republican. Comte attended the Ecole Polytechnique which was a leading scientific institution in France at the time. He was kicked out of this school for leading a student protest.

Comte's philosophy of positivism developed from historical studies of the human mind. This led to Comte's views of the three stages of the history of sciences. In order as follows, the stages are:

1. Theological — nature has a will of it's own. This stage is broken down into three stages of its own, including animism, polytheism, and monotheism.
2. Metaphysical state — though substituting ideas for a personal will.
3. Positive — a search for absolute knowledge.

When Auguste Comte claimed to have invented the new science of sociology, he said that it was going to be the science that held all other sciences together. As in the course of Positive Philosophy, he said that a science must depend on the previous science to be understood. It was also in the 47th volume of the book that he changed the name of the social physics to sociology.

When Auguste Comte claimed to have invented the new science of sociology, he said that it was going to be the science that held all other sciences together. As in the course of Positive Philosophy, he said that a science must depend on the previous science to be understood. It was also in the 47th volume of the book that he changed the name of the social physics to sociology.

HERBERT SPENCER

Herbert Spencer was born in 1820 during the period of British industrialism. One of the main reasons that Herbert Spencer was important to sociology was because of his views and ideas about evolution. Charles Darwin is always given credit for the idea of survival of the fittest, but most likely it was Spencer who coined this phrase. This phrase was almost always used to explain part of science, but in Spencer's work it took on some political meaning as well. Spencer had many very extreme political views and grew to despise government programs that were aimed to help the poor. In the end it was his harsh views on politics that held his ideas back from being accepted right away. Writings such as Principles of Sociology and others were set-aside for years. Spencer was like Darwin in some ways, but when it came down to the theory of evolution, Spencer took it one step further than Darwin by saying that it involved much more that just biology.

Herbert Spencer was born in 1820 during the period of British industrialism. One of the main reasons that Herbert Spencer was important to sociology was because of his views and ideas about evolution. Charles Darwin is always given credit for the idea of survival of the fittest, but most likely it was Spencer who coined this phrase. This phrase was almost always used to explain part of science, but in Spencer's work it took on some political meaning as well. Spencer had many very extreme political views and grew to despise government programs that were aimed to help the poor. In the end it was his harsh views on politics that held his ideas back from being accepted right away. Writings such as Principles of Sociology and others were set-aside for years. Spencer was like Darwin in some ways, but when it came down to the theory of evolution, Spencer took it one step further than Darwin by saying that it involved much more that just biology.

Herbert Spencer died in 1903. He left behind many wonderful ideas to the world of sociology, including one that states that because we are part of a society and culture we are therefore part of nature.

EMILE DURKHEIM

Emile Durkheim was born in eastern France in 1858. At the age of thirteen, he had a traditional Jewish confirmation which was soon followed by an interest in Catholicism. This did not last for long thought, he soon became totally disinterested in all religions and became an agnostic. Durkheim was always a wonderful student when he attended the College d'Epinal and then later the prestigious Ecole Normale.

Emile Durkheim.

While early on in his work, Durkheim classified social facts by exteriority and constraint, he later gave his views a 180 degree turn and said that they were internalized and a part of the consciousness of individuals.

Durkheim was highly involved with groups and structures and the characteristics that make them up. He did not want to focus on individual attributes. When studying groups, Durkheim focused on the rates that certain things occurred. This allowed him to compare separate groups and structures more effectively. One of the main things that he studied in groups were suicide rates in groups. Through these types of studies, Durkheim was able to see how different groups were integrated. Integration shows that some groups have strong control over it's members and others allow their members to have more control over their own actions.

Emile Durkheim used his own terms to describe the differences in groups and the way they think and act. He defined mechanical solidarity as members of a society being more devoted to the common good when individual differences are minimized. Organic solidarity, he said, was a product of a division of labor the developed because of differences in a group.

A brilliant man, Durkheim knew that moral unity was necessary for the survival of a group. Emile Durkheim died in 1917.

KARL MARX

Karl Marx was a social scientist and a philosopher. Although he was one of the greatest social thinkers during the 1800's, most of ideas and intellect were not recognized until after his death. Marx was born in 1818 to a middle class German family. Marx became a communist when he moved to Paris in 1843. This was when he wrote the Economic and Philosophical Manuscripts. These writings outlined communism and were not published until the 1930's. While Marx was in Paris he met the man who would become his life long friend and partner, Friedrich Engels. It was with Engels that he wrote the Communist manifesto in 1848. Engels helped Marx survive by being one of his major sources of income during the 1850's when Marx was not able to do it with only his writings. Another manuscript that was published after his death was called The German Ideology. The idea behind this discussed how an individual's nature is affected by the material conditions that determine their production.

Karl Marx.

Karl Marx believed that social change is what was needed for a better society, and to get social change there must be class conflict. Marx's major concern of social change was economic change. Marx's most well known work dealt with class conflict, the opposition between the capitalists and the working class. The capitalists are also known as the bourgeoisie. They are the ones that are responsible for controlling the land, factories, etc. The working class, which is also known as the proletariat, are the workers that are being exploited by the bourgeoisie.

One of the larger manuscripts that Marx ever wrote in his life was called The Grundrisse. The Grundrisse (which means outlines) also was not published until after Marx's death. This manuscript was 800 pages long and discussed things such as capital, labor/wages, property, etc. This was completed in 1857. It was ten years later that he finally published the first part of Capital. Capital was a work that outlined the capitalist process in detail. There were several other parts completed to this work, but they were not published until Engels did so after Marx's death.

Marx is now known as one of the founders of Communism, modern Socialism, and Sociology. Since his death Marxism has led to socialist thought and much more. Karl Marx died in 1883.

MAX WEBER

Max Weber.

Max Weber was born in 1864 and he too was considered by some to be the father of sociology. Weber looked at sociology in terms of it being an extensive science of social action and in the beginning he would only focus on specific social contexts. Somewhat in contrast to this belief, he later believed that one of the most distinguishing characteristics of a society is their change or shift in motivation that is caused by structural or historical forces.

The concept of the ideal-type came about so the sociologists and others would have a method to do historical-comparative studies. The ideal-type is mainly discussing Moral ideals. Weber used this method to form an ideal-type bureaucracy with the following: hierarchy, impersonality, written rules of conduct, promotion based on achievement, specialized division of labor, and efficiency. Weber defined such bureaucracies as goal oriented organizations designed according to rational principles in order to efficiently attain their goals (Verstehen). Weber saw many advantages in bureaucracies but he also saw that sometimes the power shifted only to those at the top and resulted in an oligarchy.

Rationalization is a process in which a person enters, applying practical knowledge to achieve an end. Rationalization is a large part of Weber's theories on bureaucracy. This is also where Weber and Marx begin to agree on some of the models of organization and rationalization. Both socialism and capitalism are the rational forms of sciences and organizations.

Weber also discussed authority. Weber sought to know what gave the power to one individual to be able to claim authority over another individual, such as man over woman. He also used the ideal-type to explain this in terms of traditional authority (pre-modern), rational-legal authority (modern), and charismatic.

Max Weber said that sociology is a science that is concerned with a social action and the course and/or consequences of the action. He had a large influence on many of the ideas that are used in sociology today. Max Weber died in 1920.

HARRIET MARTINEAU

Harriet Martineau.

Harriet Martineau was born in 1802 into a large upper middle class English family. Most of Harriet's education was done at home, although early on, she had some exposure to subjects that were taught only to males. But, at the time, university study was barred to women. Harriet was forced to support herself early on as an adult after the death of her father and the end of the relationship between her and he husband. She felt free when she was faced with this challenge and did sucessfully support herself as an author. She wrote essays, novels, biographies, news columns, and more including many informed writings on sociology.

Martineau began a two-year study of the United States when she visited the country in 1834. She reported her findings of this trip in two sets of writings: Society in America and Retrospect of Western Travel. In 1837, Society of America was released. She used this work to compare moral principles and social patterns and it became her most well known work to sociologists in the United States. One year later in 1838, How to Observe Morals and Manners was released and examined the correspondence problem between intersubjectivity, verifiable observable, and unobservable theoretical issues and provided a positivist solution.

Harriett later took a trip to the Mid-East and in 1848 had a work published on it called, Eastern Life Past and Present. At this point, Martineau became an atheist and lost the support of many, including her family. Another writing that Harriet is most well known for was her translation in 1851 of Auguste Comte's Cours de philosophic positive into English. This translation allowed positivism to be introduced into American thought.

Throughout her life, Harriet Martineau wrote more than 1,500 columns and pioneered methodological studies that are now known as sociology. Unfortunately, because of the male academic system at this time, most of her writings on sociology, literature, etc. were forgotten.

Harriett Martineau died of an illness in 1876, but can now be remembered as the first woman sociologist.

IBN KHALDUN (1332-1395 C.E.)

Abd al-Rahman Ibn Mohammad is generally known as Ibn Khaldun after a remote ancestor. His parents, originally Yemenite Arabs, had settled in Spain, but after the fall of Seville, had migrated to Tunisia. He was born in Tunisia in 1332 C.E., where he received his early education and where, still in his teens, he entered the service of the Egyptian ruler Sultan Barquq. His thirst for advanced knowledge and a better academic setting soon made him leave this service and migrate to Fez. This was followed by a long period of unrest marked by contemporary political rivalries affecting his career. This turbulent period also included a three year refuge in a small village Qalat Ibn Salama in Algeria, which provided him with the opportunity to write Muqaddimah, the first volume of his world history that won him an immortal place among historians, sociologists and philosophers. The uncertainty of his career still continued, with Egypt becoming his final abode where he spent his last 24 years. Here he lived

Ibn Khaldun.

a life of fame and respect, marked by his appointment as the Chief Malakite Judge and lecturing at the Al-Azhar University, but envy caused his removal from his high judicial office as many as five times.

Ibn Khaldun's chief contribution lies in philosophy of history and sociology. He sought to write a world history preambled by a first volume aimed at an analysis of historical events. This volume, commonly known as Muqaddimah or 'Prolegomena', was based on Ibn Khaldun's unique approach and original contribution and became a masterpiece in literature on philosophy of history and sociology. The chief concern of this monumental work was to identify psychological, economic, environmental and social facts that contribute to the advancement of human civilization and the currents of history. In this context, he analysed the dynamics of group relationships and showed how group-feelings, al-'Asabiyya, give rise to the ascent of a new civilisation and political power and how, later on, its diffusion into a more general civilization invites the advent of a still new 'Asabiyya in its pristine form. He identified an almost rhythmic repetition of rise and fall in human civilization, and analysed factors contributing to it. His contribution to history is marked by the fact that, unlike most earlier writers interpreting history largely in a political context, he emphasised environmental, sociological, psychological and economic factors governing the apparent events. This revolutionised the science of history and also laid the foundation of Umraniyat (Sociology).

Apart from the Muqaddimah that became an important independent book even during the lifetime of the author, the other volumes of his world history Kitab al-I'bar deal with the history of Arabs, contemporary Muslim rulers, contemporary European rulers, ancient history of Arabs, Jews, Greeks, Romans, Persians, etc., Islamic history, Egyptian history and North-African history, especially that of Berbers and tribes living in the adjoining areas. The last volume deals largely with the events of his own life and is known as Al-Tasrif. This was also written in a scientific manner and initiated a new analytical tradition in the art of writing autobiography. A book on mathematics written by him is not extant.

Ibn Khaldun's influence on the subject of history, philosophy of history, sociology, political science and education has remained paramount ever since his life. His books have been translated into many languages, both in the East and the West, and have inspired subsequent development of these sciences. For instance, Prof. Gum Ploughs and Kolosio consider Muqaddimah as superior in scholarship to Machiavelli's The Prince written a century later, as the forrner bases the diagnosis more on cultural, sociological, economic and psychological factors.

RACE, ETHNICITY AND MIGRATION

Introduction. What is Racism. RACISM—Traditional and Modern. Sociological Evolution of Racism. Minorities. Problems of Religious Minority in India. Various Religious Minorities: *Muslims, Christians, Sikhs.* ***National Commission for Minorities:*** *Functions and Powers of the Commission.* ***Functions of the National Commission for Minority:*** *Composition of the Commission, State Minorities Commissions.* ***Problems of Religious Minorities. Ethnic Minorities in the Labour Market:*** *The Research.* ***Ethnic Diversity. Prejudice and Discrimination. Native Americans. African Americans. The Civil Rights Movement:*** *Affirmative Action, Blacks Today.* ***Asian Americans. Migration in a Globalized World:*** *Migration and Development, Facilitated Migration, Replacement Migration, Migration Control, Forced Migration.* ***Globalization and Migration:*** *Gender Perspective in Migration.*

INTRODUCTION

The term race refers to groups of people who have differences and similarities in biological traits deemed by society to be socially significant, meaning that people treat other people differently because of them. For instance, while differences and similarities in eye colour have not been treated as socially significant, differences and similarities in skin colour have.

Although some scholars have attempted to establish dozens of racial groupings for the peoples of the world, others have suggested four or five. An example of a racial category is Asian (or Mongoloid), with its associated facial, hair colour, and body type features. Yet too many exceptions to this sort of racial grouping have been found to make any racial categorizations truly viable. This fact has led many sociologists to indicate that no clear-cut races exist—only assorted physical and genetic variations across human individuals and groups.

Certainly, obvious physical differences—some of which are inherited—exist between humans. But how these variations form the basis for social prejudice and discrimination has nothing to do with genetics but rather with a social phenomenon related to outward appearances. Racism, then, is prejudice based on socially significant physical features. A racist believes that certain people are superior, or inferior, to others in light of racial differences. Racists approve of segregation, or the social and physical separation of classes of people.

Ethnicity refers to shared cultural practices, perspectives, and distinctions that set apart one group of people from another. That is, ethnicity is a shared cultural heritage. The most common characteristics distinguishing various ethnic groups are ancestry, a sense of history, language, religion, and forms of dress. Ethnic differences are not inherited; they are learned.

Most countries today consist of different ethnic groups. Ideally, countries strive for pluralism, where people of all ethnicities and races remain distinct but have social equality. As an example, the United States is exceptionally diverse, with people representing groups from all over the globe, but lacking in true pluralism. The same can be said of the ethic diversity of the former Soviet Union with its more than 100 ethnic groups, some having more than a million members.

***Race*:** A major subdivision of the species homosapiens consisting of a large number of people who form a distinct genetic entity because they have similar physical traits which they had inherited from common ancestors. Though such a definition has the value of precision it has the important disadvantage of being indemonstrable with present techniques of anthropological analysis and research. The term is generally used to refer to a biologically defined category of people which is to be distinguished from all culturally defined categories of people.

***Migration*:** Migration has become a universal phenomenon in modern times. Due to the expansion of transport and communication, it has become a part of worldwide process of urbanization and industrialization. In most countries, it has been observed that industrialization and economic development has been accompanied by large-scale movements of people from villages to towns, from towns to other towns and from one country to another country.

From the demographic point of view, migration is one of the three basic components of population growth of any area, the other being fertility and mortality. But whereas both fertility and mortality operate within the biological framework, migration does not. It influences size, composition and distribution of population. More importantly, migration influences the social, political and economic life of the people. Indian constitution provides basic freedom to move to any part of the country, right to reside and earn livelihood of their choice. Thus, migrants are not required to register either at the place of origin or at the place of destination. A number of economic, social, cultural and political factors play an important role in the decision to move. The effects of these factors vary over time and place.

WHAT IS RACISM

Racism is the belief that a particular race is superior or inferior to another, that a person's social and moral traits are predetermined by his or her inborn biological characteristics. Racial separatism is the belief, most of the time based on racism, that different races should remain segregated and apart from one another.

Racism has existed throughout human history. It may be defined as the hatred of one person by another—or the belief that another person is less than human—because of skin colour, language, customs, place of birth or any factor that supposedly reveals the basic nature of that person. It has influenced wars, slavery, the formation of nations, and legal codes.

Racism alive in America.

During the past 500-1000 years, racism on the part of Western powers toward non-Westerners has had a far more significant impact on history than any other form of racism (such as racism among Western groups or among Easterners, such as Asians, Africans, and others). The most notorious example of racism by the West has been slavery, particularly the enslavement of Africans in the New World (slavery itself dates back thousands of years). This enslavement was accomplished because of the racist belief that Black Africans were less fully human than white Europeans and their descendants.

One important feature of racism, especially toward Blacks and immigrant groups, is clear in attitudes regarding slaves and slavery. Jews are usually seen by anti-Semites as subhuman but also superhuman: devilishly cunning, skilled, and powerful. Blacks and others are seen by racists as merely subhuman, more like beasts than men. If the focus of anti-Semitism is evil, the focus of racism is inferiority—directed toward those who have sometimes been considered to lack even the ability to be evil (though in the 20th century, especially, victims of racism are often considered morally degraded).

Racism.

In the second half of the 19th century, Darwinism, the decline of Christian belief, and growing immigration were all perceived by many white Westerners as a threat to their cultural control. European and, to a lesser degree, American scientists and philosophers devised a false racial "science" to "prove" the supremacy of non-Jewish whites. While the Nazi annihilation of Jews discredited most of these supposedly scientific efforts to elevate one race over another, small numbers of scientists and social scientists have continued throughout the 20th century to argue the inborn shortcomings of certain races, especially Blacks. At the same time, some public figures in the American Black community have championed the supremacy of their own race and the inferiority of whites - using nearly the identical language of white racists.

All of these arguments are based on a false understanding of race; in fact, contemporary scientists are not agreed on whether race is a valid way to classify people. What may seem to be significant "racial" differences to some people—skin colour, hair, facial shape—are not of much scientific significance. In fact, genetic differences within a so-called race may be greater than those between races. One philosopher writes: "There are few genetic characteristics to be found in the population of England that are not found in similar proportions in Zaire or in China.... Those differences that most deeply affect us in our dealings with each other are not to any significant degree biologically determined.

Racism is the belief that characteristics and abilities can be attributed to people simply on the basis of their race and that some racial groups are superior to others. Racism and discrimination have been used as powerful weapons encouraging fear or hatred of others in times of conflict and war, and even during economic downturns.

Racism is also a very touchy subject for some people, as issues concerning free speech and Article 19 of the Universal Declaration of Human Rights come into play. Some people argue that talking about supporting racial discrimination and prejudice is just words and that free speech should allow such views to be aired without restriction.

RACISM—TRADITIONAL AND MODERN

The Department of Fisheries and Oceans (DFO) recently advertised a 100,000-dollar-a-year position that was restricted to non-whites. "DFO believes it is important to ensure that our senior management team represents diversity," they wrote. "Competitions such as this one are aimed to help increase the involvement of Canadians within specific demographic groups..." Call it whatever you want: racism, reverse racism, or corrective racism.

Racism is a community concern.

The concept of racism—It is almost invariably assumed that racism is racism when the victim is not white. And then, today's political correctness prevents any contrary opinion. And if you did express any contrary opinion, you could be assured that your social and professional life will hit rock bottom. The same Statistics Canada report says that 5% of those not part of visible minority said they had been discriminated against or treated unfairly sometimes or often.

Imagine as a title of a book: Stupid Asian and Black Men. It would sound very racist, and it is unlikely that anyone would dare to buy it, let alone read it. But somehow the dishonest political correctness of today means that Stupid White Men is all right as a title. Actually, there is such a book on the bestsellers lists. The author – Michael Moore – is seen as a hero, and his readers as believers in equality and diversity.

Most areas outside the Western world have yet to even start conceptualizing the concept of racism. The major democracies of India, Thailand, and Russia officially charge non-citizens higher admission prices in museums, accommodation and transportation. Racism is written into their laws. The Indian government refuses to admit that the caste system is racist, but adopts a lazy way out: an affirmative action policy to reserve university places and jobs for the "lower" caste.

The consequence that follows there is not very different from what happens in Canada (and the USA): achievements of a person from a favoured minority are viewed with suspicion, for he could have got his position because of affirmative action. It is here that affirmative action policy makes the society racist.

Alas, instead of recommending that we nudge out of the affirmative action policy, Canadian Race Relations Foundation, a federal government funded foundation, says: Employment equity measures should move beyond recruitment to "focus on retention and promotion".

SOCIOLOGICAL EVOLUTION OF RACISM

Race has always been a significant sociological theme, from the founding of the field and the formulation of classical theoretical statements to the present. Since the nineteenth century, sociological perspectives on race have developed and changed, always reflecting shifts in large-scale political processes. In the classical period, colonialism and biologistic racism held sway. As the twentieth century dawned, sociology came to be dominated by US-based figures. DuBois and the Chicago School presented the first notable challenges to the field's racist assumptions. In the aftermath of World War II, with the destruction of European colonialism, the rise of the civil rights movement, and the surge in migration on a world scale, the sociology of race became a central topic. The field moved toward a more critical, more egalitarian awareness of race, focused particularly on the overcoming of prejudice and discrimination. Although the recognition of these problems increased and political reforms made some headway in combatting them, racial injustice and inequality were not surmounted. As the global and domestic politics of race entered a new period of crisis and uncertainty, so too has the field of sociology. To tackle the themes of race and racism once again in the new millennium, sociology must develop more effective racial theory. Racial formation approaches can offer a starting point here. The key tasks will be the formulation of a more adequate comparative historical sociology of race, the development of a deeper understanding of the micro-macro linkages that shape racial issues, and the recognition of the pervasiveness of racial politics in contemporary society. This is a challenging but also exciting agenda. The field must not shrink from addressing it.

MINORITIES

Racial and ethnic groups whose members are especially disadvantaged in a given society may be referred to as minorities. This term has more to do with social factors than with numbers. For example, while people with green eyes may be in the minority, they are not considered to be "true" mino-rities. From a sociological perspective, minorities generally have a sense of group identity ("belonging together") and separateness ("being isolated from others"). They are also disadvantaged in some way when compared to the majority of the population. Of course, not all minorities experience all three of these characteristics; some people are able to transcend their master status, or social identity as defined by their race or ethnicity.

Most minority groups are locked in to their minority standing, regardless of their achieved level of personal success. They live in certain regions of a country, certain cities, and certain neighbourhoods—the poorest areas, more often than not. That is, ethnicity is often associated with social inequalities of power, prestige, and wealth—all of which can lead to hostility between groups within a society. Finally, to preserve their cultural identity, most minorities value endogamy, or marriage within the group. Put another way, intermarriage between minority and majority groups, or even between different minority groups, is not always sanctioned by both groups. Prohibiting intermarriage reduces the possibility of assimilation, or gradual adoption of the dominant culture's patterns and practices.

PROBLEMS OF RELIGIOUS MINORITY IN INDIA

A minority is a sociological group that does not constitute a politically dominant voting majority of the total population of a given society. A sociological minority is not necessarily a numerical minority — it may include any group that is subnormal with respect to a dominant group in terms of social status, education, employment, wealth and political power.

Minority' as a smaller number or part; a number or part representing less than half of the whole; a relatively small group of people, differing from others in race, religion, language or political persuasion".

To avoid confusion, some writers prefer the terms "subordinate group" and "dominant group" rather than "minority" and "majority", respectively. In socioeconomics, the term "minority" typically refers to a socially subordination ethnic group (understood in terms of language, nationality, religion and/or culture). Other minority groups include people with disabilities, "economic minorities" (working poor or unemployed), "age minorities" (who are younger or older than a typical working age) and sexual minorities.

The term "minority group" often occurs alongside a discourse of civil rights and collective rights which gained prominence in the 20th century. Members of minority groups are prone to different treatment in the countries and societies in which they live. This discrimination may be directly based on an individual's perceived membership of a minority group, without consideration of that individual's personal achievement. It may also occur indirectly, due to social structures that are not equally accessible to all. Activists campaigning on a range of issues may use the language of minority rights, including student rights, consumer rights and animal rights. In recent years, some members of social groups traditionally perceived as dominant have attempted to present themselves as an oppressed minority, such as white, middle-class heterosexual males.

Muslims, Sikhs, Christians, Buddhists and Zoroastrians (Parsis) have been notified as minority communities under Section 2 (c). Minorities in the country is about 18.4% of the total population of the country, of which Muslims are 13.4%; Christians 2.3%; Sikhs 1.9%, Buddhists 0.8% and Parsis 0.007%.

VARIOUS RELIGIOUS MINORITIES

MUSLIMS

According to the 2001 Census, India's Muslim population was over 138 million, next only to that of Pakistan and Indonesia. As the final figures from the Census 2011 have not been disclosed yet, the current Muslim population, with 30% decadal growth rate, is estimated at 180 million, which is roughly 15% of India's population of 1.2 billion. But the story of 180 million Indian Muslims, however, is much bitter and less sweet.

Moreover, it is larger than the total populations of most countries of the world. India is considered an overpopulated country and India's population policy seeks to achieve replacement level fertility by 2010.

In celebration of 'National Day of Minority Rights,' Mohammed Khalil Ullah met with a group of the top Muslim clerics of India and briefed them on the human rights campaign Scientologists are carrying out in India and around the world.

The Muslims are the majorities among the minorities, which means Muslims constitute a large part of the minority community both in India and in Delhi. Going through various researches and surveys its prominently seen that education is one of the most lacking aspect in the Muslim community. Its because of this that after so many years after independence the community lacks in major fields in the country even though they constitute the second largest group in the population.

Major Problems for the Muslim Community

1. Muslims are behind other religious communities in the area of literacy and education, industrial promotion and economic pursuits. They lack technical and vocational education as well as training in trades in demand.
2. The village and districts having concentration of Muslim populations often lack markets for their products.
3. The Muslims in Delhi are not able to avail of the facilities of Wakf resources in the absence of proper management. Only 2.3% rate is been returned by the registered 4.9 lakh wakfs in India.
4. The work participation rate among Muslim women is found to be low affecting the quality of their life.

CHRISTIANS

The Christians constitute about 2.3% of the total Indian population, in which 34% are urban residents. Christians have a higher literacy level (80%) as compared to other religious minorities and above national literacy rate of 65%. They are generally engaged in service sector except in some states. Christians are more concerned about health and have better level of wellbeing.

The Christians have the highest per capita income and per capita expenditure among the minorities. Unemployment among Christian community is also significantly lower than amongst Muslims and Sikhs. Though Christianity does not recognize a caste system, nonetheless caste system is practised among Christians in large parts of the country.

The Major Problems for the Christian Community

Christian being very less in number are neglected by both the state and the Delhi Minority Commission. But with the help of individual organizations associated with the churches the socio-economic conditions of the community is taken care of.

Another issue is the allocation of land for religious constructions. Its well seen that due to the lack of institutional land in the city the DDA is very strict in land allocation, and according to Rev Fr. Dominic Immanuel, the Catholic representative, the DDA should allocate land on the basis of their need. According to him the Christian community comes in large numbers and have a tradition of congregational worship so the need for larger land is there. Although this issue has been raised a number of times in the DDA but yet no consideration has been shown.

Another important problem is lack of burial grounds in Delhi. Presently there are 3 main cemeteries in Delhi—one in Paharganj, another at Prithviraj Road and the war cemetery near Dhaula Kuan. But the major problem is the lack of space in these cemeteries. Discussions are going on for the procurement of more lands for burials which is nearly impossible in Delhi due to lack of land in the city.

Members of Pakistan's Christian community rally to condemn the killing of Shahbaz Bhatti in Lahore.

One of the alternatives would be the installation of cell like structure inside the cemeteries to accommodate more and more dead bodies within a less space. This cell structure is very well working in many southern states especially in all parts of Kerala.

Due to the lack of land in Delhi this would be an apt solution to the existing problem of lack of burial grounds. A major problem is also faced by the recognised minority institutions. Even though they are given the minority status, no rules and policy consideration has been given to them and these institutions, especially schools, are considered same as other public schools.

SIKHS

Sikhism is a monotheistic faith which was founded in the 15th century in the region of Punjab, northwest India. It is recognized as the youngest of world religions.

Sikh community.

The Sikh religion today has a following of over 20 million people worldwide and is ranked as the world's fifth largest religion.

One of the major problem faced by the Sikh community in Delhi is the declining sex ratio in the community. It is especially high in a particular section of the community called the jatthedars.

Some of the suggestions to support the girl child would be to implement the medical scheme in government hospitals and financial support for girl child in primary and secondary level education.

Another major problem is rehabilitation of riot victims of 1984; the government has not yet made arrangements for the rehabilitation of or compensation to the riot victims.

NATIONAL COMMISSION FOR MINORITIES

The National Commission for Minorities (NCM) is a body consti-tuted by the Government of India to monitor and evaluate the progress of people classified as minorities by the Indian government. Essentially the minorities in India consist of followers of all religions other than Hinduism and weaker sections in the Hindu community. The Commission is also referred to as the Minority Commission. It was formed as a result of an act of the Indian Parliament in 1993. The NCM adheres to the UN Declaration of 18 December 1992 which states that States shall protect the existence of the National or Ethnic, Cultural, Religious and Linguistic identity of minorities within their respective territories and encourage conditions for the promotion of that identity.

FUNCTIONS AND POWERS OF THE COMMISSION

The Commission has the following *functions*:

- Evaluate the progress of the development of Minorities under the Union and States.
- Monitor the working of the safeguards provided in the Constitution and in laws enacted by Parliament and the State Legislatures.
- Make recommendations for the effective implementation of safeguards for the protection of the interests of Minorities by the Central Governments or the State Governments.
- Look into specific complaints regarding deprivation of rights and safeguards of the Minorities and take up such matters with the appropriate authorities.

The Commission has the following *powers*:

- Summoning and enforcing the attendance of any person from any part of India and examining him on oath.
- Requiring the discovery and production of any document.
- Receiving evidence on affidavit.
- Requisitioning any public record or copy thereof from any court or office.

– Issuing commissions for the examination of witnesses and documents.

FUNCTIONS OF THE NATIONAL COMMISSION FOR MINORITY

The main functions of the Commission are to evaluate the progress of the development of minorities, monitor the working of the safeguards provided in the Constitution and in laws enacted by the Central Government/State Governments for the protection of the interests of minorities and look into specific complaints regarding deprivation of rights of the minorities. It also initiates studies, research and analysis to be undertaken on the issues relating to the socio-economic and educational development of minorities and make recommendations for the effective implementation of the safeguards for the protection of the interests of minorities.

COMPOSITION OF THE COMMISSION

The Commission consists of Chairman, Vice-Chairman and five Members to be nominated by the Central Government.

STATE MINORITIES COMMISSIONS

Thirteen State Governments of Andhra Pradesh, Assam, Bihar, Chhattisgarh, Delhi, Jharkhand, Karnataka, Maharashtra, Madhya Pradesh, Rajasthan, Uttar Pradesh, Tamil Nadu and West Bengal have set up statutory State Minorities Commissions. The State Governments of Manipur and Uttarakhand have set up non-statutory Commissions. The Ministry has also requested the remaining State Governments/Union Territory Administrations to set up such Commissions. The subjects allocated to this Ministry under the Allocation of Business Rules, 1961 are listed below:

– Overall policy, planning, coordination, evaluation and review of the regulatory and developmental programmes of the minority communities.
– All matters relating to the minority communities except matters relating to law and order.
– Policy initiatives for protection of minorities and their security in consultation with other Central Government Ministries and State Governments.
– Matters relating to linguistic minorities and of the office of the Commissioner for Linguistic Minorities.
– Matters relating to the National Commission for Minorities Act.
– Work relating to the evacuee Wakf properties under the Administration of Evacuee Property Act, 1950 (31 of 1950) (since repealed).
– Representation of the Anglo-Indian Community.

- Protection and preservation of non-Muslim shrines in Pakistan and Muslim shrines in India in terms of the Pant-Mirza Agreement of 1955, in consultation with the Ministry of External Affairs.
- Questions relating to the minority communities in neighbouring Countries, in consultation with the Ministry of External Affairs.
- The ministry of minority affairs ministry under the central government does provide a number of schemes to all states and union territories of India.

PROBLEMS OF RELIGIOUS MINORITIES

The problems of minorities, who are relatively lesser in numerical strength than the majority community, have been gaining too much importance in the politics of many nations in the world. Both the developed and developing countries are also caught in the problems associated with the minorities. In many third world nations, nowadays, racial tensions, communal violence and ethnic clashes make headlines almost daily. For instance, the ethnic conflict between the Buddhists and the Tamils is still going on in Sri Lanka, which has put a major obstacle in the way of economic development of that country.

India, which is known as a peace-loving nation, is also not spared by the problems of minorities. India is a multi-religious country and her society is pluralistic in nature from the religious and other points of view. Since a very long time, people belonging to various religious communities have been living together in this country. Not only major religious communities are spread all over the country, but the people belonging to all religious communities reside in each village and town in the country. Religious minority groups in India are chiefly the Muslims, the Christians, the Sikhs, the Jains and the Buddhists, who have been able to preserve their group identities and have also stayed in the mainstream of national politics.

A nation-wide alliance of church leaders, denominations, mission groups and other Christian organizations in India urged all political parties to make defending religious minorities a key priority ahead of upcoming general elections, amid concerns over spreading anti-Christian violence in the country.

The Muslims in India constitute the largest religious minority in the country. Though a minority in its numerical strength, it is as big as to make it the second biggest Muslim population in the world, next to Indonesia. The Muslims constituted 180 millions of the Indian population according to the 2011 census, and form an important segment in the social fabric of the country. But economically, Muslims are the most backward community with the lowest employment rate. With such backward economic status, there was hardly any incentive for a modern secular education.

Violence against Christians and other religious minorities continues unabated five months after Congress Party won the Indian federal elections and Prime Minister Manmohan Singh's govern-ment took office.

Unlike the Muslims, the Christians are the second largest and oldest religious minority in the country. It is chiefly spread in South India, particularly in Kerala. Consistent with the social philosophy of their religion, the Christians, in India are well represented in the social welfare activities of the country with particular concern for the service of the unprivileged. Their role in the sphere of health and education is well recognised. But recently, some Christian missionaries of the country have been alleged to be involved in conversion activities that led to communal conflicts which witnessed large scale attacks on the churches and Christians in Gujarat, Orissa and several other states. The very recent attacks on Christians and churches in the Kandhamal district of Orissa shook the entire Christian community of the world.

Similarly, the early part of the 20th century witnessed the rise of numerous Sikh sectarian organisations that emphasised the distinct Sikh identity. Sikhism is another important religion in India which is spread in different parts of the country, especially in Punjab, Delhi, Haryana, Bihar, etc. Claiming Punjab as their motherland, the Sikhs have developed a very strong sub-national identity, carrying with them the vital elements of the Punjabi culture. The Sikhs are excellent cultivators in the rural areas; they have played a very significant role in the Green Revolution of the country. In urban areas, most of them earn their livelihood in the trade and commerce sectors. They have always maintained a larger share in defence forces of the country. Like the Muslims, Sikhs and Christians, other religious minorities of the country, such as the Jains and the Buddhists have also stayed in the mainstream of Indian politics.

The Constitution of India has provided the minority groups with some safeguards. The Preamble of the Constitution describes the concept of secularism which means that the State has no religion of its own, and there is equal respect for and protection to all religions. No one is to be discriminated on grounds of religion and everyone is guaranteed full and equal freedom of religion. Article 30 of the Indian Constitution states that the minorities have rights to establish and administer educational institutions of their choice. This includes the right to choose the medium of instruction, curricula, and subject to be taught. Minorities can impart instructions to their children in their own languages. The National Commission for Minorities undertakes review of the implementation of the policies formulated by the Union and state governments with regard to minorities. It looks into specific complaints regarding deprivation of rights and safeguards of minorities, and conducts research and analysis on the question of avoidance of discrimination against the minorities.

The minority communities have to face several problems in India. The minorities are not able to integrate properly in the Hindu-dominated society. There is apprehension among some sections that for enlarging its base, the Christian community is involved in converting the low caste Hindus or tribes to its own community or religion, resulting in the killing and intense conflict between the majority Hindus and the Christian minority. This has created too much insecurity and fear among the Christian minority in India. The minorities claim that unlike their Hindu counterpart, they are relatively deprived in areas like employment, politics and social facilitation. According to them, they are poorly represented in civil services as well as in medical and engineering colleges. The serious communal riots especially after 1960s have instilled a sense of insecurity among the Muslims and tend to push them into their narrow communal shell. The anti-Muslim violence in Gujarat during February-May 2002 supposedly in retaliation to the Godhra incident has shaken not only the Indian Muslims, but all the concerned Indian citizens. During the caste conflicts, communal violence, etc., the minority groups seek police protection. But the government in power also finds it difficult to provide such protection for all the members of minorities. For instance, the Modi Government in Gujarat was unable to provide protection for the Muslims after the Gujarat massacre, in which huge numbers of Muslims were killed. Again, the then Rajiv Gandhi government at the Centre was severely criticised for its failure to provide adequate security for the Sikh community of Delhi because of the communal riots that broke out after the assassination of Indira Gandhi in 1984. Now, secularism began to be used merely as a slogan of opportunism. The politicians found it easy to align a large number of multi-cultural citizens into culturally distinct groups for the realization of their vested interests. Most of the communal riots in the country have been the handiwork of disgruntled politicians, anti-social elements and criminals. Demolition of the Babri Masjid in December 1992, the Mumbai riots, and the Godhra carnage and subsequent massacres in 2002 revealed the serious weakness and susceptibility of India's commitments towards democracy and secularism. Thus, the condition of religious minorities in India continues to be very complex and critical.

In order to improve the condition of the religious minorities in India, the government in power should make every effort to restore their confidence. It is also necessary to create conditions in which the minorities are assured that their constitutional and legal rights are safeguarded. The government should seriously respond to the real needs and requirements of the poor and needy minority groups. The government should seriously consider the Sachar Committee Report without any delay and implement its recommendations. People-to-people contact, social consciousness, abolition of illiteracy etc. may prove useful confidence-building measures. The secular values must be internalised by the people and political parties. No political party should be permitted to contest election by exploiting the emotions of a particular community. Efforts should also be made to promote liberal social reforms to deal effectively with communalism and the influence of communalist leaders. The secular political class of India should campaign for widening the base of education for Muslims. The religious minorities have to be empowered educationally and economically. The progress of the country can be achieved if all the religious communities in India live in perfect harmony.

ETHNIC MINORITIES IN THE LABOUR MARKET

- Although the position of ethnic minority groups in the labour market improved over a 10-year period, from 1991 to 2001, people from those groups continued to experience lower rates of employment than white people. While some ethnic groups have improved their labour market position relative to white people, substantial disadvantage remains, both in access to jobs and in earnings when in employment.
- The proportion of employees with managerial jobs increased for all ethnic groups, with the biggest increases for black Caribbean, black African, Indian men, and Indian women. It appears that these increases were attributable to increased levels of education among these groups.
- All ethnic minority groups experienced lower earnings than white people, and the earnings disadvantage for men from ethnic minorities is a pervasive feature of the British labour market.

The research shows that people from ethnic minority groups who have higher educational qualifications receive lower rewards than those from white British backgrounds who have similar qualifications. While there has been some improvement in the labour market situation of ethnic minorities in Britain, the research findings reveal that substantial differences remain between the employment and earnings of white people and some other ethnic groups. For example:

- only 20% of Bangladeshis, 30% of Pakistanis and 40% of black Africans of working age are in full-time work (compared with over 50% of white British people of working age);
- even with a degree, Pakistani and Bangladeshi men are less likely to be employed than someone who is white with the same types of qualification;
- despite a rapid growth in the number of Pakistani and Bangladeshi women going to university, they suffer high unemployment and are much less likely than Indian or white British women to be in professional or managerial jobs;
- the problem is not confined to first-generation immigrants: British-born people from ethnic minority backgrounds, especially Indian, black, Pakistani and Bangladeshi groups, are less likely to get jobs than their white equivalents; and
- while poverty levels among white British people are the same whether they live in London or elsewhere in the UK, rates among ethnic minority groups are far worse for those living in London.

THE RESEARCH

Using individual records from the 1991 and 2001 Censuses, supplemented with more recent data from the Labour Force Survey, the research focused on: white, black Caribbean, black African, Indian, Pakistani, Bangladeshi and Chinese ethnic groups. It also examined differences by gender.

The labour market performance of these groups was investigated according to employment rates (excluding students), occupational attainment, earnings and self-employment rates. The findings highlight the diversity of experience of Britain's ethnic minorities and the change in the relative positions of ethnic groups between 1991 and 2001.

ETHNIC DIVERSITY

India is a fascinating country where people of many different communities and religions live together in unity. Indian Population is polygenetic and is an amazing amalgamation of various races and cultures.

It is impossible to find out the exact origin of Indian People. The species known as Ramapithecus was found in the Siwalik foothills of north western Himalayas. The species believed to be the first in the line of hominids (Human Family) lived some 14 million years ago. Researchers have found that a species resembling the Austrapithecus lived in India some 2 million years ago. Even this discovery leaves an evolutionary gap of as much as

12 million years since Ramapithecus. There are many diverse ethnic groups among the people of India. The 6 main ethnic groups are as follows:

(i) *Negroids*: The Negritos or the Brachycephalic (broad headed) from Africa were the earliest people to have come to India. They have survived in their original habitat in Andaman and Nicobar Islands. The Jarawas, Onges, Sentinelese and the Great Andamanese are some of the examples. Some hill tribes like Irulas, Kodars, Paniyans and Kurumbas are found in some patches in Southern part of mainland India.

(ii) *Pro-Australoids or Austrics:* These groups were the next to come to India after the Negritos. They are people with wavy hair lavishly distributed all over their brown bodies, long headed with low foreheads and prominent eye ridges, noses with low and broad roots, thick jaws, large palates and teeth and small chins. The Austrics of India represent a race of medium height, dark complexion with long heads and rather flat noses but otherwise of regular features. Miscegenation with the earlier Negroids may be the reason for the dark or black pigmentation of the skin and flat noses.

The Austrics laid the foundation of Indian civilization. They cultivated rice and vegetables and made sugar from sugarcane. Now these people are found in some parts of India, Myanmar and the islands of South East Asia. Their languages have survived in the Central and Eastern India.

(iii) *Mongoloids*: These people are found in the North eastern part of India in the states of Assam, Nagaland, Mizoram, Meghalaya, Arunachal Pradesh, Manipur, and Tripura. They are also found in Northern parts of West Bengal, Sikkim, and Ladakh. Generally they are people with yellow complexion, oblique eyes, high cheekbones, sparse hair and medium height.

(iv) *Dravidians: These* are the people of South India. They have been believed to come before the Aryans. They have different sub-groups like the Paleo-Mediterranean, the true Mediterranean, and the Oriental Mediterranean. They appear to be people of the same stock as the peoples of Asia Minor and Crete and pre-Hellenic Aegean's of Greece. They are reputed to have built up the city civilization of the Indus valley, whose remains have been found at Mohenjodaro and Harappa and other Indus cities.

(v) *Western Bracycephals:* These include the Alpinoids, Dinarics and Armenoids. The Parsis and Kodavas also fall in this category. They are the broad headed people living mainly on the western side of the country such as the Ganga Valley and the delta, parts of Kashmir, Kathiawar, Gujarat, Maharashtra, Karnataka and Tamil Nadu.

(vi) *Nordics or the Indo-Aryans*: This group were the last one to immigrate to India. They came to India somewhere between 2000 and 1500 B.C. They are now mainly found in the northern and central part of India.

PREJUDICE AND DISCRIMINATION

Prejudice and discrimination have been prevalent throughout human history. Prejudice has to do with the inflexible and irrational attitudes and opinions held by members of one group about another, while discrimination refers to behaviours directed against another group. Being prejudiced usually means having preconceived beliefs about groups of people or cultural practices. Prejudices can either be positive or negative—both forms are usually preconceived and difficult to alter. The negative form of prejudice can lead to discrimination, although it is possible to be prejudiced and not act upon the attitudes. Those who practice discrimination do so to protect opportunities for themselves by denying access to those whom they believe do not deserve the same treatment as everyone else.

It is unfortunate that prejudices against racial and ethnic minorities exit, and continue to flourish, despite the "informed" modern mind. One well-known example of discrimination based on prejudice involves the Jews, who have endured mistreatment and persecution for thousands of years. The largest scale attempt to destroy this group of people occurred during World War II, when millions of Jews were exterminated in German concentration camps in the name of Nazi ideals of "racial purity." The story of the attempted genocide, or systematic killing, of the Jews—as well as many other examples of discrimination and oppression throughout human history—has led sociologists to examine and comment upon issues of race and ethnicity.

The Sources of Prejudice

Sociologists and psychologists hold that some of the emotionality in prejudice stems from subconscious attitudes that cause a person to ward off feelings of inadequacy by projecting them onto a target group. By using certain people as scapegoats—those without power who are unfairly blamed—anxiety and uncertainty are reduced by attributing complex problems to a simple cause: "Those people are the source of all my problems." Social research across the globe has shown that prejudice is fundamentally related to low self-esteem. By hating certain groups (in this case, minorities), people are able to enhance their sense of self-worth and importance.

Social scientists have also identified some common social factors that may contribute to the presence of prejudice and discrimination:

- *Socialization*: Many prejudices seem to be passed along from parents to children. The media—including television, movies, and advertising—also perpetuate demeaning images and stereotypes about assorted groups, such as ethnic minorities, women, gays and lesbians, the disabled, and the elderly.

- *Conforming behaviours*: Prejudices may bring support from significant others, so rejecting prejudices may lead to losing social support. The pressures to conform to the views of families, friends, and associates can be formidable.
- *Economic benefits*: Social studies have confirmed that prejudice especially rises when groups are in direct competition for jobs. This may help to explain why prejudice increases dramatically during times of economic and social stress.
- *Authoritarian personality*: In response to early socialization, some people are especially prone to stereotypical thinking and projection based on unconscious fears. People with an authoritarian personality rigidly conform, submit without question to their superiors, reject those they consider to be inferiors, and express intolerant sexual and religious opinions. The authoritarian personality may have its roots in parents who are unloving and aloof disciplinarians. The child then learns to control his or her anxieties via rigid attitudes.
- *Ethnocentrism*: Ethnocentrism is the tendency to evaluate others' cultures by one's own cultural norms and values. It also includes a suspicion of outsiders. Most cultures have their ethnocentric tendencies, which usually involve stereotypical thinking.
- *Group closure*: Group closure is the process whereby groups keep clear boundaries between themselves and others. Refusing to marry outside an ethnic group is an example of how group closure is accomplished.
- *Conflict theory*: Under conflict theory, in order to hold onto their distinctive social status, power, and possessions, privileged groups are invested in seeing that no competition for resources arises from minority groups. The powerful may even be ready to resort to extreme acts of violence against others to protect their interests. As a result, members of underprivileged groups may retaliate with violence in an attempt to improve their circumstances.

Solutions to Prejudice

For decades, sociologists have looked to ways of reducing and eliminating conflicts and prejudices between groups:

- One theory, the self-esteem hypothesis, is that when people have an appropriate education and higher self-esteem, their prejudices will go away.
- Another theory is the contact hypothesis, which states that the best answer to prejudice is to bring together members of different groups so they can learn to appreciate their common experiences and backgrounds.

- A third theory, the cooperation hypothesis, holds that conflicting groups need to cooperate by laying aside their individual interests and learning to work together for shared goals.
- A fourth theory, the legal hypothesis, is that prejudice can be eliminated by enforcing laws against discriminative behaviour.

To date, solutions to prejudice that emphasize change at the individual level have not been successful. In contrast, research sadly shows that even unprejudiced people can, under specific conditions of war or economic competition, become highly prejudiced against their perceived "enemies." Neither have attempts at desegregation in schools been successful. Instead, many integrated schools have witnessed the formation of ethnic cliques and gangs that battle other groups to defend their own identities.

Changes in the law have helped to alter some prejudiced attitudes. Without changes in the law, women might never have been allowed to vote, attend graduate school, or own property. And racial integration of public facilities in America might never have occurred. Still, laws do not necessarily change people's attitudes. In some cases, new laws can increase antagonism toward minority groups.

Finally, cooperative learning, or learning that involves collaborative interactions between students, while surely of positive value to students, does not assure reduction of hostility between conflicting groups. Cooperation is usually too limited and too brief to surmount all the influences in a person's life.

To conclude, most single efforts to eliminate prejudice are too simplistic to deal with such a complex phenomenon. Researchers, then, have focused on more holistic methods of reducing ethnocentrism and cultural conflicts. They have noted that certain conditions must be met before race relations will ever improve:

- A desire to become better acquainted.
- A desire to cooperate.
- Equal economic standing and social status.
- Equal support from society.

Sociologists speculate that one reason prejudice is still around is the fact that these conditions rarely coincide.

NATIVE AMERICANS

Native Americans, or "American Indians," settled in North America long before any Europeans arrived. Yet they have now lived as foreigners and forgotten members of their own land for more than 200 years. In the 1800s, they were corralled onto "reservations" where they had few opportunities for growing food, hunting animals, or obtaining work. Only in this decade has the Native-American population grown to more than 2 million. Most live on reservations or in rural areas primarily located in the Western states. In recent decades, though, there has been an influx of Native Americans into urban areas.

American Indians are the poorest ethnic group in America. The vast majority live in substandard housing, and about 30 percent live in utter poverty, meaning they are very prone to malnutrition and diseases. The average Native American attends school less than 10 years, and the drop-out rate is double the national average. The rate of Indian unemployment is as high as 80 percent in some parts of the country. Further complicating these matters is the fact that the rate of alcoholism for Native Americans is more than five times that of other Americans.

Native Americans remain a tightly knit and culturally minded people. Neither urban nor rural Indians have necessarily lost their original tribal identities. For instance, the Navajo—who have the most populated and largest reservation in this country—have held fast to their cultural patterns, even though many Navajo have worked in industrial cities.

Native Americans.

Inspired in part by the civil rights movement, Native Americans have become politically active in recent years. The American Indian Movement (AIM) is one example of how Indians from various tribes have organized to preserve their authentic culture, prevent further violations of their territorial rights, and pursue other legal matters. Although some goals have been attained, the small number of Native Americans in the United States limits their lobbying power and legal pull.

AFRICAN AMERICANS

Perhaps more than that of any other minority, the history of African Americans in this country has been a long and complex story. During the slave trade in the early history of the United States, millions of blacks were brought from Africa. By the late 1700s, almost 4 million slaves lived in the southern states. While some slave masters may have tried to treat their black slaves humanely, the slaves felt deeply their loss of homeland, family, and freedom. In addition, harsh working conditions, physical beatings, manacles, branding, and castration were common. Nor did the slaves always passively give in to their masters' whims; sometimes slaves rebelled against their masters. Out of all of this oppression evolved a variety of uniquely African-American forms of art and music, including gospel, jazz, and the blues.

African Americans.

The formal abolition of slavery during the Civil War forever altered the life of blacks, especially in the South. Yet the one form of group closure—slavery—was replaced by another—discrimination. The behaviour of the former slaves was closely monitored, and they were quickly punished for their "transgressions." The result was continual denial of black people's political and civil rights. Legislation was also passed legalizing segregation of blacks from whites in public places like trains and restaurants. However, following the Civil War, most states in the South passed legislation against the interests of blacks, which became known as the Jim Crow laws. The laws, for example, prohibited blacks from attending white schools, theatres, restaurants, and hotels.

During the early decades of the 20th century, thousands of southern blacks moved to the North because of increased job opportunities. However, this migration did not always set well with northerners. Race riots exploded, and blacks encountered numerous forms of discrimination in housing, work, and politics.

This migration north continued both during and after World War II, especially with the increased automation being used on southern plantations. But blacks migrating north after World War II soon found the opportunities for work slim. Increased automation coupled with unions that exerted control over many occupations added to the prejudice and discrimination experienced by blacks.

THE CIVIL RIGHTS MOVEMENT

Blacks were largely denied opportunities for education and personal advancement until the early 1950s and 1960s. It was only then that the National Urban League and the National Association for the Advancement of Colored People (NAACP) began to have an effect on black civil rights.

Even before World War II, social advocates began challenging segregation in the military, as well as on buses and in schools, restaurants, swimming pools, and other public places. In 1954, in Brown v. Board of Education of Topeka, Kansas, the Supreme Court declared that "separate educational facilities are inherently unequal"—a decision that formed the basis of the civil rights movement of the 1950s to the 1970s. The decision was strongly opposed in some states, and groups like the Ku Klux Klan (KKK), which had formed during reconstruction, organized to intimidate and persecute blacks.

In 1955 in Montgomery, Alabama, a 42-year-old African-American woman—Rosa Parks—refused to surrender her seat on a bus so that white people could sit. She was subsequently arrested, which spawned mass demonstrations and bus boycotts. Eventually, a Baptist minister, Martin Luther King, Jr., organized and led marches and campaigns of nonviolent resistance to discrimination. But responses to the movement were far from nonviolent. As examples, the National Guard would prohibit black students from entering public facilities, and police would disperse protesters with clubs, fire hoses, and attack dogs. Still, the demonstrations continued until, in 1964, Congress passed a Civil Rights bill banning discrimination in education, employment, public facilities, and in governmental agencies. Additional bills in later years were passed to outlaw discrimination in housing and to ensure the rights of blacks to vote. As might be expected, a great deal of resistance arose to the implementation of the new laws protecting blacks' civil rights. Civil rights leaders were threatened, beaten up, and even killed—as was the case of Martin Luther King, Jr., in 1968. During the remainder of the 1960s, major race riots broke out in cities across the nation.

AFFIRMATIVE ACTION

The 1960s and 1970s witnessed the beginnings of affirmative action, or action taken to provide equal opportunity, to end discrimination. Most instances of affirmative action have proven to be controversial. An example is forced school busing, in which children were taken by bus to schools outside their normal school districts in an attempt to force integration in school systems. Other examples of affirmative action attempted in the 1970s and 1980s included having "quotas" (percentages of represented groups) employed in public agencies and colleges. Critics of affirmative action argued that the resulting "reverse discrimination," or action taken to provide opportunity only to under represented groups, was not a cure for social ills. Fixed quotas were finally declared illegal.

BLACKS TODAY

Sociologists debate the actual effects of the civil rights movement. Although the movement seems to have had some impact, the degree to which that impact has caused lasting social change remains in question.

The unemployment rate of blacks compared to whites is the same as it was in the early 1960s. Employment opportunities for black men have worsened, and a greater percentage of black men have given up on the work force. Likewise, little seems to have improved in terms of neighbourhood segregation. Research has reaffirmed that blacks continue to be victims of discrimination in the real estate market.

On a more positive note, black and white children now attend the same schools, and black and white students attend the same colleges. Some urban schools and colleges, however, have larger numbers of black students because of the movement of whites to suburban and rural areas. Blacks have also made some gains in elective politics; the number of black public officials has increased dramatically since the 1960s.

ASIAN AMERICANS

About 5 million Ameri-cans are of Asian heritage, the majority being Chinese, Japanese, and Filipino. Other Asian Americans include people from Korea, Vietnam, Pakistan, and India.

Most Japanese and Chin-ese workers were brought into the United States by their employers beginning in the late 1800s. Japanese immi-grants tended to settle in Pacific states, especially California. In one of America's darker moments, following the Japanese attack on Pearl Harbour during World War II, all Japanese-American citizens were forced to report to "relocation centres," which were nothing more than concentration camps. After the war, these Japanese Americans integrated into larger American society rather than returning to segregated neighbourhoods. Over the years, this minority group has rivalled the education and income levels of whites.

Asian Americans.

Chinese immigrants also settled in California and worked in such industries as railroad construction and mining. Working- and lower- class whites viewed these immigrants as a potential threat to their jobs, and so began an intense campaign of prejudice and discrimination against these people. The Chinese responded by forming distinct cultural neighbourhoods, or "Chinatowns," where they had a fighting chance to protect themselves from white aggression.

The Immigration Act of 1965 brought about increased immigration of Asians into the United States. Immigrant Chinese Americans now tend to avoid the "Chinatowns" of the native-born Chinese Americans. Many of these foreign-born Chinese work in menial occupations, but ever-growing numbers are working in professional positions. Today, Chinese

Americans continue to integrate into mainstream society, where they often work, live, and socialize alongside whites and other groups.

MIGRATION IN A GLOBALIZED WORLD

Migration is one of the defining global issues of the early twenty-first century. Approximately 175 million people, including 10.4 million refugees, reside outside their home country, or put another way, one out of every 35 persons in the world is a migrant. There is no longer a single State that can claim to be untouched by human mobility.

The reasons behind this increase in population mobility are numerous, but globalization is often held up as a convenient (although not necessarily satisfactory) explanatory coverall for factors as diverse as the development of cheap and accessible transnational means of transport, the creation of real-time networks of electronic communication, the redefinition of individual and family identities across continents, and the income differences between developed and developing countries.

But while in the field of trade enormous steps have been taken towards liberalization of the exchange of capital, goods and services, there have not been equivalent advances in the field of migration.

An analysis of the nature – both present and future – of the relationship between globalization and migration is needed, as well as the necessary policy responses. This analysis can be facilitated by clustering issues into major policy areas for migration management: (1) migration and development; (2) facilitated migration; (3) migration control; and (4) forced migration. While forced and abusive types of migration should be prevented, most migration, if properly managed, can be positive for individuals and societies. Regular/facilitated migration is an established feature of today's mobile world. In terms of the global impact of migration, nowhere is this more strikingly apparent than in the area of migration and development where the potential of migration is attracting renewed attention.

MIGRATION AND DEVELOPMENT

Globalization can be seen as a facilitator for migration and development. Through advances in communications technology and the decline in travel costs, globalization has made it easier for migrants to "keep in contact" with their country of origin and to establish lasting links with diasporas and transnational networks. There is a growing focus on return of talent and skills, even where individual migrants may not necessarily physically or permanently return to their countries of origin. How can the circulation and return of knowledge, that qualified nationals hold, be furthered? How can links with migrant communities be developed, maintained and usefully promoted?

Globalization is seen by some, however, as playing a role in reinforcing disparities in economic structures, social conditions and political stability between industrialized countries and most of the rest of the world. If this is the case, what will be its likely long-term impact on the magnitude and nature of migratory flows?

In the emerging global labour market, the migration of highly-skilled individuals and their families can have positive and negative consequences for both countries of origin and destination. For example, countries of origin might benefit from the transfer of remittances and skills gained abroad, while deploring the loss of home-grown talent. On the other hand, countries of destination might welcome the arrival of highly-skilled workers as a way to satisfy growing demand for qualified personnel while acknowledging that excessive reliance on the importation of skills may discourage investment in national training systems. How can policy makers manage better the movement of highly-skilled workers between developing and developed countries to ensure that benefits are maximized and disadvantages minimized?

In a globalized world, migratory movement is increasingly circular. While many migrants still make a permanent unidirectional move with their families, an increasing proportion of migratory movements is temporary in nature. Increasingly countries of origin expect that migrants will maintain financial, cultural and sometimes political links with their home country, which may be difficult to reconcile with the expectation for migrants to integrate on the part of the host country. How can these expectations be balanced? How will individual migrants and their communities meet the challenge of managing multiple identities? Will it be necessary to define and design integration programmes differently in future?

FACILITATED MIGRATION

A growing number of countries are pursuing policies of increasing and facilitating the flow of regular labour migrants as a response to migration pressures, in recognition of real labour market needs and to service an increasingly global economy. The dynamism that migrants can bring to economies and societies is likely to become more important, especially as demographic trends in some countries project a sharp rise in the demand for workers and professionals. How can regular labour migration be established and managed to be positive for individuals and societies?

The emergence of new global partners involved in managing migration – official and private – are affecting every region of the world. This can be seen in the international recruitment of labour and the increasing, often unregulated, role of private agencies and the business community in this process. How can these new players be identified and encouraged to cooperate in effective migration management and in respecting migrants' rights? How might private agencies, such as recruitment and employment agencies, be better included in policy development?

In addition to the issues raised above with regard to the migration of the highly skilled, a set of competing interests may exist with regard to the migration of lower-skilled individuals and families. Often they accept jobs that nationals do not want, or do so at lower wages and with fewer social benefits than nationals. What global approaches might be needed to reduce the level of vulnerability of these migrants and to ensure that their human rights are protected?

Once migrants live in a new society, new challenges arise in terms of integration – and are relevant for some temporary as well as most permanent migrants. The challenges are multiplied where there is migration of both highly-skilled and lower-skilled migrants or temporary and permanent migrants at the same time. Particular problems can arise when large numbers are involved and migrants are concentrated in certain geographical areas.

Until 2050, decreases of up to 40 per cent of the working-age population are predicted for, among others, Germany, Poland, Italy and Spain, because of consistently low fertility rates in these countries.

REPLACEMENT MIGRATION

Is it a Solution to Declining and Ageing Populations? Flourishing cultural diversity can be one result; inter-ethnic conflict and xenophobia can be another. How can systems, such as those developed by States but also, for example, those at the local or city level, deal with the number and variety of migrants they are receiving?

MIGRATION CONTROL

Over the last decades, the ability to ensure the free-flow of bona fide visitors and migrants, while also ensuring effective control over the entry and stay of migrants, has become more complex. Irregular migration is escalating and technological advancements provide more refined tools for trafficking and smuggling networks to circumvent government efforts to monitor and control movement. In addition, challenges to national security have become more complex. Recent efforts to combat terrorism have put State security concerns at the forefront of the discussion on international migration. The involvement of transnational organized crime in facilitating irregular movement is also affecting strategies and policy responses.

While the flow of persons across borders has always been monitored with respect to State security, the current discussion is focusing on the possibilities of pre-checking personal profiles and more meticulous efforts to prevent persons identified as possible security threats from crossing borders. How can these security concerns be satisfied while fully respecting migrants' rights and the need for a mobile international workforce?

FORCED MIGRATION

Refugees and displaced persons remain a distinct category of people on the move deserving special attention. These issues have been and are being addressed in different forums. But even in the field of forced migration new challenges are emerging in a globalized world.

Internal conflicts have overtaken international ones as major threats to international peace and security. How can adequate solutions be found for internally displaced persons (IDPs)? How can effective programmes for post-conflict recovery be established?

Numerous issues cut across each of the above four pillars of migration management. The challenges posed by these issues should be addressed in the context of each pillar.

GLOBALIZATION AND MIGRATION

During the 1870-1910 wave of globalization, 60 million people migrated from Europe—primarily from less developed regions—to the United States and other parts of the new world. These flows were a powerful force for wage convergence. Emigration is estimated to have raised Irish wages by 32 percent, Italian by 28 percent, and Norwegian by 10 percent. Meanwhile, immigration lowered Argentine wages by 22 percent, Australian by 15 percent, Canadian by 16 percent, and U.S. by 8 percent. Labour flows between developing countries were also extensive in the early periods of globalization, though they are less well documented. About 10 percent of the world's population moved permanently to a new country, and even more migrated from rural to urban areas within countries.

The same forces operate today. A study following individual, legal migrants from Mexico to the United States found that on average they left jobs paying $31 a week and on arrival in the United States could immediately earn $278 a week—nine times as much. Similarly, Indonesian workers earn 28 cents a day at home, compared with $2 a day or more in neighbouring Malaysia. Thus there are huge real gains to workers who migrate to more developed economies.

Although there are strong economic pressures for migration, legal migration is highly restricted. Thus when it comes to labour flows, today's world is much less globalized than it was a hundred years ago. Only about 2 percent of the world's population consists of migrants living in countries not of their citizenship. At the same time, pressures for migration are mounting. The labour force in OECD countries is aging, while the labour force in the developing world is surging because of high birth rates. Each year 83 million people are added to the world's population—82 million of them in developing countries. Without more migration, the ratio of workers to retirees in Japan and the European Union will fall from five to one today to three to one in 2015, straining social security systems.

Combining OECD capital and technology with developing country labour has the potential to generate mutual economic benefits. Some of those benefits can come through the flow of capital and production to developing countries. But geographic factors make it unlikely that capital flows and trade will eliminate the economic rationale for migration. Too many parts of the developing world have poor institutions and weak infrastructure that will not attract production. Moreover, some production networks in industrial countries are too deeply rooted to move. Institutional and policy reforms and infrastructure investments in lagging developing countries could address the first concern and reduce—though not eliminate—economic pressures for migration.

The experiences of Mexico and the United States illustrate how migration can benefit both economies. About 7 million Mexican citizens live legally in the United States, along with another 3 million undocumented Mexican workers. These workers represent about 10 percent of Mexico's population and an even larger share of its labour force. Their work in the United States takes pressure off Mexico's labour market (raising wages there) and generates a significant flow of remittances to relatives back home. In the United States this labour inflow was a key factor in the sustained growth with low inflation of the 1990s. Still, migration is estimated to have reduced the relative wages of unskilled U.S. workers by 5 percent—highlighting again that globalization typically produces winners and losers.

OECD countries not only tend to be highly restrictive about migration, they also tend to discriminate in favour of educated workers (causing a "brain drain" from developing countries). Labour flows would do more to reduce poverty in developing countries if immigration policies in industrial countries were more neutral and allowed more unskilled workers to immigrate.

GENDER PERSPECTIVE IN MIGRATION

Earlier studies in migration have ignored the role of women. The presence of women was usually attached to family reunification, hence dependent upon the husband. Current trends, however, show that women are migrating independently. New migratory flows are no longer male-dominated. There is a growing demand for female labour and new social needs have created a demand for services in which only immigrant women are prepared to work. Observers are keeping close watch at the feminization of migration.

It is very important to include women-specific issues in migration discourses. There exists a division of labour— structured activities in a society are gendered. Not only do men and women undertake different tasks, but women are responsible for activities in the domestic sphere. These different tasks are the basis for the social construction of gender in which women are excluded from some activities, confined to others, dependent on males, docile, subservient and assigned secondary status in the labour market. They often take up the menial and low-paid occupations, with particularly difficult working conditions. We find women migrants working in sweat shops, as domestic servants, as entertainers exposing them to sexual exploitation. Women migrants face degradation due to stereotypes that devalue women and women's work.

Recognizing the gender issue in migration would also recognize human rights for women. Migrant women are vulnerable to gender-related violence like rape, sexual harassment and physical abuse. One other serious global problem is trafficking in women. Yet, how serious are governments in dealing with this problem? Migration is very much in the core of trafficking in women – in the entertainment industry, domestic workers, child prostitutes – all of which violate fundamental human rights.

The important economic contribution by migrant women, particularly the invisible work of the domestic helpers, must be recognized. Migrant women should enjoy the same privileges and opportunities as other women in the same society. The gender-agenda should be top priority in shaping migration politics. As one politician said, "if we want to change the world, change the women".

At the NGO Forum on Women in Huiaro, China, migration was a hot and contested issue. At the 4th World Congress on Women in Beijing just 50 km away, migration was hardly discussed by the official delegates. They simply want to procrastinate - hoping that the problem will go away? We are sitting on a time bomb! Migration will be one of the major issues in the 21st Century.

SCIENCE AND TECHNOLOGY

Introduction. Indian Contributions to Science and Technology: *Civil Engineering, Water Management, Textiles, Iron and Steel, Zinc Metallurgy, Shipping and Shipbuilding, Forest Management, Farming Techniques, Traditional Medicine, Mathematics, "Folk" Sciences.* ***Relationship with Inner Sciences. Meaning and Definition of Science. Nature of Science. Characteristics of Science. Meaning of Technology. The Nature of Technology. Technology is Related to Science:*** *Technology, Science.* ***Norms of Science:*** *Universalism, "Communism", Disinterestedness, Organized Skepticism.* ***Social Process of Innovation:*** *Defining Innovation, Social Foundations of Innovation, Need for Innovation in Social Policy, Role of Governments in the Innovation System—Global Experience, Creating an Innovation Infrastructure in India and the Need for a National Innovation Policy.* ***Social Control of Science and Technology:*** *Six Social Engineering Strategies.* ***Some Other Social Control Dimensions. Some Social and Ethical Implications. Success of science and technology.***

INTRODUCTION

Science and technology has been in the forefront of transforming the Indian economic structure helping India evolve as a globally competitive economic powerhouse. With the available scientific manpower--which is third largest in the world—the Indian science and technology has been growing well above world average.

While the Indian output of science, as measured by the quality and quantity of Science Citation Index (SCI) papers, has been growing at a CAGR of 8 per cent in the past three years, the world average was only 4 per cent. Also, the number of technical workforce is also increasing at a rapid clip and is set to cross the 2 million mark, with the march from one million to two million happening in just about three years.

A number of world-class institutions have instrumental in this: 162 universities award 4,000 doctorates and 35,000 postgraduate degrees and the Council of Scientific and Industrial Research runs 40 research laboratories that have made some significant achievements.

India is one of the few countries with expertise to conceptualise, design and manufacture satellites and the capability to launch them into space. In fact, it has the largest constellation of remote sensing satellites in the world. Also, the Indian Space Research Organisation (ISRO) is the world's third non-US supplier of 1-metre imageries and holds nearly 25 per cent of the US$ 120-million global free-play imageries market.

The year 2007 saw several major accomplishments being made in the Indian space programme: successful orbiting and recovery of a space capsule (which is a prelude to the development of space recovery capsule), launch of Cartosat-2 (a remote sensing satellite with a resolution capacity below 1 metre) and successfully testing indigenously developed cryogenic upper stage among others.

India has also lined up some interesting projects for the future: a lunar mission, a project for manned space outing around 2015, development of space recovery capsule (which would lay the foundation for future returning missions) and establishing indigenous regional GPS by 2012 among others.

INDIAN CONTRIBUTIONS TO SCIENCE AND TECHNOLOGY

The depth and breadth of Indian science and technology is staggering, and this section gives just a glimpse into the genius of India's scientists and engineers.

CIVIL ENGINEERING

From complex Harappan towns to Delhi's Qutub Minar, India's indigenous technologies were very sophisticated. They included the design and planning of water supply, traffic flow, natural air conditioning, complex stone work, and construction engineering.

Most students learn about the ancient cities of the Middle East and China. How many have even a basic understanding of the world's oldest and most advanced civilization – the Harappan or Indus-Sarasvati Valley Civilization in India? The Indus-Sarasvati Civilization was the world's first to build planned towns with underground drainage, civil sanitation, hydraulic engineering, and air-cooling architecture. While the other ancient civilizations of the world were small towns with one central complex, this civilization had the distinction of being spread across many towns, covering a region about half the size of Europe. Weights and linguistic symbols were standardized across this vast geography, for a period of over 1,000 years, from around 3,000 BCE to 1500 BCE. Oven-baked bricks were invented in India in approximately 4,000 BCE. Over 900 of the 1,500 known settlement sites discovered so far are in India.

Civil Engineering.

Since the Indus-Sarasvati script is yet to be decoded, it remains a mystery as to how these people could have achieved such high levels of sophistication and uniformity in a dispersed complex and with no visible signs of centralized power.

For instance, all bricks in this civilization are of the ratio 1:2:4 regardless of their size, location or period of construction. There are many pioneering items of civil engineering, such as drainage systems for water (open and closed), irrigation systems, river dams, water storage tanks carved out of rock, moats, middle-class style homes with private bathrooms and drainage and even a dockyard; there is evidence of stairs for multiple-storied buildings; many towns have separate citadels, upper and lower towns, and fortified sections; there are separate worker quarters near copper furnaces; granaries have ducts and platforms; and archeologists have found geometric compasses, linear scales made of ivory. Indians also pioneered many engineering tools for construction, surgery, warfare, etc. These included the hollow drill, the true saw, and the needle with the hole on its pointed end.

WATER MANAGEMENT

Given the importance of fresh water in India, it is no surprise that the technologies to manage water resources were highly advanced from Harappan times onwards. For example, in Gujarat, Chandragupta built the Sudarshan Lake in late 4th century BCE, and was later repaired in 150 BCE by his grandson. Bhopal's Raja Bhoj Lake, built in 1014-1053,

Water Management.

is so massive that it shows up in satellite images. The Vijayanagar Empire built such a large lake in 14th–15th century CE that it has more construction material than the Great Wall of China. What some historians call the "Persian Wheel" is actually pre-Mughal and indigenous to India.

Scientists estimate there were 1.3 million man-made water lakes and ponds across India, some as large as 250 square miles. These are now being rediscovered using satellite imagery. These enabled rain water to be harvested and used for irrigation, drinking, etc. till the following year's rainfall.

TEXTILES

Indian textiles have been legendary since ancient times. The Greeks and Romans extensively imported textiles from India. Roman archives record official complaints about massive cash drainage due to these imports from India.

Textiles.

One of the earliest industries relocated from India to Britain was textiles and it became the first major success of the Industrial Revolution, with Britain replacing India as the world's leading textile exporter. What is suppressed in the discourse about India and Europe is the fact that the technology, designs and even raw cotton were initially imported from India while, in parallel, India's indigenous textile mills were outlawed by the British. India's textile manufacturers were de-licensed, even tortured in some cases, over-taxed and regulated, to 'civilize' them into virtual extinction. Textiles and steel were the mainstays of the British Industrial Revolution. Both had their origins in India. The Ahmedabad textile museum is a great resource for scholarly material.

IRON AND STEEL

Iron is found in countries neighboring India, leading European scholars to assume that it came from outside India. Given the similarities between the Vedas and Avesta (a Zoroastrian text), some saw this as supporting the theory of diffusion of iron and Vedas into India from the outside. Refuting this, Vibha Tripathi finds that iron in India is much older. Cemeteries in present-day Baluchistan have iron objects. The earlier iron found in Middle Eastern archeological sites was essentially meteorite material sculptured as rock/stone carvings, and was not metallurgically processed at all. Since iron can be a by-product of copper technology, this could be its likely origin in India because copper was a well-known technology in many parts of ancient India. A smelting furnace dated 800 BCE is found in Naikund (Maharashtra), India. Recent discoveries reveal that iron was known in the Ganga valley in mid second millennium BCE. In the mid-first millennium BCE, the Indian steel was very popular in Persian courts for making swords.

Iron and Steel.

Rust-free steel was an Indian invention, and remained an Indian skill for centuries. Delhi's famous iron pillar, dated 402 CE, is considered a metallurgical marvel and shows minimal signs of rust. The famous Damascus steel swords, now displayed in museums across Europe, were made from Indian steel imported by Europeans. The acclaimed Sheffield steel in UK was Indian crucible steel. The best brains of European science worked for decades to learn to reverse-engineer how Indians made crucible steel, and in this process, modern alloy design and physical metallurgy was developed in Europe.

Indian industry was dealt a death blow by the colonial masters who banned the production and manufacture of iron and steel at several places in India, fearing their use in making swords and other arms. In addition, they also ensured India would depend upon iron and steel imported from Europe.

ZINC METALLURGY

Another important Indian contribution to metallurgy was in the isolation, distillation and use of zinc. From natural sources, zinc content in alloys such as brass can go no higher than 28 per cent. These primitive alloys with less than 28 per cent zinc were prevalent in many parts of the world before India. However, to increase the zinc content beyond this threshold, one must first separate the zinc into 100 per cent pure form and then mix the pure zinc back into an alloy. A major breakthrough in the history of metallurgy was India's discovery of zinc distillation whereby the metal was vaporized and then condensed back into pure metal.

Brass in Taxashila has been dated from third century BCE to fifth century CE. A vase from Taxashila is of particular interest because of its 34 per cent zinc content and has been dated to the third century BCE. Recently two brass bangles belonging to the Kushana period have been discovered from Senuwar (Uttar Pradesh, India). They are also made of metallic zinc as they have 35 per cent zinc content. Experts are unsure if this zinc was made by distillation process.

There is evidence of zinc ore mining at Zawar in Rajasthan from the fifth century BCE, but unfortunately there is lack of evidence of regular production of metallic zinc until the eighth century CE. The earliest confirmed evidence of zinc smelting by distillation is dated back to 840 +110 from Zawar. This is the earliest date for zinc smelting and production of metallic zinc by distillation process anywhere in the world.

Alloy Trading owns a major percentage of the shares in zinc smelters like IZMDC Group (CALCIMINE, NILZ, Qeshm Zinc, Bander Abbas Zinc, Bafg Smelter, Faravari Zinc), Negin Roy, Nau Sazan and Zanjan Zinc.

Europeans learnt it for the first time in 1743, when know-how was transferred from India. Until then, India had been exporting pure zinc for centuries on an industrial scale. At archeological sites in Rajasthan, retorts used for the distillation are found in very large numbers even today.

Once zinc had become separated into a pure metal, alloys could be made with the required zinc component to provide the required properties. For instance, strength and durability increase with higher zinc component. Also, copper alloys look like gold when the zinc component is higher than 28 per cent. Most early brass objects found in other countries had less than 10 per cent zinc component, and therefore, these were not based on zinc distillation technology.

Alloys that exceed 10 per cent zinc are found earliest in Taxashila in the fourth century BCE. However, while Taxashila was distilling and manufacturing zinc on a small scale, it was in Zawar, Rajasthan, where this first became industrialized on a large scale. Zinc mines have been found in Dariba (11th century BCE), Agucha (sixth century BCE) and Zawar (fifth century BCE). These mines have pots and other manufacturing tools of these dates, but the mining could be even older.

Three important items are now proven about the history of zinc metallurgy:

(i) zinc distillation and metallurgical usage was pioneered in India;
(ii) industrial scale production was pioneered in Rajasthan;
(iii) England transferred the technology of zinc from India in 1736. British metallurgy documents do not mention zinc at all prior to this transfer.

SHIPPING AND SHIPBUILDING

Shipbuilding was one of India's major export industries until the British dismantled it and formally banned it. Medieval Arab sailors purchased their boats in India. The Portuguese also continued to get their boats from India and not Europe. Some of the world's largest and most sophisticated ships were built in India and China.

Shipbuilding and ship repair.

The compass and other navigation tools were already in use in the Indian Ocean long before Europe. ("Nav" is the Sanskrit word for boat, and is the root word in "navigation" and "navy".) Using their expertise in the science of seafaring, Indians participated in the earliest-known ocean-based trading system.

Few people know that an Indian naval pilot, named Kanha, was hired by Vasco da Gama to captain his ships and take him to India. Some of Europe's acclaimed "discoveries" in navigation were in fact appropriations of a well-established thriving trade system in the Indian Ocean. Contrary to European portrayals that Indians knew only coastal navigation, deep-sea shipping had existed in India as Indian ships had been sailing to islands such as the Andamans, Lakshdweep and Maldives around 2,000 years ago. Kautilya describes the times that are good and bad for seafaring. There is also extensive archival material on the Indian Ocean trade in Greek, Roman, and Southeast Asian sources.

FOREST MANAGEMENT

Many interesting findings have recently come out about the way forests and trees were managed by each village and how a careful method was applied to harvest medicines, firewood and building material in accordance with natural renewal rates. There is now a database being built of 'sacred groves' across India. Once again, it's a story of an economic asset falling into disuse and abuse because of the dismantling of local governance and disrespect for traditional systems.

Furthermore, when scholars try to explain India's current ecological disasters, they seldom mention the large-scale logging of Indian timber by the British in order to fund the two world wars and various other industrial programs of the empire.

Forest Management.

FARMING TECHNIQUES

Indian farmers developed non-chemical, eco-friendly pesticides and fertilizers that have modern applications. These traditional pesticides have been recently revived in India with excellent results, replacing Union Carbide's products in certain markets. Crop rotation and soil technology that has been passed down for thousands of years are traditional practices which India pioneered.

Farming Techniques.

Historically, India's agricultural production was large and sustained a huge population compared to other parts of the world. Surpluses were stored for use in a drought year. But the British turned this industry into a cash cow, exporting very large amounts of grain even during food shortages. This caused tens of millions of Indians to die of starvation in the 19th century.

TRADITIONAL MEDICINE

Much re-legitimizing of traditional Indian medicine has already started, thanks in part to many Western labs and scientists. Many multinationals no longer denigrate traditional medicine and have in fact been trying to secure patents on Indian medicine without acknowledging the source. Traditional medicine is now a well-known and respected field.

MATHEMATICS

Prof. C.K Raju, a renowned scholar, has researched the "clash of epistemologies" that occurred in European ideas about numbers. When Europeans started to import Indian ideas about mathematics, what had been natural to Indian thinkers for a long time was very hard for Europeans to accept. He divides this into three periods:

The first math war in Europe was from 10th to 16th centuries, during which time it took Europe 500 years to accept the zero, because the Church considered it to be heresy.

The second math war was over the Indian concept of indivisibles, which led to the theory of real numbers and infinitesimals, paving the way for the development of calculus. This war lasted three centuries, from the 17th to 19th centuries.

The third math war is now under way and is between computational math (Indian algorithmic approach) and formal math (Western approach).

Additionally, Indians developed many important concepts including the base-ten decimal system, now in global use, and crucial trigonometry and algebra formulae. They made several astronomical discoveries. Diverse schools of logic and philosophy proliferated.

Mathematical thought was intertwined with linguistics. India's Panini is acknowledged as the founder of linguistics, and his Sanskrit grammar is still the most complete and sophisticated of any language in the world.

"FOLK" SCIENCES

Besides the above examples of Indian contributions to the origins of the so-called "Western" science, there is another category of traditional knowledge called non-literate folk science. Western science as a whole has condemned and ignored anything that it did not either appropriate or develop, by branding it as magic and superstition. However, in countries such as India, which boast of cultural continuity, ancient traditions survive with a rich legacy of folk science.

Natural resources and products in folk medicine.

In North America and Australia, where original populations have been largely decimated, such continuity of folk tradition was disrupted. In Western nations with large colonies in the Old and New Worlds, such knowledge systems were looked down upon once they had been successfully plundered. The process of contrasting Western science with folk knowledge systems has led to the imposition of contrived hegemonic categories.

The distinction between elite and folk science was non-existent in ancient times. India's advanced metallurgy and civil engineering was researched and practiced by artisan guilds. Western science seldom realized that non-literate folk science preserves the wisdom gained through millennia of experience and direct observation, and has been transmitted by word of mouth.

For instance, modern scientists have humbly admitted that the ecological management practiced today by the tribes of India's Northeast is far superior to anything they could teach them. A good example is the use of alder (Alnus nepalensis), which has been cultivated in the jhum (shifting cultivation) fields by the Khonoma farmers in Nagaland for centuries. It has multiple usages for the farmers, since it is a nitrogen-fixing tree and helps to retain the soil fertility. Its leaves are used as fodder and fertilizer, and it is also utilized as timber. One could cite numerous such examples.

The vast majority of modern medicines patented by Western pharmaceutical firms are based on tropical plants. The most common method to select candidates for detailed testing has been for Western firms to scout tropical societies, seek out established "folk" remedies and subject these to testing by "Western science". In many cases, patents owned by multinationals are largely for isolating the active ingredients in a lab and going through rigorous protocols of testing and patent filing. While this is an important and expensive task that deserves credit, these are seldom truly independent discoveries from scratch. Never has the society that has discovered them through centuries of empirical trial and error received any recognition, much less any share of royalty.

Colin Scott writes: "With the upsurge of multidisciplinary interest in 'traditional ecological knowledge,' models explicitly held by indigenous people in areas as diverse as forestry, fisheries, and physical geography are being paid increasing attention by Western scientists, who have in some cases established extremely productive long-term dialogues with local experts. The idea that local experts are often better informed than their Western peers is at last receiving significant acknowledgment beyond the boundaries of anthropology."

Myths and legends sometimes represent the attempts of our ancestors to explain the scientific observations they made about the world around them and transmitted these to the future. They chose different models to interpret the observations, but the observations were empirical. Theorizing the possible role of myths, Scott writes: "The complementarity of the literal and the figurative helps us to realize that the distinction between myth and science is not structural, but procedural ... Myths in a broader, paradigmatic sense are condensed expressions of root metaphors that reflect the genius of particular knowledge traditions ... Numerous studies have found that the "anthropomorphic" paradigms of egalitarian hunters and horticulturalists not only generate practical knowledge consistent with the insights of scientific ecology, but simultaneously cultivate an ethic of environmental responsibility that for western societies has proven elusive."

Despite these acknowledgments, in too many cases Western scholars reduce India's experts to "native informants" who are seen located below the glass ceiling: the pandit as native informant to the Western Sanskritist; the poor woman in Rajasthan as native informant to the Western feminist seeking to cure her of her native tradition; the herbal farmer as native informant to the Western pharmaceutical firm appropriating medicines for patents. Given their poverty in modern times, these 'native informants' dish out whatever the Western scholar expects to hear in order to fit his/her thesis, because in return they receive rewards. Rarely have Western scholars acknowledged India's knowledge bearers as equal partners. The obsession to make 'original' discoveries and to put one's name on publications has exacerbated the tendency to appropriate with one hand, while denigrating the source with other hand. This deserves to be called 'academic arson'.

RELATIONSHIP WITH INNER SCIENCES

India's inner sciences of mind and consciousness are simultaneously (a) being appropriated by the West and (b) being depicted as anti-progressive and irrational. In fact, inner and outer realms of inquiry are often viewed as opposites that can, at best, be balanced but not unified. This falsely assumes that the inner sciences make a person and society less productive, creative, and competitive in the outer realm. However, contradicting this, India's inner sciences and outer development coexisted in a mutually symbiotic relationship.

A strong inner science will definitely strengthen the outer science since it is the inner world which provides the inspiration, creativity, and knowledge that is necessary in the development of a sound outer science. A strong outer science allows the freedom for the exploration of the inner science. Without the use of technology of some form, man will be forced to dwell in his lower nature to satisfy his basic needs of survival.

The divorce of 'religion' and science is a strictly Western construct due to the dogmatic and rigid nature of the Abrahamic religions. History-centric religions (such as Judaism, Christianity, and Islam) are often not compatible with the human tendency towards freedom of thought, intellectual originality, and non-conformity of thought which are necessary in scientific innovation. The tradition of spiritual experimentation in India, however, is compatible with the material and intellectual experimentation required by science.

MEANING AND DEFINITION OF SCIENCE

The word science comes from the Latin "scientia," meaning knowledge. Science is a particular way of understanding the natural world. It extends the intrinsic curiosity with which we are born. It allows us to connect the past with the present. Science is based on the premise that our senses, and extensions of those senses through the use of instruments, can give us accurate information about the Universe. Science follows very specific "rules" and its results are always subject to testing and, if necessary, revision. Even with such constraints science does not exclude, and often benefits from, creativity and imagination.

What does that really mean? Science refers to a system of acquiring knowledge. This system uses observation and experimentation to describe and explain natural phenomena. The term science also refers to the organized body of knowledge people have gained using that system. Less formally, the word science often describes any systematic field of study or the knowledge gained from it.

What is the purpose of science? Perhaps the most general description is that the purpose of science is to produce useful models of reality.

Science as defined above is sometimes called *pure science* to differentiate it from applied science, which is the application of research to human needs. Fields of science are commonly classified along two major lines:

- Natural sciences, the study of the natural world, and
- Social sciences, the systematic study of human behavior and society.

NATURE OF SCIENCE

In general, the nature of science refers to key principles and ideas which provide a description of science as a way of knowing, as well as characteristics of scientific knowledge. Many of these intrinsic ideas are lost in the everyday aspects of a science classroom, resulting in students learning skewed notions about how science is conducted.

What are the main ideas regarding the nature of science?

1. **Scientific knowledge is tentative:** Although scientific knowledge is supported by a wealth of data from repeated trials, it is not considered the final word. Scientific knowledge is at the same time stable and malleable. Scientists continually test and challenge previous assumptions and findings. After all, science is a human endeavor, and we know human perspective is limited and fallible. This idea of fundamental uncertainty is vital to scientific studies and is the basis of great scientific discoveries.

2. **Nature of facts/hypotheses/theories:** Some key words in science are often misinterpreted.
   - ***Facts*:** Students often think of the pieces of scientific knowledge they learn as "facts." As mentioned in the last section, we should not refer to scientific knowledge as fact, because that would tend to perpetuate the idea that scientific knowledge is inalterable. Scientific facts are observable phenomenon in a particular situation. "Dinosaurs were cold-blooded" is not a scientific fact, because this phenomenon cannot be observed. "The caterpillar is 2.6 cm in length" is an example of a fact, because the phenomenon was observed in a particular situation.
   - ***Hypotheses*:** If you ask a student to tell you what a hypothesis is, you will likely receive the following response: "A hypothesis is an educated guess." Although a hypothesis is partly a "guess" in the sense that it is an idea, this inevitable definition is not adequate. A hypothesis is a statement, based on previous observations, that can be tested scientifically. The idea that a scientific hypothesis must be testable often eludes students.
   - ***Theories*:** In the colloquial, theories are often ideas that have not been validated. In science, a theory has a much stronger meaning. Scientific theories are broadly based concepts that make sense of a large body of observations and experimentation. Because theories successfully tie together such a huge amount of information, they are among the most important ideas in science.
3. **Scientific methods:** In the first chapter of most science textbooks, there will be a section laying out "the scientific method," a step-by-step process that apparently must be followed in order to conduct scientific studies. The danger in this approach is not only that learning the scientific method is a bummer to students, but that it is also quite restrictive in its scope. Scientists usually do not walk through the method sequentially. They often bounce around, perhaps forming a new hypothesis during experimentation. Studies in which no experimentation is performed are also valid scientific studies, but do not follow the scientific method. For example: Jane Goodall observed the behavior of the apes in Africa and did not experiment on them, yet her research is still considered science. This butterfly study is a good example of an observational study which does not follow the scientific method, yet students record scientific data and create scientific conclusions.
4. **Observations and inferences:** It is important for students to understand the difference between observation and inference. However, this knowledge in itself is not enough. Students should also learn to make good observations and inferences, and understand

the role that observations and inferences play in the development of scientific knowledge.

- ***Observations***: When we describe an environment based on our five senses, it is called an observation. For example, "Upon magnification, the painted lady eggs appear bluish and barrel-shaped." Observations are direct enough that most would make the same observation in the same situation.
- ***Inferences***: When we bring our past experience into making a judgment based on an observation, it is an inference. For example, "The caterpillar appears as if it is about to form its chrysalis" is an inference, because you are interpreting observations according to knowledge from past experience. Inferences are important in science in making explanations, but one must be careful not to confuse observations with inferences when conducting a study.

5. ***Human error:*** Although we take steps not to make errors in observation or experimentation, scientists are still human and make mistakes. It is important to challenge students to view their mistakes or unexpected results as potentially helpful. Scientific studies are most often riddled with problems that must be addressed. Often, scientists do not find the answer they expect, but if they do not allow their expectations to cloud their judgment, they may be able to approach the problem in a more appropriate manner.

CHARACTERISTICS OF SCIENCE

"Science is a system of ideas, a body of statements about the material universe. Only logical consistency and especially the evidence of our sense can serve as a check, a way of assessing the accuracy of our ideas about the world around us. It is a procedural norm of science -- though, curiously enough, a dictum honored most often in the breach -- that when one's thoughts about the way things are supposed to be conflict with what seems to be the actual truth of the matter, we reexamine those notions which led us to erroneous predictions...."

- Science is logical (utilizing the appropriate form of logic), reasonable, and rational.
- Science makes well-defined claims based upon the best available evidence.
- Scientific hypothesis must be falsifable.
- Scientific experiments should be repeatable under similar circumstances.
- Science requires that claims be examined by qualified peers.
- Science views unexplained gaps in theories or evidence with suspicion.

- Science requires caution both in performing experiments, and in examining and evaluating evidence.
- Science requires efforts at objectivity, both in control of variables and of biases.
- Science does not accept coincidence or unlinked or unproven correlations as proofs.
- Science does not accept undocumented anecdotal evidence as good proof by itself.
- Science demands extraordinarily good evidence for extraordinary unconventional claims.
- Scientific favors parsimony: that the simplest adequate explanation is preferred.
- Science assumes that the Laws of Nature are universal, if relative.
- Science demands the honest use of the scientific method and truthful reports.
- Science demands every effort be made to control or assess all variables.
- Science needs the uninhibited exchange of ideas and greatest possible discourse of the material.

MEANING OF TECHNOLOGY

The purposeful application of information in the design, production, and utilization of goods and services, and in the organization of human activities. Technology is generally divided into five categories:

- ***Tangible:*** blueprints, models, operating manuals and prototypes.
- ***Intangible:*** consultancy, problem-solving and training methods.
- ***High:*** entirely or almost entirely automated and intelligent technology that manipulates ever finer matter and ever powerful forces.
- ***Intermediate:*** semiautomated partially intelligent technology that manipulates refined matter and medium level forces.
- ***Low:*** labor-intensive technology that manipulates only coarse or gross matter and weaker forces.

Throughout the twentieth century the uses of the term have increased to the point where it now encompasses a number of "classes" of technology:

- ***Technology as objects:*** Tools, machines, instruments, weapons, appliances - the physical devices of technical performance.
- ***Technology as knowledge:*** The know-how behind technological innovation.
- ***Technology as activities:*** What people do - their skills, methods, procedures, routines.

- ***Technology as a process:*** Begins with a need and ends with a solution.
- ***Technology as a sociotechnical system:*** The manufacture and use of objects involving people and other objects in combination.

THE NATURE OF TECHNOLOGY

Technology has a number of distinct characteristics:

1. It is Related to Science?

Although there is certainly a relationship between science and technology, there is, except in certain high technology industries, very little technology that could be classified as applied science. Technology is marked by different purposes, different processes a different relationship to established knowledge and a particular relationship to specific contexts of activity. Change in the material environment is the explicit purpose of technology, and not, as is the case with science, the understanding of nature; accordingly its solutions are not right or wrong, verifiable or falsifiable, but more or less effective from different points of view.

2. It Involves Design

At the centre of technology lies design. That "design is the very core of engineering" is affirmed by the requirement that all degree engineering courses should embody it. The design process in technology is a sequential process which begins with the perception of a need, continues with the formulation of a specification, the generation of ideas and a final solution, and ends with an evaluation of the solution.

3. It Involves Making

The motivating factor behind all technological activity is the desire to fulfil a need. For this reason all designs should be made or realised—whether that be through prototype, batch-or mass-production or some form of three-dimensional or computer model—if the need is to be truly fulfilled, the design is to be legitimately evaluated, and the design activity is to have been purposeful and worthwhile.

4. It is Multi-Dimensional

Not only may design and production involve co-operation between different specialisms (between, for example, designer, production engineer and materials scientist), but may involve "technologists" in performing a multitude of functions, such as working with others, operating within budgets, persuading decision makers, communicating to clients and working to deadlines.

5. It is Concerned with Values

Technology is informed by values at every point. Value decisions may be called for not only in relation to the specific design criteria, (i.e., aesthetic, ergonomic and economic judgements, suitability for purpose and ease of manufacture) but also in relation to the rightness or wrongness of a particular solution in ethical terms.

6. It is Socially Shaped/Shaping

Technological enterprises are determined not by advances in knowledge nor simply by the identification of needs, but by social interests. Of the potential new technologies available at any one time only a few are developed and become widely implemented. In this way technology is shaped by society, by consumer choice. yet it could also be argued that technology shapes society - the technology of the motor car, for example, has shaped our environment and our whole way of life.

TECHNOLOGY IS RELATED TO SCIENCE

Bigelow's phrase "the practical applications of science" points to the root of much of the current confusion as to the meaning of technology. In using this phrase to describe technology he effectively placed technology beneath the umbrella of science to such an extent that science and technology are now, as Rose described, seen by many as an "indivisible pair" with technology as the subservient and dependant partner. Thus, for much of the time the pair are wrapped together into a single conceptual package known simply as "science". This point is emphasised when surfing the Internet for technology-related teaching resources. A plethora of lesson plans exist at sites dedicated to science education. The problem is, though, that many of these lessons should properly be termed "technology" but are all too often referred to as "applied science".

Relationship between Science and Technology.

One source of confusion is the undoubted relationship that exists between science and technology. Sparkes illustrated this relationship and pointed out that even though science and technology overlap in an area which might be referred to as "applied science", there are a number of important differences between the two (Table 1), even though these differences might not be self-evident to an average member of the general public who, through neglect and through repeated use of the phrase "science and technology" has lost the distinction between "science" and between "technology". The two cannot be told apart. Which is hardly surprising given that, as Mayr put it: " . . . practical usable criteria for making sharp neat distinctions between science and technology do not exist."

Table 1: Differences between Science and Technology

Science can broadly be defined as the study of "things" such as: Chemistry, Biology, Physics, Genetics, Geology, Psychology, Sociology, and other fields of study that analyze interactions, behaviors, physical properties, effects, causes, etc. in order to rationalize or establish given properties, behaviors and interactions about such "things". The basis of Science is the conducting of experiments. Basically, a theory is made (stated), analysis and testing are performed with the use of various controls, and when a specific, measurable result occurs, and can be reproduced or proven time and time again, the theory then becomes Scientific law, or a truism of sorts.

Technology, refers generally to items of use, created from "Applied Science". A good example of this is the production of Solar panels. Solar Panels are used in a variety of different technologies, but the simplest example is a Solar Powered Calculator. It was proposed long ago that the Sun emits two types of energy, heat energy and light energy. The Sun's heat energy is what warms the Earth's atmosphere so that life as we know it can exist, by warming the atmosphere to a tolerable temperature that the Human Body can function in. (Space is somewhere around –230 degrees Fahrenheit, and at those temperatures, plants could not grow, and the Human body would not be able to carry on normal functions such as breathing in that cold of temperature.) The sun's light energy is absorbed by Solar Panels (and Solar Cells), and converts that energy to electricity so that the calculator can perform mathematical functions. To test this, put a piece of electrical tape over your calculator for 15 minutes, and then see if you can turn it on. If you can not then you know the light energy is being converted to electricity.

In short, science is the study of forces and interactions between different "things", both animate and inanimate. Technology can be referred to as things which we make, but were developed by applying Scientific law, knowing what such "things" are capable of doing.

TECHNOLOGY

- Goal: the creation of artfacts and systems to meet people's needs.
- Key Technological Processes.
- Design, invention, production.
- Analysis and synthesis of design.
- Holism, involving the integration of many competing demands, theories, data and ideas.
- Activities always value-laden.
- The search for and theorizing about new processes (e.g. control; information).

- Pursuit of sufficient accuracy in modelling to achieve success.
- Taking good decisions based on incomplete data and approximate models.
- Design, construction, testing, planning, quality assurance, problem solving, decision making, interpersonal and communication skills.
- Trying to ensure, by subsequent action, that even poor decisions turn out to be successful.

SCIENCE

- Goal: the pursuit of knowledge and understanding for its own sake.
- Correseponding Scientific Processes.
- Discovery (controlled by experimentation).
- Analysis, generalization and creation of theories.
- Reductionism, involving the isolation and definition of distinct concepts.
- Making virtually value-free statements.
- The search for and theorizing about cause (e.g., gravity; electromagnetism).
- Pursuit of accuracy in modelling.
- Drawing correct conclusions based on good theories and accurate data.
- Experimental and logical skills.
- Using predictions that turn out to be incorrect to falsify or improve the theories or data on which they were based.

NORMS OF SCIENCE

The ethos of science is that affectively toned complex of values and norms which is held to be binding on the man of science. The norms are expressed in the form of prescriptions, proscriptions, preferences, and permissions. They are legitimatized in terms of institutional values. These imperatives, transmitted by precept and example and reinforced by sanctions are in varying degrees internalized by the scientist, thus fashioning his scientific conscience or, if one prefers the latter-day phrase, his superego. Although the ethos of science has not been codified, it can be inferred from the moral consensus of scientists as expressed in use and wont, in countless writings on the scientific spirit and in moral indignation directed toward contraventions of the ethos. Let's break that down:

The norms Merton has in mind are statements of what scientists believe they ought to do, and what they believe they are allowed to do, and what it would be good for them to do. In other words, by "norms" we are not identifying whatever it is scientists normally do; sometimes what scientists normally do falls short of what they know they should do.

Scientists are not handed a rule book that includes the norms Merton is about to describe. Rather, they figure them out by paying attention to other scientists in their community to see what behaviors they reward and what behaviors they punish.

Members of the scientific community do spend some time talking about the norms—or at least, gnashing their teeth at what they view as egregious violations of the norms. But mostly scientists talk about the norms either when a scientist violates them or when someone outside the community of science attacks that community's reputation. When scientists are more or less living by the norms, scientists tend not to talk about them.

As a sociologist, Merton was interested in understanding science as a social group. He was not primarily concerned with providing some independent justification for how scientists conduct their research. It's worth noting, though, that he seemed to think the norms of science were good ones to have if you are interested in building good knowledge about the world:

The ***institutional goal of science*** is the extension of certified knowledge. The technical methods employed toward this end provide the relevant definition of knowledge: empirically confirmed and logically consistent statements of regularities (which are, in effect, predictions). The institutional imperatives (mores) derive from the goals and the methods. The entire structure of technical and moral norms implements the final objective. The technical norm or empirical evidence, adequate and reliable, is a prerequisite for sustained true prediction; the technical norm of logical consistency, a prerequisite for systematic and valid prediction. The mores of science possess a methodological rationale but they are binding, not only because they are procedurally efficient, but because they are believed right and good. They are moral as well as technical prescriptions.

If the tribe of science is a community defined by a common project—building a body of reliable knowledge about the world and how it works—the norms. Merton identifies are something like the shared values of that community, values that are taken to be essential to the project of the community. *Merton* thinks the values of modern science boil down to a set of ***four norms***:

UNIVERSALISM

This is the idea that the important issue for scientists is the content of claims about the world (or about the phenomena being studied), not the particulars about the people making those claims.

In other words, the tribe of science is committed to investigating knowledge claims made by graduate students as well as those made by Nobel Prize winners, those made by scientists at small colleges as well as those made at famous universities with huge endowments and buckets of grant money, those made by scientists in other countries as well as those made by scientists in one's own country. Since the shared goal is building a reliable body of knowledge about the world we share, all the scientists engaged in that project are to be treated as capable to contribute. Disregarding another scientist's report because of who he is, then, is a breach of the norm of universalism.

"COMMUNISM"

Writing in 1942, Merton was careful to put this in scare-quotes. He's not talking about Marxist-Leninist Communism, but about the view that scientific knowledge is a resource to be shared by the whole tribe of science, regardless of which individual scientists produced which particular bits of knowledge.

In other words, ideally, if you establish a finding, you get recognition within the tribe for finding it, you may even get your name on an equation, but then that finding is public knowledge that anyone in the tribe of science can use to build additional knowledge (which itself is to be shared by the tribe of science).

One of the things a scientist needs to do to live up to this norm is to communicate her findings to other scientists. If a result stays in your head, or even your lab notebook, it's not ending up in the shared body of scientific knowledge. Knowledge that is not made public does not help the tribe with its shared project.

DISINTERESTEDNESS

One way to think about the norm of disinterestedness is that scientists are not doing science primarily to get the big bucks, or fame, or attractive dates. Merton's description of this community value is a bit more subtle. He notes that disinterestedness is different from altruism, and that scientists need not be saints.

The best way to understand disinterestedness might be to think of how a scientist working within her tribe is different from an expert out in the world dealing with laypeople. The expert, knowing more than the layperson, could exploit the layperson's ignorance or his tendency to trust the judgment of the expert. The expert, in other words, could put one over on the layperson for her own benefit. This is how snake oil gets sold.

The scientist working within the tribe of science can expect no such advantage. Thus, trying to put one over on other scientists is a strategy that should not get you far. By necessity, the knowledge claims you advance are going to be useful primarily in terms of what they add to the shared body of scientific knowledge, if only because your being accountable to the other scientists in the tribe means that there is no value added to the claims from using them to play your scientific peers for chumps.

ORGANIZED SKEPTICISM

This is the value that balances universalism. Everyone in the tribe of science can advance knowledge claims, but every such claims that is advanced is scrutinized, tested, tortured to see if it really holds up. The claims that do survive the skeptical scrutiny of the tribe get to take their place in the shard body of scientific knowledge. This is also the norm that makes disinterestedness work — without organized skepticism, you might actually have a reasonable expectation of putting one over on your scientific peers for personal gain.

Merton sees these four norms as the values that scientists themselves take to be definitive of the scientific enterprise. However, Merton himself identified tendencies pulling in the opposite directions from these norms. He thought instances of scientists criticizing other scientists for not resisting these pulls were good evidence that scientists as a group were serious about the norms.

SOCIAL PROCESS OF INNOVATION

Everybody starts from the same place with respect to innovation. We know that innovation drives productivity growth, and, as a result, we focus our attention on the world of commercial enterprise. We do not think much about innovation in other sectors of the economy – the non-profit sector, the social sector, or, heaven forbid, the public sector. And yet each one of these sectors consumes resources and produces outputs. And every one of them is being reshaped by technology and by knowledge-based activity. So our productive potential, writ large, depends on the capacity for innovation across markets, governments, communities, and even families.

DEFINING INNOVATION

The most widely used definition of innovation comes from the Organisation for Economic Co-operation and Development (OECD). Paraphrased, this definition states that "Innovation is new or significantly improved products or processes introduced to the market".

According to the Oslo Manual, "Technological product and process (TPP) innovations comprise implemented technologically new products and processes and significant technological improvements in products and processes. A TPP innovation has been implemented if it has been introduced on the market (product innovation) or used within a production process (process innovation).... The TPP innovating firm is one that has implemented technologically new or significantly technologically improved products or processes during the period under review."

For the market and technology notion of innovation, the macro debate includes such issues as the under-investment in research and development (R&D), shortages of faculty to teach information technology, the number of patent applications in Canada compared to other countries, tax rates, exchange rates, consumer protection and government regulation. These are the subjects that tend to dominate the speeches of Canadian opinion leaders. But there are also micro issues which are the subtext for those speeches. They include innovation on the shop floor, workplace training, trade in intellectual property, and participation in IP networks involving suppliers, customers, educators, and researchers.

The dialogue image of innovation is also present in these speeches. Business leaders talk about skills, labour shortages, the war for talent. They talk about collaboration, behaviour change, entrepreneurship, ambition, and risk taking. They sometimes refer to good management and organizational culture.

But this discussion of the second image of innovation is too narrow. It focuses mainly on the supply of talent and the rhetoric of management science and does not pay enough attention to the subtleties or the importance of the processes at work in innovation. One important reason for this is that they tend to focus on codified knowledge, as opposed to tacit knowledge.

SOCIAL FOUNDATIONS OF INNOVATION

Susan McDaniel has written about "the macro-social contexts of risks, uncertainties, insecurities, education, health, environment and community." (There is also the micro context of the people interacting with each other in neighbourhoods, schools, and parks.) Now McDaniel's definition of the macro context is very broad, and perhaps hard for you to accept at first blush. So let me give you a practical example.

When the federal government was setting goals for the education system and for early childhood development, it was focussing on achievement – graduating with good literacy, numeracy, and problem-solving skills. But, when we look at the Employability Skills Profile created by a group of employers convened by the Conference Board in Canada, we find much more than traditional school achievement. The profile tells us that employers are looking for people who can work in teams and also autonomously, people who understand risk-taking and can make good judgement calls on risk.

So where do young people learn these social and interaction skills? Certainly they learn some of them in the classroom, but they also learn them through good recreation – sports, music, dance, and parks with mid-night basketball.

Young people need safe places to play, because that is where they learn to make rules, settle disputes, and take a leadership role. So recreation is an important part of the social infrastructure for innovation. Most middle class and well-to-do families are able to provide these opportunities, but the barriers to recreation for low-income families can be insuperable.

NEED FOR INNOVATION IN SOCIAL POLICY

Since Independence, India has endeavoured to bring economic and social change through science and technology. The effort has been both on upgrading the traditional skills to make them relevant and competitive and developing advanced capabilities in frontier areas of science and technology. The visionaries who led the growth of science and technology (S&T) in India were convinced that S&T could play an important role in transforming India in to a modern, industrialized society. Experience and results show that this confidence was well placed. Science, technology, and innovation are even more relevant today. Scientific knowledge and expertise, innovation, high technology, industrial infrastructure and skilled workforce are the currencies of this new era.

ROLE OF GOVERNMENTS IN THE INNOVATION SYSTEM—GLOBAL EXPERIENCE

There is a wide spectrum with regard to the extent to which governments can influence the innovation system. To a large extent, the approaches adopted by various nations in the direction of innovation systems have varied depending on the overall national economic orientation.

These approaches have ranged from a 'directed or coordinated' model such as the one selected by Japan, to a much more laissez faire model employed in the USA. Countries such as Canada and others in the European Union (EU) region have adopted models that fall in between those of Japan and the US, at least in terms of strategy and sector identification for leveraging innovations. Thus, from the standpoint of a national planning process, there are several approaches to directing and shaping the innovation-led development processes. Although there may be varying levels of the directed or coordinated functions of the governments in shaping the innovation infrastructure, most nations have recognized the similarity of needs for creating an innovation infrastructure.

CREATING AN INNOVATION INFRASTRUCTURE IN INDIA AND THE NEED FOR A NATIONAL INNOVATION POLICY

Often missing within discussions of innovation in the developed countries is the role of innovation for directly improving the livelihood or quality of life of the poor. The general assumption is that the market mechanism will take care of this. However, innovation may also be important for the delivery of, and access to, services that are essential for a quality of life; whether it is clean water, modern energy or affordable health care. In terms of an innovation policy for India, this may be an important and distinguishing feature.

The forward plan of India is towards faster and more inclusive growth. Faster growth in a globally competitive market environment demands a national innovation infrastructure that connects knowledge systems to wealth creation efficiently and effectively. In the Indian social context, there is a need to ensure that innovative growthlinked processes do not bypass the poor and leave them out of developmental choices emanating from the benefits of globally competitive innovations. Therefore, the Indian model for innovation should be unique. The innovation infrastructure of India should aim to bridge the internal asymmetries and serve the dual purpose associated with global competitiveness and inclusive growth.

Both pro-poor and global competitiveness objectives should be embedded in the search for innovations. The number of grass-root innovators in the informal sector in India is large. However, grass-root innovations are not able to reap sufficient economic benefits for want of backing with adequate resources. The innovation infrastructure in the formal sector is thin. It requires deepening by referencing to global best practices and market demands. Such an innovation infrastructure would depend strongly upon a vibrant and gainful PPP in research and development as well as commercialization of innovations.

The prevailing asymmetry between inventors and investors is required to be bridged. Financing systems for backing up early-stage innovations with risk capital are required. Provisions for exiting from non-profitable innovations also need to be made. Innovations created at the expense of considerable investment of resources would demand a matching Intellectual Property Rights (IPR) regime. While the legal framework for protecting IPR is in place, infrastructure for capturing and protecting IPR is still evolving in India. Use of technology tools and capacity building in the area of IPR management require scaling up. New approaches and programmes are essential for unleashing India's innovation potential. Competitiveness innovation cluster has emerged as a successful global concept. Such innovation clusters in which academia, research and industry partner under viable and equitable PPP are the way forward.

The design and development of a sustainable innovation infrastructure should take into account global best practices, attraction, attachment, retention and renovation of talent within the research and development streams, PPPs, venture and angel financing and capacity building. The realization of Indian Vision 2025 to emerge as a major economic power in the global knowledge economy would call for a sustainable innovation infrastructure.

At the root of innovation is invention, which is an essential creative step that cannot really be directed or forced. However, there is much that can be done to facilitate this initial step and the many subsequent steps that will ultimately yield the value to society from the invention. These steps are not isolated or distinct from one another; therefore it is more appropriate to think of a comprehensive innovation policy, rather than a policy that is aimed at only one of the steps in the process or elements of the innovation system. Innovation policy needs to be placed within the broader social and economic context, informed by goals and aspirations of development and should reflect a fair and effective balance between public and private interests, social and economic goals and inclusiveness versus rapidity.

In order to unleash our full innovative potential, we need to put in place a National Innovation policy, which encourages competition among enterprises, greater diffusion of knowledge and increased support to early stage technology development initiatives and grass root level innovators. We need to foster increased collaboration among R&D institutes, universities and private sector enterprises and leverage upon their cumulative strengths in designing and implementing various innovation programmes. There is also a need for an appropriate legislative framework for incentivizing the innovators and commercialization of public funded R&D, where the government, the recipient(s) of funds, the inventor, as well as the public benefit from the protection and commercialization of IP.

SOCIAL CONTROL OF SCIENCE AND TECHNOLOGY

The last half of the 20th century has seen a significant increase in the use of science and technology for purposes of social control. Examples include video and audio surveillance, heat, light, motion, sound and olfactory sensors, electronic tagging of consumer items, animals and humans, biometric access codes, drug testing, DNA analysis and the use of computer techniques such as expert systems, matching and profiling, data mining, mapping, network analysis, and simulation. Control technologies have become available that previously existed only in the dystopic imaginations of science fiction writers. Many technologies developed for the military such as spy and global positioning satellites and night vision scopes have become commercially available.

As used here social control refers to efforts to enforce norms by preventing violations or discovering and apprehending violators, rather than to other aspects of social control such as the creation of norms, processes of adjudication and sanctioning, or the broad societal guidance and integration which was of concern to early theorists of industrialization and urbanization. The engineering of social control can be differentiated from related control forms such as the creation and manipulation of culture and socialization, the redistributive rewards of the welfare state and interpersonal influences. The increased prominence of social control via engineering is related to concerns over issues such as crime, terrorism, drug abuse, border controls, AIDS and economic competitiveness and to technical developments in electronics, computerization, artificial intelligence, bio-chemistry, architecture and materials science. The scale, mobility and anonymity of mass society and ironically, increased expectations of, an protections for privacy, have furthered reliance on external, impersonal, distance-mediated, secondary technical means and data-base memories that locate, identify, register, record, classify and validate or generate grounds for suspicion. The perception of catastrophic risks in an interdependent world relying on complex technologies and the entrepreneurial efforts of the security industry and governments such as the United States with its' war on drugs, have helped spread the technologies internationally.

There is a magisterial, legitimacy-granting aura around both law and science (Ericson and Shearing). Too often they serve as their own justification divorced from broader critical questions. Technological controls, presumably being science based, are justified as valid, objective, neutral, universal, consensual and fair. This view tends to overlook the fact that results are socially interpreted (and thus potentially disputable) and it overlooks the personal interests of control agents and the sectarian, socially constructed interests agents may represent. This legitimacy is strengthened in free market societies where the tactics can often be used by citizens (e.g., video cameras to record police behavior or DNA analysis offered by a criminal defendant) and internally by police managers for guarding the guards.

Of course the inventors and builders of the first locks, safes, moats and castles and the developers of early biometric identification systems (e.g., the Italian criminologist Cesare Lombroso 1835-1909) were engaged in the engineering of social control. What is new is the scale and relatively greater scientific precision, continual invention and experimentation and rapid global diffusion. Technical means of control saturate modern society, colonizing and documenting ever more areas of life. The roots of contemporary social control lie in the development of large organizations and standardized control technologies (Beniger). They are one strand of broad processes of rationalization, professionalization and specialization occuring with modernization.

The ratio of machines as protectors, monitors and controllers relative to humans continues to increase. Control has become softer and less visible partly because it is built-in (e.g., software that sends an internet message or shuts down if it is misused or that monitors work—such as the number of keystrokes entered or the driving behavior of truckers), and partly because of more sophisticated uses of deception (complex undercover operations and disguised video cameras). Much contemporary control is better symbolized by manipulation than coercion, by computer chips than prison bars, and by remote and invisible tethers and filters, than by handcuffs, straitjackets and physical walls. Being more covert, embedded and remote, it is often involuntary, occuring without the awareness or consent of its subject. Controllers are increasingly able to know things about subjects that the latter do not know about themselves and to make decisions affecting their life chances of which they are unaware.

Contemporary social control has become more extensive and casts a much wider net than at mid-twentieth century, continuing an expansionary trend that began with industrialization and the rise of the nation-state. Control involves ever more integrated information-sharing networks, blurring many traditional institutional and organizational borders (e.g., within and between agencies and levels of government, banks, insurance, health care, education, work, telecommunications and sales and marketing organizations). This data-sharing is taken further in the United States than in Canada or Europe. Technical controls are capital rather than labour-intensive and hence the cost of control per unit of information has decreased. More objects and areas are subjected to inspection and control and there is a broadening from the traditional targeting of a specific suspect, to categorical suspicion (e.g., the computer search, video camera, or metal detector capture information on all those within their province) and from individuals to networks and organizations.

Control has also become more intensive, probing deeply beneath protective surfaces. Many contemporary controls transcend boundaries of distance, darkness, physical barriers and time factors which traditionally protected liberty, as well as malfeasance. Data can be easily stored, retrieved, combined (from different places and in different forms such as visual, auditory, print and numerical), analyzed and communicated. Control may be remote and deterritorialized, with buffers between controllers and those controlled. Control and knowledge of other's behavior are no longer restricted to what the senses directly reveal through interaction, nor to a bounded physical place.

Contemporary social control themes are seen in their most extreme form in the maximum security prison (e.g., continuous surveillance, extensive use of computer dossiers, decisions about individuals based on actuarial data, the engineering of control). However with the spread of such controls throughout the society, we may ask if we are not moving toward becoming a maximum security society (Marx). The surveillance society's more omniscient and omnipresent technical social control is seen in a broad variety of rule enforcement contexts beyond public policing or prisons. The original 18th century French notion of an all-knowing, absorbent political police (Brodeur) to protect the state, has become generalized across institutions and applied by new users and for new goals.

A reliance on technology for social control is a hallmark of private police who, in the United States (although not in Europe), far out number public police. It is also seen in the workplace, the marketplace, schools and even among friends and family members. In the case of children for example there are at home video and audio room monitors, geographic location devices for tracking teenagers in cars, drug tests, beepers, records of phone and computer use and internet content filters that censor what can be accessed. Consider also "intelligent highway systems" or the "smart homes" that are appearing on the market in which all data flows into, and out of, the home are part of an integrated, continuously monitored system.

SIX SOCIAL ENGINEERING STRATEGIES

Target Removal: The logic of prevention is clearest and most effective here. Something that is not there can not be taken. The move toward a cashless society is one example. Merchants who only accept credit or debit cards, or whose registers never have more than a modest amount of cash are unlikely to be conventionally robbed. Furniture built into the wall cannot be stolen. Subway and bus exteriors built with graffiti resistant metals are hard to draw upon. Through software programming, computers and telephones can be blocked from sending or receiving messages to, or from, selected locations.

Target Devaluation: Here the goal is to reduce or eliminate the value of a potential target to anyone but authorized users. The target remains, but its uselessness makes it unattractive to predators. Examples include products which self-destruct, as with some car radios when stolen, or which leave clear proof of theft, as with exploding red dye packs that stain money taken in bank robberies. Encrypted messages can often be easily intercepted, however absent the decryption code, the data are useless. Telephones, computers, automobiles and even guns are increasingly available which can only be used with access devices such as a unique biometric identifier (e.g., retinal, voice or geometric hand pattern), card or access code.

Target Insulation: With this ancient technique the object of desire remains, but it is protected. Perimeter maintaining strategies such as fences, walls, moats, guards, and guards dogs can be separated from more specific protections surrounding an object such as safes, chastity belts, goods that are in locked cases or chained to an immovable object and the hiding or disguising of valuables. High security, gated communities in which access and egress is carefully controlled and the use of networked sensors, alarms, and in some cases even internet video of public areas, are becoming more common . The architectural development of "skywalks" linking downtown private buildings creates "sanitary zones" more subject to control than the potentially disorderly public streets below.

Offender Incapacitation: This classic strategy seeks to render potential offenders harmless with respect to the will, or ability, to violate the norm in question. The means may act directly on the body by permanently altering it and making certain offenses impossible – literal or chemical castration for sex offenders, cutting off the hands of thieves. Passivity may be created by tranquilizers and other medications such as Depo-Provera or psycho-surgery for the violent. A variety of non-lethal restraining or blocking devices from pepper spray to straight jackets to a net fired over a disruptive person are available. Related efforts deal not with the body of the offender but with the instrumentalities involved in the offense. The goal is to render useless or unavailable something that is essential for the violation. For example anti-drunk driving interlock systems which require passing a breath analyzer test attached to the automobile ignition system before a car will start, or limiting gun purchases to those who have undergone computer checks for purchase eligibility (e.g., no felony conviction) and not permitting adolescents to purchase magic markers that can be used for graffiti, or mixing a bad smelling chemical into a product to prevent it from being inhaled for its' hallucinatory effects.

Exclusion: Potential offenders have traditionally been kept away from targets or tempting environments by exile, prison, curfew and place or activity exclusions (e.g., bars for juveniles or the home of an ex-spouse for an abusing husband). The ultimate form is capital punishment. A related form is the visible warning offered by a stigma such as the brand or clipped ear of offenders in medieval Europe, which encouraged others to stay away. Electronic monitoring or location devices based on Global Positioning Satellites are contemporary examples. In one form alarms go off and messages are sent to authorities if an adjudicated person wearing a transmitter gets too close to a prohibited person or area or leaves an areas they are restricted to. With the human genome project completed, eugenics will become a contentious issue. For example the belief (which ignores interactions with the environment and the socially crafted character of most rules) that DNA is linked to violence and other anti-social behavior could generate another ultimate form of exclusion—requiring a license indicating an "acceptable" genetic pattern before a child could be born.

Offense/Offender/Target Identification: Where it is not actually possible to prevent the violation physically, or where that is too expensive, it may be possible to at least know that it took place and perhaps who is responsible and where they are. The goal is to document its occurrence, and identify the violator. A major goal of nineteenth century forensic science was to develop reliable biometric measures of identity based on the analysis of fingerprints, facial measurements, and chemical properties (Thorwald 1965). One technique used by the former East Germany involved identifying individuals by their unique olifactors. Architectural design emphasizing visibility as a deterrent fits here (Newman 1972), as do video, audio, motion, and heat detection means and access codes that are presumed to document who enters an area, or is using a resource such as a computer. Hand-activated personal alarm systems, or a luggage alarm that goes off if a purse or suitcase is illegitimately moved or opened and the electronic tagging of consumer items or expensive tools at work which give off an alarm if wrongly removed are other examples. New information technologies have made it possible not only to watch everyone, but for everyone to be a watcher. This greater ease of mobilizing the law by involving citizens in social control is one characteristic of the Anglo-American police tradition, although not in the rest of Europe. Citizens are encouraged to use hot lines to report infractions (e.g., erratic highway drivers, drug dealing, poaching or "whistle-blowing" regarding organizational malfeasance) via cell and traditional telephones and e-mail. The police use mass communications media to help identify and locate wanted persons via posting warrant information on web cites and crime re-enactments on television.

SOME OTHER SOCIAL CONTROL DIMENSIONS

The six "ideal type" concepts above are based on combining several aspects such as whether the focus is on the potential offender, a resource used in the violation, the offence or the target of an offence and whether the action involves removal/exclusion, devaluation, insulation, incapacitation or identification. Such ideal types can be useful as a short hand for classification and comparison. Yet they also distort by combining sources of variation that can be analyzed separately.

Another approach starts with single dimensions which may cut across the different forms. Some other relevant dimensions include classifying based on: visibility or invisibility; openness or secrecy regarding use of the tactic both generally and specifically; control access into or out of a system; the individual, an organization or a network; a focus on the body, consciousness or the environment; the degree of reliability and validity and relative cost of errors and mistakes; the relative availability and ease or difficulty in neutralizing or using a tactic; and the presence or absence of democratic decision-making and review processes regarding the adoption and application of a tactic.

There has historically been much more research on those who violate rules than on those who enforce them. We know little about the prior social correlates and consequences of the above dimensions. While anyone who travels will see a certain international standardization of technical control (e.g., at airports, national borders, banks, nuclear power plants, or with telecommuncations) there is still much local variation. Distinctive histories, social organization and cultures mean that sweeping generalizations across all technologies and countries are unwarranted (Marx). Singapore for example appears to have taken electronic surveillance the furthest, while Japan and China are far behind (if for different reasons). In the United States drug testing, undercover operations, citizen informers and consumer and work monitoring are widespread, while in Europe these are seen much less often. Great Britain is the world leader in video surveillance and Germany has been among the most innovative in computer matching and profiling. The Scandinavian countries make the most extensive use of social census data as part of their welfare states. France, Italy and Spain have been generally slower than Anglo-American countries to adopt the new technologies. While the polygraph is rarely used in Europe because of doubts about its validity, handwriting analysis has a credibility in France that is lacking in most other countries.

SOME SOCIAL AND ETHICAL IMPLICATIONS

However ideal a technical control system may appear in the abstract from the viewpoint of those advocating it, the world of application is often much messier and more complicated. The search for the perfect technical fix is like the donkey forever chasing the carrot suspended in front of it. To the person with a hammer everything may look like a nail. The technology's narrowing of focus may come at a cost of failing to see larger systemic contexts, alternatives and longer range consequences. The complexity and fluidity of human situations makes this a rich area for the study of trade-offs, irony and paradox. There are some parallels to iatrogenetic medical practices in which one problem is cured, but at a cost of creating another. Technical efforts to insure conformity may be hindered by conflicting goals, unintended consequences, displacement, lessened equity, complacency, neutralization, invalidity, escalation, system overload, a negative image of personal dignity and the danger of the means determining, or becoming ends.

Bars over windows to keep out thieves may prevent occupants from escaping through the window in the event of a fire. In commercial settings where access to merchandise is important, attaching expensive clothes (e.g., leather jackets) to a rack with a locked cable reduces the likelihood that an item will be stolen, but also complicates trying clothes on and impulse buying.

The discovery that a target has been rendered useless to an offender may increase violence, whether as a resource to gain the needed access, or out of frustration. For example the appearance of "car-jacking" is related to more sophisticated anti-theft devices on cars. The use of access codes to activate autos and appliances may mean that the crime of burglary is converted to robbery or kidnapping, as thieves confront property owners and demand not only the property, but the code to make it work. A frustrated thief may respond to a self-destruct automobile radio by fire-bombing the car.

While the rule breaking in question may be blocked, the problem may be displaced rather than disappear or new problems may be created. In efforts to keep the homeless away from heating vents or entrances to subway systems, a variety of grates and barriers have been developed. These do nothing to solve the issue of homelessness, but move it elsewhere. Some persons manage to get off of heroin but only by becoming addicted to methadone. Equity issues are raised when displacement involves a shift to new victims. If relatively effective technical solutions are commercialized (as with embedding hidden transmitters in cars which permits locating them by remotely activating the transmitter) or gated communities to keep out would-be thieves, predators may focus greater attention on those unable to afford enhanced levels of security.

A related equity issue involves who has access to the technology and its results. Video cameras and desk top computers are potentially egalitarian in their low cost, ease of use and wide spread availability. But other technologies such as satellites and highly sophisticated computer programs are disproportionately available to the most powerful. There is the possibility of societies becoming an even more stratified based on unequal access to information in which individuals live in glass houses, while the external wall of large organizations, whether government or private, are one-way mirrors. Whether out of self-interested rule breaking or human contrariness, individuals can be very creative in neutralizing systems of control. Faith in the technology and its routinization may create complacency in control agents and a predictability that undermines effectiveness. That locks open with keys and borders require access points means they are eternally vulnerable.

The initial anti-drunk driving car interlock systems could be beaten by saving air in a balloon or by having someone else blow into it to start the car. A variety of means are available for beating drug tests—from contaminating the urine with bleach on one's hand to using a catheter to insert drug-free urine into the body. Dogs in heat have been used as antidotes to male guard dogs and debugging devices help discover hidden surveillance. In a free market economy new controls create incentives to develop means of neutralization, whether legally or available through the black market. Police use of radar detectors against speeders were soon followed by anti-radar detection devices. Police in turn developed a tool for detecting when a driver was using the latter. The guilty may now face charges for the secondary or derivative offense of possession, even if they were not speeding. Not long after anti-theft ignition protection systems appeared on automobiles, a device that permitted by-passing the lock appeared.

When systems cannot be technically defeated as with very sophisticated encryption, then their human context may be compromised, whether through coercion or deception. For example a thief who could not break a manufacturer's sophisticated encryption code, never-the-less managed to embezzle millions of dollars through generating fake invoices. He did this by having an affair with the individual who had the decryption codes.

There are also important questions around validity and reliability. Even if a measure is empirically valid that does not guarantee a socially meaningful result. Thus a DNA match between material from a crime scene and a suspect can not reveal if a death resulted from a homicide or self-defense. The sample might also have been planted, or a secure chain of evidence custody not maintained. A computer match between persons on welfare and those with bank accounts may reveal a person over the savings limits, but that is not proof of cheating since funds may be held in trust for a funeral—something legally permitted, but not built into the computer program. Audio and video recordings may reflect what was done and said, but will not necessarily reveal why, or what a suspect intended. Seeing should not automatically mean believing. Thus a suspect in an undercover scheme may have been threatened or entrapped off-camera. A threat or seeming admission of a crime may have been said in jest or as boasting. Nor is a drug test, even if "valid" indicating the presence of drug's within a person's system, a necessary indication of a violation. Depending on the assessment used, if the standard is set low enough it is possible to have a positive reading as a result of just being in a room where marijuana is being smoked (false positive).

Conversely justice issues involving false negatives may also be raised if the threshold is set too high. Drug tests may also be distorted by what an individual has eaten (e.g., poppy seeds) or by some over-the counter medications. Tests may be of doubtful validity to begin with. Concern over the validity of the polygraph led the United States Congress to greatly restrict its use (although that led to an increase in paper and pencil honesty tests whose validity has also been questioned).

New control techniques may be turned against control agents. While authorities may have an initial advantage, this is often short lived. Thus more powerful armor, bullet proof vests and sophisticated communication systems are no longer the sole property of police. There maybe something of an escalating domestic arms race in which the interaction becomes more sophisticated, but the fundamental dynamic does not change.

Documentation of all infractions may overload the control system. This may lower morale among enforcers who feel overwhelmed, or offer corrupt officials a resource (non-enforcement) to market. Since resources for acting on all the information may not be available, authorities may be accused of discriminatory enforcement.

Even if adequate resources for full enforcement action were available, organizational effectiveness could be harmed. Automatic technical solutions developed without adequate appreciation of complexity and contingency run the risk of eliminating the discretion, negotiation, compromise and informal understandings that are often central to morale and the effective working of organizations.

If technical solutions could some how be effective at eliminating all rule breaking (holding apart the conflict between, and ambiguity, and lack of consensus on, many rules), there could be some unexpected costs. Systems might become too rigid and unable to change. Much innovation is initially seen as deviance. Experimentation and risk taking can be aided by anonymity and secrecy. A socially transparent, engineered society would be more orderly, but likely less creative, dynamic and free.

If order depended primarily on technical means of blocking infractions, rather than on legitimacy, how would people behave when the means failed, as at some points they invariably would? A social order based primarily on technical fixes is likely to be as fragile over time as one based primarily on overt repression.

Even if systems could some how be made fool and fail-proof with ever more, and more advanced technology, there is a danger of viewing humans as robots, rather than as creative beings with a conscience capable of making choices about how they behave. The former image is inconsistent with belief in the dignity of the autonomous individual in a democratic society. Whatever a technology is capable of, the view of humans as volitional (and hence responsible for their behavior) and beliefs about the inviolability (absent clear justification) of the borders that protect private personal zones around one's body, mind, relationships, communications, physical space and past history are central to ideas of respect for personhood.

The search for stand-alone mechanical solutions also avoids the need to ask why some individuals break the rules and points away from examining the social conditions which may contribute to violations and the possibility of changing those conditions. Technical solutions seek to bypass the need to create consensus and a community in which individuals act responsibly as a result of voluntary commitment to the rules, not because they have no choice, or only out of fear of reprisals.

A well known, if often naïve expression given social inequality, holds that where there is a will there is a way. This speaks to the role of human effort in obtaining goals. With the control possibilities made available by science and technology this may be reversed to where there is a way there is a will. As the myth of Frankenstein implies, we must be ever vigilant to be sure that we control the technology rather than the reverse. As Jacques Ellul (1964) argues there is a danger of self-amplifying technical means silently coming to determine the ends or even becoming ends in themselves, divorced from a vision of, and the continual search for, the good society.

SUCCESS OF SCIENCE AND TECHNOLOGY

Technology permeates every level of our ever changing, advancing society. Today's employment outlook suggests the value of math, science, and technology coursework for future employment success.

Broadly defined, technology comprises the processes, devices, products, and systems through which individuals and organizations meet their needs and wants by modifying nature.

In preparation for future career success, students can benefit by being well versed in basic math, science, and technology skills. These skills form the basis for a broad array of career opportunities. The pervasive need for math, science, and technology skills across the board, no matter which of the projected top growth careers is chosen.

Basic math, science, and technology skills are essential for career success in the twenty-first century. It is not only science and computer-oriented careers that require fundamental math, science, and technology skills; in fact, many of the top growth industries require these same skills. Students, parents, and teachers should heed the value of math, science, and technology coursework and competence as elemental preparation for any career pursuit.

GENDER AND HUMAN SEXUALITY

Gender. Why Gender and Not Sex? Social Construction of Gender. Gender and Work. Gender Inequality. Changing Gender. Human Sexuality. Methods of Research in Human Sexuality: *Survey Method, Observational Method, Experimental Method, Correlational Method, Case Study Method, Biological Perspective, Cognitive Perspective, Learning Perspective.*

GENDER

Gender, race, ethnicity, and social class are the most commonly used categories in sociology. They represent the major social statuses that determine the life chances of individuals in heterogeneous societies, and together they form a hierarchy of access to property, power, and prestige.

Gender is the division of people into two categories, "men" and "women." Through interaction with caretakers, socialization in childhood, peer pressure in adolescence, and gendered work and family roles, women and men are socially constructed to be different in behaviour, attitudes, and emotions. The gendered social order is based on and maintains these differences.

In sociology, the main ordering principles of social life are called institutions. Gender is a social institution as encompassing as the four main institutions of traditional sociology—family, economy, religion, and symbolic language. Like these institutions, gender structures social life, patterns social roles, and provides individuals with identities and values. And just as the institutions of family, economy, religion, and language are intertwined and affect each other reciprocally, as a social institution, gender pervades kinship and family life, work roles and organizations, the rules of most religions, and the symbolism and meanings of language and other cultural representations of human life. The outcome is a gendered social order.

Gender in art is shown through everyday images like television, advertisements, magazines, and more. Gender has become a stereotype. Both Men and Women experience gender roles and the side effects every single day.

The source of gendered social orders lies in the evolution of human societies and their diversity in history. The gendered division of work has shifted with changing means of producing food and other goods, which in turn modifies patterns of child care and family structures. Gendered power imbalances, which are usually based on the ability to amass and distribute material resources, change with rules about property ownership and inheritance. Men's domination of women has not been the same throughout time and place; rather, it varies with political, economic, and family structures, and is differently justified by religions and laws. As an underlying principle of how people are categorized and valued, gender is differently constructed throughout the world and has been throughout history. In societies with other major social divisions, such as race, ethnicity, religion, and social class, gender is intricately intertwined with these other statuses.

As pervasive as gender is, it is important to remember that it is constructed and maintained through daily interaction and therefore can be resisted, reformed, and even rebelled against. The social construction perspective argues that people create their social realities and identities, including their gender, through their actions with others—their families, friends, colleagues. It also argues that their actions are hemmed in by the general rules of social life, by their culture's expectations, their workplace's and occupation's norms, and their government's laws. These social restraints are amenable to change—but not easily.

Gender is deeply rooted in every aspect of social life and social organization in Western-influenced societies. The Western world is a very gendered world, consisting of only two legal categories—"men" and "women." Despite the variety of playful and serious attempts at blurring gender boundaries with androgynous dress and desegregating gender-typed jobs, third genders and gender neutrality are rare in Western societies. Those who cross gender boundaries by passing as a member of the opposite gender, or by sex-change surgery, want to be taken as a "normal" man or woman.

Although it is almost impossible to be anything but a "woman" or a "man," a "girl" or a "boy" in Western societies, this does not mean that one cannot have three, four, five, or more socially recognized genders—there are societies that have at least three. Not all societies base gender categories on male and female bodies— Native Americans, for example, have biological males whose gender status is that of women. Some African societies have females with the gender status of sons or husbands. Others use age categories as organizing principles, not gender statuses. Even in Western societies, where there are only two genders, we can think about restructuring families and workplaces so they are not as rigidly gendered as they are today.

WHY GENDER AND NOT SEX?

Gender was first conceptualized as distinct from sex in order to highlight the social and cultural processes that constructed different social roles for females and males and that prescribed sexappropriate behaviour, demeanor, personality characteristics, and dress. However, sex and gender were often conflated and interchanged, to the extent that this early usage was called "sex roles" theory. More recently, gender has been conceptually separated from sex and also from sexuality.

Understanding gender practices and structures is easier if what is usually conflated as sex/gender or sex/sexuality/gender is split into three conceptually distinct categories—sex (or biology, physiology), sexuality (desire, sexual preference, sexual orientation, sexual behaviour), and gender (social status, position in the social order, personal identity). Each is socially constructed but in different ways. Gender is an overarching category—a major social status that organizes almost all areas of social life. Therefore bodies and sexuality are gendered—biology and sexuality, in contrast, do not add up to gender.

Conceptually separating sex and gender makes it easier to explain how female and male bodies are socially constructed to be feminine and masculine through sports and in popular culture. In medicine, separating sex from gender helps to pinpoint how much of the differences in longevity and propensity to different illnesses is due to biology and how much to socially induced behaviour, such as alcohol and drug abuse, which is higher among men than women. The outcome is a greater number of recorded illnesses but longer life expectancy for women of all races, ethnicities, and social classes when compared to men with the same social characteristics. This phenomenon is known in social epidemiology as "women get sicker, but men die quicker."

SOCIAL CONSTRUCTION OF GENDER

As with any other aspect of social life, gender is shaped by an individual's genetic heritage, physical body, and physiological development. Socially, however, gendering begins as soon as the sex of the fetus is identified. At birth, infants are placed in one of two sex categories, based on the appearance of the genitalia. In cases of ambiguity, since Western societies do not have a third gender for hermaphrodites as some cultures do, the genitalia are now "clarified" surgically, so that the child can be categorized as a boy or a girl. Gendering then takes place through interaction with parents and other family members, teachers, and peers ("significant others"). Through socialization and gendered personality development, the child develops a gendered identity that, in most cases, reproduces the values, attitudes, and behaviour that the child's social milieu deems appropriate for a girl or a boy.

Borrowing from Freudian psychoanalytic theory, Nancy Chodorow developed an influential argument for the gendering of personalities in the two-parent, heterogendered nuclear family. Because women are the primary parents, infants bond with them. Boys have to separate from their mothers and identify with their fathers in order to establish their masculinity. They thus develop strong ego boundaries and a capacity for the independent action, objectivity, and rational thinking so valued in Western culture. Women are a threat to their independence and masculine sexuality because they remind men of their dependence on their mothers. However, men need women for the emotional sustenance and intimacy they rarely give each other. Their ambivalence toward women comes out in heterosexual love–hate relationships and in misogynistic depictions of women in popular culture and in novels, plays, and operas.

Girls continue to identify with their mothers, and so they grow up with fluid ego boundaries that make them sensitive, empathic, and emotional. It is these qualities that make them potentially good mothers and keep them open to men's emotional needs. But because the men in their lives have developed personalities that make them emotionally guarded, women want to have children to bond with. Thus, psychological gendering of children is continually reproduced.

To develop nurturing capabilities in men and to break the cycle of the reproduction of gendered personality structures would, according to this theory, take fully shared parenting. There is little data on whether the same psychic processes produce similarly gendered personalities in singleparent families, in households where both parents are the same gender, or in differently structured families in non-Western cultures.

Children are also gendered at school, in the classroom, where boys and girls are often treated differently by teachers. Boys are encouraged to develop their math abilities and science interests; girls are steered toward the humanities and social sciences. The result is that women students in the United States outnumber men students in college, but only in the liberal arts; in science programs, men still outnumber women. Men also predominate in enrollment in the elite colleges, which prepare for high-level careers in finance, the professions, and government.

This data on gender imbalance, however, when broken down by race, ethnicity, and social class, is more complex. In the United States, upper- and middle-class boys are pushed ahead of girls in school and do better on standardized tests, although girls of all social statuses get better grades than boys. African-American, Hispanic, and white working-class and poor boys do particularly badly, partly because of a peer culture that denigrates"book learning" and rewards defiance and risk taking. In the context of an unresponsive educational structure, discouraged teachers, and crowded, poorly maintained school buildings, the pedagogical needs of marginal students do not get enough attention; they are also much more likely to be treated as discipline problems.

Children's peer culture is another site of gender construction. On playgrounds, girls and boys divide up into separate groups whose borders are defended against opposite-gender intruders. Within the group, girls tend to be more cooperative and play people-based games. Boys tend to play rulebased games that are competitive. These tendencies have been observed in Western societies; anthropological data about children's socialization shows different patterns of gendering. Everywhere, children's gender socialization is closely attuned to expected adult behaviour.

GENDER AND WORK

Whether they have fully internalized Western society's gender binarism and social construction of gender differences or rebelled against gender typing, adults encounter a gendered work world. The workplaces in industrialized societies are either gender-segregated or composed of all one gender. During the 1970s and 1980s, decades in which women were thought to have made inroads into many occupations previously dominated by men in the United States, about 6 percent of occupations saw an increase of women workers that was significantly greater than the increase of women overall in the paid labour force during that period. Rather than desegregating occupations, most of the new women workers went into occupations where most of the employees were women, and those who went into occupations where the employees were predominantly men soon found that their coworkers became predominantly women. Some U.S. occupations that went from having a predominance of workers who were men to mostly women workers were personnel, training, and labour relations specialists; computer operators; and insurance adjusters, examiners, and investigators. These occupations had resegregated. When women and men work in nontraditional occupations, gender typing is often maintained symbolically, as when policewomen view their work as social work and men nurses emphasize the technical and physical strength aspects of what they do.

The processes that sort women and men of different racial and ethnic groups into different types of work include a matching of ranked workers and jobs, or queues of workers and jobs. Workers are ranked by employers from their first picks to their last. Jobs are ranked by workers similarly. Lower-ranked workers get the chance to move into better jobs than they have held in the past when these jobs are abandoned by favored workers or there are too few of these workers to go around, such as in wartime. The process works the other way, too; when there are too few of the best jobs for the preferred workers, as in a recession, only the best qualified or experienced among them will be hired; those with fewer credentials and less seniority move down the queue, bumping out lower-ranked workers. When workers are moving up, the most preferred on the basis of race, ethnicity, and gender usually get the better jobs. If gender segregation is so rigid that men will not apply or be hired for "women's work," when manufacturing jobs decline or are taken elsewhere, women in service, sales, and clerical work may continue to work as men's unemployment rates rise.

Workers rank jobs on the basis of payoff for education and experience in salaries and also in fringe benefits, prestige, autonomy, security, and chances of promotion. For some workers, having any job may be an improvement over economic dependency. Employers' preferences for workers, however, are not so uniform. Some will rank gender and race above qualifications; others will choose the most highly qualified of the preferred race and gender and then go down the line, looking for the most qualified each time. Another variable employers factor in is the going pay scale for the workers they want; they may have to settle for less preferred workers to see more of a profit or sacrifice some profits to avoid protests from highly paid entrenched workers.

Although worker demographics, industry growth, and employer preferences produce changes in occupational gender composition, the main factor that redistributes workers of different races and genders is change in the structure of the work process and in the quality of particular jobs within occupations, which can be manipulated by employers. That is, jobs can be automated and deskilled or made part time or home based to justify reducing labour costs, with a few better-paid workers retained in supervisory positions.

During shifts of labour queues up and down the job ladder, the potential for conflict between women and men as well as between members of dominant and subordinated racial and ethnic groups is high. Dominant men want to perpetuate the work conditions that justify their high pay; employers who want to reduce their labour costs degrade the work process so they can hire cheaper labour, and then these new workers are accused of depressing the job's qualifications and skills. Gender segregation of jobs is historically the way employers have kept their men workers satisfied, while expanding the number of cheaper women workers. Such job divisions undercut unions that want to organize women and demand the same pay for them as similarly situated men workers. In a growing or stable job market, dominant men are much less resistant to incoming new types of workers, since they do not see them as competition. In those cases, the job may come closer to being integrated along lines of gender and race.

Occupational gender segregation does not result in separate but equal jobs. Rather, women's work tends to be lower in pay, prestige, and fringe benefits, such as health insurance. Workers themselves rate jobs where most of the employees are women as inferior to jobs where most of the employees are men. The criteria are number and flexibility of hours, earnings, educational requirements, on-the-job training, having a union contract, extent of supervision and place in the hierarchy, repetitiveness, risk of job loss, and being a government employee. Workers rate women's jobs as better in vacation days and not getting dirty at work, even though changing bedpans is as "dirty" as changing oil pans. If wages were used to compensate for unattractive nonmonetary job characteristics, women's jobs would have to pay four times as much as men's jobs for workers to rate them equally. Nor is there a trade-off of pay for compatibility with child care—most full-time jobs held by mothers are incompatible with parenting demands; flexibility of schedules and control and timing of work-related tasks are the prerogatives of men managers, not their women secretaries.

The best-paid jobs are shaped on an ideal, dominant man's career—long-term, continuous work in the same occupation, with steady pay raises and a pension at retirement. Men's gender status is an advantage to them as workers; they are expected to earn more money when they marry and when they have children, so employers tend to view them as better workers than women. Women workers are felt to be entitled only to supplementary wages, whether they are married or single, because they are not considered legitimate workers but primarily wives and mothers. In actuality, research has shown that married women with children work harder and are more productive than married men with children.

The structured patterns of opportunities and access far override most individual employers' tastes or individual workers' motivations, ambitions, personal desires, and material needs. By the 1970s in the United States, adolescent girls were considerably less likely than in previous years to plan on entering an occupation in which most of the workers were women, especially if they lived in a woman-headed household. But they continued to value working with people, helping others, using their abilities, and being creative; boys wanted jobs with status, high earnings, freedom from supervision, and leadership potential. The jobs women are likely to end up in are more gender typed and less fulfilling than their occupational aspirations, but ambitious and hard-working men can often reach their early goals.

Women of all educational levels and men disadvantaged because of race, immigrant status, lack of education, or outmoded job skills are profitable workers because they tend to receive low wages; they also get promoted less frequently and therefore receive fewer raises. Many work part time and get no benefits. They can be paid little because the pool of such workers is larger that of privileged men workers. The size and social characteristics of the pool of low-waged workers are affected by state policies encouraging or discouraging the employment of women, the influx of immigrants, and the flight of capital from one area of a country to another or offshore.

Other processes that segregate and stratify occupations are segmentation and ghettoization. Segmented occupations are horizontally or vertically divided into sectors with different educational or credential requirements for hiring, different promotion ladders, different work assignments, and different pay scales. Typically, these segments are gendered and frequently also exhibit racial and ethnic clustering. However, occupations in which almost all the workers are of one gender can also be segmented. For instance, in the United States, doctors and nurses are gender-segregated segments in hospitals. Physicians are segmented between those in primary care and those who are hospital-based specialists, who have more prestige and power and higher incomes. Women physicians are often found in primary care. Nursing is also segmented into registered nurses, licensed practical nurses, nurses' aides, and home health workers. Nurses are virtually all women, but the segments are racially differentiated: The majority of registered nurses tend to be white or Asian-American; most of the lower-paid health workers tend to be black or Hispanic. Men who go into nursing tend to specialize in the more lucrative specializations and become administrators.

Segmentation is legitimized by bureaucratic rules or legal requirements for qualifying credentials, but ghettoization separates the lower-paid "women's" jobs from the better-paid "men's" jobs within an occupation through informal gender typing. What is dubbed "women's work" or "men's work" has a sense of normality and naturalness, an almost moral quality, even though the justification for such typing is usually an after-the-fact rationalization. The assumption is that the skills, competence, strength, and other qualities needed to do a job are tied up with masculinity and femininity, but gendered identities as workers are constructed in the gendered organization of the workplace and reinforced in training and organizational sociability, such as company golf games and sports teams. Within gender-typed occupations, jobs or specialties may be gender typed in the opposite direction. For example, the majority of physicians are men in the United States and women in Russia, but the same specialties are seen as appropriate for one gender—pediatrics for women and neurosurgery for men. In both countries, neurosurgery pays better and has more prestige than pediatrics.

Both structural segmentation and gender typing that puts some jobs into a low-wage ghetto have the same results. They limit the extent of competition for the better positions, make it easier for privileged workers to justify their advantageous salary scales, and create a group of workers whose lack of credentials or requisite skills legitimate their lower pay. Credentials and skills, however, as well as experience, are manipulated or circumvented to favor workers with certain social characteristics, as when men with less lower-rank experience in women's jobs are hired as supervisors. In addition, femaleness and maleness are stereotypically linked to certain capabilities, such as finger dexterity and physical strength; gender then becomes the discriminant criterion for hiring, not what potential employees can actually do with their hands, backs, and heads.

Promotion ladders are also gender segregated. Women and men who are not of the dominant racial or ethnic group tend not to rise to the top in their work organization, unless practically all the workers are women or men of the same racial or ethnic group. White men tend to dominate positions of authority whether or not they are numerically predominant. This pattern is known as the glass ceiling—the lid on women's rise to the top of their work organizations. In occupations where the majority of the workers are women, positions of authority tend to be held by men—elementary school teachers are predominantly women in the United States, but principals and superintendents are predominantly men. That is, token men in a woman's occupation tend to be promoted faster than the women workers. This parallel phenomenon has been dubbed the glass escalator.

These pervasive patterns of occupational segregation and stratification are the result of deliberate actions and also inaction on the part of governments, owners and managers, and organized groups of workers—and change has to come from the same sources. Since gender segregation involves occupations and professions, job titles, and specific work sites, integration has to involve more than simply increasing the numbers of women. True occupational gender equality would mean that women and men would have the same opportunities to obtain professional credentials and occupational training, and would be distributed in the same proportions as they are in the paid work force across workplaces, job titles, occupations, and hierarchical positions. Instead, in most industrialized countries, women are overrepresented in clerical and service jobs, low-prestige professional and technical work, and sales. In developing countries, and in areas of industrialized countries where there are concentrations of poor people and recent immigrants, women tend to be concentrated in labour-intensive factory work, agriculture, and the informal (off-the-books) economy.

This gendered organization of paid labour dovetails with the gendered organization of domestic labour. Low pay, uninteresting jobs, and the glass ceiling encourage single women to marry and married women to devote energy and attention to child rearing and domestic work. The job market encourages women to be a reserve army of labour—available for full-time work in times of scarce labour, but fired or put on part-time schedules when there is less work. Better job opportunities are offered to men of the dominant racial and ethnic groups to encourage them to give their all to the job. Employers (mostly men) benefit from women's cheap labour and men's need to earn more to support a family; men who live with women benefit from women's unpaid labour at home. Highly educated and professional women are caught in the structural conflicts of these two forms of labour; in order to compete with the men of their status, they have to hire "wives"—other women to do their domestic work. This pool of paid domestic labour historically is made up of the least advantaged women—native poor and recent immigrants of a variety of racial and ethnic groups.

Women empowerment and gender equality.

GENDER INEQUALITY

Gender inequality takes many different forms, depending on the economic structure and social organization of a particular society and on the culture of any particular group within that society. Although we speak of gender inequality, it is usually women who are disadvantaged when compared to similarly situated men. In the job market, women often receive lower pay for the same or comparable work and are frequently blocked in their chances for advancement, especially to top positions. There is usually an imbalance in the amount of housework and child care a wife does compared to her husband, even when both spend the same amount of time in waged work outside the home. When women professionals are matched with men of comparable productiveness, men get greater recognition for their work and move up career ladders faster. On an overall basis, work most often done by women, such as teaching small children and nursing, is paid less than work most often done by men, such as computer programming and engineering. Gender inequality also takes the form of girls getting less education than boys of the same social class. It often means an unequal distribution of health care services between women and men, and research priorities that focus on diseases men are more likely to get than women.

Gender inequality takes even more oppressive and exploitative forms. Throughout the world, women are vulnerable to beatings, rape, and murder—often by their husbands or boyfriends, and especially when they try to leave an abusive relationship. The bodies of girls and women are used in sex work—pornography and prostitution. They undergo cosmetic surgery and are on display in movies, television, and advertising in Western cultures. In other cultures, their genitals are mutilated and their bodies are covered from head to toe in the name of chastity. They may be forced to bear children they do not want or have abortions or be sterilized against their will. In countries with overpopulation, infant girls are much more often abandoned in orphanages than infant boys. In cultural groups that value boys over girls, if the sex of the fetus can be determined, it is girls who are aborted.

Gender inequality can also disadvantage men. In many countries, only men serve in the armed forces, and in most countries, only men are sent into direct combat. It is mostly men who do the more dangerous work, such as firefighting and policing. Although women have fought in wars and are entering police forces and fire departments, the gender arrangements of most societies assume that women will do the work of bearing and caring for children, while men do the work of protecting them and supporting them economically.

Most women in industrial and postindustrial societies do not spend their lives having and caring for babies, and most women throughout the world do paid and unpaid work to supply their families with food, clothing, and shelter, even while they are taking care of children. The modern forms of gender inequality are not a complementary exchange of responsibilities, but a social system within which women are exploitable. In a succinct summary of gender inequality, it was estimated by a United Nations report in 1980 that women do two-thirds of the world's work, receive 10 percent of the world's income, and own 1 percent of the world's property.

The major social and cultural institutions support this system of gender inequality. Religions legitimate the social arrangements that produce it, justifying them as right and proper. Laws support the status quo and also often make it impossible to redress the outcomes—to prosecute husbands for beating their wives, or boyfriends for raping their girlfriends. In the arts, women's productions are so often ignored that they are virtually invisible, which led Virginia Woolf to conclude that Anonymous must have been a woman. Much scientific research assumes that differences between women and men are genetic or hormonal and looks for data to support these beliefs, ignoring findings that show gender overlaps or input from the social environment. In the social sciences, gender is entered into research designs only as a binary, erasing the effects of racial, social class, and ethnic variations.

Except for the Scandinavian countries, which have the greatest participation of women in government and the most gender-equal laws and state policies, most governments are run by socially dominant men, and their policies reflect their interests. In every period of change, including those of revolutionary upheaval, men's interests, not women's, have prevailed, and many men, but few women, have benefited from progressive social policies. Equality and justice for all usually means for men only. Women have never had their revolution because the structure of gender as a social institution has never been seriously challenged. Therefore, all men benefit from the "patriarchal dividend"—women's unpaid work maintaining homes and bringing up children; women's low-paid work servicing hospitals, schools, and myriad other workplaces.

Gender inequality is deeply ingrained in the structure of Western, industrialized societies. It is built into the organization of marriage and families, work and the economy, politics, religion, sports, the arts and other cultural productions, and the very language we speak. Making women and men equal, therefore, necessitates social, not individual, solutions.

CHANGING GENDER

Changing a gendered society entails structural and institutional change. Attitudes and values must change, too, but these are often altered when social policies and practices shift. Which changes have occurred since the beginning of the feminist movement of the early 1970s and which have not? What kind of programs target institutions and social structures? What is still needed for gender equality?

Affirmative action and comparable worth pay scales were two efforts to effect structural change—one to desegregate occupations and the other to distribute economic rewards for work on a genderneutral basis. Affirmative action (hiring women in occupations dominated by men and men for work usually done by women) was widely implemented in the United States and did desegregate some occupations, but without continuous effort, gender segregation reestablishes itself as jobs and work organizations change. Another effort to establish gender-neutral work policies was comparable worth pay scales—assessing the characteristics of the job and paying on the basis of type of work done, not on who does the work. These programs were not widely implemented; women's work continues to be paid less than men's even when a man does the work. Women have entered the professions, especially medicine and the law, in large numbers and have moved up career ladders, but in most large-scale corporations and professional organizations, the top positions of authority are still held by men.

Sexual harassment guidelines have been another effective effort at changing thinking about acceptable behaviour, and again, while the results are imperfect (and the guidelines are being used in ways that do not empower women), thinking about what was "normal" behaviour in the workplace did change drastically.

In Europe, but not in the United States, subsidized parental leave for either parent and child care for every mother has changed mothering from a full-time occupation to something that can be combined with paid work out of the home without a constant struggle. The Scandinavian countries provide "daddy days"—leave time in the first year of a newborn's life that the father must take or it is forfeited.

A radical effort at restructuring government has taken place in France—a proposed program for mandating equal numbers of women and men representatives at the national level of government. Parity is not likely to become a widespread policy, but even redressing gender imbalance would give women and men a more equal opportunity to make laws and influence social policy. Gender differences in voting patterns in the United States indicate that women do have a different perspective on many issues. For women to be elected in greater numbers, powerful men now in politics would have to encourage young women to consider a career in politics, foster their advancement through mentoring, nominate them for national offices, and campaign with them and raise money for them when they run for office. Paradoxically, it has seemed easier for women to become heads of state than for these same states to vote in an equal number of women and men in their governing bodies. It has also been easier for women to become heads of parliamentary governments, where a party chooses the prime minister. The appointment of women to high positions, such as Madeleine Albright as U.S. Secretary of State, has also been welcomed. Yet when it comes to directly putting women into leadership positions of great authority, whether in government or in major corporations, there is still a public reluctance to grant women as much power as men.

On a more personal level, some people have structured their families to be gender-equal on every level—domestic work, child care, and financial contribution to the household economy. However, as long as work is structured for a marriedman-with-wife career pattern, and men's work is paid better than women's work, gender-equal families will be very hard to attain by the majority of people. Other heterosexual couples have reversed roles—the woman is the breadwinner and the man cares for the children and keeps house. Here, the problem is that the domestic world is so gendered that male househusbands suffer from ostracism and isolation, as well as from a suspicion of homosexuality. Oddly, lesbian and gay couples who have reared children in a variety of family arrangements have blended more easily into hetero-coupled social worlds, at least in some communities. Corporate and government policies that offer health insurance and other benefits to any couple in a long-term household arrangement have also helped to restructure family life in ways that do not assume heterosexuality and marriage. Note, however, that communal domestic households have waned in popularity in Western countries, although they are the norm in polygamous cultures.

Least amenable to change have been the gendered divisions of work in the global economy. Financed by capital from developed countries, work organizations around the world exploit the labour of young, unmarried women under sweatshop-like conditions, while reserving better-paid jobs and support for entrepreneurship to men. The policies of the International Monetary Fund and other financial restructuring agencies do not include among their goals gender desegregation or encouraging women's education and access to health resources. In many developing countries, violence and sexual exploitation, as well as the heterosexual spread of AIDS, seriously undermine efforts to upgrade the lives of women and girls.

In sum, to change gendered social orders to be more equal (or, alternatively, less gendered) will take individual effort and modification of gender-stereotyped attitudes and values, but most of all, a restructuring of work and family through the policies and practices of large-scale corporations and the governments of dominant nations.

HUMAN SEXUALITY

Human sexuality is a very complex behaviour that is affected by many facets of our lives including our physiology, cognition, and learning. These are just a few of the components that this paper focused on for the sake of brevity. Otherwise, many other factors could have been discussed, such as, the culture, personal and general history, and the humanistic perspective. The point here is that human sexuality, like us, is multi-dimensional and one can only begin to get a sense of what it is by the inclusion of many perspectives and ideas.

Human sexuality plays a major role in everyone's life. Regardless, whether we are young or old, man or woman, American or Japanese, it is an integral part of what we do and who we are. There has been much done by way of research and scholarly writing examining human sexuality. This chapter will explore the topic of human sexuality as a motivation. Of course, there are many emotions associated with human sexuality, but the primary aim of this particular chapter will be a general overview of sexuality with special attention to the various perspectives, including the:

- Biological perspective
- Cognitive perspective
- Learning perspective

Human sexuality.

All the while, the lens through which we summarize these perspectives will be with the understanding that human sexual behaviour is a motivation.

Next to sleeping and eating, it seems that it is one of the most important drives we have to deal with as humans. That is, it takes up so much of our time in thought and behaviour that it sometimes seems that every facet of our life revolves around this to a certain extent.

Human sexual behaviour is different from the sexual behaviour of other animals, in that, it seems to be governed by a variety and interplay of different factors. That is, while "lower" animals or species are driven by a "force" to reproduce and therefore partake in sexual behaviour. Humans are not sexually active just for the sake of reproduction, rather, there are a variety of complex factors that lead people to have sex.

Human sexuality is the way in which we experience and express ourselves as sexual beings. There are many factors that help develop our sexuality, arguably one of the most important, is our actual gender. Whether, I am a male or female will likely have a major influence on the development of my individual sexuality. Furthermore, sexuality is an integral part of our personalities whether we are aware of it or not.

METHODS OF RESEARCH IN HUMAN SEXUALITY

There are numerous ways of gathering scientific evidence about human sexuality. While, some methods focus on description, others methods concentrate on identifying relationships between variables, and still others in identifying causal relationships. The following are general summaries as to the various data collection methods.

SURVEY METHOD

Surveys collect information about behaviour through interviews with participants or questionnaires. The aim of this particular method is to gather information on the sexual attitudes and behaviour of a particular population or group of people. This particular method does have limitations. For example, drawbacks of this method are that surveys require self-report from the participants, therefore, it is likely that the data collected might contain a plethora of inaccuracies. Depending on the question posed to the individual they may want to present themselves in a socially acceptable way or be to embarrassed to answer truthfully. In addition, many people refuse to even participate in human sexuality survey studies, thus, you may get a selection bias because the sample attained may not be representative of the population you want to generalize to.

Arguably, one of the seminal studies in human sexuality employing the survey method was that completed by Kinsey and colleagues. Kinsey and colleagues interviewed about 5300 men and 5900 women between 1938 through 1949 and asked them a variety of questions about their sexual behaviour and attitudes. This approach was well advised since Kinsey was particularly interested in the frequency of certain sexual behaviours (e.g., oral sex, masturbation, and intercourse) rather than the underlying causes.

OBSERVATIONAL METHOD

In the observational method the investigator is a direct observer of sexual behaviour. These observations may take place in field settings or in labouratories. This particular method, however, has had a very limited application so far because of the requirement of privacy that shrouds sexual experience in many cultures. An example of observational research is when psychologists observe the patterns of nonverbal communication and body language among couples in dating situations. Researchers can also interact with the people whose behaviour they are recording, this is deemed the participant observation method. One major limitation of this method is the possibility that the behaviour under study may be altered by the participant because of the presence of the observer (i.e., observer effect). In other words, the participants' behaviour may consciously be changed to "fit" with what they believe the observer is seeking.

Human Sexual Response by William Masters and Virginia Johnson is one of the seminal studies examining the sexual behaviour of humans via the observation method. Despite the controversy engendered by the method of their study, it gave a reliable picture of what happens to the body during sexual behaviour.

EXPERIMENTAL METHOD

Experiments permit researchers to draw causal conclusions between the independent variable and dependent variable. One example of this method is exposing participants to sexually arousing materials while instruments monitor physiological responses. The particular limitations of this study seem obvious, in that, one cannot manipulate many variables of interest directly because of ethical standards.

CORRELATIONAL METHOD

Allows the researcher to examine the relationship between variables of interest. For example, a researcher may be interested in the variables that relate to sexual satisfaction in couples. Therefore, he/she may look at the variables of partner compatibility, communication skills, and number of years the couple has been together. The major limitation of this method is that correlation does not equal causation.

CASE STUDY METHOD

The intensive study of one particular participant. A vast amount of descriptive information is gathered about one particular individual, therefore, giving a much more detailed picture of that individual than would otherwise normally be attained. The major shortcoming of this method is that generalization to a population is out of the question. In addition, participants may also have "gaps" in their memories and ways of thinking which bias results.

BIOLOGICAL PERSPECTIVE

One cannot truly begin a dialogue about human sexuality without addressing the biological perspective, in particular, hormones. Hormones may be viewed as one of the major "driving forces" of sexual behaviour. Over the past several years, there has been much research examining the various roles that hormones play in the sexual behaviour of humans. Hormones are produced by the gonads (i.e., testes and ovaries), the adrenal cortex, the pituitary gland, and the hypothalamus. In addition, the hormones of androgens, estrogens, and progestins all exist in both males and females. They exist in different concentrations, however, within males and females.

Males have a higher concentration of androgens and females have a higher concentration of estrogens and progestins. Incidentally, androgens are responsible for the sexual differentiation of the male reproductive system before birth and the sexual maturation of boys at puberty. Testosterone, a specific androgen, is associated with the male sexual drive and possibly with aggressive behaviour. Estrogens and progestins, found in higher concentrations within females, regulate the menstrual cycle and are essential for reproduction. The relationship of these hormones to the female sexual drive and behaviour are unclear. Hormone levels are usually correlated with sexual behaviour, but in humans this is not necessarily true because of intervening variables. Thus, an individual may be physiologically ready to participate in sexual behaviour, but does not because of factors that supercede any biological reason.

COGNITIVE PERSPECTIVE

A comprehension of the processes of sexual arousal is an important element in understanding sexual responses. The notion that our most erogenous sex organ lies between our ears should not be dismissed. The cognitive activity of the brain can quickly either augment or inhibit a sexual response cycle. Walen & Roth pointed out that perceptions and evaluations are the two major types of cognitive activity. That is, how a stimulus or situation is interpreted determines how the individual will respond to the stimulus.

According to Walen & Roth, perception includes at least three components: detection, labeling, and attribution. Detection is defined by an individual's ability to note the presence of a stimulus or to discriminate it from other stimuli. Next, labeling is the descriptors that an individual uses to categorize the stimulus event. Third, attribution is an explanation for the perception. Individuals may of course rely heavily on situational cues when making attributions. How may all three of these factors affect sexual behaviour? Well, the inability to detect sexual stimuli, incorrect labeling, or misattribution may significantly impede sexual performance. The second major cognitive factor is evaluation, which is a process of rating events from good to bad. For example, the cognitive theory of Rational Emotive Therapy (RET) has focused primarily on evaluative beliefs. The general point to take away from this particular theory is that "when an individual evaluates a sexual stimulus as good or positive, sexual arousal may be enhanced. On the other hand, when a stimulus is evaluated negatively, sexuality will be diminished. Even more destructive are the exaggerated negative evaluations that Ellis refers to as catastrophic".

LEARNING PERSPECTIVE

To what extent does sexual behaviour reflect experience? Would you hold the same sexual attitudes and behaviours if you had been reared in another culture? Even within the same society, family and personal experiences can shape unique sexual attitudes and behaviours. Learning theory focuses on environmental factors that shape behaviour. Within this context, learning theory examines the environmental factors that shape sexual behaviour. Behaviourism emphasizes the importance of rewards and punishments in the learning process. Events (such as rewards) that increase the frequency or likelihood of particular behaviour are termed reinforcements. When applied to sexual behaviour, children left to explore their bodies without parental condemnation will learn what feels good and tend to repeat it.

However, when sexual behaviour (like masturbation) feels pleasurable, but parents connect it with feelings of guilt and shame, the child is placed in conflict. Conversely, punishment tends to suppress behaviour in circumstances in which it is expected to occur. Thus, if young people are severely punished for sexual exploration, we may come to associate sexual stimulation in general with feelings of guilt or anxiety. Social Learning Theory uses the concepts of rewards and punishment, but it also emphasizes the importance of cognitive activity (i.e., anticipations, thoughts, and plans) and learning by observation. Observational learning or modeling refers to acquiring knowledge and skills through observing others. Observational learning may also take place when exposed to certain films, books, or music. According to social learning theory children acquire the gender roles deemed appropriate in society through reinforcement of gender-appropriate behaviour. In addition, individuals duplicate behaviours of those they respect and hold as models.

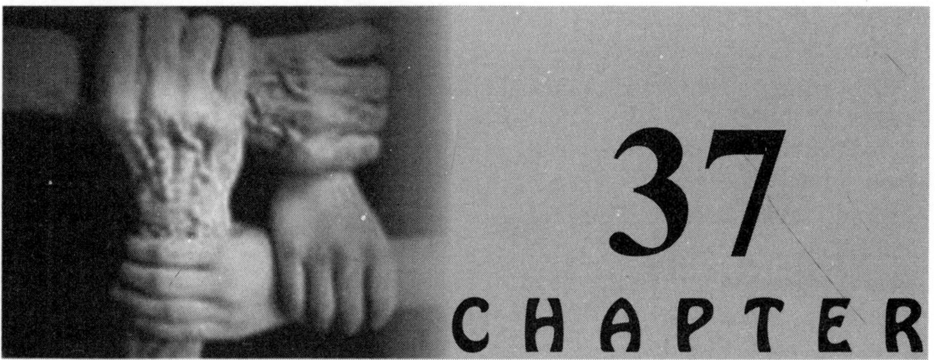

AGING AND THE LIFE COURSE

Introduction. History of Ssocial Gerontology: *The Age-period-cohort Problem, Aged Hetrogeneity, Life-course Dynamic, The Intersection of History and Personal Biography, The Persisting Effects of Early Traumas and Deprivations, The Persisting Effects of Early Life Decisions.* ***Life-course Trajectories and Person-centred Research:*** *Life-Course Trajectories, Person-centered Research.*

INTRODUCTION

Social gerontology, or the sociology of aging, has two primary foci:

(a) social factors during late life, and

(b) social antecedents and consequences of aging.

Thus, social gerontology includes examination of both the status of being old and the process of becoming old. Increasingly, theories and methods of the life course are replacing the earlier emphasis on late life as a separate topic of inquiry. This is a vast arena, and the sociology of aging is appropriately informed by the theories and methods of many sociological subspecialities ranging from macrohistorical and demographic perspectives to the microorientations of social psychology and interpretive sociology.

HISTORY OF SOCIAL GERONTOLOGY

Historically, social gerontology emerged from a social-problems orientation and focused on the deprivations and losses that were expected to characterize late life. Early research in the field focused on issues such as poverty during late life; old age as a marginal status, reflecting problems of social integration; the negative effects of institutionalization and poor quality of long-term care; and ageism and age discrimination. Early on, however, some investigators saw the dangers of allowing a crisis orientation to dominate the study of aging and focused attention on patterns of "normal" and "successful" aging. A significant proportion of research also focuses on the problems of late life. Investigators remain concerned about social integration and adaptation to loss. The majority of funding for aging research is provided by the National Institute on Aging, which is mandated to support health-related research. Consequently, much aging research focuses on illness and the health care delivery system. The dramatic aging of the population — a trend that will peak with the aging of the Baby Boom cohorts — leads to questions about the capacities of social institutions and public policies to meet the needs of an unprecedented number and proportion of older adults. Scholars using political economy theories focus on the ways in which societies respond to the dependency needs of older adults and the social implications of those responses.

Although much research remains focused on the problems of late life, sociologists now recognize the broader importance and implications of old age and aging. Two primary factors appear to have been the driving forces that account for this broader and more complex view. First, despite the social-problems orientation of most early research, empirical data failed to confirm a uniformly bleak picture of old age. For example, in spite of higher rates of illness and disability, the vast majority of older adults are competent and able to live independent lives. Similarly, rather than representing involuntary loss of a treasured role, retirement is actively sought by the majority of older workers and seldom poses adaptive problems. In addition, some of the problems observed in early studies of older adults have been remedied by the increased resources that recent cohorts have brought to late life, as well as to effective public policies. Thus, although health care costs remain a burden for many older adults, Medicare and Medicaid substantially reduced barriers to health care among older people. Similarly, as a result of improvements in Social Security benefits and increased participation in private pensions, older Americans now are no more likely to live in poverty than younger adults and, indeed, are less likely to live in poverty than children. Such findings pushed social gerontology toward more complex and empirically defensible perspectives on old age and aging.

Second, sociologists came to recognize that age plays a fundamental role in social structure and social organization. As a parameter of social organization, age affects the allocation of social resources and social roles. Along with sex and race, age is an ascribed status. But age is unique among ascribed statuses in that it changes over time, and movement across age categories results in changing expectations for behavior, changing access to social resources, and changing personal and social responsibilities. The structural quality of age is best articulated in age stratification theory. Age stratification refers to the division of society into meaningful age groups that differ in social value and the allocation of social resources. The concept of age stratification has proven to be useful in a variety of ways. At the broadest level, it reminds us that age is a fundamental parameter of social organization. Age stratification has been particularly useful in highlighting age-related roles and norms. It has a social-psychological facet as well: age consciousness or awareness and identification with members of one's age group. Moreover, the structural and individual facets of age stratification operate in both directions. On the one hand, the structural component of age stratification allocates roles and resources and assigns differential social value to age strata. Thus, ageism is largely an effect of age stratification. On the other hand, by promoting age consciousness, age stratification sets the stage for age-based public policies and collective efforts by older adults to protect or increase their share of societal resources (e.g., voting and lobbying efforts based on the self-interests of the elderly).

In the 1990s, the sociology of aging focused on change and stability across the life course. Lifecourse perspectives have enriched aging research in several ways. First, a life-course approach is attractive because it recognizes that the past is prologue to the future. That is, status and personal well-being in late life depend in large part on events and achievements experienced earlier in the life course. Second, lifecourse perspectives emphasize relationships across life domains, recognizing that, for example, family events affect and are affected by work and health. Traditionally, sociological research has focused on specific life domains (e.g., the sociology of work, the sociology of the family); life-course perspectives, in contrast, are person-centered rather than domain-centered. Third, life-course perspectives focus on the intersection of history and personal biography. Although the macro-micro schism remains difficult to bridge, life-course research has documented some of the complex ways that historical conditions affect personal lives both contemporaneously and over subsequent decades.

THE AGE-PERIOD-COHORT PROBLEM

Isolating the effects of age and characterizing the aging process are difficult tasks. Because many factors affect social structure and individual behavior, it is always difficult to isolate the effects of a specific factor. But this task is especially difficult with regard to age, because it is inherently confounded with the effects of two other factors: cohort and period. Age, of course, refers to time since birth, and age effects refers to patterns resulting from the passage of time or sheer length of life. Cohort refers to the group of persons born at approximately the same time (e.g., the 1920 cohort, the 1940–1944 cohort). There are two primary kinds of cohort effects. One type results from historical factors. For example, cohorts who lived through the Great Depression or World War II had different life experiences than cohorts who were not exposed to those historical events. And, as a further complication, the effects of historical events vary depending on the ages of those who experience them. The second type of cohort effect reflects compositional characteristics. For example, large cohorts (such as the Baby Boomers) may face greater competition for social resources than smaller cohorts (e.g., those born during the Great Depression, when fertility rates were low). Both types of cohort effects can have persistent effects on the life course, and, hence, late life. Period effects (also called time of measurement effects) result from events or situations that happen at a specific time, and tend to affect individuals regardless of age or cohort. For example, faith in government decreased in all Americans (regardless of age or cohort) at the time of the Watergate scandal.

Age, cohort, and period effects are intertwined. If one knows when an individual was born and also knows the time of measurement, simple subtraction provides accurate information about the individual's age. Similarly, if one knows an individual's age and time of measurement, one can easily calculate date of birth or birth cohort. Statistically, there are no easy methods for disentangling age, period, and cohort. In general, however, the most compelling research results are those that are based on examination of multiple cohorts at multiple times of measurement. If the same age patterns are observed across different cohorts measured at different times, those patterns are likely to reflect age effects. If patterns are not similar across cohorts and times of measurement, however, they are likely to reflect cohort or period effects.

The issue of age-period-cohort effects has lost some of its appeal; critics point out that simply knowing, for example, that there is a cohort effect leaves unanswered what it is about those cohorts that generated the observed differences. This is an appropriate criticism; nonetheless, it is immensely helpful in searching for causal explanations to know whether the underlying mechanism is consistent across time and place (an aging effect), had strong contemporaneous effects on persons of all ages (a period effect), or affected only specific cohorts (a cohort effect). Age, cohort, and period effects are all important in aging research. Age effects provide information about human development as it unfolds in social context. Cohort effects permit us to observe the social implications of shared history and cohort composition. Period effects provide information about the effects of contemporaneous events and situations on social structure and individual behavior. Distinguishing among age, period, and cohort effects also has important implications for the generalization of research results. Age effects are the same or highly similar across time and place; thus, they are generalizable. In contrast, cohort and period effects are, by definition, variable across time. Consequently, generalization is limited.

Examination of age-period-cohort effects requires large data bases in which multiple cohorts are observed on multiple occasions over long periods of time. Because of these stringent requirements, few aging studies focus specifically on disentangling these confounded factors. But recognition of these sources of confounding appropriately temper investigators' generalizations. In addition, this issue has sensitized researchers to the need to examine change over time, with the result that longitudinal studies have become the dominant research design in efforts to characterize the aging process.

No single theme nor easily summarized list of topics does justice to the scope and diversity of research on aging and the life course. However, three major research domains can provide a general sense of the current major avenues of aging and life-course research: aged heterogeneity, lifecourse dynamics, and life-course trajectories.

AGED HETROGENEITY

The majority of research on older adults focuses on heterogeneity in that population. In many ways, this is the legacy of the problem orientation upon which initial aging research in the social sciences rested. Even now, most aging research focuses on differences among older adults and the complex configurations of social factors that can account for individual differences during late life. And, although there are many exceptions, a majority of research in this domain focuses on the social factors that explain individual behavior and personal well-being.

The specific topics that are examined in research on aged heterogeneity are extensive. Health and disability are major concerns in this research tradition, including physical illness; mental illness, especially depression; cognitive status and dementing illness; functional status and disability; and health behaviors. Health service utilization is a corollary emphasis; there are numerous studies on both utilization in general (e.g., doctors visits, hospitalizations) and specialized health care settings and providers (e.g., long-term care facilities, emergency room visits, screening programs and other preventative services, mental health professionals, dentists). There also has been extensive research on the use of social and community services and living arrangements—both of which are strongly driven by health during late life.

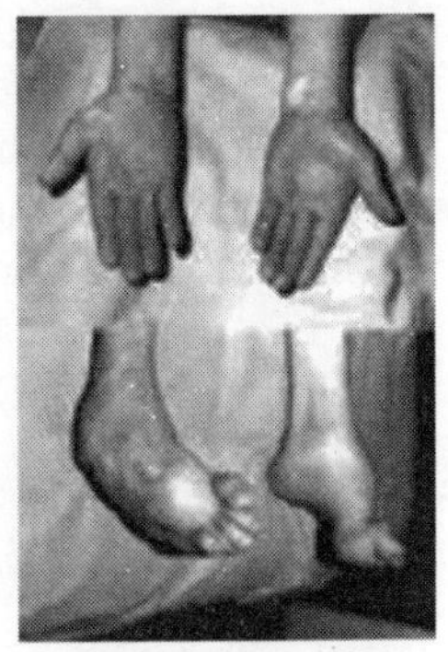

Aged Hetrogeneity.

Along with health, socioeconomic status has been a high-volume, longstanding focus in research on aged heterogeneity. Economic status, in the form of income and, to a lesser extent, assets has been the primary emphasis of this research, with studies of the antecedents and consequences of retirement ranking as a close second. Pensions have been shown to have strong effects upon the adequacy of postretirement income, which has spurred substantial investigation of the determinants of pension acquisition and value.

From a more social-psychological perspective, there are strong research traditions examining multiple psychosocial states that can be subsumed under the umbrella of "quality of life." Life satisfaction and morale have received paramount attention in this regard. But several dimensions of the self (e.g., self-esteem, locus of control, sense of mastery) also have rich research traditions.

Two common elements of the wide range of research conducted on the topic of aged heterogeneity merit note. First, a common thread in this research is the desire to understand the processes that render some older adults advantaged and others disadvantaged. This is often described as the "applied" character of aging research. However, it also is a focus on stratification in the broadest sense, which is one of the most persistent and cherished issues in mainstream sociology. Research on aging and the life course has contributed much to our understanding of how broadly life chances and life quality are linked to social factors, as well as to the multiple powerful social bases of stratification.

Second, examination of heterogeneity among the elderly has proven to be a strategic site for testing and refining multiple middle-range theories and concepts that are central to sociological research. A few examples will illustrate this point. Research on health and disability during late life has been enriched by attention to issues of social stress and social support; conversely, the older population has proven to be ideal for testing theoretical propositions about the effects of stress and social support. Similarly, the issue of social integration, which has an honored tradition in sociology, has been reactivated in studies of older adults, who vary widely in number and quality of links to social structure. And issues such as the "feminization of poverty" and the "double/triple jeopardy hypothesis" (i.e., the potential interacting deprivations associated with being female, nonwhite, and old) have highlighted the extent to which socioeconomic stratification rests on ascribed rather than achieved statuses.

LIFE-COURSE DYNAMIC

While the issue of heterogeneity focuses attention on differences across individuals, life-course dynamics focus on the persisting effects of social factors over time and stages of life; that is, on intraindividual change. At least three types of lifecourse studies have received substantial attention in aging research.

THE INTERSECTION OF HISTORY AND PERSONAL BIOGRAPHY

There now is substantial evidence that historical events can permanently alter personal lives. Most research to date has focused on two historical events: the Great Depression and World War II; both historical events have been linked to life circumstances during late life. Elder has compellingly documented, for example, that entering the labor market during the Depression had a permanent negative effect on occupation and income, which in turn affected socioeconomic status during late life. In contrast, younger men, who entered the labour force immediately after World War II experienced historically unparalled occupational opportunities (and, if they were veterans, government-subsidized college educations).

Other studies by Elder and colleagues focused on the life-course consequences of combat experience during World War II. Exposure to combat was strongly related to subsequent health problems, not only immediately after the war, but also during late life. Social factors loom large in these dynamics. First, social factors were strongly predictive of which soldiers were exposed to combat. Second, social resources and deprivations were strong predictors of the onset or avoidance of health problems.

The effects of historical events on the life course appear on two levels. When an historical event is pervasive, one method of observing its effects is via cohort differences. That is, an event with wide-ranging effects will render those who experience it discernibly different from cohorts that come before and after it. At the same time, historical events do not have the same immediate or long-term consequences for all members of a cohort. For example, families were differentially affected by the economic dislocations of the Depression, with some suffering extensive economic deprivation and others experiencing little or no change in their economic fortunes. Thus, not everyone who "lives through" a major historical event will experience serious life-course consequences. One of the tasks of the life-course scholar is to identify the social factors that determine whether or not an historical event alters personal biography.

THE PERSISTING EFFECTS OF EARLY TRAUMAS AND DEPRIVATIONS

A second research focus that illustrates the power of life-course perspectives is investigation of the consequences of early traumas and deprivations on well-being in middle and late life. A growing body of research documents the far-reaching effects of severe childhood experiences — including parental divorce and, to a lesser extent, parental death; childhood poverty; and childhood physical and sexual abuse—on the course of adulthood. Most research to date has focused on the implications of these traumas and deprivations on physical and mental health. The robust relationships between events experienced during childhood and health fifty to sixty years later, controlling on contemporaneous risk factors for morbidity, is strong evidence of the power of fateful events to alter the life course.

Again, social factors are strongly implicated in the processes that account for the relationships between childhood traumas and health and wellbeing during late life. First, the availability of social resources at the time of the trauma can dampen its negative effects in both the short and the long term. For example, financial security and adequate supervision ameliorate most of the negative effects of parental divorce on subsequent socioeconomic achievements and physical and mental health. Second, two of the primary mechanisms by which childhood traumas generate poor health in later life are socioeconomic achievement and high-quality social relationships. That is, childhood traumas are often associated with lower socioeconomic status and poor-quality relationships during adulthood—both of which are risk factors for physical and mental illness. If, however, individuals who experienced childhood traumas manage to achieve adequate financial resources and supportive social ties during adulthood, their excess risk of illness in middle and late life is reduced substantially.

THE PERSISTING EFFECTS OF EARLY LIFE DECISIONS

There now is substantial evidence that the decisions that individuals make during early adulthood have important consequences for their life circumstances in late life. Studies of retirement income provide perhaps the best illustration of this research domain. The strongest predictor of retirement income is occupational history. Throughout adulthood, individuals "sort themselves" into jobs that differ not only in income, but also in benefits (i.e., total compensation packages). Of these, the availability and quality of pensions is most important for retirement income. There is strong evidence that the provision of pensions differs not only by occupation, but also by industrial sector. Thus, when individuals make occupational choices—including job changes throughout adulthood—they are inevitably determining, in part, their retirement incomes.

Research on women's retirement income has broadened our understanding of the life-course consequences of early decisions. Women and men tend to be concentrated in different occupations and different industrial sectors—and those in which women dominate have, on average, lower earnings and lower likelihood of pension coverage. Moreover, family formation decisions strongly affect women's job histories. Compared to men, women are less likely to work full-time and work fewer total years, largely as a result of parental responsibilities. All of these factors combine to produce substantially lower retirement incomes for women than for men.

LIFE-COURSE TRAJECTORIES AND PERSON-CENTRED RESEARCH

The two research domains described above focus on interindividual differences in late life and intraindividual change over the life course. A third domain, less developed than the others but exciting in its scope, attempts to examine interindividual differences and intraindividual change simultaneo-usly. At this point, two emerging research traditions illustrate the nature and potential of this approach.

LIFE-COURSE TRAJECTORIES

Trajectories refer to long-term patterns of stability and change. They can be examined at both the aggregate (e.g., the "typical" career, the modal pathway to nursing home placement) and individual levels. Thus, trajectories capture patterns of intraindividual change. Examination of heterogeneity can be pursued in two ways. In the first, the trajectory that best describes the sample or population is constructed. Subsequently, using techniques such as hierarchical linear modeling or growth-curve analysis, investigators can examine the extent to which factors of interest alter the shape of the trajectory. For example, a trajectory of earnings across adulthood can be constructed for a given sample. Investigators can then examine the degree to which factors such as sex, education, and race affect the shape of the earnings trajectory. In the second approach, multiple common trajectories are identified and investigators then determine the characteristics associated with those trajectories. Using this approach, for example, several common trajectories of earnings during adulthood could be identified (e.g., consistently increasing earnings, earnings peaking during mid-life and then decreasing, consistently decreasing earnings, a relatively flat earnings history). Factors such as sex, education, and race could then be examined to determine their association with these distinctive earnings trajectories.

Trajectory-based research, with its focus on both interindividual differences and intraindividual change, is very attractive. The major limitation to the use of this approach is the availability of data, because longitudinal data covering long periods of time are required if one wishes to understand lifecourse patterns. It should be noted, however, that trajectory-based research can also be useful for studying shorter processes (e.g., patterns of illness outcome, with relatively short-term trajectories of death, chronicity, recovery, and relapse).

Trajectory-based research relevant to our understanding of middle and late life is gradually accumulating. This is especially true for long-term patterns of health and functioning, providing evidence about both the dynamics of disability during late life and long-term patterns of stability, improvement, and decline in health over the course of adulthood. Important trajectorybased research on pathways to retirement and place of death is also available.

The concept of trajectories has been valuable in theoretical development, as well as empirical inquiry. The theory of cumulative advantage/disadvantage has intersected well with studies of lifecourse trajectories. This theory posits that heterogeneity is greater in late life than earlier in the life course as a result of the accumulation of assets (advantage) or liabilities (disadvantage) over time. The theory of cumulative advantage/disadvantage has been especially useful in understanding socioeconomic heterogeneity in late life, especially differences in total net worth. However, it can be applied to other sources of heterogeneity in late life as well (e.g., health). Investigators who prefer examination of the multiple distinctive trajectories within a sample would offer a caution to cumulative advantage/disadvantage theory, however. They would note that although trajectories of increasing and decreasing advantage are undoubtedly common, there are likely to be other important trajectories as well—e.g., a trajectory of cumulating advantage that is reversed as a result of a personal (e.g., serious illness) or societal (e.g., severe economic downturn) catastrophic event.

PERSON-CENTERED RESEARCH

A more recent contribution to the sociological armamentarium for understanding aging and the life course is person-centered research. As the label implies, the focus of this emerging research strategy is to analyze "people" rather than "variables." In practice, this means that members of a sample are first grouped into subsets on the dependent variable of interest. Subsequently, those categories are further disaggregated into groups based on distinctive pathways or life histories associated with the outcome of interest.

Work by Singer, Ryff, and Magee provides the richest example of person-centered aging research to date. The dependent variable of interest was mental health. In the first stage of their research, groups of middle-aged women were divided into groups that differed on levels of mental health. Subsequently, the large archive on longitudinal data obtained from these women over the previous three decades was examined to identify distinctive pathways associated with mid-life mental health. For example, the group of women who exhibited high levels of mental health and well-being were further subdivided into two groups that Singer et al. labeled the healthy and the resilient. Healthy women were those who had life histories that were relatively free of major stressors or traumas, enjoyed adequate or higher levels of social and economic resources, and exhibited stable patterns of robust mental health. Resilient women were those who had achieved robust mental health at mid-life despite earlier evidence of poor mental health and/or histories of stress and/or inadequate social and economic resources. Clearly the life histories of women who were mentally healthy at mid-life varied in important ways. Moreover, the healthy women illustrate the benefits of leading relatively "charmed" lives, while the resilient women help us to understand the circumstances under which "risky" life histories can be turned around to produce health and personal growth.

There are clear similarities between personcentered research and trajectory-based research. Both are based on long-term patterns of change and stability and both are designed to understand both life-course dynamics and heterogeneity in those dynamics. But there also are important differences between the two approaches. In trajectory-based research, the trajectory or pathway itself is the "dependent variable" of interest and the "independent variables" are factors that have the potential to alter the shape(s) of those pathways. In person-centered research, the "dependent variable" is an outcome of interest (e.g., mental health), and trajectories of the "independent variables" are constructed to explain that outcome. Both are currently at the cutting edge of research that attempts to simultaneously examine life-course dynamics and life-course heterogeneity.

Aging and the life course is an important sociological specialty. It provides us with information about aging and being "old," and about the antecedents and consequences of stability and change during late life. The increasing life-course focus of aging research is especially important in that it concentrates sociologists' attention on the dynamics of intraindividual change and on the intersections of social structure, social change, and personal biography. At its best, aging and lifecourse research effectively link processes and dynamics at the macrohistorical and societal levels with individual attitudes and behaviors. In addition, the life course in general, and late life in particular, provide excellent contexts for testing and, indeed, challenging some commonly held assumptions and hypotheses about the dynamics of social influence. In this way, it offers valuable contributions to the larger sociological enterprise.

INDEX

D

E

F

T

U

V

W

WORKING NOTES

WORKING NOTES